SUPERMAN'S PAL

JIMMY OLSEN

WHO KILLED JIMMY OLSEN?

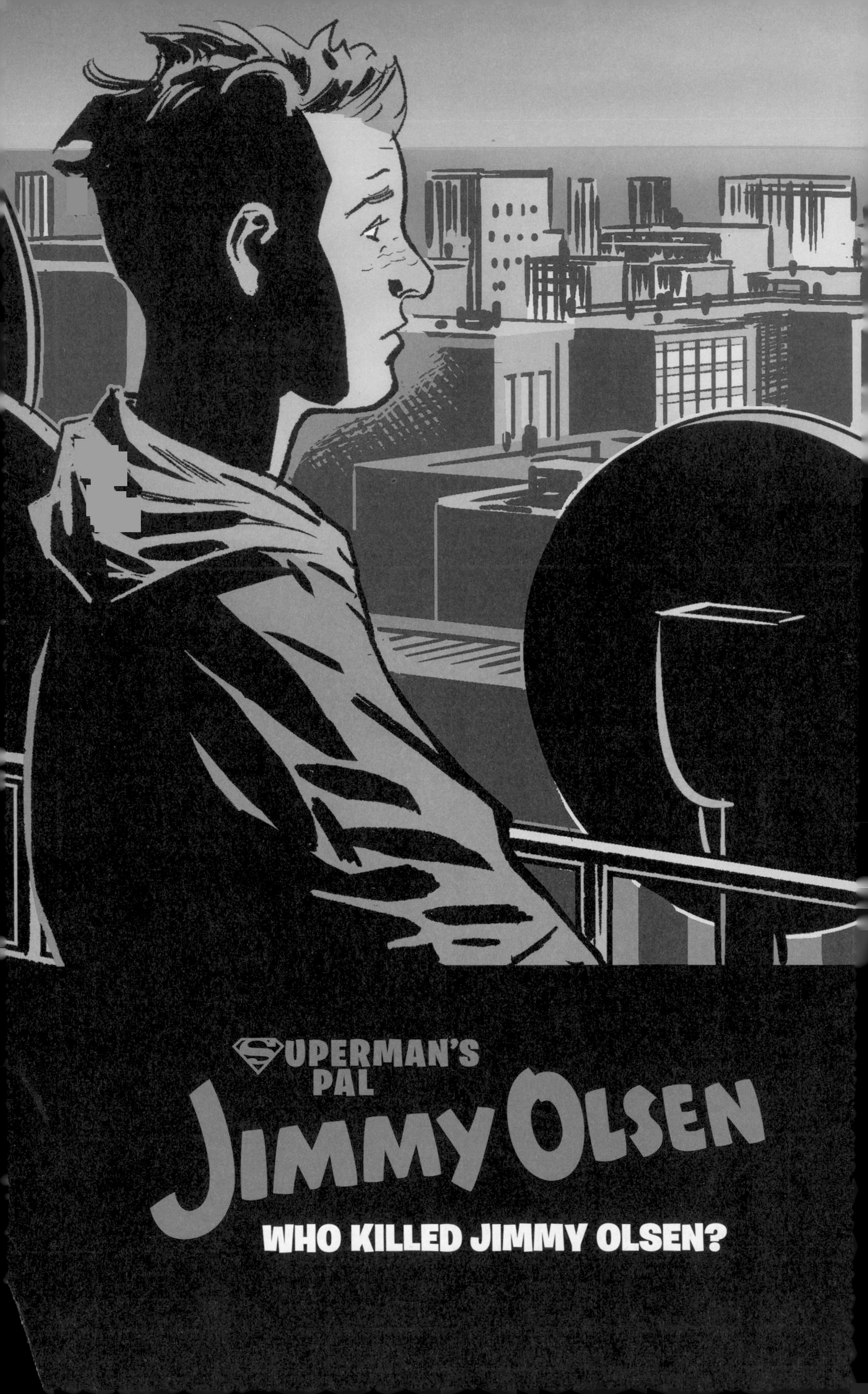

SUPERMAN'S PAL
JIMMY OLSEN
WHO KILLED JIMMY OLSEN?

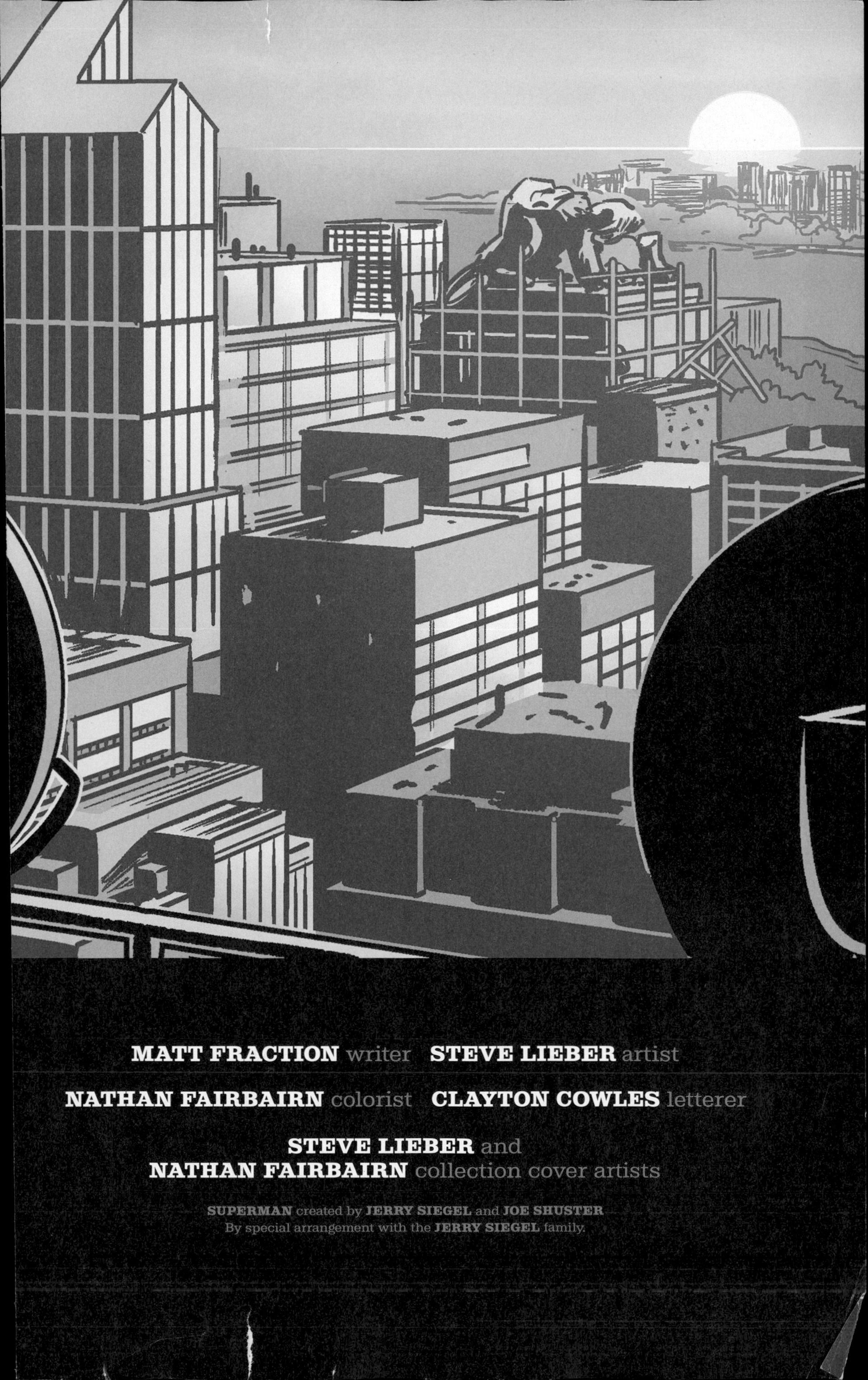

MATT FRACTION writer **STEVE LIEBER** artist

NATHAN FAIRBAIRN colorist **CLAYTON COWLES** letterer

STEVE LIEBER and
NATHAN FAIRBAIRN collection cover artists

MIKE COTTON
JESSICA CHEN
ALEX ANTONE
JESSICA CHEN (again)   Editors – Original Series
BIXIE MATHIEU   Assistant Editor – Original Series
JEB WOODARD   Group Editor – Collected Editions
SCOTT NYBAKKEN   Editor – Collected Edition
STEVE COOK   Design Director – Books
                                and Publication Design
CHRISTY SAWYER   Publication Production

BOB HARRAS   Senior VP – Editor-in-Chief, DC Comics

JIM LEE   Publisher & Chief Creative Officer
BOBBIE CHASE   VP – Global Publishing Initiatives & Digital Strategy
DON FALLETTI   VP – Manufacturing Operations & Workflow Management
LAWRENCE GANEM   VP – Talent Services
ALISON GILL   Senior VP – Manufacturing & Operations
HANK KANALZ   Senior VP – Publishing Strategy & Support Services
DAN MIRON   VP – Publishing Operations
NICK J. NAPOLITANO   VP – Manufacturing Administration & Design
NANCY SPEARS   VP – Sales
JONAH WEILAND   VP – Marketing & Creative Services
MICHELE R. WELLS   VP & Executive Editor, Young Reader

SUPERMAN'S PAL JIMMY OLSEN: WHO KILLED JIMMY OLSEN?

DC Comics, 2900 West Alameda Ave., Burbank, CA 91505
Printed by LSC Communications, Owensville, MO, USA. 9/4/20. First Printing.
ISBN: 978-1-77950-462-3

Library of Congress Cataloging-in-Publication Data is available.

PROLOGUE

From *Superman: Leviathan Rising Special* #1

Cover art by YANICK PAQUETTE and NATHAN FAIRBAIRN

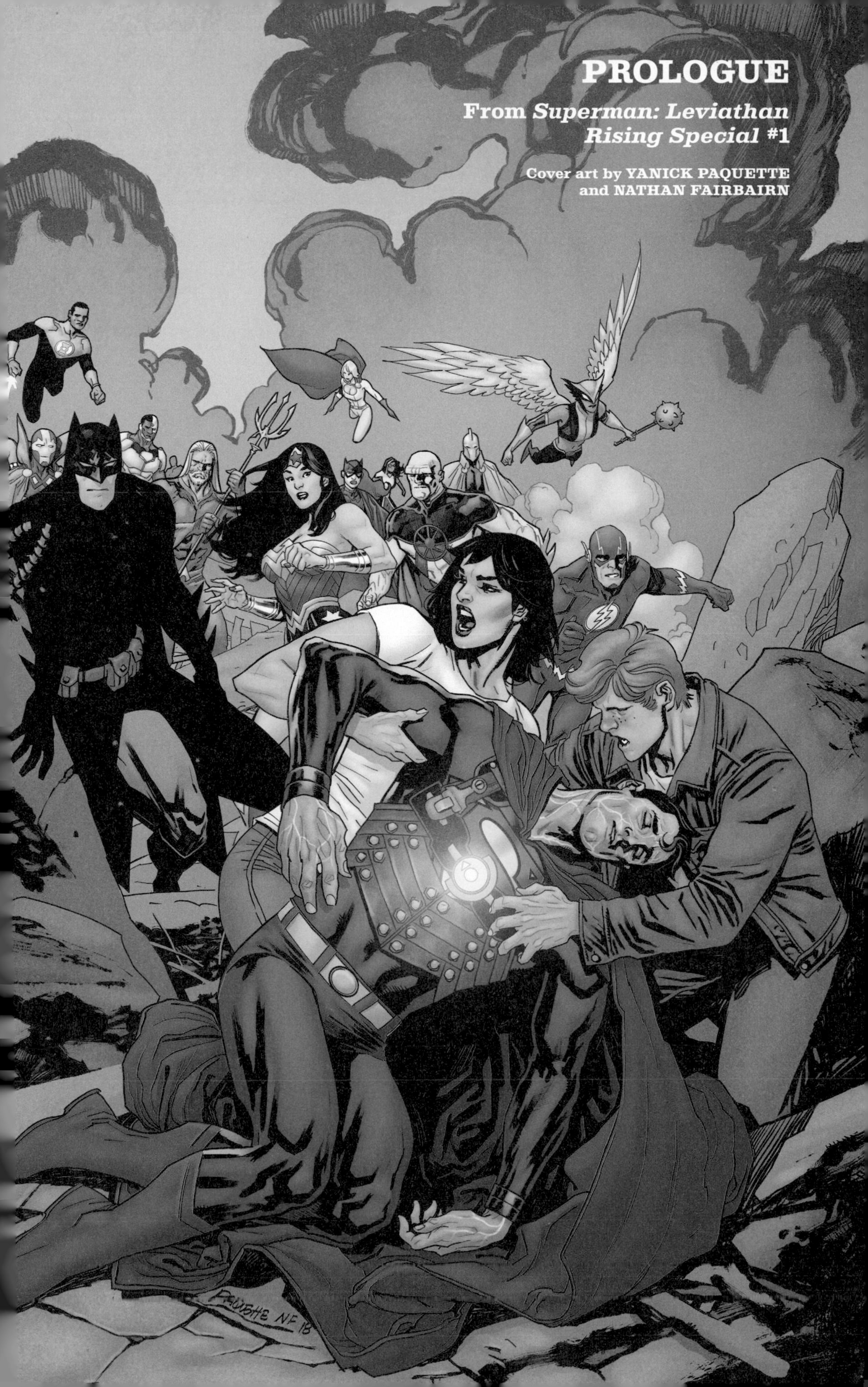

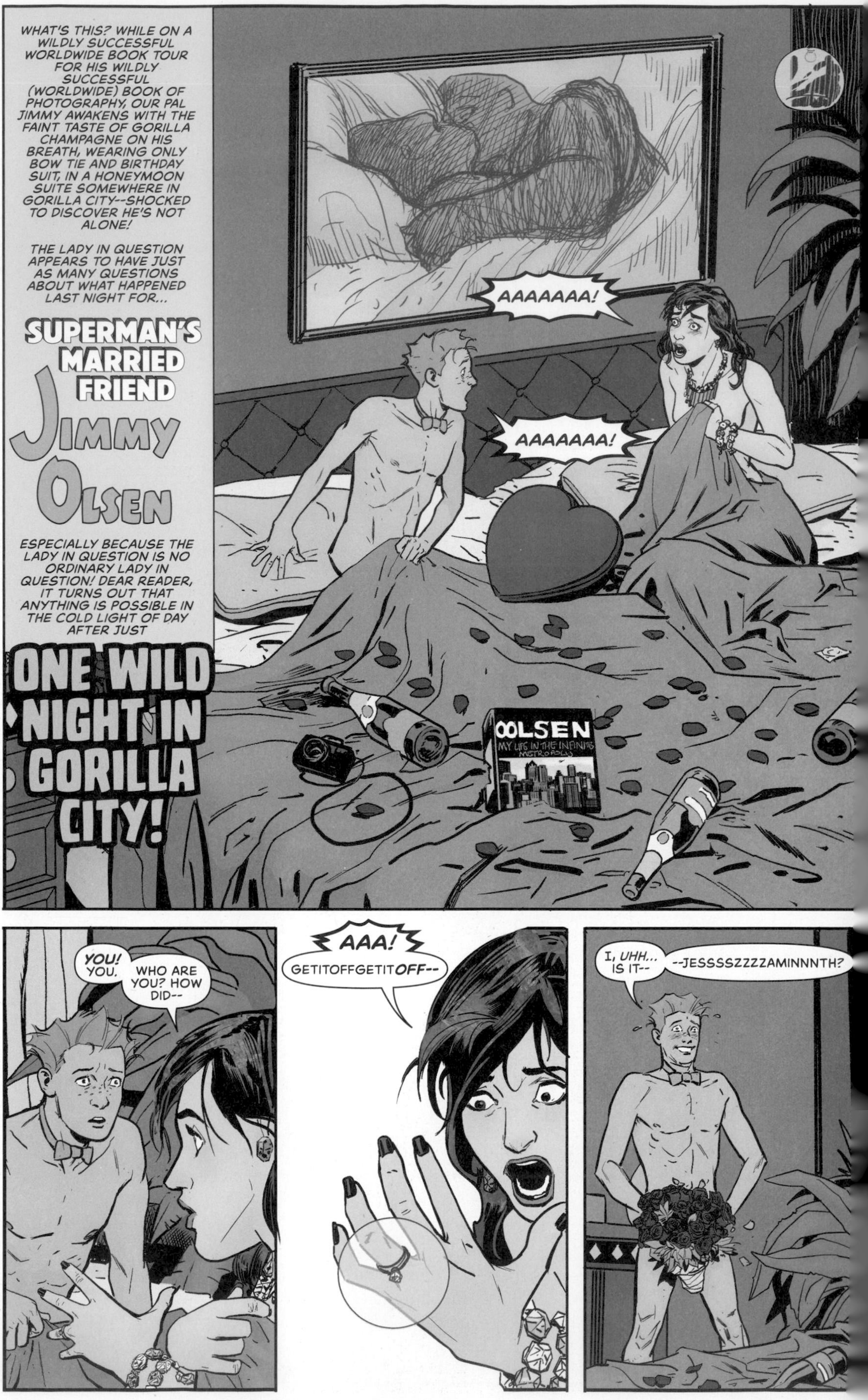
WHAT'S THIS? WHILE ON A WILDLY SUCCESSFUL WORLDWIDE BOOK TOUR FOR HIS WILDLY SUCCESSFUL (WORLDWIDE) BOOK OF PHOTOGRAPHY, OUR PAL JIMMY AWAKENS WITH THE FAINT TASTE OF GORILLA CHAMPAGNE ON HIS BREATH, WEARING ONLY BOW TIE AND BIRTHDAY SUIT, IN A HONEYMOON SUITE SOMEWHERE IN GORILLA CITY--SHOCKED TO DISCOVER HE'S NOT ALONE!
THE LADY IN QUESTION APPEARS TO HAVE JUST AS MANY QUESTIONS ABOUT WHAT HAPPENED LAST NIGHT FOR...
SUPERMAN'S MARRIED FRIEND JIMMY OLSEN
ESPECIALLY BECAUSE THE LADY IN QUESTION IS NO ORDINARY LADY IN QUESTION! DEAR READER, IT TURNS OUT THAT ANYTHING IS POSSIBLE IN THE COLD LIGHT OF DAY AFTER JUST
ONE WILD NIGHT IN GORILLA CITY!
AAAAAAA!
AAAAAAA!
OLSEN
MY LIFE IN THE INFINITE METROPOLIS
YOU! YOU.
WHO ARE YOU? HOW DID--
AAA!
GETITOFFGETITOFF--
I, UHH... IS IT--
--JESSSSZZZZAMINNNTH?

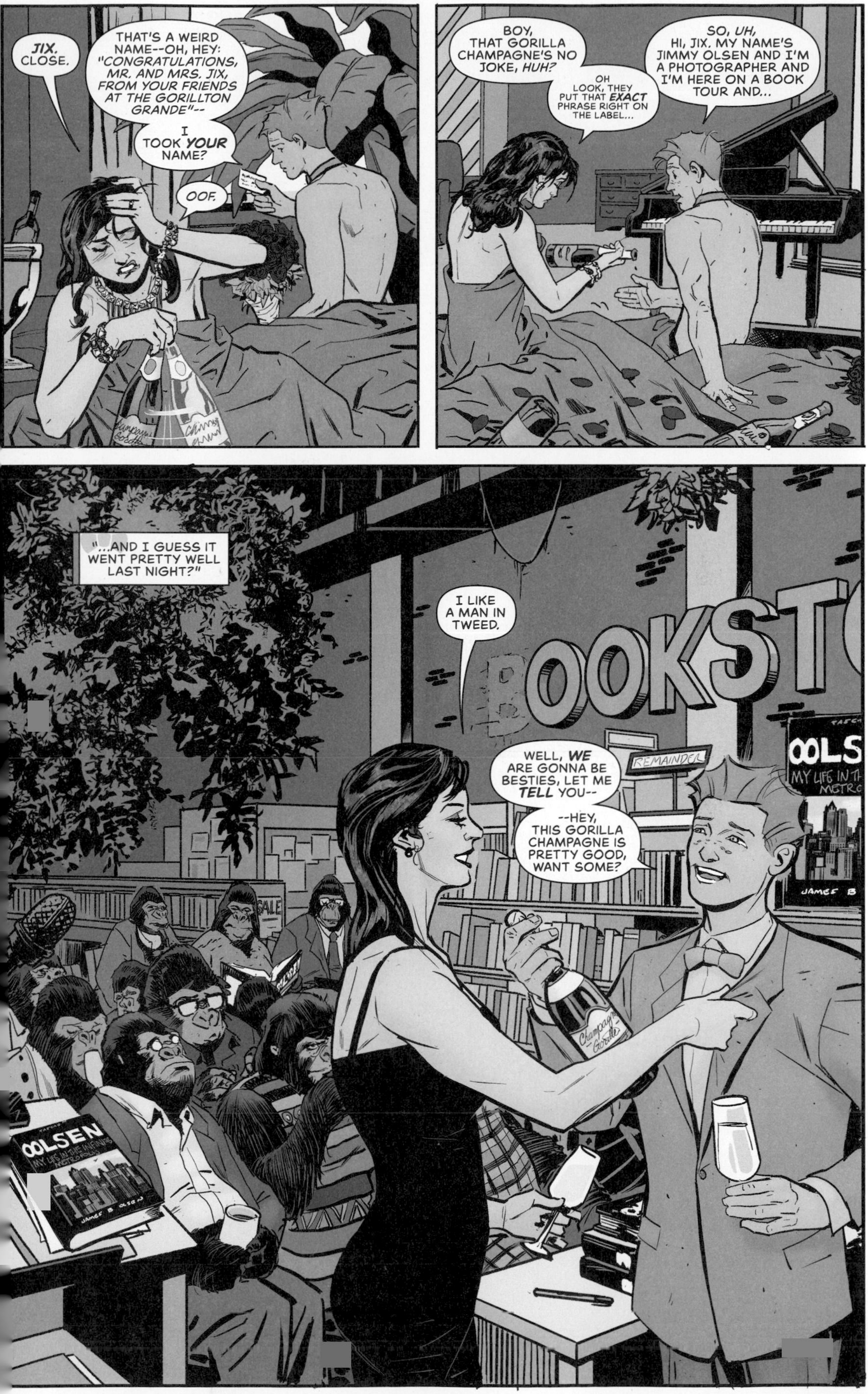
JIX. CLOSE.
THAT'S A WEIRD NAME--OH, HEY: "CONGRATULATIONS, MR. AND MRS. JIX, FROM YOUR FRIENDS AT THE GORILLTON GRANDE"--
I TOOK YOUR NAME?
OOF.
BOY, THAT GORILLA CHAMPAGNE'S NO JOKE, HUH?
OH LOOK, THEY PUT THAT EXACT PHRASE RIGHT ON THE LABEL...
SO, UH, HI, JIX. MY NAME'S JIMMY OLSEN AND I'M A PHOTOGRAPHER AND I'M HERE ON A BOOK TOUR AND...
"...AND I GUESS IT WENT PRETTY WELL LAST NIGHT?"
I LIKE A MAN IN TWEED.
WELL, WE ARE GONNA BE BESTIES, LET ME TELL YOU--
--HEY, THIS GORILLA CHAMPAGNE IS PRETTY GOOD, WANT SOME?

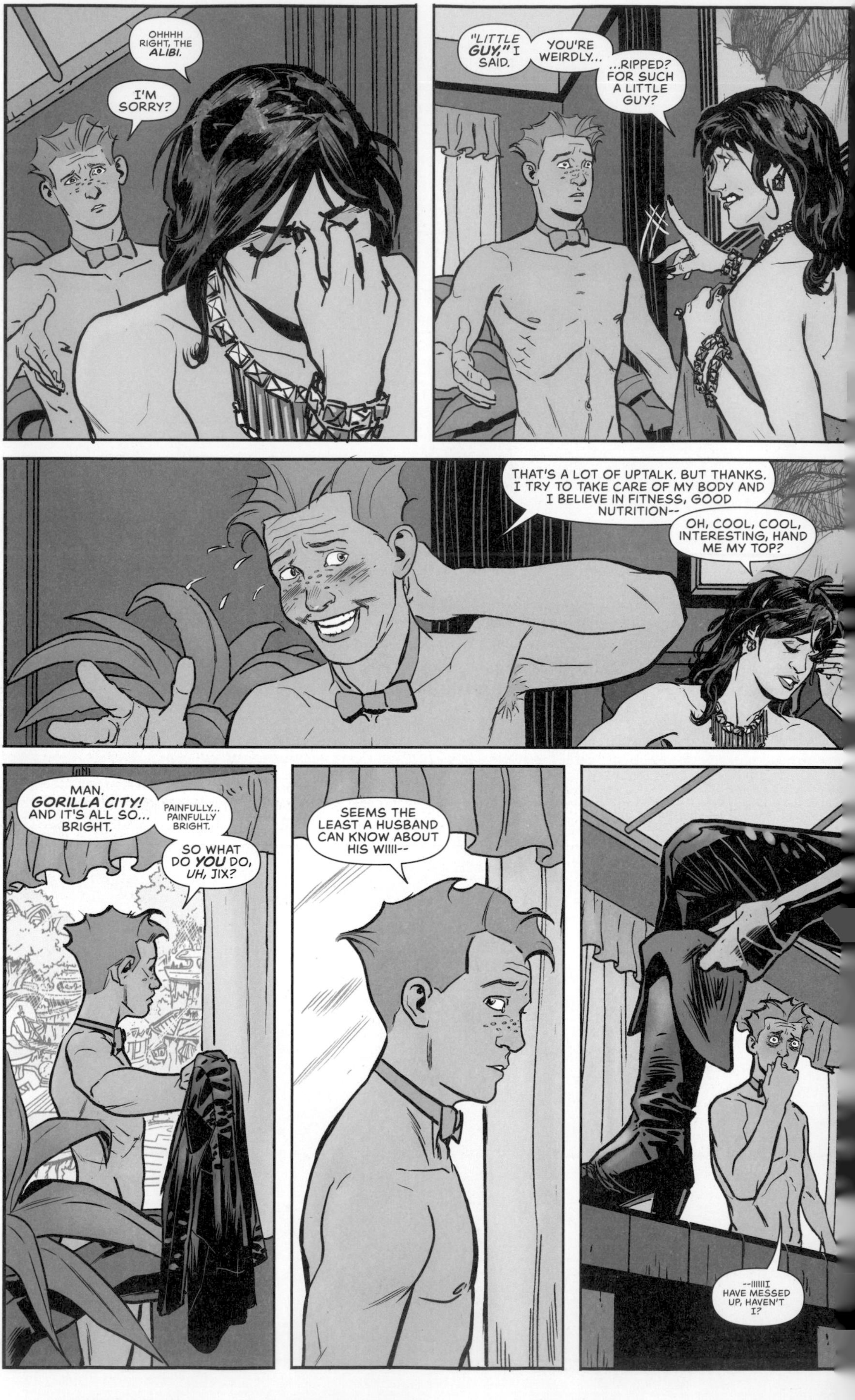
OHHHH RIGHT, THE *ALIBI.*
I'M SORRY?
"LITTLE *GUY*," I SAID.
YOU'RE WEIRDLY...
...RIPPED? FOR SUCH A LITTLE GUY?
THAT'S A LOT OF UPTALK. BUT THANKS. I TRY TO TAKE CARE OF MY BODY AND I BELIEVE IN FITNESS, GOOD NUTRITION--
OH, COOL, COOL, INTERESTING, HAND ME MY TOP?
MAN. *GORILLA CITY!* AND IT'S ALL SO... BRIGHT.
PAINFULLY... PAINFULLY BRIGHT.
SO WHAT DO *YOU* DO, UH, JIX?
SEEMS THE LEAST A HUSBAND CAN KNOW ABOUT HIS WIIII--
--IIIIIII HAVE MESSED UP, HAVEN'T I?

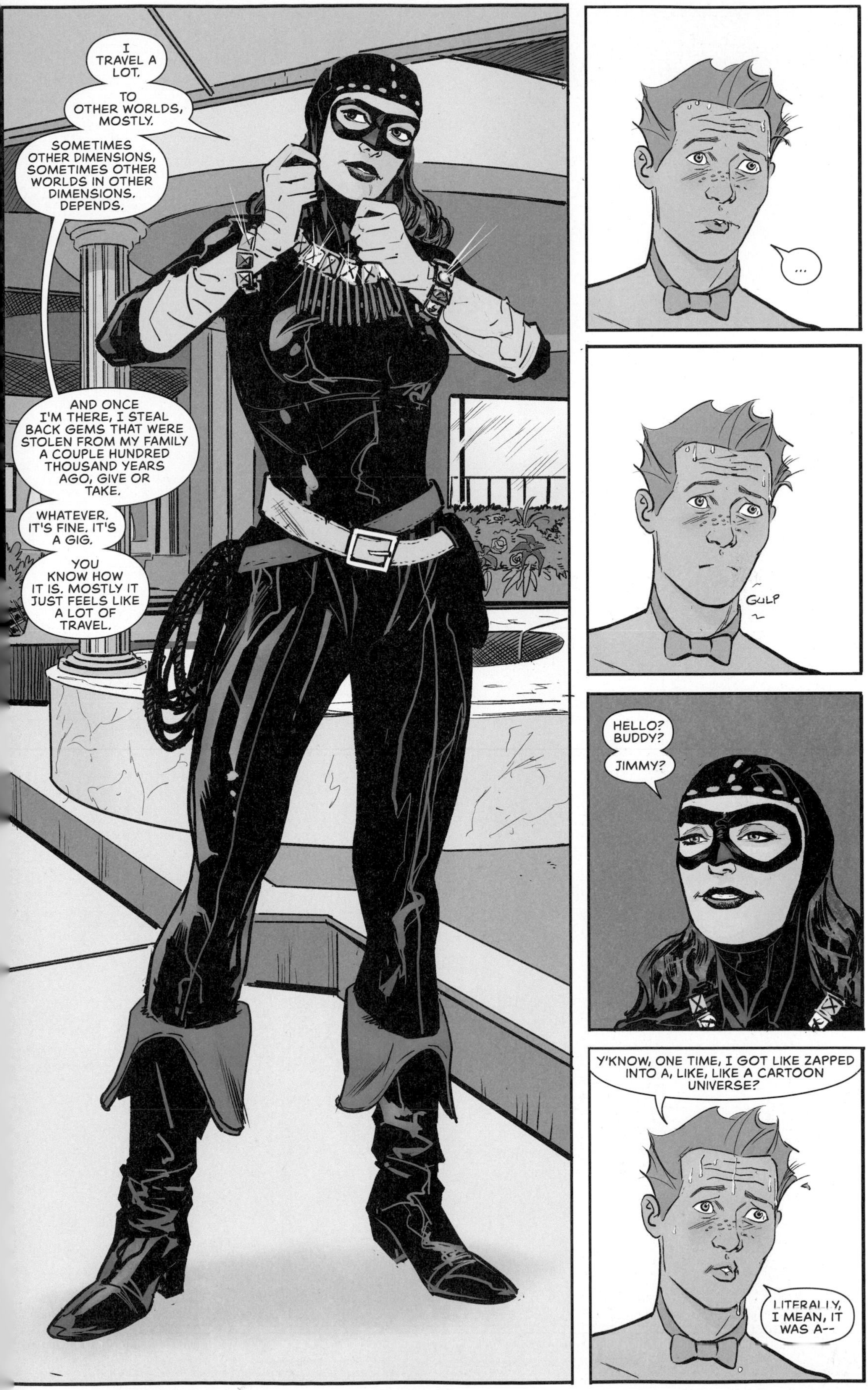
I TRAVEL A LOT.
TO OTHER WORLDS, MOSTLY.
SOMETIMES OTHER DIMENSIONS, SOMETIMES OTHER WORLDS IN OTHER DIMENSIONS. DEPENDS.
AND ONCE I'M THERE, I STEAL BACK GEMS THAT WERE STOLEN FROM MY FAMILY A COUPLE HUNDRED THOUSAND YEARS AGO, GIVE OR TAKE.
WHATEVER. IT'S FINE. IT'S A GIG.
YOU KNOW HOW IT IS. MOSTLY IT JUST FEELS LIKE A LOT OF TRAVEL.
...
GULP
HELLO? BUDDY?
JIMMY?
Y'KNOW, ONE TIME, I GOT LIKE ZAPPED INTO A, LIKE, LIKE A CARTOON UNIVERSE?
LITERALLY, I MEAN, IT WAS A--

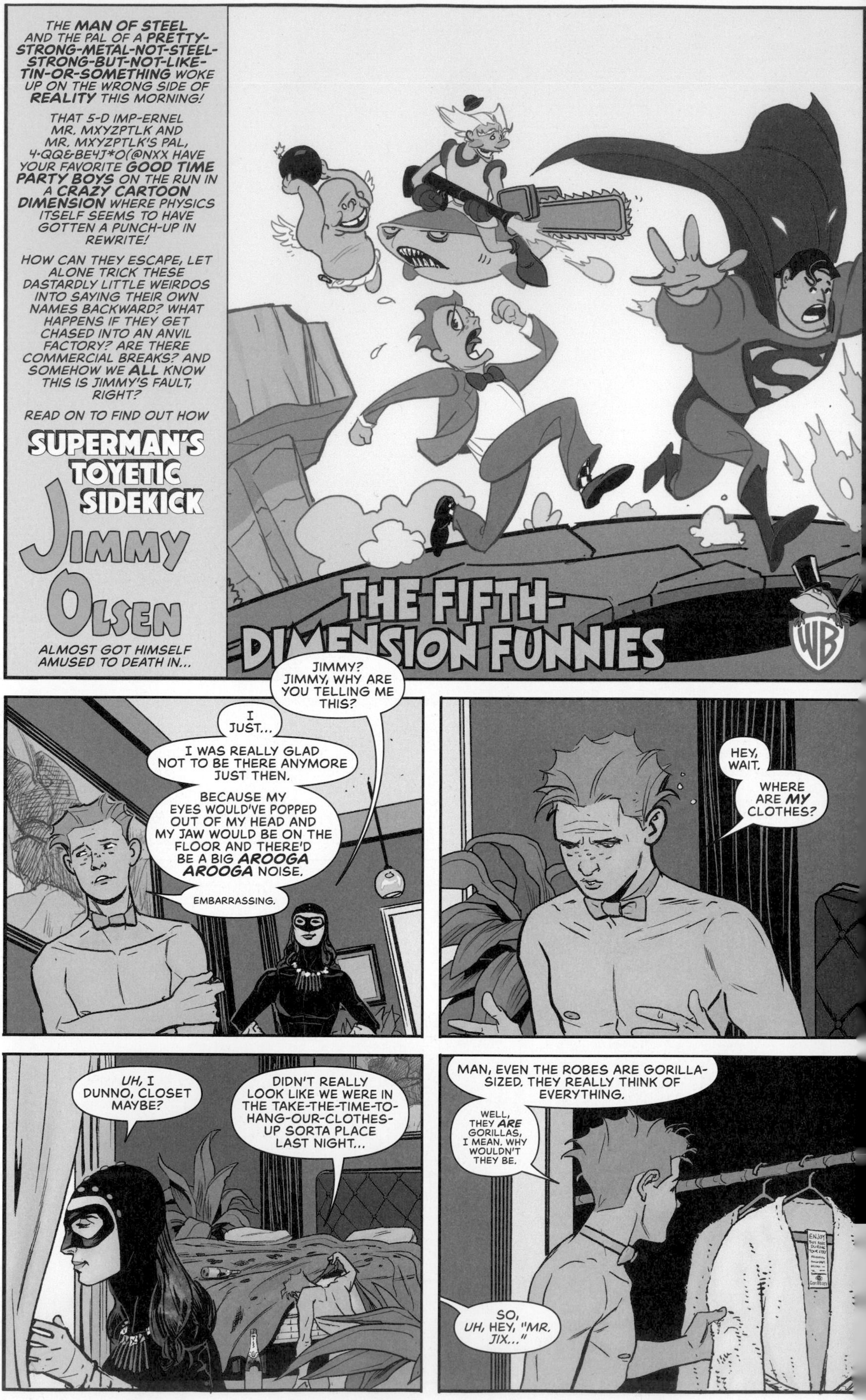
THE MAN OF STEEL AND THE PAL OF A PRETTY-STRONG-METAL-NOT-STEEL-STRONG-BUT-NOT-LIKE-TIN-OR-SOMETHING WOKE UP ON THE WRONG SIDE OF REALITY THIS MORNING!
THAT 5-D IMP-ERNEL MR. MXYZPTLK AND MR. MXYZPTLK'S PAL, 4-QQ&BE4J*O(@NXX HAVE YOUR FAVORITE GOOD TIME PARTY BOYS ON THE RUN IN A CRAZY CARTOON DIMENSION WHERE PHYSICS ITSELF SEEMS TO HAVE GOTTEN A PUNCH-UP IN REWRITE!
HOW CAN THEY ESCAPE, LET ALONE TRICK THESE DASTARDLY LITTLE WEIRDOS INTO SAYING THEIR OWN NAMES BACKWARD? WHAT HAPPENS IF THEY GET CHASED INTO AN ANVIL FACTORY? ARE THERE COMMERCIAL BREAKS? AND SOMEHOW WE ALL KNOW THIS IS JIMMY'S FAULT, RIGHT?
READ ON TO FIND OUT HOW
SUPERMAN'S TOYETIC SIDEKICK
JIMMY OLSEN
ALMOST GOT HIMSELF AMUSED TO DEATH IN...
THE FIFTH-DIMENSION FUNNIES
WB
JIMMY? JIMMY, WHY ARE YOU TELLING ME THIS?
I JUST...
I WAS REALLY GLAD NOT TO BE THERE ANYMORE JUST THEN.
BECAUSE MY EYES WOULD'VE POPPED OUT OF MY HEAD AND MY JAW WOULD BE ON THE FLOOR AND THERE'D BE A BIG AROOGA AROOGA NOISE.
EMBARRASSING.
HEY, WAIT.
WHERE ARE MY CLOTHES?
UH, I DUNNO, CLOSET MAYBE?
DIDN'T REALLY LOOK LIKE WE WERE IN THE TAKE-THE-TIME-TO-HANG-OUR-CLOTHES-UP SORTA PLACE LAST NIGHT...
MAN, EVEN THE ROBES ARE GORILLA-SIZED. THEY REALLY THINK OF EVERYTHING.
WELL, THEY ARE GORILLAS, I MEAN. WHY WOULDN'T THEY BE.
SO, UH, HEY, "MR. JIX..."

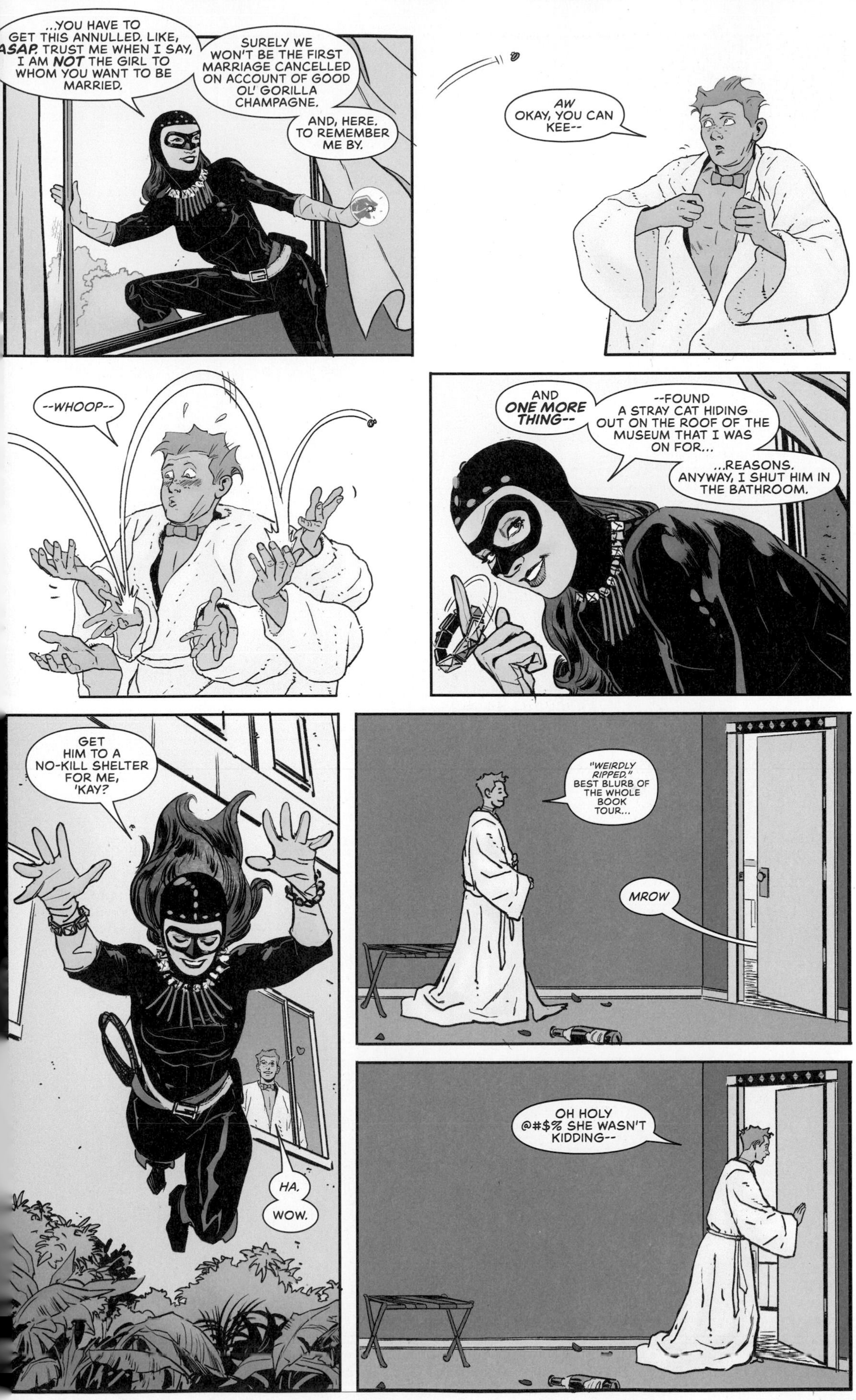
...YOU HAVE TO GET THIS ANNULLED. LIKE, ASAP. TRUST ME WHEN I SAY, I AM NOT THE GIRL TO WHOM YOU WANT TO BE MARRIED.
SURELY WE WON'T BE THE FIRST MARRIAGE CANCELLED ON ACCOUNT OF GOOD OL' GORILLA CHAMPAGNE.
AND, HERE. TO REMEMBER ME BY.
AW OKAY, YOU CAN KEE--
--WHOOP--
AND ONE MORE THING--
--FOUND A STRAY CAT HIDING OUT ON THE ROOF OF THE MUSEUM THAT I WAS ON FOR...
...REASONS. ANYWAY, I SHUT HIM IN THE BATHROOM.
GET HIM TO A NO-KILL SHELTER FOR ME, 'KAY?
HA.
WOW.
"WEIRDLY RIPPED." BEST BLURB OF THE WHOLE BOOK TOUR...
MROW
OH HOLY @#$% SHE WASN'T KIDDING--

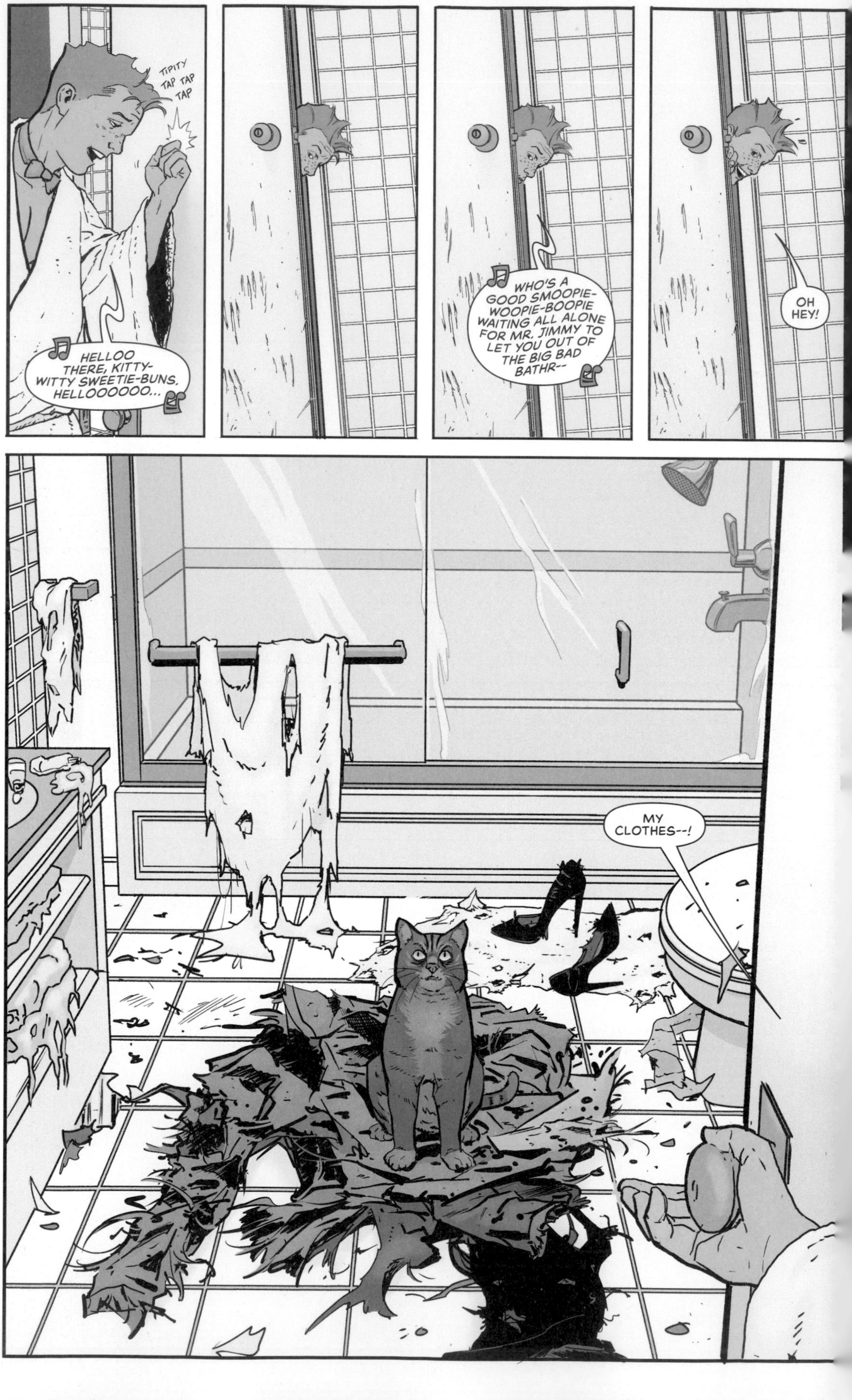
TIPITY TAP TAP TAP
HELLOO THERE, KITTY-WITTY SWEETIE-BUNS. HELLOOOOOO...
WHO'S A GOOD SMOOPIE-WOOPIE-BOOPIE WAITING ALL ALONE FOR MR. JIMMY TO LET YOU OUT OF THE BIG BAD BATHR--
OH HEY!
MY CLOTHES--!

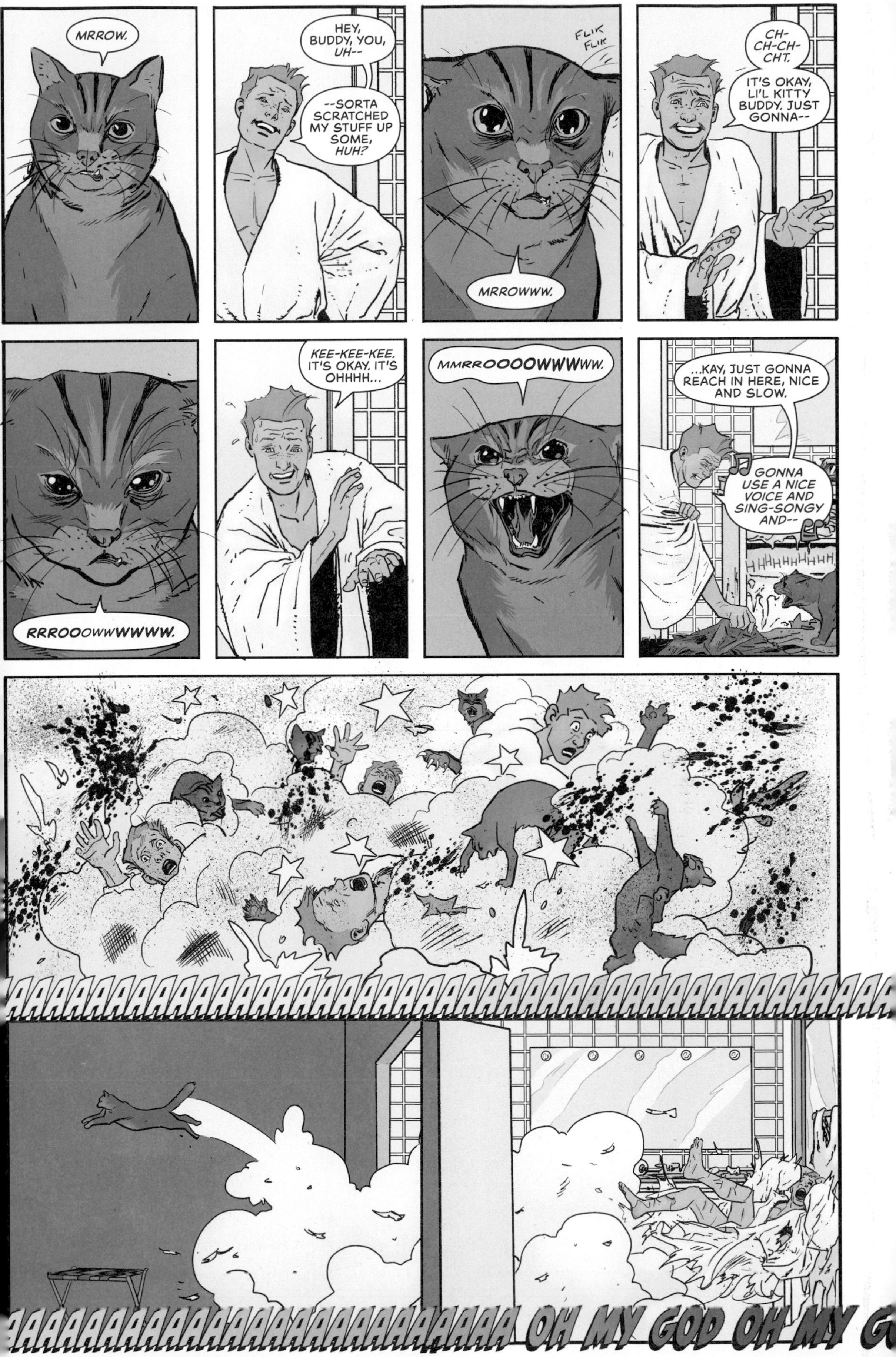
MRROW.
HEY, BUDDY, YOU, UH--
--SORTA SCRATCHED MY STUFF UP SOME, HUH?
FLIK FLIK
MRROWWW.
CH- CH-CH-CHT.
IT'S OKAY, LI'L KITTY BUDDY. JUST GONNA--
RRROOOWWWWWW.
KEE-KEE-KEE. IT'S OKAY. IT'S OHHHH...
MMRROOOOWWWWW.
...KAY, JUST GONNA REACH IN HERE, NICE AND SLOW.
GONNA USE A NICE VOICE AND SING-SONGY AND--
AAAAAAAAAAAAAAAAAAAAAAAAAAAAAAAAAAAAAAAAAA
AAAAAAAAAAAAAAAAAAAAAAAAAAAA OH MY GOD OH MY G

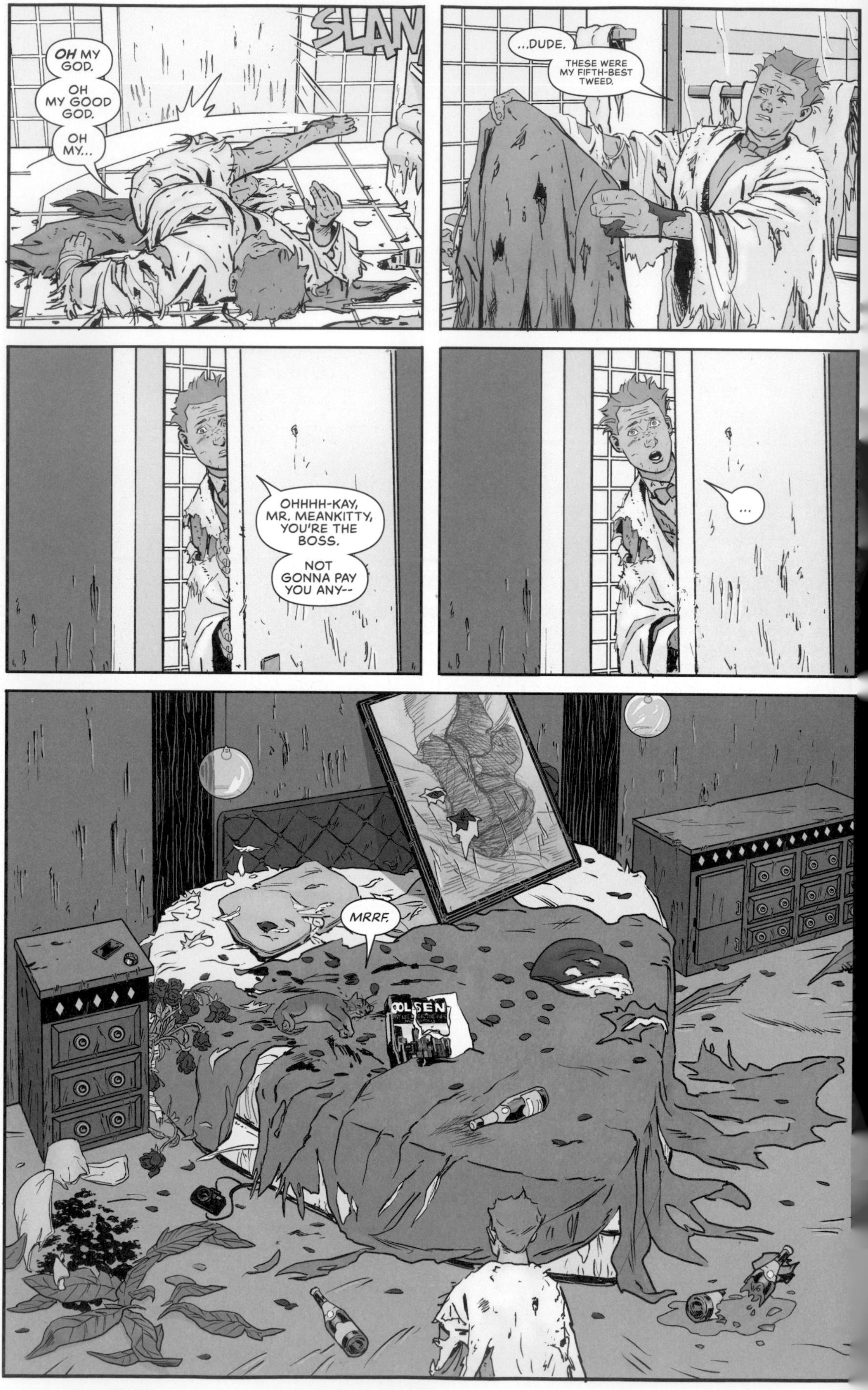
SLAM
OH MY GOD.
OH MY GOOD GOD.
OH MY...
...DUDE.
THESE WERE MY FIFTH-BEST TWEED.
OHHHH-KAY, MR. MEANKITTY, YOU'RE THE BOSS.
NOT GONNA PAY YOU ANY--
...
MRRF.

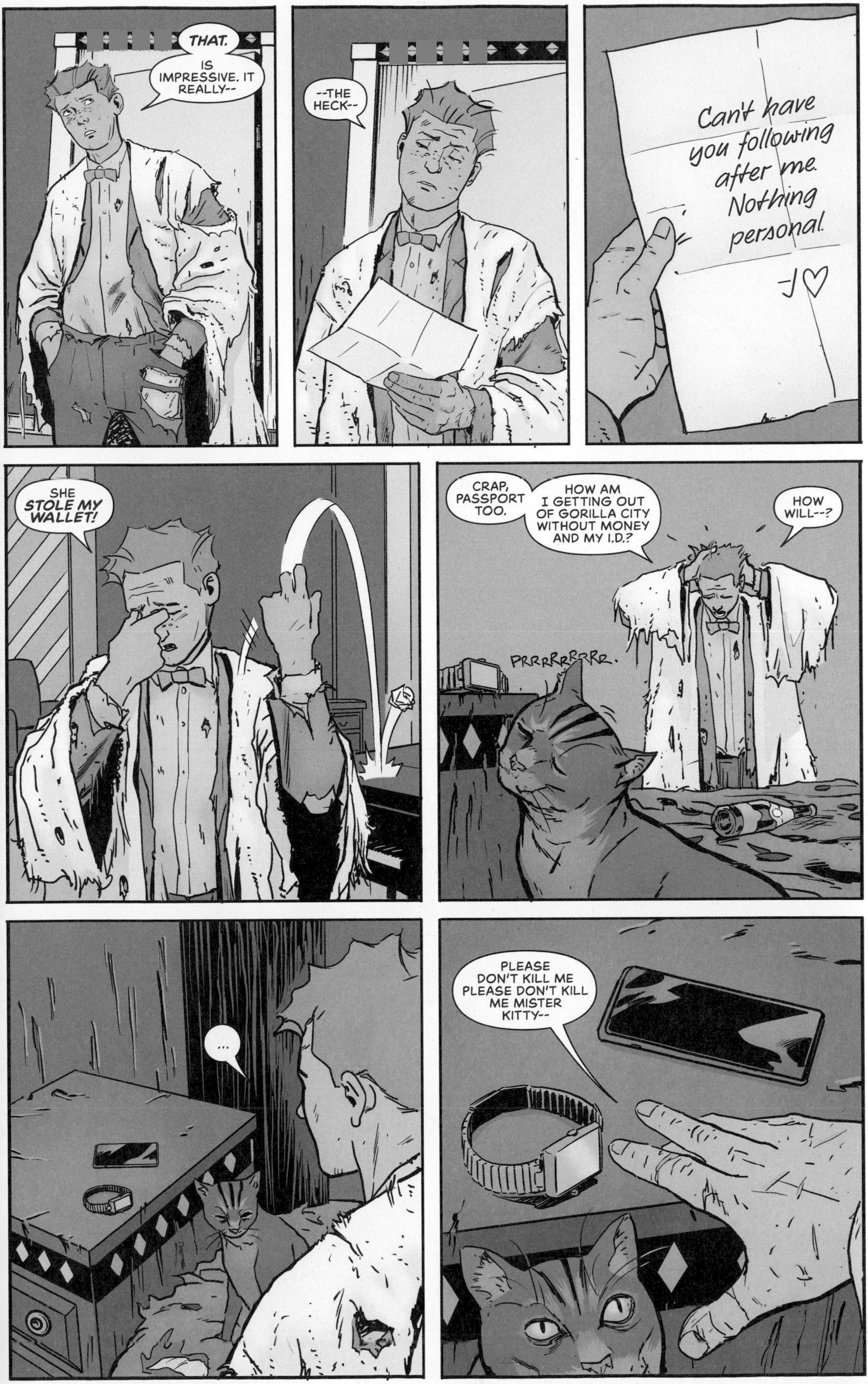
THAT.
IS IMPRESSIVE. IT REALLY--
--THE HECK--
Can't have you following after me. Nothing personal.
-J ♡
SHE STOLE MY WALLET!
CRAP, PASSPORT TOO.
HOW AM I GETTING OUT OF GORILLA CITY WITHOUT MONEY AND MY I.D.?
HOW WILL--?
PRRRRRRRRRR.
...
PLEASE DON'T KILL ME PLEASE DON'T KILL ME MISTER KITTY--

YOINK!

THIS DOESN'T EVEN RATE IN MY, LIKE, TOP *TWENTY* CALLS OF SHAME, MR. SHREDDIE VEDDER.

SO DON'T YOU JUDGE ME.

WORRF.

ZEEZEEZEEZEEZEEZEEZEEZEEZE

OH NO! HANG ON HANG ON--

HRRK   HRRK

HHHRRRPH

RRPPH.

KK   KK

--NONONONONO DON'T BARF ON THE--

EEZEEZEEZEEZEEZEEZEEZEEZEEZEEZEEZEEZE

BUUUOOOKRGG

*JIMMY OLSEN'S SUPERMAN SIGNAL WATCH WAS PATCHED WITH A KRYPTONITE PROXIMITY FIRMWARE UPGRADE, ALERTING THE MAN OF STEEL THAT PAL WHENEVER SOMEONE IS CAUSING HIM TROUBLE WITH A CAPITAL K! --Editor

RT.RRT.RRTRRT.RRT.RRTRRT.RRTRRT.RRTRRT.R

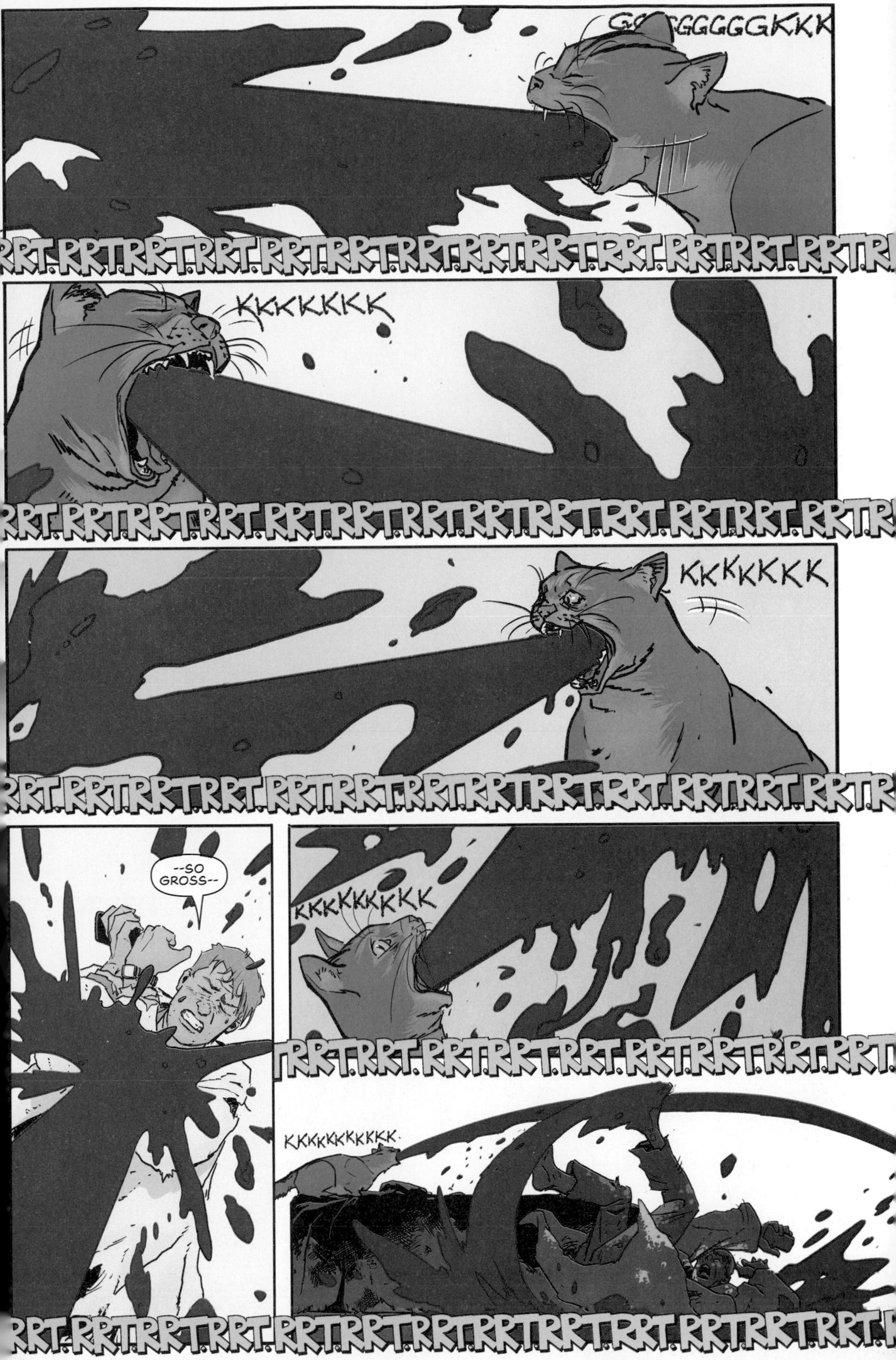

GGGGGGGKKK
RRT. RRT. RRT. RRT. RRT. RRT. RRT. RRT. RRT. RRT. RRT. RRT. RRT.
KKKKKKK
RRT. RRT. RRT. RRT. RRT. RRT. RRT. RRT. RRT. RRT. RRT. RRT. RRT.
KKKKKKK
RRT. RRT. RRT. RRT. RRT. RRT. RRT. RRT. RRT. RRT. RRT. RRT. RRT.
--SO GROSS--
KKKKKKKKK
RRT. RRT. RRT. RRT. RRT. RRT. RRT. RRT. RRT. RRT.
KKKKKKKKKK
RRT. RRT. RRT. RRT. RRT. RRT. RRT. RRT. RRT. RRT. RRT. RRT. RRT. RRT.

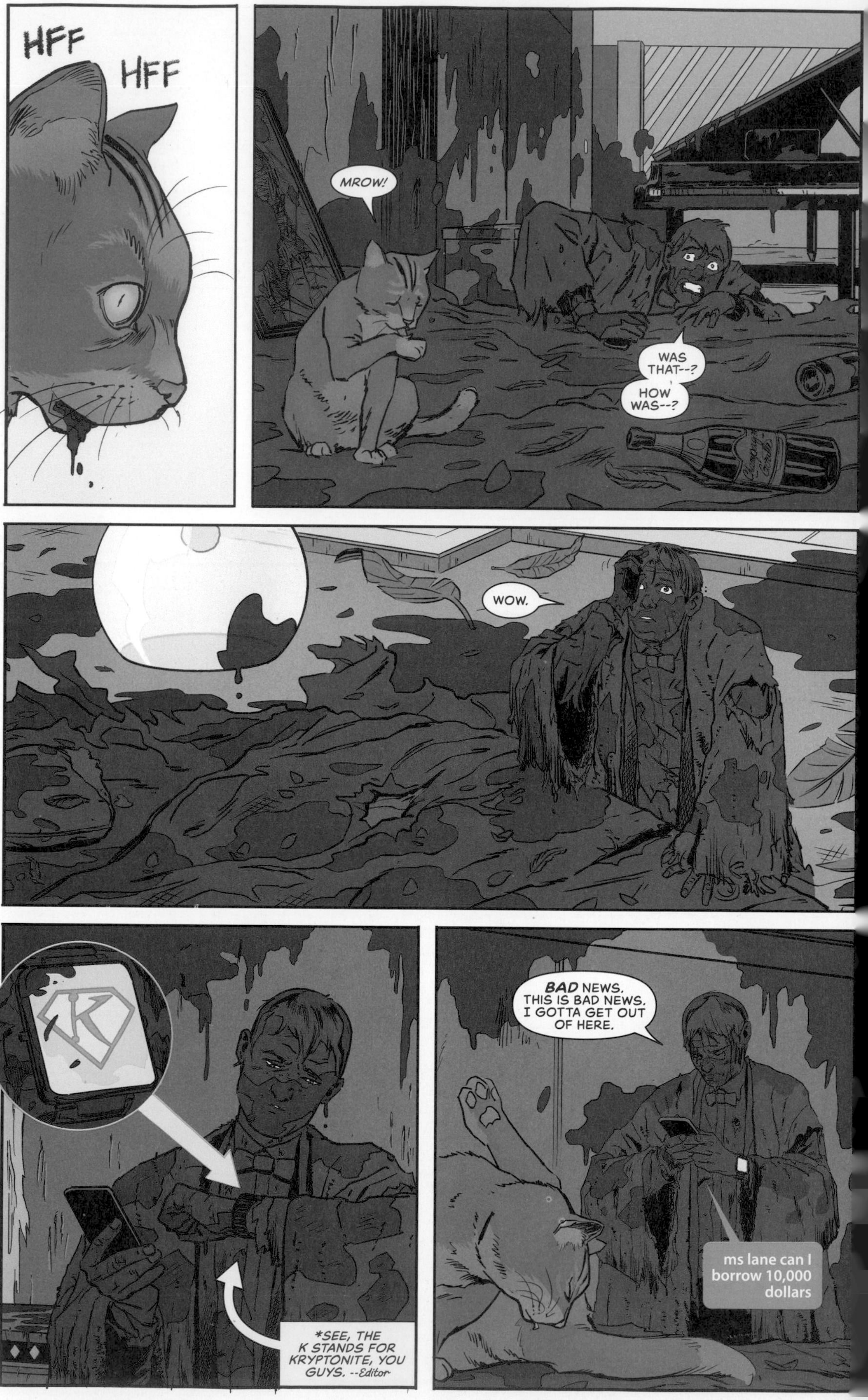
HFF
HFF
MROW!
WAS THAT--?
HOW WAS--?
WOW.
*SEE, THE K STANDS FOR KRYPTONITE, YOU GUYS. --Editor
BAD NEWS. THIS IS BAD NEWS. I GOTTA GET OUT OF HERE.
ms lane can I borrow 10,000 dollars

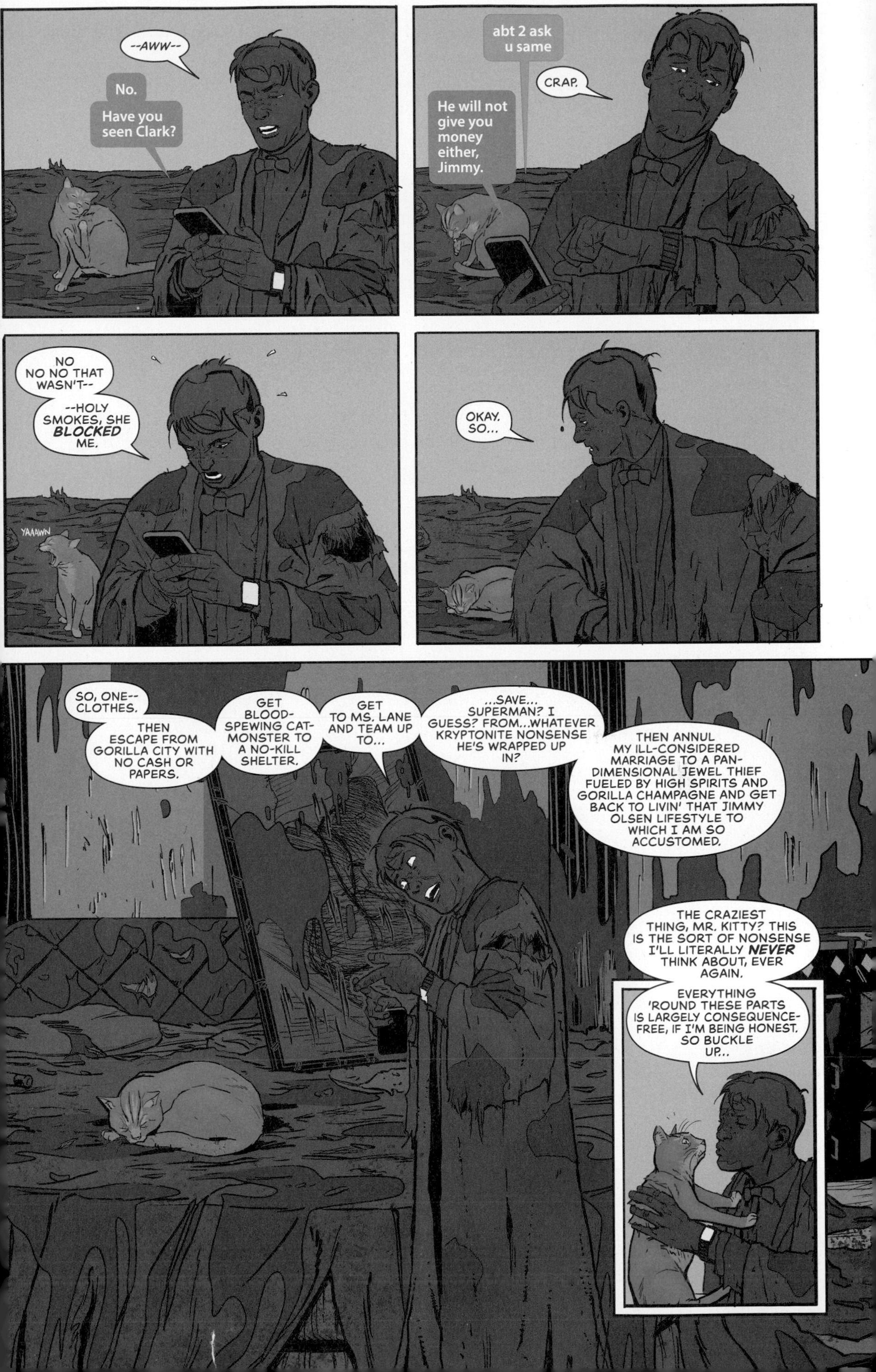
--AWW--
No.
Have you seen Clark?
abt 2 ask u same
He will not give you money either, Jimmy.
CRAP.
NO NO NO THAT WASN'T--
--HOLY SMOKES, SHE *BLOCKED* ME.
YAAAWN
OKAY. SO...
SO, ONE-- CLOTHES.
THEN ESCAPE FROM GORILLA CITY WITH NO CASH OR PAPERS.
GET BLOOD-SPEWING CAT-MONSTER TO A NO-KILL SHELTER.
GET TO MS. LANE AND TEAM UP TO...
...SAVE... SUPERMAN? I GUESS? FROM...WHATEVER KRYPTONITE NONSENSE HE'S WRAPPED UP IN?
THEN ANNUL MY ILL-CONSIDERED MARRIAGE TO A PAN-DIMENSIONAL JEWEL THIEF FUELED BY HIGH SPIRITS AND GORILLA CHAMPAGNE AND GET BACK TO LIVIN' THAT JIMMY OLSEN LIFESTYLE TO WHICH I AM SO ACCUSTOMED.
THE CRAZIEST THING, MR. KITTY? THIS IS THE SORT OF NONSENSE I'LL LITERALLY *NEVER* THINK ABOUT, EVER AGAIN.
EVERYTHING 'ROUND THESE PARTS IS LARGELY CONSEQUENCE-FREE, IF I'M BEING HONEST. SO BUCKLE UP...

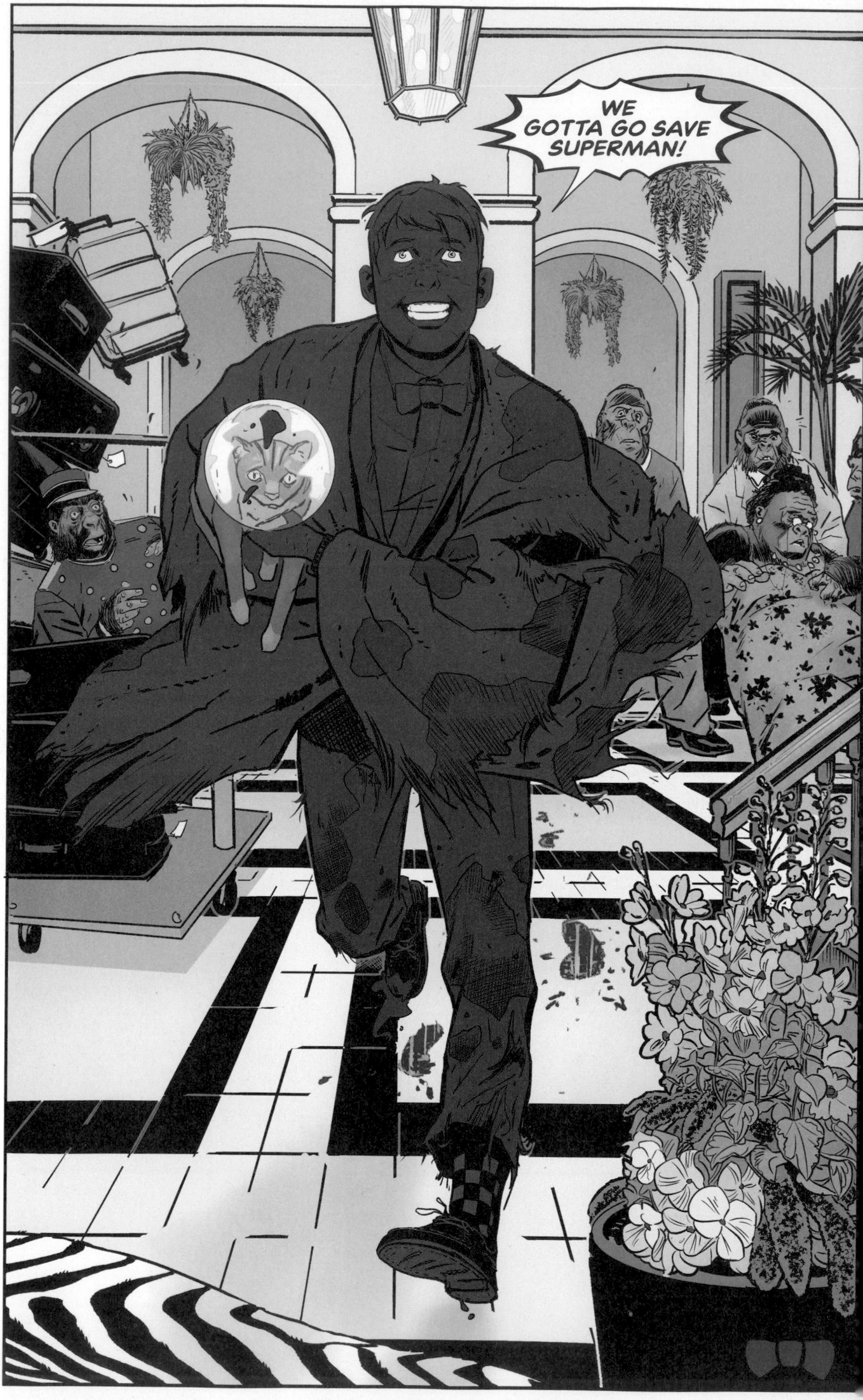
WE GOTTA GO SAVE SUPERMAN!

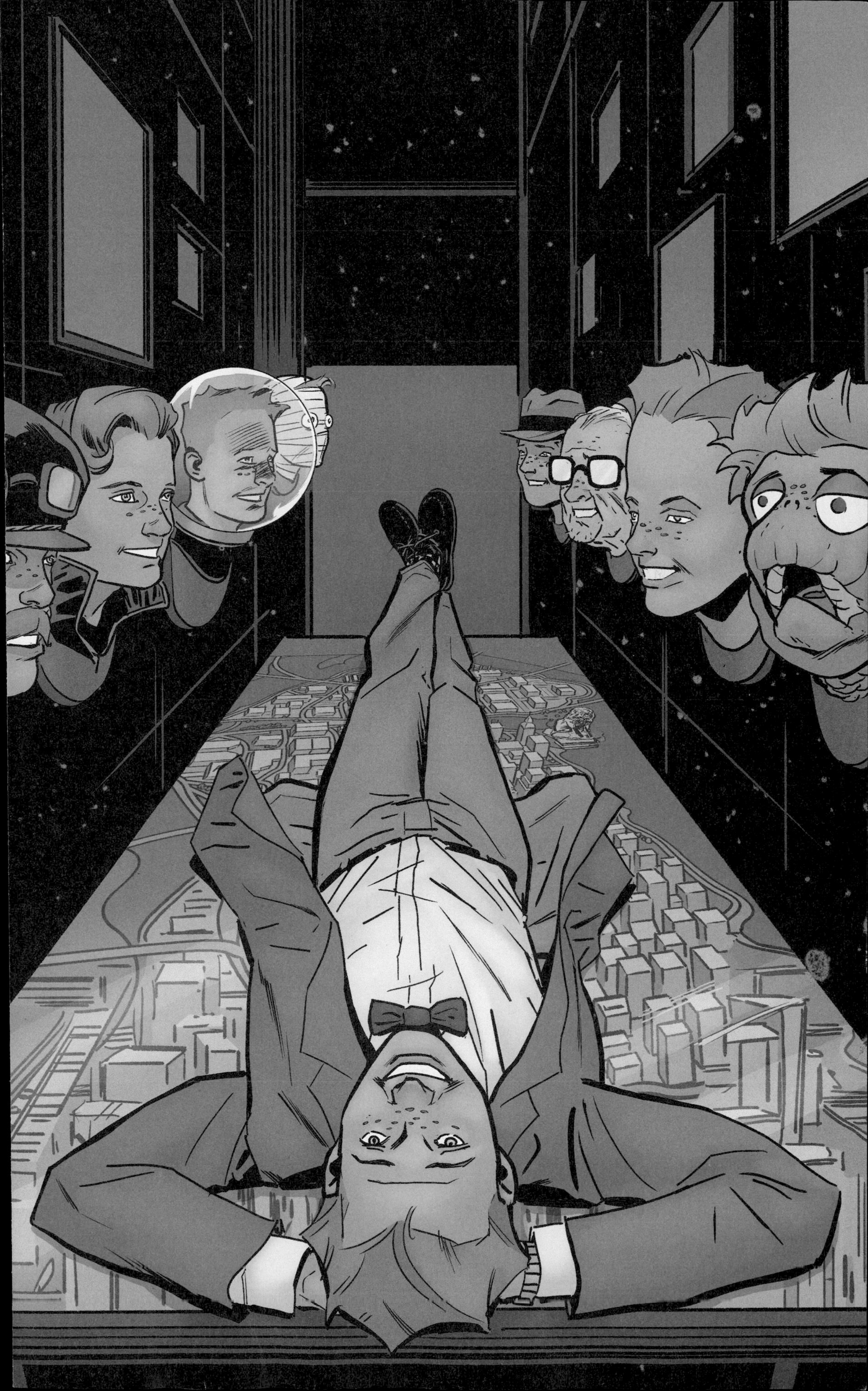

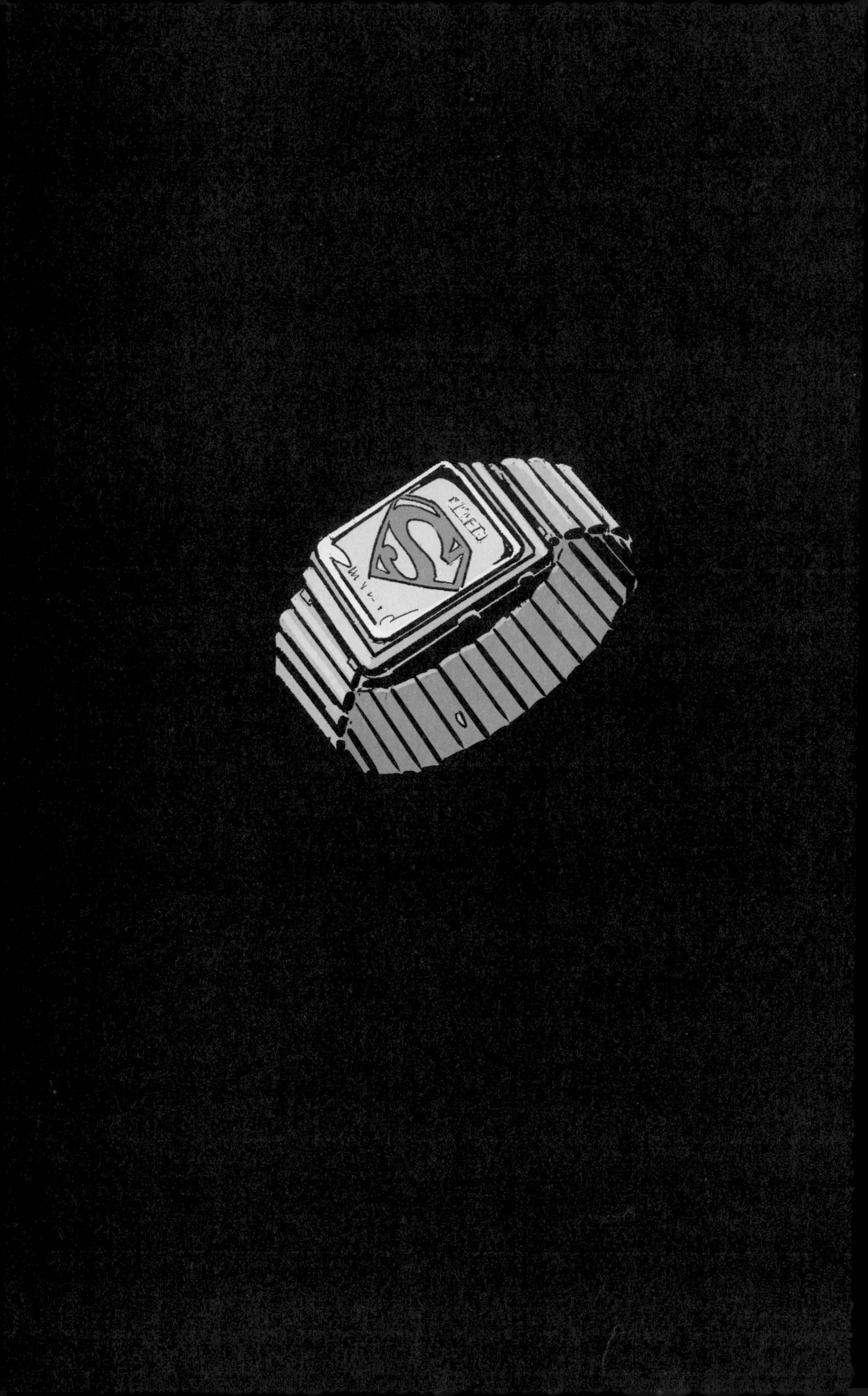

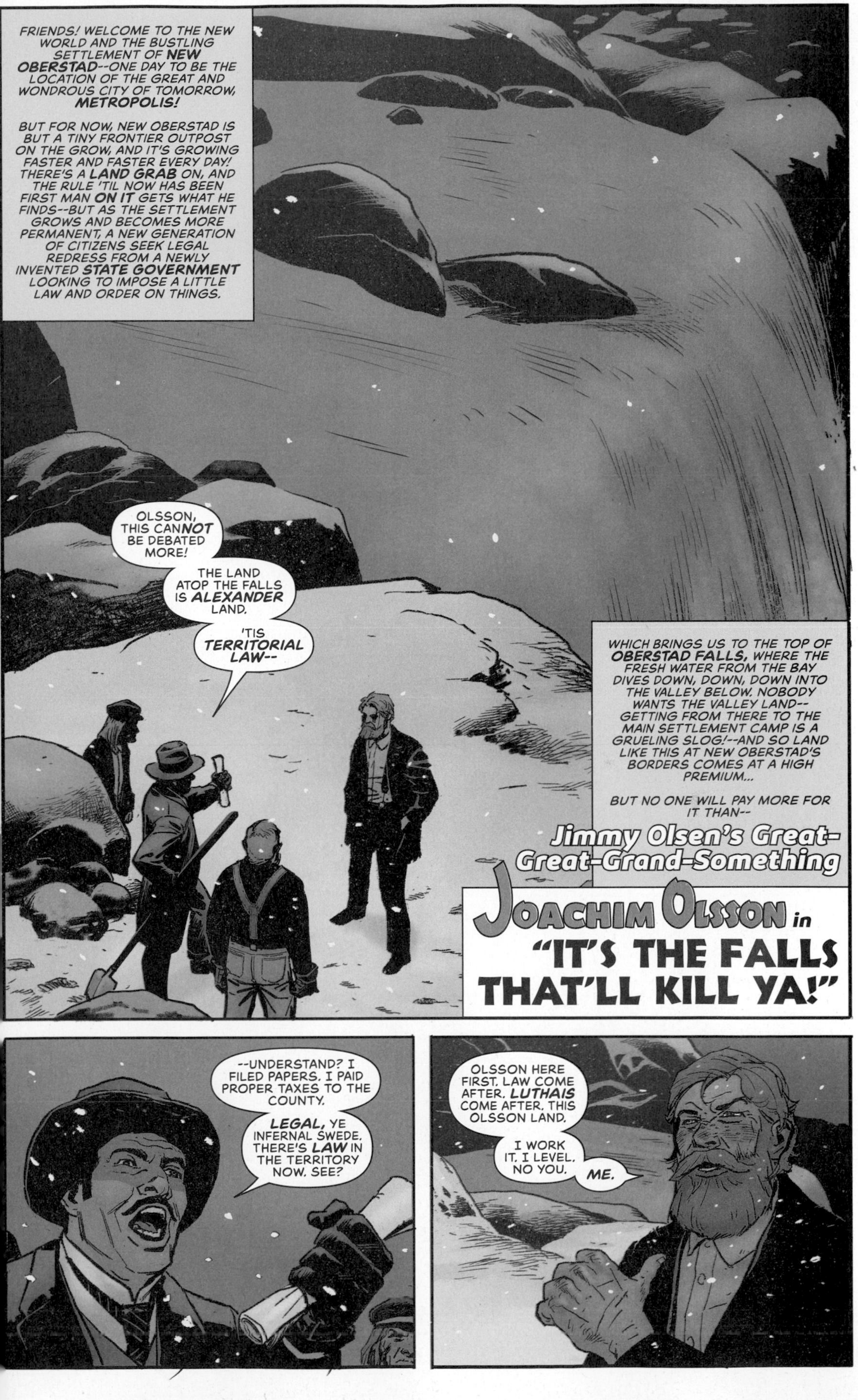
FRIENDS! WELCOME TO THE NEW WORLD AND THE BUSTLING SETTLEMENT OF NEW OBERSTAD--ONE DAY TO BE THE LOCATION OF THE GREAT AND WONDROUS CITY OF TOMORROW, METROPOLIS!
BUT FOR NOW, NEW OBERSTAD IS BUT A TINY FRONTIER OUTPOST ON THE GROW, AND IT'S GROWING FASTER AND FASTER EVERY DAY! THERE'S A LAND GRAB ON, AND THE RULE 'TIL NOW HAS BEEN FIRST MAN ON IT GETS WHAT HE FINDS--BUT AS THE SETTLEMENT GROWS AND BECOMES MORE PERMANENT, A NEW GENERATION OF CITIZENS SEEK LEGAL REDRESS FROM A NEWLY INVENTED STATE GOVERNMENT LOOKING TO IMPOSE A LITTLE LAW AND ORDER ON THINGS.
OLSSON, THIS CANNOT BE DEBATED MORE!
THE LAND ATOP THE FALLS IS ALEXANDER LAND.
'TIS TERRITORIAL LAW--
WHICH BRINGS US TO THE TOP OF OBERSTAD FALLS, WHERE THE FRESH WATER FROM THE BAY DIVES DOWN, DOWN, DOWN INTO THE VALLEY BELOW. NOBODY WANTS THE VALLEY LAND--GETTING FROM THERE TO THE MAIN SETTLEMENT CAMP IS A GRUELING SLOG!--AND SO LAND LIKE THIS AT NEW OBERSTAD'S BORDERS COMES AT A HIGH PREMIUM...
BUT NO ONE WILL PAY MORE FOR IT THAN--
Jimmy Olsen's Great-Great-Grand-Something
JOACHIM OLSSON in
"IT'S THE FALLS THAT'LL KILL YA!"
--UNDERSTAND? I FILED PAPERS. I PAID PROPER TAXES TO THE COUNTY.
LEGAL, YE INFERNAL SWEDE. THERE'S LAW IN THE TERRITORY NOW. SEE?
OLSSON HERE FIRST. LAW COME AFTER. LUTHAIS COME AFTER. THIS OLSSON LAND.
I WORK IT. I LEVEL. NO YOU.
ME.

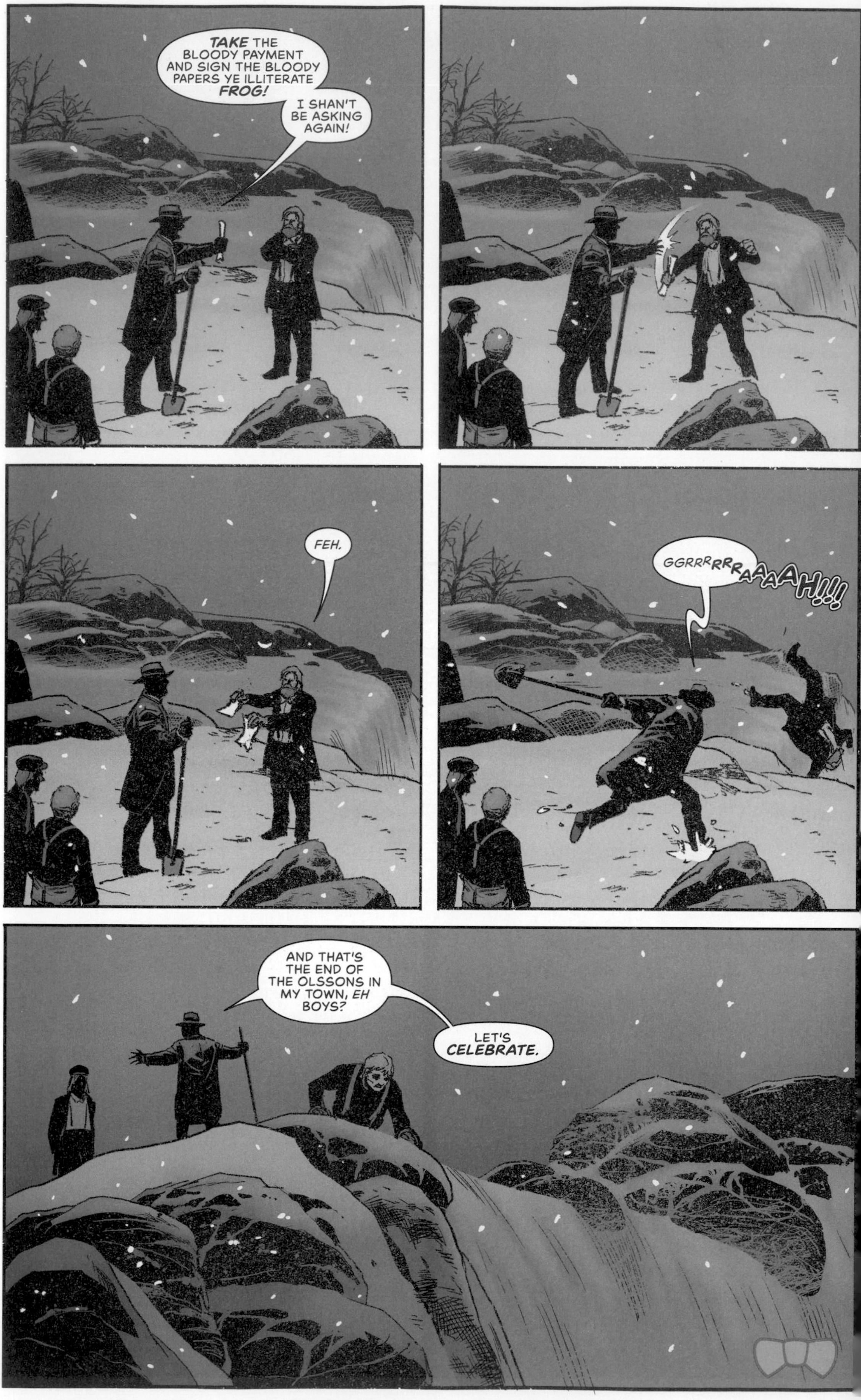
TAKE THE BLOODY PAYMENT AND SIGN THE BLOODY PAPERS YE ILLITERATE FROG!
I SHAN'T BE ASKING AGAIN!
FEH.
GGRRRRRRAAAAH!!!
AND THAT'S THE END OF THE OLSSONS IN MY TOWN, EH BOYS?
LET'S CELEBRATE.

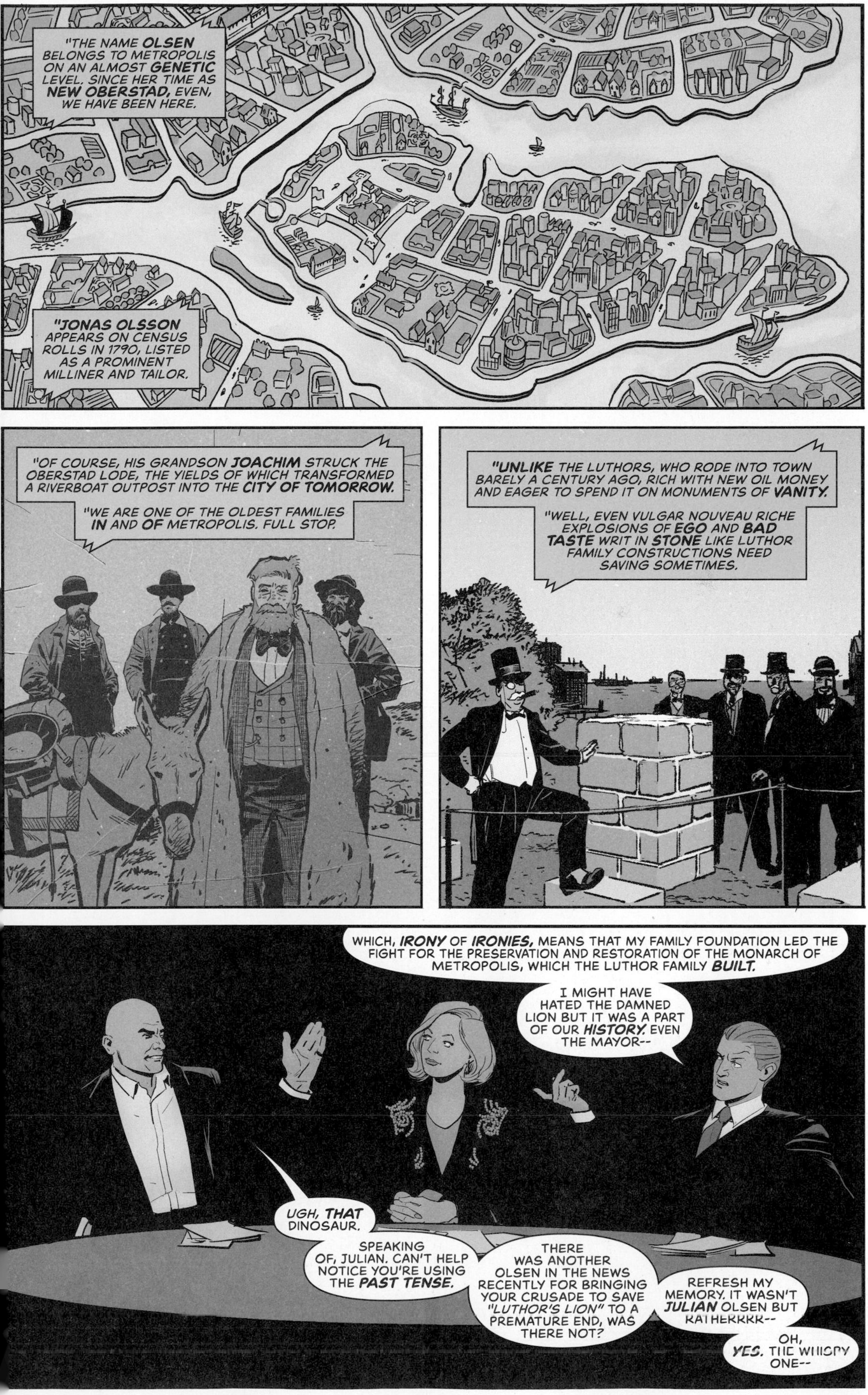
"THE NAME OLSEN BELONGS TO METROPOLIS ON AN ALMOST GENETIC LEVEL. SINCE HER TIME AS NEW OBERSTAD, EVEN, WE HAVE BEEN HERE.
"JONAS OLSSON APPEARS ON CENSUS ROLLS IN 1790, LISTED AS A PROMINENT MILLINER AND TAILOR.
"OF COURSE, HIS GRANDSON JOACHIM STRUCK THE OBERSTAD LODE, THE YIELDS OF WHICH TRANSFORMED A RIVERBOAT OUTPOST INTO THE CITY OF TOMORROW.
"WE ARE ONE OF THE OLDEST FAMILIES IN AND OF METROPOLIS. FULL STOP.
"UNLIKE THE LUTHORS, WHO RODE INTO TOWN BARELY A CENTURY AGO, RICH WITH NEW OIL MONEY AND EAGER TO SPEND IT ON MONUMENTS OF VANITY.
"WELL, EVEN VULGAR NOUVEAU RICHE EXPLOSIONS OF EGO AND BAD TASTE WRIT IN STONE LIKE LUTHOR FAMILY CONSTRUCTIONS NEED SAVING SOMETIMES.
WHICH, IRONY OF IRONIES, MEANS THAT MY FAMILY FOUNDATION LED THE FIGHT FOR THE PRESERVATION AND RESTORATION OF THE MONARCH OF METROPOLIS, WHICH THE LUTHOR FAMILY BUILT.
I MIGHT HAVE HATED THE DAMNED LION BUT IT WAS A PART OF OUR HISTORY. EVEN THE MAYOR--
UGH, THAT DINOSAUR.
SPEAKING OF, JULIAN. CAN'T HELP NOTICE YOU'RE USING THE PAST TENSE.
THERE WAS ANOTHER OLSEN IN THE NEWS RECENTLY FOR BRINGING YOUR CRUSADE TO SAVE "LUTHOR'S LION" TO A PREMATURE END, WAS THERE NOT?
REFRESH MY MEMORY. IT WASN'T JULIAN OLSEN BUT RATHERRRR--
OH, YES. THE WHISPY ONE--

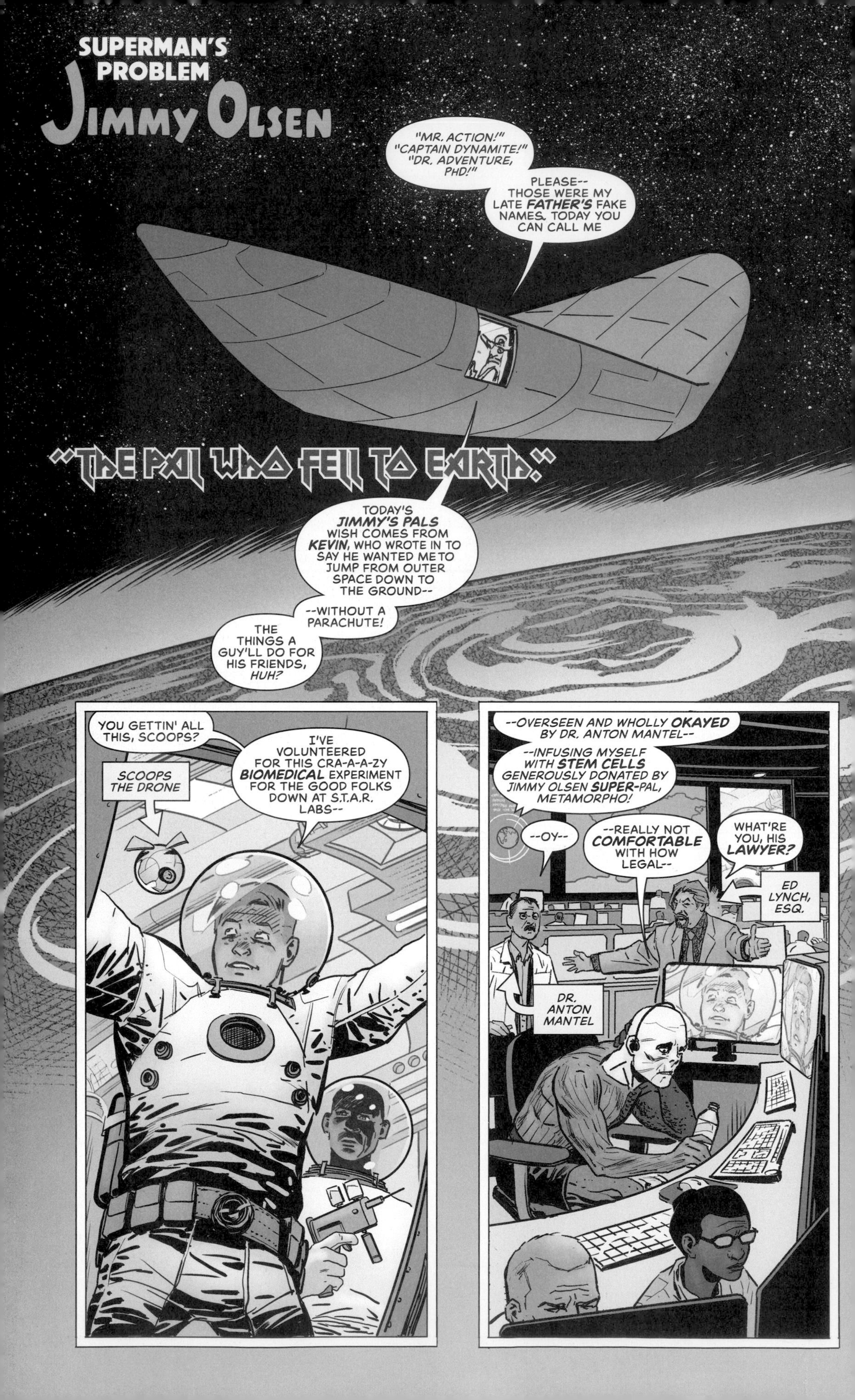
SUPERMAN'S PROBLEM
JIMMY OLSEN
"MR. ACTION!" "CAPTAIN DYNAMITE!" "DR. ADVENTURE, PHD!"
PLEASE-- THOSE WERE MY LATE FATHER'S FAKE NAMES. TODAY YOU CAN CALL ME
"THE PAL WHO FELL TO EARTH."
TODAY'S JIMMY'S PALS WISH COMES FROM KEVIN, WHO WROTE IN TO SAY HE WANTED ME TO JUMP FROM OUTER SPACE DOWN TO THE GROUND--
--WITHOUT A PARACHUTE!
THE THINGS A GUY'LL DO FOR HIS FRIENDS, HUH?
YOU GETTIN' ALL THIS, SCOOPS?
SCOOPS THE DRONE
I'VE VOLUNTEERED FOR THIS CRA-A-A-ZY BIOMEDICAL EXPERIMENT FOR THE GOOD FOLKS DOWN AT S.T.A.R. LABS--
--OVERSEEN AND WHOLLY OKAYED BY DR. ANTON MANTEL--
--INFUSING MYSELF WITH STEM CELLS GENEROUSLY DONATED BY JIMMY OLSEN SUPER-PAL, METAMORPHO!
--OY--
--REALLY NOT COMFORTABLE WITH HOW LEGAL--
WHAT'RE YOU, HIS LAWYER?
ED LYNCH, ESQ.
DR. ANTON MANTEL

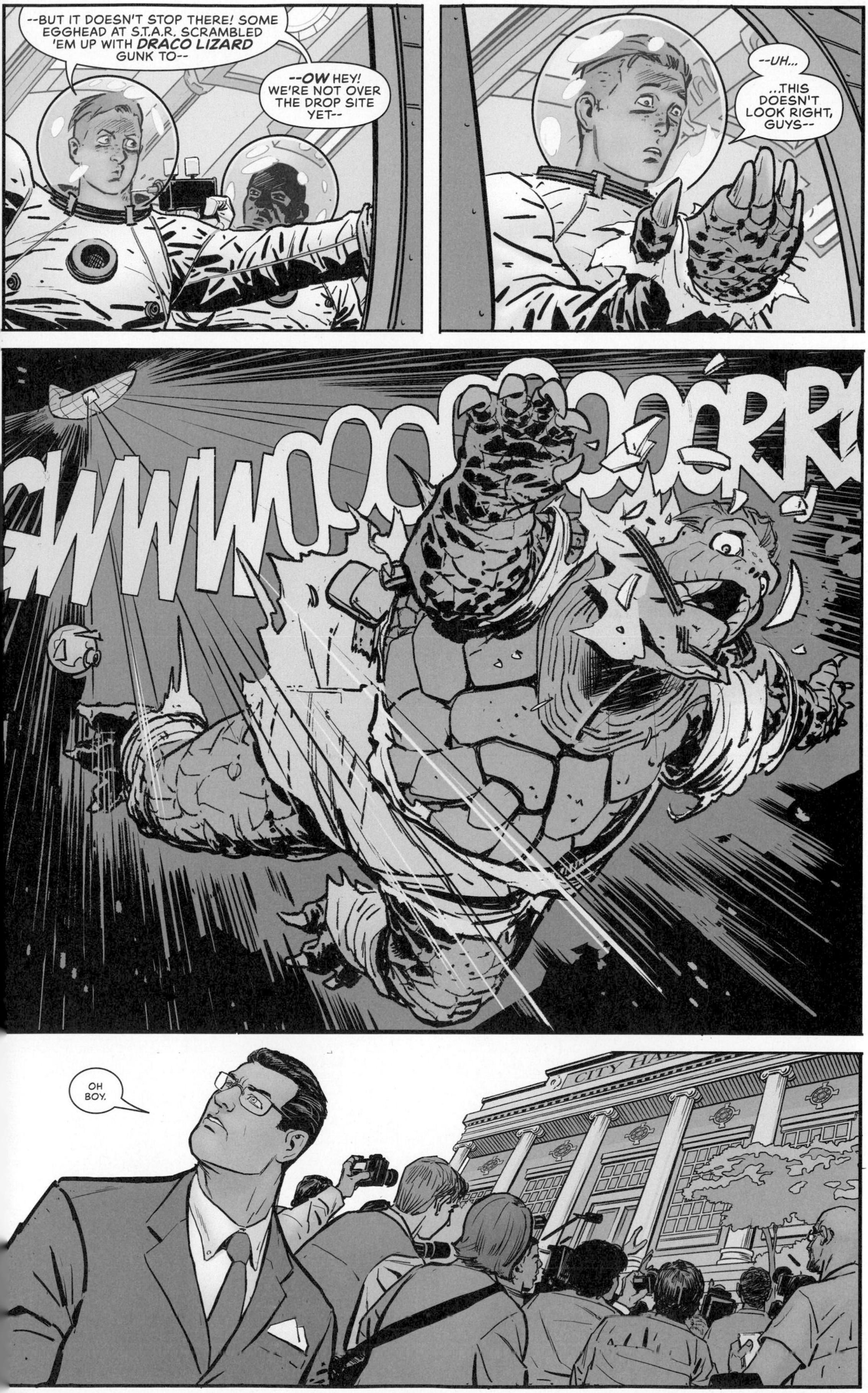
--BUT IT DOESN'T STOP THERE! SOME EGGHEAD AT S.T.A.R. SCRAMBLED 'EM UP WITH DRACO LIZARD GUNK TO--
--OW HEY! WE'RE NOT OVER THE DROP SITE YET--
--UH...
...THIS DOESN'T LOOK RIGHT, GUYS--
GWWWOOOOOOORR
OH BOY.
CITY HA

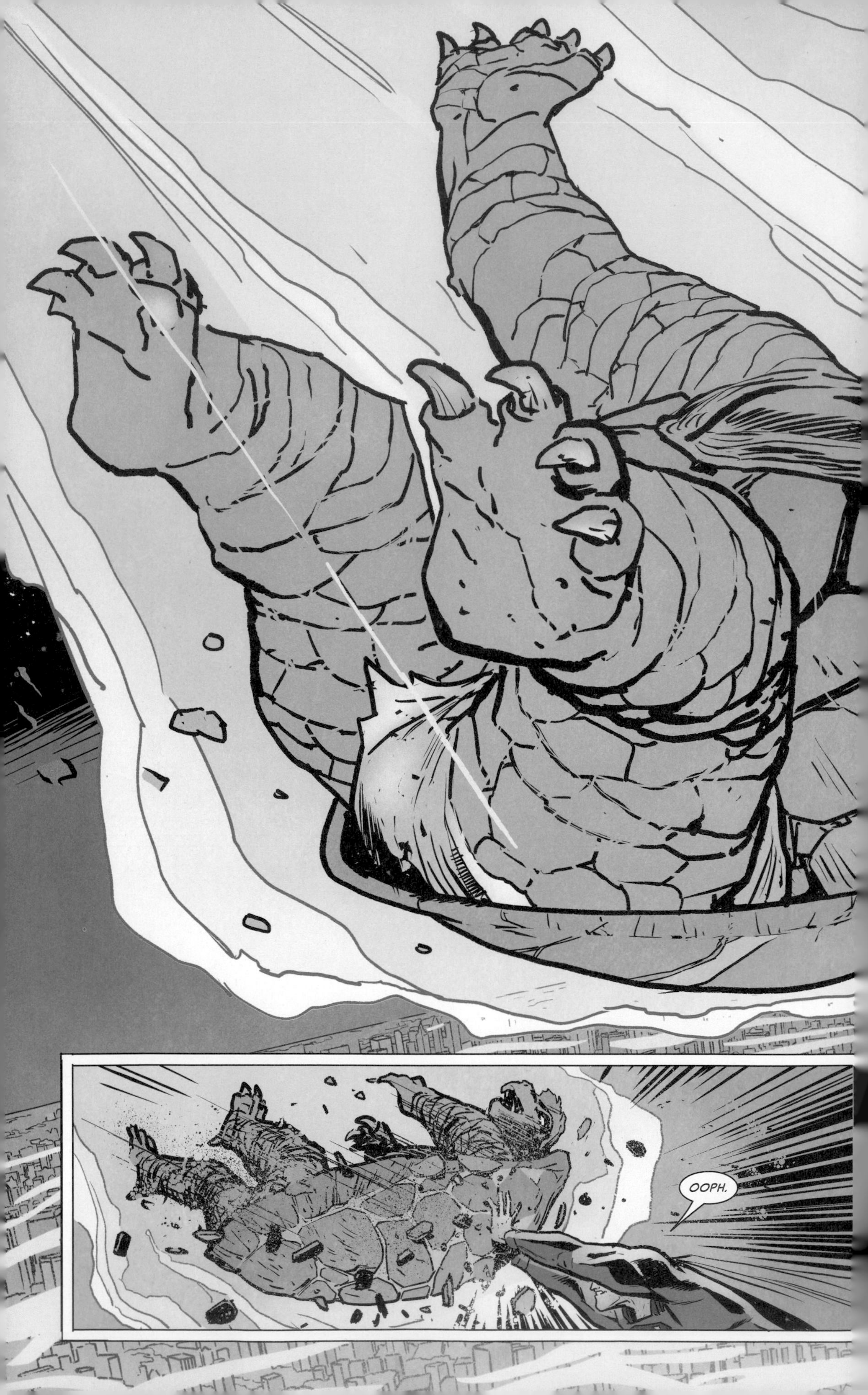
OOPH.

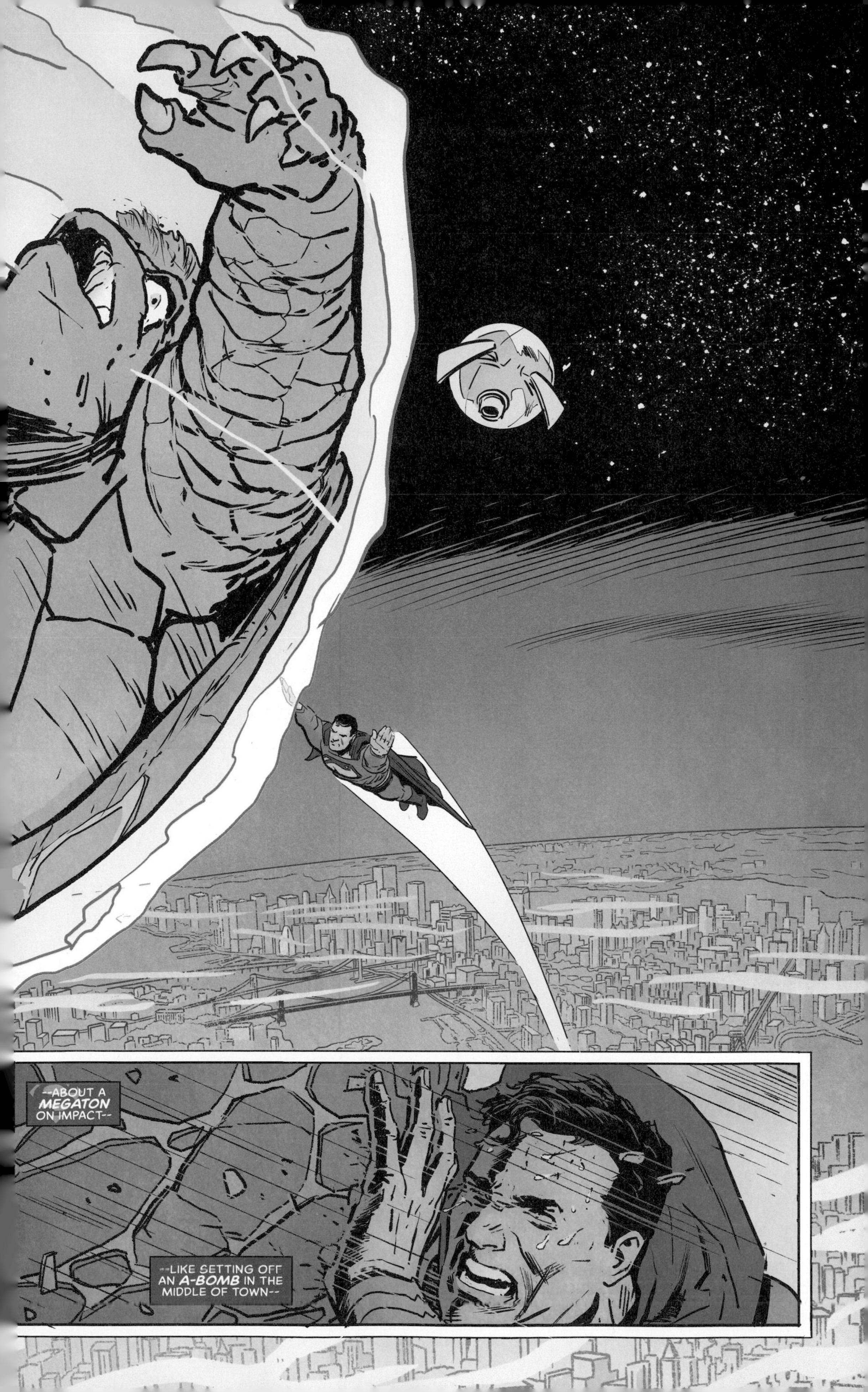
--ABOUT A *MEGATON* ON IMPACT--
--LIKE SETTING OFF AN *A-BOMB* IN THE MIDDLE OF TOWN--

--BETTER AIM US TOWARD THE *BAY*--

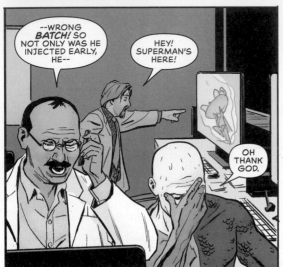

--WRONG *BATCH!* SO NOT ONLY WAS HE INJECTED EARLY, HE--

HEY! SUPERMAN'S HERE!

OH THANK GOD.

LOOKS LIKE THEY'RE HEADED TOWARD THE MONARCH OF METROPOLIS, THOUGH.

OH GOD, NO.

$A = 4\pi r^2$ AND $V = 4/3 \pi r^2$ BUT THAT'S A *SPHERE,* NOT--

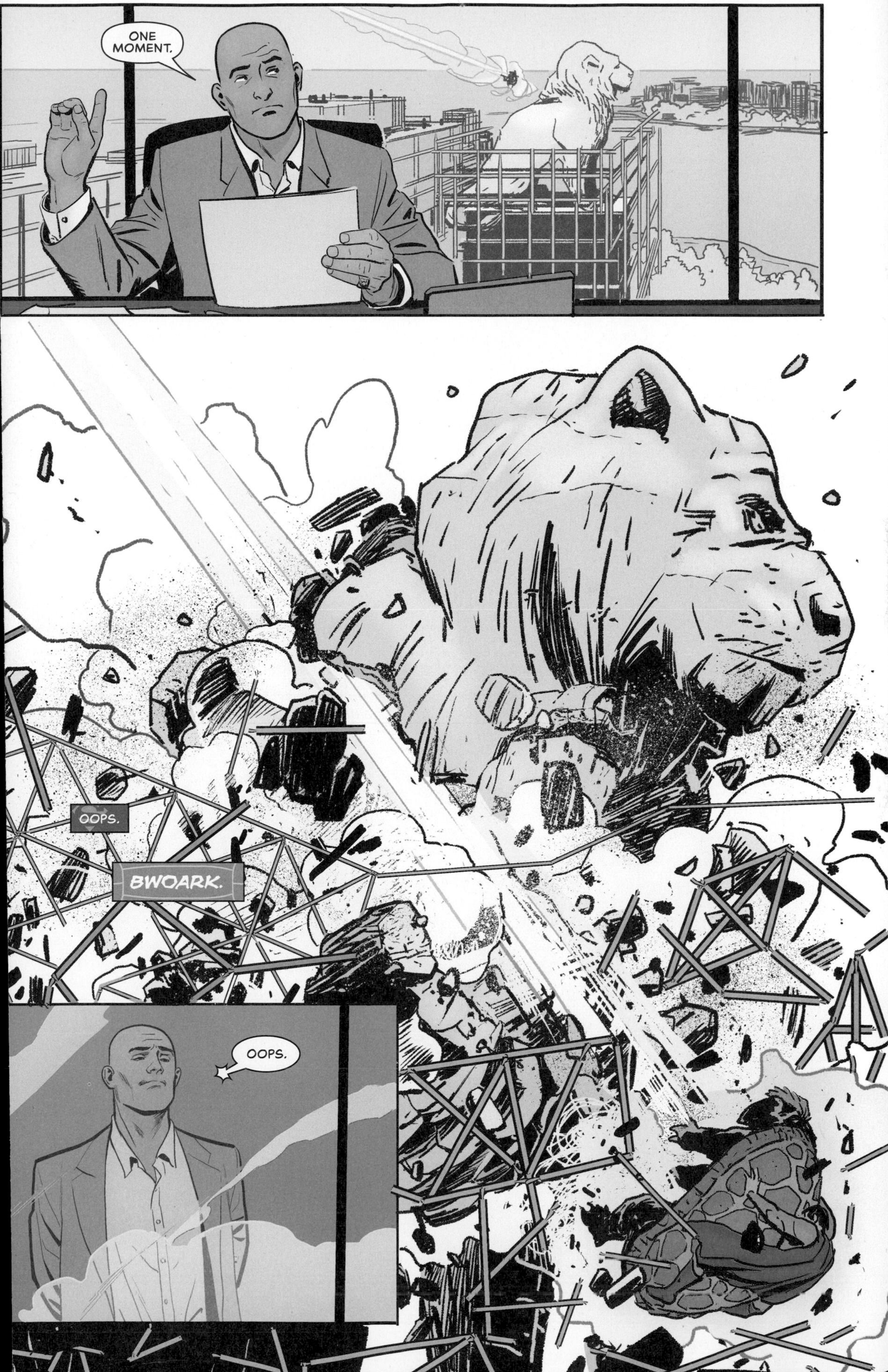
ONE MOMENT.
OOPS.
BWOARK.
OOPS.

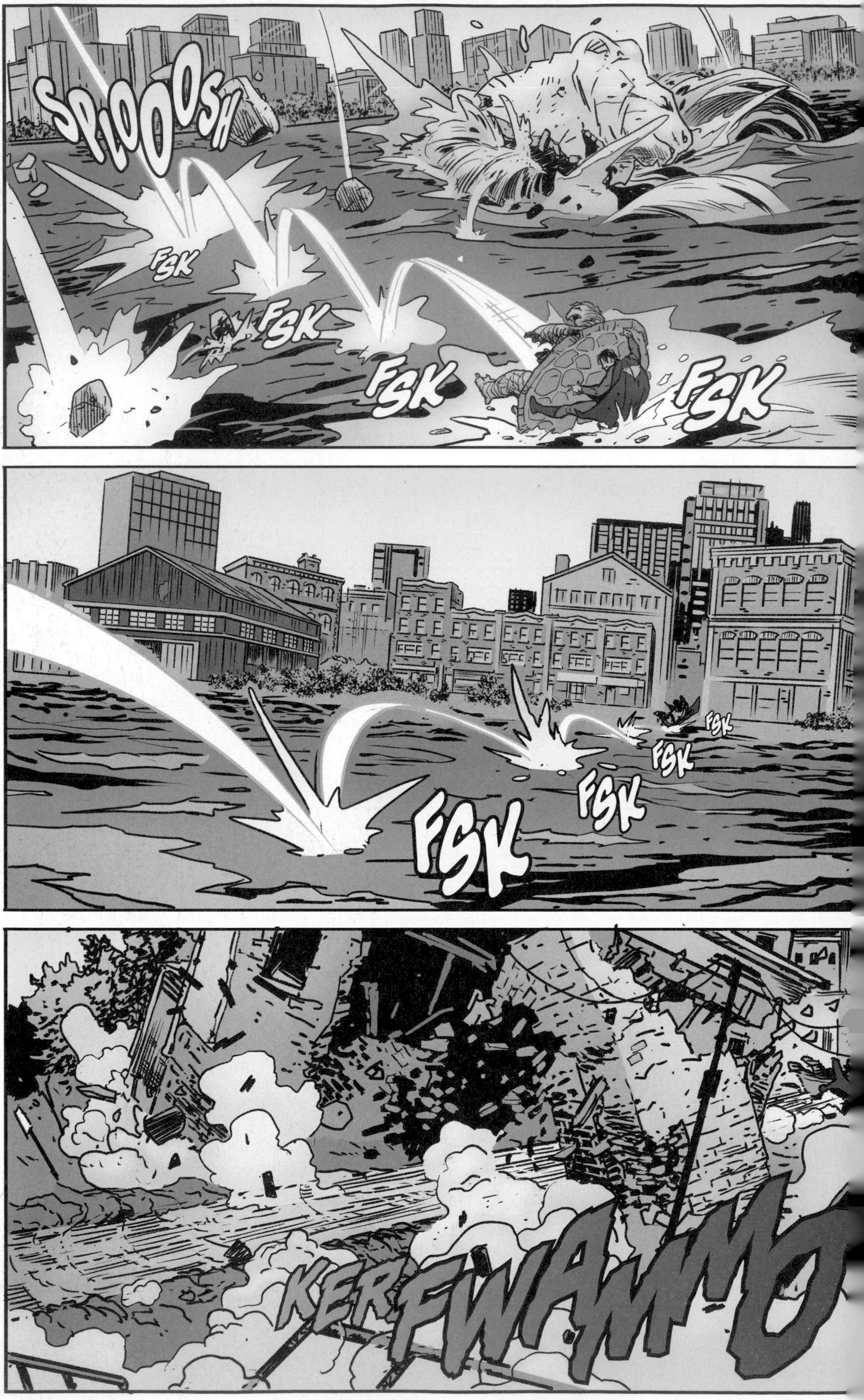
SPLOOOSH
FSK
FSK
FSK
FSK
FSK
FSK
FSK
FSK
KERFWAMMO

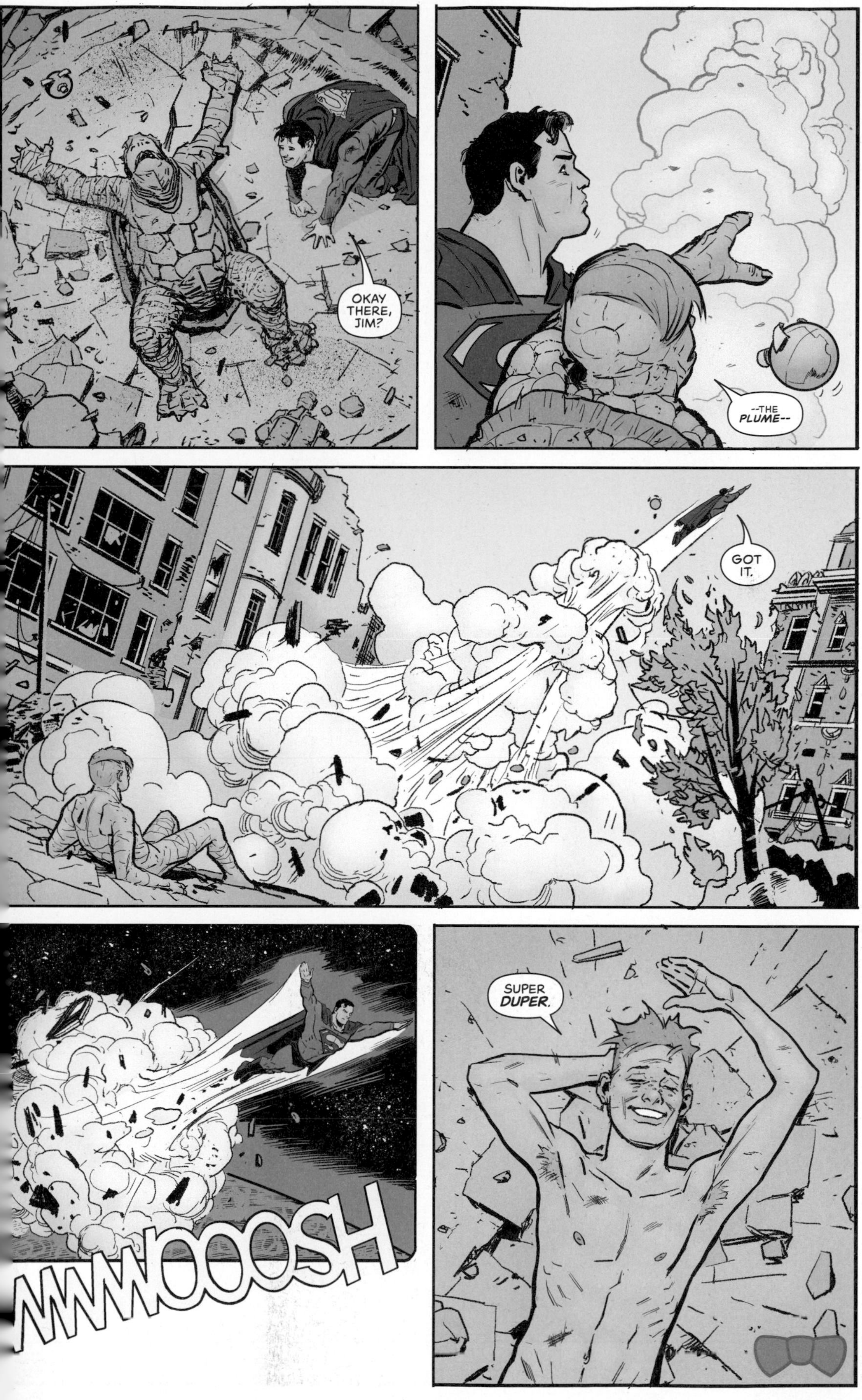
OKAY THERE, JIM?
--THE PLUME--
GOT IT.
MMMOOOSH
SUPER DUPER.

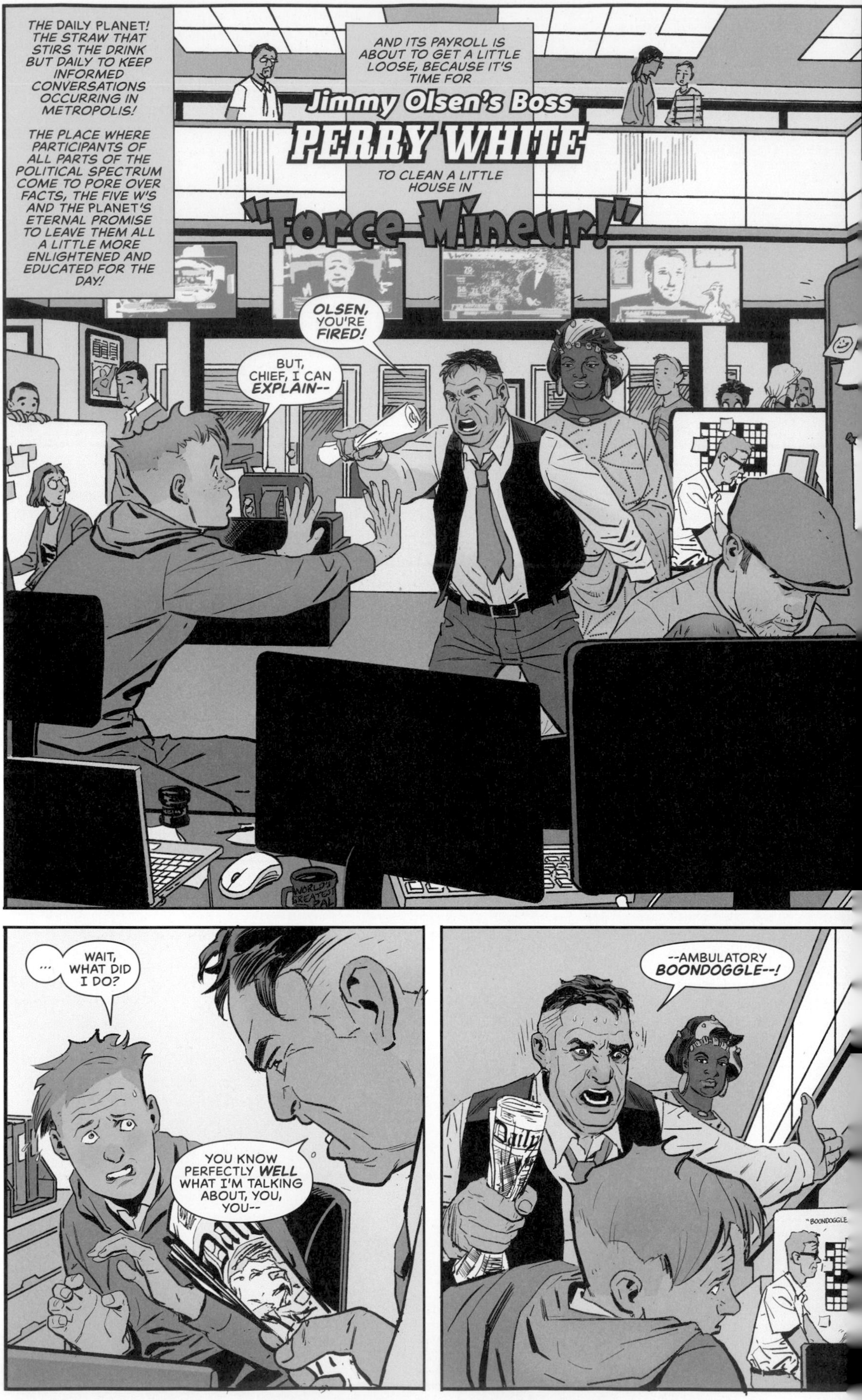
THE DAILY PLANET! THE STRAW THAT STIRS THE DRINK BUT DAILY TO KEEP INFORMED CONVERSATIONS OCCURRING IN METROPOLIS!
THE PLACE WHERE PARTICIPANTS OF ALL PARTS OF THE POLITICAL SPECTRUM COME TO PORE OVER FACTS, THE FIVE W'S AND THE PLANET'S ETERNAL PROMISE TO LEAVE THEM ALL A LITTLE MORE ENLIGHTENED AND EDUCATED FOR THE DAY!
AND ITS PAYROLL IS ABOUT TO GET A LITTLE LOOSE, BECAUSE IT'S TIME FOR
Jimmy Olsen's Boss
PERRY WHITE
TO CLEAN A LITTLE HOUSE IN
"Force Mineur!"
OLSEN, YOU'RE FIRED!
BUT, CHIEF, I CAN EXPLAIN--
...
WAIT, WHAT DID I DO?
YOU KNOW PERFECTLY WELL WHAT I'M TALKING ABOUT, YOU, YOU--
--AMBULATORY BOONDOGGLE--!
"BOONDOGGLE

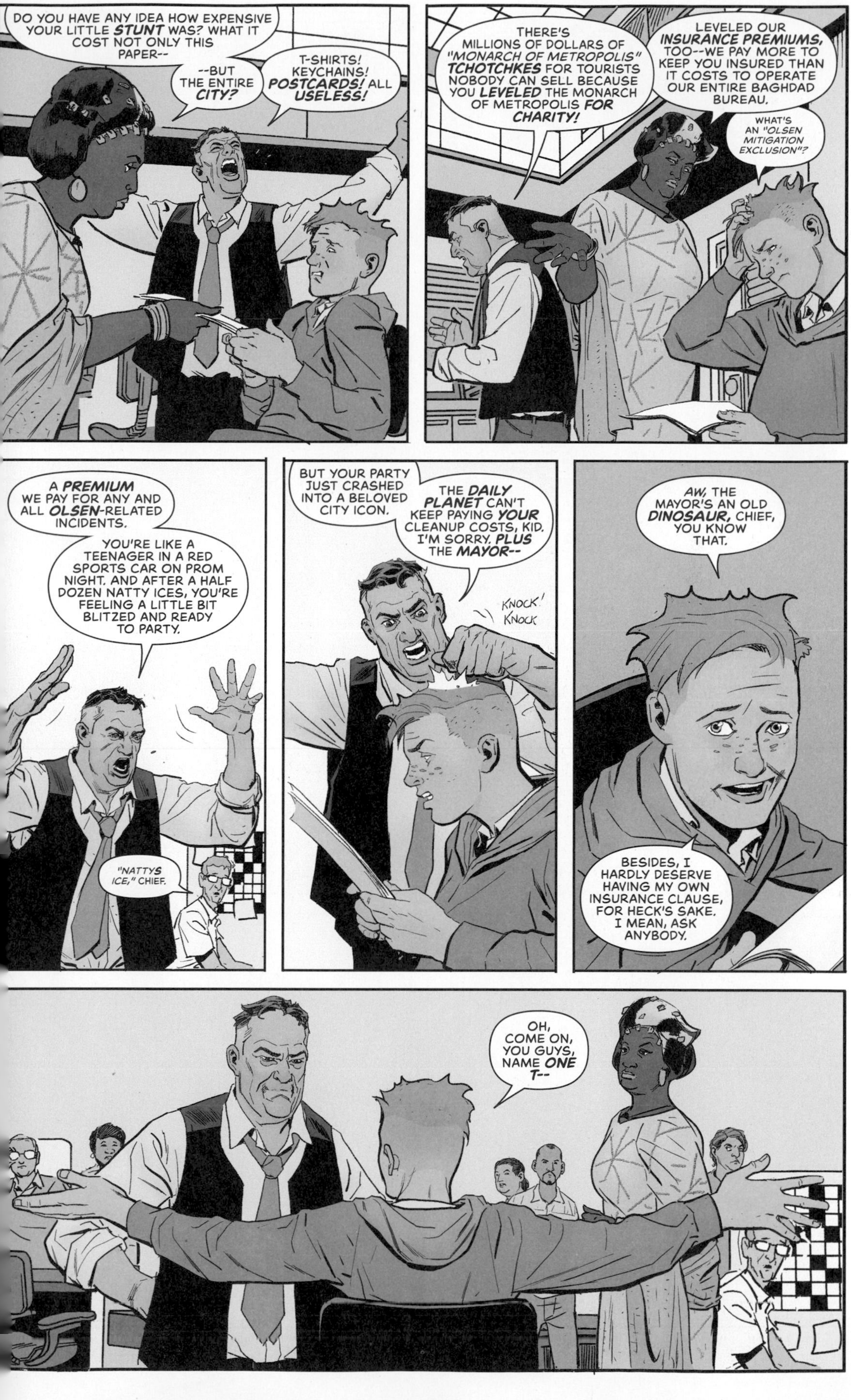
DO YOU HAVE ANY IDEA HOW EXPENSIVE YOUR LITTLE STUNT WAS? WHAT IT COST NOT ONLY THIS PAPER--
--BUT THE ENTIRE CITY?
T-SHIRTS! KEYCHAINS! POSTCARDS! ALL USELESS!
THERE'S MILLIONS OF DOLLARS OF "MONARCH OF METROPOLIS" TCHOTCHKES FOR TOURISTS NOBODY CAN SELL BECAUSE YOU LEVELED THE MONARCH OF METROPOLIS FOR CHARITY!
LEVELED OUR INSURANCE PREMIUMS, TOO--WE PAY MORE TO KEEP YOU INSURED THAN IT COSTS TO OPERATE OUR ENTIRE BAGHDAD BUREAU.
WHAT'S AN "OLSEN MITIGATION EXCLUSION"?
A PREMIUM WE PAY FOR ANY AND ALL OLSEN-RELATED INCIDENTS.
YOU'RE LIKE A TEENAGER IN A RED SPORTS CAR ON PROM NIGHT, AND AFTER A HALF DOZEN NATTY ICES, YOU'RE FEELING A LITTLE BIT BLITZED AND READY TO PARTY.
"NATTYS ICE," CHIEF.
BUT YOUR PARTY JUST CRASHED INTO A BELOVED CITY ICON.
THE DAILY PLANET CAN'T KEEP PAYING YOUR CLEANUP COSTS, KID. I'M SORRY. PLUS THE MAYOR--
KNOCK! KNOCK
AW, THE MAYOR'S AN OLD DINOSAUR, CHIEF, YOU KNOW THAT.
BESIDES, I HARDLY DESERVE HAVING MY OWN INSURANCE CLAUSE, FOR HECK'S SAKE. I MEAN, ASK ANYBODY.
OH, COME ON, YOU GUYS, NAME ONE T--

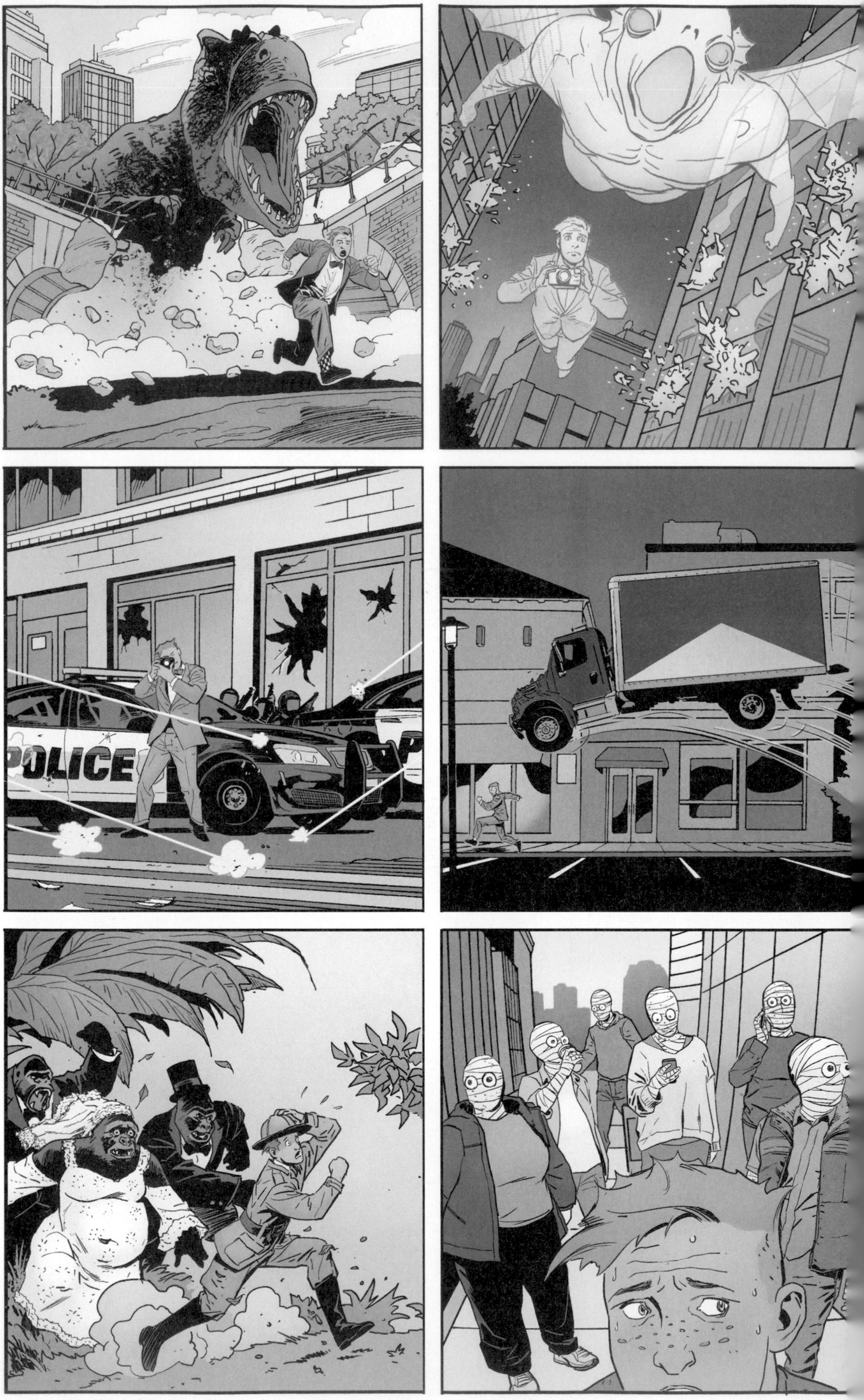
POLICE

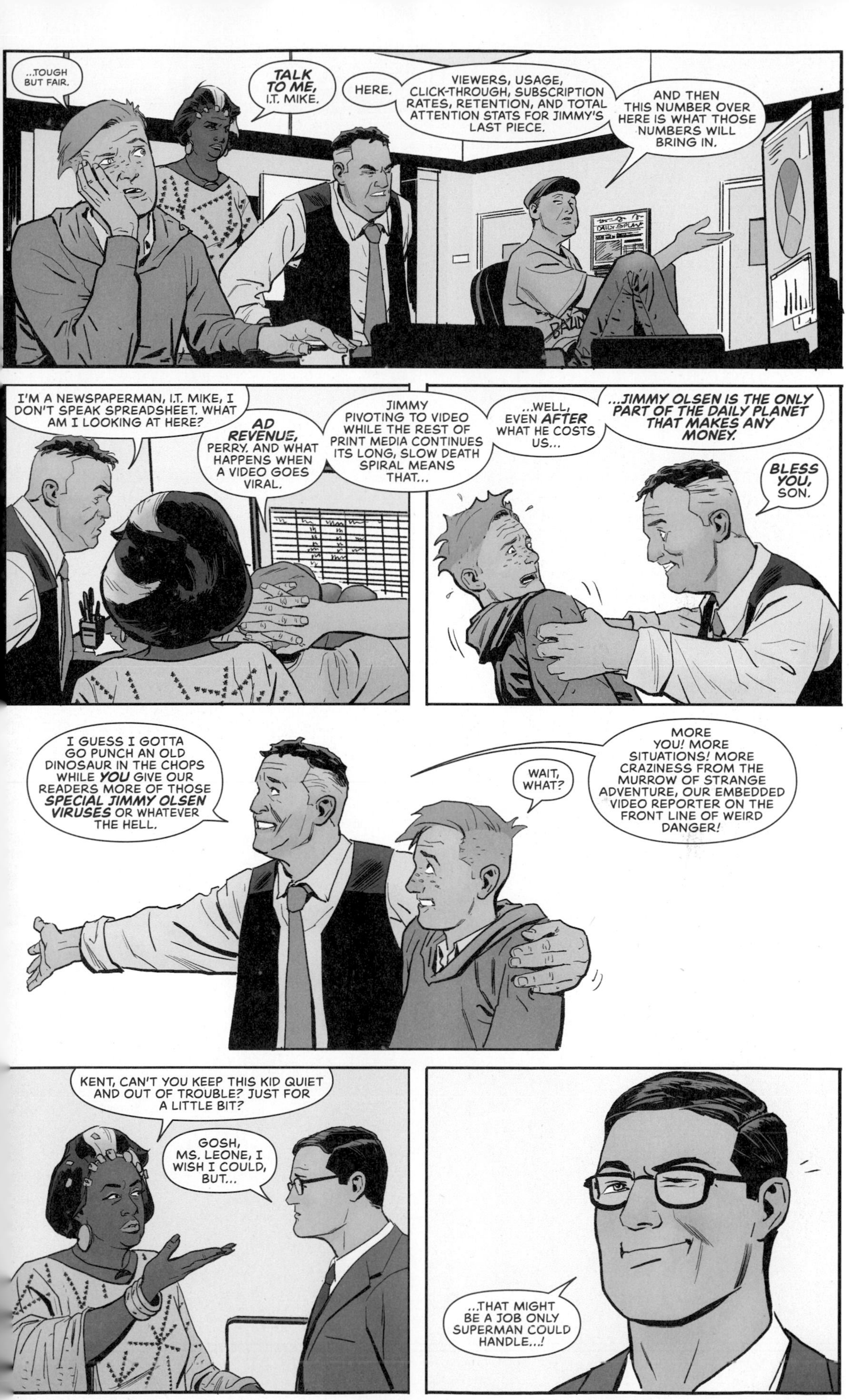

...TOUGH BUT FAIR.
TALK TO ME, I.T. MIKE.
HERE.
VIEWERS, USAGE, CLICK-THROUGH, SUBSCRIPTION RATES, RETENTION, AND TOTAL ATTENTION STATS FOR JIMMY'S LAST PIECE.
AND THEN THIS NUMBER OVER HERE IS WHAT THOSE NUMBERS WILL BRING IN.
I'M A NEWSPAPERMAN, I.T. MIKE, I DON'T SPEAK SPREADSHEET. WHAT AM I LOOKING AT HERE?
AD REVENUE, PERRY. AND WHAT HAPPENS WHEN A VIDEO GOES VIRAL.
JIMMY PIVOTING TO VIDEO WHILE THE REST OF PRINT MEDIA CONTINUES ITS LONG, SLOW DEATH SPIRAL MEANS THAT...
...WELL, EVEN AFTER WHAT HE COSTS US...
...JIMMY OLSEN IS THE ONLY PART OF THE DAILY PLANET THAT MAKES ANY MONEY.
BLESS YOU, SON.
I GUESS I GOTTA GO PUNCH AN OLD DINOSAUR IN THE CHOPS WHILE YOU GIVE OUR READERS MORE OF THOSE SPECIAL JIMMY OLSEN VIRUSES OR WHATEVER THE HELL.
WAIT, WHAT?
MORE YOU! MORE SITUATIONS! MORE CRAZINESS FROM THE MURROW OF STRANGE ADVENTURE, OUR EMBEDDED VIDEO REPORTER ON THE FRONT LINE OF WEIRD DANGER!
KENT, CAN'T YOU KEEP THIS KID QUIET AND OUT OF TROUBLE? JUST FOR A LITTLE BIT?
GOSH, MS. LEONE, I WISH I COULD, BUT...
...THAT MIGHT BE A JOB ONLY SUPERMAN COULD HANDLE...!

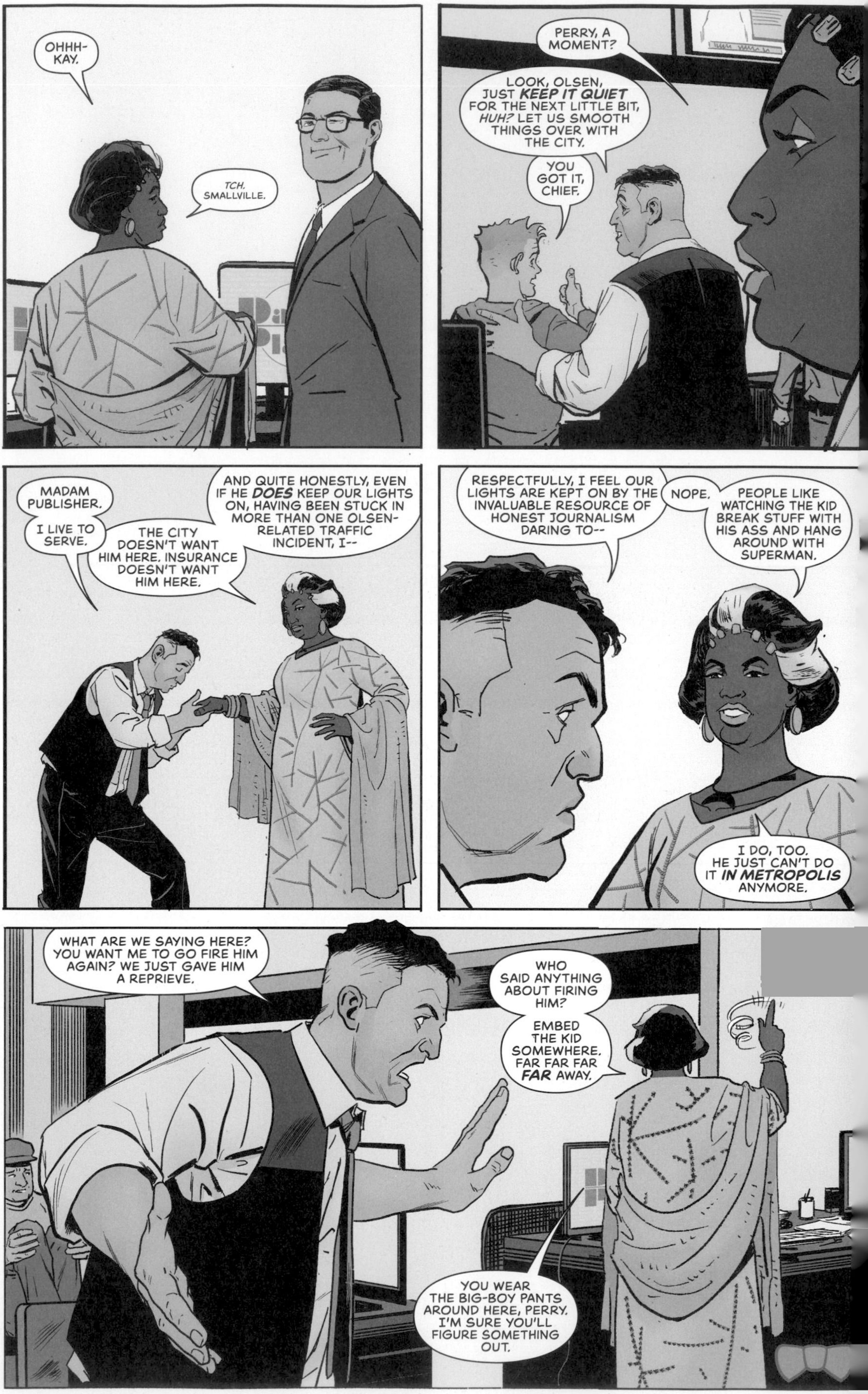
OHHH-KAY.
TCH. SMALLVILLE.
PERRY, A MOMENT?
LOOK, OLSEN, JUST KEEP IT QUIET FOR THE NEXT LITTLE BIT, HUH? LET US SMOOTH THINGS OVER WITH THE CITY.
YOU GOT IT, CHIEF.
MADAM PUBLISHER.
I LIVE TO SERVE.
THE CITY DOESN'T WANT HIM HERE. INSURANCE DOESN'T WANT HIM HERE.
AND QUITE HONESTLY, EVEN IF HE DOES KEEP OUR LIGHTS ON, HAVING BEEN STUCK IN MORE THAN ONE OLSEN-RELATED TRAFFIC INCIDENT, I--
RESPECTFULLY, I FEEL OUR LIGHTS ARE KEPT ON BY THE INVALUABLE RESOURCE OF HONEST JOURNALISM DARING TO--
NOPE.
PEOPLE LIKE WATCHING THE KID BREAK STUFF WITH HIS ASS AND HANG AROUND WITH SUPERMAN.
I DO, TOO. HE JUST CAN'T DO IT IN METROPOLIS ANYMORE.
WHAT ARE WE SAYING HERE? YOU WANT ME TO GO FIRE HIM AGAIN? WE JUST GAVE HIM A REPRIEVE.
WHO SAID ANYTHING ABOUT FIRING HIM?
EMBED THE KID SOMEWHERE. FAR FAR FAR FAR AWAY.
YOU WEAR THE BIG-BOY PANTS AROUND HERE, PERRY. I'M SURE YOU'LL FIGURE SOMETHING OUT.

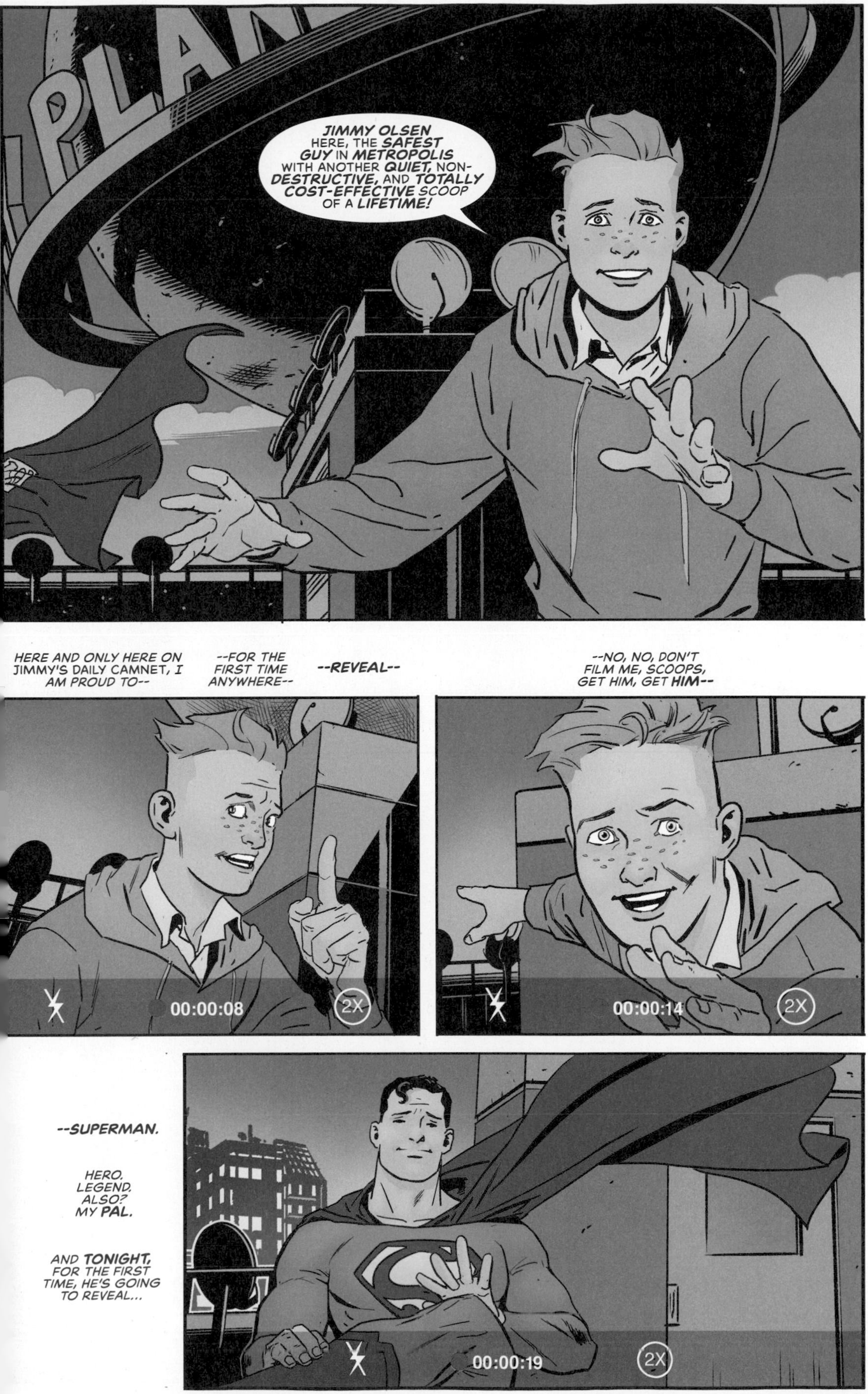
JIMMY OLSEN HERE, THE SAFEST GUY IN METROPOLIS WITH ANOTHER QUIET, NON-DESTRUCTIVE, AND TOTALLY COST-EFFECTIVE SCOOP OF A LIFETIME!
HERE AND ONLY HERE ON JIMMY'S DAILY CAMNET, I AM PROUD TO--
--FOR THE FIRST TIME ANYWHERE--
--REVEAL--
00:00:08
2X
--NO, NO, DON'T FILM ME, SCOOPS, GET HIM, GET HIM--
00:00:14
2X
--SUPERMAN.
HERO. LEGEND. ALSO? MY PAL.
AND TONIGHT, FOR THE FIRST TIME, HE'S GOING TO REVEAL...
00:00:19
2X

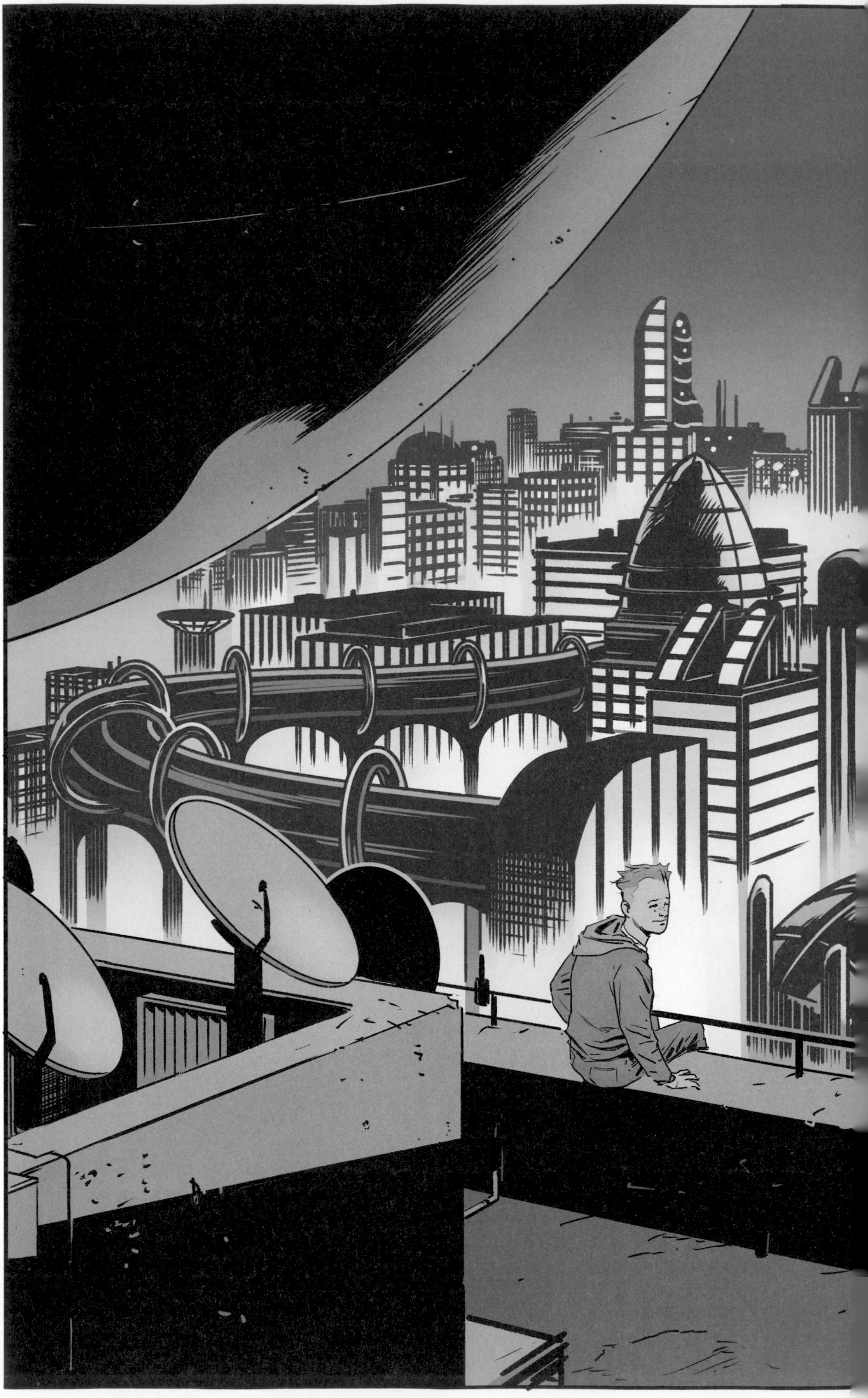

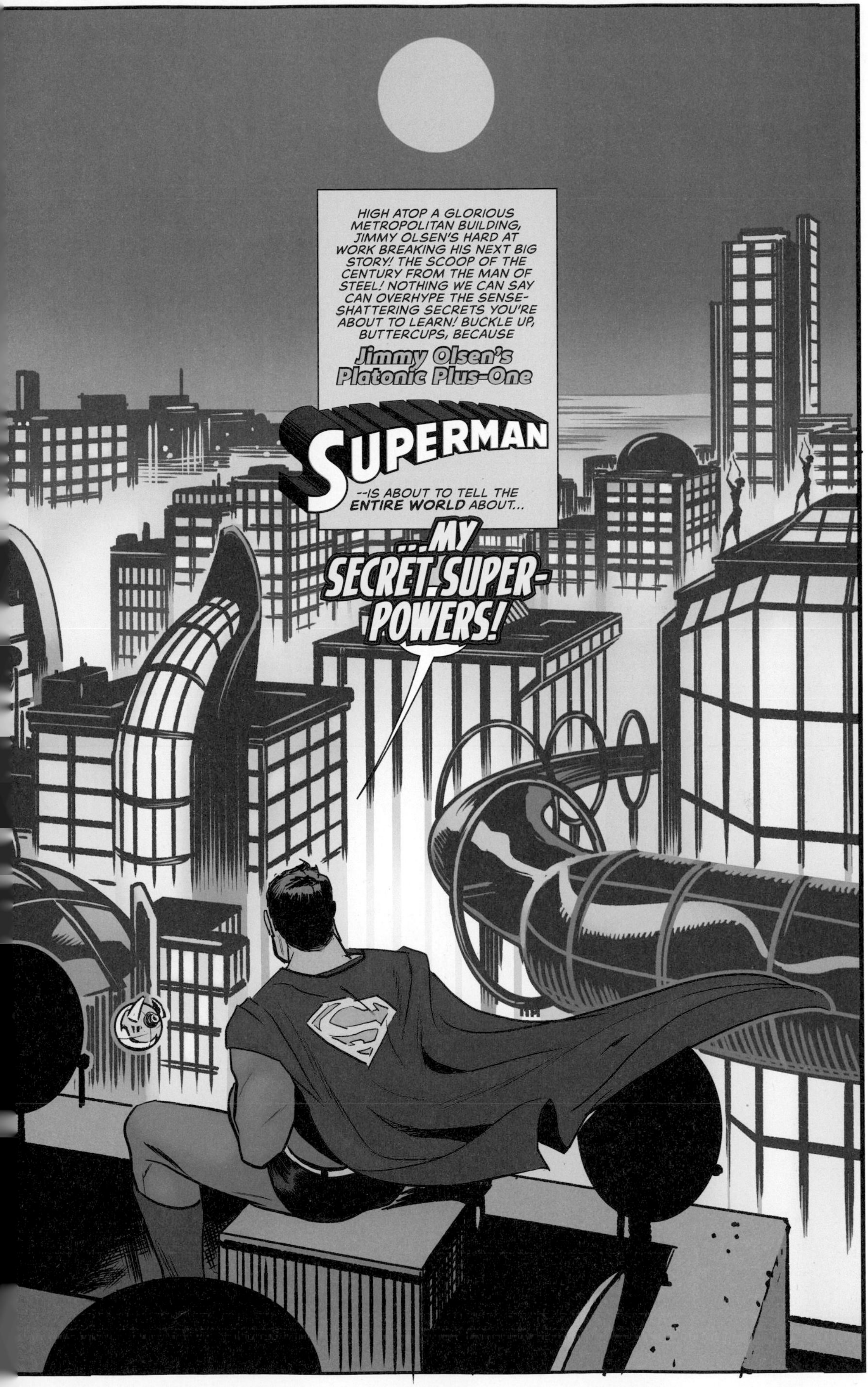
HIGH ATOP A GLORIOUS METROPOLITAN BUILDING, JIMMY OLSEN'S HARD AT WORK BREAKING HIS NEXT BIG STORY! THE SCOOP OF THE CENTURY FROM THE MAN OF STEEL! NOTHING WE CAN SAY CAN OVERHYPE THE SENSE-SHATTERING SECRETS YOU'RE ABOUT TO LEARN! BUCKLE UP, BUTTERCUPS, BECAUSE
Jimmy Olsen's Platonic Plus-One
SUPERMAN
--IS ABOUT TO TELL THE ENTIRE WORLD ABOUT...
...MY SECRET SUPER-POWERS!

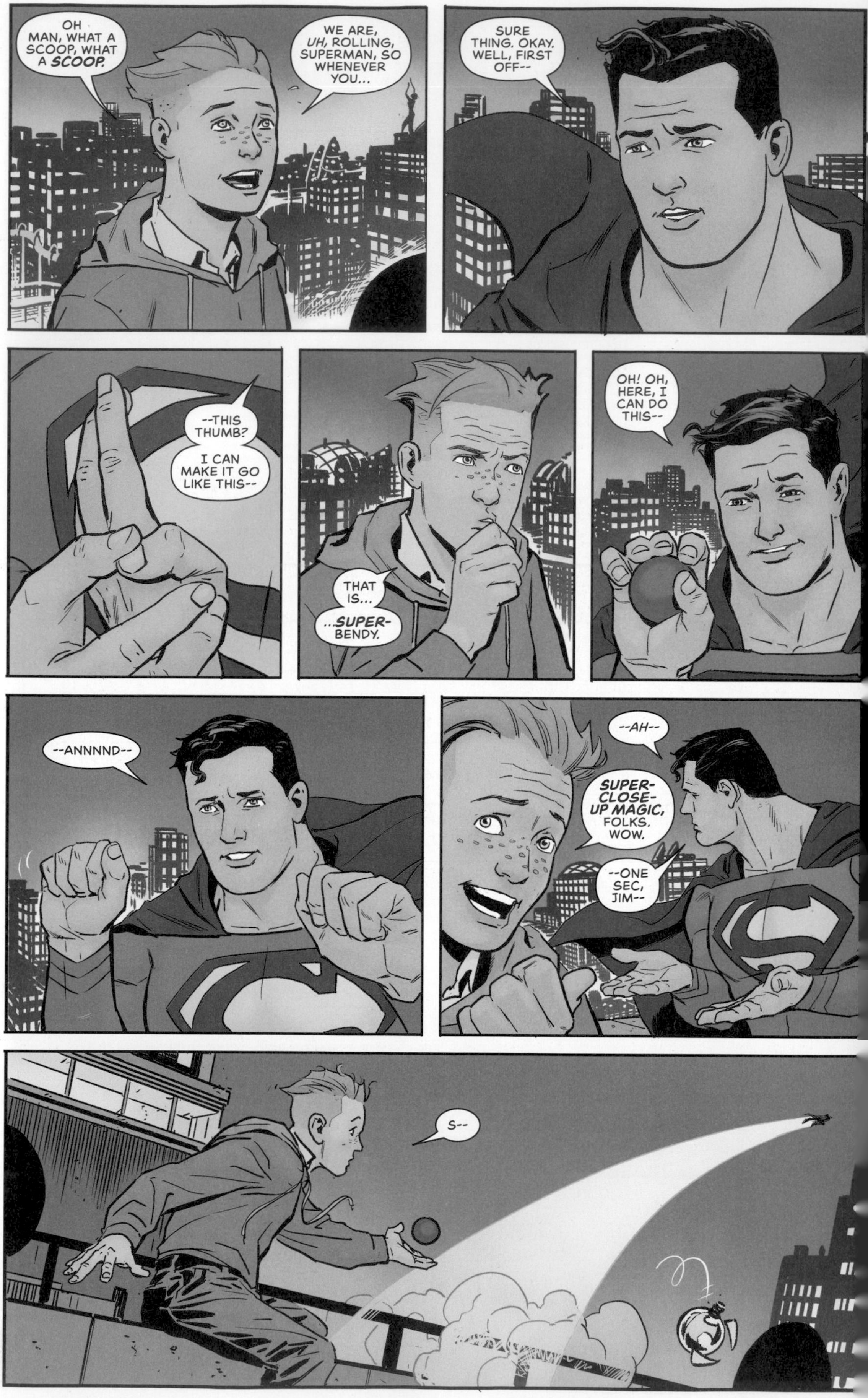
OH MAN, WHAT A SCOOP, WHAT A **SCOOP.**
WE ARE, *UH,* ROLLING, SUPERMAN, SO WHENEVER YOU...
SURE THING. OKAY. WELL, FIRST OFF--
--THIS THUMB?
I CAN MAKE IT GO LIKE THIS--
THAT IS...
...**SUPER-**BENDY.
OH! OH, HERE, I CAN DO THIS--
--ANNNND--
--AH--
SUPER-CLOSE-UP MAGIC, FOLKS. WOW.
--ONE SEC, JIM--
S--

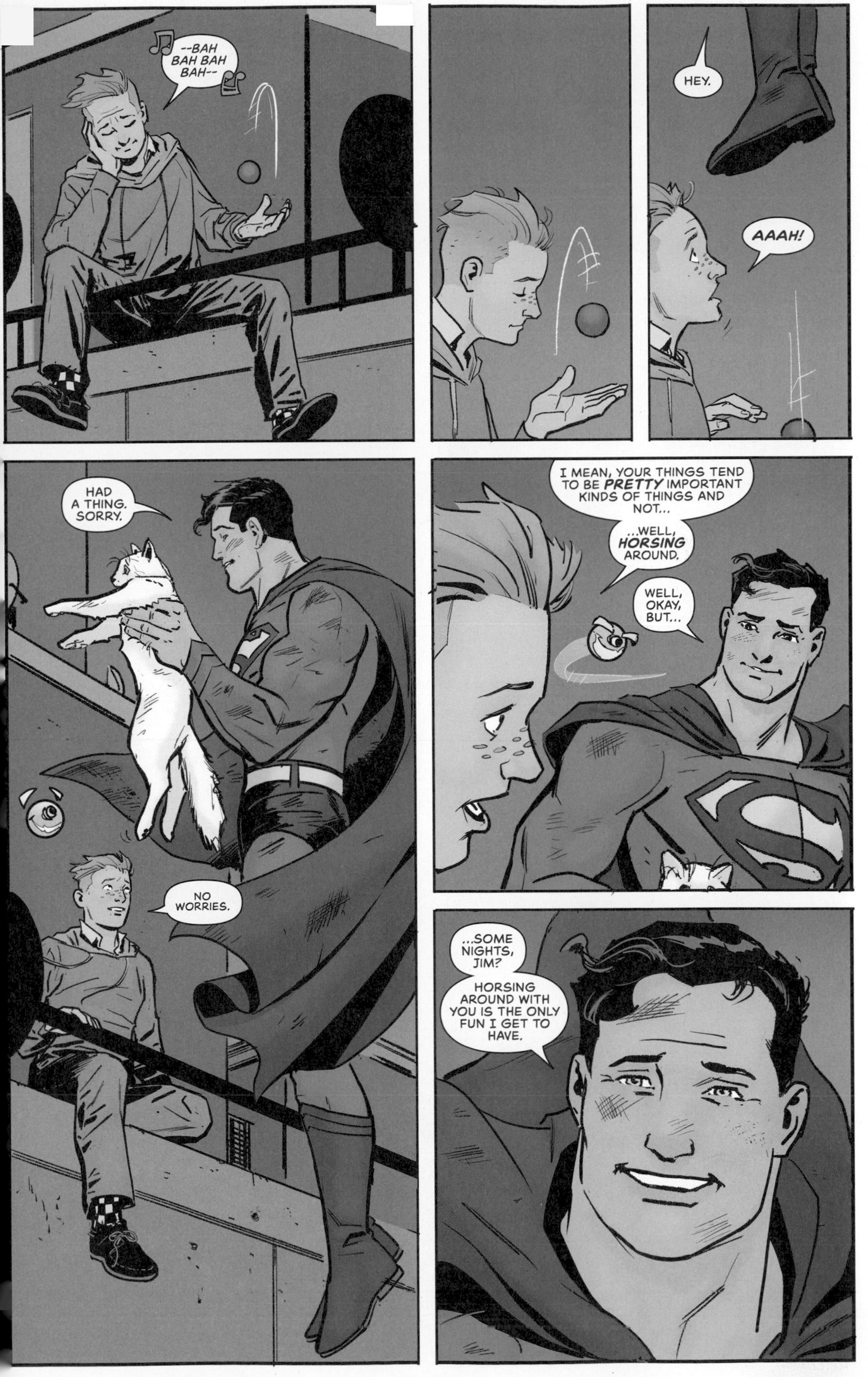
--BAH BAH BAH BAH--
HEY.
AAAH!
HAD A THING. SORRY.
NO WORRIES.
I MEAN, YOUR THINGS TEND TO BE PRETTY IMPORTANT KINDS OF THINGS AND NOT...
...WELL, HORSING AROUND.
WELL, OKAY, BUT...
...SOME NIGHTS, JIM?
HORSING AROUND WITH YOU IS THE ONLY FUN I GET TO HAVE.

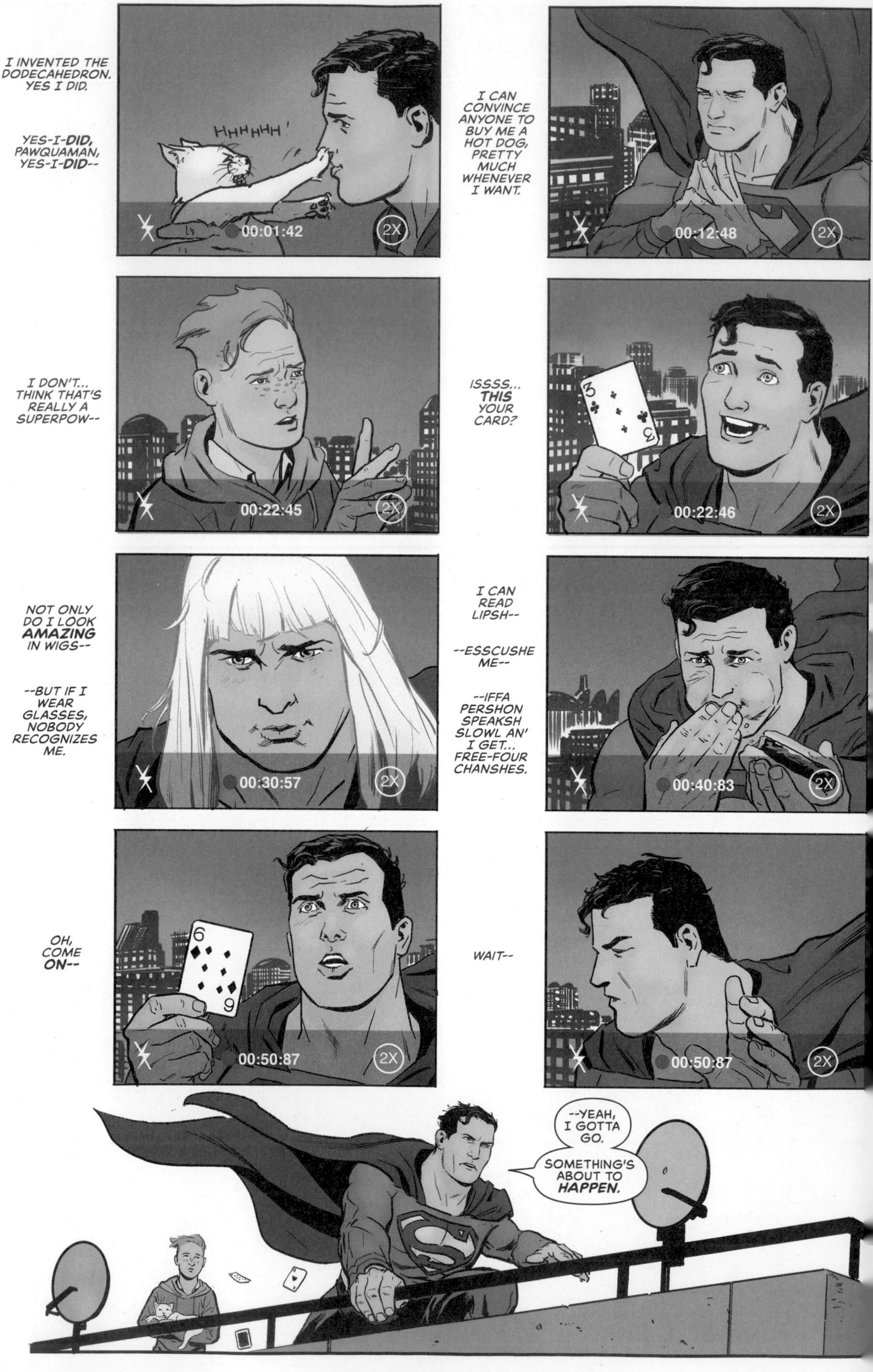
I INVENTED THE DODECAHEDRON. YES I DID.
YES-I-**DID,** PAWQUAMAN, YES-I-**DID**--
HHHHHH!
00:01:42
2X
I CAN CONVINCE ANYONE TO BUY ME A HOT DOG, PRETTY MUCH WHENEVER I WANT.
00:12:48
2X
I DON'T... THINK THAT'S REALLY A SUPERPOW--
00:22:45
2X
ISSSS... **THIS** YOUR CARD?
00:22:46
2X
NOT ONLY DO I LOOK **AMAZING** IN WIGS--
--BUT IF I WEAR GLASSES, NOBODY RECOGNIZES ME.
00:30:57
2X
I CAN READ LIPSH--
--ESSCUSHE ME--
--IFFA PERSHON SPEAKSH SLOWL AN' I GET... FREE-FOUR CHANSHES.
00:40:83
2X
OH, COME **ON--**
00:50:87
2X
WAIT--
00:50:87
2X
--YEAH, I GOTTA GO.
SOMETHING'S ABOUT TO **HAPPEN.**

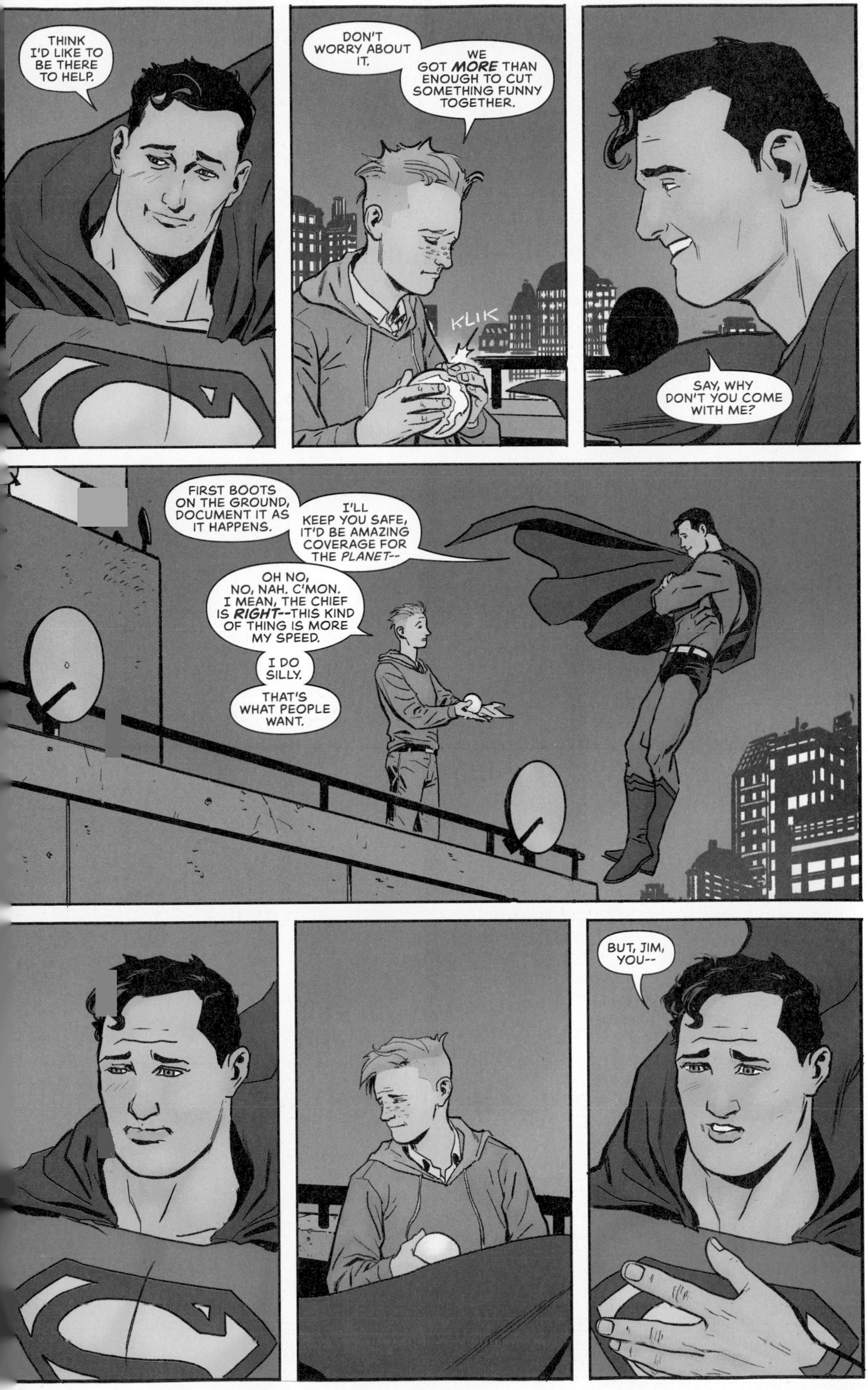
THINK I'D LIKE TO BE THERE TO HELP.
DON'T WORRY ABOUT IT.
WE GOT **MORE** THAN ENOUGH TO CUT SOMETHING FUNNY TOGETHER.
KLIK
SAY, WHY DON'T YOU COME WITH ME?
FIRST BOOTS ON THE GROUND, DOCUMENT IT AS IT HAPPENS.
I'LL KEEP YOU SAFE, IT'D BE AMAZING COVERAGE FOR THE *PLANET*--
OH NO, NO, NAH. C'MON. I MEAN, THE CHIEF IS **RIGHT**--THIS KIND OF THING IS MORE MY SPEED.
I DO SILLY.
THAT'S WHAT PEOPLE WANT.
BUT, JIM, YOU--

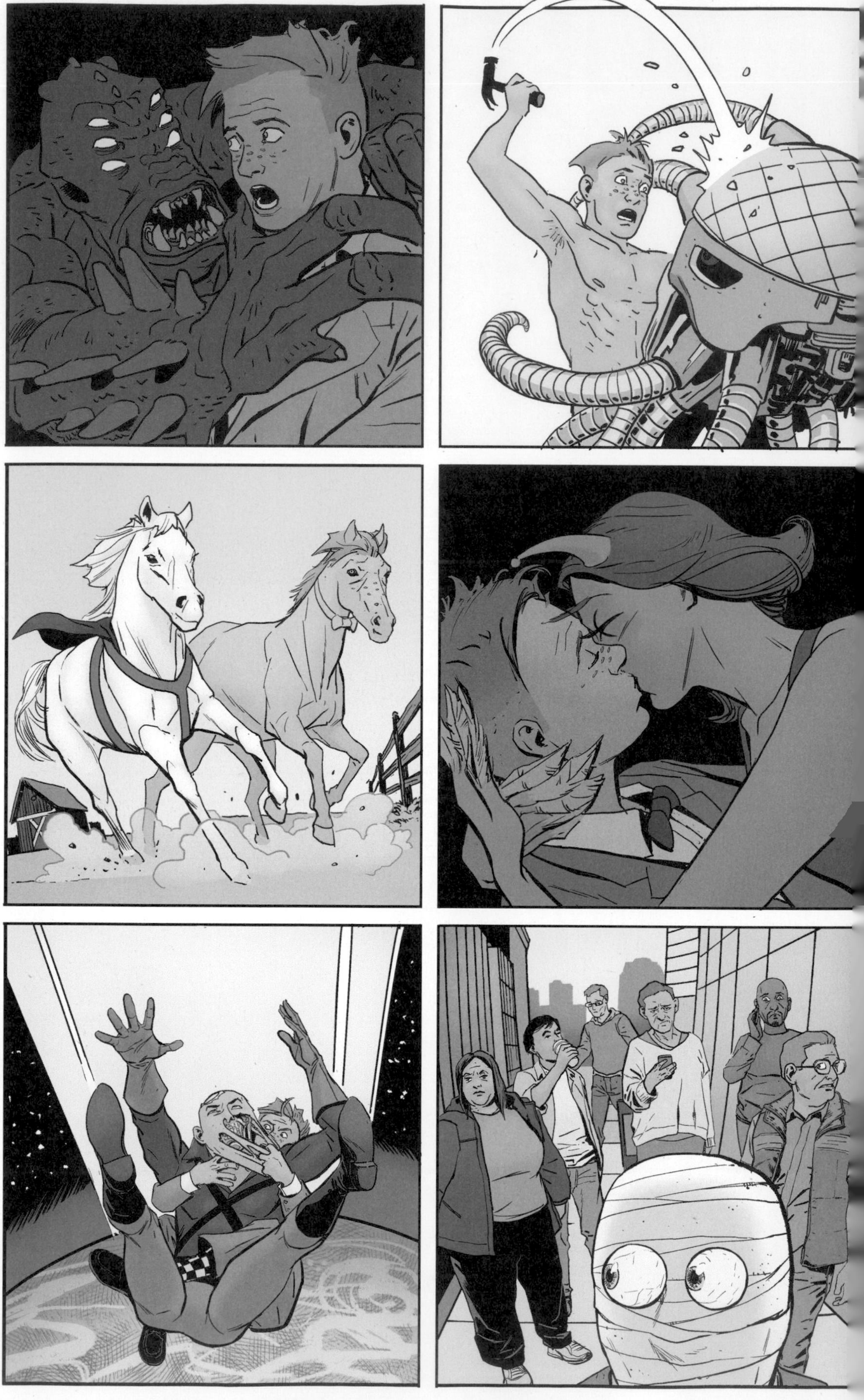

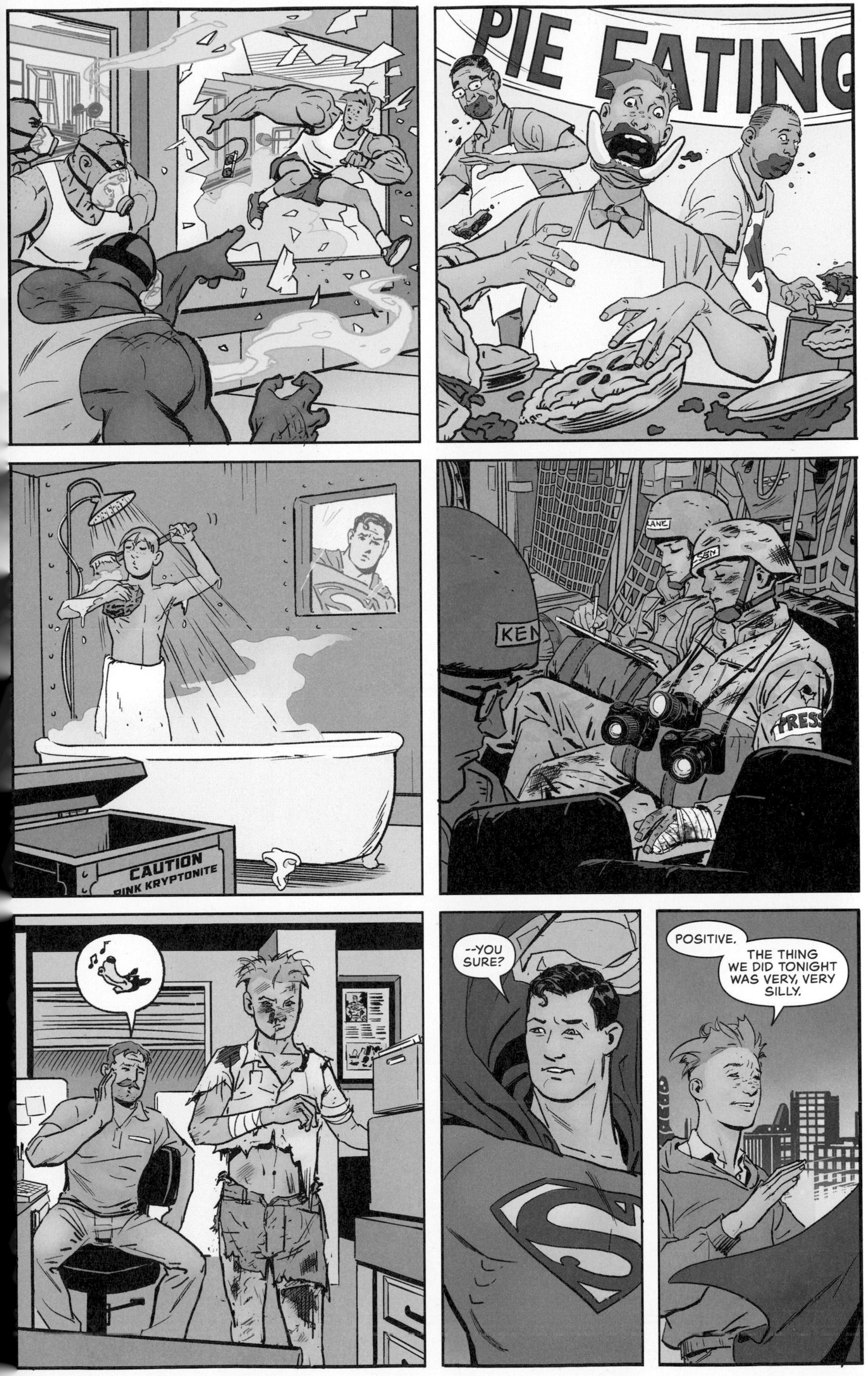

PIE EATING
LANE
PRESS
CAUTION
PINK KRYPTONITE
--YOU SURE?
POSITIVE.
THE THING WE DID TONIGHT WAS VERY, VERY SILLY.

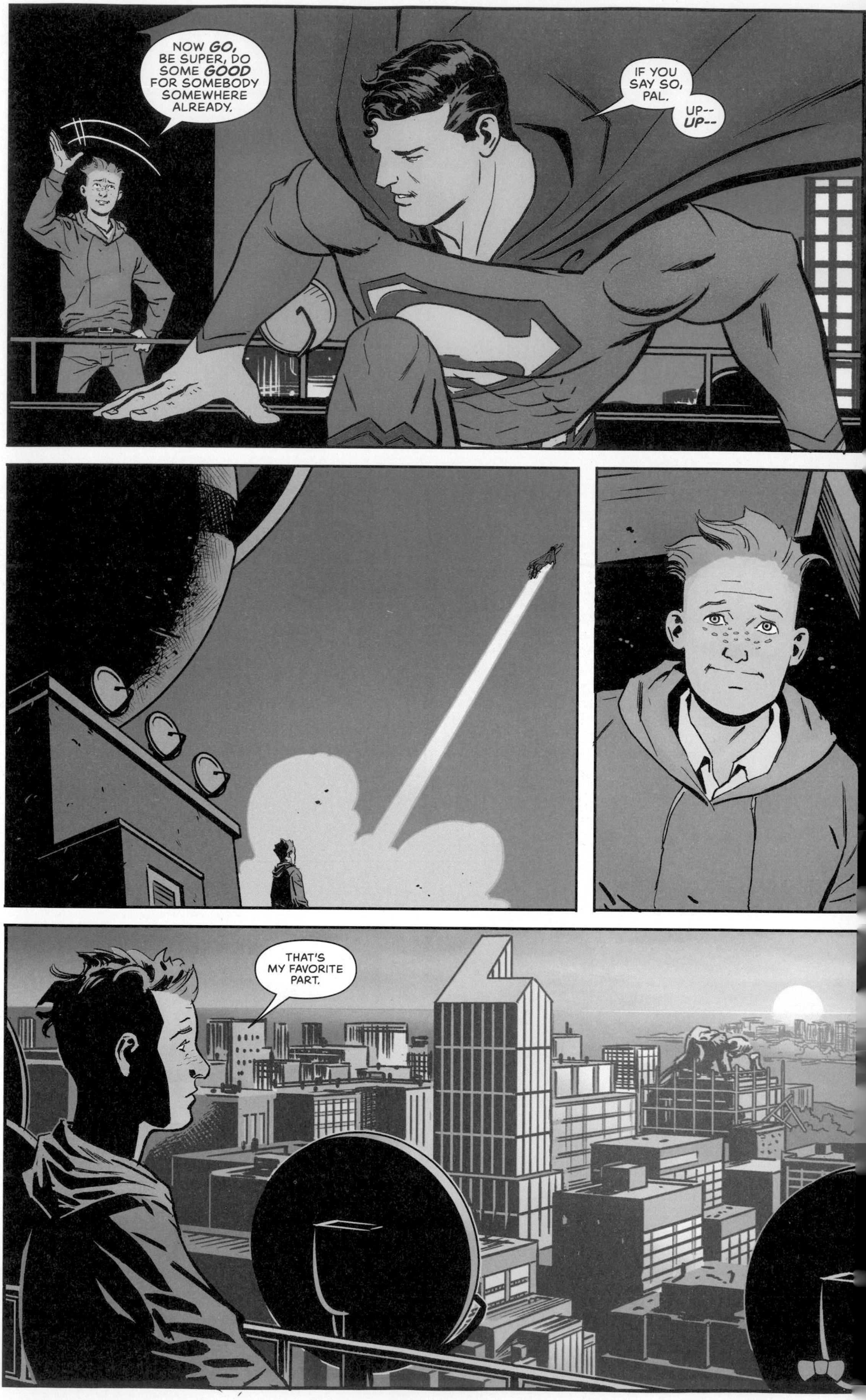
NOW GO, BE SUPER, DO SOME GOOD FOR SOMEBODY SOMEWHERE ALREADY.
IF YOU SAY SO, PAL.
UP-- UP--
THAT'S MY FAVORITE PART.

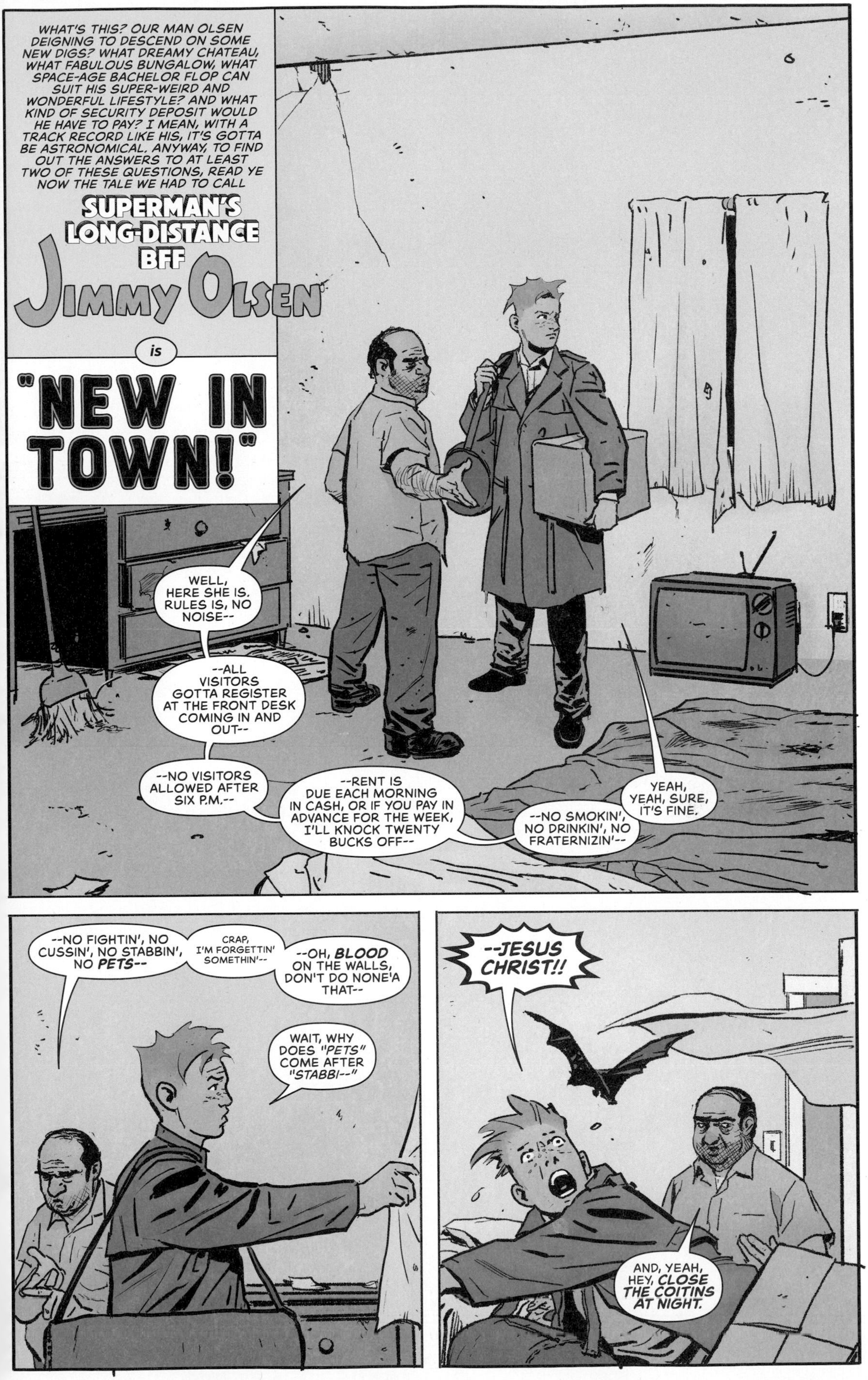
WHAT'S THIS? OUR MAN OLSEN DEIGNING TO DESCEND ON SOME NEW DIGS? WHAT DREAMY CHATEAU, WHAT FABULOUS BUNGALOW, WHAT SPACE-AGE BACHELOR FLOP CAN SUIT HIS SUPER-WEIRD AND WONDERFUL LIFESTYLE? AND WHAT KIND OF SECURITY DEPOSIT WOULD HE HAVE TO PAY? I MEAN, WITH A TRACK RECORD LIKE HIS, IT'S GOTTA BE ASTRONOMICAL. ANYWAY, TO FIND OUT THE ANSWERS TO AT LEAST TWO OF THESE QUESTIONS, READ YE NOW THE TALE WE HAD TO CALL
SUPERMAN'S LONG-DISTANCE BFF
JIMMY OLSEN
is
"NEW IN TOWN!"
WELL, HERE SHE IS. RULES IS, NO NOISE--
--ALL VISITORS GOTTA REGISTER AT THE FRONT DESK COMING IN AND OUT--
--NO VISITORS ALLOWED AFTER SIX P.M.--
--RENT IS DUE EACH MORNING IN CASH, OR IF YOU PAY IN ADVANCE FOR THE WEEK, I'LL KNOCK TWENTY BUCKS OFF--
--NO SMOKIN', NO DRINKIN', NO FRATERNIZIN'--
YEAH, YEAH, SURE, IT'S FINE.
--NO FIGHTIN', NO CUSSIN', NO STABBIN', NO PETS--
CRAP, I'M FORGETTIN' SOMETHIN'--
--OH, BLOOD ON THE WALLS, DON'T DO NONE'A THAT--
WAIT, WHY DOES "PETS" COME AFTER "STABBI--"
--JESUS CHRIST!!
AND, YEAH, HEY, CLOSE THE COITINS AT NIGHT.

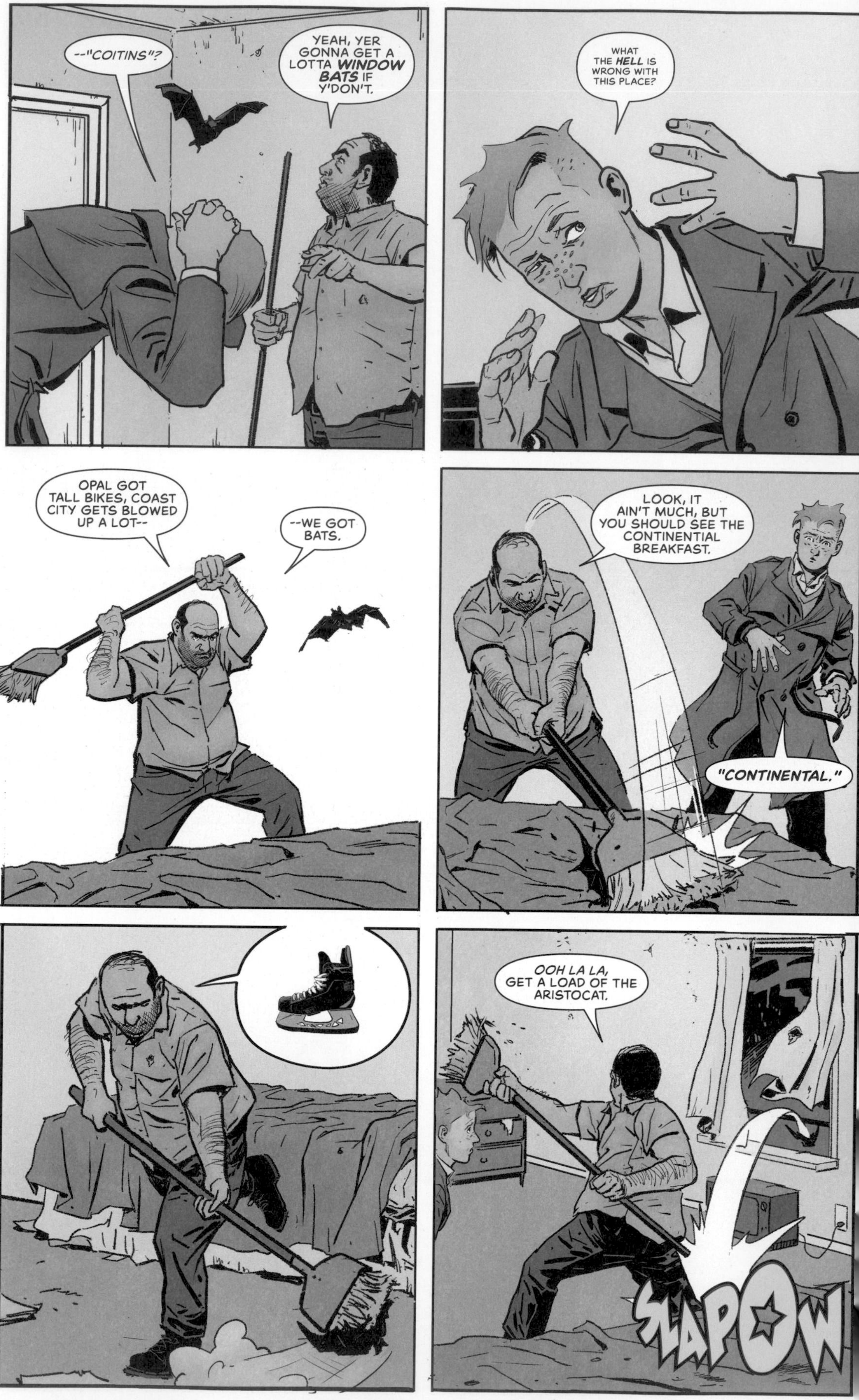
--"COITINS"?
YEAH, YER GONNA GET A LOTTA WINDOW BATS IF Y'DON'T.
WHAT THE HELL IS WRONG WITH THIS PLACE?
OPAL GOT TALL BIKES, COAST CITY GETS BLOWED UP A LOT--
--WE GOT BATS.
LOOK, IT AIN'T MUCH, BUT YOU SHOULD SEE THE CONTINENTAL BREAKFAST.
"CONTINENTAL."
OOH LA LA, GET A LOAD OF THE ARISTOCAT.
SLAPOW

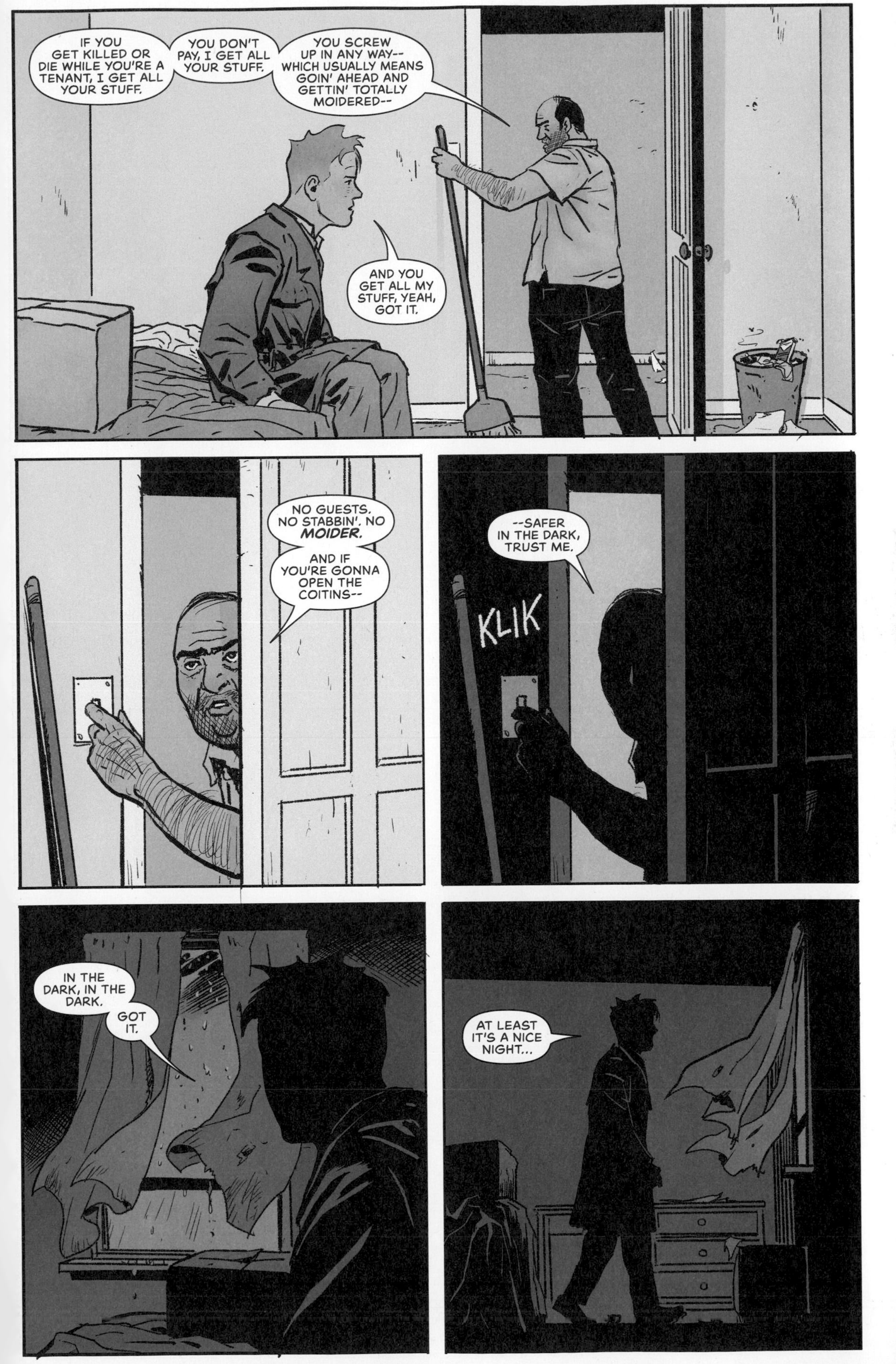
IF YOU GET KILLED OR DIE WHILE YOU'RE A TENANT, I GET ALL YOUR STUFF.
YOU DON'T PAY, I GET ALL YOUR STUFF.
YOU SCREW UP IN ANY WAY-- WHICH USUALLY MEANS GOIN' AHEAD AND GETTIN' TOTALLY MOIDERED--
AND YOU GET ALL MY STUFF, YEAH, GOT IT.
NO GUESTS. NO STABBIN'. NO *MOIDER.*
AND IF YOU'RE GONNA OPEN THE COITINS--
--SAFER IN THE DARK, TRUST ME.
KLIK
IN THE DARK, IN THE DARK.
GOT IT.
AT LEAST IT'S A NICE NIGHT...

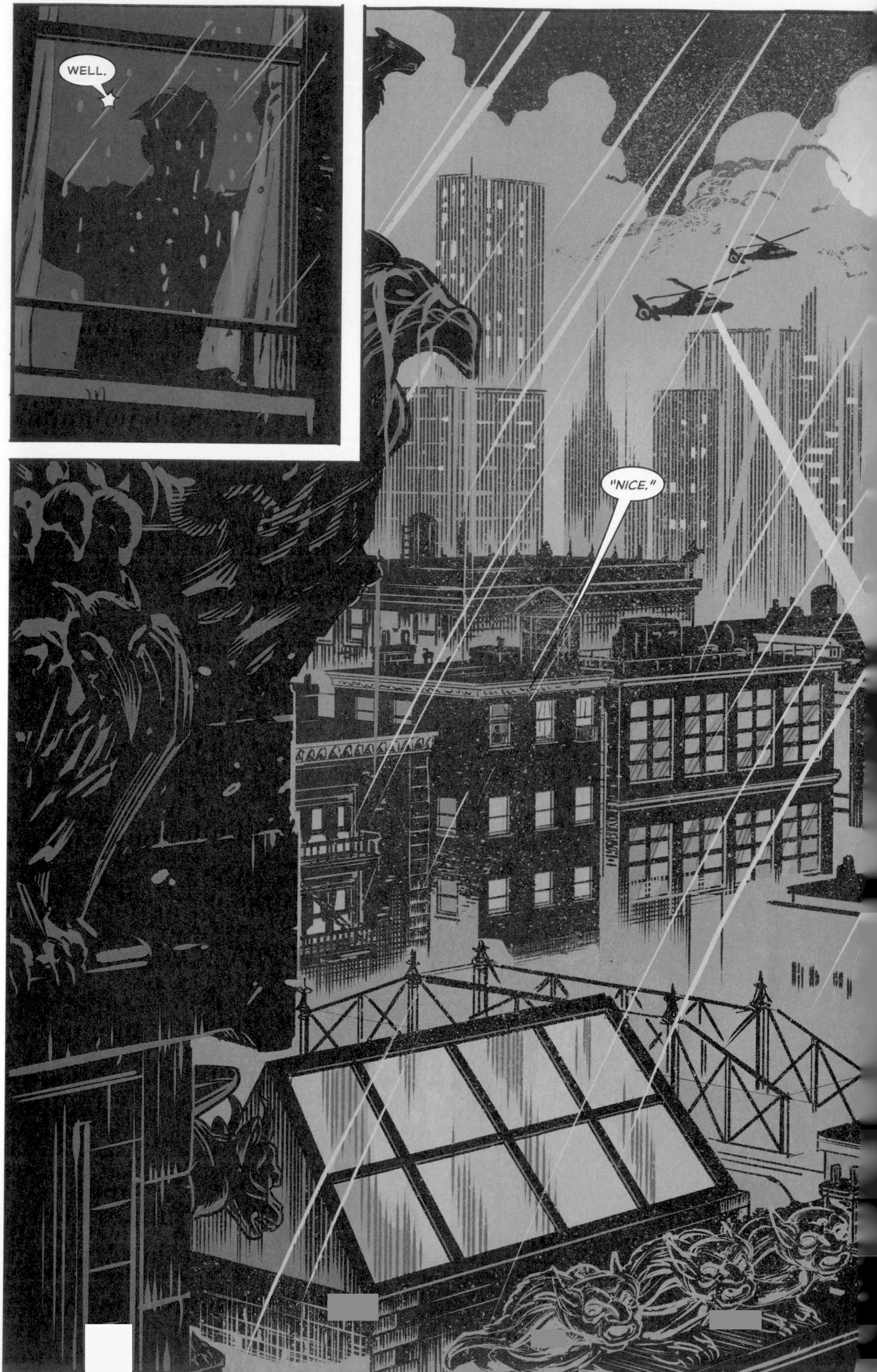
WELL.
"NICE."

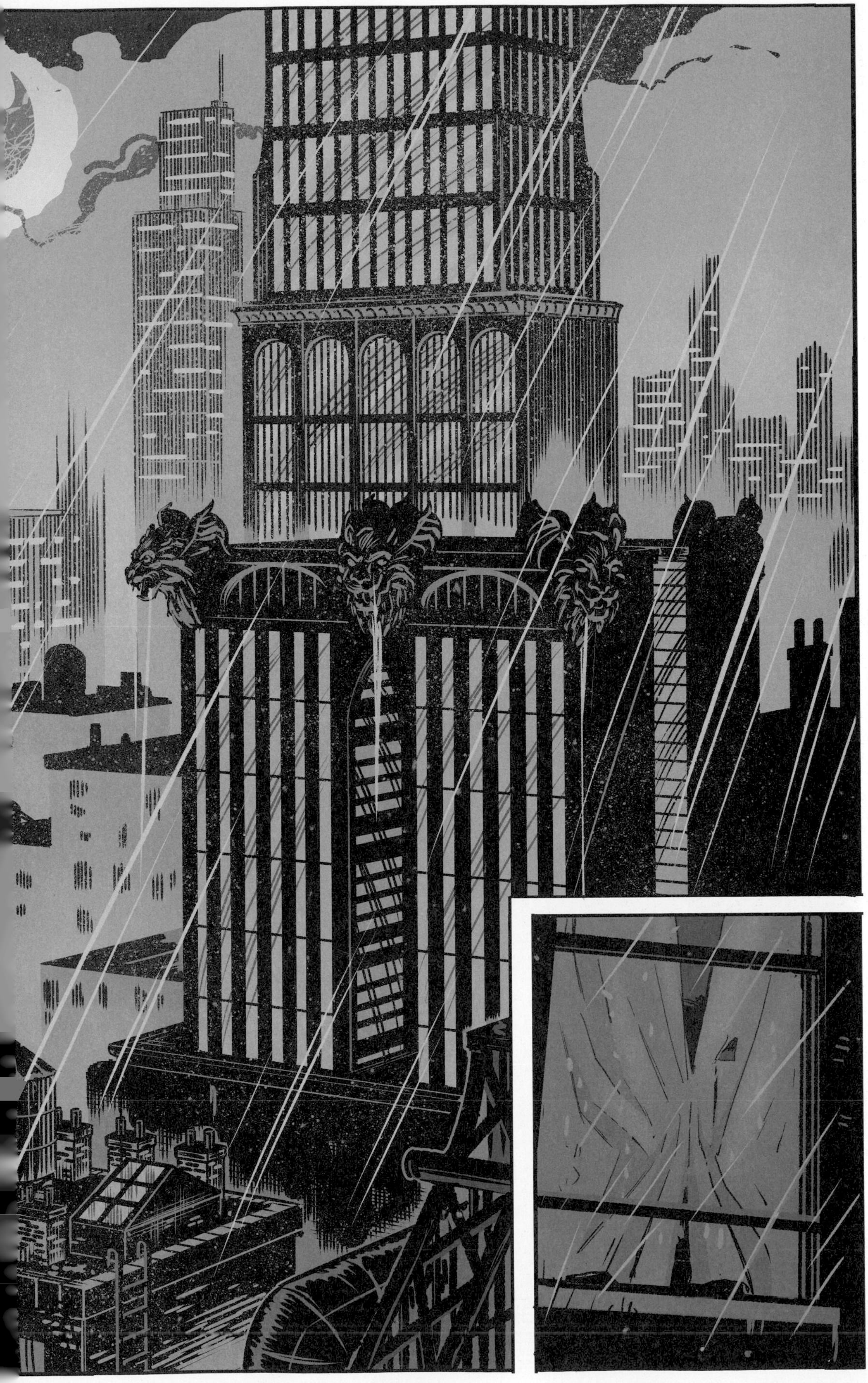

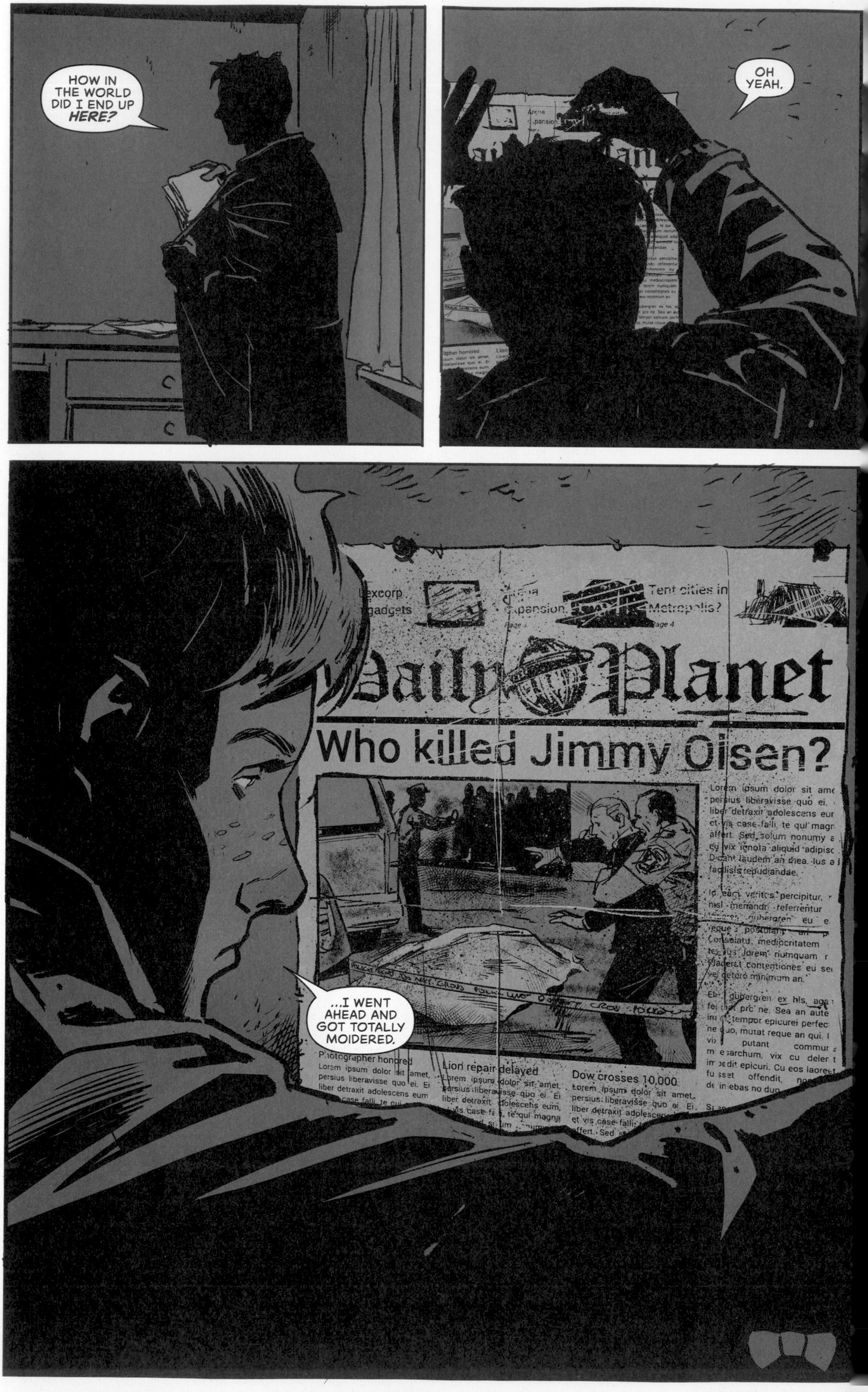
HOW IN THE WORLD DID I END UP HERE?
OH YEAH.
Tent cities in Metropolis?
Daily Planet
Who killed Jimmy Olsen?
...I WENT AHEAD AND GOT TOTALLY MOIDERED.
Photographer honored
Lion repair delayed
Dow crosses 10,000

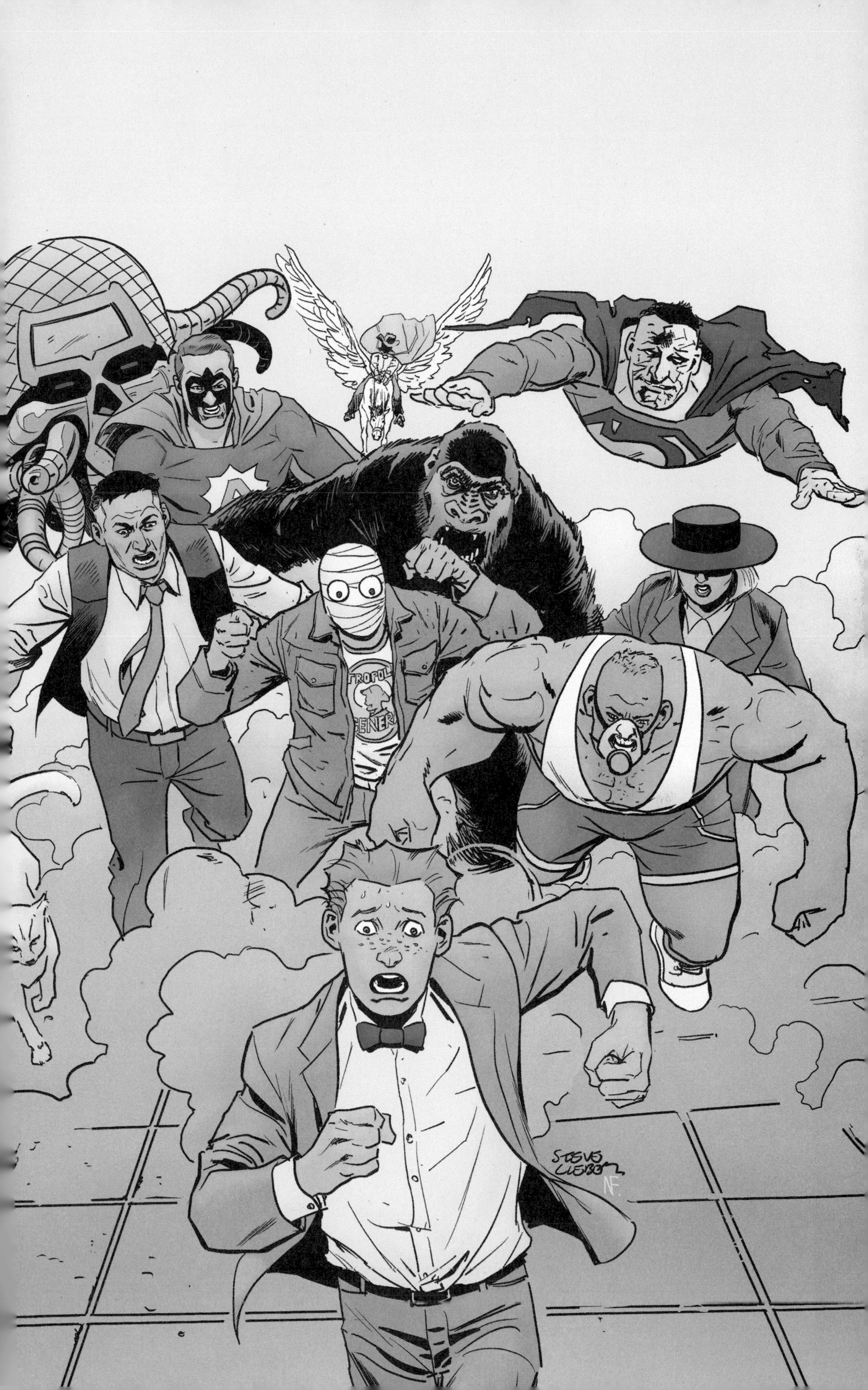

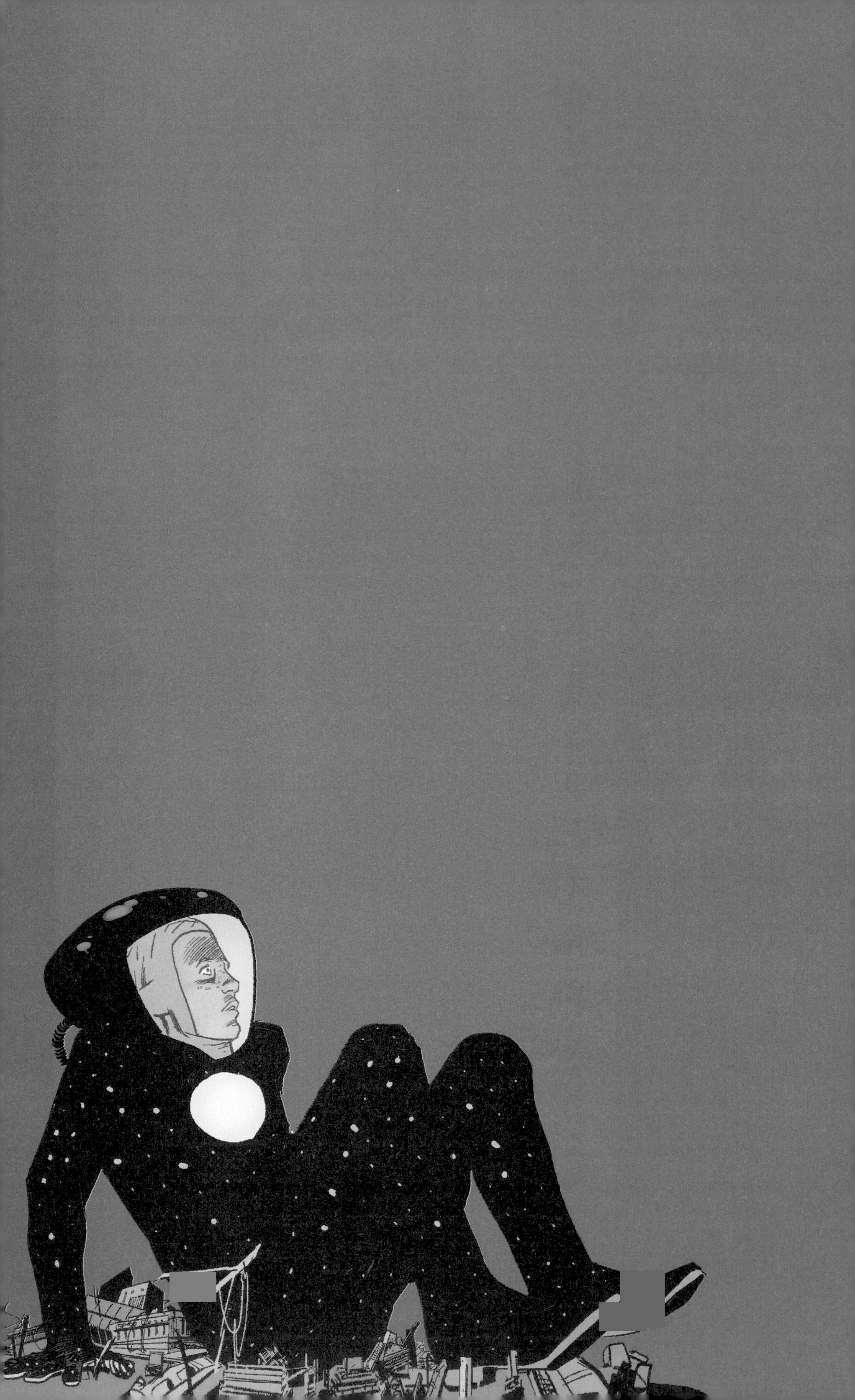

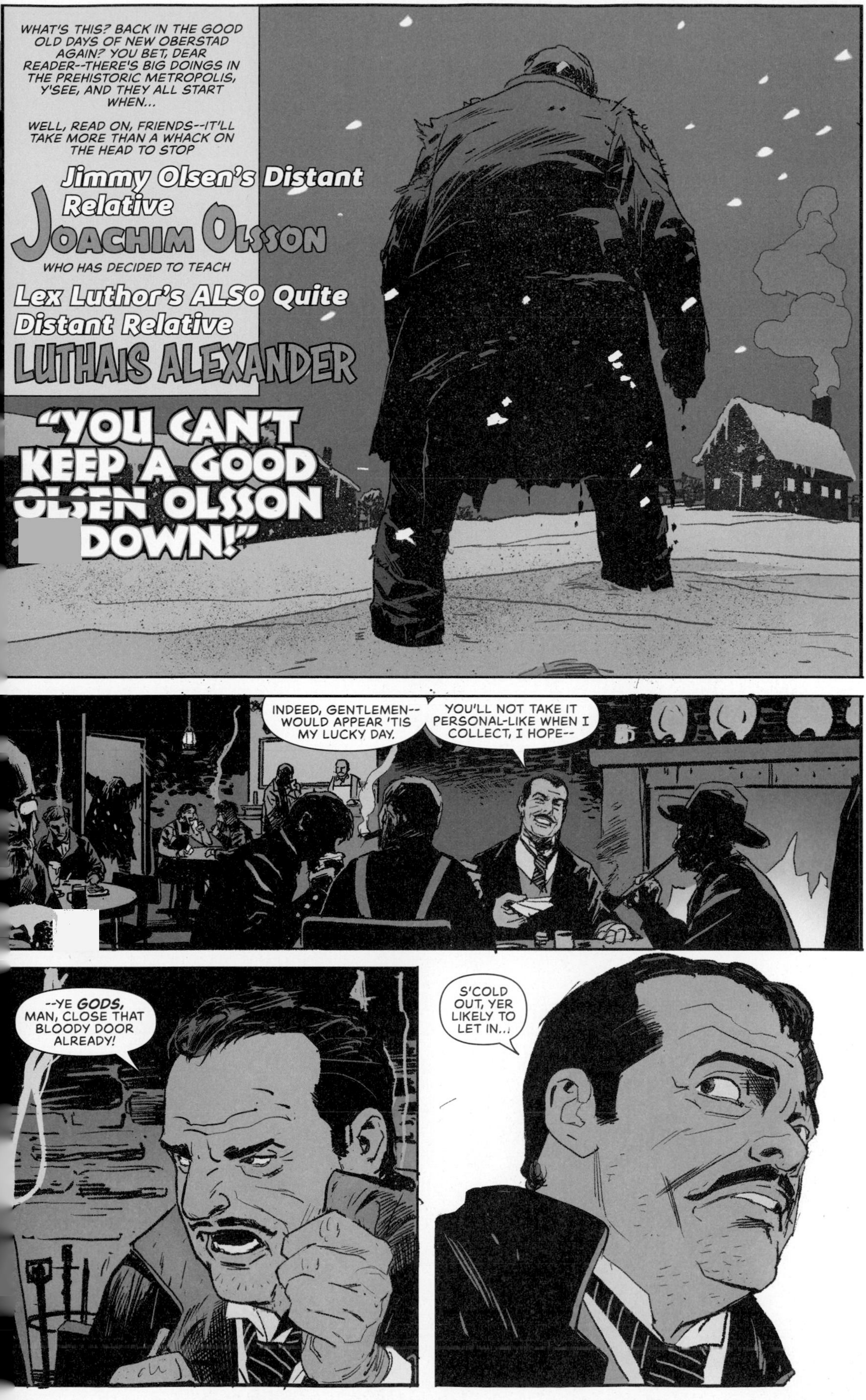
WHAT'S THIS? BACK IN THE GOOD OLD DAYS OF NEW OBERSTAD AGAIN? YOU BET, DEAR READER--THERE'S BIG DOINGS IN THE PREHISTORIC METROPOLIS, Y'SEE, AND THEY ALL START WHEN...
WELL, READ ON, FRIENDS--IT'LL TAKE MORE THAN A WHACK ON THE HEAD TO STOP
Jimmy Olsen's Distant Relative
JOACHIM OLSSON
WHO HAS DECIDED TO TEACH
Lex Luthor's ALSO Quite Distant Relative
LUTHAIS ALEXANDER
"YOU CAN'T KEEP A GOOD ~~OLSEN~~ OLSSON DOWN!"
INDEED, GENTLEMEN--WOULD APPEAR 'TIS MY LUCKY DAY.
YOU'LL NOT TAKE IT PERSONAL-LIKE WHEN I COLLECT, I HOPE--
--YE GODS, MAN, CLOSE THAT BLOODY DOOR ALREADY!
S'COLD OUT, YER LIKELY TO LET IN...

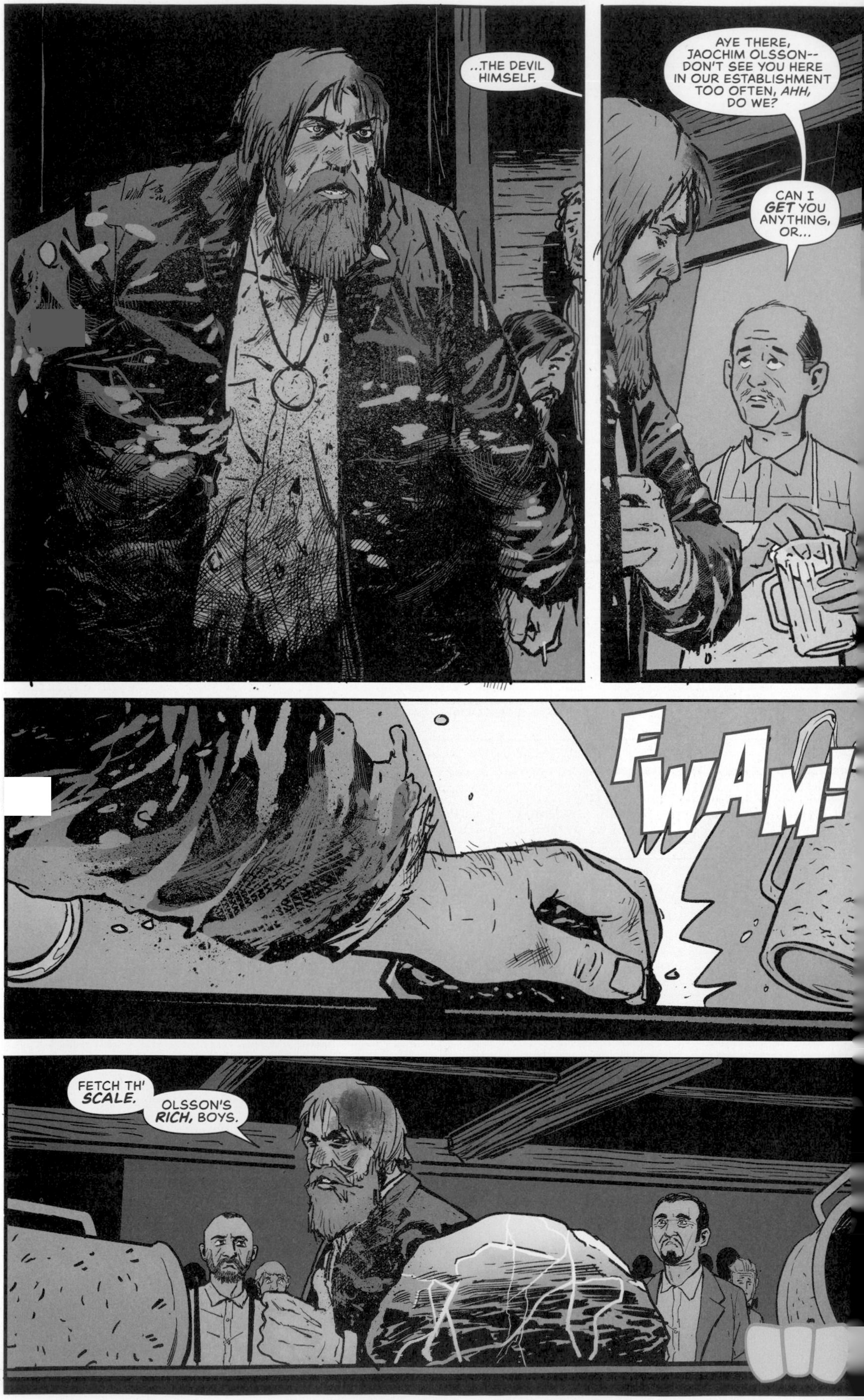
...THE DEVIL HIMSELF.
AYE THERE, JAOCHIM OLSSON-- DON'T SEE YOU HERE IN OUR ESTABLISHMENT TOO OFTEN, AHH, DO WE?
CAN I GET YOU ANYTHING, OR...
FWAM!
FETCH TH' SCALE.
OLSSON'S RICH, BOYS.

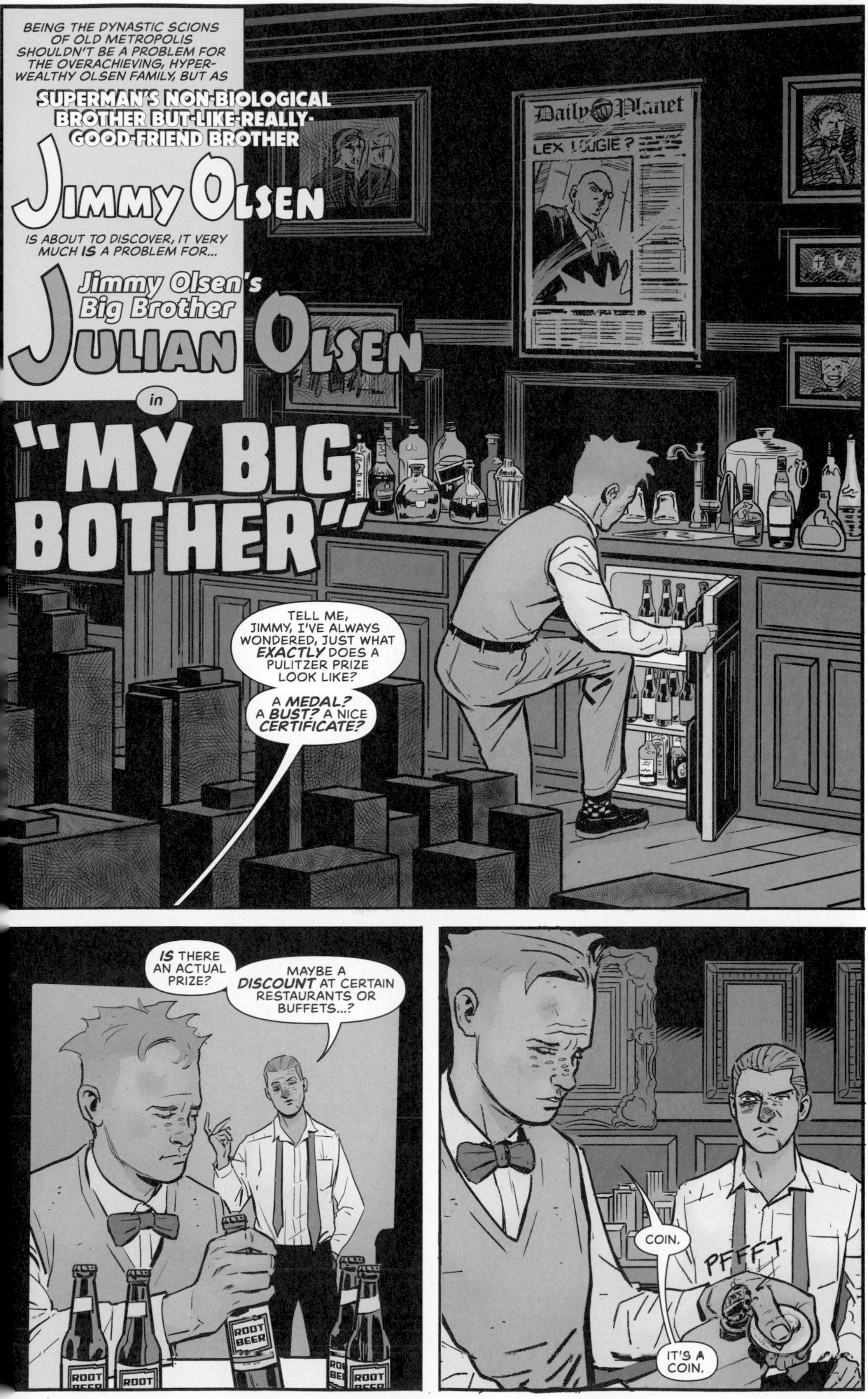
BEING THE DYNASTIC SCIONS OF OLD METROPOLIS SHOULDN'T BE A PROBLEM FOR THE OVERACHIEVING, HYPER-WEALTHY OLSEN FAMILY, BUT AS
SUPERMAN'S NON-BIOLOGICAL BROTHER BUT-LIKE-REALLY-GOOD-FRIEND BROTHER
JIMMY OLSEN
IS ABOUT TO DISCOVER, IT VERY MUCH IS A PROBLEM FOR...
Jimmy Olsen's Big Brother
JULIAN OLSEN
in
"MY BIG BOTHER"
Daily Planet
TELL ME, JIMMY, I'VE ALWAYS WONDERED, JUST WHAT EXACTLY DOES A PULITZER PRIZE LOOK LIKE?
A MEDAL? A BUST? A NICE CERTIFICATE?
IS THERE AN ACTUAL PRIZE?
MAYBE A DISCOUNT AT CERTAIN RESTAURANTS OR BUFFETS...?
ROOT BEER
COIN.
PFFFT
IT'S A COIN.

SEE?

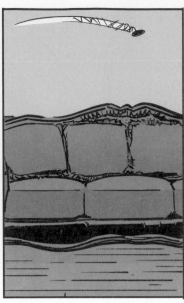

AH. WELL, YES.

I MEAN, THERE'S A CERTIFICATE, TOO, AND STUFF...

Daily Planet

LEX LOOGIE?

SAY, DID I EVER TELL YOU HOW I *GOT* THAT SHOT?

WHY YES, YOU HAVE, ABOUT SEVENTEEN *MILLION*

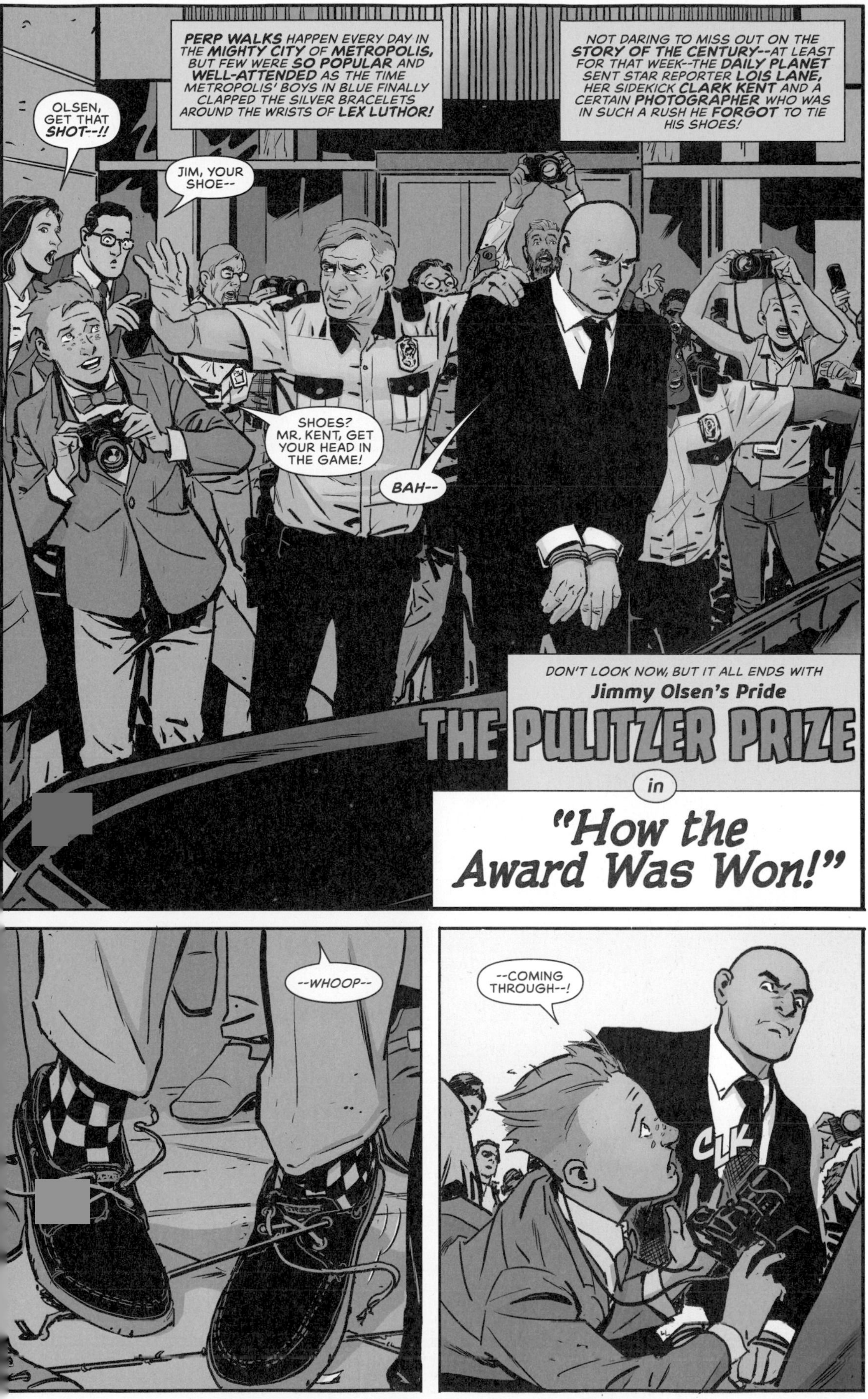
PERP WALKS HAPPEN EVERY DAY IN THE MIGHTY CITY OF METROPOLIS, BUT FEW WERE SO POPULAR AND WELL-ATTENDED AS THE TIME METROPOLIS' BOYS IN BLUE FINALLY CLAPPED THE SILVER BRACELETS AROUND THE WRISTS OF LEX LUTHOR!
NOT DARING TO MISS OUT ON THE STORY OF THE CENTURY--AT LEAST FOR THAT WEEK--THE DAILY PLANET SENT STAR REPORTER LOIS LANE, HER SIDEKICK CLARK KENT AND A CERTAIN PHOTOGRAPHER WHO WAS IN SUCH A RUSH HE FORGOT TO TIE HIS SHOES!
OLSEN, GET THAT SHOT--!!
JIM, YOUR SHOE--
SHOES? MR. KENT, GET YOUR HEAD IN THE GAME!
BAH--
DON'T LOOK NOW, BUT IT ALL ENDS WITH
Jimmy Olsen's Pride
THE PULITZER PRIZE
in
"How the Award Was Won!"
--WHOOP--
--COMING THROUGH--!
CLIK

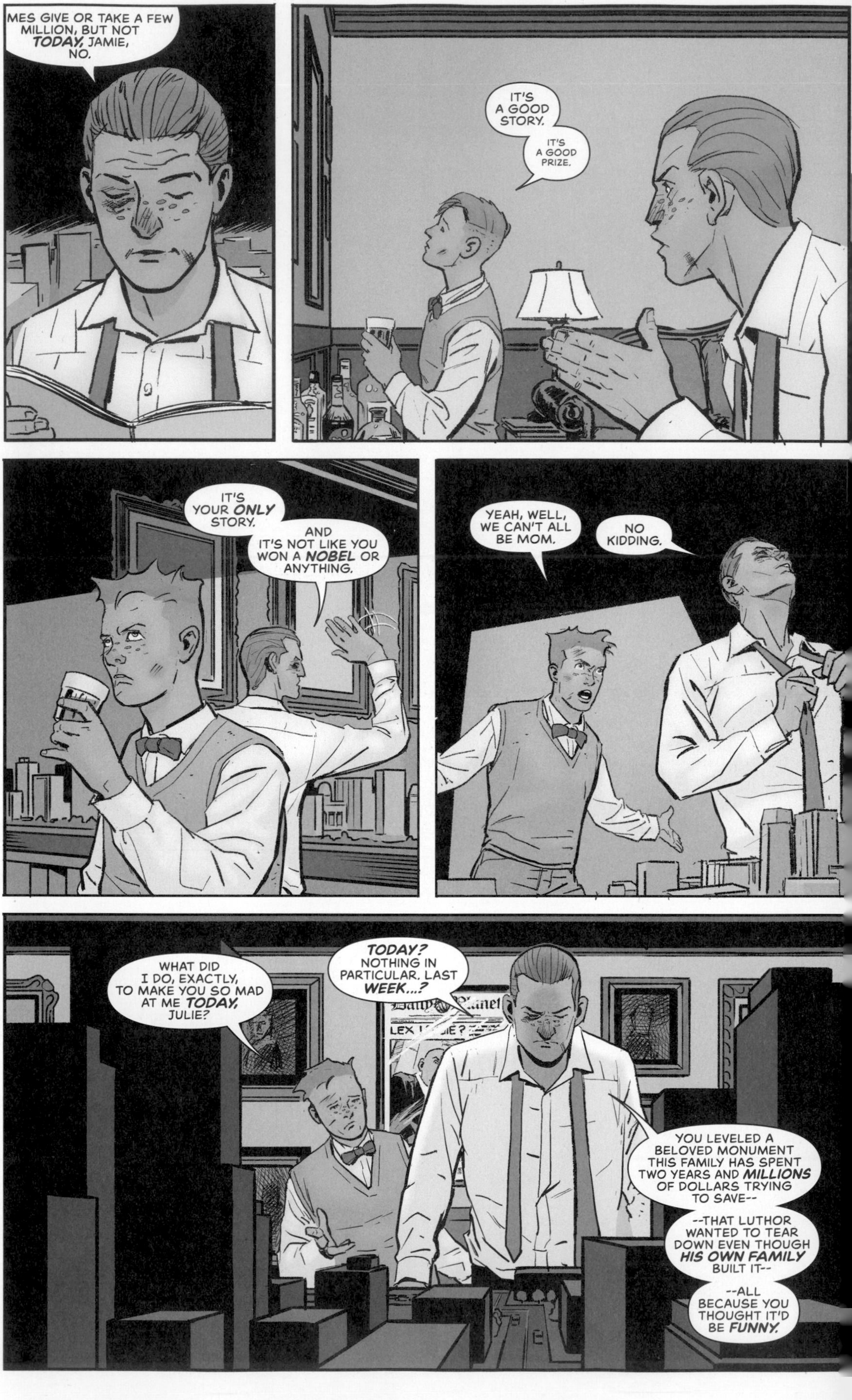
MES GIVE OR TAKE A FEW MILLION, BUT NOT TODAY, JAMIE, NO.
IT'S A GOOD STORY.
IT'S A GOOD PRIZE.
IT'S YOUR ONLY STORY.
AND IT'S NOT LIKE YOU WON A NOBEL OR ANYTHING.
YEAH, WELL, WE CAN'T ALL BE MOM.
NO KIDDING.
WHAT DID I DO, EXACTLY, TO MAKE YOU SO MAD AT ME TODAY, JULIE?
TODAY? NOTHING IN PARTICULAR. LAST WEEK...?
YOU LEVELED A BELOVED MONUMENT THIS FAMILY HAS SPENT TWO YEARS AND MILLIONS OF DOLLARS TRYING TO SAVE--
--THAT LUTHOR WANTED TO TEAR DOWN EVEN THOUGH HIS OWN FAMILY BUILT IT--
--ALL BECAUSE YOU THOUGHT IT'D BE FUNNY.

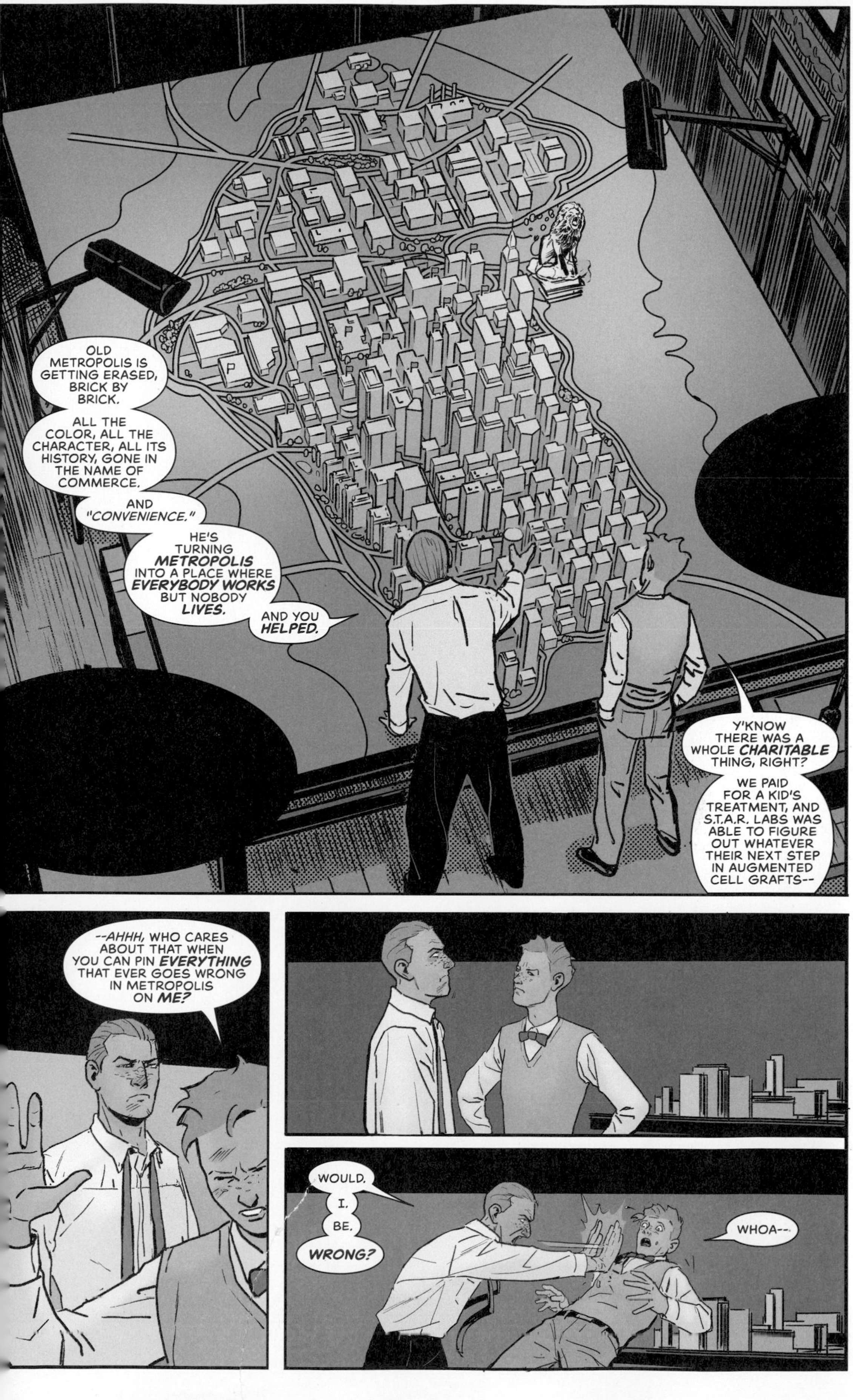

OLD METROPOLIS IS GETTING ERASED, BRICK BY BRICK.
ALL THE COLOR, ALL THE CHARACTER, ALL ITS HISTORY, GONE IN THE NAME OF COMMERCE.
AND "CONVENIENCE."
HE'S TURNING METROPOLIS INTO A PLACE WHERE EVERYBODY WORKS BUT NOBODY LIVES.
AND YOU HELPED.
Y'KNOW THERE WAS A WHOLE CHARITABLE THING, RIGHT?
WE PAID FOR A KID'S TREATMENT, AND S.T.A.R. LABS WAS ABLE TO FIGURE OUT WHATEVER THEIR NEXT STEP IN AUGMENTED CELL GRAFTS--
--AHHH, WHO CARES ABOUT THAT WHEN YOU CAN PIN EVERYTHING THAT EVER GOES WRONG IN METROPOLIS ON ME?
WOULD.
I.
BE.
WRONG?
WHOA--

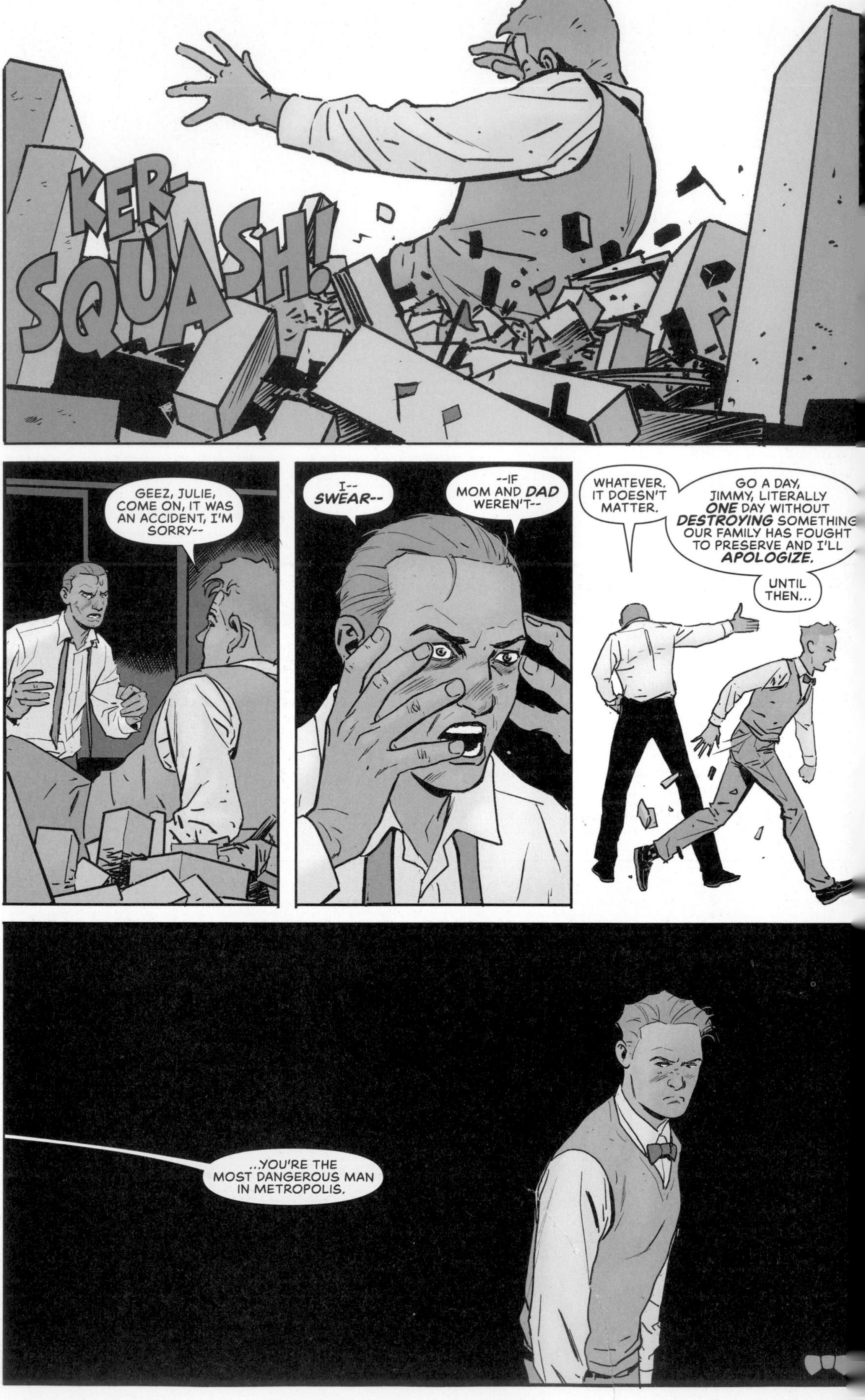
KER-SQUASH!
GEEZ, JULIE, COME ON, IT WAS AN ACCIDENT, I'M SORRY--
I-- SWEAR--
--IF MOM AND DAD WEREN'T--
WHATEVER. IT DOESN'T MATTER.
GO A DAY, JIMMY, LITERALLY ONE DAY WITHOUT DESTROYING SOMETHING OUR FAMILY HAS FOUGHT TO PRESERVE AND I'LL APOLOGIZE.
UNTIL THEN...
...YOU'RE THE MOST DANGEROUS MAN IN METROPOLIS.

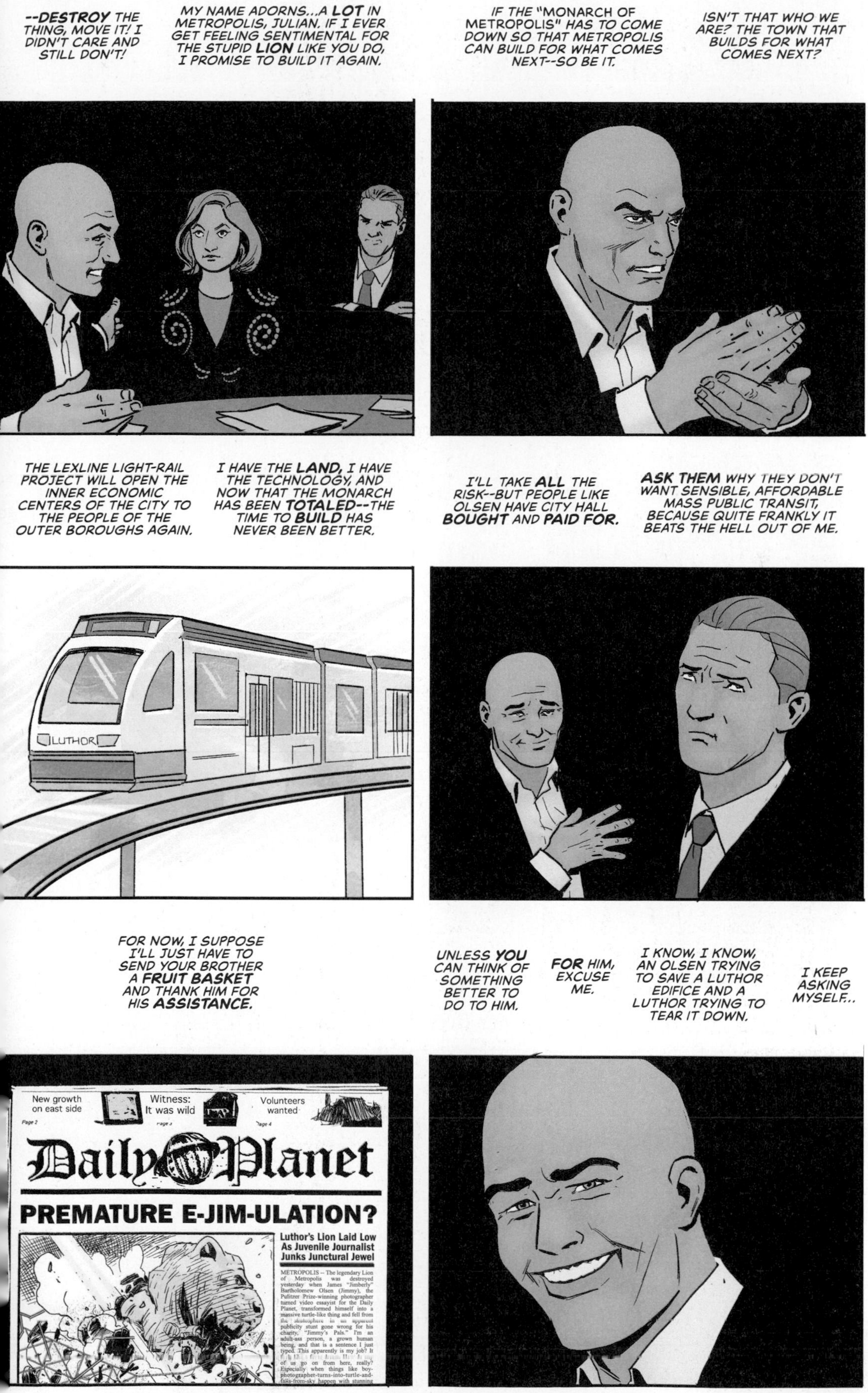
--DESTROY THE THING, MOVE IT! I DIDN'T CARE AND STILL DON'T!
MY NAME ADORNS...A LOT IN METROPOLIS, JULIAN. IF I EVER GET FEELING SENTIMENTAL FOR THE STUPID LION LIKE YOU DO, I PROMISE TO BUILD IT AGAIN.
IF THE "MONARCH OF METROPOLIS" HAS TO COME DOWN SO THAT METROPOLIS CAN BUILD FOR WHAT COMES NEXT--SO BE IT.
ISN'T THAT WHO WE ARE? THE TOWN THAT BUILDS FOR WHAT COMES NEXT?
THE LEXLINE LIGHT-RAIL PROJECT WILL OPEN THE INNER ECONOMIC CENTERS OF THE CITY TO THE PEOPLE OF THE OUTER BOROUGHS AGAIN.
I HAVE THE LAND, I HAVE THE TECHNOLOGY, AND NOW THAT THE MONARCH HAS BEEN TOTALED--THE TIME TO BUILD HAS NEVER BEEN BETTER.
LUTHOR
I'LL TAKE ALL THE RISK--BUT PEOPLE LIKE OLSEN HAVE CITY HALL BOUGHT AND PAID FOR.
ASK THEM WHY THEY DON'T WANT SENSIBLE, AFFORDABLE MASS PUBLIC TRANSIT, BECAUSE QUITE FRANKLY IT BEATS THE HELL OUT OF ME.
FOR NOW, I SUPPOSE I'LL JUST HAVE TO SEND YOUR BROTHER A FRUIT BASKET AND THANK HIM FOR HIS ASSISTANCE.
New growth on east side
Page 2
Witness: It was wild
Volunteers wanted
Daily Planet
PREMATURE E-JIM-ULATION?
Luthor's Lion Laid Low As Juvenile Journalist Junks Junctural Jewel
METROPOLIS -- The legendary Lion of Metropolis was destroyed yesterday when James "Jimberly" Bartholomew Olsen (Jimmy), the Pulitzer Prize-winning photographer turned video essayist for the Daily Planet, transformed himself into a massive turtle-like thing and fell from
publicity stunt gone wrong for his charity, "Jimmy's Pals." I'm an adult-ass person, a grown human being, and that is a sentence I just typed. This apparently is my job? It
of us go on from here, really? Especially when things like boy-photographer-turns-into-turtle-and-falls-from-sky happen with stunning
UNLESS YOU CAN THINK OF SOMETHING BETTER TO DO TO HIM.
FOR HIM, EXCUSE ME.
I KNOW, I KNOW, AN OLSEN TRYING TO SAVE A LUTHOR EDIFICE AND A LUTHOR TRYING TO TEAR IT DOWN.
I KEEP ASKING MYSELF...

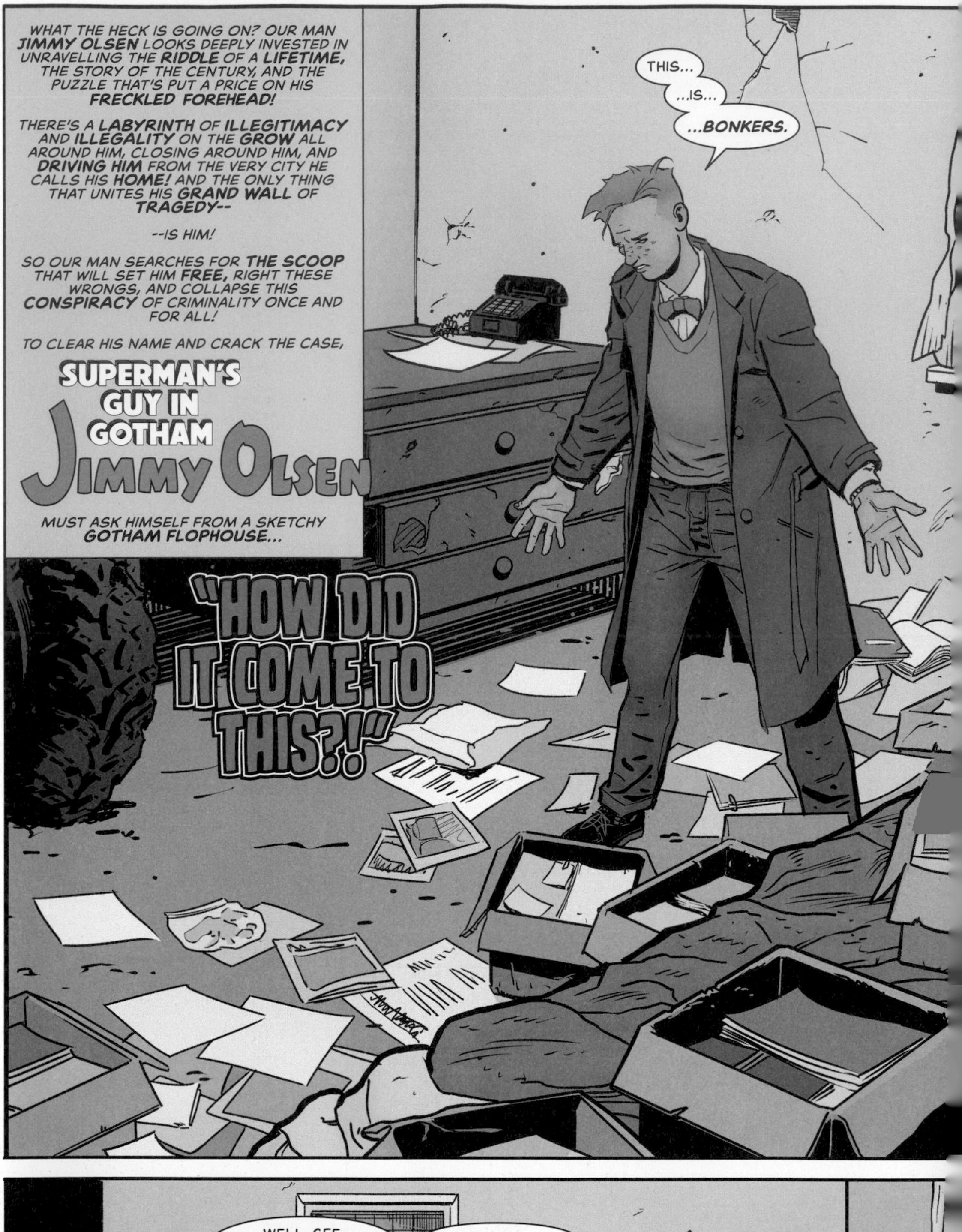
WHAT THE HECK IS GOING ON? OUR MAN JIMMY OLSEN LOOKS DEEPLY INVESTED IN UNRAVELLING THE RIDDLE OF A LIFETIME, THE STORY OF THE CENTURY, AND THE PUZZLE THAT'S PUT A PRICE ON HIS FRECKLED FOREHEAD!
THERE'S A LABYRINTH OF ILLEGITIMACY AND ILLEGALITY ON THE GROW ALL AROUND HIM, CLOSING AROUND HIM, AND DRIVING HIM FROM THE VERY CITY HE CALLS HIS HOME! AND THE ONLY THING THAT UNITES HIS GRAND WALL OF TRAGEDY--
--IS HIM!
SO OUR MAN SEARCHES FOR THE SCOOP THAT WILL SET HIM FREE, RIGHT THESE WRONGS, AND COLLAPSE THIS CONSPIRACY OF CRIMINALITY ONCE AND FOR ALL!
TO CLEAR HIS NAME AND CRACK THE CASE,
SUPERMAN'S GUY IN GOTHAM
JIMMY OLSEN
MUST ASK HIMSELF FROM A SKETCHY GOTHAM FLOPHOUSE...
THIS...
...IS...
...BONKERS.
"HOW DID IT COME TO THIS?!"
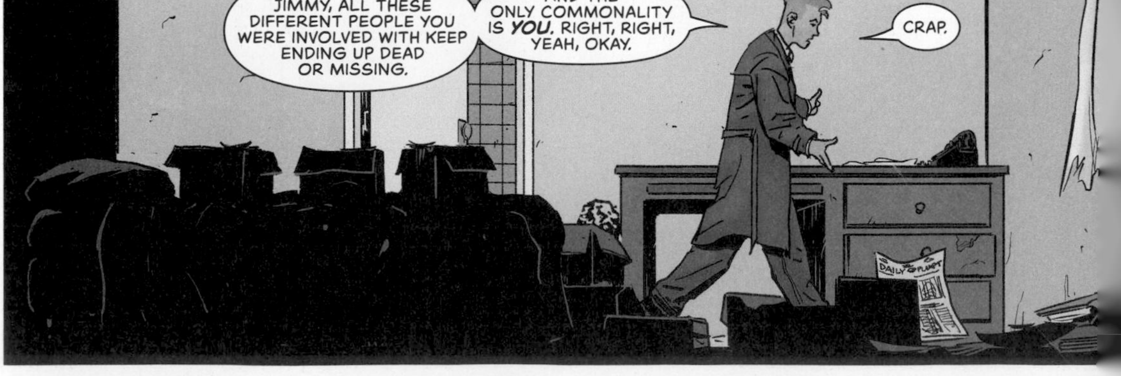
WELL, SEE, JIMMY, ALL THESE DIFFERENT PEOPLE YOU WERE INVOLVED WITH KEEP ENDING UP DEAD OR MISSING.
AND THE ONLY COMMONALITY IS YOU. RIGHT, RIGHT, YEAH, OKAY.
CRAP.

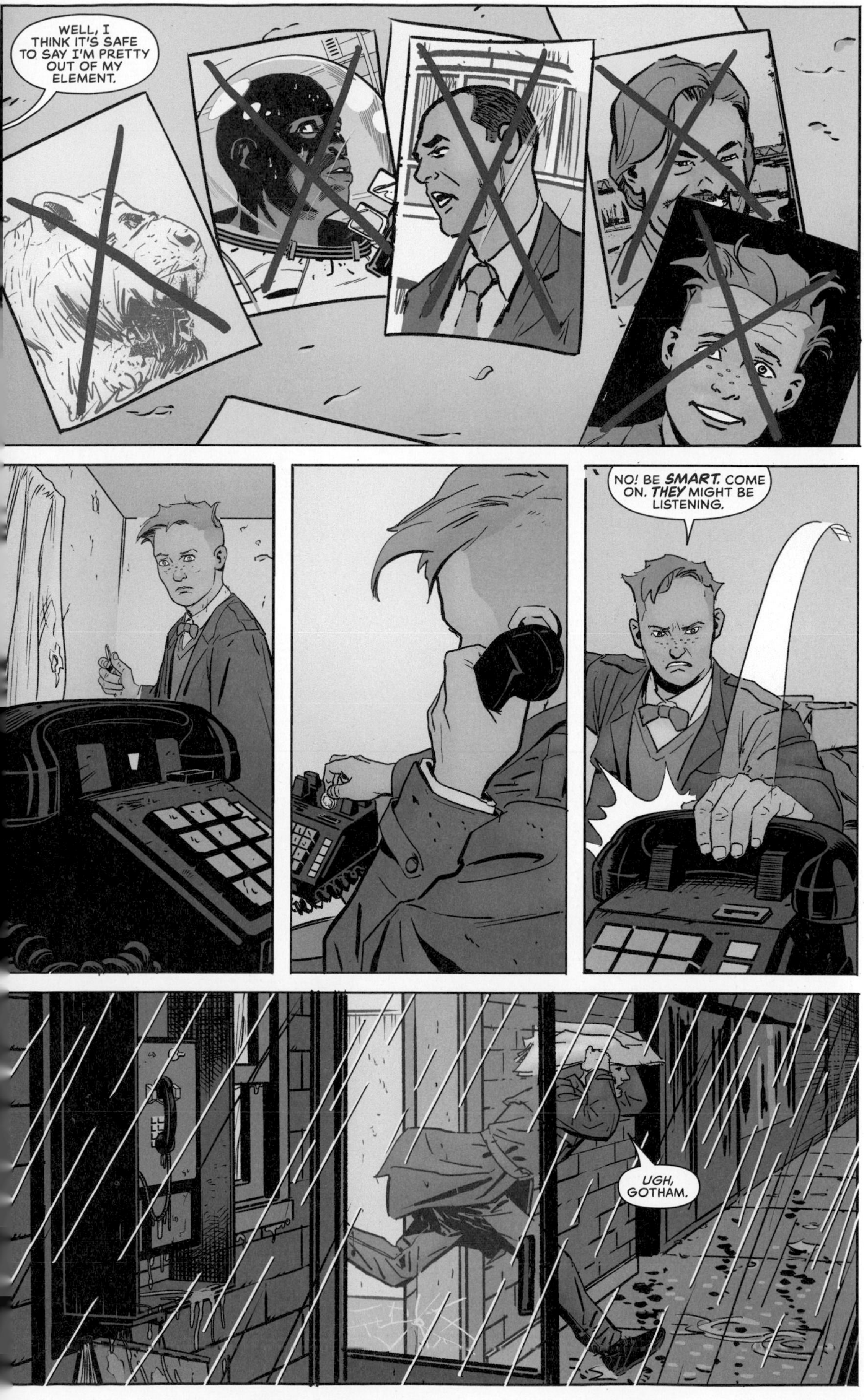
WELL, I THINK IT'S SAFE TO SAY I'M PRETTY OUT OF MY ELEMENT.
NO! BE **SMART.** COME ON. ***THEY*** MIGHT BE LISTENING.
UGH, GOTHAM.

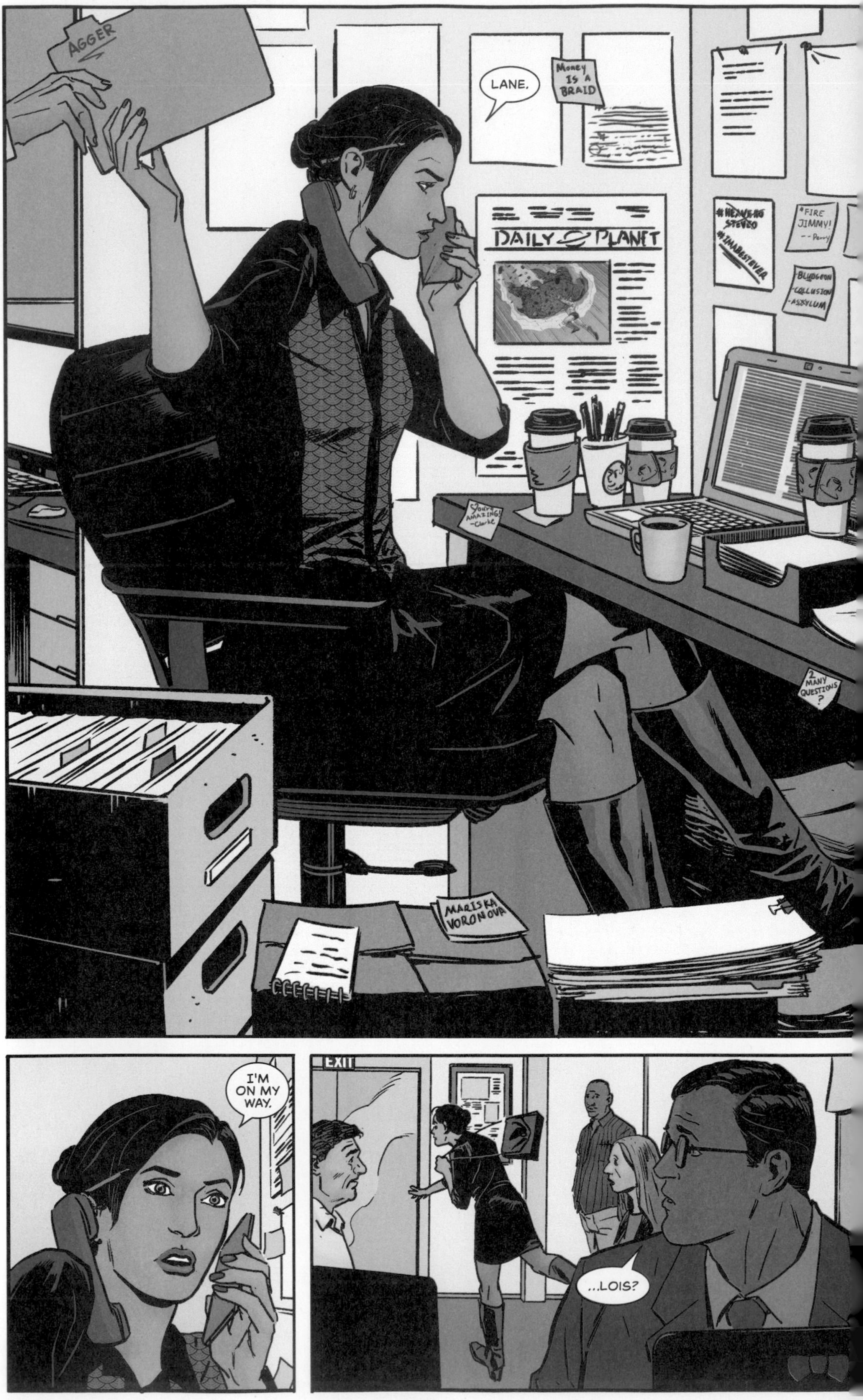

AGGER
LANE.
Money Is a Braid
DAILY PLANET
*FIRE JIMMY! --Perry
-BLUDGEON -COLLUSION -ASSYLUM
You're AMAZING! -Clark
2 MANY QUESTIONS ?
MARISKA VORONOVA
I'M ON MY WAY.
EXIT
...LOIS?

WHO
SHOT
THE DECOY CORPSE OF SUPERMAN'S PAL
JIMMY
OLSEN?

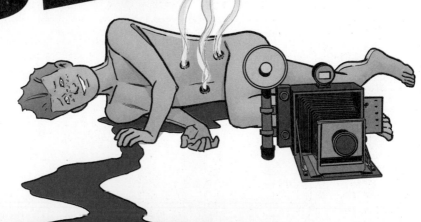

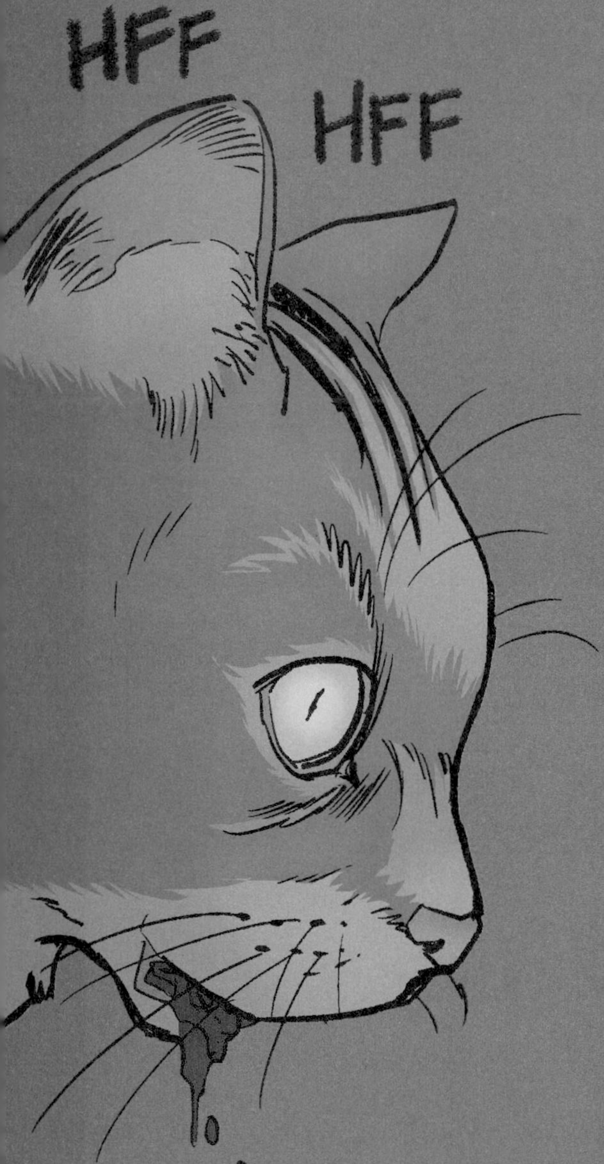
HFF
HFF

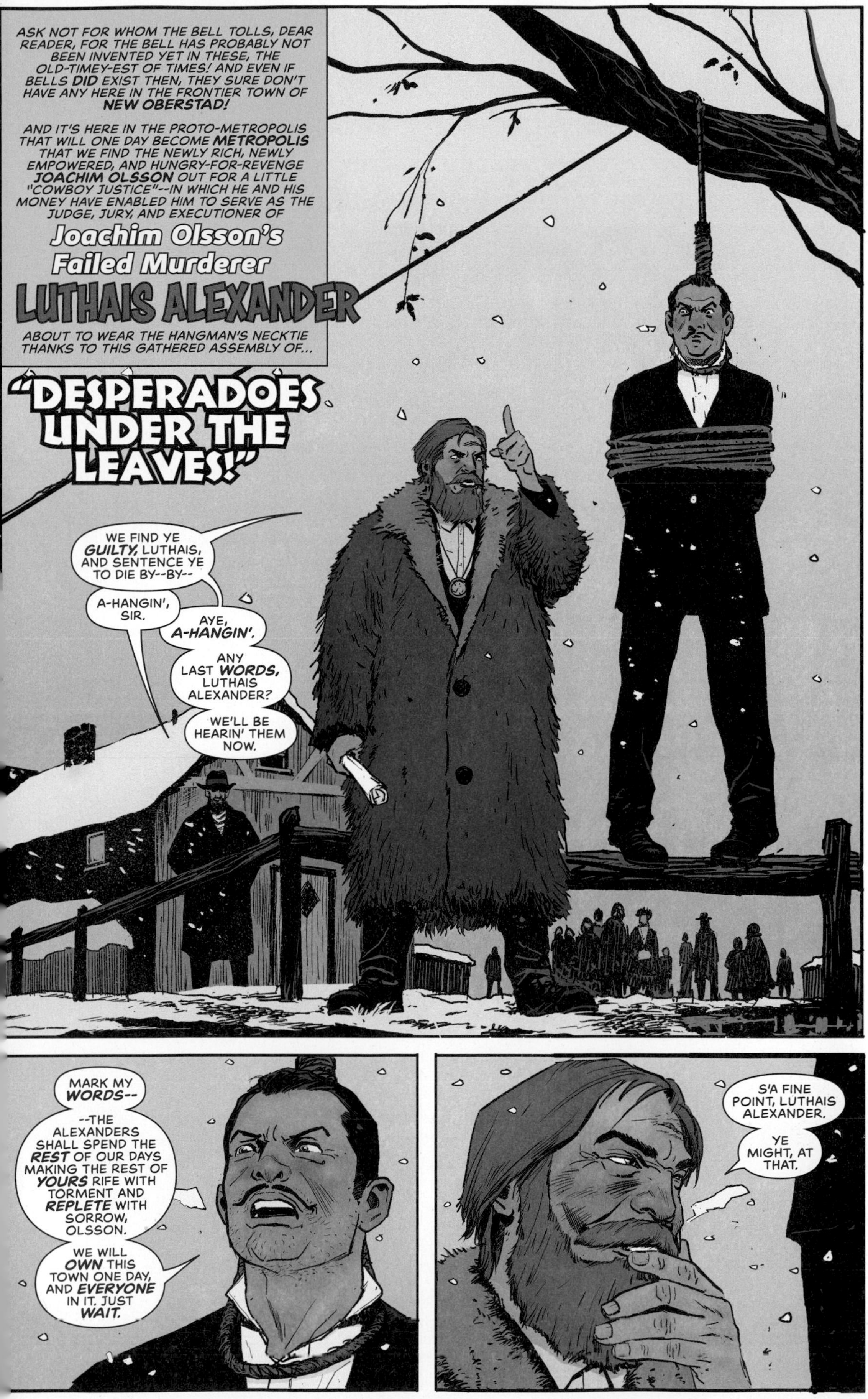
ASK NOT FOR WHOM THE BELL TOLLS, DEAR READER, FOR THE BELL HAS PROBABLY NOT BEEN INVENTED YET IN THESE, THE OLD-TIMEY-EST OF TIMES! AND EVEN IF BELLS DID EXIST THEN, THEY SURE DON'T HAVE ANY HERE IN THE FRONTIER TOWN OF NEW OBERSTAD!
AND IT'S HERE IN THE PROTO-METROPOLIS THAT WILL ONE DAY BECOME METROPOLIS THAT WE FIND THE NEWLY RICH, NEWLY EMPOWERED, AND HUNGRY-FOR-REVENGE JOACHIM OLSSON OUT FOR A LITTLE "COWBOY JUSTICE"--IN WHICH HE AND HIS MONEY HAVE ENABLED HIM TO SERVE AS THE JUDGE, JURY, AND EXECUTIONER OF
Joachim Olsson's Failed Murderer
LUTHAIS ALEXANDER
ABOUT TO WEAR THE HANGMAN'S NECKTIE THANKS TO THIS GATHERED ASSEMBLY OF...
"DESPERADOES UNDER THE LEAVES!"
WE FIND YE GUILTY, LUTHAIS, AND SENTENCE YE TO DIE BY--BY--
A-HANGIN', SIR.
AYE, A-HANGIN'.
ANY LAST WORDS, LUTHAIS ALEXANDER?
WE'LL BE HEARIN' THEM NOW.
MARK MY WORDS--
--THE ALEXANDERS SHALL SPEND THE REST OF OUR DAYS MAKING THE REST OF YOURS RIFE WITH TORMENT AND REPLETE WITH SORROW, OLSSON.
WE WILL OWN THIS TOWN ONE DAY, AND EVERYONE IN IT. JUST WAIT.
S'A FINE POINT, LUTHAIS ALEXANDER.
YE MIGHT, AT THAT.

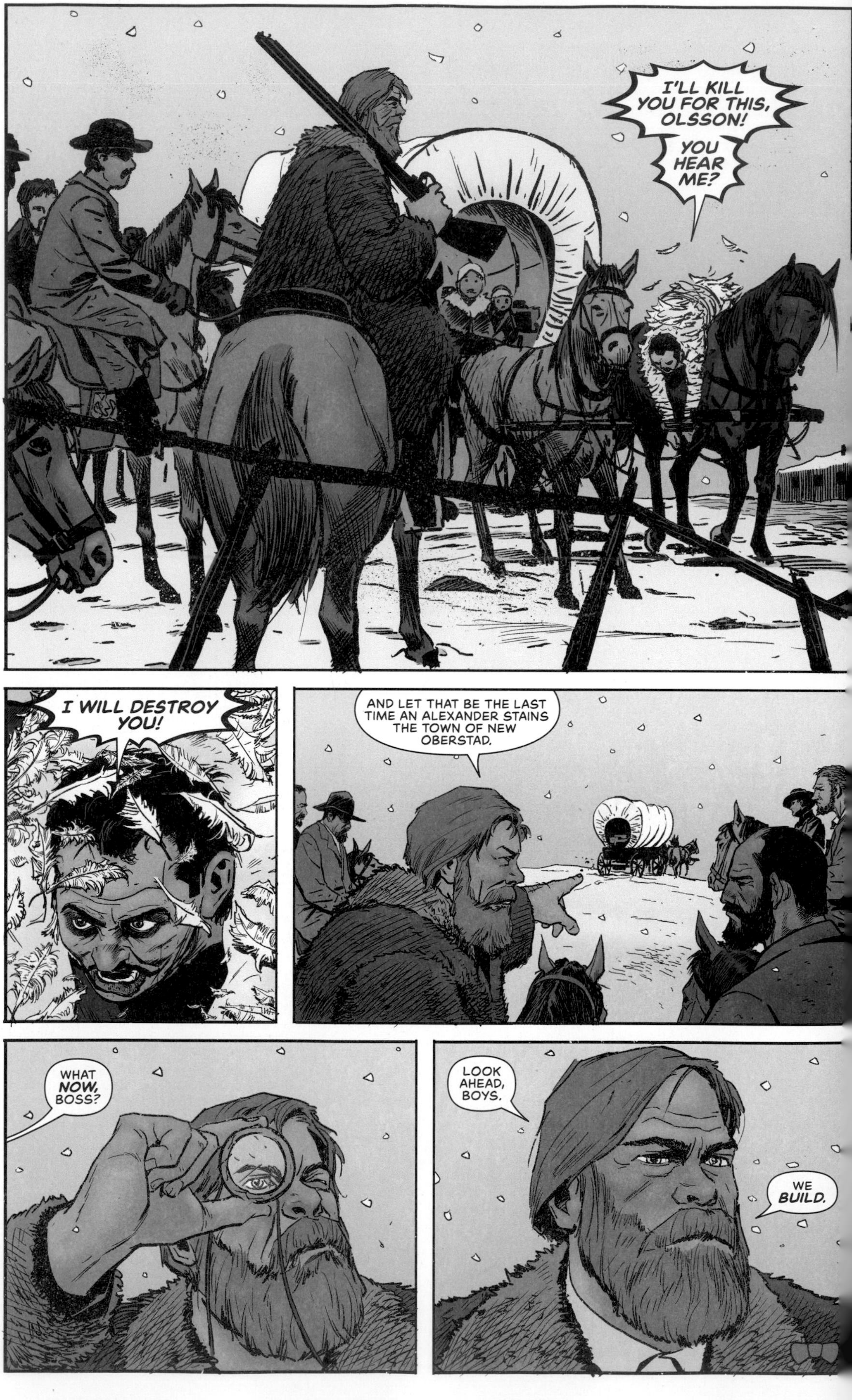
I'LL KILL YOU FOR THIS, OLSSON!
YOU HEAR ME?
I WILL DESTROY YOU!
AND LET THAT BE THE LAST TIME AN ALEXANDER STAINS THE TOWN OF NEW OBERSTAD.
WHAT NOW, BOSS?
LOOK AHEAD, BOYS.
WE BUILD.

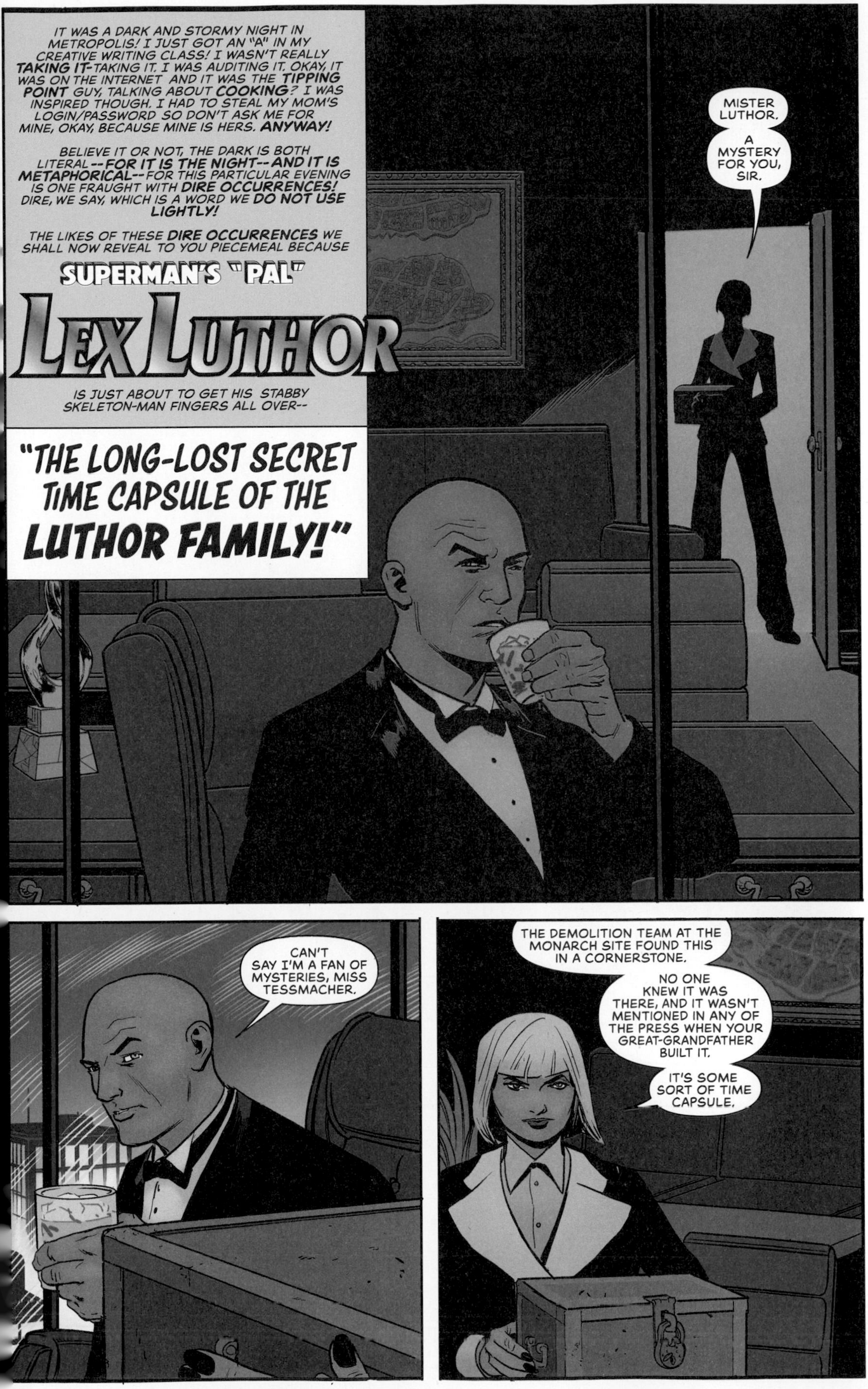
IT WAS A DARK AND STORMY NIGHT IN METROPOLIS! I JUST GOT AN "A" IN MY CREATIVE WRITING CLASS! I WASN'T REALLY TAKING IT-TAKING IT. I WAS AUDITING IT. OKAY, IT WAS ON THE INTERNET AND IT WAS THE TIPPING POINT GUY, TALKING ABOUT COOKING? I WAS INSPIRED THOUGH. I HAD TO STEAL MY MOM'S LOGIN/PASSWORD SO DON'T ASK ME FOR MINE, OKAY, BECAUSE MINE IS HERS. ANYWAY!
BELIEVE IT OR NOT, THE DARK IS BOTH LITERAL--FOR IT IS THE NIGHT--AND IT IS METAPHORICAL--FOR THIS PARTICULAR EVENING IS ONE FRAUGHT WITH DIRE OCCURRENCES! DIRE, WE SAY, WHICH IS A WORD WE DO NOT USE LIGHTLY!
THE LIKES OF THESE DIRE OCCURRENCES WE SHALL NOW REVEAL TO YOU PIECEMEAL BECAUSE
SUPERMAN'S "PAL"
LEX LUTHOR
IS JUST ABOUT TO GET HIS STABBY SKELETON-MAN FINGERS ALL OVER--
"THE LONG-LOST SECRET TIME CAPSULE OF THE LUTHOR FAMILY!"
MISTER LUTHOR.
A MYSTERY FOR YOU, SIR.
CAN'T SAY I'M A FAN OF MYSTERIES, MISS TESSMACHER.
THE DEMOLITION TEAM AT THE MONARCH SITE FOUND THIS IN A CORNERSTONE.
NO ONE KNEW IT WAS THERE, AND IT WASN'T MENTIONED IN ANY OF THE PRESS WHEN YOUR GREAT-GRANDFATHER BUILT IT.
IT'S SOME SORT OF TIME CAPSULE.

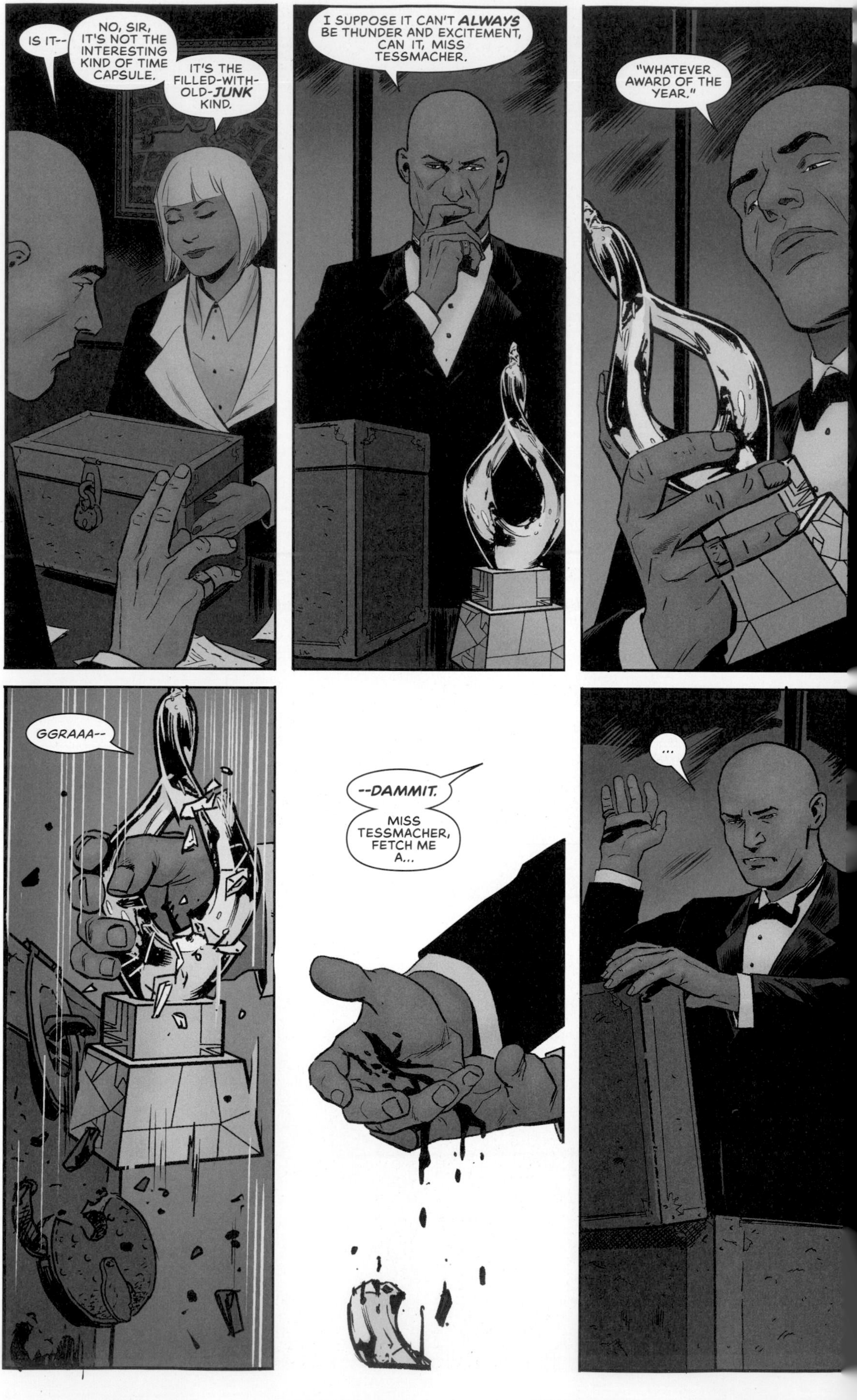
IS IT--
NO, SIR, IT'S NOT THE INTERESTING KIND OF TIME CAPSULE.
IT'S THE FILLED-WITH-OLD-JUNK KIND.
I SUPPOSE IT CAN'T ALWAYS BE THUNDER AND EXCITEMENT, CAN IT, MISS TESSMACHER.
"WHATEVER AWARD OF THE YEAR."
GGRAAA--
--DAMMIT.
MISS TESSMACHER, FETCH ME A...
...

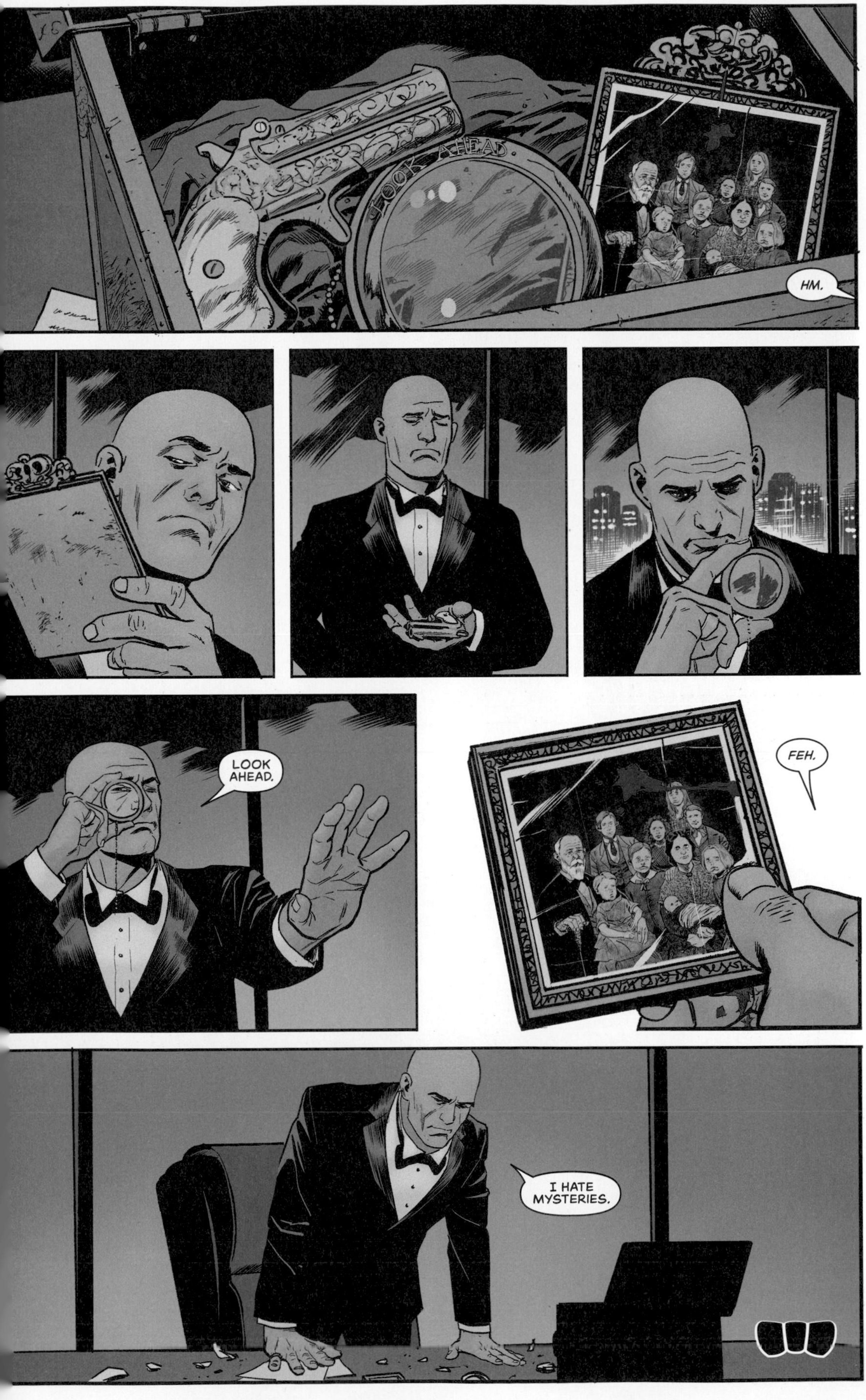
LOOK AHEAD
HM.
LOOK AHEAD.
FEH.
I HATE MYSTERIES.

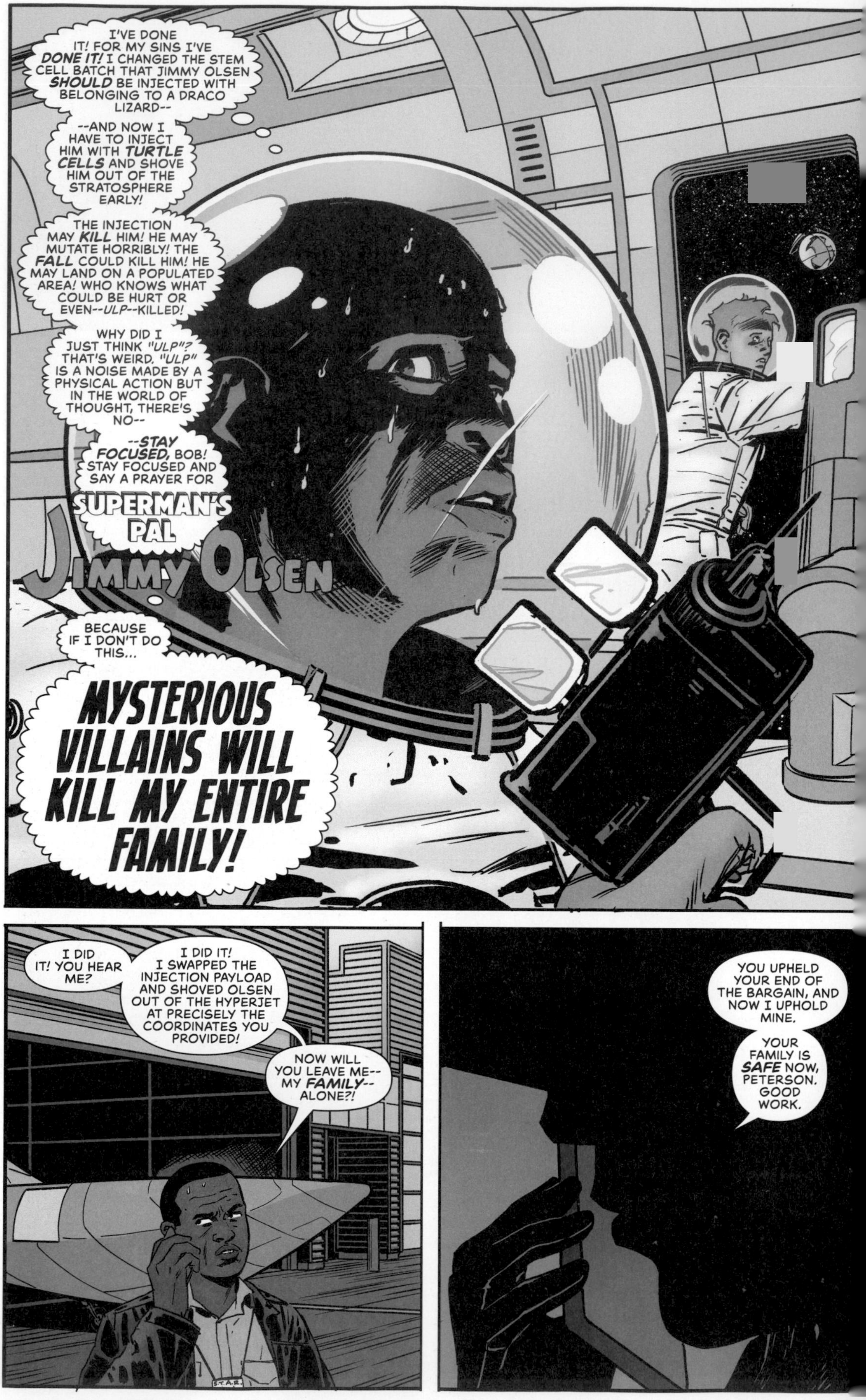
I'VE DONE IT! FOR MY SINS I'VE DONE IT! I CHANGED THE STEM CELL BATCH THAT JIMMY OLSEN SHOULD BE INJECTED WITH BELONGING TO A DRACO LIZARD--
--AND NOW I HAVE TO INJECT HIM WITH TURTLE CELLS AND SHOVE HIM OUT OF THE STRATOSPHERE EARLY!
THE INJECTION MAY KILL HIM! HE MAY MUTATE HORRIBLY! THE FALL COULD KILL HIM! HE MAY LAND ON A POPULATED AREA! WHO KNOWS WHAT COULD BE HURT OR EVEN--ULP--KILLED!
WHY DID I JUST THINK "ULP"? THAT'S WEIRD. "ULP" IS A NOISE MADE BY A PHYSICAL ACTION BUT IN THE WORLD OF THOUGHT, THERE'S NO--
--STAY FOCUSED, BOB! STAY FOCUSED AND SAY A PRAYER FOR
SUPERMAN'S PAL JIMMY OLSEN
BECAUSE IF I DON'T DO THIS...
MYSTERIOUS VILLAINS WILL KILL MY ENTIRE FAMILY!
I DID IT! YOU HEAR ME?
I DID IT! I SWAPPED THE INJECTION PAYLOAD AND SHOVED OLSEN OUT OF THE HYPERJET AT PRECISELY THE COORDINATES YOU PROVIDED!
NOW WILL YOU LEAVE ME--MY FAMILY--ALONE?!
S.T.A.R.
YOU UPHELD YOUR END OF THE BARGAIN, AND NOW I UPHOLD MINE.
YOUR FAMILY IS SAFE NOW, PETERSON. GOOD WORK.

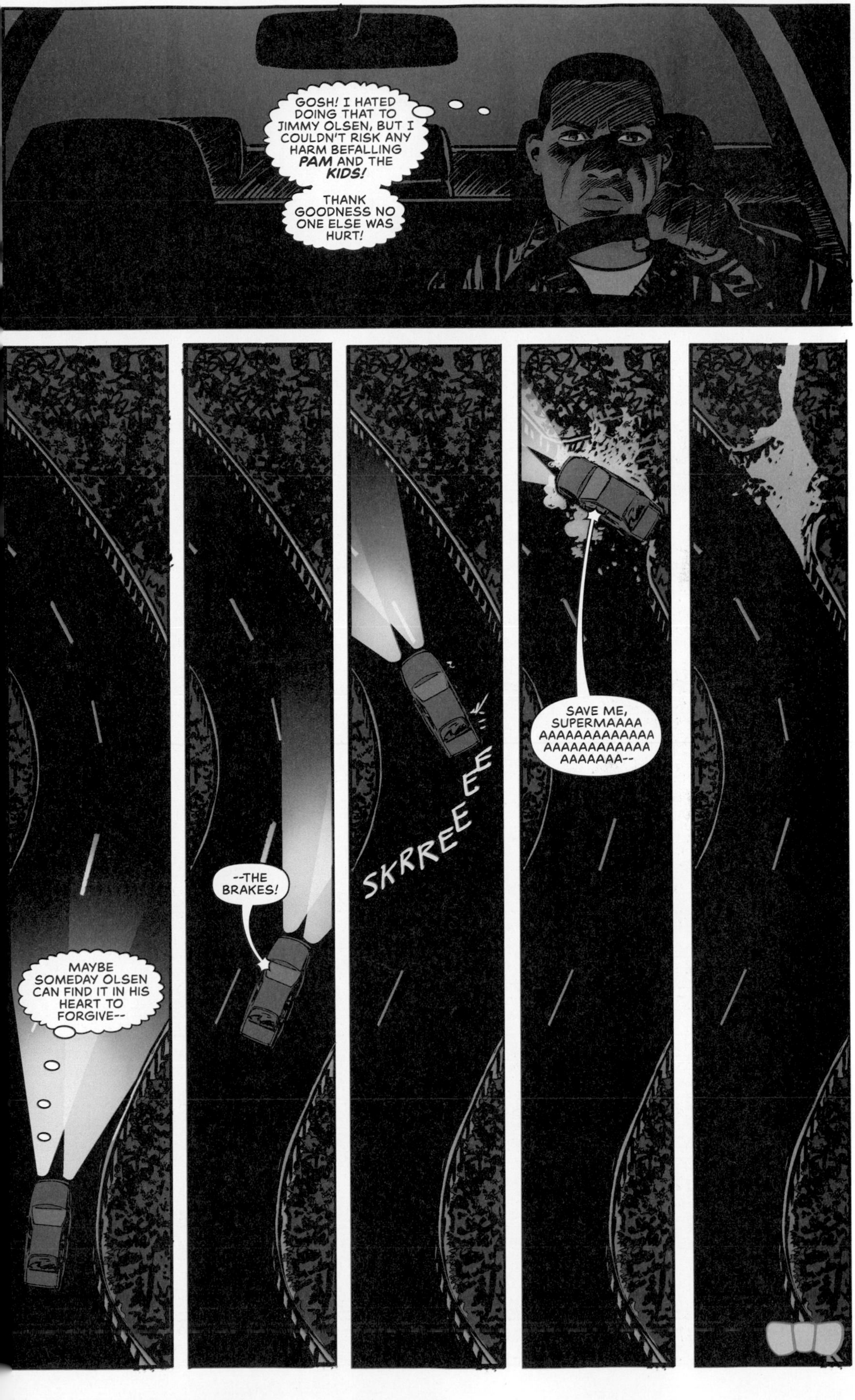
GOSH! I HATED DOING THAT TO JIMMY OLSEN, BUT I COULDN'T RISK ANY HARM BEFALLING PAM AND THE KIDS!
THANK GOODNESS NO ONE ELSE WAS HURT!
MAYBE SOMEDAY OLSEN CAN FIND IT IN HIS HEART TO FORGIVE--
--THE BRAKES!
SKRREEEE
SAVE ME, SUPERMAAAAA AAAAAAAAAAAAA AAAAAAAAAAAA AAAAAAA--

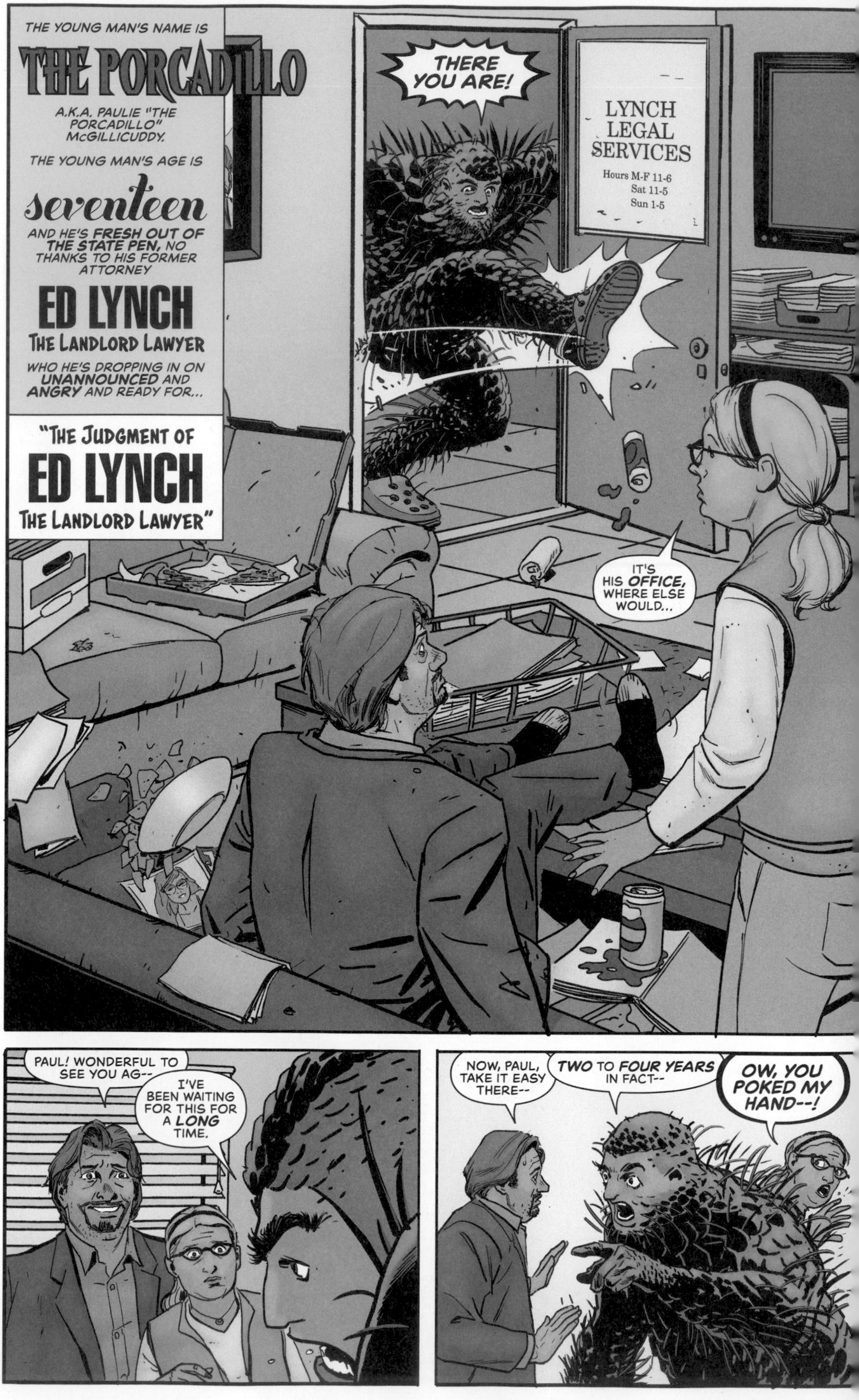
THE YOUNG MAN'S NAME IS
THE PORCADILLO
A.K.A. PAULIE "THE PORCADILLO" McGILLICUDDY.
THE YOUNG MAN'S AGE IS
seventeen
AND HE'S FRESH OUT OF THE STATE PEN, NO THANKS TO HIS FORMER ATTORNEY
ED LYNCH
THE LANDLORD LAWYER
WHO HE'S DROPPING IN ON UNANNOUNCED AND ANGRY AND READY FOR...
"THE JUDGMENT OF
ED LYNCH
THE LANDLORD LAWYER"
THERE YOU ARE!
LYNCH LEGAL SERVICES
Hours M-F 11-6
Sat 11-5
Sun 1-5
IT'S HIS OFFICE, WHERE ELSE WOULD...
PAUL! WONDERFUL TO SEE YOU AG--
I'VE BEEN WAITING FOR THIS FOR A LONG TIME.
NOW, PAUL, TAKE IT EASY THERE--
TWO TO FOUR YEARS IN FACT--
OW, YOU POKED MY HAND--!

MS. DENISE, I'M SO SORRY--

STAY AWAY--

OW, NOW YOU POKED IT AGAIN IN THE SAME PLACE!

YOU TRIED TOUCHING ME!

OH NO! HELP! HELP!

LYNCH LEGAL SERVICES

Hours M-F 11-6
Sat 11-5
Sun 1-5

SLAM

LYNCH LEGAL SERVICES

Hours M-F 11-6
Sat 11-5
Sun 1-5

STAY BACK--

--STAY-- AAARG!

NO-- OH NO!

KKRSSHH

AND JUST LIKE THAT, THE PORCADILLO IS GONE IN A SMASHING OF DRYWALL AND LEGAL BRIEFS! IS THERE NO LOVE FOR LANDLORDS OR LAWYERS IN THIS COLD AND MODERN WORLD? WHAT FATE SHALL BEFALL JIMMY'S LEGAL REPRESENTATION?

WHO CARES?

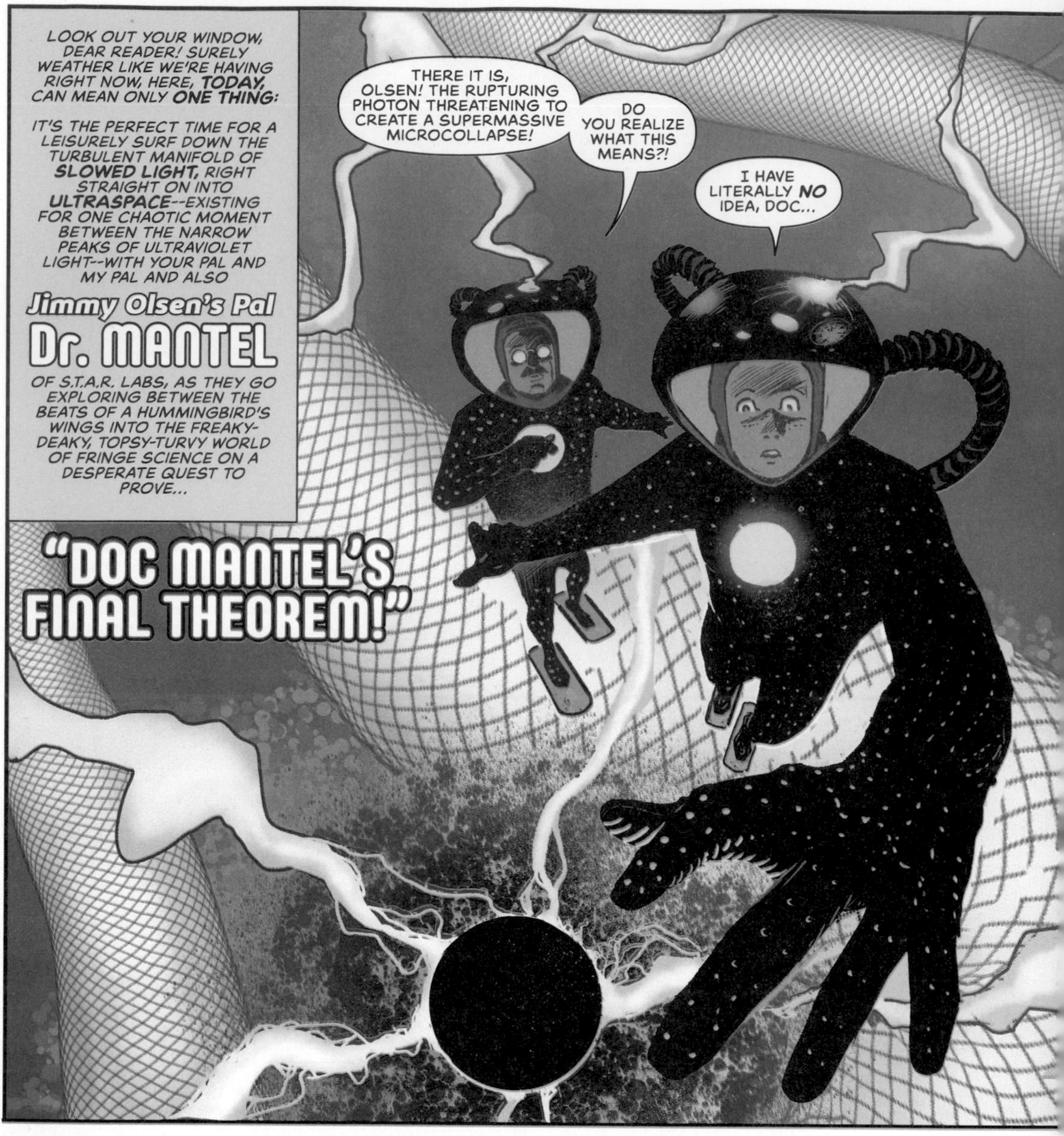
LOOK OUT YOUR WINDOW, DEAR READER! SURELY WEATHER LIKE WE'RE HAVING RIGHT NOW, HERE, TODAY, CAN MEAN ONLY ONE THING:
IT'S THE PERFECT TIME FOR A LEISURELY SURF DOWN THE TURBULENT MANIFOLD OF SLOWED LIGHT, RIGHT STRAIGHT ON INTO ULTRASPACE--EXISTING FOR ONE CHAOTIC MOMENT BETWEEN THE NARROW PEAKS OF ULTRAVIOLET LIGHT--WITH YOUR PAL AND MY PAL AND ALSO
Jimmy Olsen's Pal
Dr. MANTEL
OF S.T.A.R. LABS, AS THEY GO EXPLORING BETWEEN THE BEATS OF A HUMMINGBIRD'S WINGS INTO THE FREAKY-DEAKY, TOPSY-TURVY WORLD OF FRINGE SCIENCE ON A DESPERATE QUEST TO PROVE...
"DOC MANTEL'S FINAL THEOREM!"
THERE IT IS, OLSEN! THE RUPTURING PHOTON THREATENING TO CREATE A SUPERMASSIVE MICROCOLLAPSE!
DO YOU REALIZE WHAT THIS MEANS?!
I HAVE LITERALLY NO IDEA, DOC...

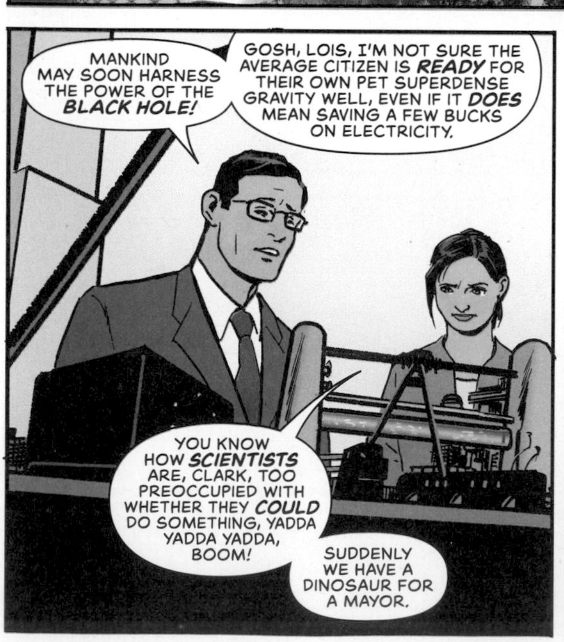
MANKIND MAY SOON HARNESS THE POWER OF THE BLACK HOLE!
GOSH, LOIS, I'M NOT SURE THE AVERAGE CITIZEN IS READY FOR THEIR OWN PET SUPERDENSE GRAVITY WELL, EVEN IF IT DOES MEAN SAVING A FEW BUCKS ON ELECTRICITY.
YOU KNOW HOW SCIENTISTS ARE, CLARK, TOO PREOCCUPIED WITH WHETHER THEY COULD DO SOMETHING, YADDA YADDA YADDA, BOOM!
SUDDENLY WE HAVE A DINOSAUR FOR A MAYOR.

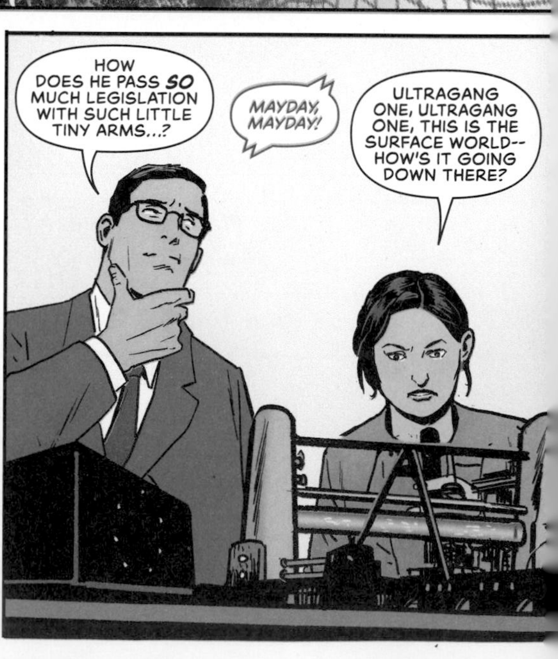
HOW DOES HE PASS SO MUCH LEGISLATION WITH SUCH LITTLE TINY ARMS...?
MAYDAY, MAYDAY!
ULTRAGANG ONE, ULTRAGANG ONE, THIS IS THE SURFACE WORLD--HOW'S IT GOING DOWN THERE?

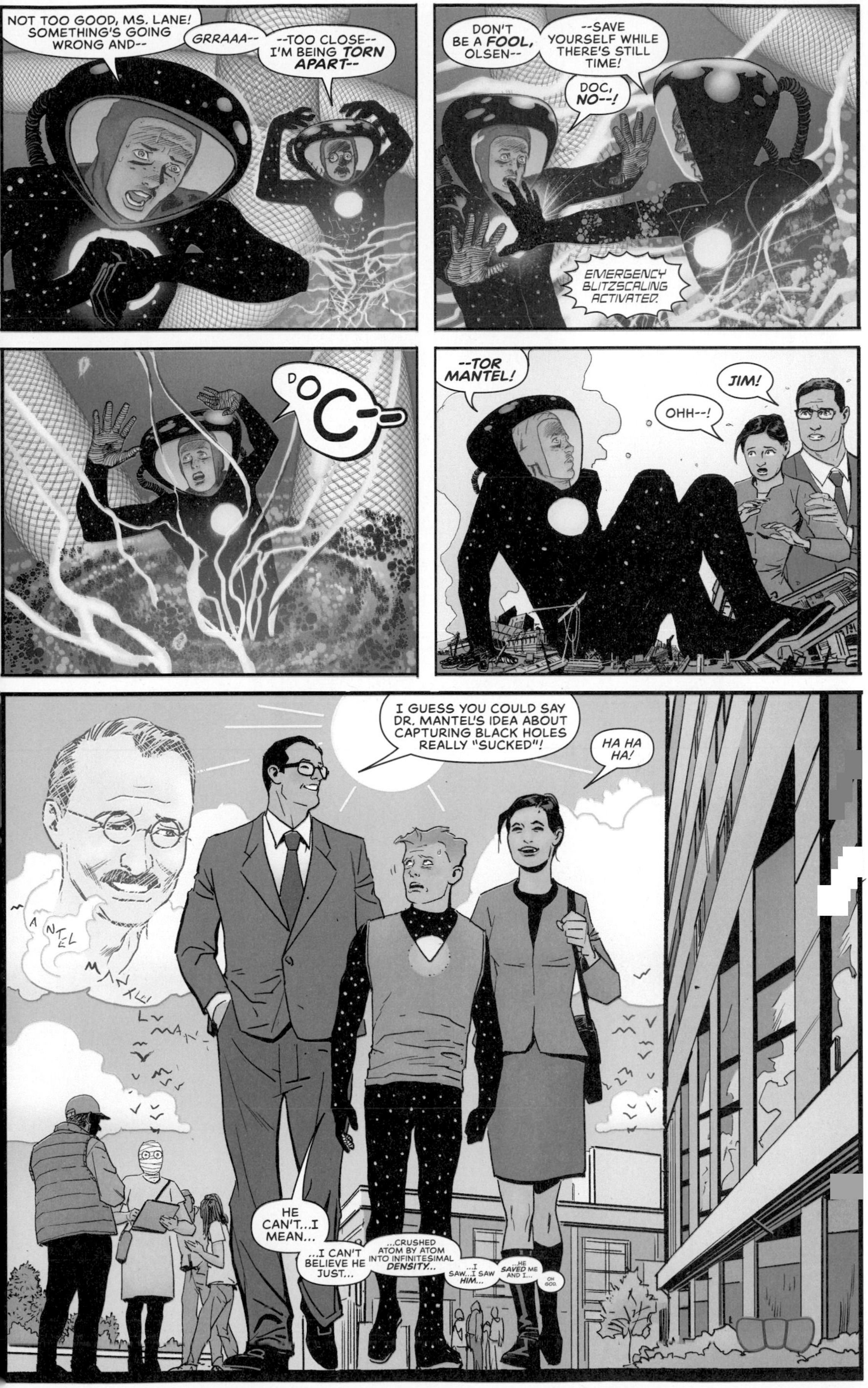
NOT TOO GOOD, MS. LANE! SOMETHING'S GOING WRONG AND--
GRRAAA--
--TOO CLOSE-- I'M BEING *TORN APART*--
DON'T BE A *FOOL,* OLSEN--
--SAVE YOURSELF WHILE THERE'S STILL TIME!
DOC, *NO--!*
EMERGENCY BLITZSCALING ACTIVATED.
DOC--
--TOR MANTEL!
JIM!
OHH--!
I GUESS YOU COULD SAY DR. MANTEL'S IDEA ABOUT CAPTURING BLACK HOLES REALLY "SUCKED"!
HA HA HA!
HE CAN'T...I MEAN...
...I CAN'T BELIEVE HE JUST...
...CRUSHED ATOM BY ATOM INTO INFINITESIMAL *DENSITY...*
...I SAW...I SAW *HIM...*
...HE *SAVED* ME AND I...
OH GOD.

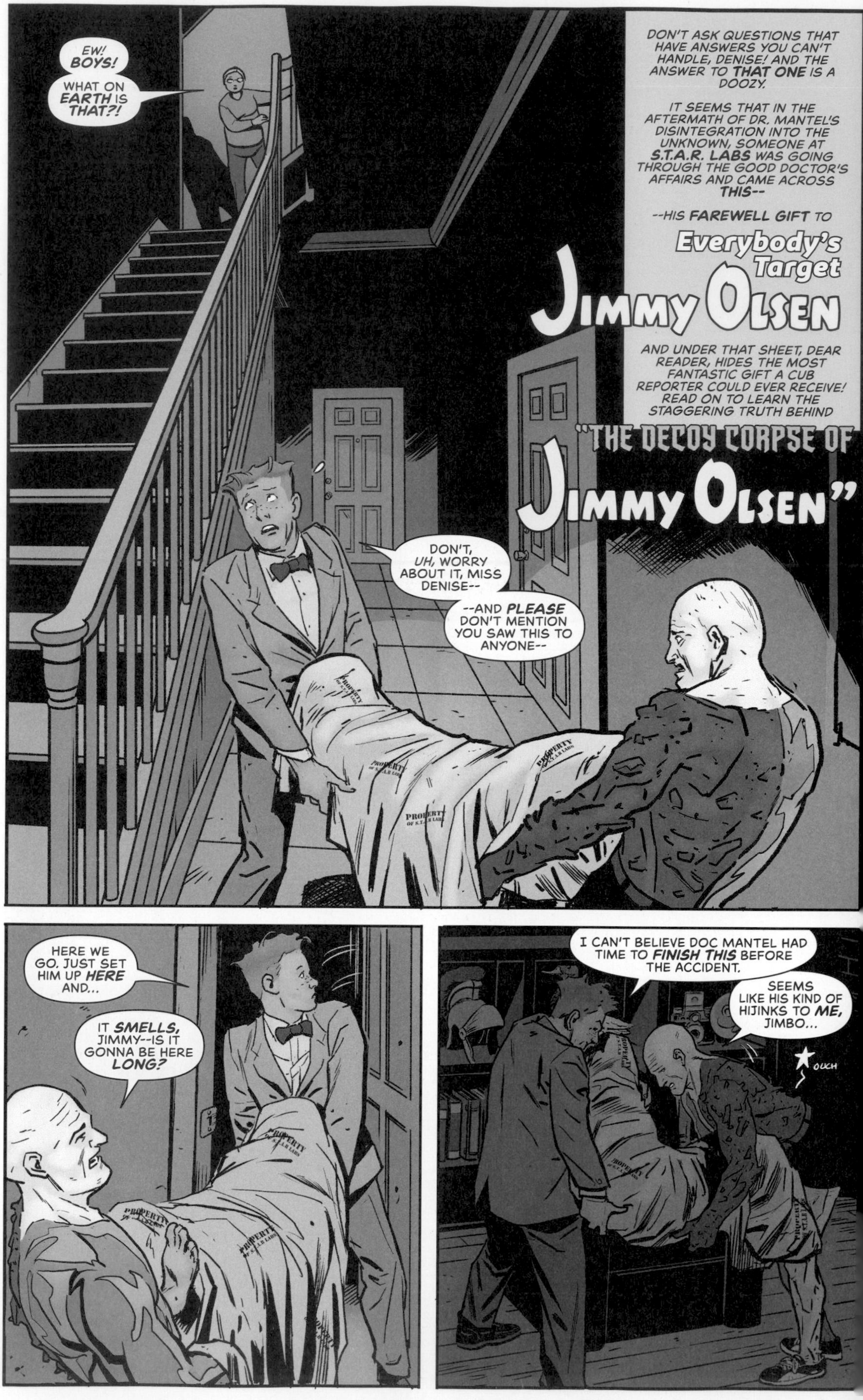

EW! BOYS!
WHAT ON EARTH IS THAT?!
DON'T ASK QUESTIONS THAT HAVE ANSWERS YOU CAN'T HANDLE, DENISE! AND THE ANSWER TO THAT ONE IS A DOOZY.
IT SEEMS THAT IN THE AFTERMATH OF DR. MANTEL'S DISINTEGRATION INTO THE UNKNOWN, SOMEONE AT S.T.A.R. LABS WAS GOING THROUGH THE GOOD DOCTOR'S AFFAIRS AND CAME ACROSS THIS--
--HIS FAREWELL GIFT TO
Everybody's Target JIMMY OLSEN
AND UNDER THAT SHEET, DEAR READER, HIDES THE MOST FANTASTIC GIFT A CUB REPORTER COULD EVER RECEIVE! READ ON TO LEARN THE STAGGERING TRUTH BEHIND
"THE DECOY CORPSE OF JIMMY OLSEN"
DON'T, UH, WORRY ABOUT IT, MISS DENISE--
--AND PLEASE DON'T MENTION YOU SAW THIS TO ANYONE--
PROPERTY OF S.T.A.R LABS
HERE WE GO. JUST SET HIM UP HERE AND...
IT SMELLS, JIMMY--IS IT GONNA BE HERE LONG?
I CAN'T BELIEVE DOC MANTEL HAD TIME TO FINISH THIS BEFORE THE ACCIDENT.
SEEMS LIKE HIS KIND OF HIJINKS TO ME, JIMBO...
OUCH

AW, THAT'S JUST NEW BODY SMELL, REX. YOU GET USED TO IT, ESPECIALLY WHEN IT COMES FROM--
--TA-DA! MY VERY OWN ASSASSINATION DECOY!
A PERFECT CLONE THAT'D PASS ANY IDENTIFICATION TEST! NEVER ROTS! NEVER DECAYS! WHAT A SWELL GOODBYE GIFT FROM OL' DOC MANTEL!
I GOTTA GET A NEW PLACE.
WHY WOULD YOU NEED TO HAVE AN ASSASSINATION DECOY JUST... READY LIKE THAT?
DO THAT MANY PEOPLE WANT TO KILL YOU?
ACTUALLY, YEAH, REX, NOW THAT YOU MENTION IT--
JESUS CHRIST--!
FIP! FIP! FIP!

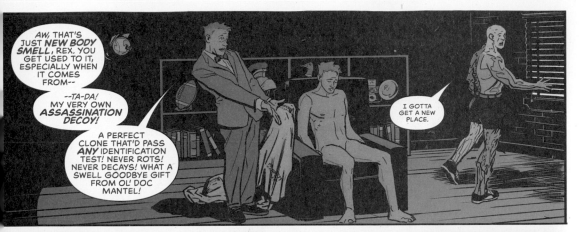

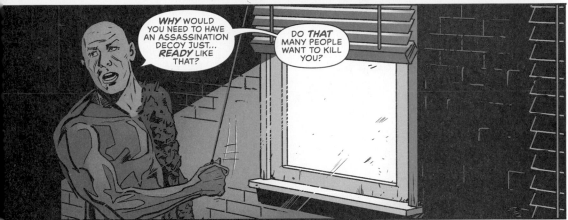

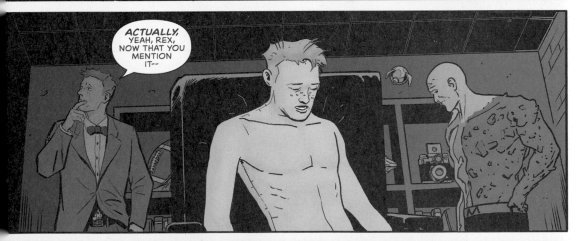

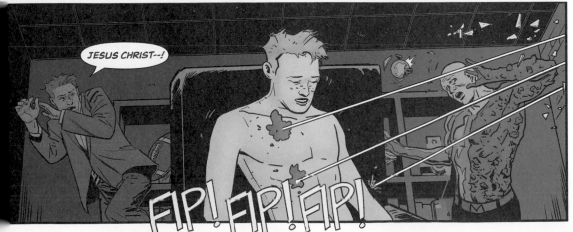

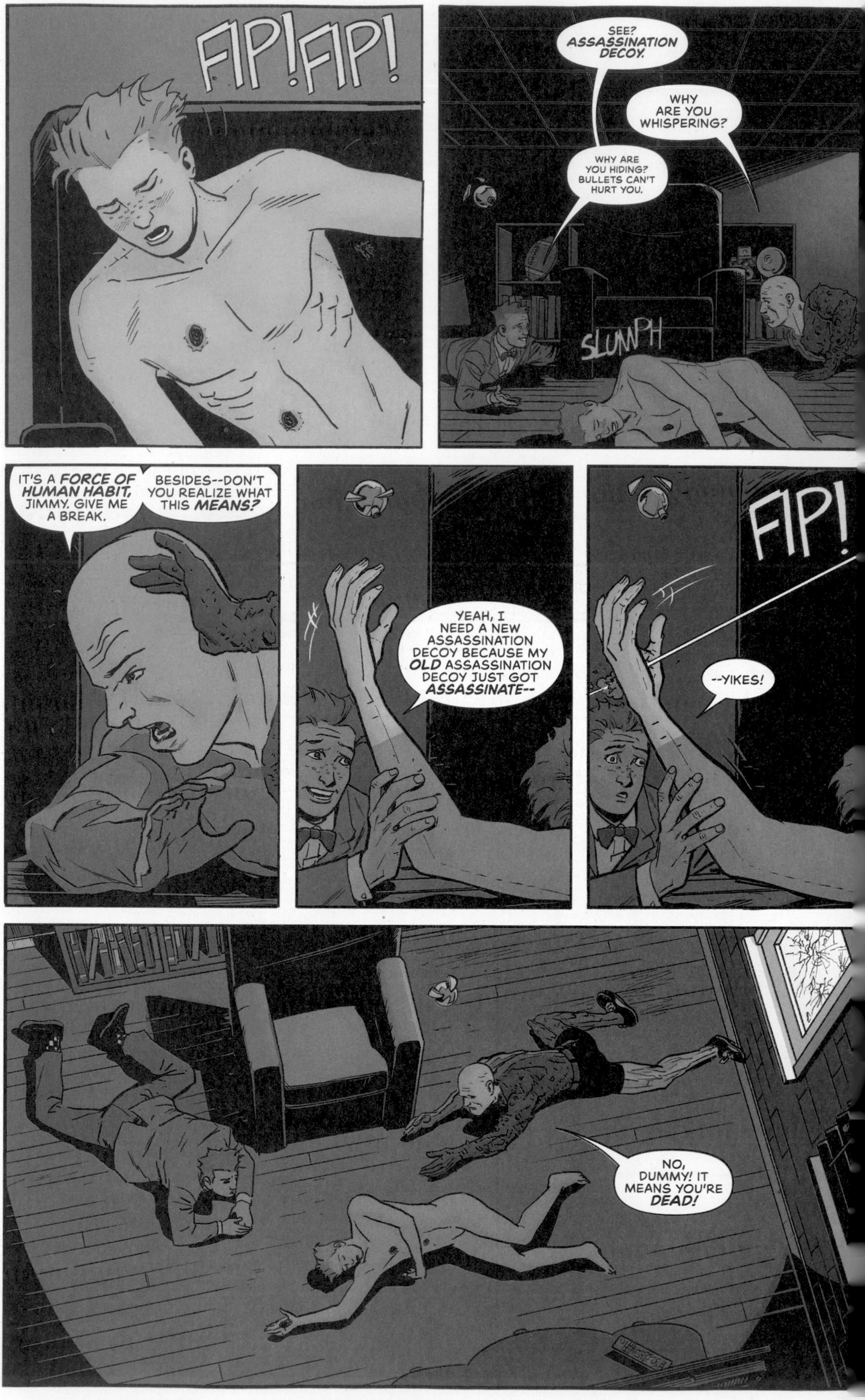
FIP! FIP!
SEE? ASSASSINATION DECOY.
WHY ARE YOU WHISPERING?
WHY ARE YOU HIDING? BULLETS CAN'T HURT YOU.
SLUMPH
IT'S A FORCE OF HUMAN HABIT, JIMMY. GIVE ME A BREAK.
BESIDES--DON'T YOU REALIZE WHAT THIS MEANS?
YEAH, I NEED A NEW ASSASSINATION DECOY BECAUSE MY OLD ASSASSINATION DECOY JUST GOT ASSASSINATE--
FIP!
--YIKES!
NO, DUMMY! IT MEANS YOU'RE DEAD!

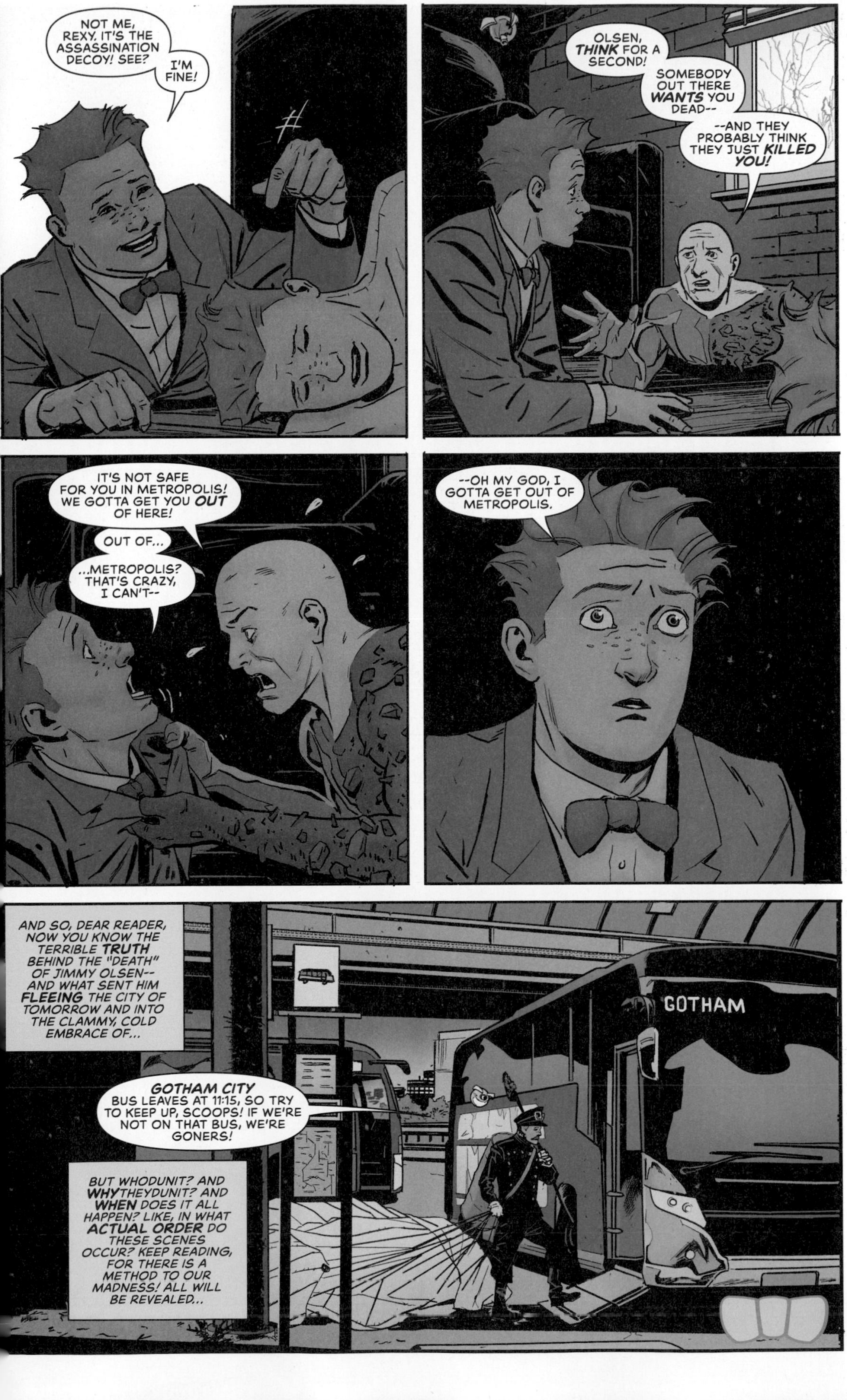
NOT ME, REXY, IT'S THE ASSASSINATION DECOY! SEE?
I'M FINE!
OLSEN, THINK FOR A SECOND!
SOMEBODY OUT THERE WANTS YOU DEAD--
--AND THEY PROBABLY THINK THEY JUST KILLED YOU!
IT'S NOT SAFE FOR YOU IN METROPOLIS! WE GOTTA GET YOU OUT OF HERE!
OUT OF...
...METROPOLIS? THAT'S CRAZY, I CAN'T--
--OH MY GOD, I GOTTA GET OUT OF METROPOLIS.
AND SO, DEAR READER, NOW YOU KNOW THE TERRIBLE TRUTH BEHIND THE "DEATH" OF JIMMY OLSEN-- AND WHAT SENT HIM FLEEING THE CITY OF TOMORROW AND INTO THE CLAMMY, COLD EMBRACE OF...
GOTHAM
GOTHAM CITY
BUS LEAVES AT 11:15, SO TRY TO KEEP UP, SCOOPS! IF WE'RE NOT ON THAT BUS, WE'RE GONERS!
BUT WHODUNIT? AND WHYTHEYDUNIT? AND WHEN DOES IT ALL HAPPEN? LIKE, IN WHAT ACTUAL ORDER DO THESE SCENES OCCUR? KEEP READING, FOR THERE IS A METHOD TO OUR MADNESS! ALL WILL BE REVEALED...

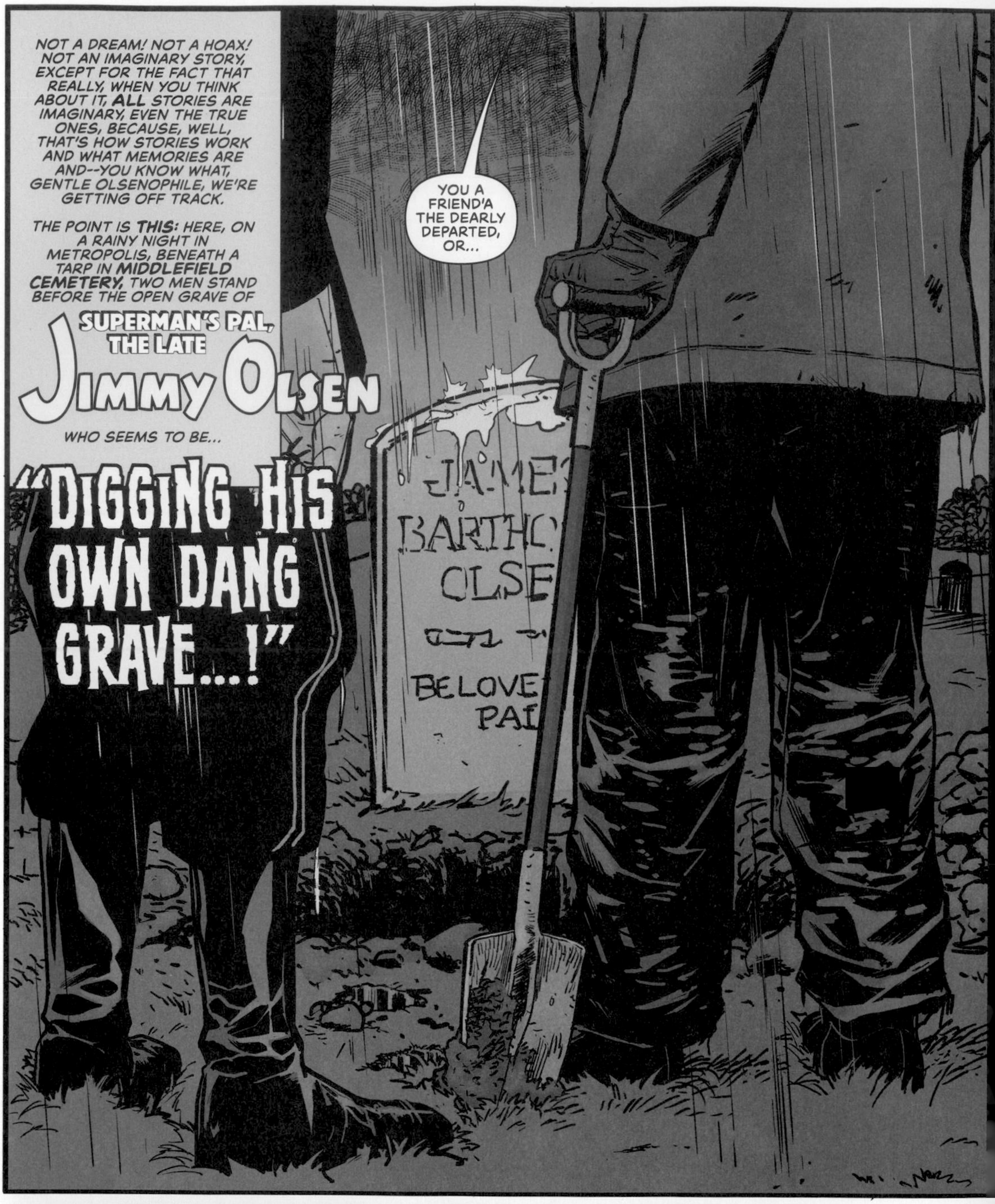
NOT A DREAM! NOT A HOAX! NOT AN IMAGINARY STORY, EXCEPT FOR THE FACT THAT REALLY, WHEN YOU THINK ABOUT IT, **ALL** STORIES ARE IMAGINARY, EVEN THE TRUE ONES, BECAUSE, WELL, THAT'S HOW STORIES WORK AND WHAT MEMORIES ARE AND--YOU KNOW WHAT, GENTLE OLSENOPHILE, WE'RE GETTING OFF TRACK.
THE POINT IS **THIS:** HERE, ON A RAINY NIGHT IN METROPOLIS, BENEATH A TARP IN **MIDDLEFIELD CEMETERY,** TWO MEN STAND BEFORE THE OPEN GRAVE OF
SUPERMAN'S PAL, THE LATE
JIMMY OLSEN
WHO SEEMS TO BE...
"DIGGING HIS OWN DANG GRAVE...!"
YOU A FRIEND'A THE DEARLY DEPARTED, OR...

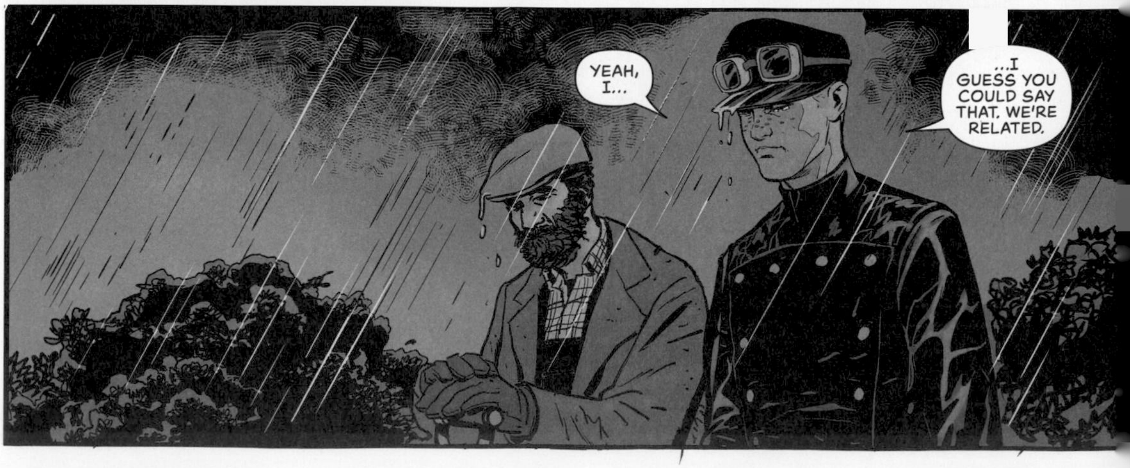
YEAH, I...
...I GUESS YOU COULD SAY THAT. WE'RE RELATED.

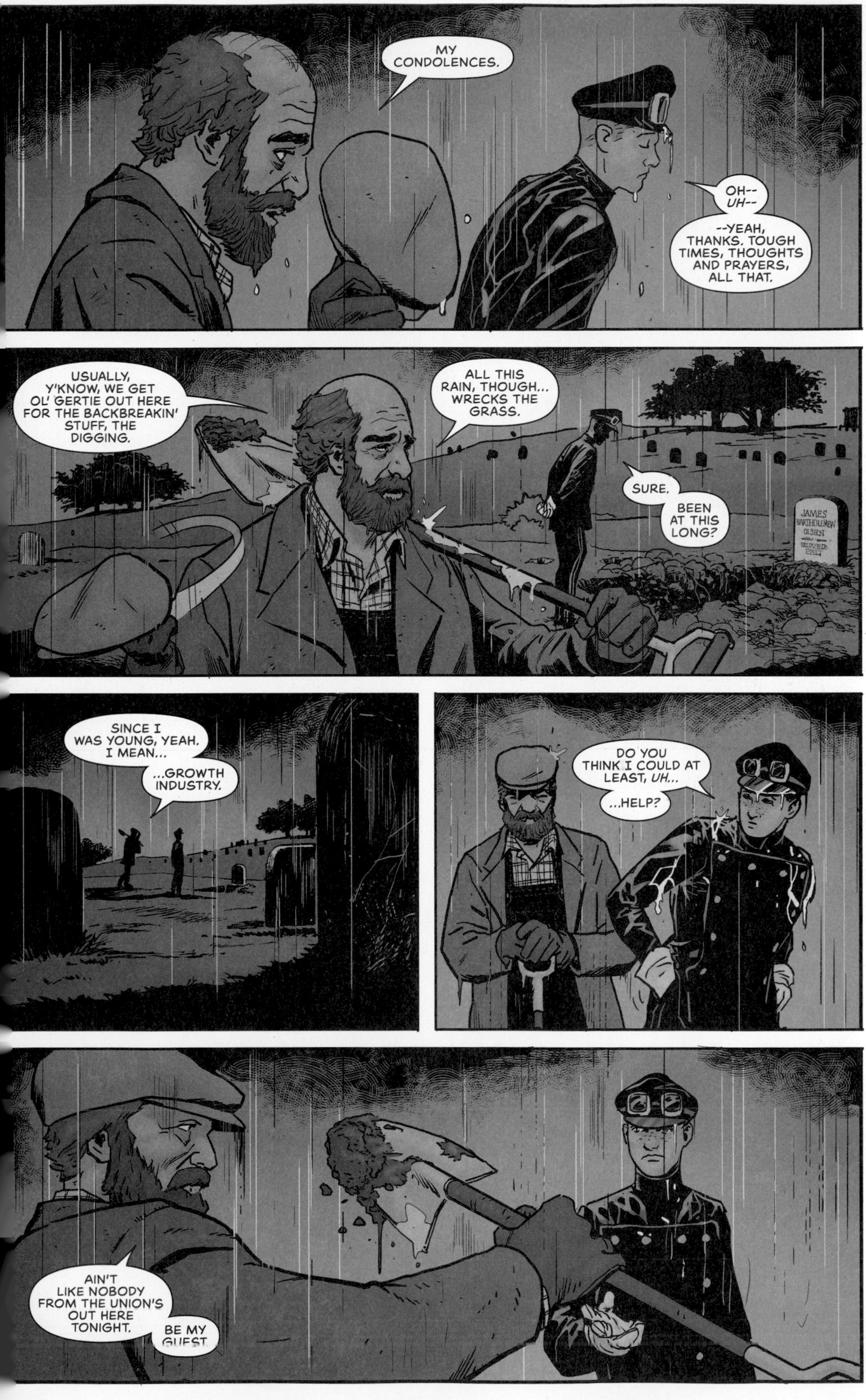
MY CONDOLENCES.
OH-- UH--
--YEAH, THANKS. TOUGH TIMES, THOUGHTS AND PRAYERS, ALL THAT.
USUALLY, Y'KNOW, WE GET OL' GERTIE OUT HERE FOR THE BACKBREAKIN' STUFF, THE DIGGING.
ALL THIS RAIN, THOUGH... WRECKS THE GRASS.
SURE.
BEEN AT THIS LONG?
JAMES BARTHOLOMEW OLSEN
SINCE I WAS YOUNG, YEAH. I MEAN...
...GROWTH INDUSTRY.
DO YOU THINK I COULD AT LEAST, UH...
...HELP?
AIN'T LIKE NOBODY FROM THE UNION'S OUT HERE TONIGHT.
BE MY GUEST.

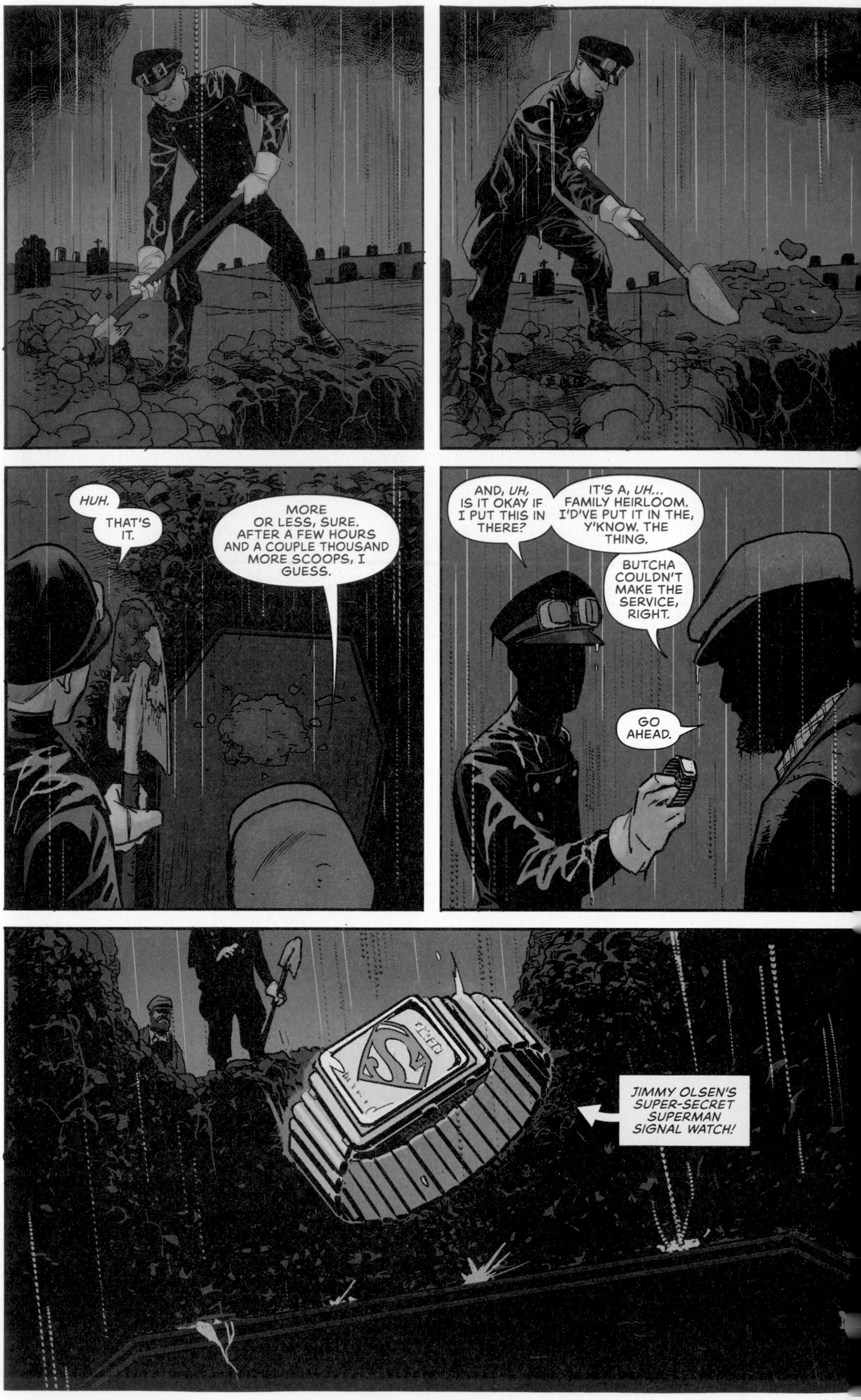
HUH.
THAT'S IT.
MORE OR LESS, SURE. AFTER A FEW HOURS AND A COUPLE THOUSAND MORE SCOOPS, I GUESS.
AND, UH, IS IT OKAY IF I PUT THIS IN THERE?
IT'S A, UH... FAMILY HEIRLOOM. I'D'VE PUT IT IN THE, Y'KNOW. THE THING.
BUTCHA COULDN'T MAKE THE SERVICE, RIGHT.
GO AHEAD.
JIMMY OLSEN'S SUPER-SECRET SUPERMAN SIGNAL WATCH!

I'LL, *UH*, I'LL GIVE YOU SOME TIME.

THANKS.

I KNOW YOU CAN HEAR ME. I KNOW THAT I COULD FIRE THE WATCH TO SATURN AND YOU'D STILL BE ABLE TO HEAR ME.

I--THIS IS TRICKY, BUT WE WORKED IT OUT A LITTLE AND...

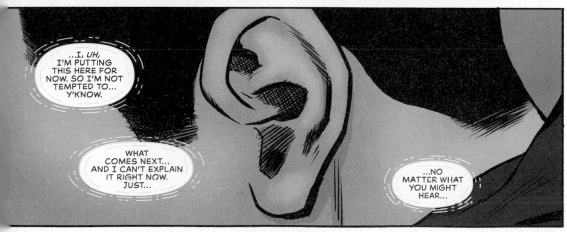

...I, *UH*, I'M PUTTING THIS HERE FOR NOW. SO I'M NOT TEMPTED TO... Y'KNOW.

WHAT COMES NEXT... AND I CAN'T EXPLAIN IT RIGHT NOW. JUST...

...NO MATTER WHAT YOU MIGHT HEAR...

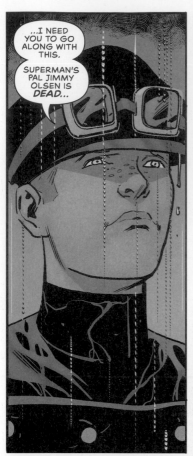

...I NEED YOU TO GO ALONG WITH THIS.

SUPERMAN'S PAL JIMMY OLSEN IS *DEAD*...

...LONG *LIVE* Irresponsible Blogger

TIMMY OLSEN

---WHO *MIGHT* HAVE A MUSTACHE, I HAVEN'T DECIDED YET.

HEY!

YOU ONLY DID THE ONE SCOOP? YOU AIN'T GONNA HELP? DAT'S MY SHOVEL! *HEY!*

WHAT? WHO? HOW?

THE UNBELIEVABLE TRUTH WOULD BE--UH--UNBELIEVABLE IF WE SIMPLY *TOLD YOU* WHAT'S GOING ON IN DEAR JIMMY/TIMMY'S LIFE TO LEAD TO THIS DRAMATIC DEPARTURE!

YOU'LL JUST HAVE TO *KEEP READING*, AND LIKE JIMMY...

...KEEP *DIGGING!*

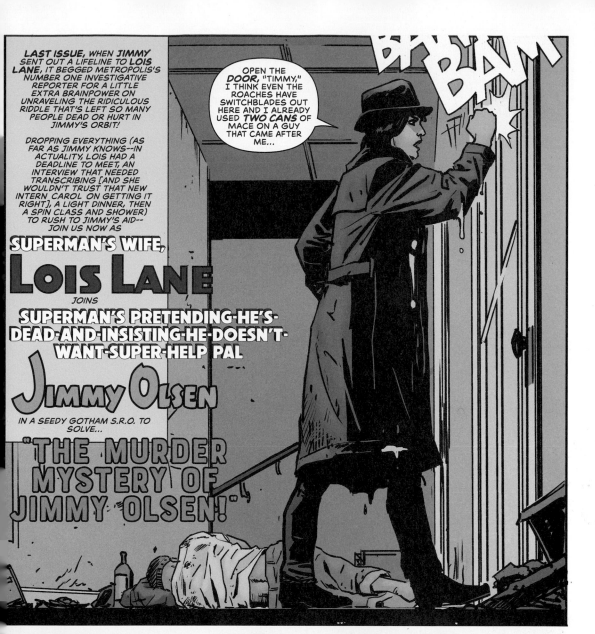

LAST ISSUE, WHEN JIMMY SENT OUT A LIFELINE TO LOIS LANE, IT BEGGED METROPOLIS'S NUMBER ONE INVESTIGATIVE REPORTER FOR A LITTLE EXTRA BRAINPOWER ON UNRAVELING THE RIDICULOUS RIDDLE THAT'S LEFT SO MANY PEOPLE DEAD OR HURT IN JIMMY'S ORBIT!

DROPPING EVERYTHING (AS FAR AS JIMMY KNOWS--IN ACTUALITY, LOIS HAD A DEADLINE TO MEET, AN INTERVIEW THAT NEEDED TRANSCRIBING [AND SHE WOULDN'T TRUST THAT NEW INTERN CAROL ON GETTING IT RIGHT], A LIGHT DINNER, THEN A SPIN CLASS AND SHOWER) TO RUSH TO JIMMY'S AID-- JOIN US NOW AS

SUPERMAN'S WIFE,

LOIS LANE
JOINS

SUPERMAN'S PRETENDING-HE'S-DEAD-AND-INSISTING-HE-DOESN'T-WANT-SUPER-HELP PAL

JIMMY OLSEN
IN A SEEDY GOTHAM S.R.O. TO SOLVE...

"THE MURDER MYSTERY OF JIMMY OLSEN!"

OPEN THE **DOOR,** "TIMMY," I THINK EVEN THE ROACHES HAVE SWITCHBLADES OUT HERE AND I ALREADY USED **TWO CANS** OF MACE ON A GUY THAT CAME AFTER ME...

BAM BAM

WERE YOU FOLLOWED?

YEAH, I SAID I USED TWO CANS OF MACE ON A GUY--IS THAT **PAPER?**

MY CHAIN!

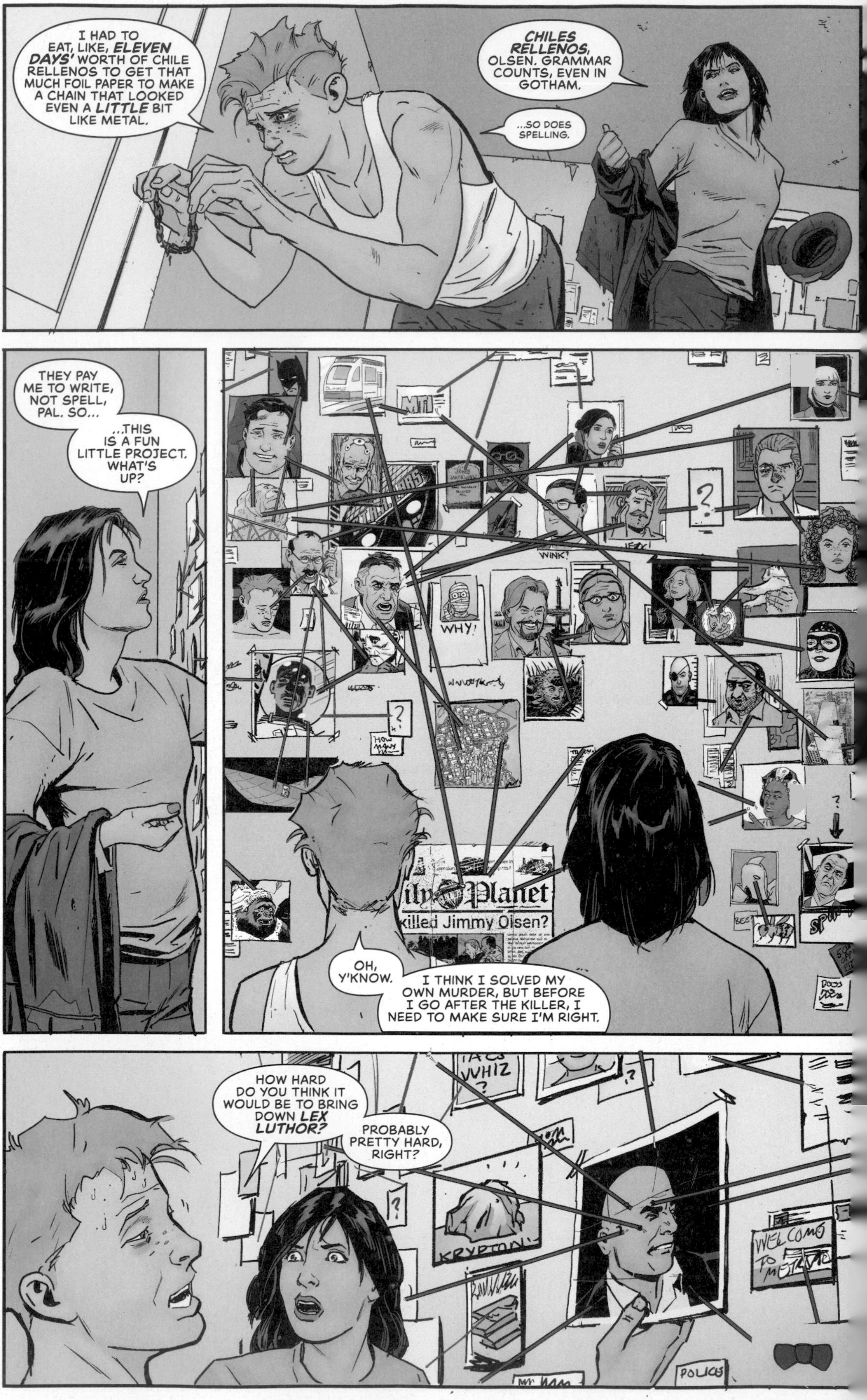
I HAD TO EAT, LIKE, ELEVEN DAYS' WORTH OF CHILE RELLENOS TO GET THAT MUCH FOIL PAPER TO MAKE A CHAIN THAT LOOKED EVEN A LITTLE BIT LIKE METAL.
CHILES RELLENOS, OLSEN. GRAMMAR COUNTS, EVEN IN GOTHAM.
...SO DOES SPELLING.
THEY PAY ME TO WRITE, NOT SPELL, PAL. SO...
...THIS IS A FUN LITTLE PROJECT. WHAT'S UP?
WINK!
WHY!
killed Jimmy Olsen?
OH, Y'KNOW.
I THINK I SOLVED MY OWN MURDER, BUT BEFORE I GO AFTER THE KILLER, I NEED TO MAKE SURE I'M RIGHT.
HOW HARD DO YOU THINK IT WOULD BE TO BRING DOWN LEX LUTHOR?
PROBABLY PRETTY HARD, RIGHT?
KRYPTON
POLICE

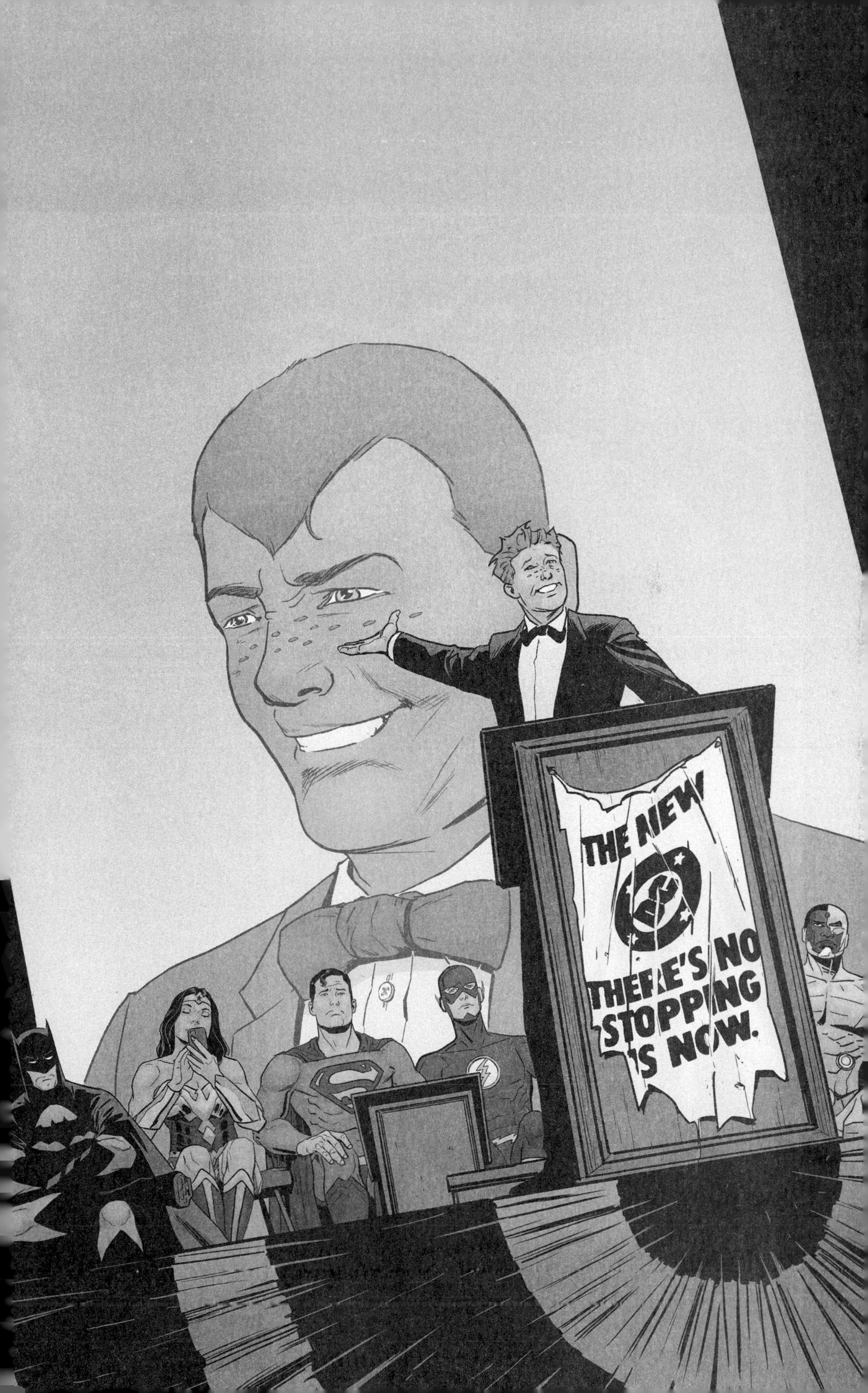
THE NEW
THERE'S NO STOPPING IS NOW.

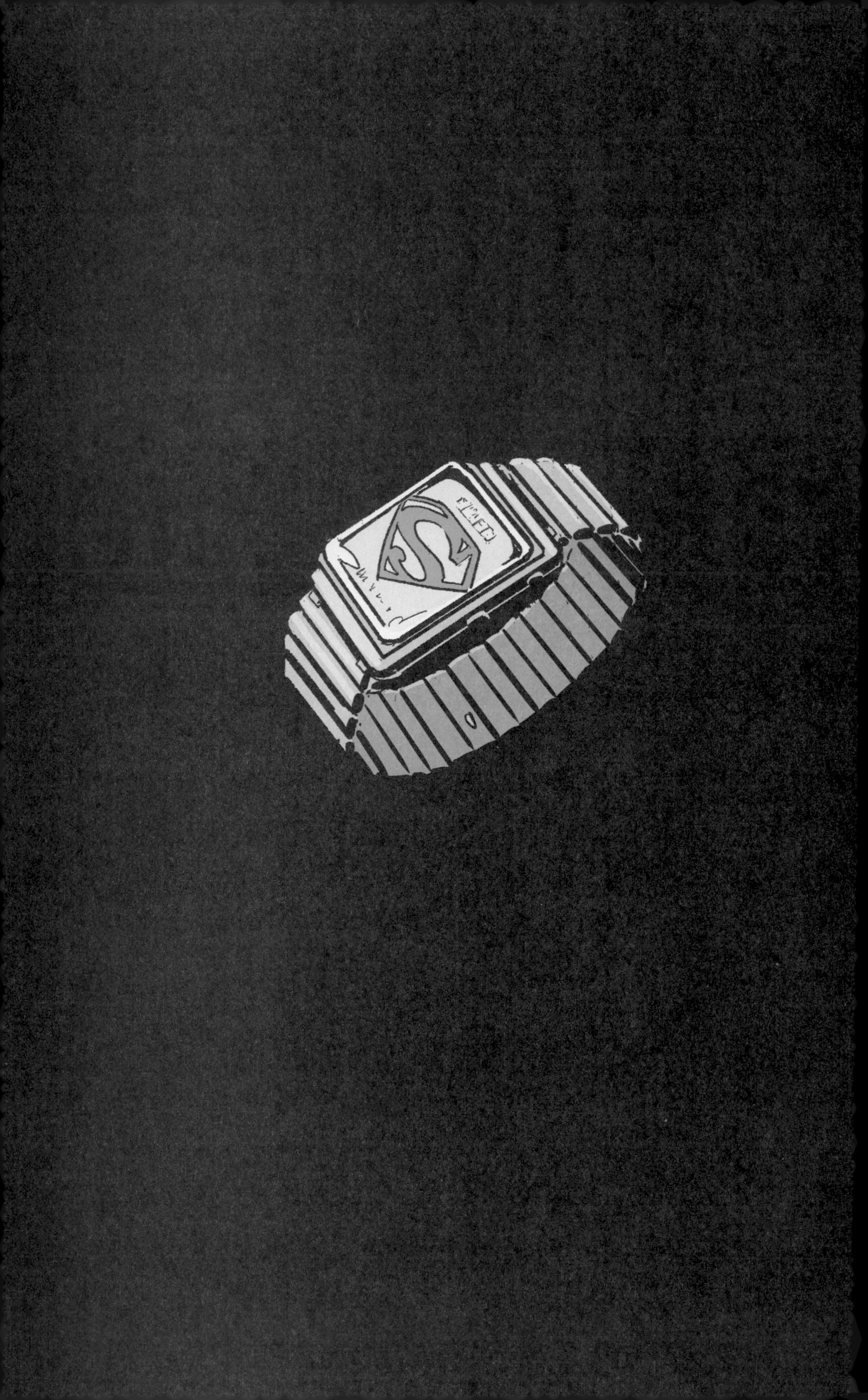

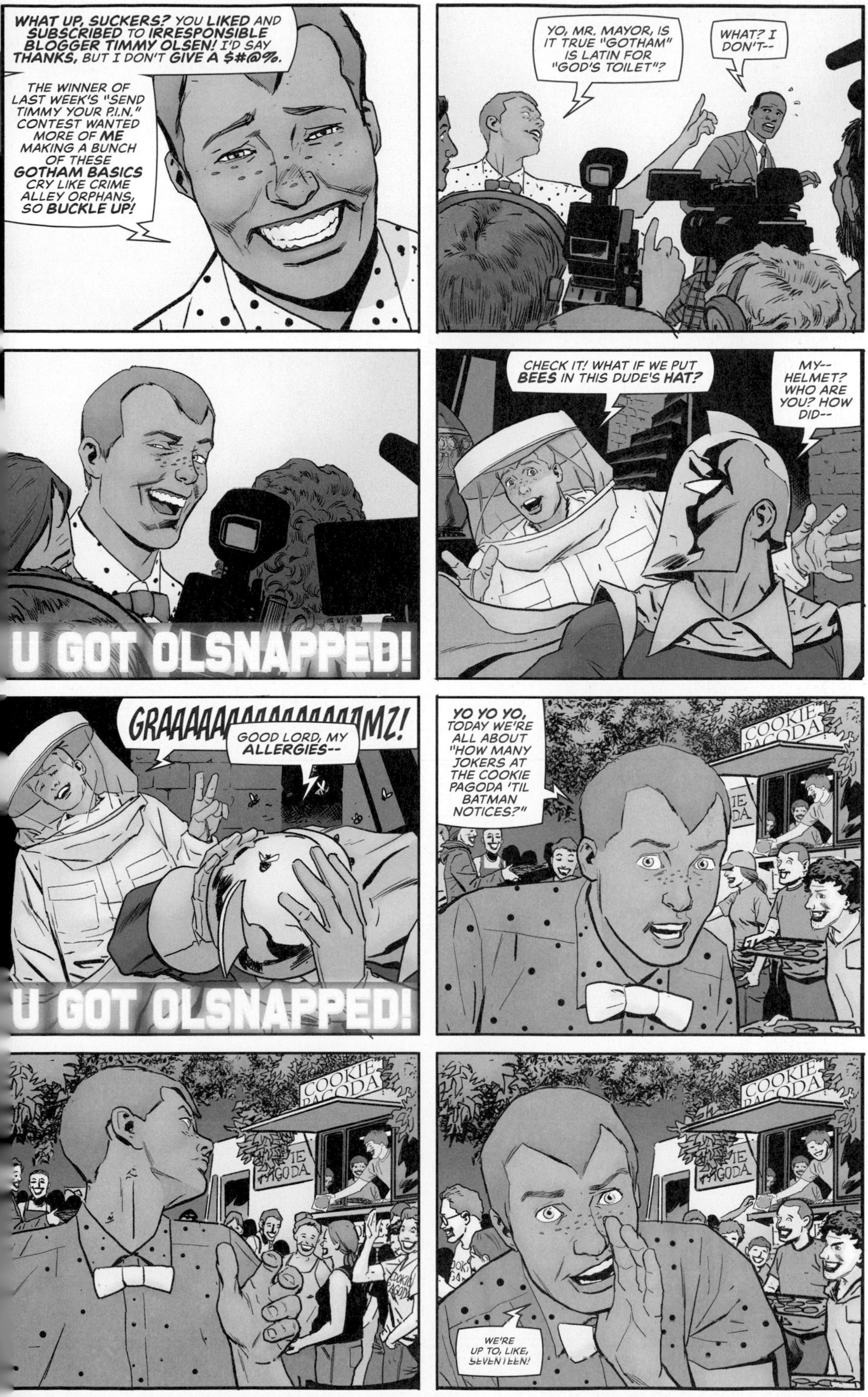
WHAT UP, SUCKERS? YOU LIKED AND SUBSCRIBED TO IRRESPONSIBLE BLOGGER TIMMY OLSEN! I'D SAY THANKS, BUT I DON'T GIVE A $#@%.
THE WINNER OF LAST WEEK'S "SEND TIMMY YOUR P.I.N." CONTEST WANTED MORE OF ME MAKING A BUNCH OF THESE GOTHAM BASICS CRY LIKE CRIME ALLEY ORPHANS, SO BUCKLE UP!
YO, MR. MAYOR, IS IT TRUE "GOTHAM" IS LATIN FOR "GOD'S TOILET"?
WHAT? I DON'T--
U GOT OLSNAPPED!
CHECK IT! WHAT IF WE PUT BEES IN THIS DUDE'S HAT?
MY-- HELMET? WHO ARE YOU? HOW DID--
GRAAAAAAAAAAAAAAAMZ!
GOOD LORD, MY ALLERGIES--
U GOT OLSNAPPED!
YO YO YO, TODAY WE'RE ALL ABOUT "HOW MANY JOKERS AT THE COOKIE PAGODA 'TIL BATMAN NOTICES?"
COOKIE PAGODA
WE'RE UP TO, LIKE, SEVENTEEN!

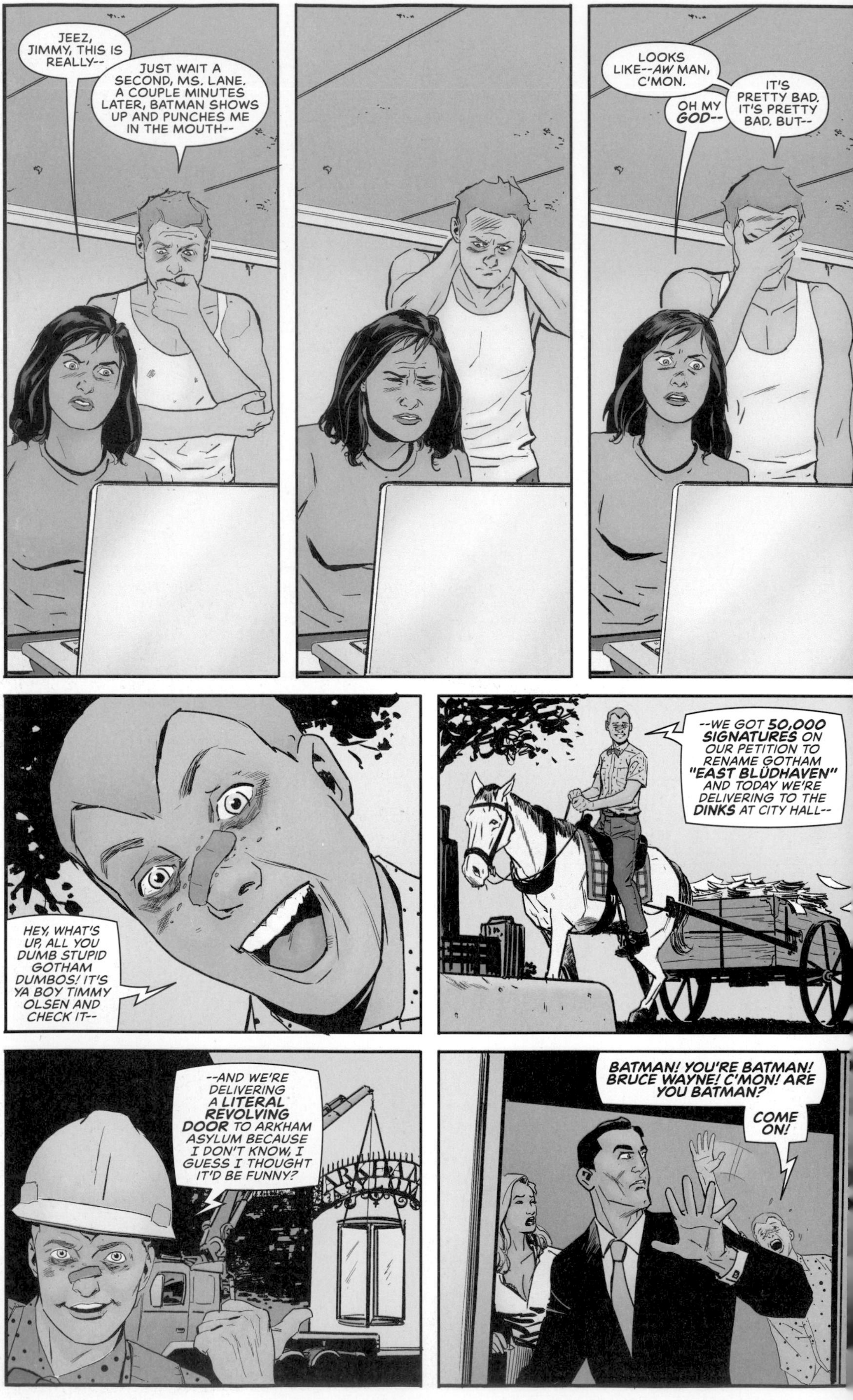
JEEZ, JIMMY, THIS IS REALLY--
JUST WAIT A SECOND, MS. LANE. A COUPLE MINUTES LATER, BATMAN SHOWS UP AND PUNCHES ME IN THE MOUTH--
LOOKS LIKE--AW MAN, C'MON.
OH MY GOD--
IT'S PRETTY BAD. IT'S PRETTY BAD. BUT--
HEY, WHAT'S UP, ALL YOU DUMB STUPID GOTHAM DUMBOS! IT'S YA BOY TIMMY OLSEN AND CHECK IT--
--WE GOT 50,000 SIGNATURES ON OUR PETITION TO RENAME GOTHAM "EAST BLÜDHAVEN" AND TODAY WE'RE DELIVERING TO THE DINKS AT CITY HALL--
--AND WE'RE DELIVERING A LITERAL REVOLVING DOOR TO ARKHAM ASYLUM BECAUSE I DON'T KNOW, I GUESS I THOUGHT IT'D BE FUNNY?
BATMAN! YOU'RE BATMAN! BRUCE WAYNE! C'MON! ARE YOU BATMAN?
COME ON!

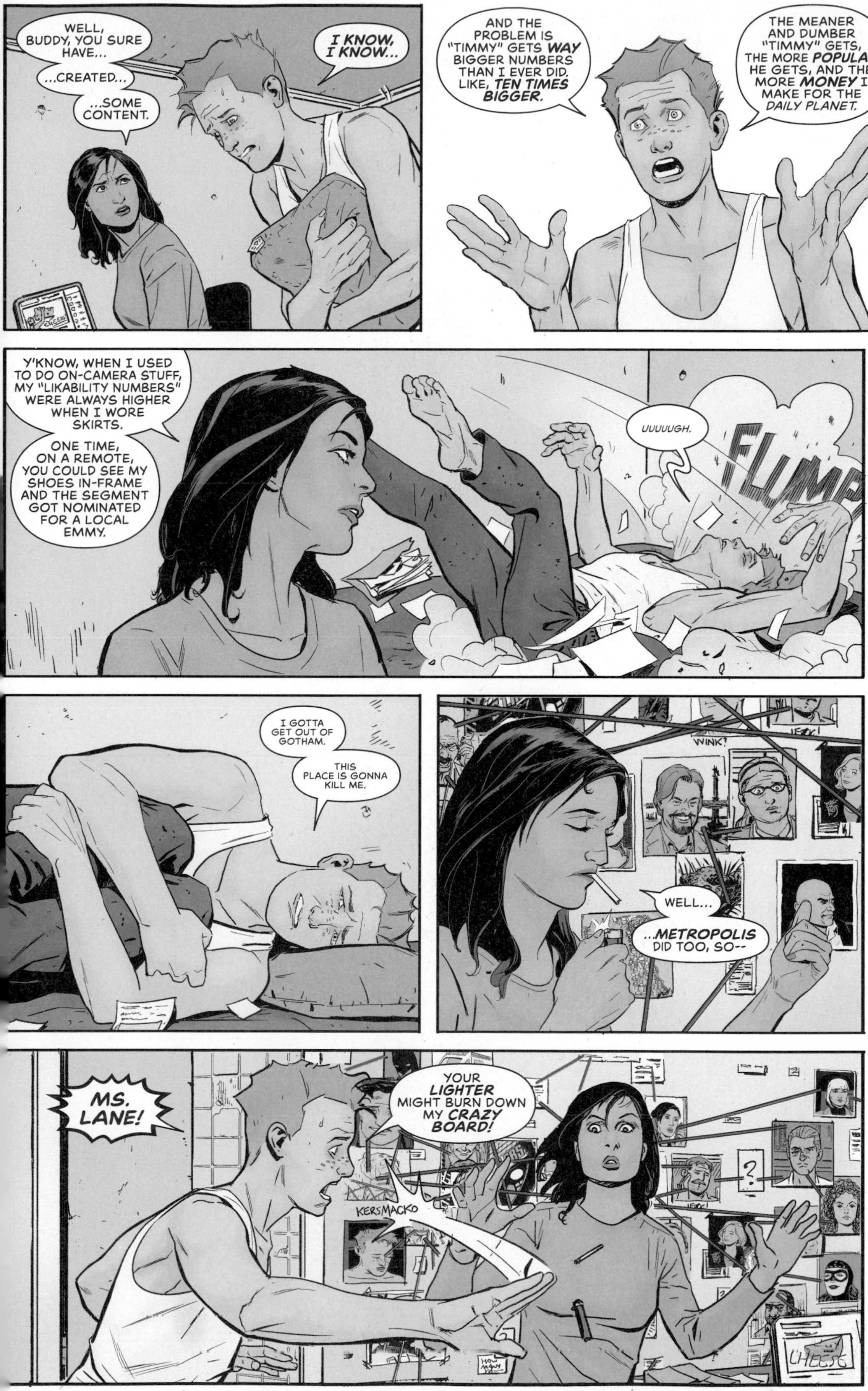
WELL, BUDDY, YOU SURE HAVE...
...CREATED...
...SOME CONTENT.
I KNOW, I KNOW...
AND THE PROBLEM IS "TIMMY" GETS WAY BIGGER NUMBERS THAN I EVER DID. LIKE, TEN TIMES BIGGER.
THE MEANER AND DUMBER "TIMMY" GETS, THE MORE POPULAR HE GETS, AND THE MORE MONEY I MAKE FOR THE DAILY PLANET.
Y'KNOW, WHEN I USED TO DO ON-CAMERA STUFF, MY "LIKABILITY NUMBERS" WERE ALWAYS HIGHER WHEN I WORE SKIRTS.
ONE TIME, ON A REMOTE, YOU COULD SEE MY SHOES IN-FRAME AND THE SEGMENT GOT NOMINATED FOR A LOCAL EMMY.
UUUUUGH.
FLUMP
I GOTTA GET OUT OF GOTHAM.
THIS PLACE IS GONNA KILL ME.
WINK!
WELL...
...METROPOLIS DID TOO, SO--
MS. LANE!
YOUR LIGHTER MIGHT BURN DOWN MY CRAZY BOARD!
KERSMACKO
CHEESE

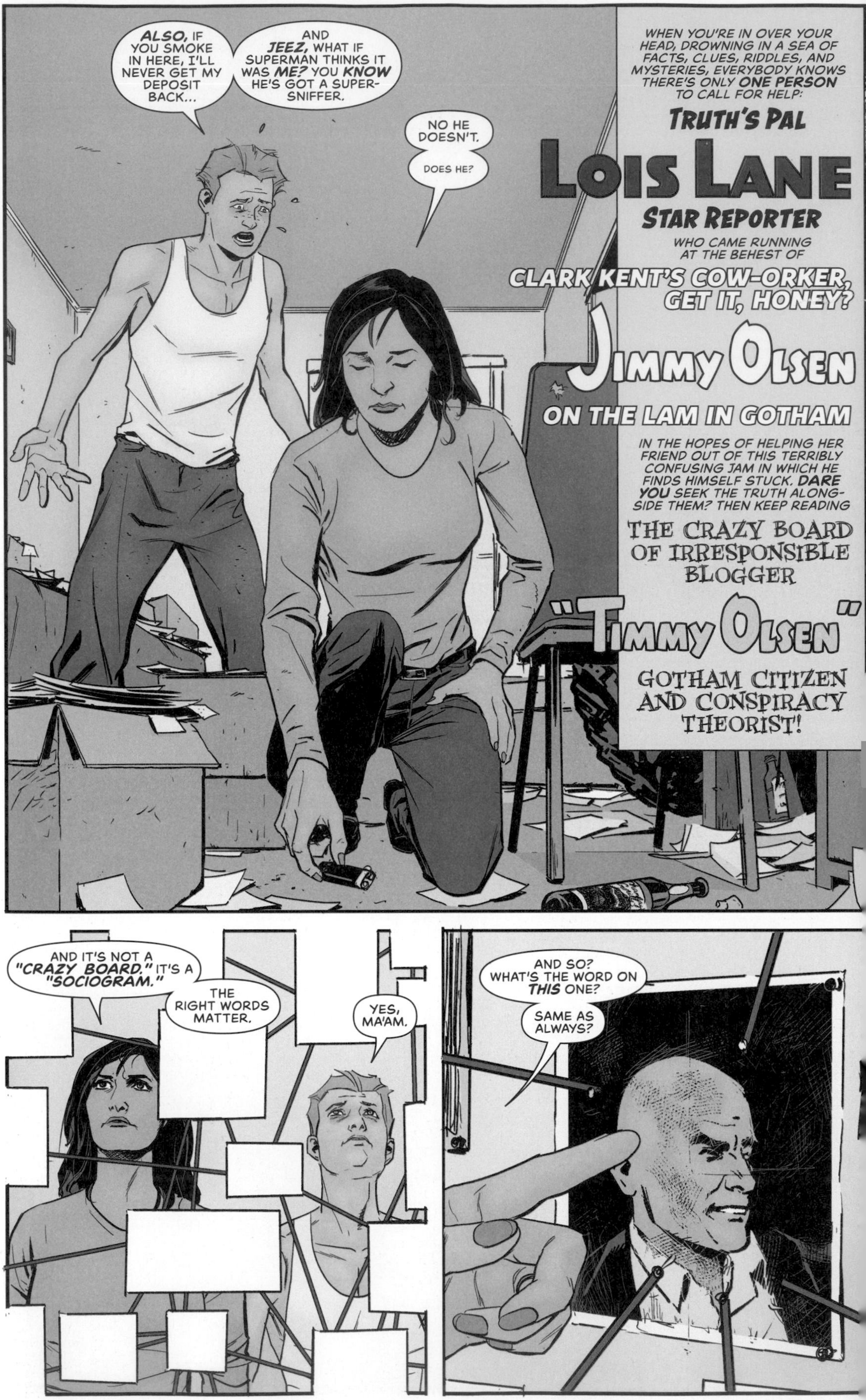
ALSO, IF YOU SMOKE IN HERE, I'LL NEVER GET MY DEPOSIT BACK...
AND JEEZ, WHAT IF SUPERMAN THINKS IT WAS ME? YOU KNOW HE'S GOT A SUPER-SNIFFER.
NO HE DOESN'T.
DOES HE?
WHEN YOU'RE IN OVER YOUR HEAD, DROWNING IN A SEA OF FACTS, CLUES, RIDDLES, AND MYSTERIES, EVERYBODY KNOWS THERE'S ONLY ONE PERSON TO CALL FOR HELP:
TRUTH'S PAL
LOIS LANE
STAR REPORTER
WHO CAME RUNNING AT THE BEHEST OF
CLARK KENT'S COW-ORKER, GET IT, HONEY?
JIMMY OLSEN
ON THE LAM IN GOTHAM
IN THE HOPES OF HELPING HER FRIEND OUT OF THIS TERRIBLY CONFUSING JAM IN WHICH HE FINDS HIMSELF STUCK. DARE YOU SEEK THE TRUTH ALONG-SIDE THEM? THEN KEEP READING
THE CRAZY BOARD OF IRRESPONSIBLE BLOGGER
"TIMMY OLSEN"
GOTHAM CITIZEN AND CONSPIRACY THEORIST!
AND IT'S NOT A "CRAZY BOARD." IT'S A "SOCIOGRAM."
THE RIGHT WORDS MATTER.
YES, MA'AM.
AND SO? WHAT'S THE WORD ON THIS ONE?
SAME AS ALWAYS?

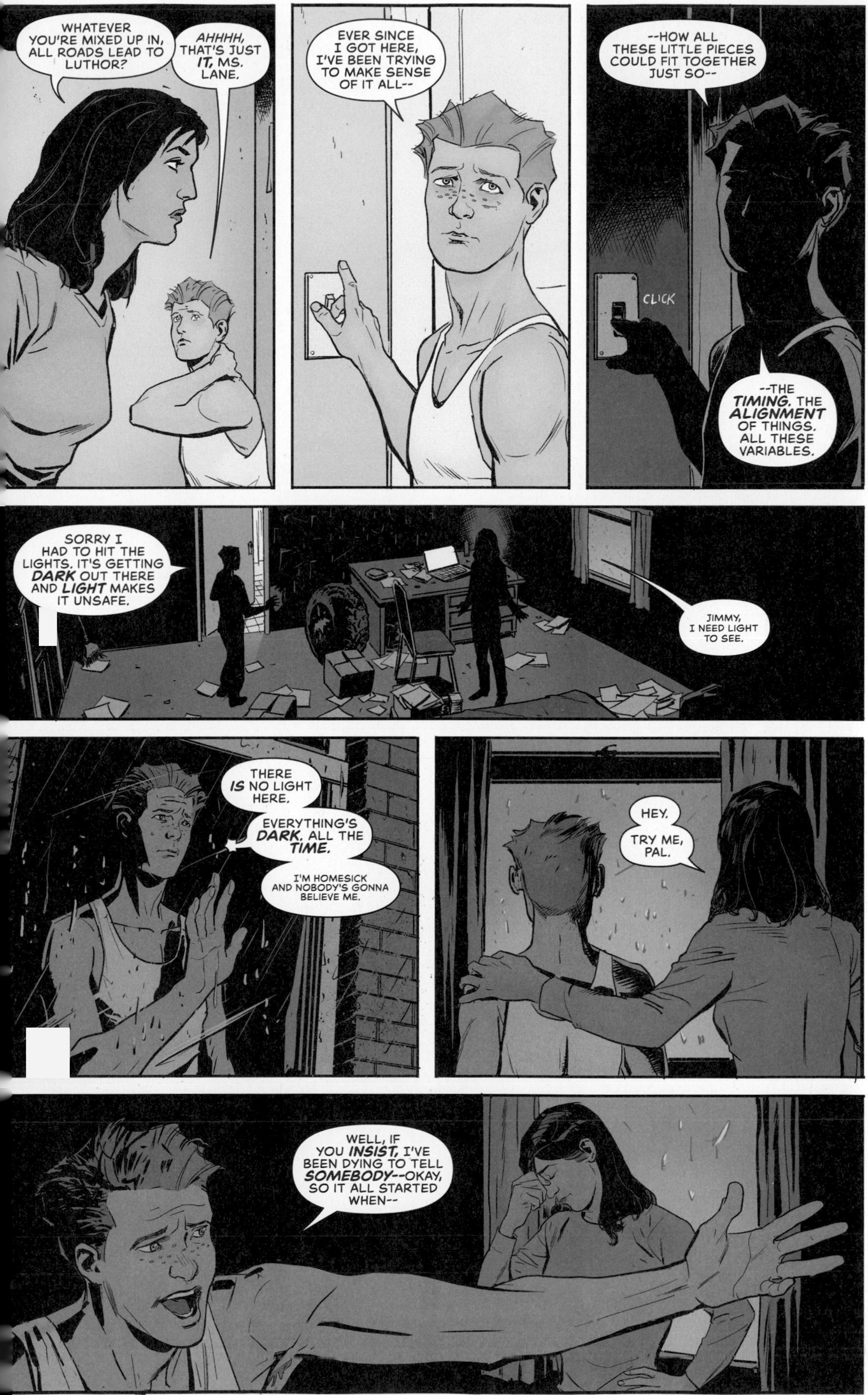
WHATEVER YOU'RE MIXED UP IN, ALL ROADS LEAD TO LUTHOR?
AHHHH, THAT'S JUST IT, MS. LANE.
EVER SINCE I GOT HERE, I'VE BEEN TRYING TO MAKE SENSE OF IT ALL--
--HOW ALL THESE LITTLE PIECES COULD FIT TOGETHER JUST SO--
CLICK
--THE TIMING. THE ALIGNMENT OF THINGS. ALL THESE VARIABLES.
SORRY I HAD TO HIT THE LIGHTS. IT'S GETTING DARK OUT THERE AND LIGHT MAKES IT UNSAFE.
JIMMY, I NEED LIGHT TO SEE.
THERE IS NO LIGHT HERE.
EVERYTHING'S DARK. ALL THE TIME.
I'M HOMESICK AND NOBODY'S GONNA BELIEVE ME.
HEY.
TRY ME, PAL.
WELL, IF YOU INSIST, I'VE BEEN DYING TO TELL SOMEBODY--OKAY, SO IT ALL STARTED WHEN--

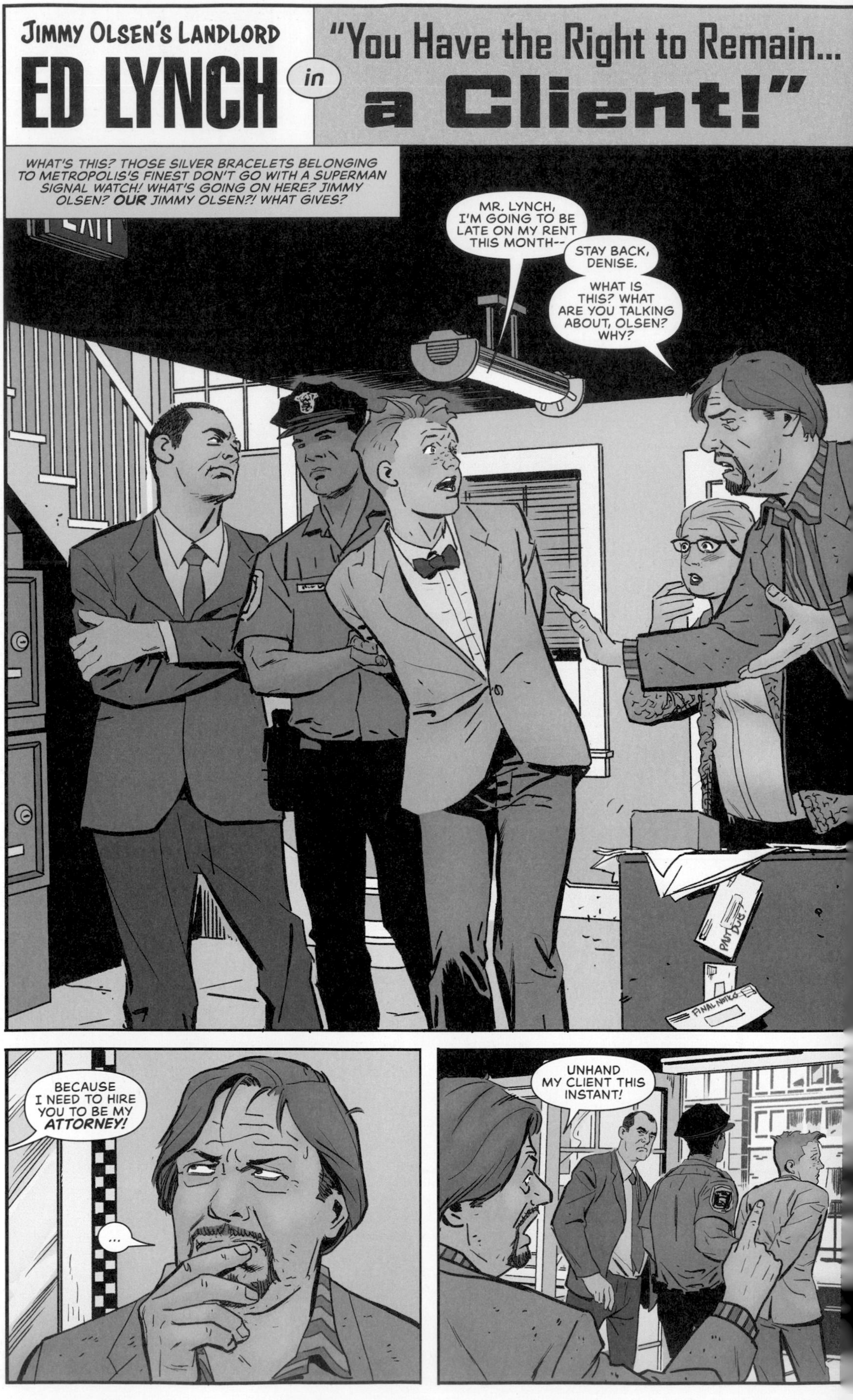
JIMMY OLSEN'S LANDLORD
ED LYNCH
in
"You Have the Right to Remain... a Client!"
WHAT'S THIS? THOSE SILVER BRACELETS BELONGING TO METROPOLIS'S FINEST DON'T GO WITH A SUPERMAN SIGNAL WATCH! WHAT'S GOING ON HERE? JIMMY OLSEN? OUR JIMMY OLSEN?! WHAT GIVES?
MR. LYNCH, I'M GOING TO BE LATE ON MY RENT THIS MONTH--
STAY BACK, DENISE.
WHAT IS THIS? WHAT ARE YOU TALKING ABOUT, OLSEN? WHY?
PAST DUE
FINAL NOTICE
BECAUSE I NEED TO HIRE YOU TO BE MY ATTORNEY!
...
UNHAND MY CLIENT THIS INSTANT!

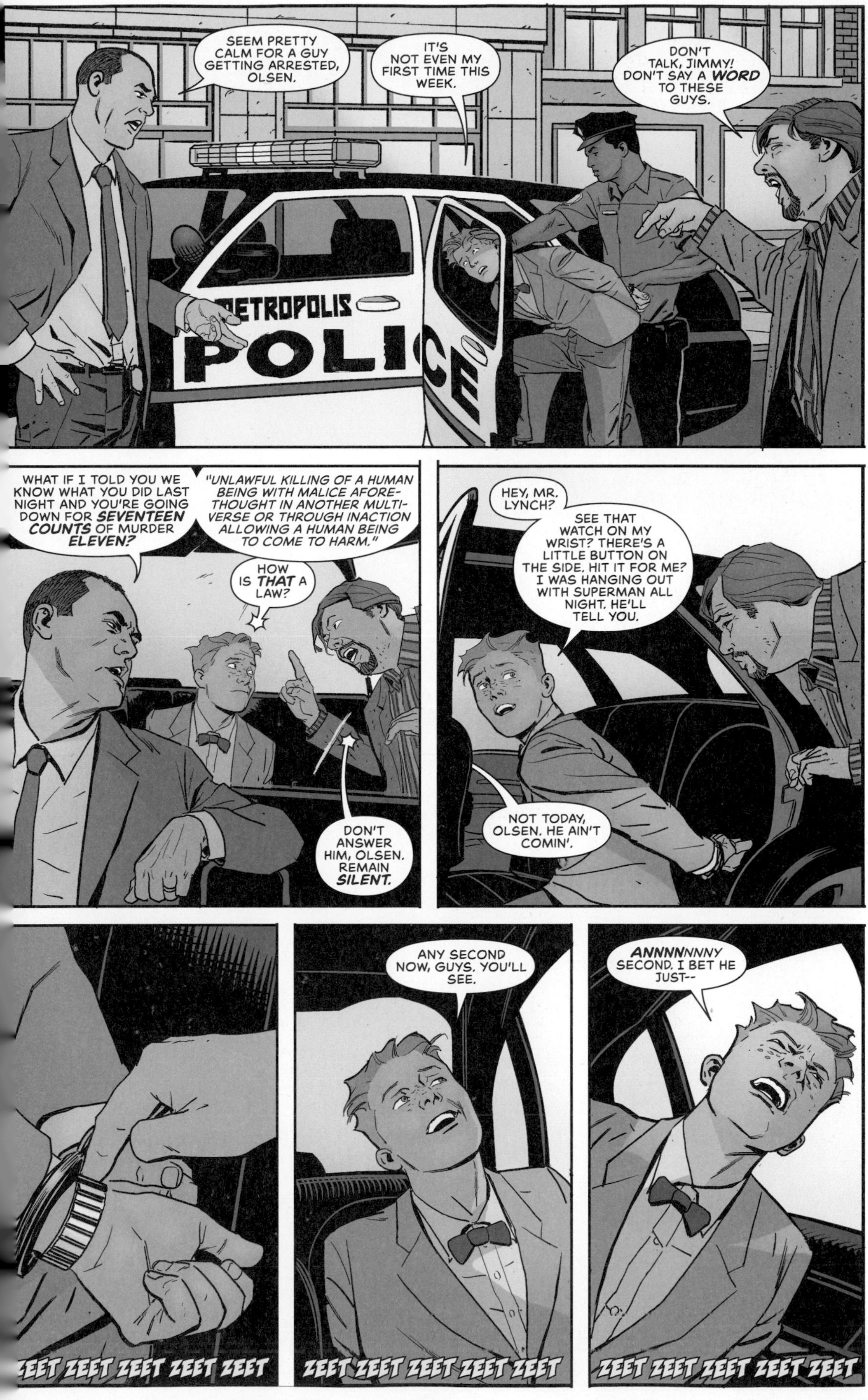
SEEM PRETTY CALM FOR A GUY GETTING ARRESTED, OLSEN.
IT'S NOT EVEN MY FIRST TIME THIS WEEK.
DON'T TALK, JIMMY! DON'T SAY A WORD TO THESE GUYS.
METROPOLIS POLICE
WHAT IF I TOLD YOU WE KNOW WHAT YOU DID LAST NIGHT AND YOU'RE GOING DOWN FOR SEVENTEEN COUNTS OF MURDER ELEVEN?
"UNLAWFUL KILLING OF A HUMAN BEING WITH MALICE AFORE-THOUGHT IN ANOTHER MULTI-VERSE OR THROUGH INACTION ALLOWING A HUMAN BEING TO COME TO HARM."
HOW IS THAT A LAW?
DON'T ANSWER HIM, OLSEN. REMAIN SILENT.
HEY, MR. LYNCH?
SEE THAT WATCH ON MY WRIST? THERE'S A LITTLE BUTTON ON THE SIDE. HIT IT FOR ME? I WAS HANGING OUT WITH SUPERMAN ALL NIGHT. HE'LL TELL YOU.
NOT TODAY, OLSEN. HE AIN'T COMIN'.
ZEET ZEET ZEET ZEET ZEET
ANY SECOND NOW, GUYS. YOU'LL SEE.
ZEET ZEET ZEET ZEET ZEET
ANNNNNNNY SECOND. I BET HE JUST--
ZEET ZEET ZEET ZEET ZEET

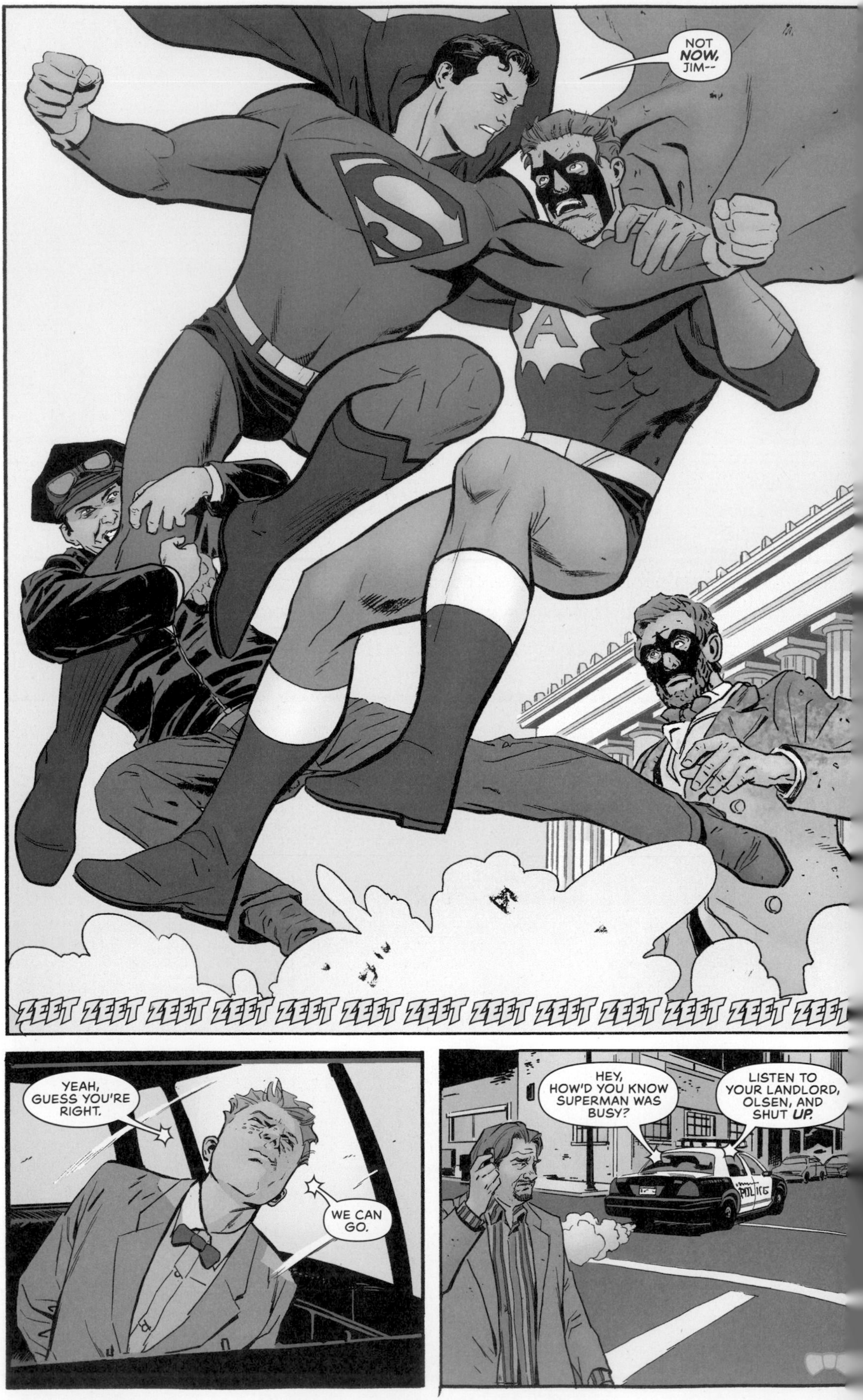
NOT NOW, JIM--
ZEET ZEET ZEET ZEET ZEET ZEET ZEET ZEET ZEET ZEET ZEET ZEET ZEET
YEAH, GUESS YOU'RE RIGHT.
WE CAN GO.
HEY, HOW'D YOU KNOW SUPERMAN WAS BUSY?
LISTEN TO YOUR LANDLORD, OLSEN, AND SHUT UP.

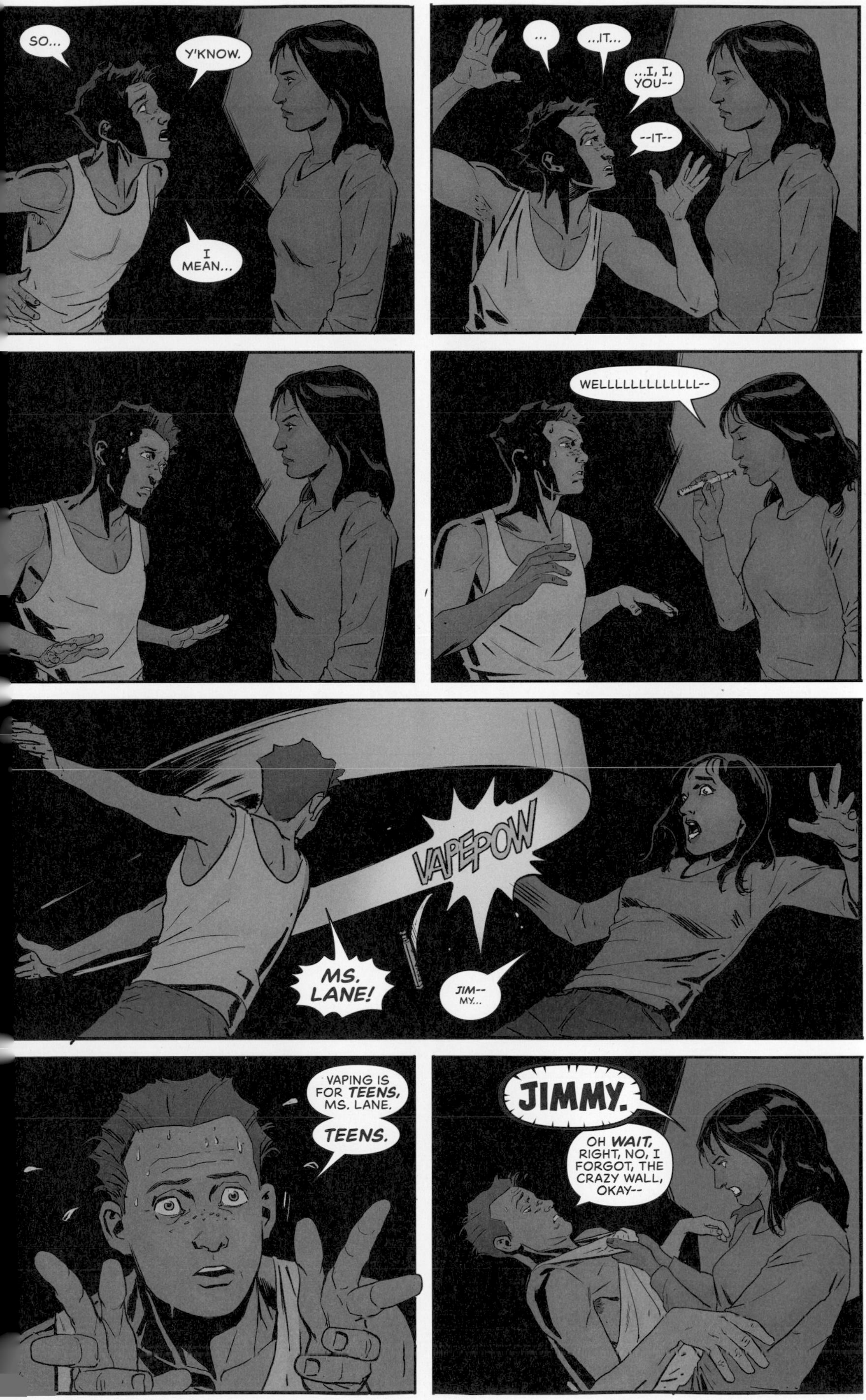
SO...
Y'KNOW.
I MEAN...
...
...IT...
...I, I, YOU--
--IT--
WELLLLLLLLLLLLLL--
VAPEPOW
MS. LANE!
JIM--MY...
VAPING IS FOR TEENS, MS. LANE.
TEENS.
JIMMY.
OH WAIT, RIGHT, NO, I FORGOT, THE CRAZY WALL, OKAY--

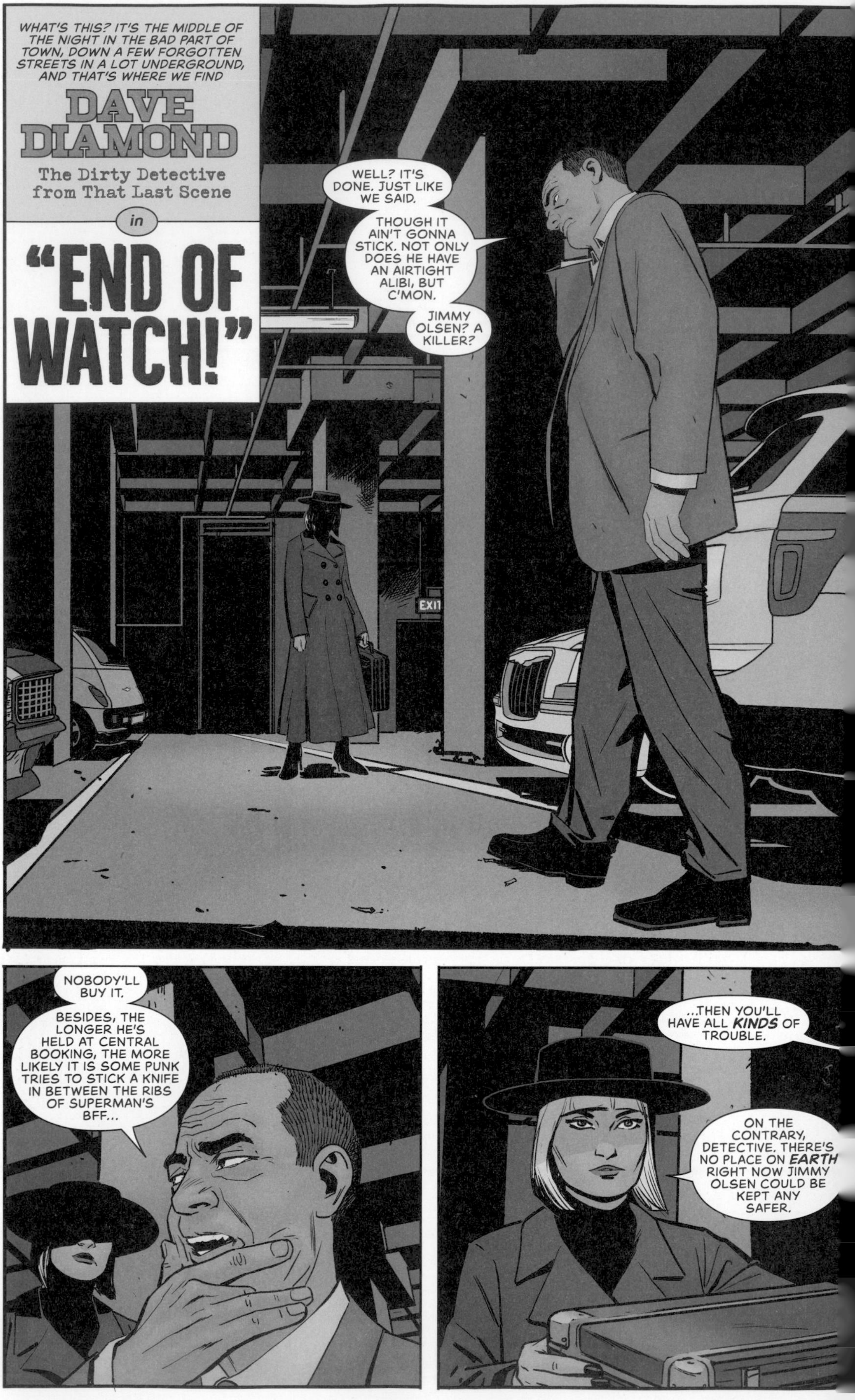
WHAT'S THIS? IT'S THE MIDDLE OF THE NIGHT IN THE BAD PART OF TOWN, DOWN A FEW FORGOTTEN STREETS IN A LOT UNDERGROUND, AND THAT'S WHERE WE FIND
DAVE DIAMOND
The Dirty Detective from That Last Scene
in
"END OF WATCH!"
WELL? IT'S DONE. JUST LIKE WE SAID.
THOUGH IT AIN'T GONNA STICK. NOT ONLY DOES HE HAVE AN AIRTIGHT ALIBI, BUT C'MON.
JIMMY OLSEN? A KILLER?
EXIT
NOBODY'LL BUY IT.
BESIDES, THE LONGER HE'S HELD AT CENTRAL BOOKING, THE MORE LIKELY IT IS SOME PUNK TRIES TO STICK A KNIFE IN BETWEEN THE RIBS OF SUPERMAN'S BFF...
...THEN YOU'LL HAVE ALL KINDS OF TROUBLE.
ON THE CONTRARY, DETECTIVE. THERE'S NO PLACE ON EARTH RIGHT NOW JIMMY OLSEN COULD BE KEPT ANY SAFER.

♪

SAFER?

I DON'T UNDERSTAND. I THOUGHT YOU WANTED--

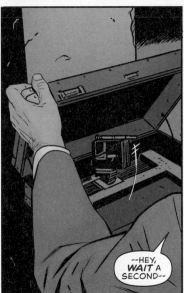

--HEY, *WAIT* A SECOND--

!!

FSSSHHHP

SHH. NEVER KNOW WHO MAY BE LISTENING.

OR EVEN *SUPER*-LISTENING, AS THE CASE MAY BE.

PLEASURE DOING BUSINESS WITH YOU, DETECTIVE.

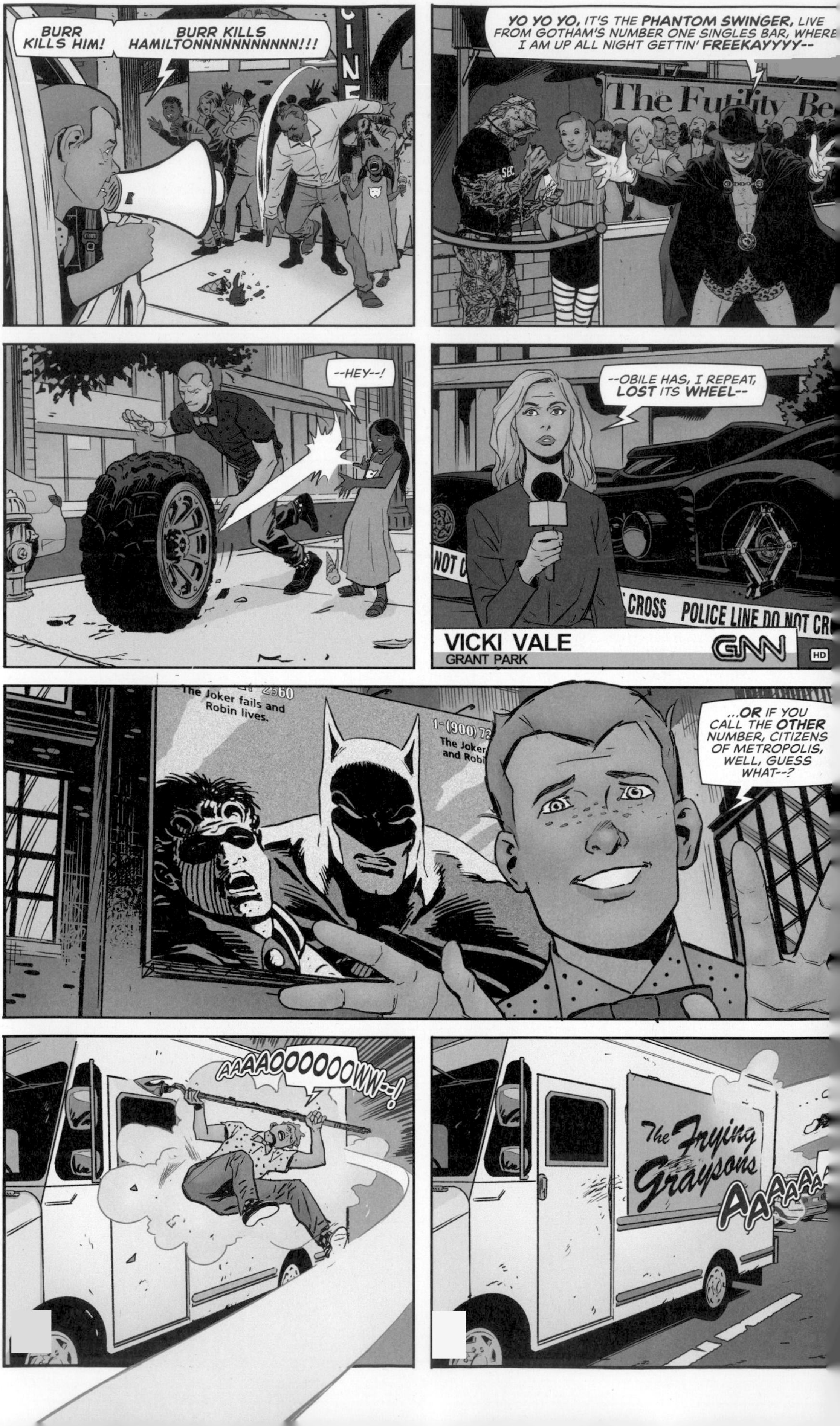
BURR KILLS HIM!
BURR KILLS HAMILTONNNNNNNNNNN!!!
YO YO YO, IT'S THE PHANTOM SWINGER, LIVE FROM GOTHAM'S NUMBER ONE SINGLES BAR, WHERE I AM UP ALL NIGHT GETTIN' FREEKAYYYY--
The Futility
--HEY--!
--OBILE HAS, I REPEAT, LOST ITS WHEEL--
CROSS
POLICE LINE DO NOT
VICKI VALE
GRANT PARK
GNN
HD
The Joker fails and Robin lives.
...OR IF YOU CALL THE OTHER NUMBER, CITIZENS OF METROPOLIS, WELL, GUESS WHAT--?
AAAAOOOOOOWW--!
The Frying Graysons

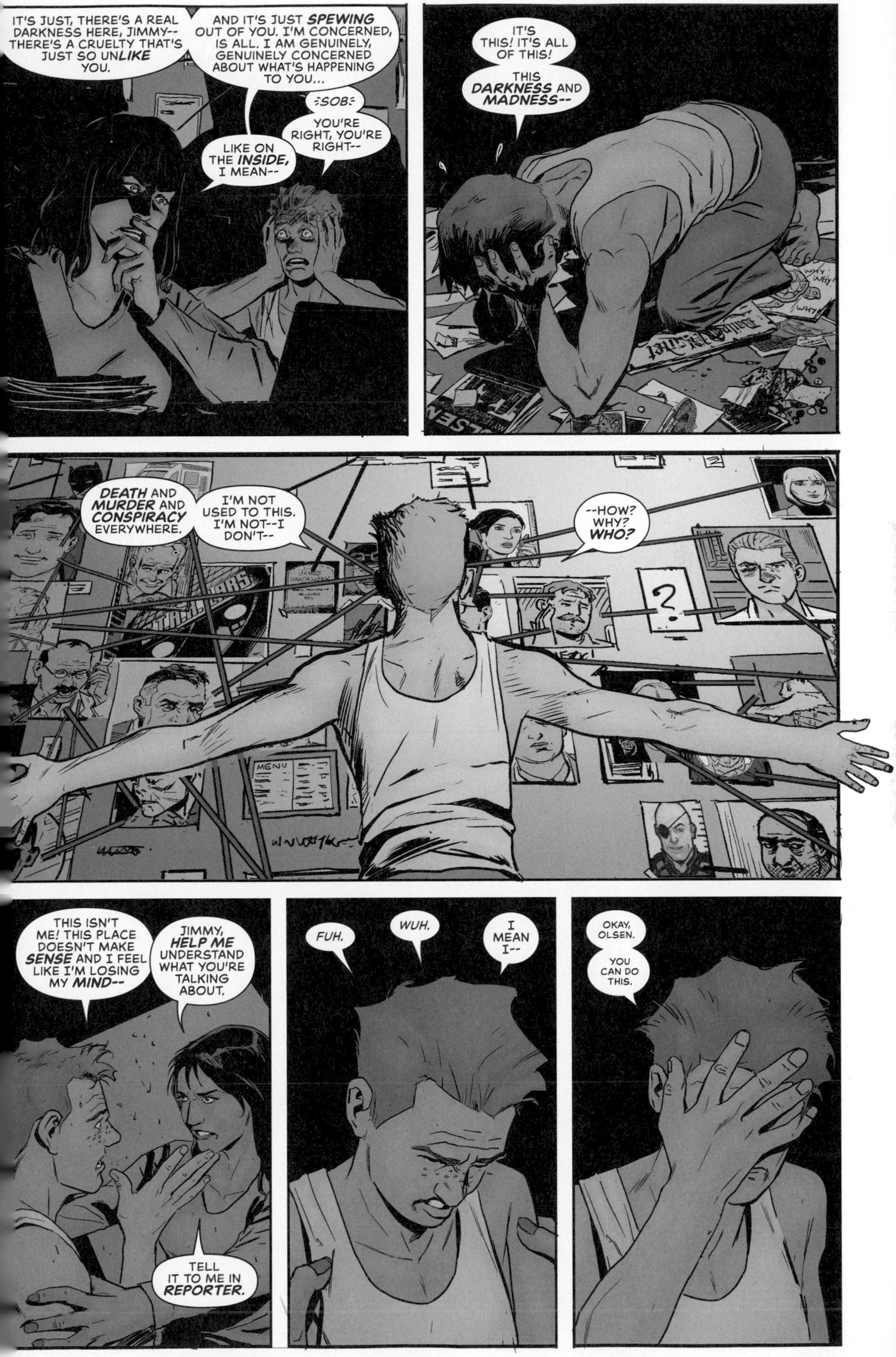
IT'S JUST, THERE'S A REAL DARKNESS HERE, JIMMY-- THERE'S A CRUELTY THAT'S JUST SO UNLIKE YOU.
AND IT'S JUST SPEWING OUT OF YOU. I'M CONCERNED, IS ALL. I AM GENUINELY, GENUINELY CONCERNED ABOUT WHAT'S HAPPENING TO YOU...
LIKE ON THE INSIDE, I MEAN--
SOB
YOU'RE RIGHT, YOU'RE RIGHT--
IT'S THIS! IT'S ALL OF THIS!
THIS DARKNESS AND MADNESS--
DEATH AND MURDER AND CONSPIRACY EVERYWHERE.
I'M NOT USED TO THIS. I'M NOT--I DON'T--
--HOW? WHY? WHO?
MENU
THIS ISN'T ME! THIS PLACE DOESN'T MAKE SENSE AND I FEEL LIKE I'M LOSING MY MIND--
JIMMY, HELP ME UNDERSTAND WHAT YOU'RE TALKING ABOUT.
TELL IT TO ME IN REPORTER.
FUH.
WUH.
I MEAN I--
OKAY, OLSEN.
YOU CAN DO THIS.

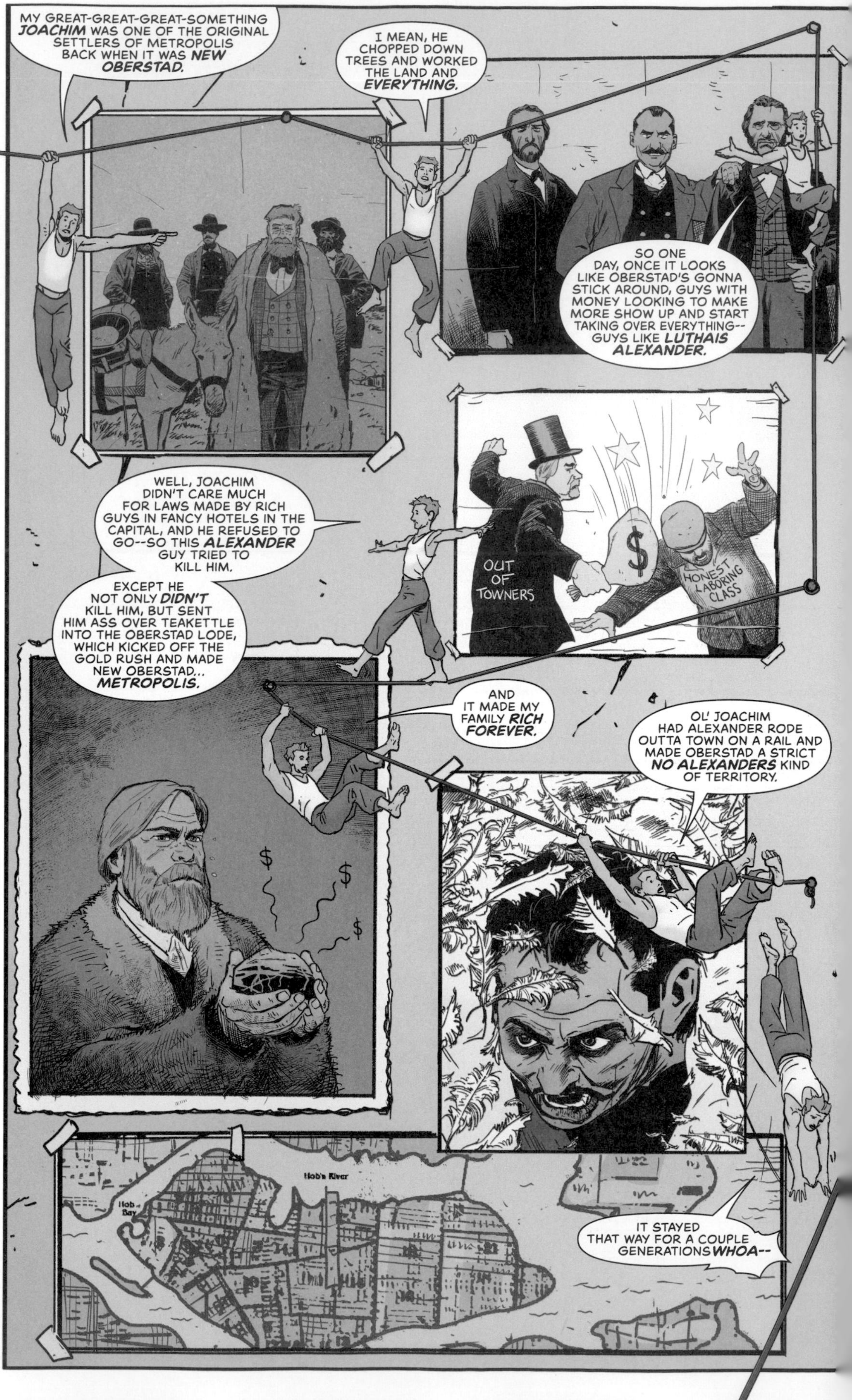
MY GREAT-GREAT-GREAT-SOMETHING JOACHIM WAS ONE OF THE ORIGINAL SETTLERS OF METROPOLIS BACK WHEN IT WAS NEW OBERSTAD.
I MEAN, HE CHOPPED DOWN TREES AND WORKED THE LAND AND EVERYTHING.
SO ONE DAY, ONCE IT LOOKS LIKE OBERSTAD'S GONNA STICK AROUND, GUYS WITH MONEY LOOKING TO MAKE MORE SHOW UP AND START TAKING OVER EVERYTHING-- GUYS LIKE LUTHAIS ALEXANDER.
WELL, JOACHIM DIDN'T CARE MUCH FOR LAWS MADE BY RICH GUYS IN FANCY HOTELS IN THE CAPITAL, AND HE REFUSED TO GO--SO THIS ALEXANDER GUY TRIED TO KILL HIM.
OUT OF TOWNERS
$
HONEST LABORING CLASS
EXCEPT HE NOT ONLY DIDN'T KILL HIM, BUT SENT HIM ASS OVER TEAKETTLE INTO THE OBERSTAD LODE, WHICH KICKED OFF THE GOLD RUSH AND MADE NEW OBERSTAD... METROPOLIS.
AND IT MADE MY FAMILY RICH FOREVER.
OL' JOACHIM HAD ALEXANDER RODE OUTTA TOWN ON A RAIL AND MADE OBERSTAD A STRICT NO ALEXANDERS KIND OF TERRITORY.
Hob's River
Hob Bay
IT STAYED THAT WAY FOR A COUPLE GENERATIONS WHOA--

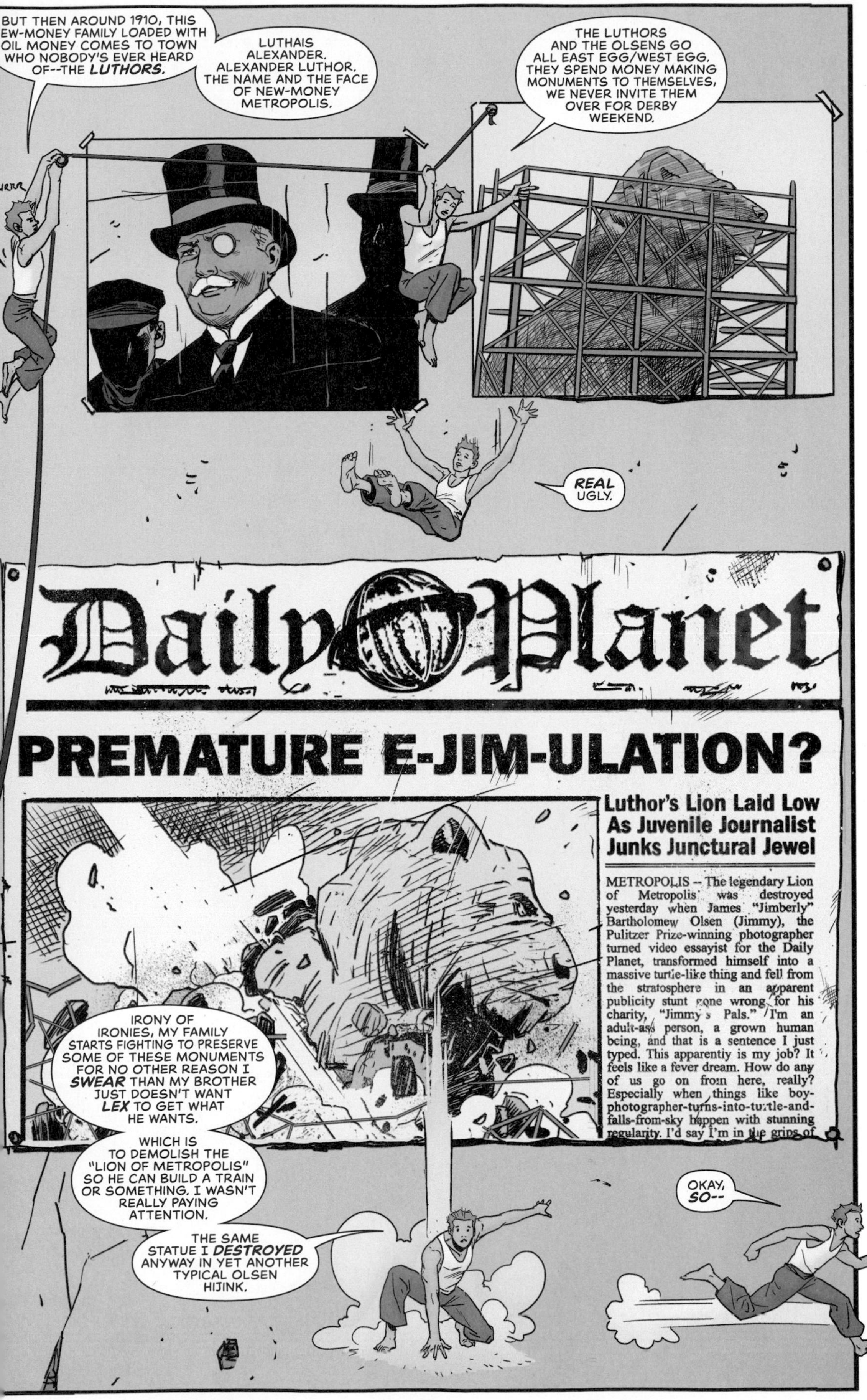
BUT THEN AROUND 1910, THIS NEW-MONEY FAMILY LOADED WITH OIL MONEY COMES TO TOWN WHO NOBODY'S EVER HEARD OF--THE LUTHORS.
LUTHAIS ALEXANDER. ALEXANDER LUTHOR. THE NAME AND THE FACE OF NEW-MONEY METROPOLIS.
THE LUTHORS AND THE OLSENS GO ALL EAST EGG/WEST EGG. THEY SPEND MONEY MAKING MONUMENTS TO THEMSELVES, WE NEVER INVITE THEM OVER FOR DERBY WEEKEND.
URRR
REAL UGLY.
Daily Planet
PREMATURE E-JIM-ULATION?
Luthor's Lion Laid Low As Juvenile Journalist Junks Junctural Jewel
METROPOLIS -- The legendary Lion of Metropolis was destroyed yesterday when James "Jimberly" Bartholomew Olsen (Jimmy), the Pulitzer Prize-winning photographer turned video essayist for the Daily Planet, transformed himself into a massive turtle-like thing and fell from the stratosphere in an apparent publicity stunt gone wrong for his charity, "Jimmy's Pals." I'm an adult-ass person, a grown human being, and that is a sentence I just typed. This apparently is my job? It feels like a fever dream. How do any of us go on from here, really? Especially when things like boy-photographer-turns-into-turtle-and-falls-from-sky happen with stunning regularity. I'd say I'm in the grips of
IRONY OF IRONIES, MY FAMILY STARTS FIGHTING TO PRESERVE SOME OF THESE MONUMENTS FOR NO OTHER REASON I SWEAR THAN MY BROTHER JUST DOESN'T WANT LEX TO GET WHAT HE WANTS.
WHICH IS TO DEMOLISH THE "LION OF METROPOLIS" SO HE CAN BUILD A TRAIN OR SOMETHING. I WASN'T REALLY PAYING ATTENTION.
THE SAME STATUE I DESTROYED ANYWAY IN YET ANOTHER TYPICAL OLSEN HIJINK.
OKAY, SO--

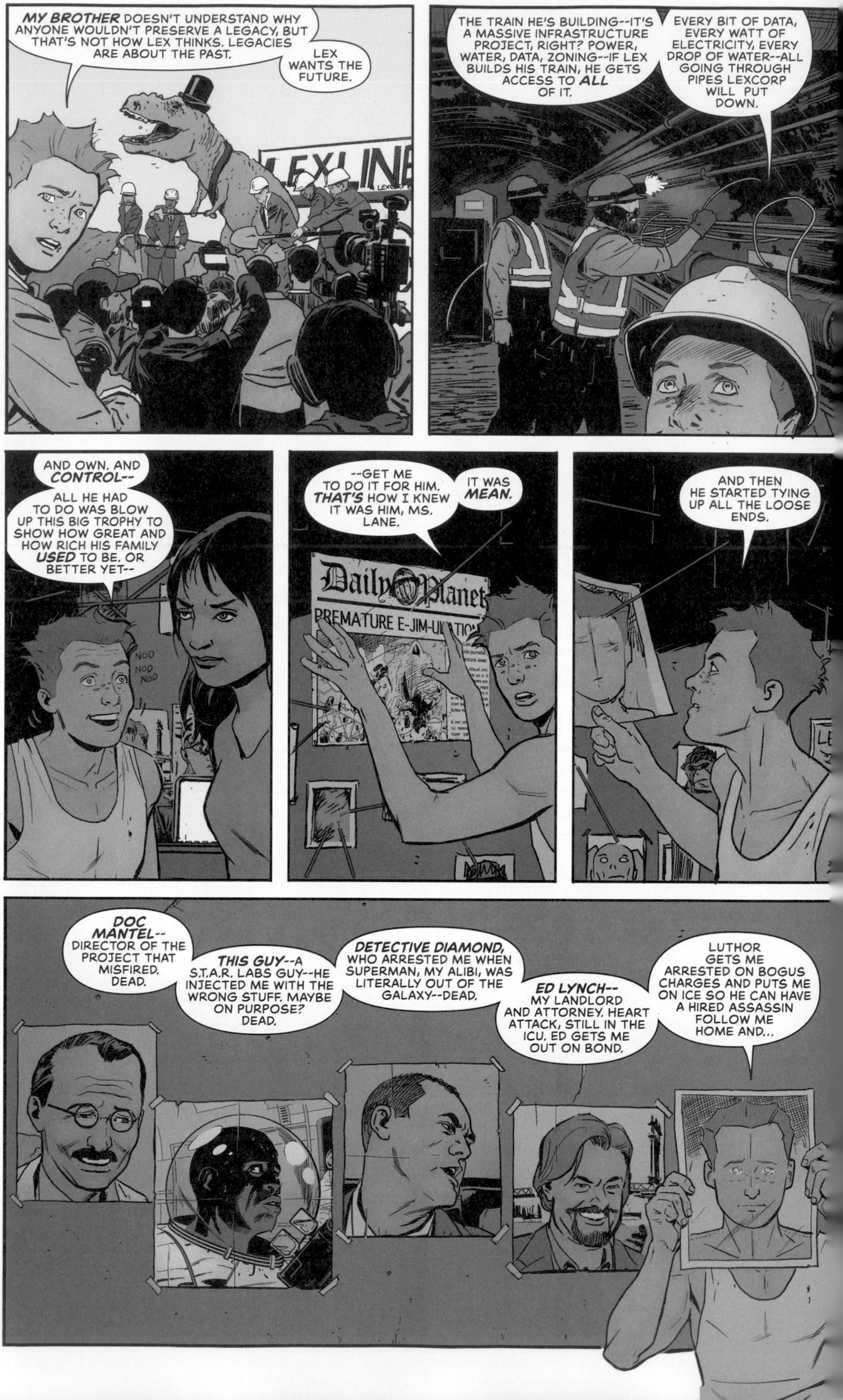
MY BROTHER DOESN'T UNDERSTAND WHY ANYONE WOULDN'T PRESERVE A LEGACY, BUT THAT'S NOT HOW LEX THINKS. LEGACIES ARE ABOUT THE PAST.
LEX WANTS THE FUTURE.
LEXLINE
LEXCORP
THE TRAIN HE'S BUILDING--IT'S A MASSIVE INFRASTRUCTURE PROJECT, RIGHT? POWER, WATER, DATA, ZONING--IF LEX BUILDS HIS TRAIN, HE GETS ACCESS TO **ALL** OF IT.
EVERY BIT OF DATA, EVERY WATT OF ELECTRICITY, EVERY DROP OF WATER--ALL GOING THROUGH PIPES LEXCORP WILL PUT DOWN.
AND OWN, AND **CONTROL**--
ALL HE HAD TO DO WAS BLOW UP THIS BIG TROPHY TO SHOW HOW GREAT AND HOW RICH HIS FAMILY **USED** TO BE. OR BETTER YET--
NOD NOD NOD
--GET ME TO DO IT FOR HIM. **THAT'S** HOW I KNEW IT WAS HIM, MS. LANE.
IT WAS **MEAN.**
Daily Planet
PREMATURE E-JIM-ULATIO
AND THEN HE STARTED TYING UP ALL THE LOOSE ENDS.
DOC MANTEL--DIRECTOR OF THE PROJECT THAT MISFIRED. DEAD.
THIS GUY--A S.T.A.R. LABS GUY--HE INJECTED ME WITH THE WRONG STUFF. MAYBE ON PURPOSE? DEAD.
DETECTIVE DIAMOND, WHO ARRESTED ME WHEN SUPERMAN, MY ALIBI, WAS LITERALLY OUT OF THE GALAXY--DEAD.
ED LYNCH--MY LANDLORD AND ATTORNEY. HEART ATTACK, STILL IN THE ICU. ED GETS ME OUT ON BOND.
LUTHOR GETS ME ARRESTED ON BOGUS CHARGES AND PUTS ME ON ICE SO HE CAN HAVE A HIRED ASSASSIN FOLLOW ME HOME AND...

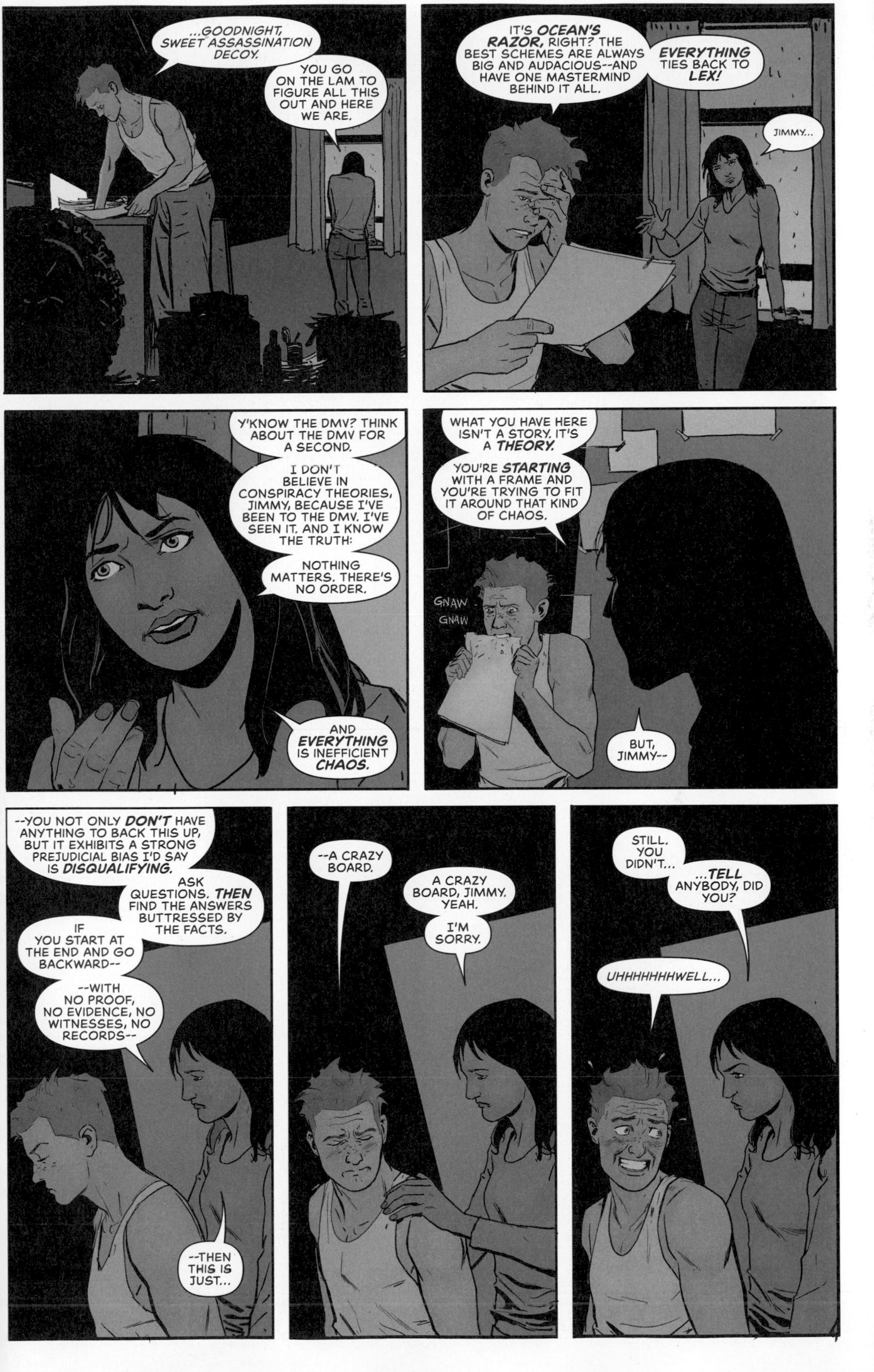
...GOODNIGHT, SWEET ASSASSINATION DECOY.
YOU GO ON THE LAM TO FIGURE ALL THIS OUT AND HERE WE ARE.
IT'S OCEAN'S RAZOR, RIGHT? THE BEST SCHEMES ARE ALWAYS BIG AND AUDACIOUS--AND HAVE ONE MASTERMIND BEHIND IT ALL.
EVERYTHING TIES BACK TO LEX!
JIMMY...
Y'KNOW THE DMV? THINK ABOUT THE DMV FOR A SECOND.
I DON'T BELIEVE IN CONSPIRACY THEORIES, JIMMY, BECAUSE I'VE BEEN TO THE DMV. I'VE SEEN IT. AND I KNOW THE TRUTH:
NOTHING MATTERS. THERE'S NO ORDER.
AND EVERYTHING IS INEFFICIENT CHAOS.
WHAT YOU HAVE HERE ISN'T A STORY. IT'S A THEORY.
YOU'RE STARTING WITH A FRAME AND YOU'RE TRYING TO FIT IT AROUND THAT KIND OF CHAOS.
GNAW GNAW
BUT, JIMMY--
--YOU NOT ONLY DON'T HAVE ANYTHING TO BACK THIS UP, BUT IT EXHIBITS A STRONG PREJUDICIAL BIAS I'D SAY IS DISQUALIFYING.
ASK QUESTIONS. THEN FIND THE ANSWERS BUTTRESSED BY THE FACTS.
IF YOU START AT THE END AND GO BACKWARD--
--WITH NO PROOF, NO EVIDENCE, NO WITNESSES, NO RECORDS--
--THEN THIS IS JUST...
--A CRAZY BOARD.
A CRAZY BOARD, JIMMY. YEAH.
I'M SORRY.
STILL. YOU DIDN'T...
...TELL ANYBODY, DID YOU?
UHHHHHHHWELL...

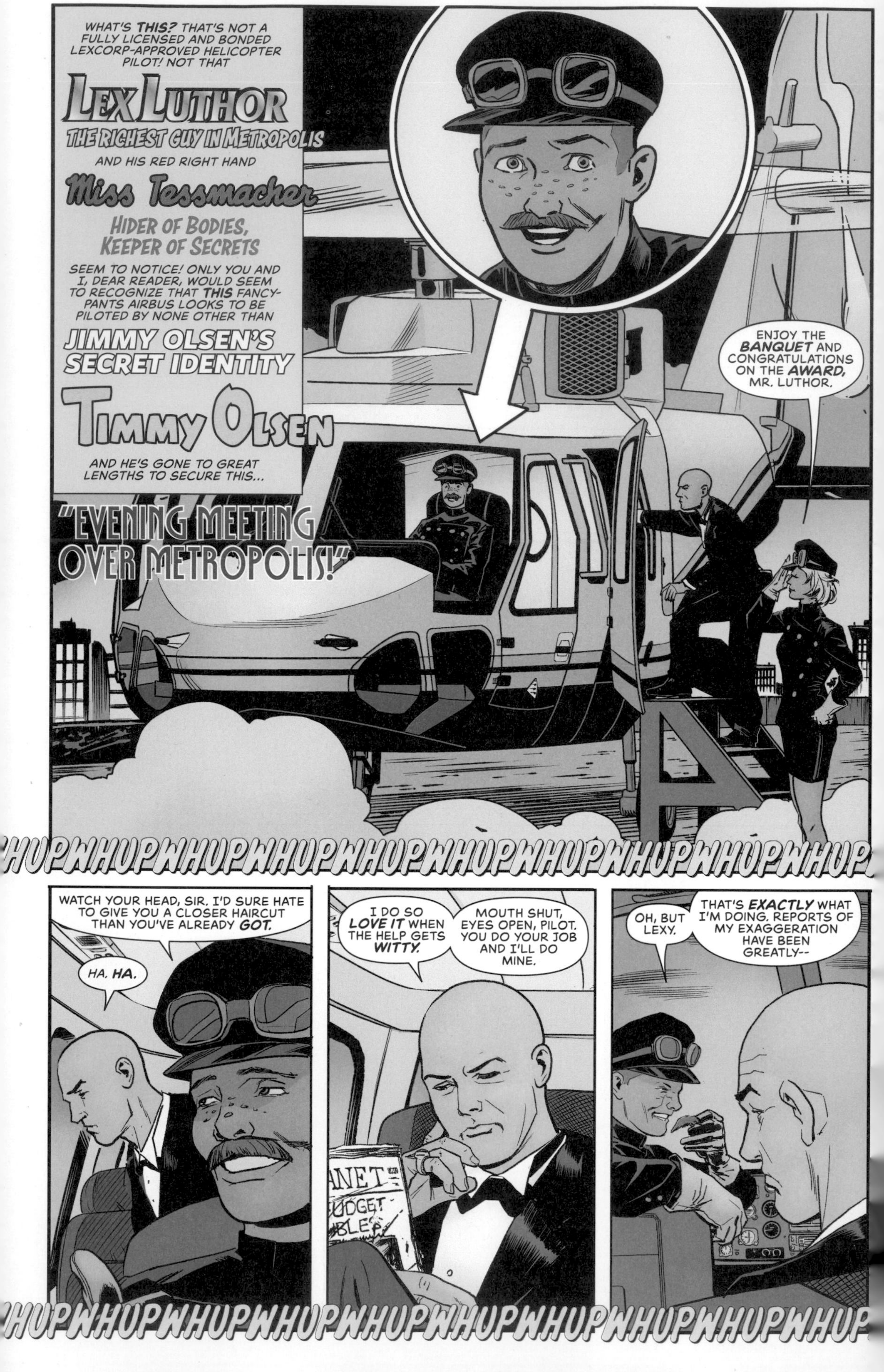
WHAT'S THIS? THAT'S NOT A FULLY LICENSED AND BONDED LEXCORP-APPROVED HELICOPTER PILOT! NOT THAT
LEX LUTHOR
THE RICHEST GUY IN METROPOLIS
AND HIS RED RIGHT HAND
Miss Tessmacher
HIDER OF BODIES, KEEPER OF SECRETS
SEEM TO NOTICE! ONLY YOU AND I, DEAR READER, WOULD SEEM TO RECOGNIZE THAT THIS FANCY-PANTS AIRBUS LOOKS TO BE PILOTED BY NONE OTHER THAN
JIMMY OLSEN'S SECRET IDENTITY
TIMMY OLSEN
AND HE'S GONE TO GREAT LENGTHS TO SECURE THIS...
"EVENING MEETING OVER METROPOLIS!"
ENJOY THE BANQUET AND CONGRATULATIONS ON THE AWARD, MR. LUTHOR.
HUPWHUPWHUPWHUPWHUPWHUPWHUPWHUPWHUPWHUP
WATCH YOUR HEAD, SIR. I'D SURE HATE TO GIVE YOU A CLOSER HAIRCUT THAN YOU'VE ALREADY GOT.
HA. HA.
I DO SO LOVE IT WHEN THE HELP GETS WITTY.
MOUTH SHUT, EYES OPEN, PILOT. YOU DO YOUR JOB AND I'LL DO MINE.
OH, BUT LEXY.
THAT'S EXACTLY WHAT I'M DOING. REPORTS OF MY EXAGGERATION HAVE BEEN GREATLY--
HUPWHUPWHUPWHUPWHUPWHUPWHUPWHUPWHUPWHUP

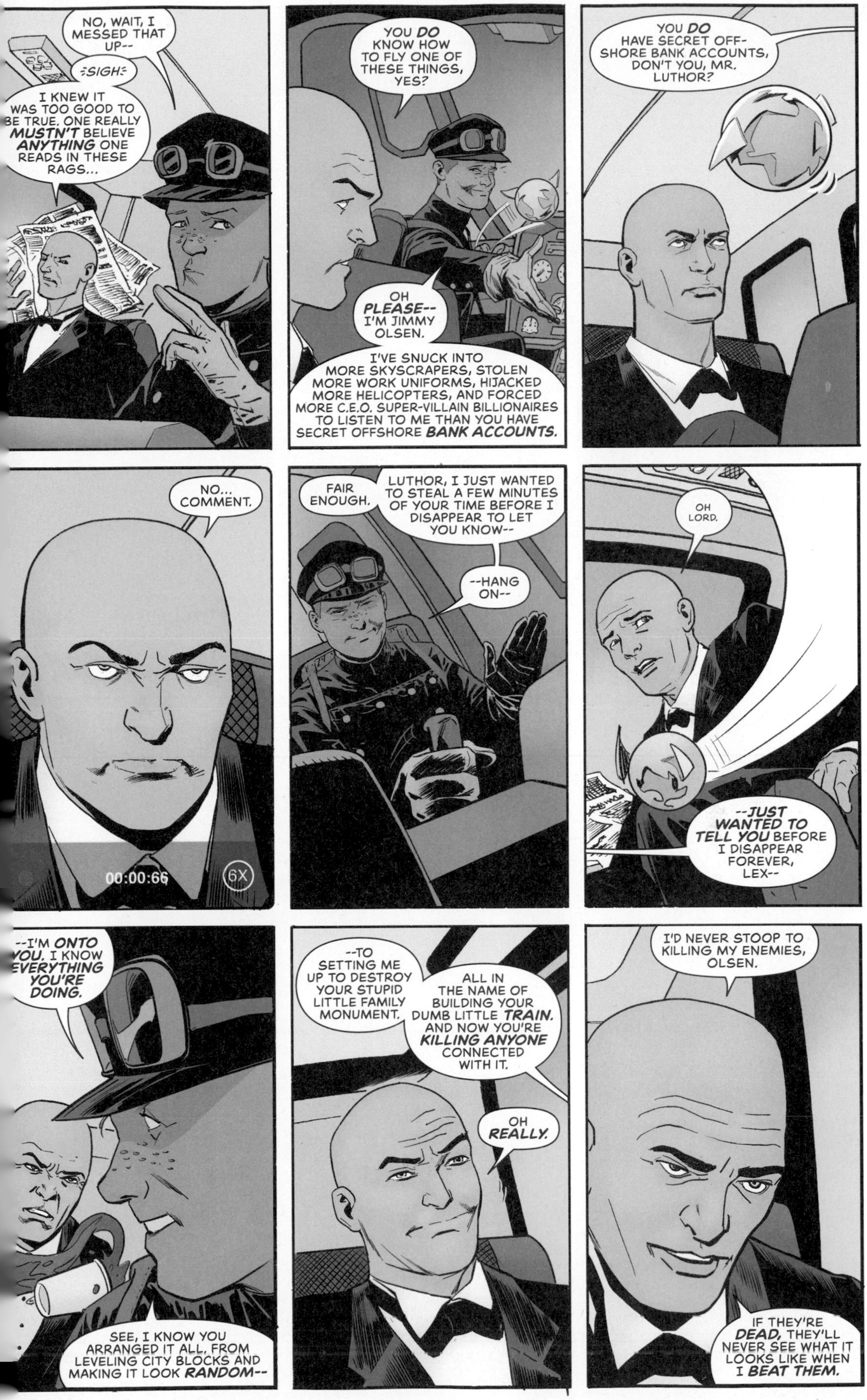
NO, WAIT, I MESSED THAT UP--
SIGH
I KNEW IT WAS TOO GOOD TO BE TRUE. ONE REALLY MUSTN'T BELIEVE ANYTHING ONE READS IN THESE RAGS...
YOU DO KNOW HOW TO FLY ONE OF THESE THINGS, YES?
OH PLEASE-- I'M JIMMY OLSEN.
I'VE SNUCK INTO MORE SKYSCRAPERS, STOLEN MORE WORK UNIFORMS, HIJACKED MORE HELICOPTERS, AND FORCED MORE C.E.O. SUPER-VILLAIN BILLIONAIRES TO LISTEN TO ME THAN YOU HAVE SECRET OFFSHORE BANK ACCOUNTS.
YOU DO HAVE SECRET OFF-SHORE BANK ACCOUNTS, DON'T YOU, MR. LUTHOR?
NO... COMMENT.
00:00:66
6X
FAIR ENOUGH.
LUTHOR, I JUST WANTED TO STEAL A FEW MINUTES OF YOUR TIME BEFORE I DISAPPEAR TO LET YOU KNOW--
--HANG ON--
OH LORD.
--JUST WANTED TO TELL YOU BEFORE I DISAPPEAR FOREVER, LEX--
--I'M ONTO YOU. I KNOW EVERYTHING YOU'RE DOING.
SEE, I KNOW YOU ARRANGED IT ALL, FROM LEVELING CITY BLOCKS AND MAKING IT LOOK RANDOM--
--TO SETTING ME UP TO DESTROY YOUR STUPID LITTLE FAMILY MONUMENT.
ALL IN THE NAME OF BUILDING YOUR DUMB LITTLE TRAIN. AND NOW YOU'RE KILLING ANYONE CONNECTED WITH IT.
OH REALLY.
I'D NEVER STOOP TO KILLING MY ENEMIES, OLSEN.
IF THEY'RE DEAD, THEY'LL NEVER SEE WHAT IT LOOKS LIKE WHEN I BEAT THEM.

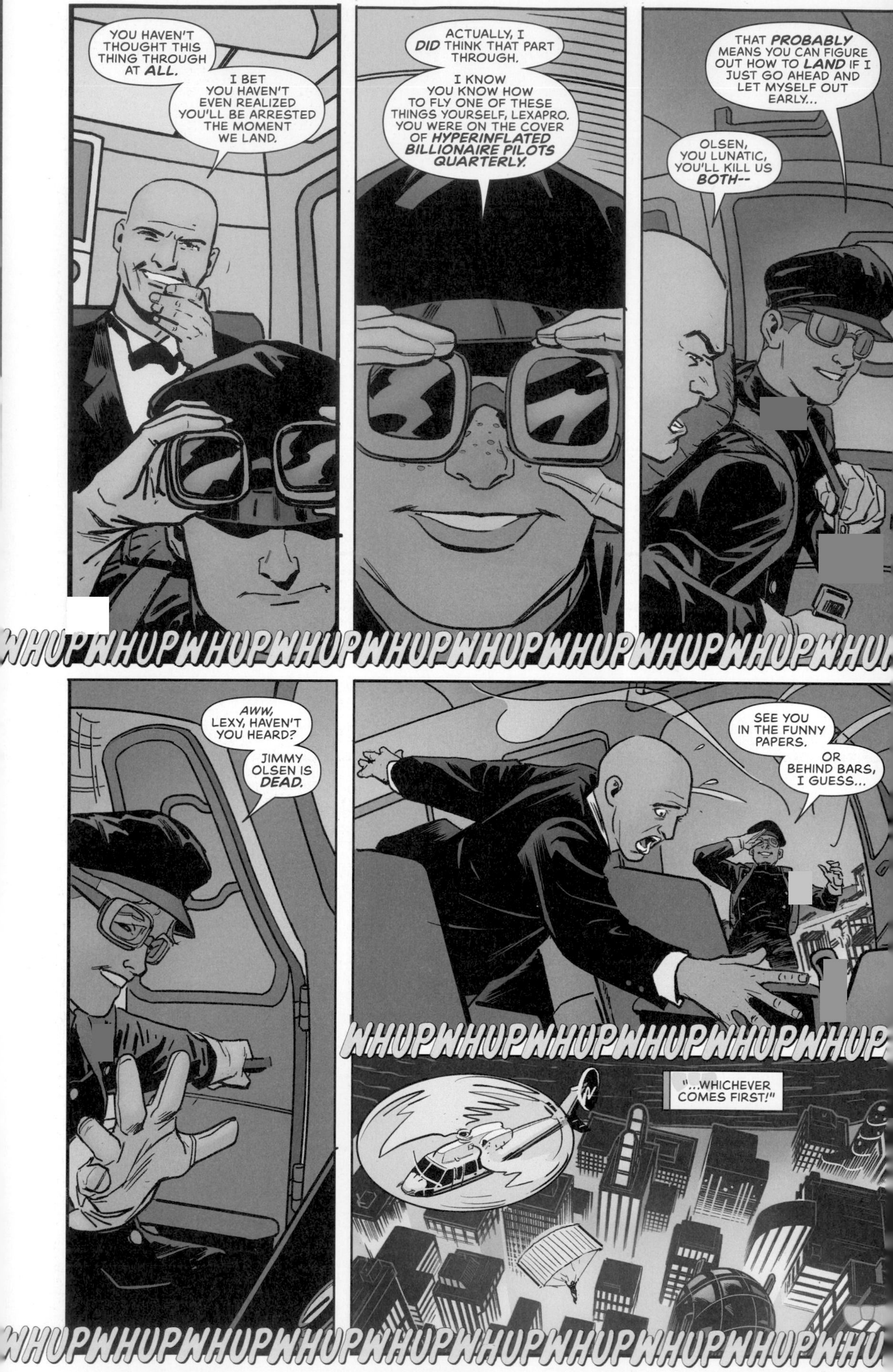
YOU HAVEN'T THOUGHT THIS THING THROUGH AT ALL.
I BET YOU HAVEN'T EVEN REALIZED YOU'LL BE ARRESTED THE MOMENT WE LAND.
ACTUALLY, I DID THINK THAT PART THROUGH.
I KNOW YOU KNOW HOW TO FLY ONE OF THESE THINGS YOURSELF, LEXAPRO. YOU WERE ON THE COVER OF HYPERINFLATED BILLIONAIRE PILOTS QUARTERLY.
THAT PROBABLY MEANS YOU CAN FIGURE OUT HOW TO LAND IF I JUST GO AHEAD AND LET MYSELF OUT EARLY...
OLSEN, YOU LUNATIC, YOU'LL KILL US BOTH--
WHUPWHUPWHUPWHUPWHUPWHUPWHUPWHUPWHUPWHU
AWW, LEXY, HAVEN'T YOU HEARD?
JIMMY OLSEN IS DEAD.
SEE YOU IN THE FUNNY PAPERS.
OR BEHIND BARS, I GUESS...
WHUPWHUPWHUPWHUPWHUPWHUP
"...WHICHEVER COMES FIRST!"
WHUPWHUPWHUPWHUPWHUPWHUPWHUPWHUPWHUPWHU

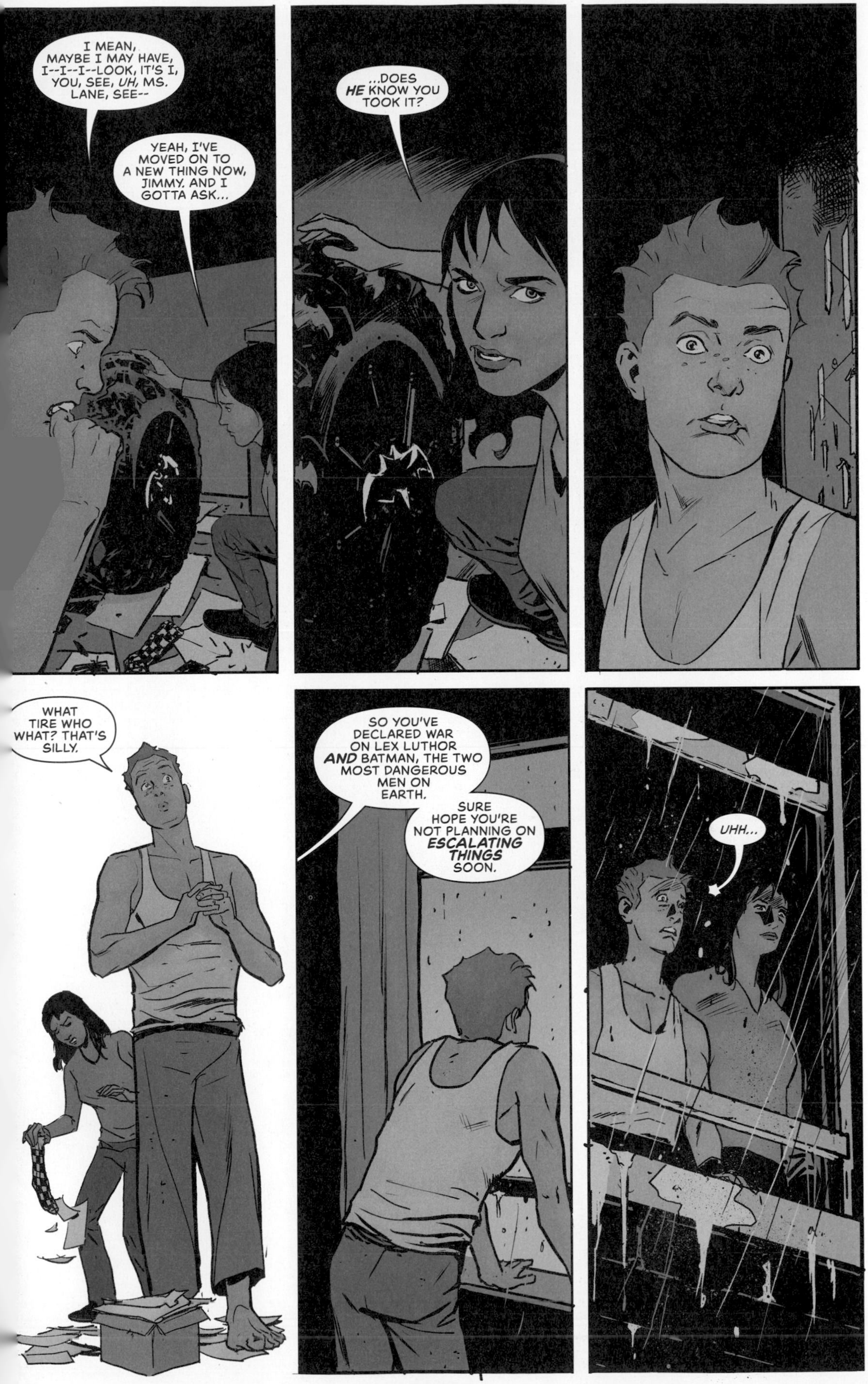
I MEAN, MAYBE I MAY HAVE, I--I--I--LOOK, IT'S I, YOU, SEE, UH, MS. LANE, SEE--
YEAH, I'VE MOVED ON TO A NEW THING NOW, JIMMY. AND I GOTTA ASK...
...DOES HE KNOW YOU TOOK IT?
WHAT TIRE WHO WHAT? THAT'S SILLY.
SO YOU'VE DECLARED WAR ON LEX LUTHOR AND BATMAN, THE TWO MOST DANGEROUS MEN ON EARTH.
SURE HOPE YOU'RE NOT PLANNING ON ESCALATING THINGS SOON.
UHH...

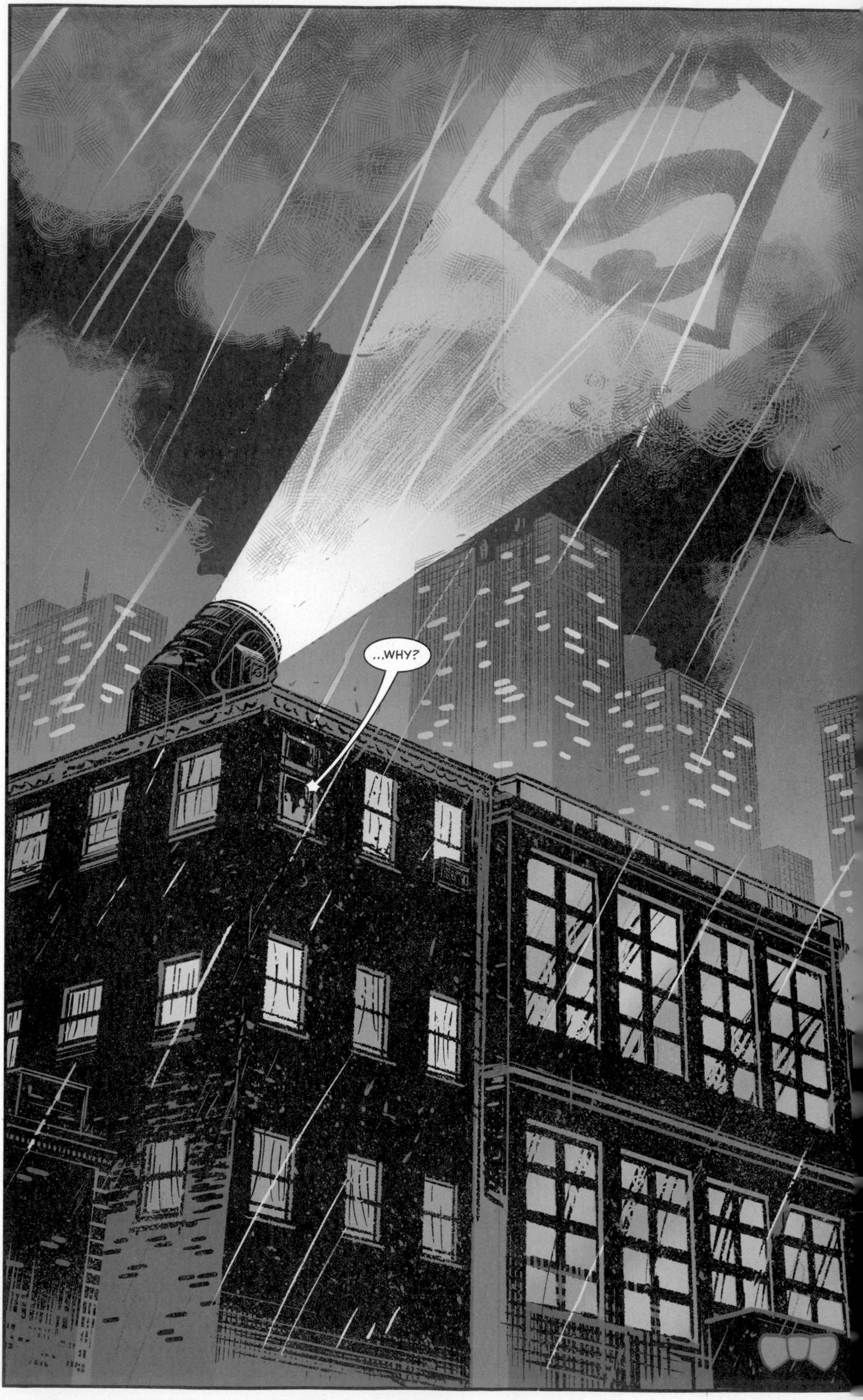
...WHY?

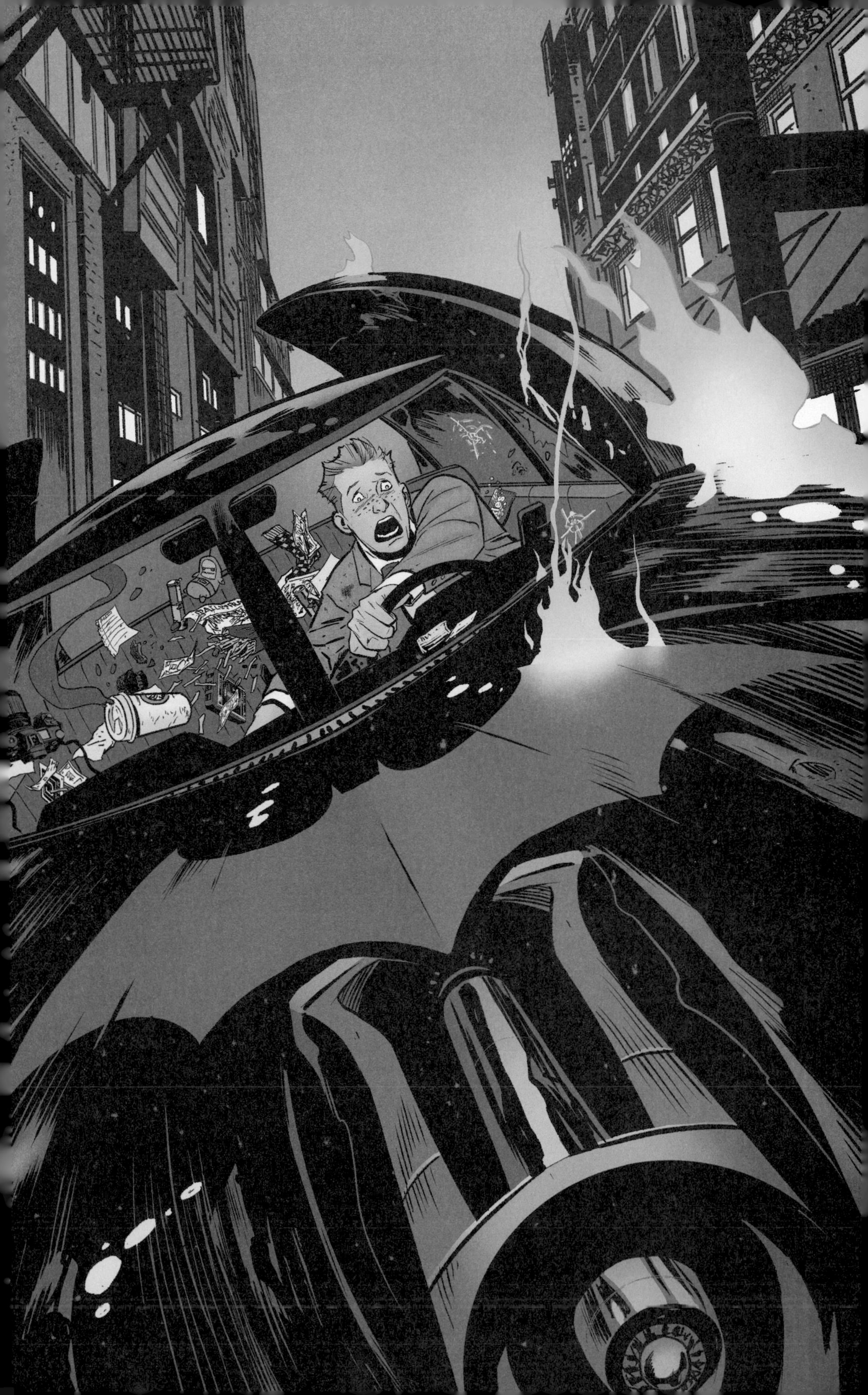

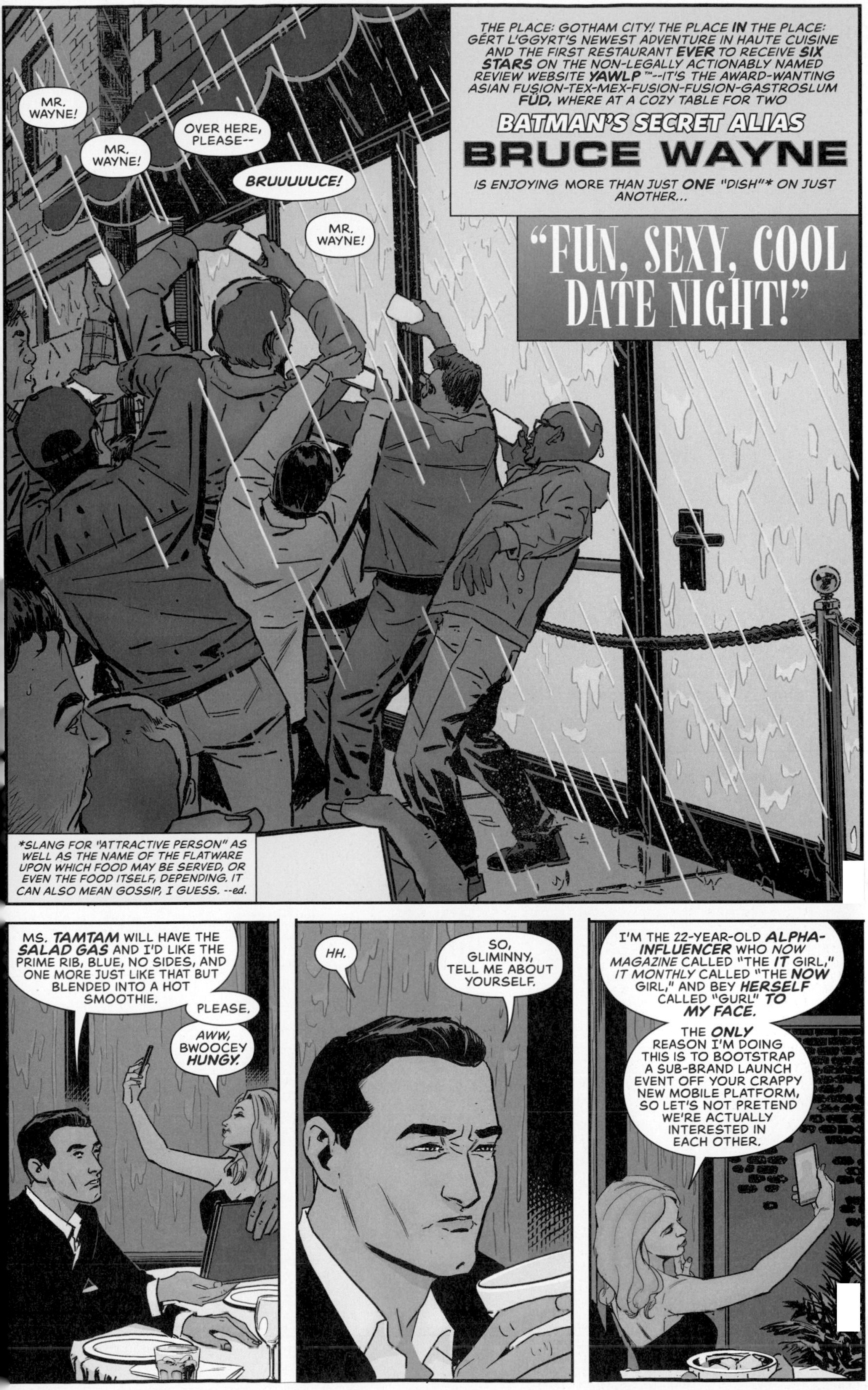
THE PLACE: GOTHAM CITY! THE PLACE IN THE PLACE: GÉRT L'GGYRT'S NEWEST ADVENTURE IN HAUTE CUISINE AND THE FIRST RESTAURANT EVER TO RECEIVE SIX STARS ON THE NON-LEGALLY ACTIONABLY NAMED REVIEW WEBSITE YAWLP™--IT'S THE AWARD-WANTING ASIAN FUSION-TEX-MEX-FUSION-FUSION-GASTROSLUM FŪD, WHERE AT A COZY TABLE FOR TWO
BATMAN'S SECRET ALIAS
BRUCE WAYNE
IS ENJOYING MORE THAN JUST ONE "DISH"* ON JUST ANOTHER...
"FUN, SEXY, COOL DATE NIGHT!"
MR. WAYNE!
MR. WAYNE!
OVER HERE, PLEASE--
BRUUUUUCE!
MR. WAYNE!
*SLANG FOR "ATTRACTIVE PERSON" AS WELL AS THE NAME OF THE FLATWARE UPON WHICH FOOD MAY BE SERVED, OR EVEN THE FOOD ITSELF, DEPENDING. IT CAN ALSO MEAN GOSSIP, I GUESS. --ed.
MS. TAMTAM WILL HAVE THE SALAD GAS AND I'D LIKE THE PRIME RIB, BLUE, NO SIDES, AND ONE MORE JUST LIKE THAT BUT BLENDED INTO A HOT SMOOTHIE.
PLEASE.
AWW, BWOOCEY HUNGY.
HH.
SO, GLIMINNY, TELL ME ABOUT YOURSELF.
I'M THE 22-YEAR-OLD ALPHA-INFLUENCER WHO NOW MAGAZINE CALLED "THE IT GIRL," IT MONTHLY CALLED "THE NOW GIRL," AND BEY HERSELF CALLED "GURL" TO MY FACE.
THE ONLY REASON I'M DOING THIS IS TO BOOTSTRAP A SUB-BRAND LAUNCH EVENT OFF YOUR CRAPPY NEW MOBILE PLATFORM, SO LET'S NOT PRETEND WE'RE ACTUALLY INTERESTED IN EACH OTHER.

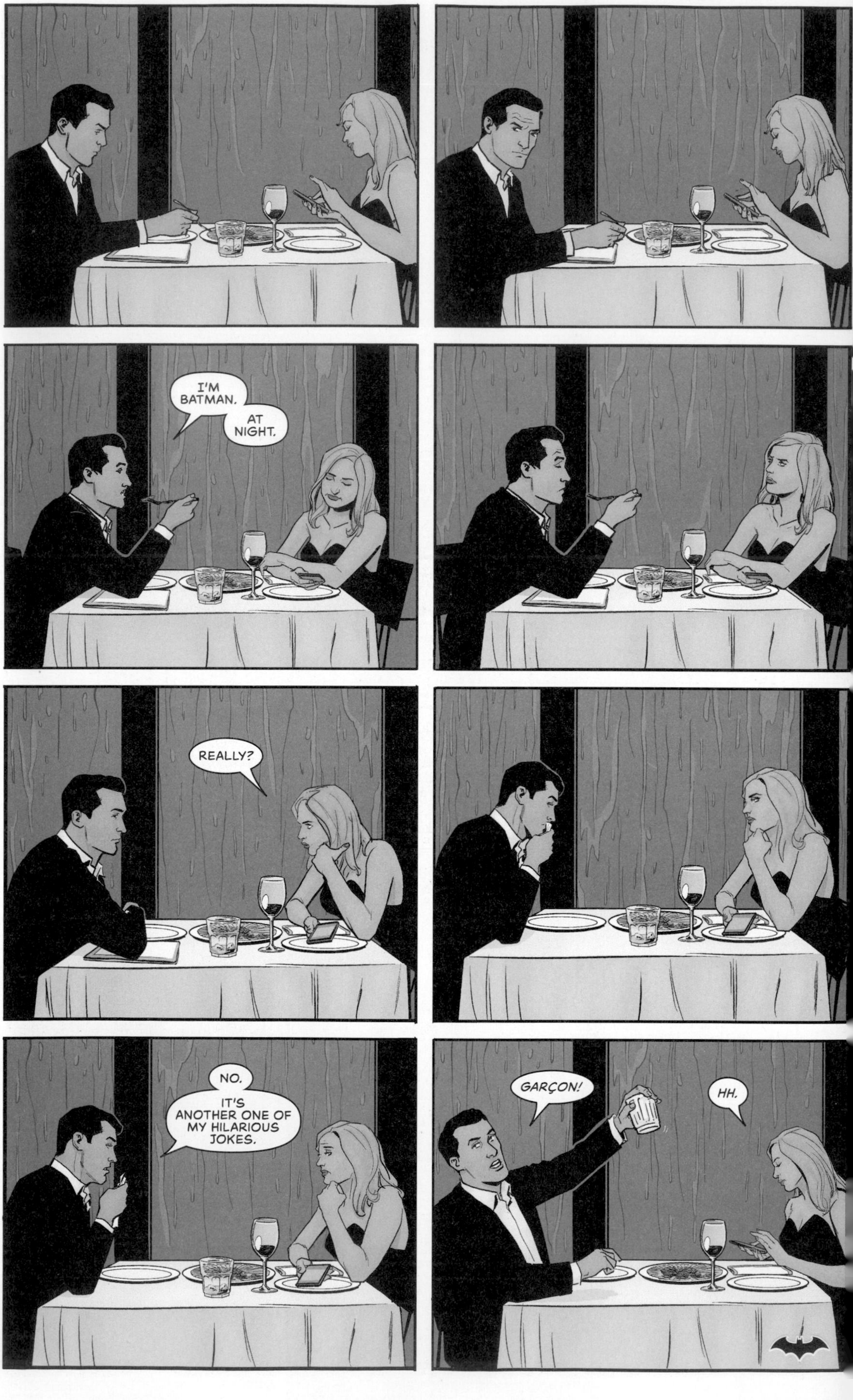
I'M BATMAN.
AT NIGHT.
REALLY?
NO.
IT'S ANOTHER ONE OF MY HILARIOUS JOKES.
GARÇON!
HH.

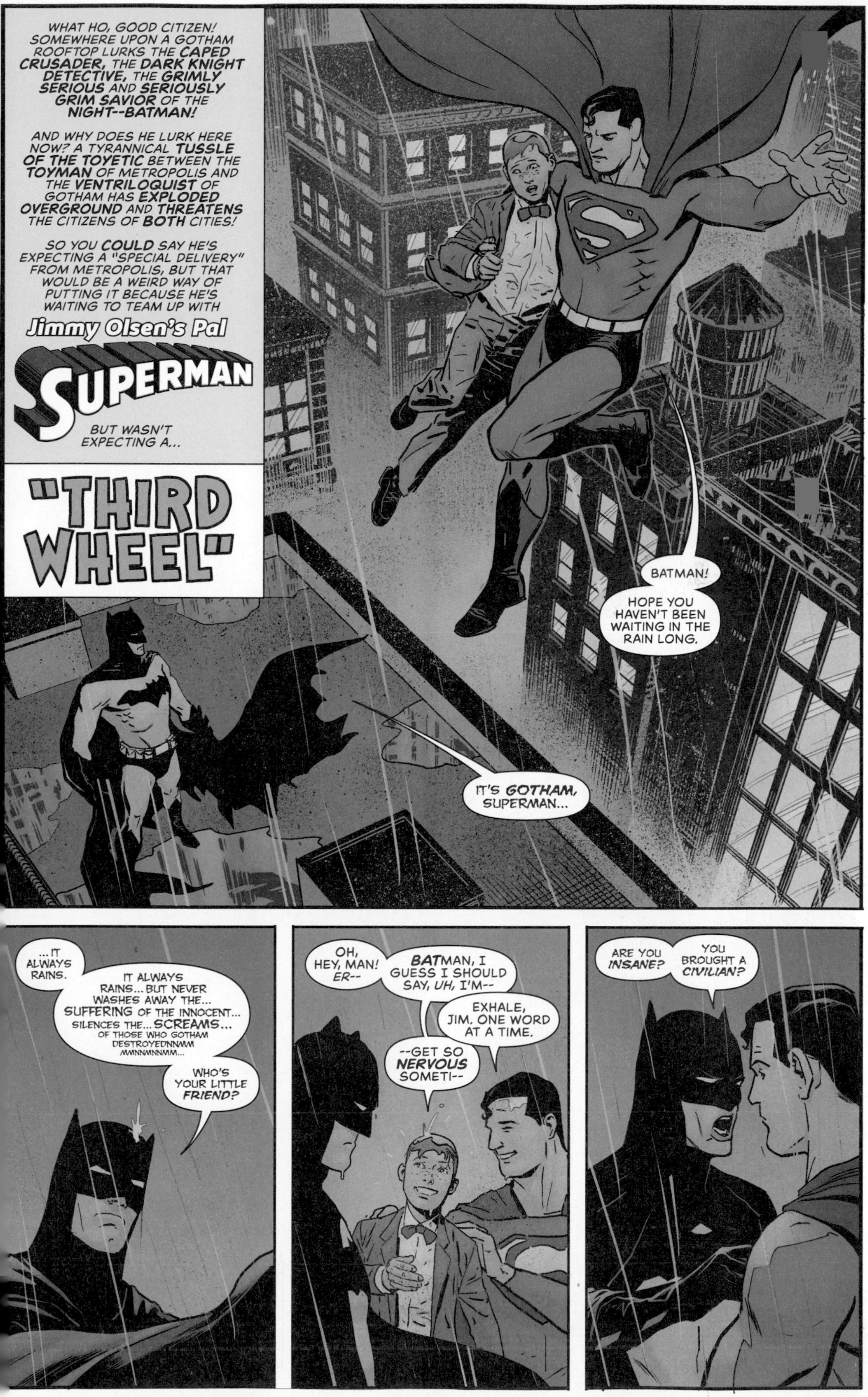

WHAT HO, GOOD CITIZEN! SOMEWHERE UPON A GOTHAM ROOFTOP LURKS THE CAPED CRUSADER, THE DARK KNIGHT DETECTIVE, THE GRIMLY SERIOUS AND SERIOUSLY GRIM SAVIOR OF THE NIGHT--BATMAN!
AND WHY DOES HE LURK HERE NOW? A TYRANNICAL TUSSLE OF THE TOYETIC BETWEEN THE TOYMAN OF METROPOLIS AND THE VENTRILOQUIST OF GOTHAM HAS EXPLODED OVERGROUND AND THREATENS THE CITIZENS OF BOTH CITIES!
SO YOU COULD SAY HE'S EXPECTING A "SPECIAL DELIVERY" FROM METROPOLIS, BUT THAT WOULD BE A WEIRD WAY OF PUTTING IT BECAUSE HE'S WAITING TO TEAM UP WITH
Jimmy Olsen's Pal
SUPERMAN
BUT WASN'T EXPECTING A...
"THIRD WHEEL"
BATMAN!
HOPE YOU HAVEN'T BEEN WAITING IN THE RAIN LONG.
IT'S GOTHAM, SUPERMAN...
...IT ALWAYS RAINS.
IT ALWAYS RAINS... BUT NEVER WASHES AWAY THE... SUFFERING OF THE INNOCENT... SILENCES THE... SCREAMS... OF THOSE WHO GOTHAM DESTROYEDNNMM MMNNMNNMM...
WHO'S YOUR LITTLE FRIEND?
OH, HEY, MAN! ER--
BATMAN, I GUESS I SHOULD SAY, UH, I'M--
EXHALE, JIM. ONE WORD AT A TIME.
--GET SO NERVOUS SOMETI--
ARE YOU INSANE?
YOU BROUGHT A CIVILIAN?

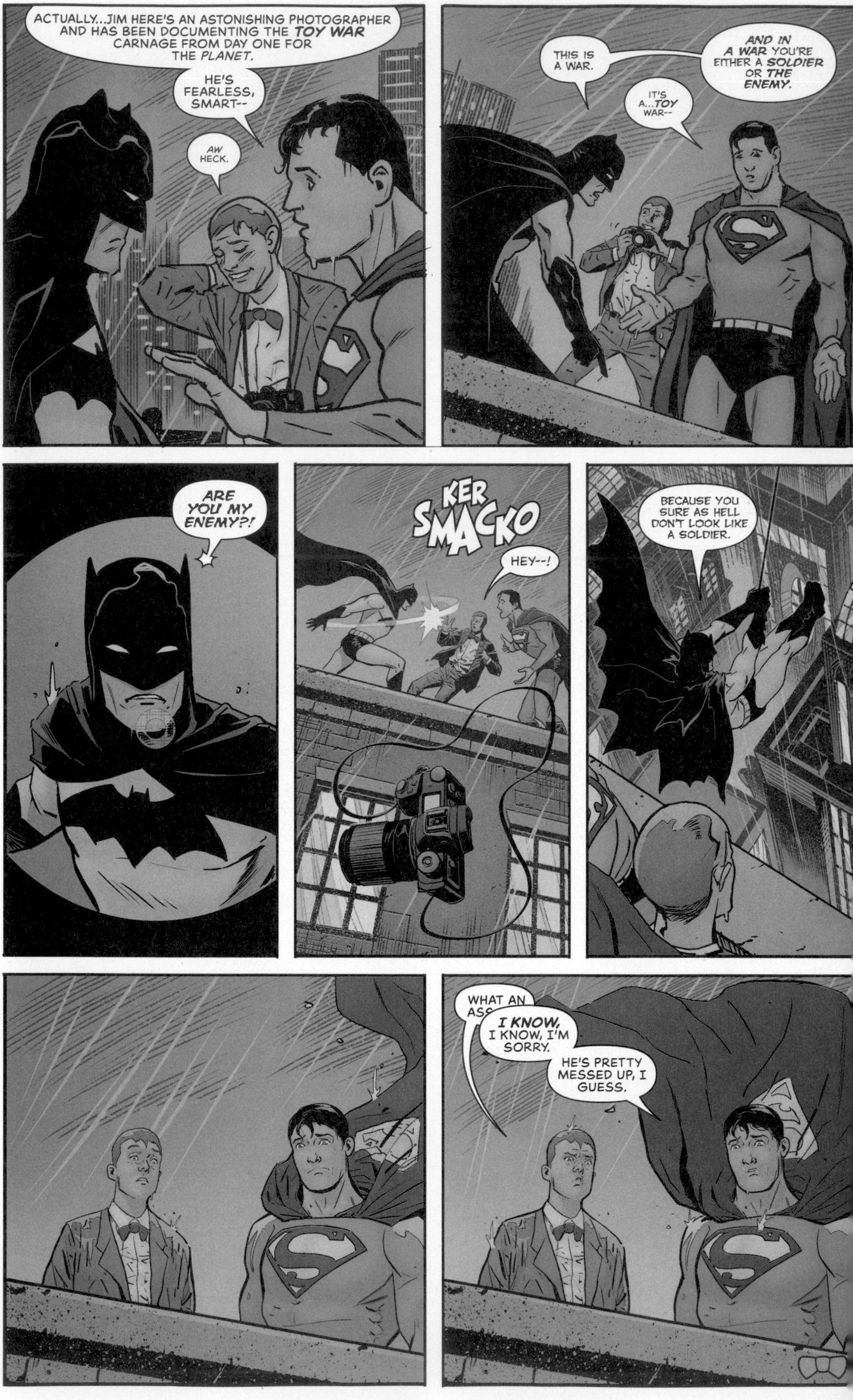
ACTUALLY...JIM HERE'S AN ASTONISHING PHOTOGRAPHER AND HAS BEEN DOCUMENTING THE TOY WAR CARNAGE FROM DAY ONE FOR THE PLANET.
HE'S FEARLESS, SMART--
AW HECK.
THIS IS A WAR.
AND IN A WAR YOU'RE EITHER A SOLDIER OR THE ENEMY.
IT'S A...TOY WAR--
ARE YOU MY ENEMY?!
KER SMACKO
HEY--!
BECAUSE YOU SURE AS HELL DON'T LOOK LIKE A SOLDIER.
WHAT AN ASS
I KNOW, I KNOW, I'M SORRY.
HE'S PRETTY MESSED UP, I GUESS.

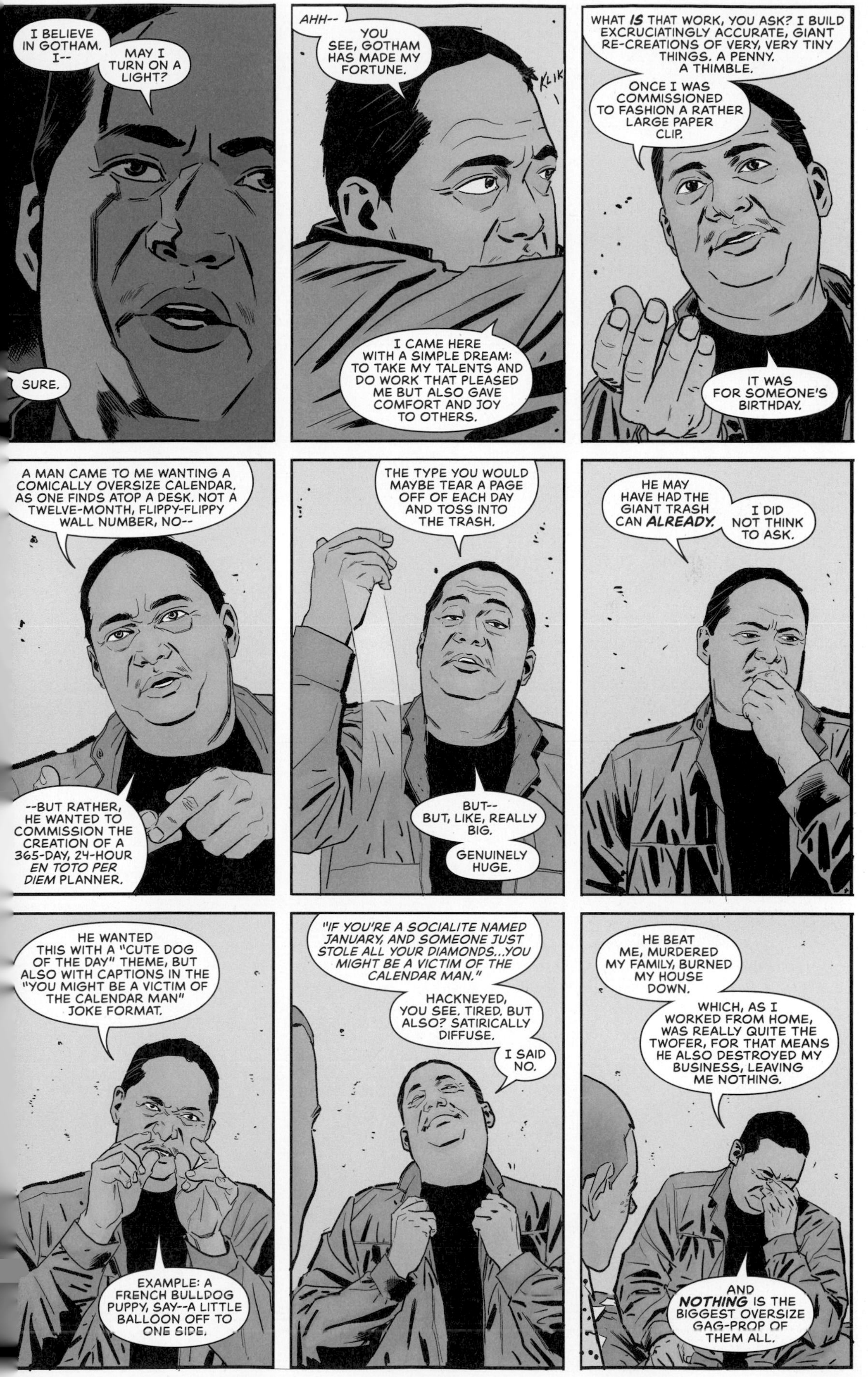
I BELIEVE IN GOTHAM. I--
MAY I TURN ON A LIGHT?
SURE.
AHH--
YOU SEE, GOTHAM HAS MADE MY FORTUNE.
KLIK
I CAME HERE WITH A SIMPLE DREAM: TO TAKE MY TALENTS AND DO WORK THAT PLEASED ME BUT ALSO GAVE COMFORT AND JOY TO OTHERS.
WHAT IS THAT WORK, YOU ASK? I BUILD EXCRUCIATINGLY ACCURATE, GIANT RE-CREATIONS OF VERY, VERY TINY THINGS. A PENNY. A THIMBLE.
ONCE I WAS COMMISSIONED TO FASHION A RATHER LARGE PAPER CLIP.
IT WAS FOR SOMEONE'S BIRTHDAY.
A MAN CAME TO ME WANTING A COMICALLY OVERSIZE CALENDAR. AS ONE FINDS ATOP A DESK. NOT A TWELVE-MONTH, FLIPPY-FLIPPY WALL NUMBER, NO--
--BUT RATHER, HE WANTED TO COMMISSION THE CREATION OF A 365-DAY, 24-HOUR EN TOTO PER DIEM PLANNER.
THE TYPE YOU WOULD MAYBE TEAR A PAGE OFF OF EACH DAY AND TOSS INTO THE TRASH.
BUT-- BUT, LIKE, REALLY BIG.
GENUINELY HUGE.
HE MAY HAVE HAD THE GIANT TRASH CAN ALREADY.
I DID NOT THINK TO ASK.
HE WANTED THIS WITH A "CUTE DOG OF THE DAY" THEME, BUT ALSO WITH CAPTIONS IN THE "YOU MIGHT BE A VICTIM OF THE CALENDAR MAN" JOKE FORMAT.
EXAMPLE: A FRENCH BULLDOG PUPPY, SAY--A LITTLE BALLOON OFF TO ONE SIDE.
"IF YOU'RE A SOCIALITE NAMED JANUARY, AND SOMEONE JUST STOLE ALL YOUR DIAMONDS...YOU MIGHT BE A VICTIM OF THE CALENDAR MAN."
HACKNEYED, YOU SEE. TIRED. BUT ALSO? SATIRICALLY DIFFUSE.
I SAID NO.
HE BEAT ME, MURDERED MY FAMILY, BURNED MY HOUSE DOWN.
WHICH, AS I WORKED FROM HOME, WAS REALLY QUITE THE TWOFER, FOR THAT MEANS HE ALSO DESTROYED MY BUSINESS, LEAVING ME NOTHING.
AND NOTHING IS THE BIGGEST OVERSIZE GAG-PROP OF THEM ALL.

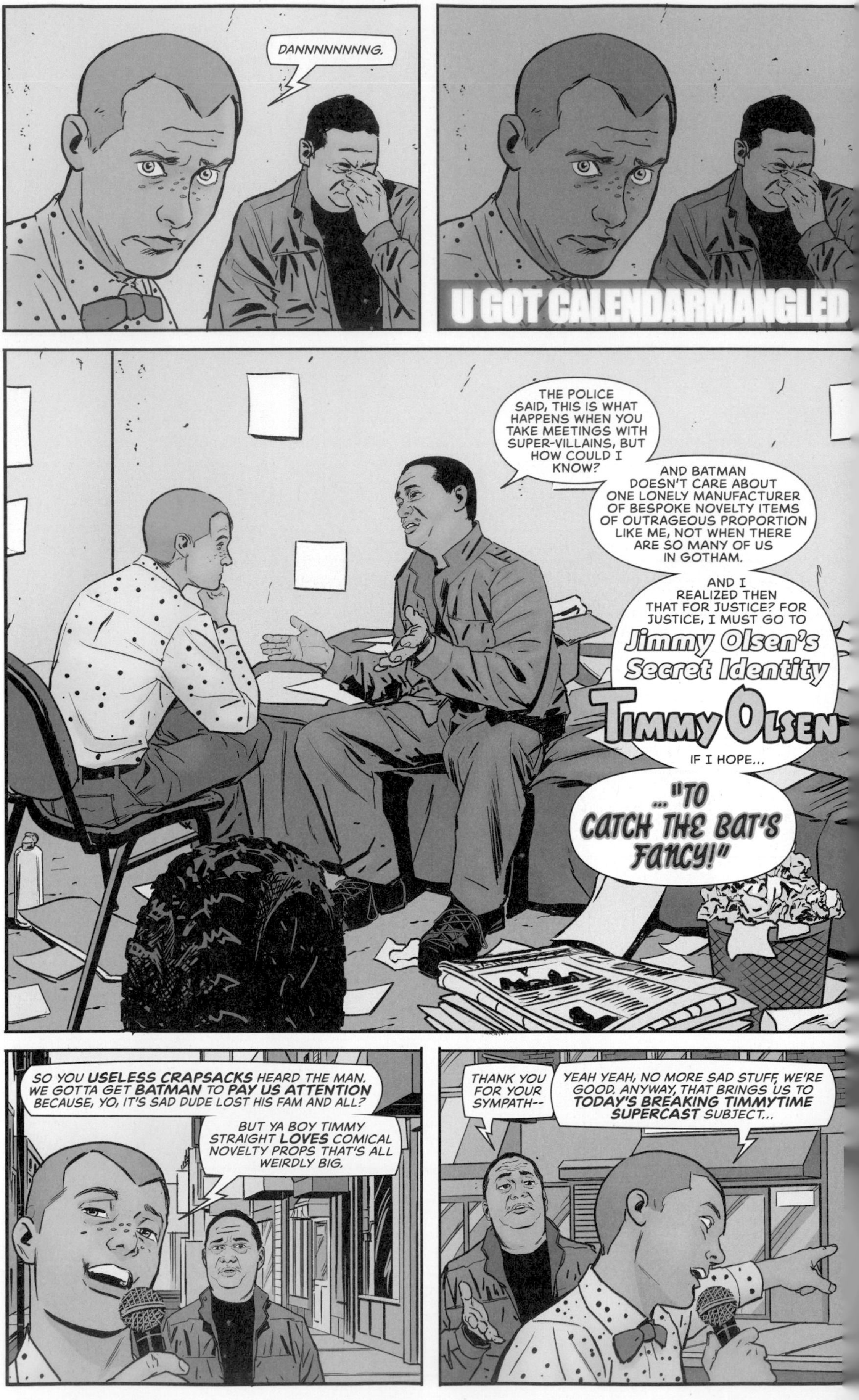
DANNNNNNNNG.
U GOT CALENDARMANGLED
THE POLICE SAID, THIS IS WHAT HAPPENS WHEN YOU TAKE MEETINGS WITH SUPER-VILLAINS, BUT HOW COULD I KNOW?
AND BATMAN DOESN'T CARE ABOUT ONE LONELY MANUFACTURER OF BESPOKE NOVELTY ITEMS OF OUTRAGEOUS PROPORTION LIKE ME, NOT WHEN THERE ARE SO MANY OF US IN GOTHAM.
AND I REALIZED THEN THAT FOR JUSTICE? FOR JUSTICE, I MUST GO TO Jimmy Olsen's Secret Identity TIMMY OLSEN IF I HOPE...
..."TO CATCH THE BAT'S FANCY!"
SO YOU USELESS CRAPSACKS HEARD THE MAN. WE GOTTA GET BATMAN TO PAY US ATTENTION BECAUSE, YO, IT'S SAD DUDE LOST HIS FAM AND ALL?
BUT YA BOY TIMMY STRAIGHT LOVES COMICAL NOVELTY PROPS THAT'S ALL WEIRDLY BIG.
THANK YOU FOR YOUR SYMPATH--
YEAH YEAH, NO MORE SAD STUFF, WE'RE GOOD. ANYWAY, THAT BRINGS US TO TODAY'S BREAKING TIMMYTIME SUPERCAST SUBJECT...

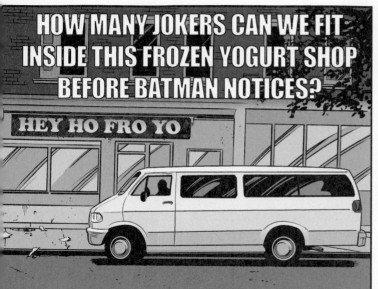

HOW MANY JOKERS CAN WE FIT INSIDE THIS FROZEN YOGURT SHOP BEFORE BATMAN NOTICES?

HEY HO FRO YO

ALL RIGHT, WE'RE READY, CLIFF.

NO PARKING

YOU HOID HIM. GO, GO--

THIS IS AN *EQUITY* GIG, RIGHT?

GO!

OKAY, OKAY...

MORE, CLIFFY, SEND IN MORE.

MAY I SEE--

NO! STOP!

NO PARKING

ALL OF 'EM, CLIFFY! SEND 'EM ALL!

NO PARKING

ROGER THAT, BOSS.

HOW IS HE NOT *SEEING* THIS...?

I JUST GOTTA GET IN THERE MYSELF AND--

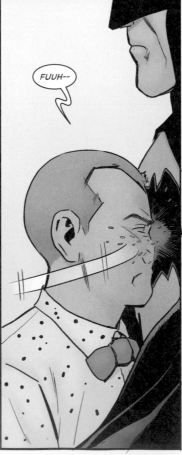

FUUH--

MR. TIMMY! MR. TIMMY! HE WAS HERE! LOOK!
OOPHA... WHAT? WHO? WHAT'RE YOU...
UHHH...
NO PARKING
squint
Tonight -B
...WHY DOES BRUCE WAYNE WANT TO MEET ME TONIGHT?
NO, NO, MISTER TIMMY, THE "B" IS FOR "BATMAN."
PARKING
BUT IT COULD BE "BRUCE," I MEAN--
NO, DUDE, LOOK AT THE STATIONERY. IT'S TOTALLY BATMAN.
SUPER... DUPER.

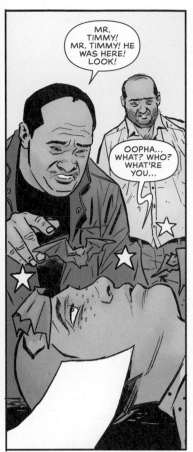

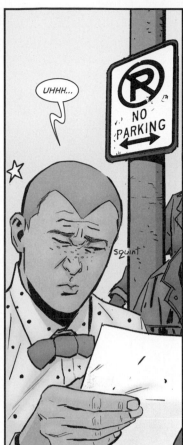

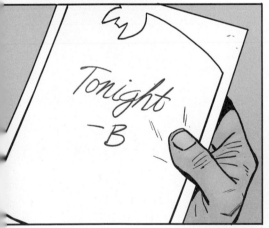

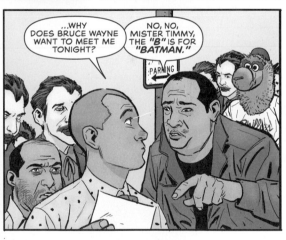

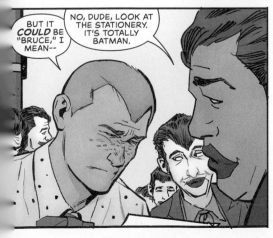

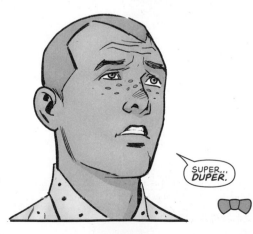

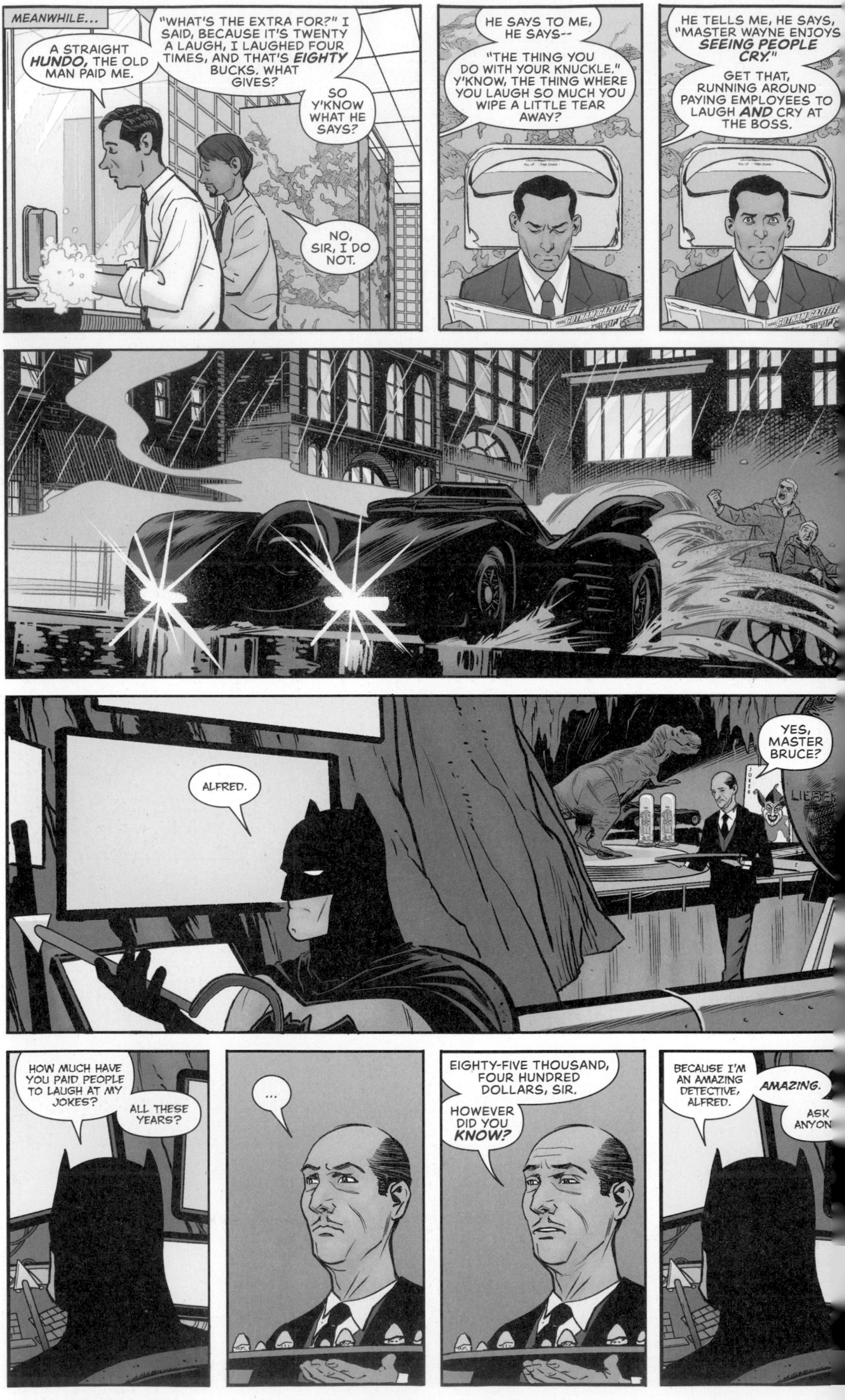
MEANWHILE...
A STRAIGHT HUNDO, THE OLD MAN PAID ME.
"WHAT'S THE EXTRA FOR?" I SAID, BECAUSE IT'S TWENTY A LAUGH, I LAUGHED FOUR TIMES, AND THAT'S EIGHTY BUCKS. WHAT GIVES?
SO Y'KNOW WHAT HE SAYS?
NO, SIR, I DO NOT.
HE SAYS TO ME, HE SAYS--
"THE THING YOU DO WITH YOUR KNUCKLE." Y'KNOW, THE THING WHERE YOU LAUGH SO MUCH YOU WIPE A LITTLE TEAR AWAY?
HE TELLS ME, HE SAYS, "MASTER WAYNE ENJOYS SEEING PEOPLE CRY."
GET THAT, RUNNING AROUND PAYING EMPLOYEES TO LAUGH AND CRY AT THE BOSS.
GOTHAM GAZETTE
ALFRED.
YES, MASTER BRUCE?
JOKER
HOW MUCH HAVE YOU PAID PEOPLE TO LAUGH AT MY JOKES?
ALL THESE YEARS?
...
EIGHTY-FIVE THOUSAND, FOUR HUNDRED DOLLARS, SIR.
HOWEVER DID YOU KNOW?
BECAUSE I'M AN AMAZING DETECTIVE, ALFRED.
AMAZING.
ASK ANYON

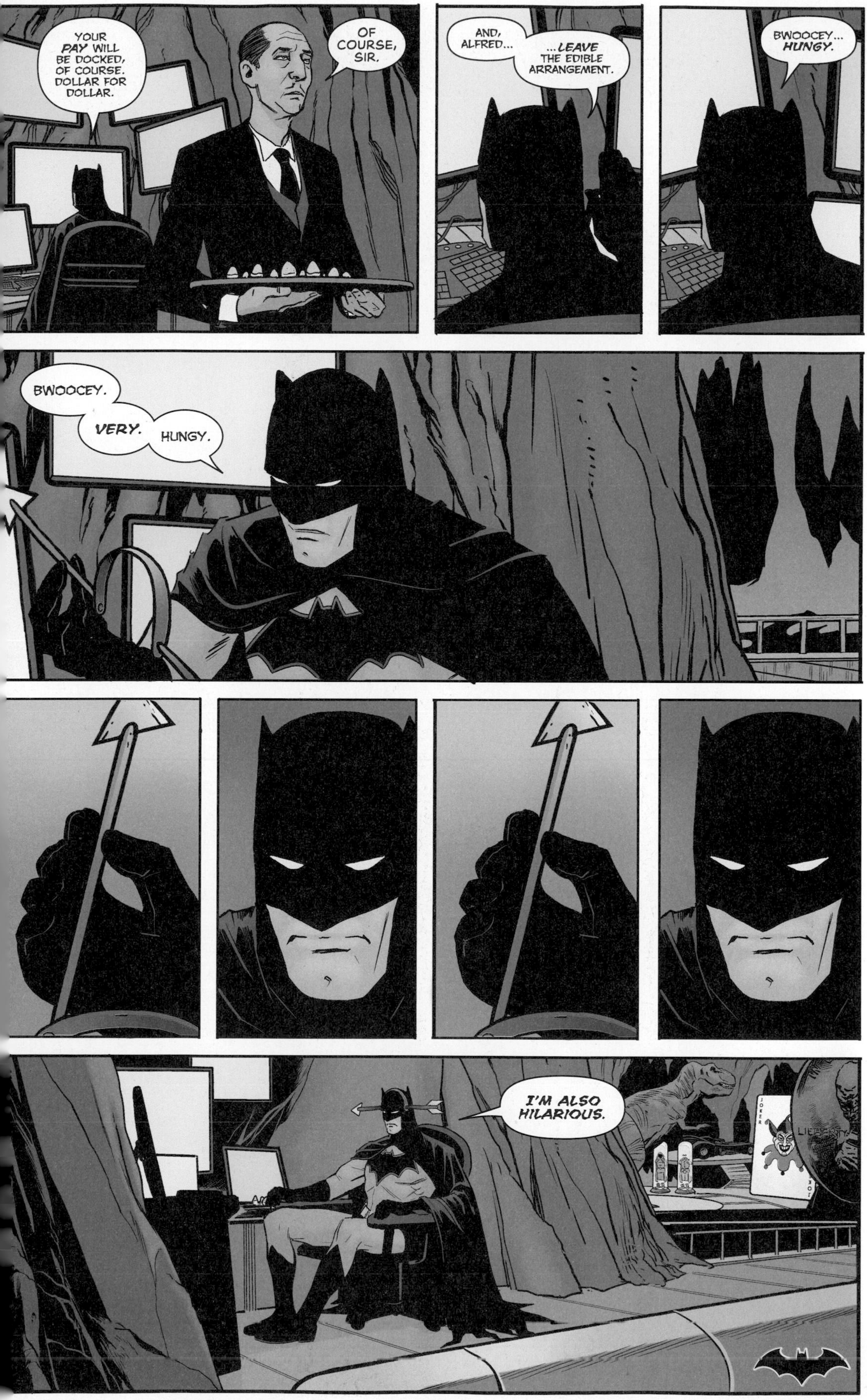
YOUR PAY WILL BE DOCKED, OF COURSE. DOLLAR FOR DOLLAR.
OF COURSE, SIR.
AND, ALFRED...
...LEAVE THE EDIBLE ARRANGEMENT.
BWOOCEY... HUNGY.
BWOOCEY.
VERY.
HUNGY.
I'M ALSO HILARIOUS.
JOKER
LIBERTY

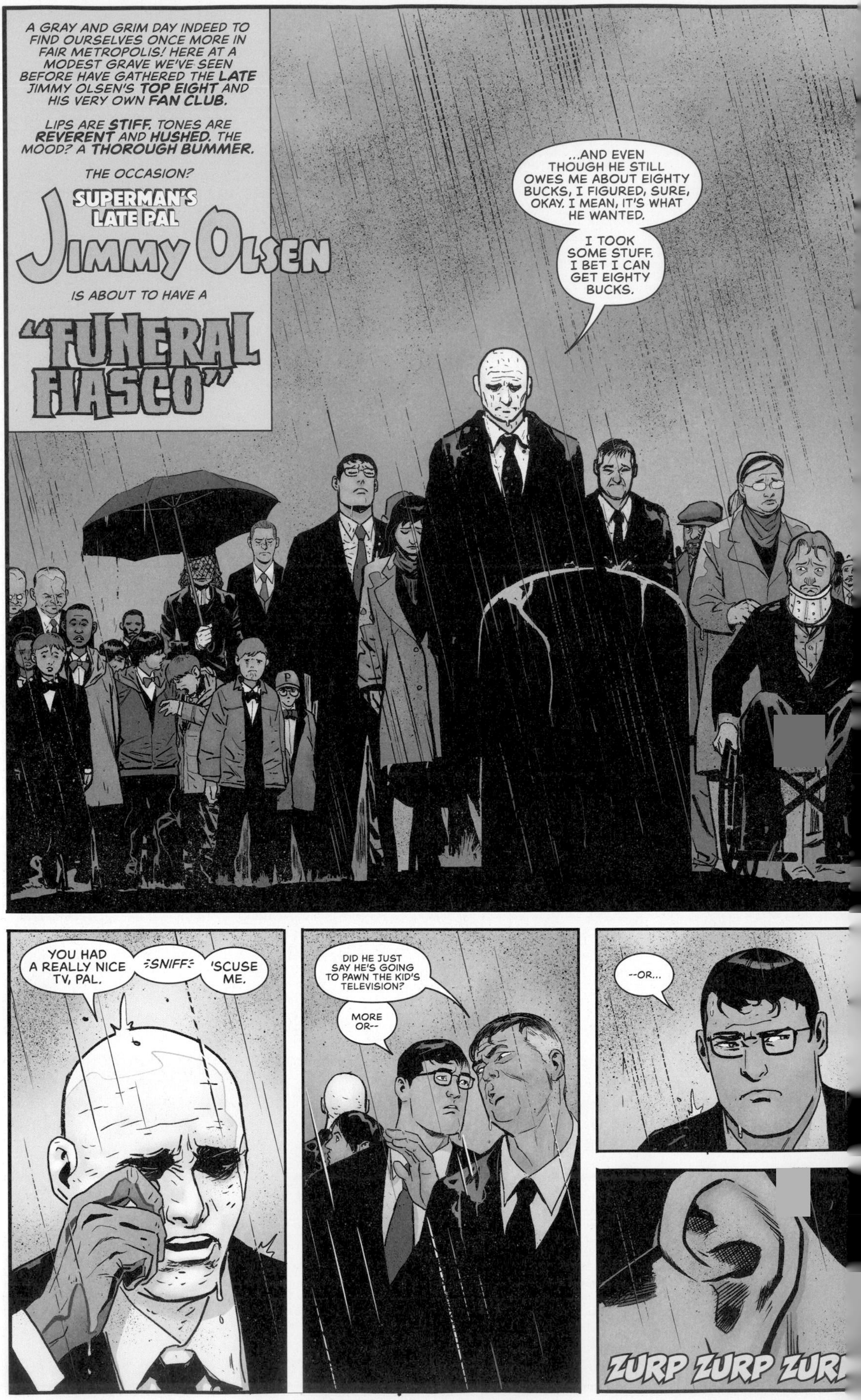
A GRAY AND GRIM DAY INDEED TO FIND OURSELVES ONCE MORE IN FAIR METROPOLIS! HERE AT A MODEST GRAVE WE'VE SEEN BEFORE HAVE GATHERED THE LATE JIMMY OLSEN'S TOP EIGHT AND HIS VERY OWN FAN CLUB.
LIPS ARE STIFF. TONES ARE REVERENT AND HUSHED. THE MOOD? A THOROUGH BUMMER.
THE OCCASION?
SUPERMAN'S LATE PAL
JIMMY OLSEN
IS ABOUT TO HAVE A
"FUNERAL FIASCO"
...AND EVEN THOUGH HE STILL OWES ME ABOUT EIGHTY BUCKS, I FIGURED, SURE, OKAY. I MEAN, IT'S WHAT HE WANTED.
I TOOK SOME STUFF. I BET I CAN GET EIGHTY BUCKS.
YOU HAD A REALLY NICE TV, PAL.
=SNIFF=
'SCUSE ME.
DID HE JUST SAY HE'S GOING TO PAWN THE KID'S TELEVISION?
MORE OR--
--OR...
ZURP ZURP ZUR

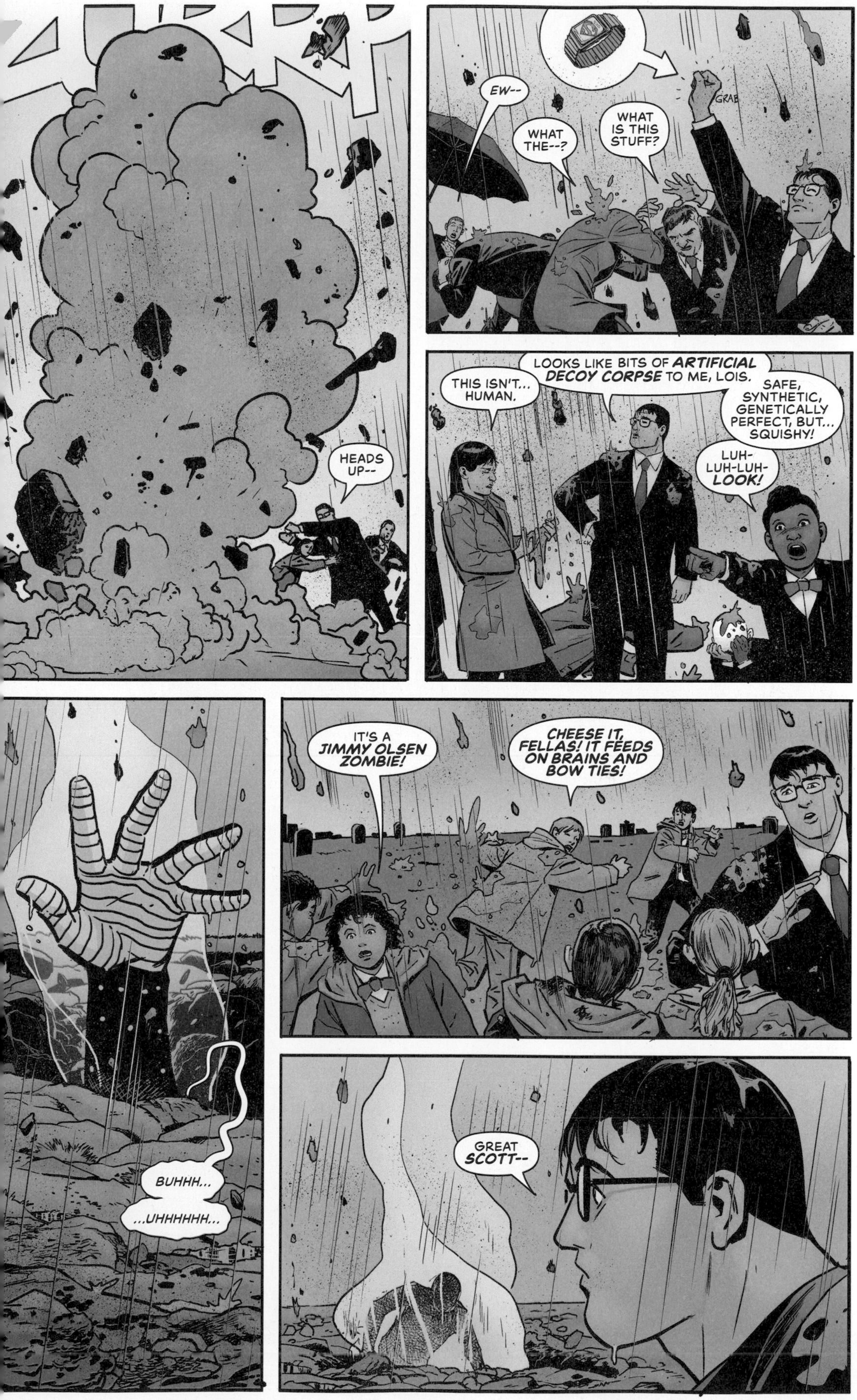
HEADS UP--
EW--
WHAT THE--?
WHAT IS THIS STUFF?
GRAB
THIS ISN'T... HUMAN.
LOOKS LIKE BITS OF ARTIFICIAL DECOY CORPSE TO ME, LOIS.
SAFE, SYNTHETIC, GENETICALLY PERFECT, BUT... SQUISHY!
LUH-LUH-LUH-LUH-LOOK!
BUHHH...
...UHHHHHH...
IT'S A JIMMY OLSEN ZOMBIE!
CHEESE IT, FELLAS! IT FEEDS ON BRAINS AND BOW TIES!
GREAT SCOTT--

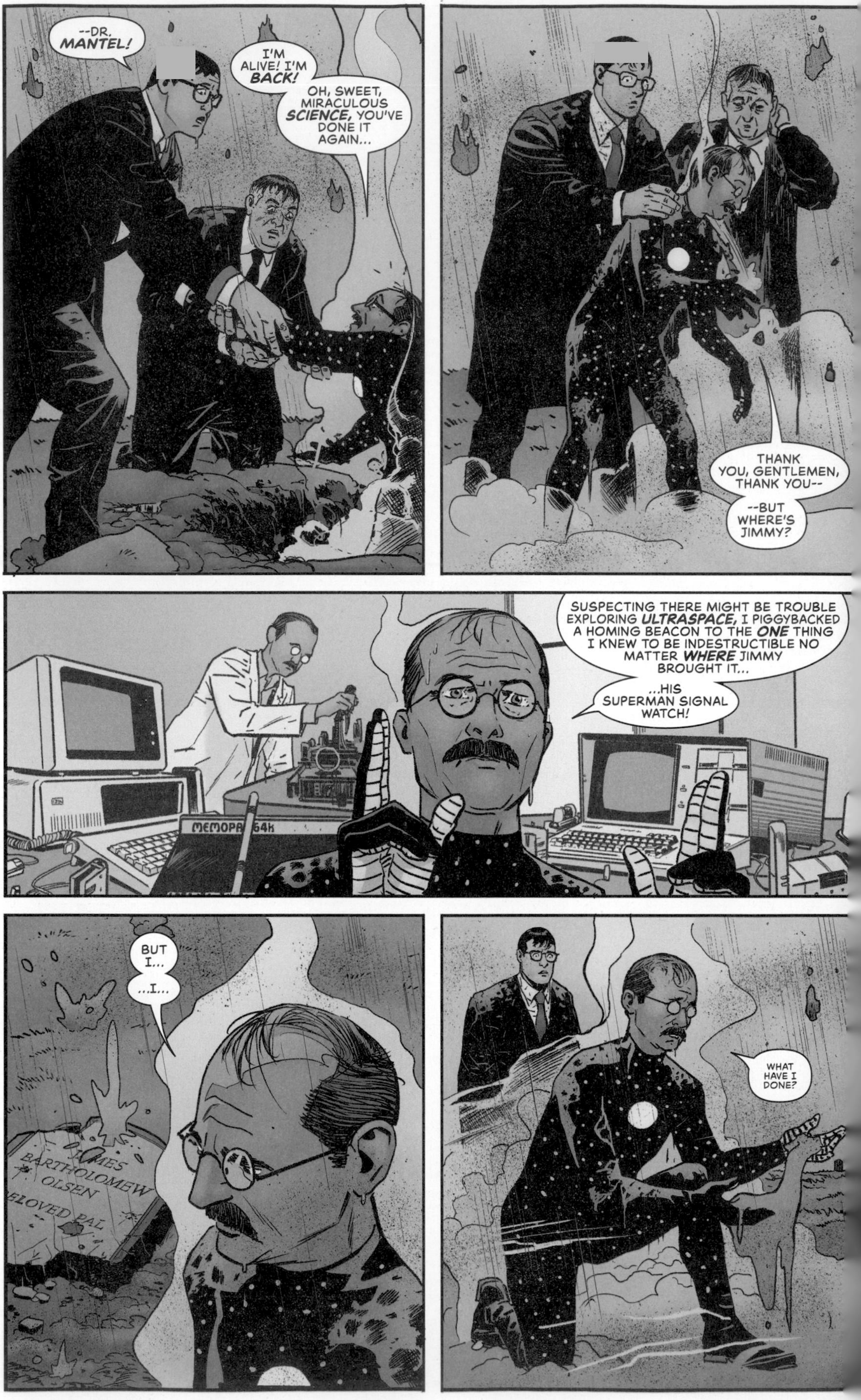
--DR. MANTEL!
I'M ALIVE! I'M BACK!
OH, SWEET, MIRACULOUS SCIENCE, YOU'VE DONE IT AGAIN...
THANK YOU, GENTLEMEN, THANK YOU--
--BUT WHERE'S JIMMY?
SUSPECTING THERE MIGHT BE TROUBLE EXPLORING ULTRASPACE, I PIGGYBACKED A HOMING BEACON TO THE ONE THING I KNEW TO BE INDESTRUCTIBLE NO MATTER WHERE JIMMY BROUGHT IT...
...HIS SUPERMAN SIGNAL WATCH!
BUT I...
...I...
JAMES
BARTHOLOMEW
OLSEN
ELOVED PAL
WHAT HAVE I DONE?

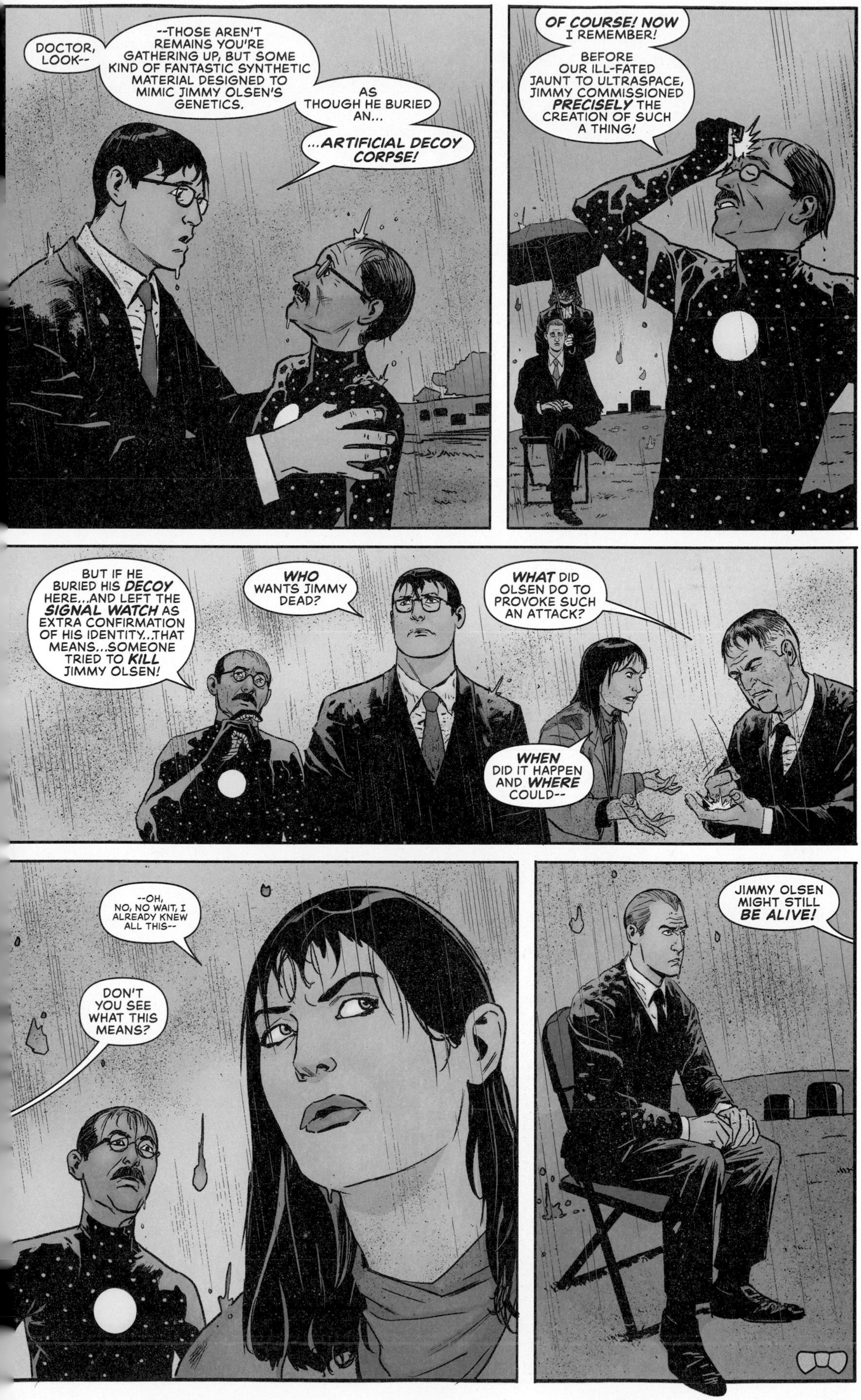
DOCTOR, LOOK--
--THOSE AREN'T REMAINS YOU'RE GATHERING UP, BUT SOME KIND OF FANTASTIC SYNTHETIC MATERIAL DESIGNED TO MIMIC JIMMY OLSEN'S GENETICS.
AS THOUGH HE BURIED AN...
...ARTIFICIAL DECOY CORPSE!
OF COURSE! NOW I REMEMBER!
BEFORE OUR ILL-FATED JAUNT TO ULTRASPACE, JIMMY COMMISSIONED PRECISELY THE CREATION OF SUCH A THING!
BUT IF HE BURIED HIS DECOY HERE...AND LEFT THE SIGNAL WATCH AS EXTRA CONFIRMATION OF HIS IDENTITY...THAT MEANS...SOMEONE TRIED TO KILL JIMMY OLSEN!
WHO WANTS JIMMY DEAD?
WHAT DID OLSEN DO TO PROVOKE SUCH AN ATTACK?
WHEN DID IT HAPPEN AND WHERE COULD--
--OH, NO, NO WAIT, I ALREADY KNEW ALL THIS--
DON'T YOU SEE WHAT THIS MEANS?
JIMMY OLSEN MIGHT STILL BE ALIVE!

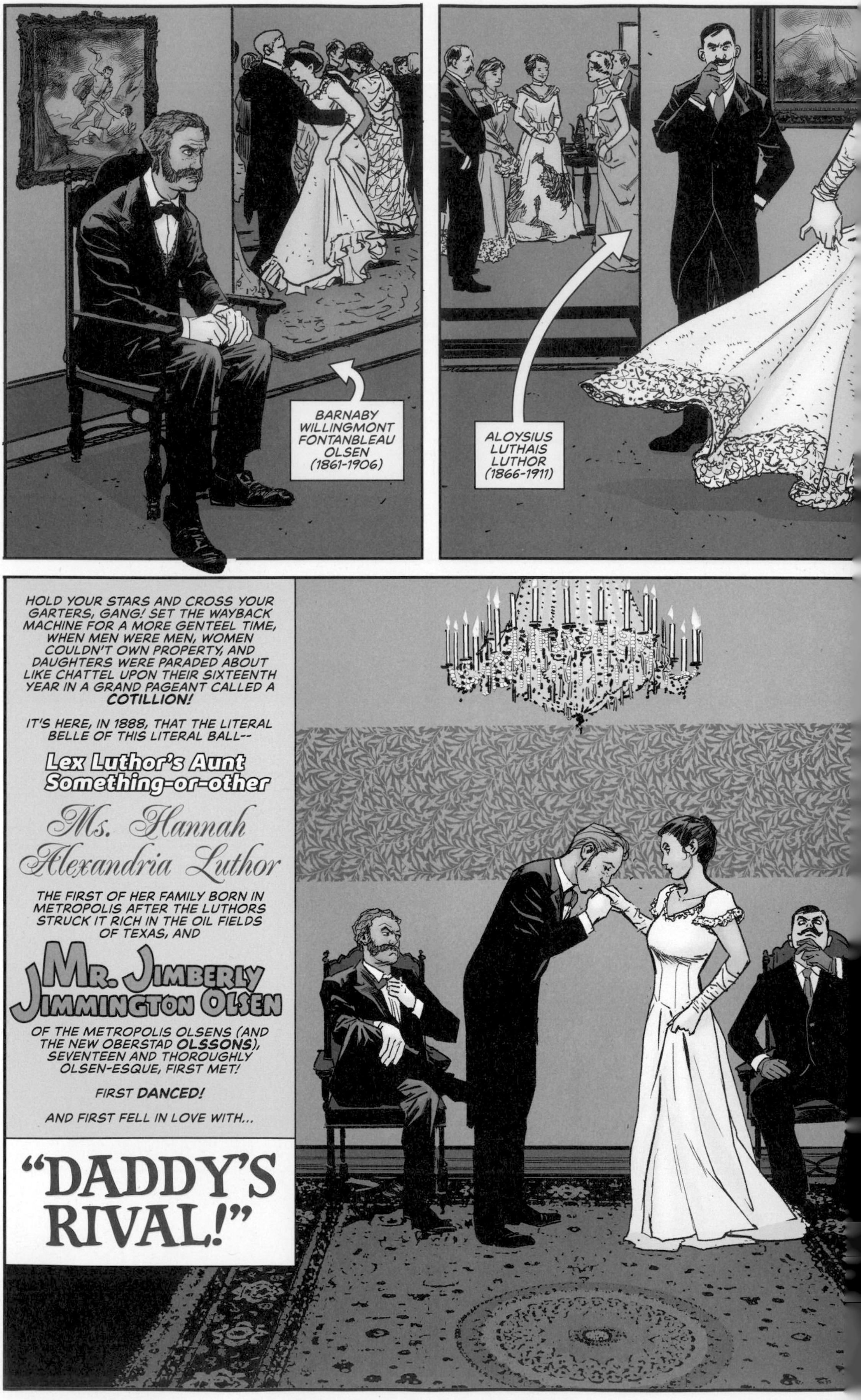
BARNABY WILLINGMONT FONTANBLEAU OLSEN (1861-1906)
ALOYSIUS LUTHAIS LUTHOR (1866-1911)
HOLD YOUR STARS AND CROSS YOUR GARTERS, GANG! SET THE WAYBACK MACHINE FOR A MORE GENTEEL TIME, WHEN MEN WERE MEN, WOMEN COULDN'T OWN PROPERTY, AND DAUGHTERS WERE PARADED ABOUT LIKE CHATTEL UPON THEIR SIXTEENTH YEAR IN A GRAND PAGEANT CALLED A COTILLION!
IT'S HERE, IN 1888, THAT THE LITERAL BELLE OF THIS LITERAL BALL--
Lex Luthor's Aunt Something-or-other
Ms. Hannah Alexandria Luthor
THE FIRST OF HER FAMILY BORN IN METROPOLIS AFTER THE LUTHORS STRUCK IT RICH IN THE OIL FIELDS OF TEXAS, AND
MR. JIMBERLY JIMMINGTON OLSEN
OF THE METROPOLIS OLSENS (AND THE NEW OBERSTAD OLSSONS), SEVENTEEN AND THOROUGHLY OLSEN-ESQUE, FIRST MET!
FIRST DANCED!
AND FIRST FELL IN LOVE WITH...
"DADDY'S RIVAL!"

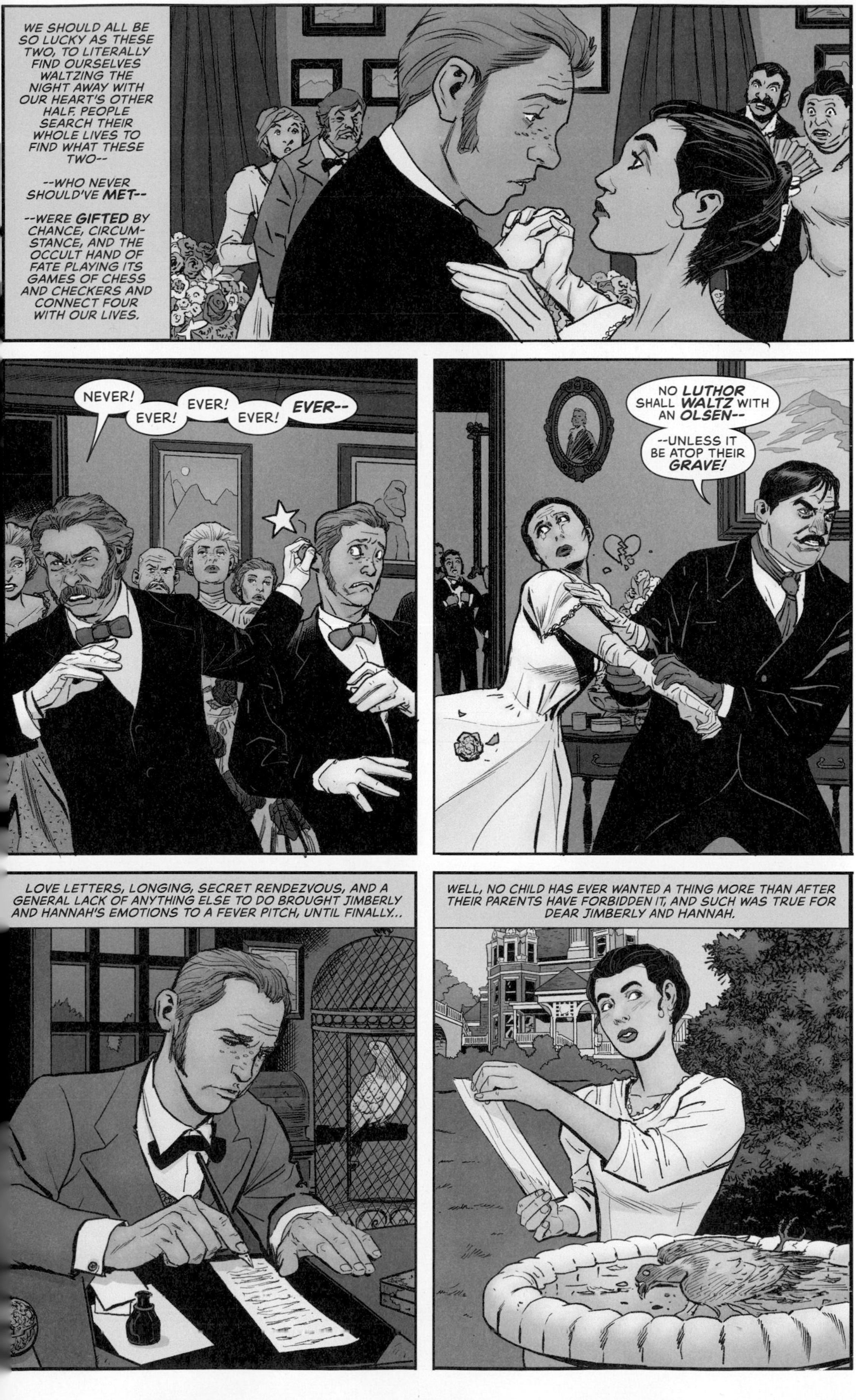
WE SHOULD ALL BE SO LUCKY AS THESE TWO, TO LITERALLY FIND OURSELVES WALTZING THE NIGHT AWAY WITH OUR HEART'S OTHER HALF. PEOPLE SEARCH THEIR WHOLE LIVES TO FIND WHAT THESE TWO--
--WHO NEVER SHOULD'VE MET--
--WERE GIFTED BY CHANCE, CIRCUMSTANCE, AND THE OCCULT HAND OF FATE PLAYING ITS GAMES OF CHESS AND CHECKERS AND CONNECT FOUR WITH OUR LIVES.
NEVER!
EVER!
EVER!
EVER!
EVER--
NO LUTHOR SHALL WALTZ WITH AN OLSEN--
--UNLESS IT BE ATOP THEIR GRAVE!
LOVE LETTERS, LONGING, SECRET RENDEZVOUS, AND A GENERAL LACK OF ANYTHING ELSE TO DO BROUGHT JIMBERLY AND HANNAH'S EMOTIONS TO A FEVER PITCH, UNTIL FINALLY...
WELL, NO CHILD HAS EVER WANTED A THING MORE THAN AFTER THEIR PARENTS HAVE FORBIDDEN IT, AND SUCH WAS TRUE FOR DEAR JIMBERLY AND HANNAH.

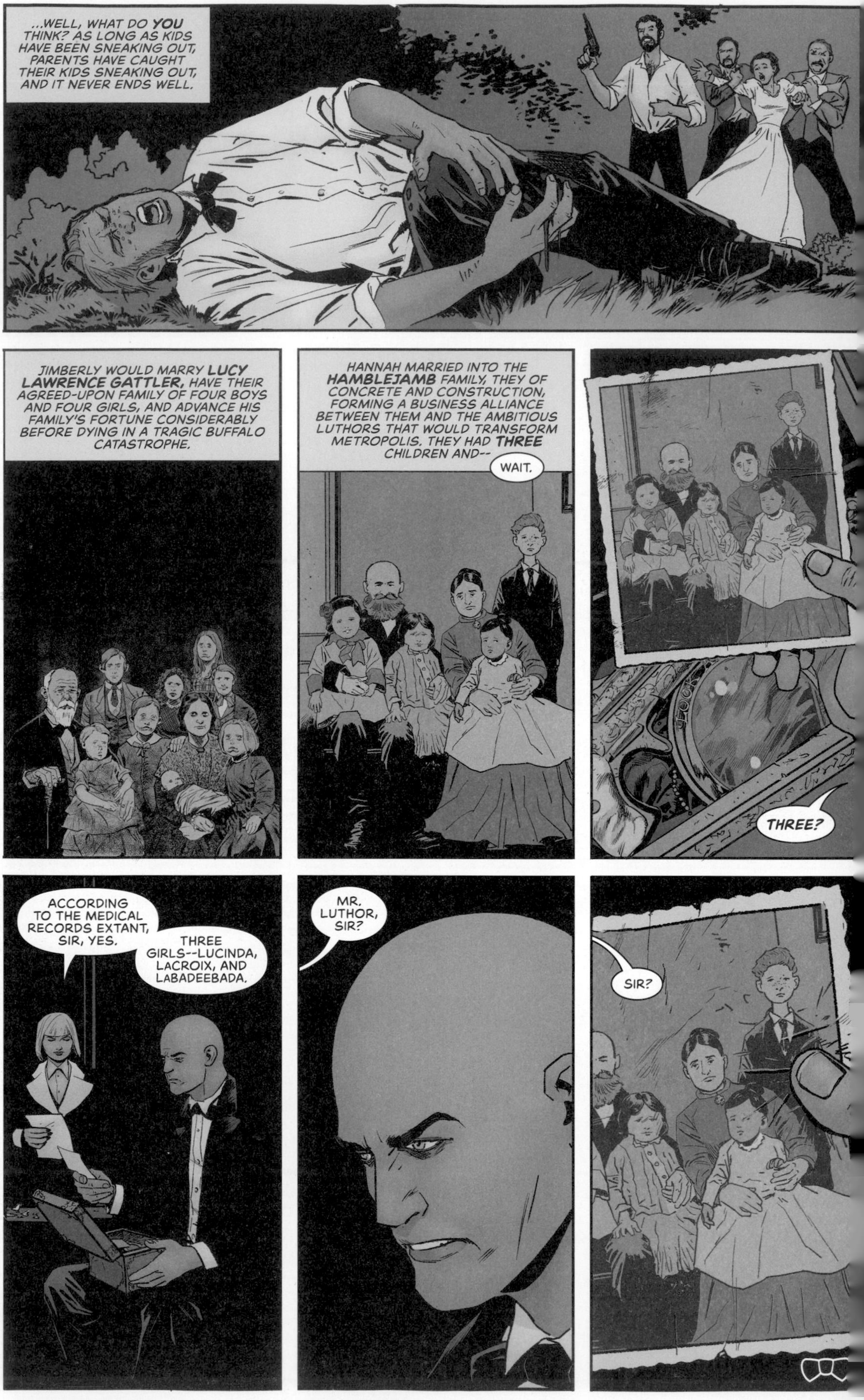
...WELL, WHAT DO YOU THINK? AS LONG AS KIDS HAVE BEEN SNEAKING OUT, PARENTS HAVE CAUGHT THEIR KIDS SNEAKING OUT, AND IT NEVER ENDS WELL.
JIMBERLY WOULD MARRY LUCY LAWRENCE GATTLER, HAVE THEIR AGREED-UPON FAMILY OF FOUR BOYS AND FOUR GIRLS, AND ADVANCE HIS FAMILY'S FORTUNE CONSIDERABLY BEFORE DYING IN A TRAGIC BUFFALO CATASTROPHE.
HANNAH MARRIED INTO THE HAMBLEJAMB FAMILY, THEY OF CONCRETE AND CONSTRUCTION, FORMING A BUSINESS ALLIANCE BETWEEN THEM AND THE AMBITIOUS LUTHORS THAT WOULD TRANSFORM METROPOLIS. THEY HAD THREE CHILDREN AND--
WAIT.
THREE?
ACCORDING TO THE MEDICAL RECORDS EXTANT, SIR, YES.
THREE GIRLS--LUCINDA, LACROIX, AND LABADEEBADA.
MR. LUTHOR, SIR?
SIR?

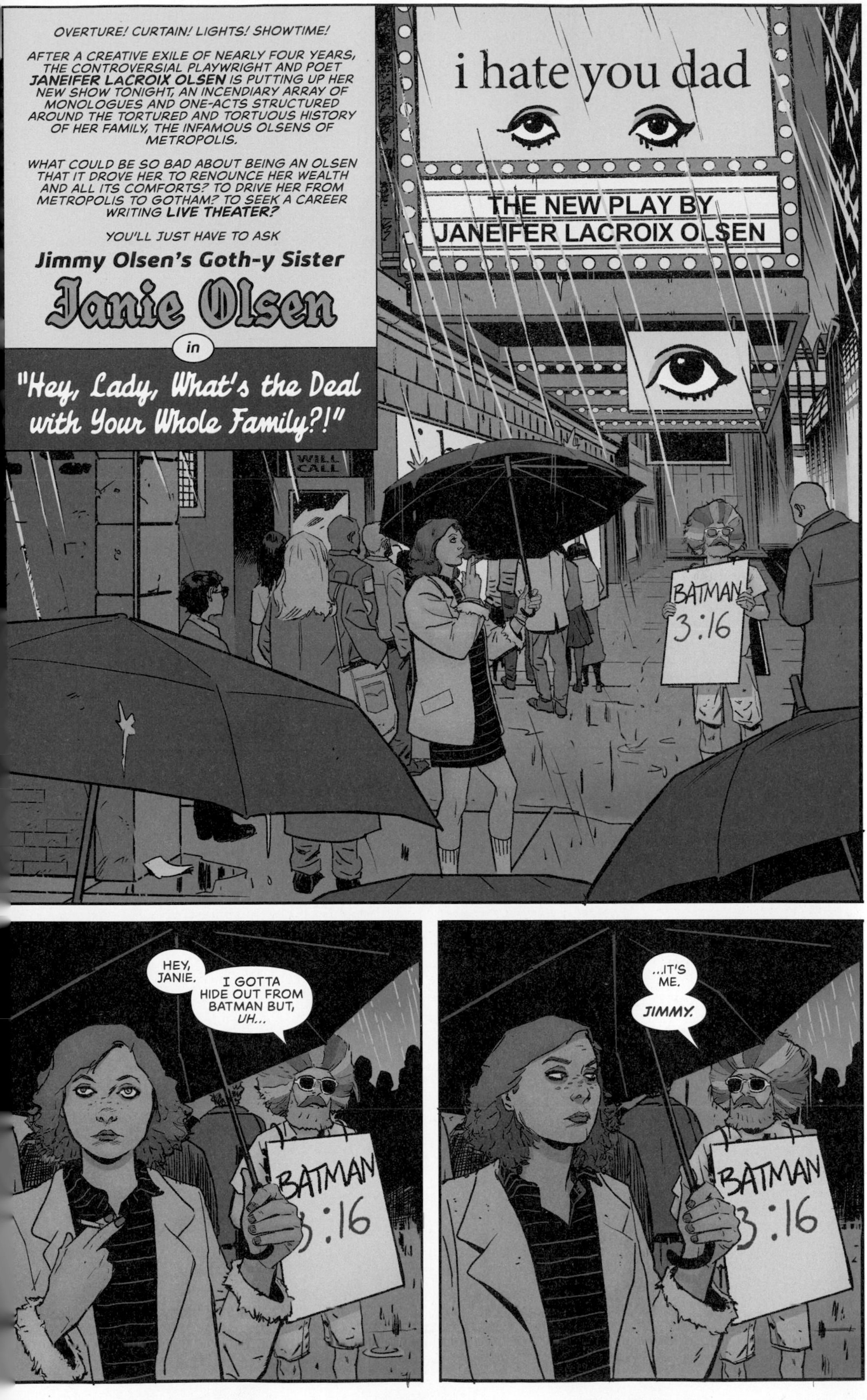
OVERTURE! CURTAIN! LIGHTS! SHOWTIME!
AFTER A CREATIVE EXILE OF NEARLY FOUR YEARS, THE CONTROVERSIAL PLAYWRIGHT AND POET JANEIFER LACROIX OLSEN IS PUTTING UP HER NEW SHOW TONIGHT, AN INCENDIARY ARRAY OF MONOLOGUES AND ONE-ACTS STRUCTURED AROUND THE TORTURED AND TORTUOUS HISTORY OF HER FAMILY, THE INFAMOUS OLSENS OF METROPOLIS.
WHAT COULD BE SO BAD ABOUT BEING AN OLSEN THAT IT DROVE HER TO RENOUNCE HER WEALTH AND ALL ITS COMFORTS? TO DRIVE HER FROM METROPOLIS TO GOTHAM? TO SEEK A CAREER WRITING LIVE THEATER?
YOU'LL JUST HAVE TO ASK
Jimmy Olsen's Goth-y Sister
Janie Olsen
in
"Hey, Lady, What's the Deal with Your Whole Family?!"
i hate you dad
THE NEW PLAY BY
JANEIFER LACROIX OLSEN
WILL CALL
BATMAN 3:16
HEY, JANIE.
I GOTTA HIDE OUT FROM BATMAN BUT, UH...
BATMAN 3:16
...IT'S ME.
JIMMY.
BATMAN 3:16

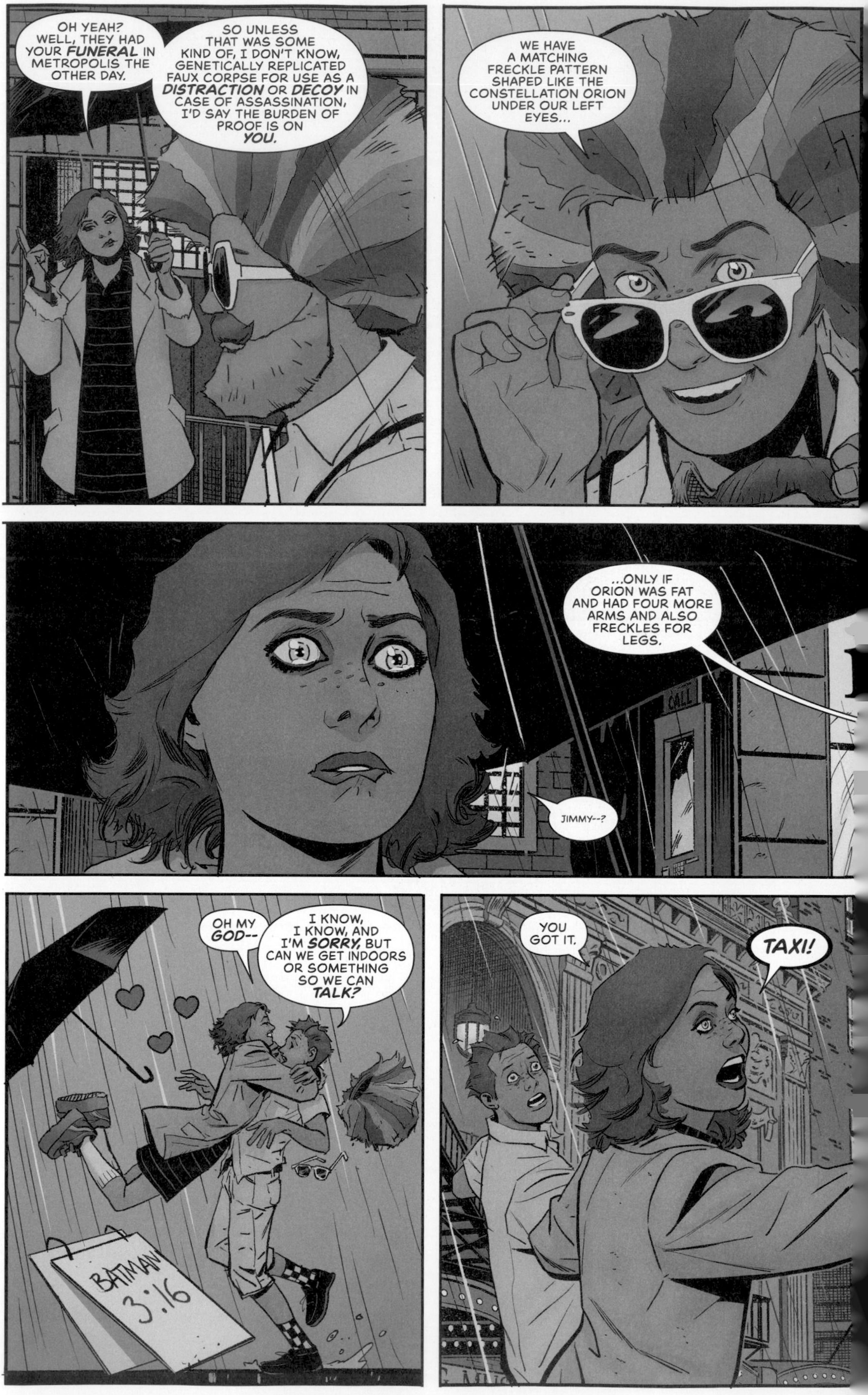
OH YEAH? WELL, THEY HAD YOUR FUNERAL IN METROPOLIS THE OTHER DAY.
SO UNLESS THAT WAS SOME KIND OF, I DON'T KNOW, GENETICALLY REPLICATED FAUX CORPSE FOR USE AS A DISTRACTION OR DECOY IN CASE OF ASSASSINATION, I'D SAY THE BURDEN OF PROOF IS ON YOU.
WE HAVE A MATCHING FRECKLE PATTERN SHAPED LIKE THE CONSTELLATION ORION UNDER OUR LEFT EYES...
...ONLY IF ORION WAS FAT AND HAD FOUR MORE ARMS AND ALSO FRECKLES FOR LEGS.
CALL
JIMMY--?
OH MY GOD--
I KNOW, I KNOW, AND I'M SORRY, BUT CAN WE GET INDOORS OR SOMETHING SO WE CAN TALK?
BATMAN 3:16
YOU GOT IT.
TAXI!

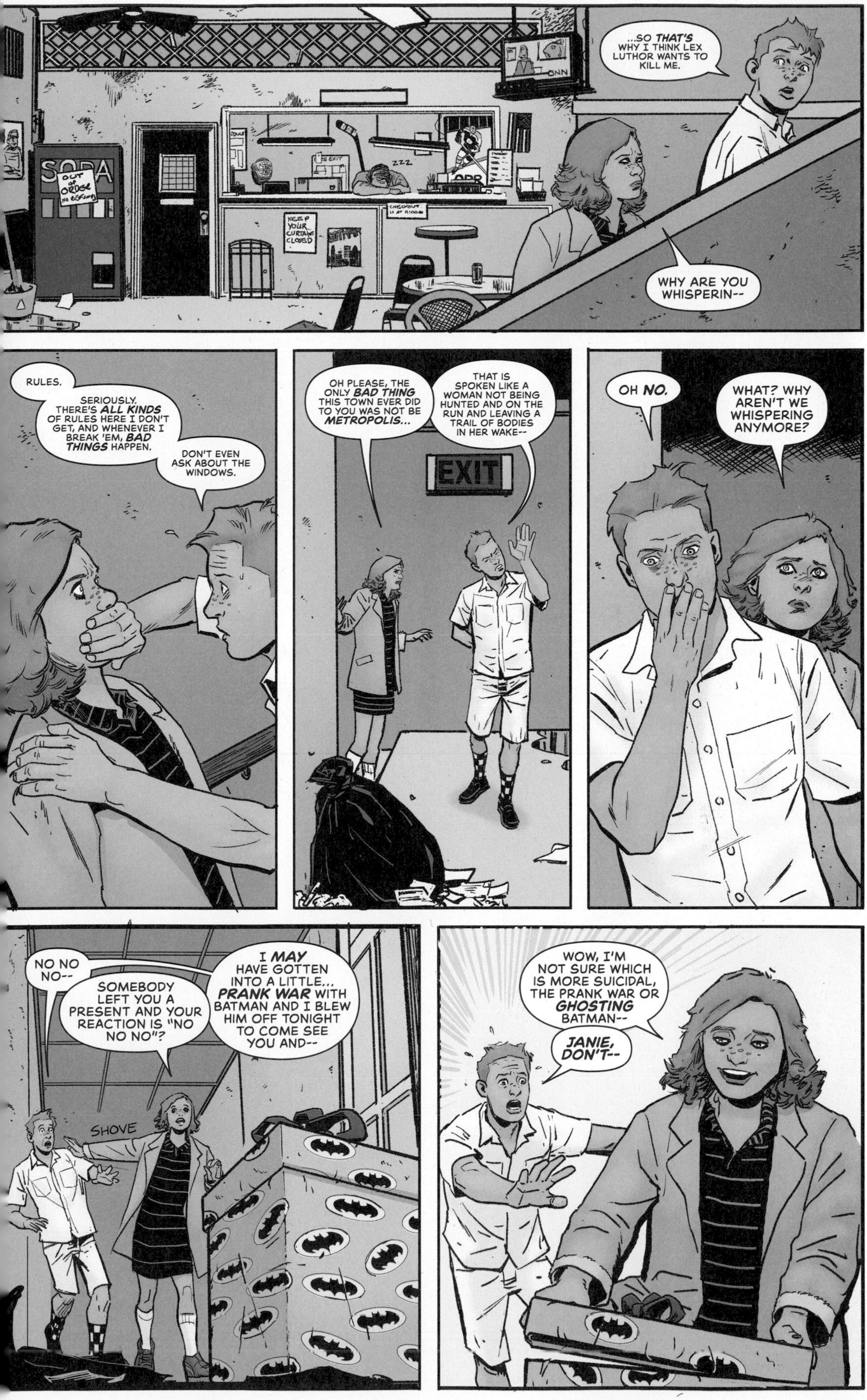
...SO THAT'S WHY I THINK LEX LUTHOR WANTS TO KILL ME.
WHY ARE YOU WHISPERIN--
RULES.
SERIOUSLY. THERE'S ALL KINDS OF RULES HERE I DON'T GET, AND WHENEVER I BREAK 'EM, BAD THINGS HAPPEN.
DON'T EVEN ASK ABOUT THE WINDOWS.
OH PLEASE, THE ONLY BAD THING THIS TOWN EVER DID TO YOU WAS NOT BE METROPOLIS...
THAT IS SPOKEN LIKE A WOMAN NOT BEING HUNTED AND ON THE RUN AND LEAVING A TRAIL OF BODIES IN HER WAKE--
EXIT
OH NO.
WHAT? WHY AREN'T WE WHISPERING ANYMORE?
NO NO NO--
SOMEBODY LEFT YOU A PRESENT AND YOUR REACTION IS "NO NO NO"?
I MAY HAVE GOTTEN INTO A LITTLE... PRANK WAR WITH BATMAN AND I BLEW HIM OFF TONIGHT TO COME SEE YOU AND--
SHOVE
WOW, I'M NOT SURE WHICH IS MORE SUICIDAL, THE PRANK WAR OR GHOSTING BATMAN--
JANIE, DON'T--

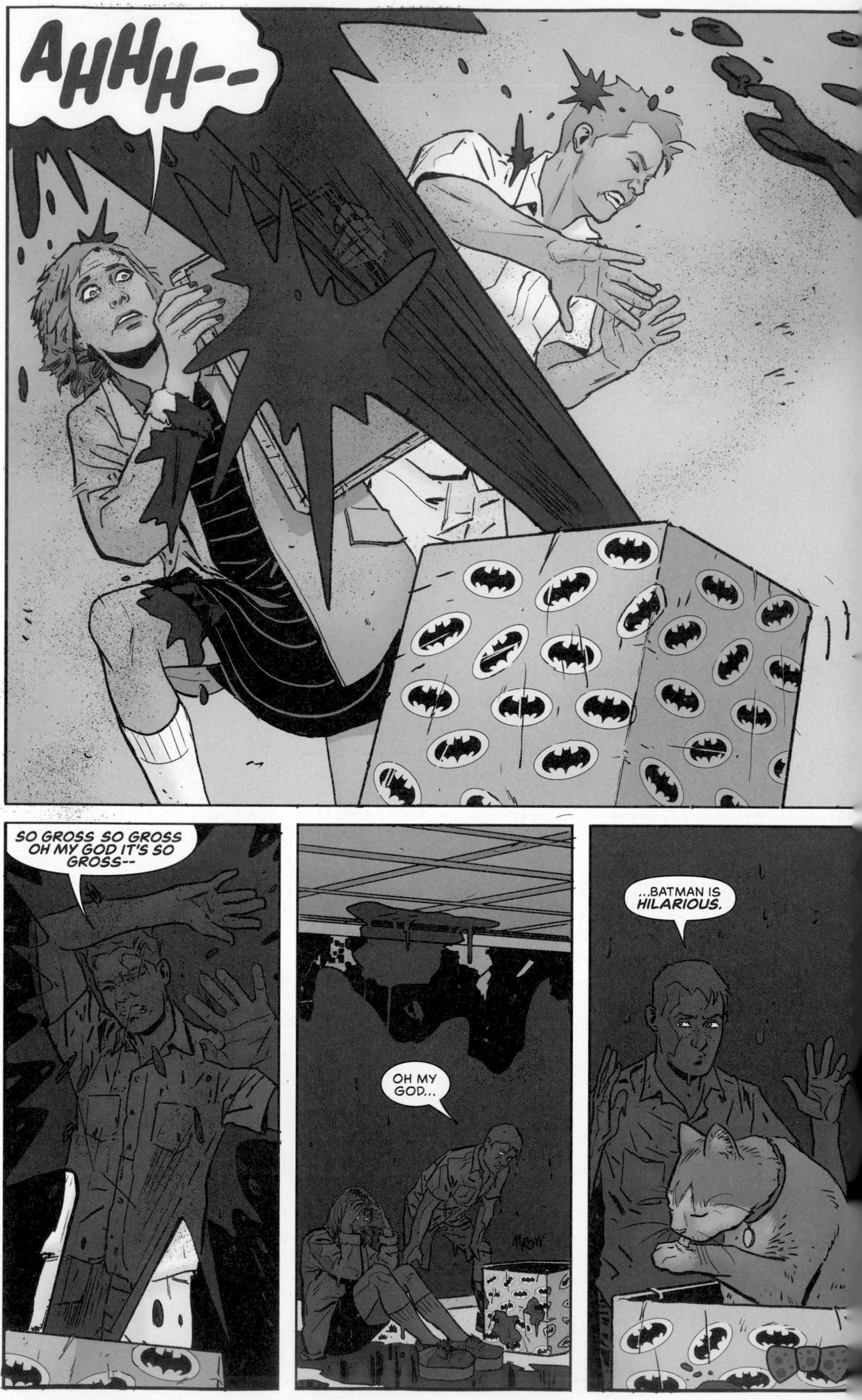
AHHH--
SO GROSS SO GROSS OH MY GOD IT'S SO GROSS--
OH MY GOD...
MROW
...BATMAN IS HILARIOUS.

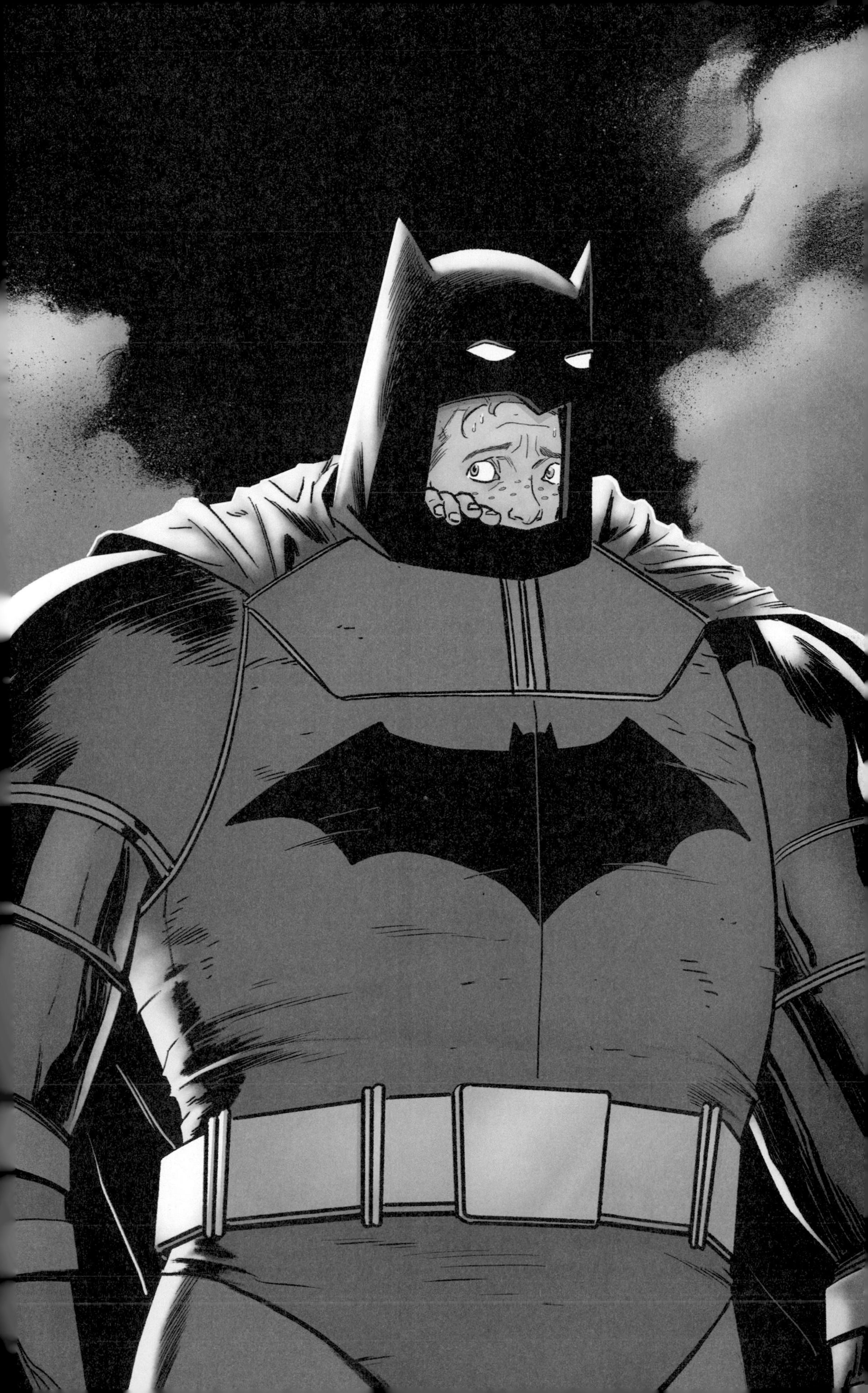

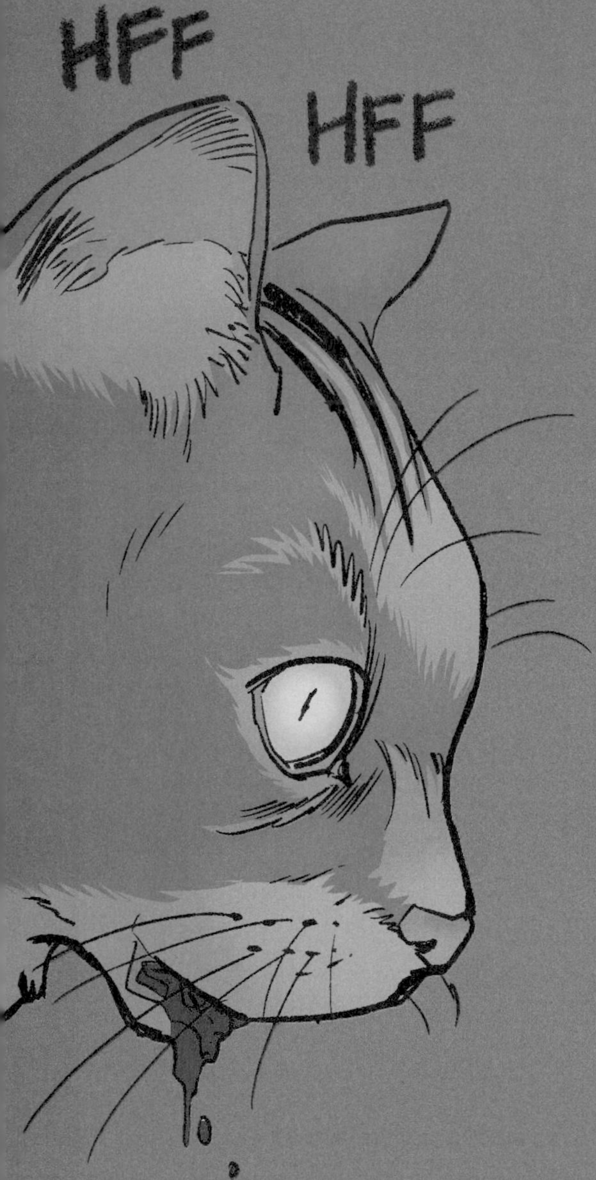
HFF
HFF

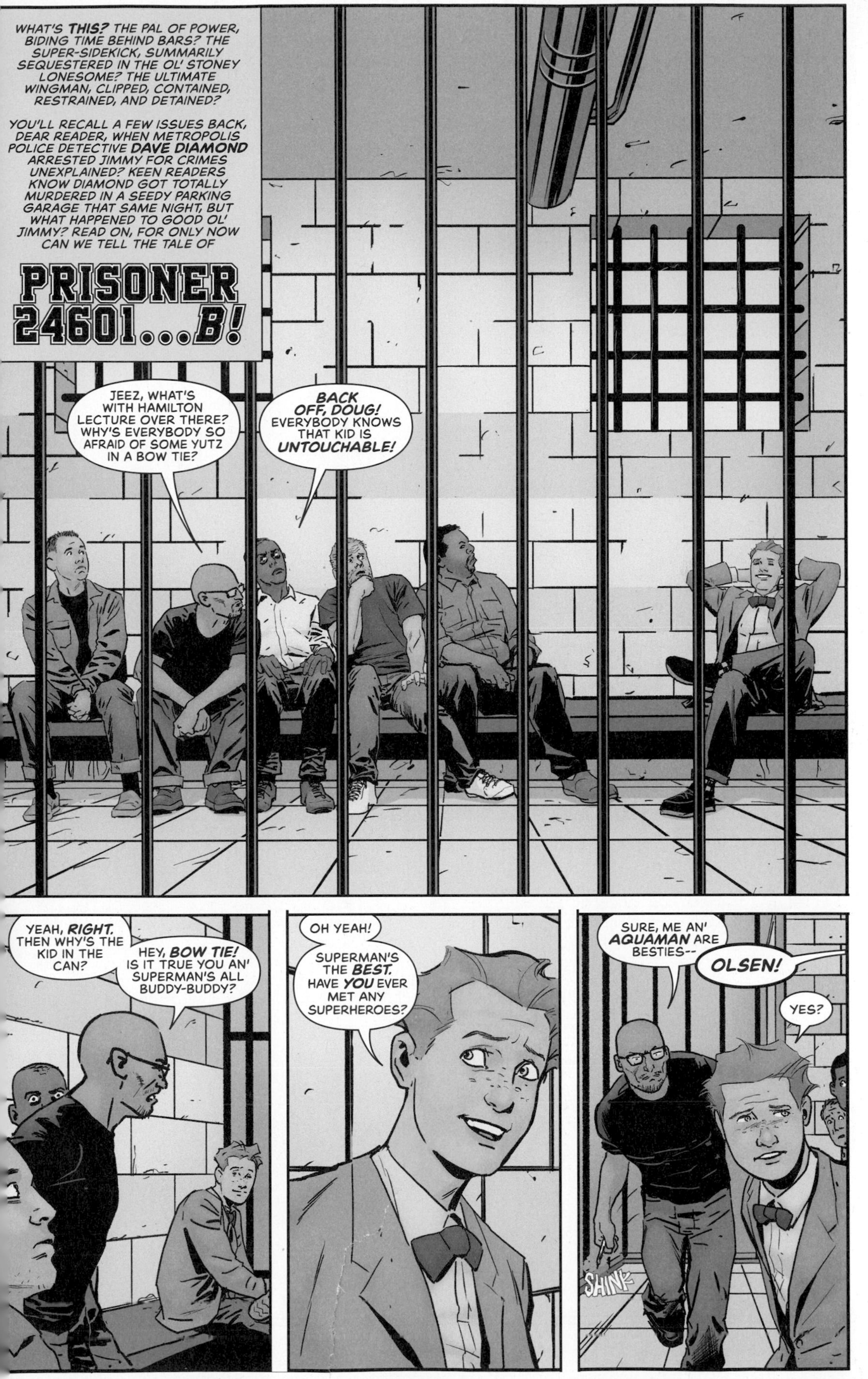
WHAT'S THIS? THE PAL OF POWER, BIDING TIME BEHIND BARS? THE SUPER-SIDEKICK, SUMMARILY SEQUESTERED IN THE OL' STONEY LONESOME? THE ULTIMATE WINGMAN, CLIPPED, CONTAINED, RESTRAINED, AND DETAINED?
YOU'LL RECALL A FEW ISSUES BACK, DEAR READER, WHEN METROPOLIS POLICE DETECTIVE DAVE DIAMOND ARRESTED JIMMY FOR CRIMES UNEXPLAINED? KEEN READERS KNOW DIAMOND GOT TOTALLY MURDERED IN A SEEDY PARKING GARAGE THAT SAME NIGHT, BUT WHAT HAPPENED TO GOOD OL' JIMMY? READ ON, FOR ONLY NOW CAN WE TELL THE TALE OF
PRISONER 24601...B!
JEEZ, WHAT'S WITH HAMILTON LECTURE OVER THERE? WHY'S EVERYBODY SO AFRAID OF SOME YUTZ IN A BOW TIE?
BACK OFF, DOUG! EVERYBODY KNOWS THAT KID IS UNTOUCHABLE!
YEAH, RIGHT. THEN WHY'S THE KID IN THE CAN?
HEY, BOW TIE! IS IT TRUE YOU AN' SUPERMAN'S ALL BUDDY-BUDDY?
OH YEAH!
SUPERMAN'S THE BEST. HAVE YOU EVER MET ANY SUPERHEROES?
SURE, ME AN' AQUAMAN ARE BESTIES--
OLSEN!
YES?
SHINK

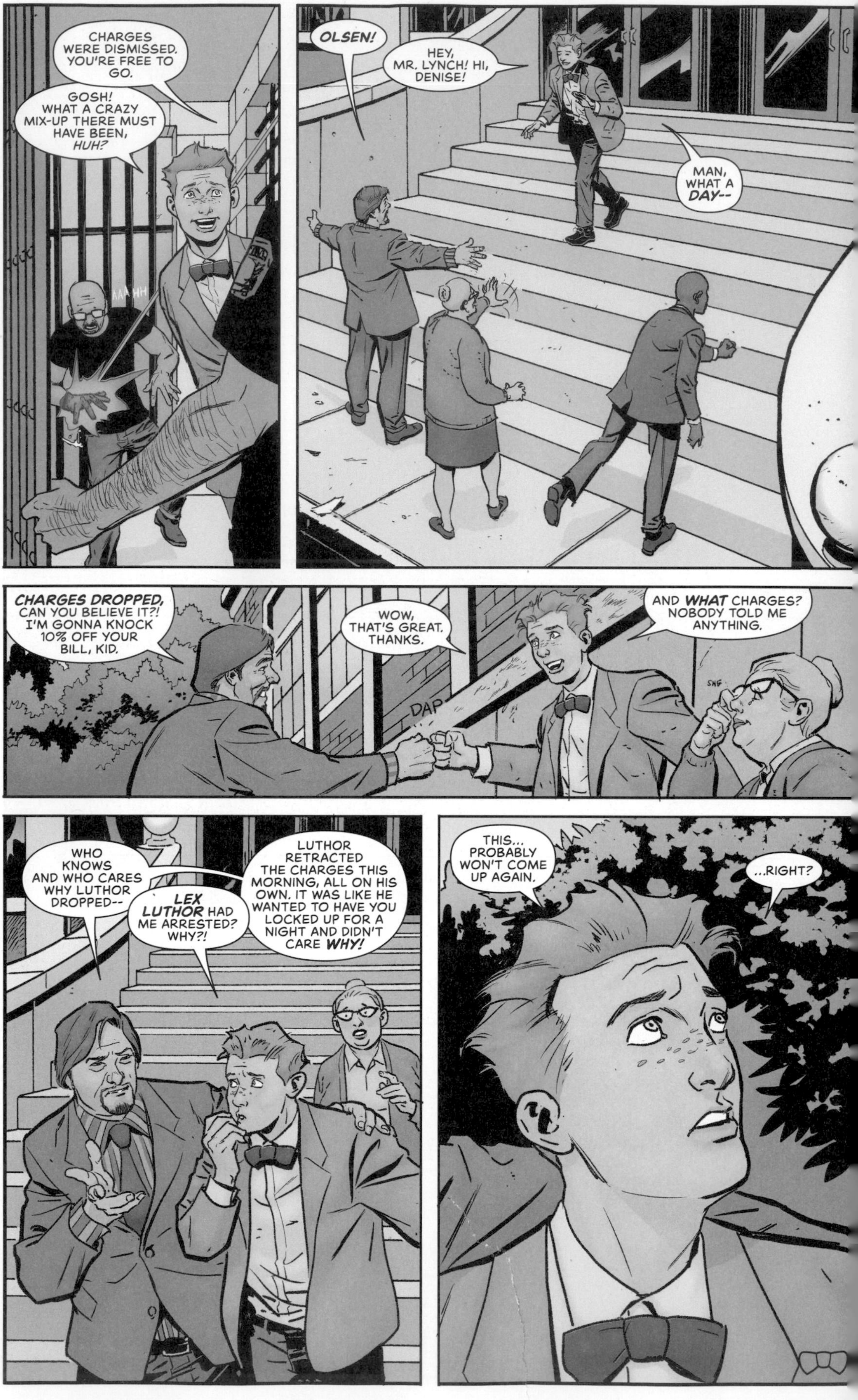
CHARGES WERE DISMISSED. YOU'RE FREE TO GO.
GOSH! WHAT A CRAZY MIX-UP THERE MUST HAVE BEEN, HUH?
AAAHH
OLSEN!
HEY, MR. LYNCH! HI, DENISE!
MAN, WHAT A DAY--
CHARGES DROPPED, CAN YOU BELIEVE IT?! I'M GONNA KNOCK 10% OFF YOUR BILL, KID.
WOW, THAT'S GREAT. THANKS.
AND WHAT CHARGES? NOBODY TOLD ME ANYTHING.
DAP
SNF
WHO KNOWS AND WHO CARES WHY LUTHOR DROPPED--
LEX LUTHOR HAD ME ARRESTED? WHY?!
LUTHOR RETRACTED THE CHARGES THIS MORNING, ALL ON HIS OWN. IT WAS LIKE HE WANTED TO HAVE YOU LOCKED UP FOR A NIGHT AND DIDN'T CARE WHY!
THIS... PROBABLY WON'T COME UP AGAIN.
...RIGHT?

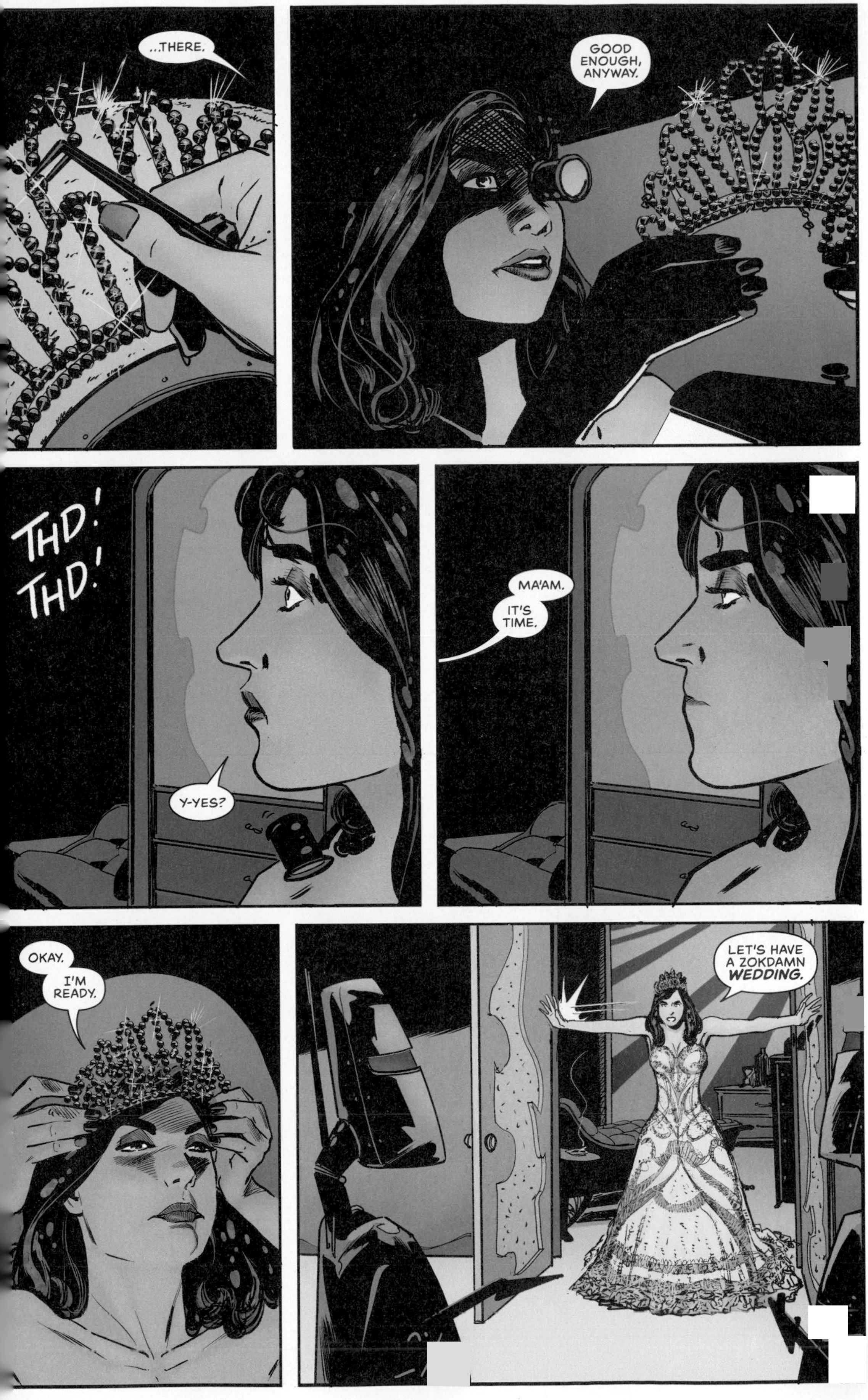
...THERE.
GOOD ENOUGH, ANYWAY.
THD! THD!
Y-YES?
MA'AM.
IT'S TIME.
OKAY.
I'M READY.
LET'S HAVE A ZOKDAMN WEDDING.

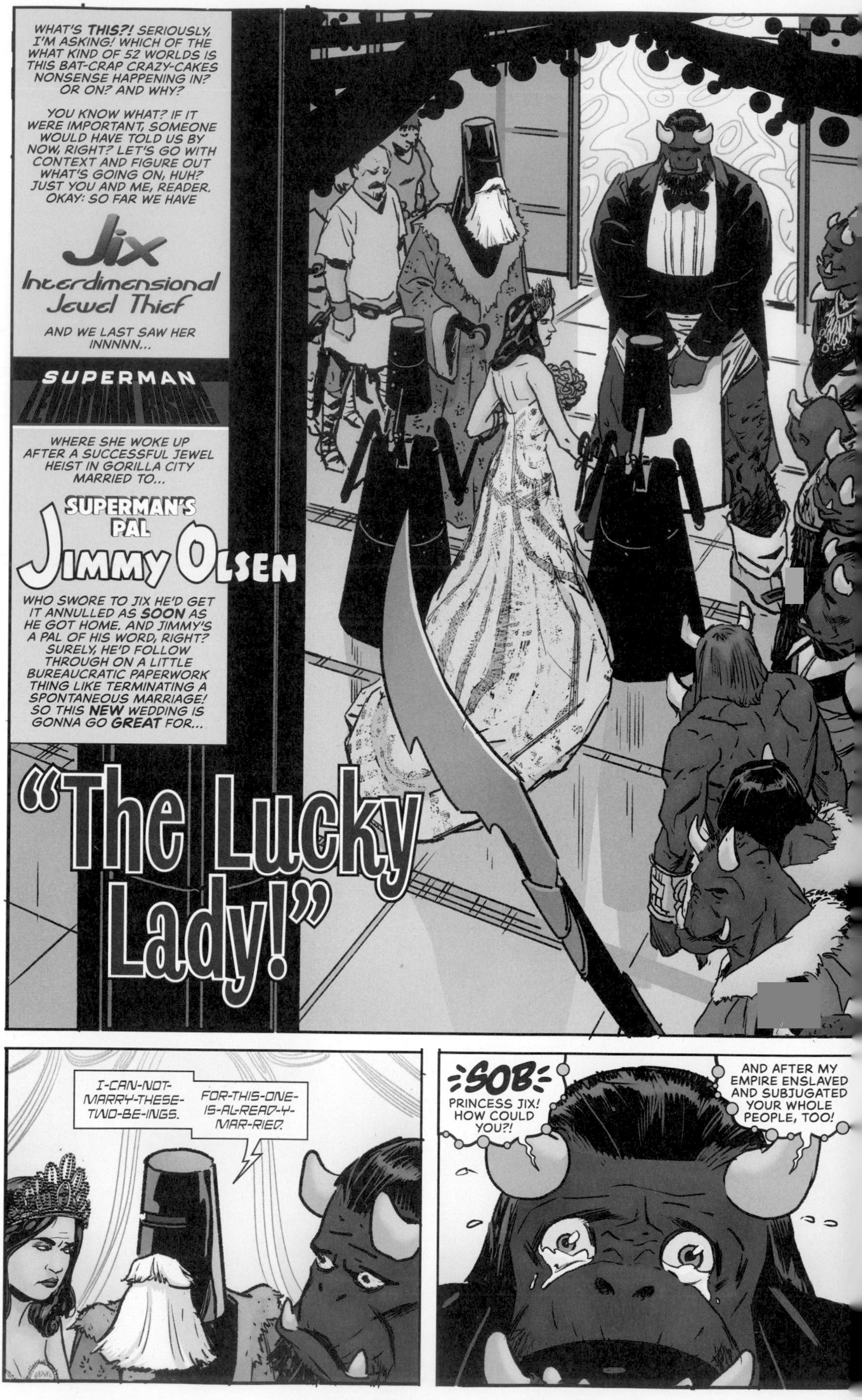

WHAT'S THIS?! SERIOUSLY, I'M ASKING! WHICH OF THE WHAT KIND OF 52 WORLDS IS THIS BAT-CRAP CRAZY-CAKES NONSENSE HAPPENING IN? OR ON? AND WHY?
YOU KNOW WHAT? IF IT WERE IMPORTANT, SOMEONE WOULD HAVE TOLD US BY NOW, RIGHT? LET'S GO WITH CONTEXT AND FIGURE OUT WHAT'S GOING ON, HUH? JUST YOU AND ME, READER. OKAY: SO FAR WE HAVE
Jix
Interdimensional Jewel Thief
AND WE LAST SAW HER INNNNN...
SUPERMAN
LEVIATHAN RISING
WHERE SHE WOKE UP AFTER A SUCCESSFUL JEWEL HEIST IN GORILLA CITY MARRIED TO...
SUPERMAN'S PAL
JIMMY OLSEN
WHO SWORE TO JIX HE'D GET IT ANNULLED AS SOON AS HE GOT HOME. AND JIMMY'S A PAL OF HIS WORD, RIGHT? SURELY, HE'D FOLLOW THROUGH ON A LITTLE BUREAUCRATIC PAPERWORK THING LIKE TERMINATING A SPONTANEOUS MARRIAGE! SO THIS NEW WEDDING IS GONNA GO GREAT FOR...
"The Lucky Lady!"
I-CAN-NOT-MARRY-THESE-TWO-BE-INGS.
FOR-THIS-ONE-IS-AL-READ-Y-MAR-RIED.
SOB
PRINCESS JIX! HOW COULD YOU?!
AND AFTER MY EMPIRE ENSLAVED AND SUBJUGATED YOUR WHOLE PEOPLE, TOO!

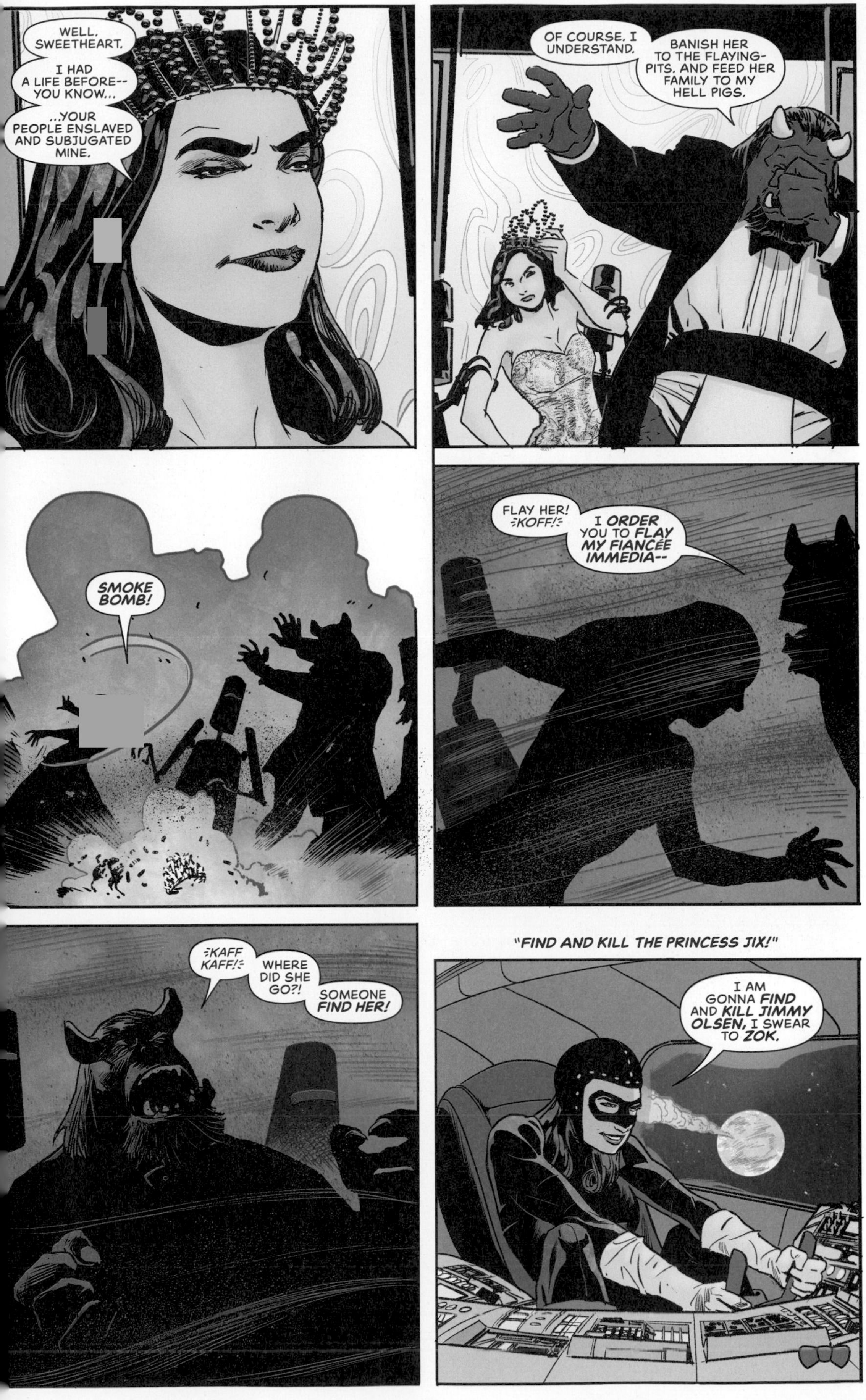
WELL. SWEETHEART.
I HAD A LIFE BEFORE-- YOU KNOW...
...YOUR PEOPLE ENSLAVED AND SUBJUGATED MINE.
OF COURSE. I UNDERSTAND.
BANISH HER TO THE FLAYING-PITS. AND FEED HER FAMILY TO MY HELL PIGS.
SMOKE BOMB!
FLAY HER! KOFF!
I ORDER YOU TO FLAY MY FIANCÉE IMMEDIA--
KAFF KAFF!
WHERE DID SHE GO?!
SOMEONE FIND HER!
"FIND AND KILL THE PRINCESS JIX!"
I AM GONNA FIND AND KILL JIMMY OLSEN, I SWEAR TO ZOK.

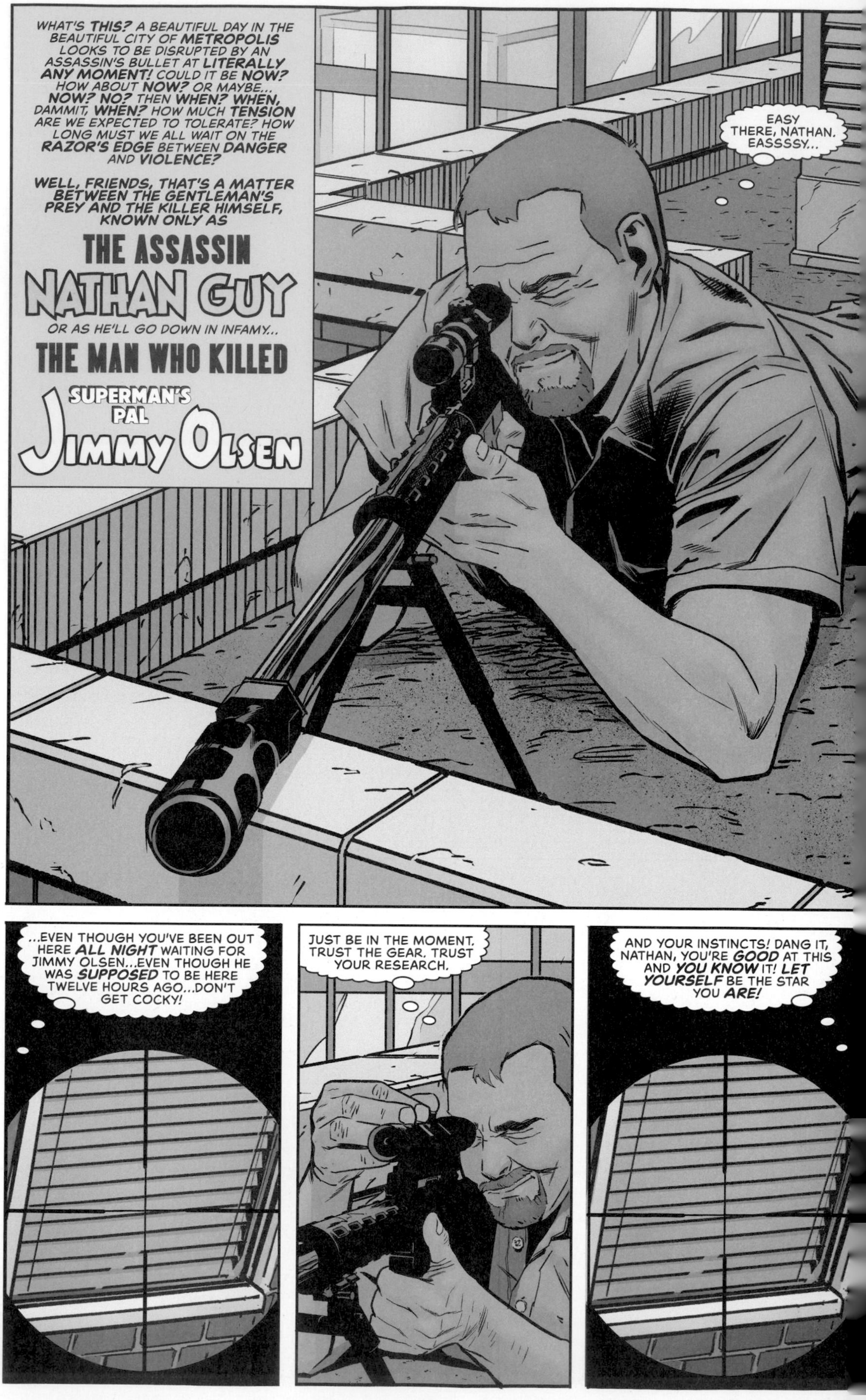
WHAT'S THIS? A BEAUTIFUL DAY IN THE BEAUTIFUL CITY OF METROPOLIS LOOKS TO BE DISRUPTED BY AN ASSASSIN'S BULLET AT LITERALLY ANY MOMENT! COULD IT BE NOW? HOW ABOUT NOW? OR MAYBE... NOW? NO? THEN WHEN? WHEN, DAMMIT, WHEN? HOW MUCH TENSION ARE WE EXPECTED TO TOLERATE? HOW LONG MUST WE ALL WAIT ON THE RAZOR'S EDGE BETWEEN DANGER AND VIOLENCE?
WELL, FRIENDS, THAT'S A MATTER BETWEEN THE GENTLEMAN'S PREY AND THE KILLER HIMSELF, KNOWN ONLY AS
THE ASSASSIN
NATHAN GUY
OR AS HE'LL GO DOWN IN INFAMY...
THE MAN WHO KILLED
SUPERMAN'S PAL
JIMMY OLSEN
EASY THERE, NATHAN. EASSSSY...
...EVEN THOUGH YOU'VE BEEN OUT HERE ALL NIGHT WAITING FOR JIMMY OLSEN...EVEN THOUGH HE WAS SUPPOSED TO BE HERE TWELVE HOURS AGO...DON'T GET COCKY!
JUST BE IN THE MOMENT. TRUST THE GEAR. TRUST YOUR RESEARCH.
AND YOUR INSTINCTS! DANG IT, NATHAN, YOU'RE GOOD AT THIS AND YOU KNOW IT! LET YOURSELF BE THE STAR YOU ARE!

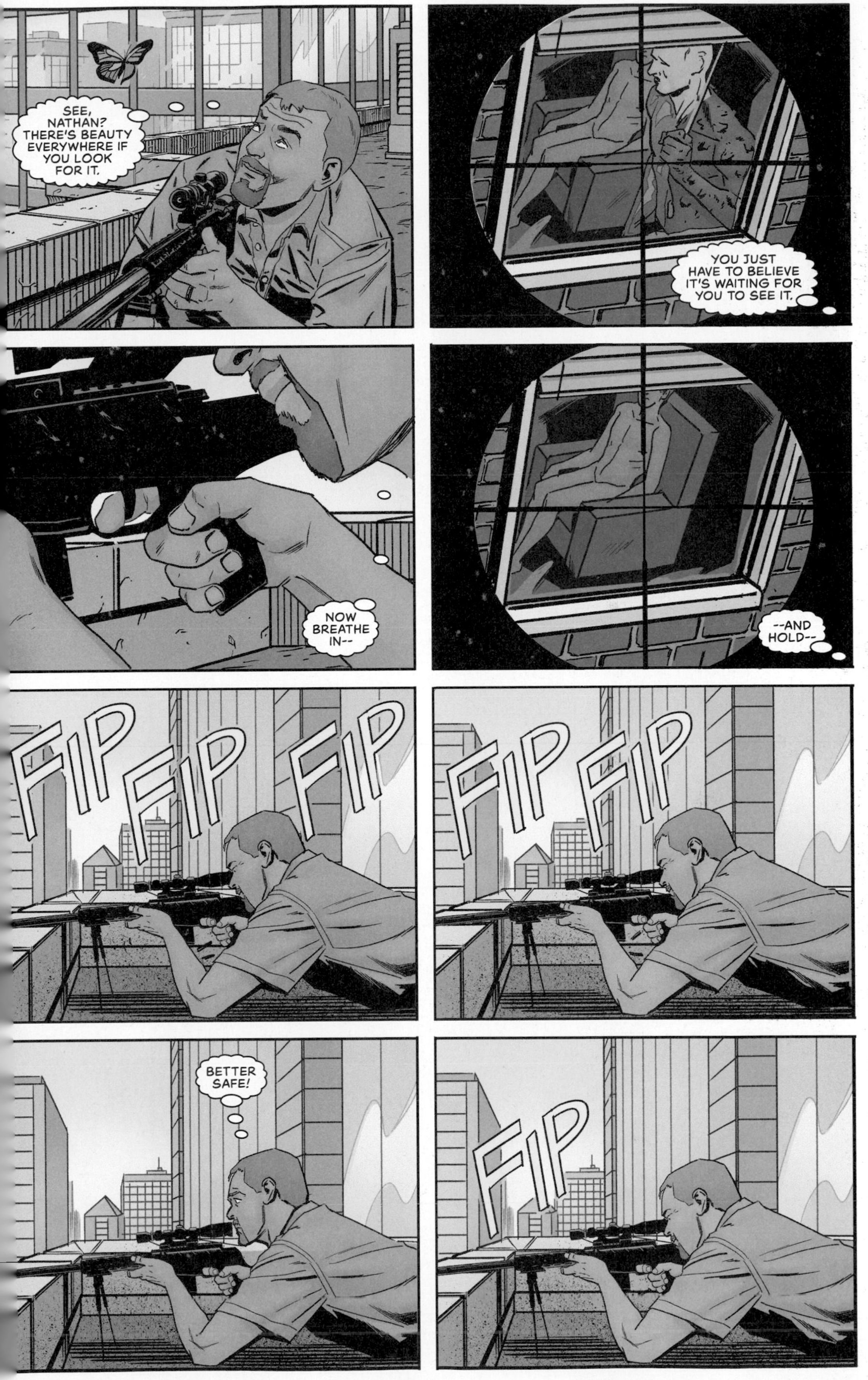
SEE, NATHAN? THERE'S BEAUTY EVERYWHERE IF YOU LOOK FOR IT.
YOU JUST HAVE TO BELIEVE IT'S WAITING FOR YOU TO SEE IT.
NOW BREATHE IN--
--AND HOLD--
FIP FIP FIP
FIP FIP
BETTER SAFE!
FIP

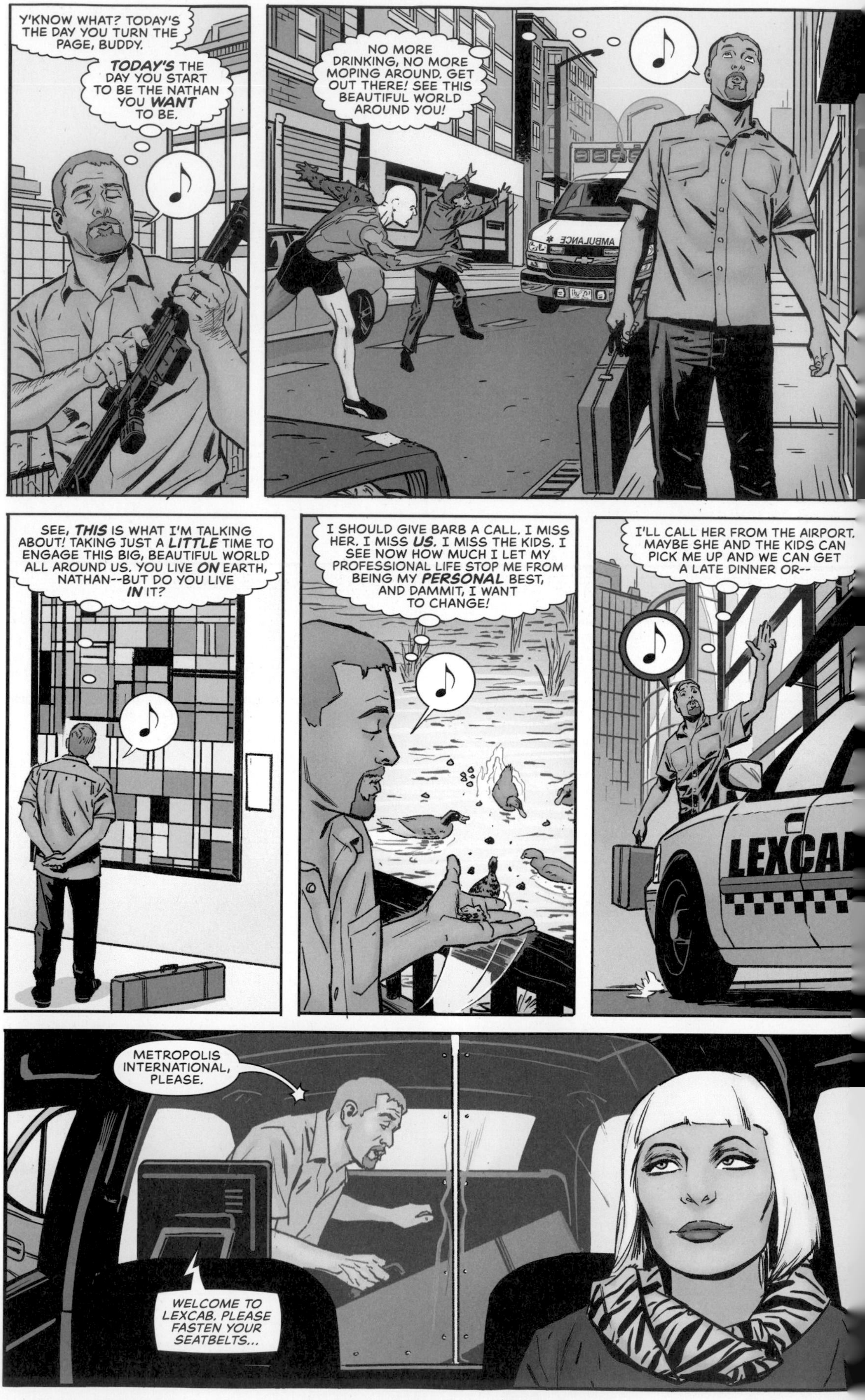

Y'KNOW WHAT? TODAY'S THE DAY YOU TURN THE PAGE, BUDDY.
TODAY'S THE DAY YOU START TO BE THE NATHAN YOU WANT TO BE.
♪
NO MORE DRINKING, NO MORE MOPING AROUND. GET OUT THERE! SEE THIS BEAUTIFUL WORLD AROUND YOU!
♪
AMBULANCE
SEE, THIS IS WHAT I'M TALKING ABOUT! TAKING JUST A LITTLE TIME TO ENGAGE THIS BIG, BEAUTIFUL WORLD ALL AROUND US. YOU LIVE ON EARTH, NATHAN--BUT DO YOU LIVE IN IT?
♪
I SHOULD GIVE BARB A CALL. I MISS HER. I MISS US. I MISS THE KIDS. I SEE NOW HOW MUCH I LET MY PROFESSIONAL LIFE STOP ME FROM BEING MY PERSONAL BEST, AND DAMMIT, I WANT TO CHANGE!
♪
I'LL CALL HER FROM THE AIRPORT. MAYBE SHE AND THE KIDS CAN PICK ME UP AND WE CAN GET A LATE DINNER OR--
♪
METROPOLIS INTERNATIONAL, PLEASE.
WELCOME TO LEXCAB. PLEASE FASTEN YOUR SEATBELTS...

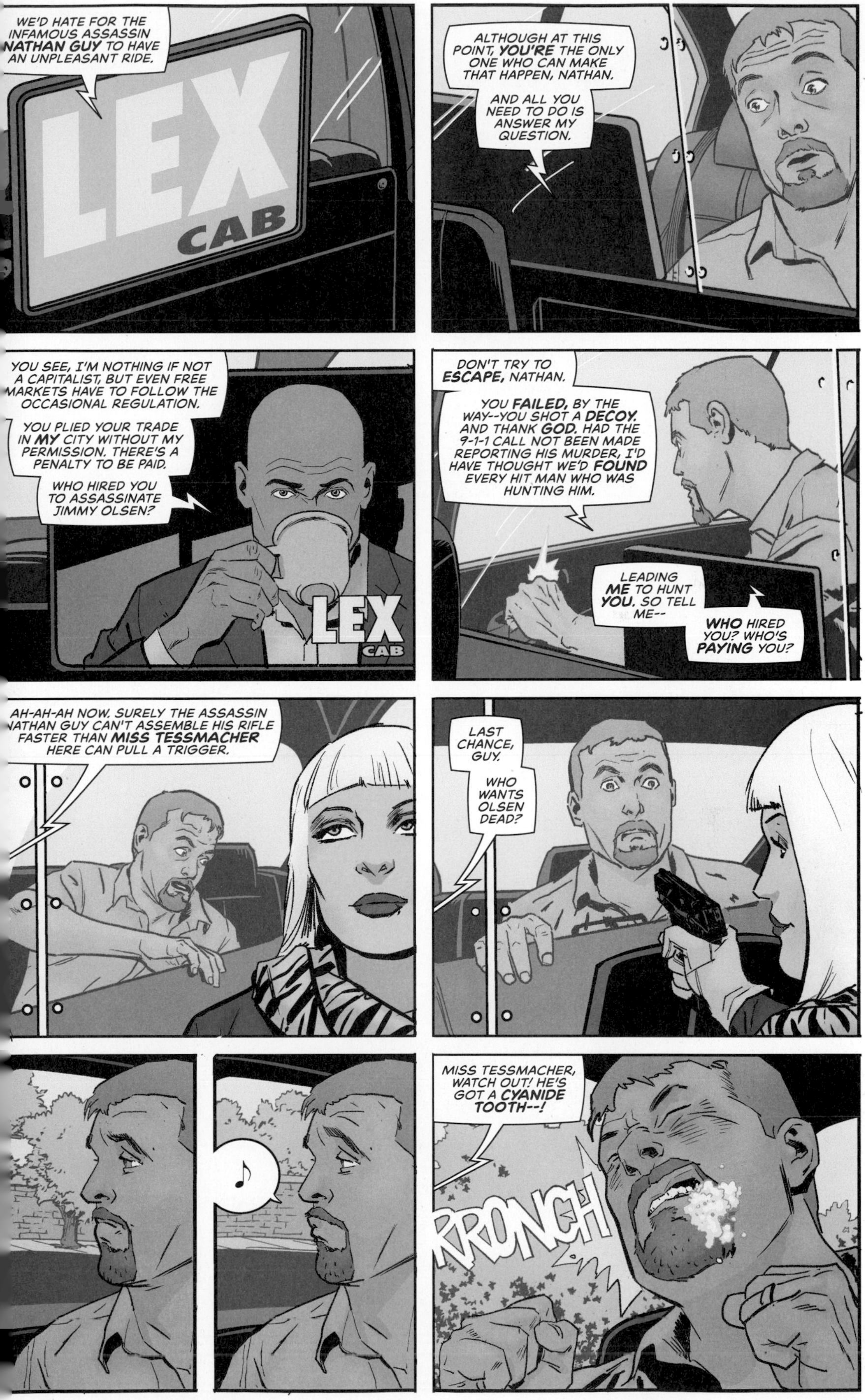
WE'D HATE FOR THE INFAMOUS ASSASSIN NATHAN GUY TO HAVE AN UNPLEASANT RIDE.
LEX CAB
ALTHOUGH AT THIS POINT, YOU'RE THE ONLY ONE WHO CAN MAKE THAT HAPPEN, NATHAN.
AND ALL YOU NEED TO DO IS ANSWER MY QUESTION.
YOU SEE, I'M NOTHING IF NOT A CAPITALIST, BUT EVEN FREE MARKETS HAVE TO FOLLOW THE OCCASIONAL REGULATION.
YOU PLIED YOUR TRADE IN MY CITY WITHOUT MY PERMISSION. THERE'S A PENALTY TO BE PAID.
WHO HIRED YOU TO ASSASSINATE JIMMY OLSEN?
LEX CAB
DON'T TRY TO ESCAPE, NATHAN.
YOU FAILED, BY THE WAY--YOU SHOT A DECOY. AND THANK GOD. HAD THE 9-1-1 CALL NOT BEEN MADE REPORTING HIS MURDER, I'D HAVE THOUGHT WE'D FOUND EVERY HIT MAN WHO WAS HUNTING HIM.
LEADING ME TO HUNT YOU. SO TELL ME--
WHO HIRED YOU? WHO'S PAYING YOU?
AH-AH-AH NOW. SURELY THE ASSASSIN NATHAN GUY CAN'T ASSEMBLE HIS RIFLE FASTER THAN MISS TESSMACHER HERE CAN PULL A TRIGGER.
LAST CHANCE, GUY.
WHO WANTS OLSEN DEAD?
♪
MISS TESSMACHER, WATCH OUT! HE'S GOT A CYANIDE TOOTH--!
KRRONCH

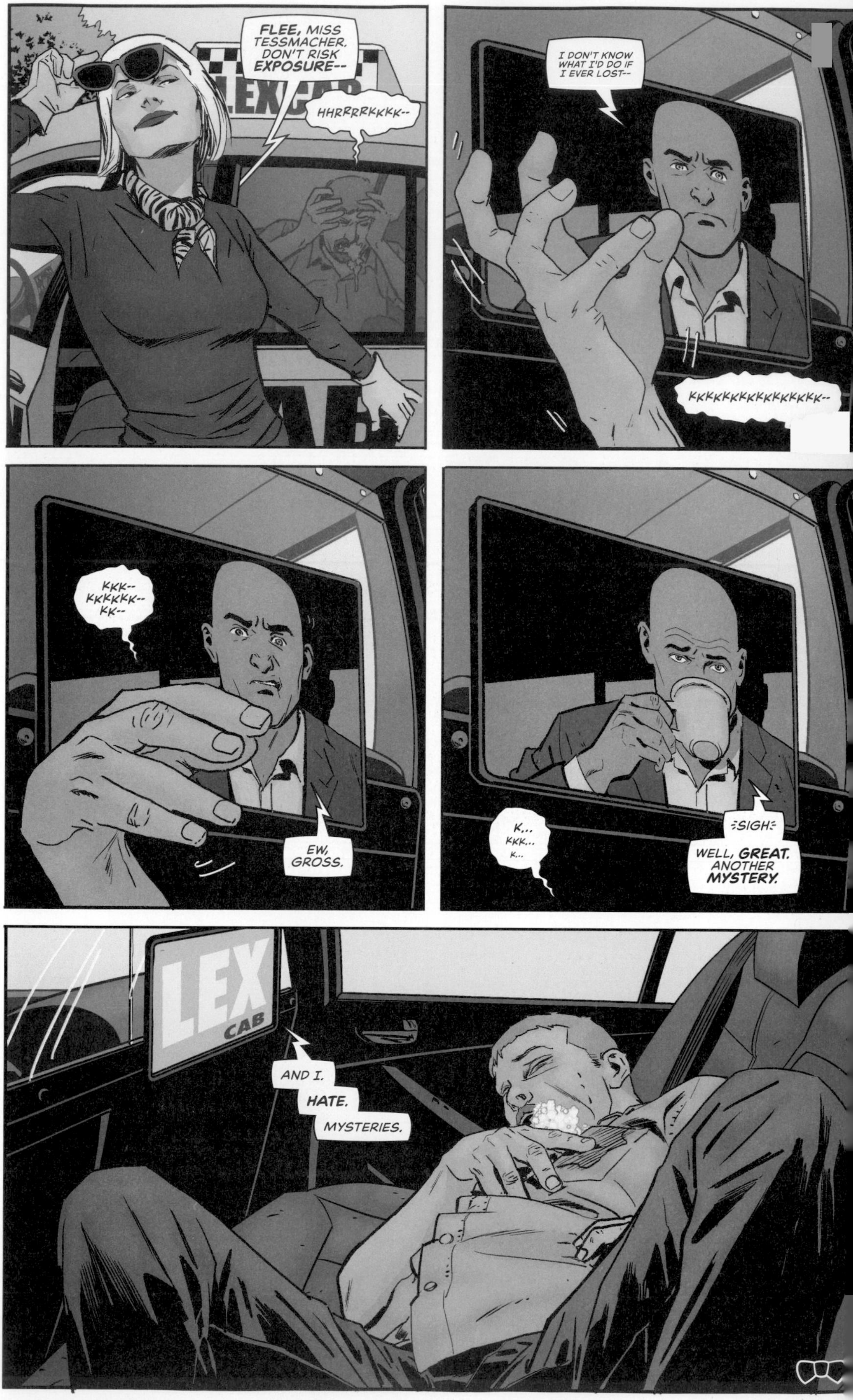
LEX CAB
FLEE, MISS TESSMACHER. DON'T RISK EXPOSURE--
HHRRRRKKKK--
I DON'T KNOW WHAT I'D DO IF I EVER LOST--
KKKKKKKKKKKKKKKK--
KKK-- KKKKKK-- KK--
EW, GROSS.
K... KKK... K...
SIGH
WELL, GREAT. ANOTHER MYSTERY.
LEX CAB
AND I.
HATE.
MYSTERIES.

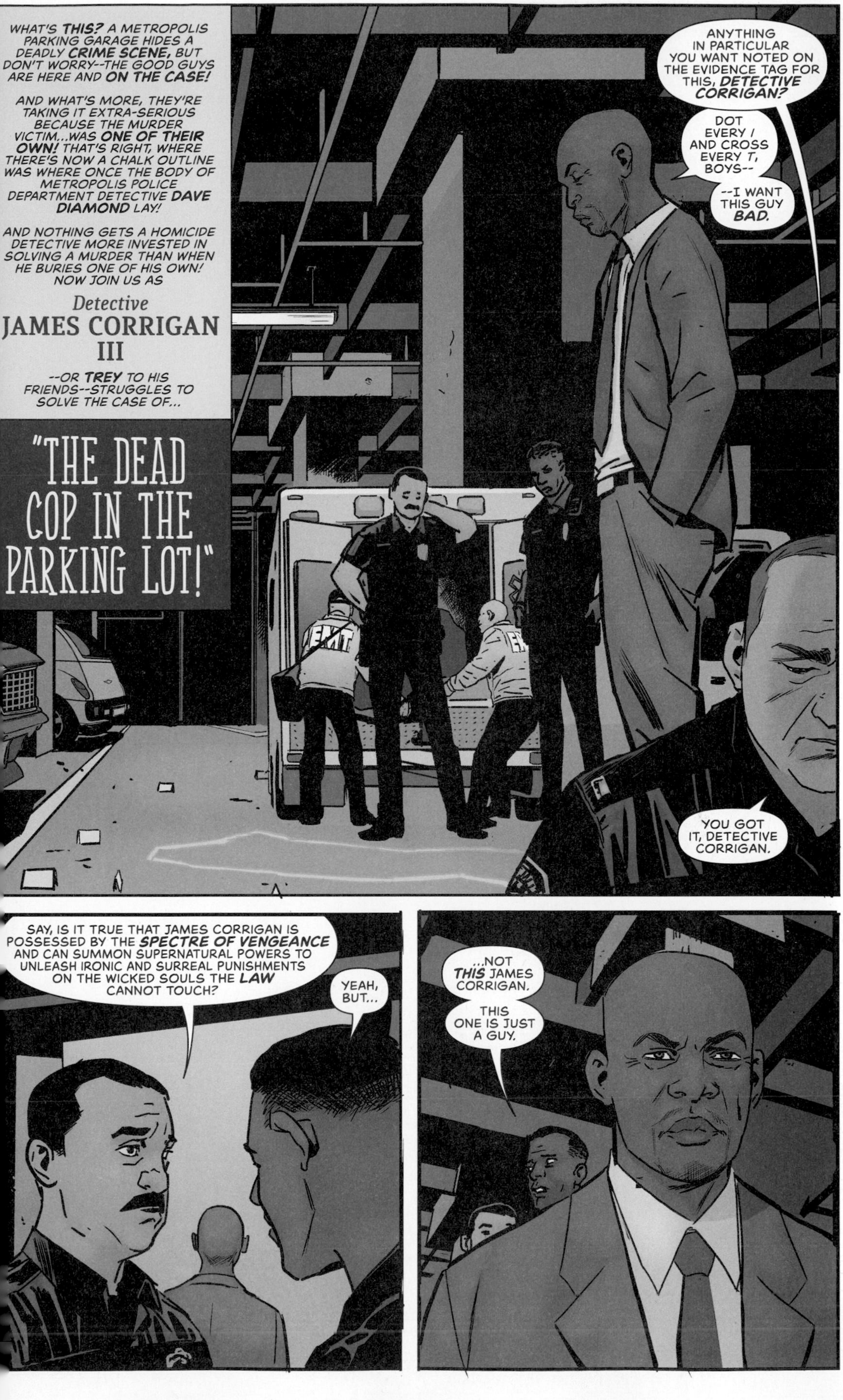
WHAT'S THIS? A METROPOLIS PARKING GARAGE HIDES A DEADLY CRIME SCENE, BUT DON'T WORRY--THE GOOD GUYS ARE HERE AND ON THE CASE!
AND WHAT'S MORE, THEY'RE TAKING IT EXTRA-SERIOUS BECAUSE THE MURDER VICTIM...WAS ONE OF THEIR OWN! THAT'S RIGHT, WHERE THERE'S NOW A CHALK OUTLINE WAS WHERE ONCE THE BODY OF METROPOLIS POLICE DEPARTMENT DETECTIVE DAVE DIAMOND LAY!
AND NOTHING GETS A HOMICIDE DETECTIVE MORE INVESTED IN SOLVING A MURDER THAN WHEN HE BURIES ONE OF HIS OWN! NOW JOIN US AS
Detective JAMES CORRIGAN III
--OR TREY TO HIS FRIENDS--STRUGGLES TO SOLVE THE CASE OF...
"THE DEAD COP IN THE PARKING LOT!"
ANYTHING IN PARTICULAR YOU WANT NOTED ON THE EVIDENCE TAG FOR THIS, DETECTIVE CORRIGAN?
DOT EVERY I AND CROSS EVERY T, BOYS--
--I WANT THIS GUY BAD.
YOU GOT IT, DETECTIVE CORRIGAN.
SAY, IS IT TRUE THAT JAMES CORRIGAN IS POSSESSED BY THE SPECTRE OF VENGEANCE AND CAN SUMMON SUPERNATURAL POWERS TO UNLEASH IRONIC AND SURREAL PUNISHMENTS ON THE WICKED SOULS THE LAW CANNOT TOUCH?
YEAH, BUT...
...NOT THIS JAMES CORRIGAN.
THIS ONE IS JUST A GUY.

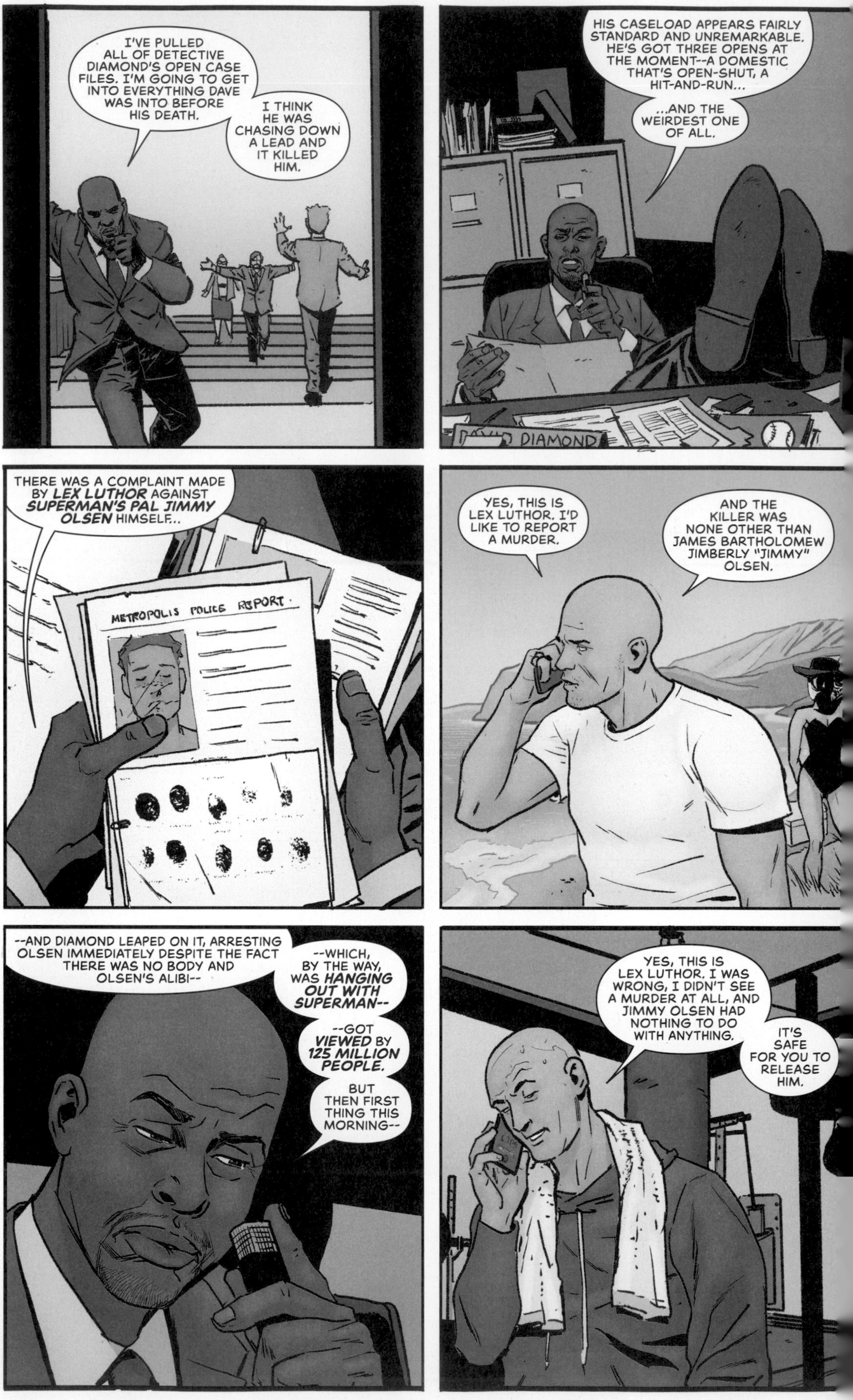
I'VE PULLED ALL OF DETECTIVE DIAMOND'S OPEN CASE FILES. I'M GOING TO GET INTO EVERYTHING DAVE WAS INTO BEFORE HIS DEATH.
I THINK HE WAS CHASING DOWN A LEAD AND IT KILLED HIM.
HIS CASELOAD APPEARS FAIRLY STANDARD AND UNREMARKABLE. HE'S GOT THREE OPENS AT THE MOMENT--A DOMESTIC THAT'S OPEN-SHUT, A HIT-AND-RUN...
...AND THE WEIRDEST ONE OF ALL.
DAVID DIAMOND
THERE WAS A COMPLAINT MADE BY LEX LUTHOR AGAINST SUPERMAN'S PAL JIMMY OLSEN HIMSELF...
METROPOLIS POLICE REPORT
YES, THIS IS LEX LUTHOR. I'D LIKE TO REPORT A MURDER.
AND THE KILLER WAS NONE OTHER THAN JAMES BARTHOLOMEW JIMBERLY "JIMMY" OLSEN.
--AND DIAMOND LEAPED ON IT, ARRESTING OLSEN IMMEDIATELY DESPITE THE FACT THERE WAS NO BODY AND OLSEN'S ALIBI--
--WHICH, BY THE WAY, WAS HANGING OUT WITH SUPERMAN--
--GOT VIEWED BY 125 MILLION PEOPLE.
BUT THEN FIRST THING THIS MORNING--
YES, THIS IS LEX LUTHOR. I WAS WRONG, I DIDN'T SEE A MURDER AT ALL, AND JIMMY OLSEN HAD NOTHING TO DO WITH ANYTHING.
IT'S SAFE FOR YOU TO RELEASE HIM.

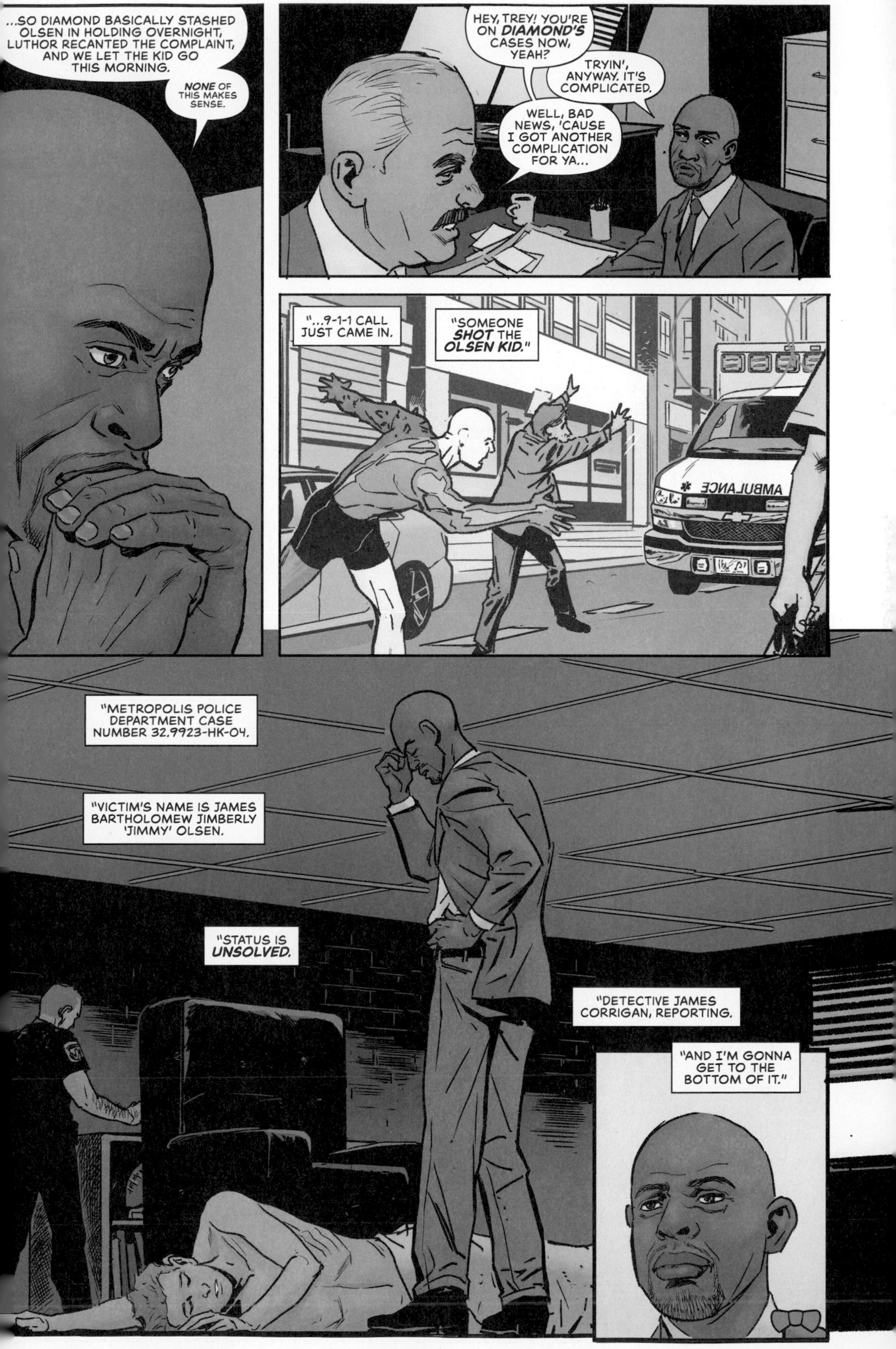
...SO DIAMOND BASICALLY STASHED OLSEN IN HOLDING OVERNIGHT, LUTHOR RECANTED THE COMPLAINT, AND WE LET THE KID GO THIS MORNING.
NONE OF THIS MAKES SENSE.
HEY, TREY! YOU'RE ON DIAMOND'S CASES NOW, YEAH?
TRYIN', ANYWAY. IT'S COMPLICATED.
WELL, BAD NEWS, 'CAUSE I GOT ANOTHER COMPLICATION FOR YA...
"...9-1-1 CALL JUST CAME IN.
"SOMEONE SHOT THE OLSEN KID."
AMBULANCE
"METROPOLIS POLICE DEPARTMENT CASE NUMBER 32.9923-HK-04.
"VICTIM'S NAME IS JAMES BARTHOLOMEW JIMBERLY 'JIMMY' OLSEN.
"STATUS IS UNSOLVED.
"DETECTIVE JAMES CORRIGAN, REPORTING.
"AND I'M GONNA GET TO THE BOTTOM OF IT."

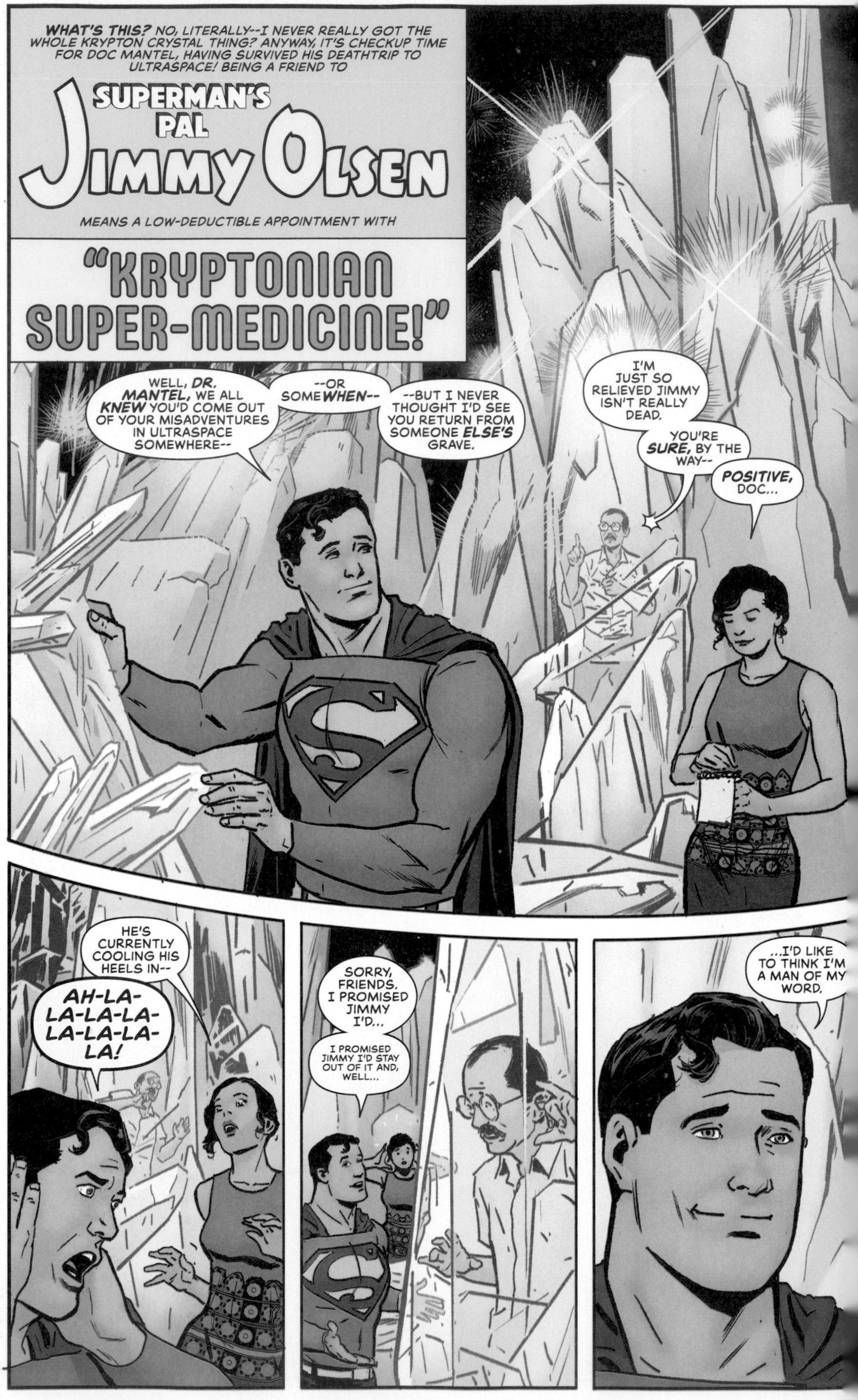
WHAT'S THIS? NO, LITERALLY--I NEVER REALLY GOT THE WHOLE KRYPTON CRYSTAL THING? ANYWAY, IT'S CHECKUP TIME FOR DOC MANTEL, HAVING SURVIVED HIS DEATHTRIP TO ULTRASPACE! BEING A FRIEND TO
SUPERMAN'S PAL JIMMY OLSEN
MEANS A LOW-DEDUCTIBLE APPOINTMENT WITH
"KRYPTONIAN SUPER-MEDICINE!"
WELL, DR. MANTEL, WE ALL KNEW YOU'D COME OUT OF YOUR MISADVENTURES IN ULTRASPACE SOMEWHERE--
--OR SOMEWHEN--
--BUT I NEVER THOUGHT I'D SEE YOU RETURN FROM SOMEONE ELSE'S GRAVE.
I'M JUST SO RELIEVED JIMMY ISN'T REALLY DEAD.
YOU'RE SURE, BY THE WAY--
POSITIVE, DOC...
HE'S CURRENTLY COOLING HIS HEELS IN--
AH-LA-LA-LA-LA-LA-LA-LA-LA!
SORRY, FRIENDS. I PROMISED JIMMY I'D...
I PROMISED JIMMY I'D STAY OUT OF IT AND, WELL...
...I'D LIKE TO THINK I'M A MAN OF MY WORD.

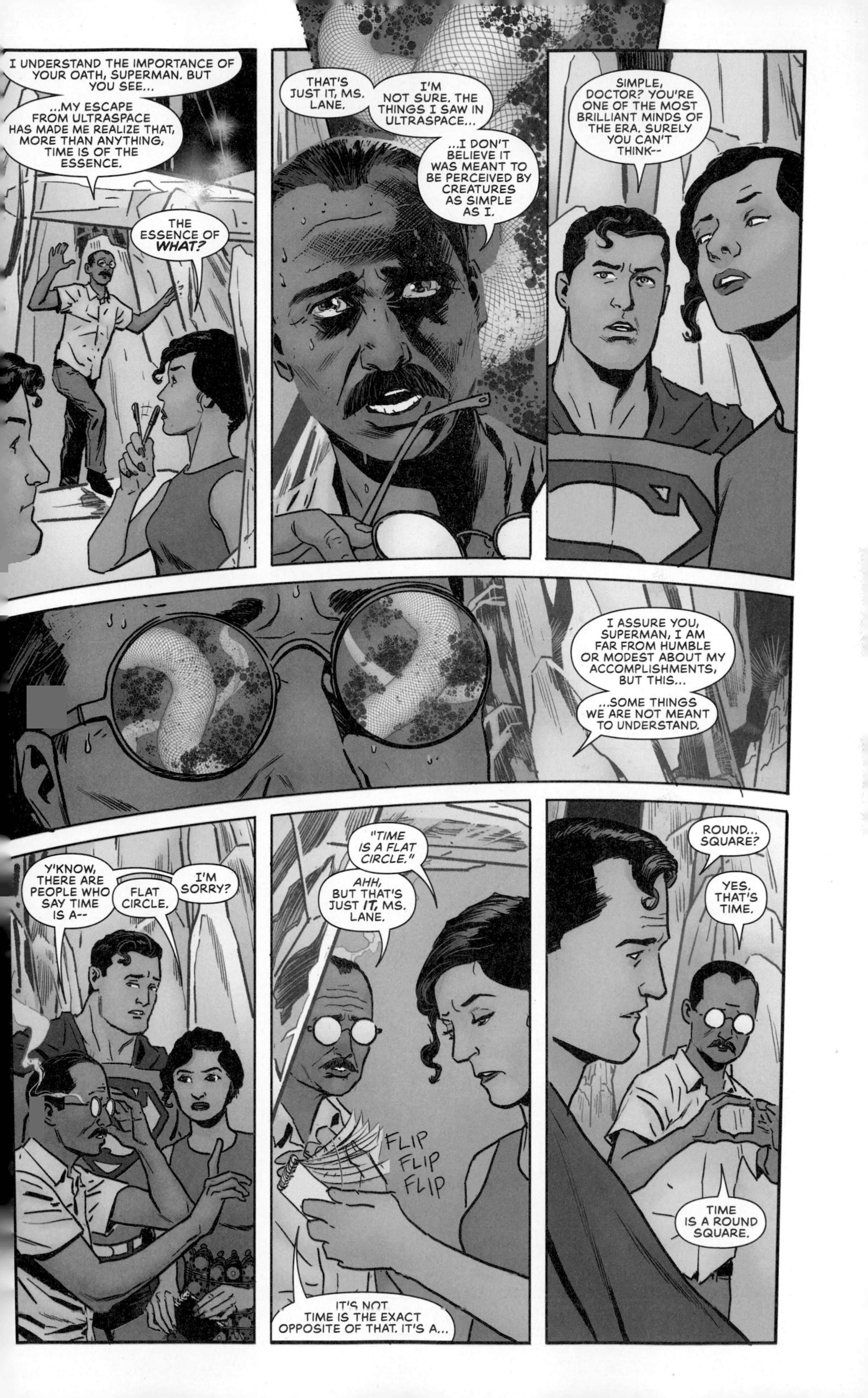

I UNDERSTAND THE IMPORTANCE OF YOUR OATH, SUPERMAN. BUT YOU SEE...
...MY ESCAPE FROM ULTRASPACE HAS MADE ME REALIZE THAT, MORE THAN ANYTHING, TIME IS OF THE ESSENCE.
THE ESSENCE OF *WHAT?*
THAT'S JUST IT, MS. LANE.
I'M NOT SURE. THE THINGS I SAW IN ULTRASPACE...
...I DON'T BELIEVE IT WAS MEANT TO BE PERCEIVED BY CREATURES AS SIMPLE AS I.
SIMPLE, DOCTOR? YOU'RE ONE OF THE MOST BRILLIANT MINDS OF THE ERA. SURELY YOU CAN'T THINK--
I ASSURE YOU, SUPERMAN, I AM FAR FROM HUMBLE OR MODEST ABOUT MY ACCOMPLISHMENTS, BUT THIS...
...SOME THINGS WE ARE NOT MEANT TO UNDERSTAND.
Y'KNOW, THERE ARE PEOPLE WHO SAY TIME IS A--
FLAT CIRCLE.
I'M SORRY?
"TIME IS A FLAT CIRCLE."
AHH, BUT THAT'S JUST IT, MS. LANE.
FLIP FLIP FLIP
IT'S NOT. TIME IS THE EXACT OPPOSITE OF THAT. IT'S A...
ROUND... SQUARE?
YES. THAT'S TIME.
TIME IS A ROUND SQUARE.

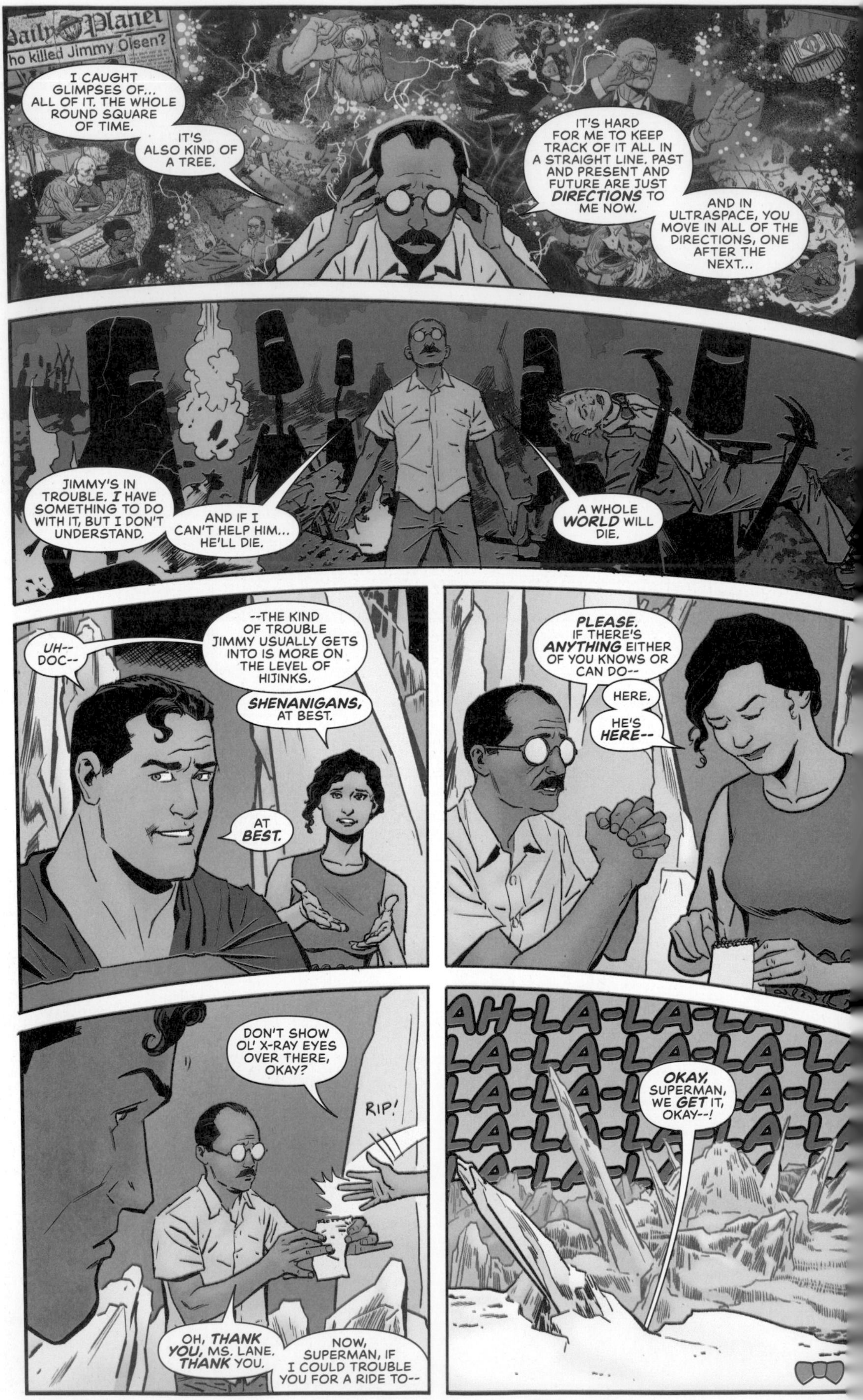
Daily Planet
Who killed Jimmy Olsen?
I CAUGHT GLIMPSES OF... ALL OF IT. THE WHOLE ROUND SQUARE OF TIME.
IT'S ALSO KIND OF A TREE.
IT'S HARD FOR ME TO KEEP TRACK OF IT ALL IN A STRAIGHT LINE. PAST AND PRESENT AND FUTURE ARE JUST DIRECTIONS TO ME NOW.
AND IN ULTRASPACE, YOU MOVE IN ALL OF THE DIRECTIONS, ONE AFTER THE NEXT...
JIMMY'S IN TROUBLE. I HAVE SOMETHING TO DO WITH IT, BUT I DON'T UNDERSTAND.
AND IF I CAN'T HELP HIM... HE'LL DIE.
A WHOLE WORLD WILL DIE.
UH-- DOC--
--THE KIND OF TROUBLE JIMMY USUALLY GETS INTO IS MORE ON THE LEVEL OF HIJINKS.
SHENANIGANS, AT BEST.
AT BEST.
PLEASE. IF THERE'S ANYTHING EITHER OF YOU KNOWS OR CAN DO--
HERE.
HE'S HERE--
DON'T SHOW OL' X-RAY EYES OVER THERE, OKAY?
RIP!
OH, THANK YOU, MS. LANE. THANK YOU.
NOW, SUPERMAN, IF I COULD TROUBLE YOU FOR A RIDE TO--
AH-LA-LA-LA
LA-LA-LA-LA-LA
LA-LA-LA-LA-LA
LA-LA-LA-LA-LA
OKAY, SUPERMAN, WE GET IT, OKAY--!

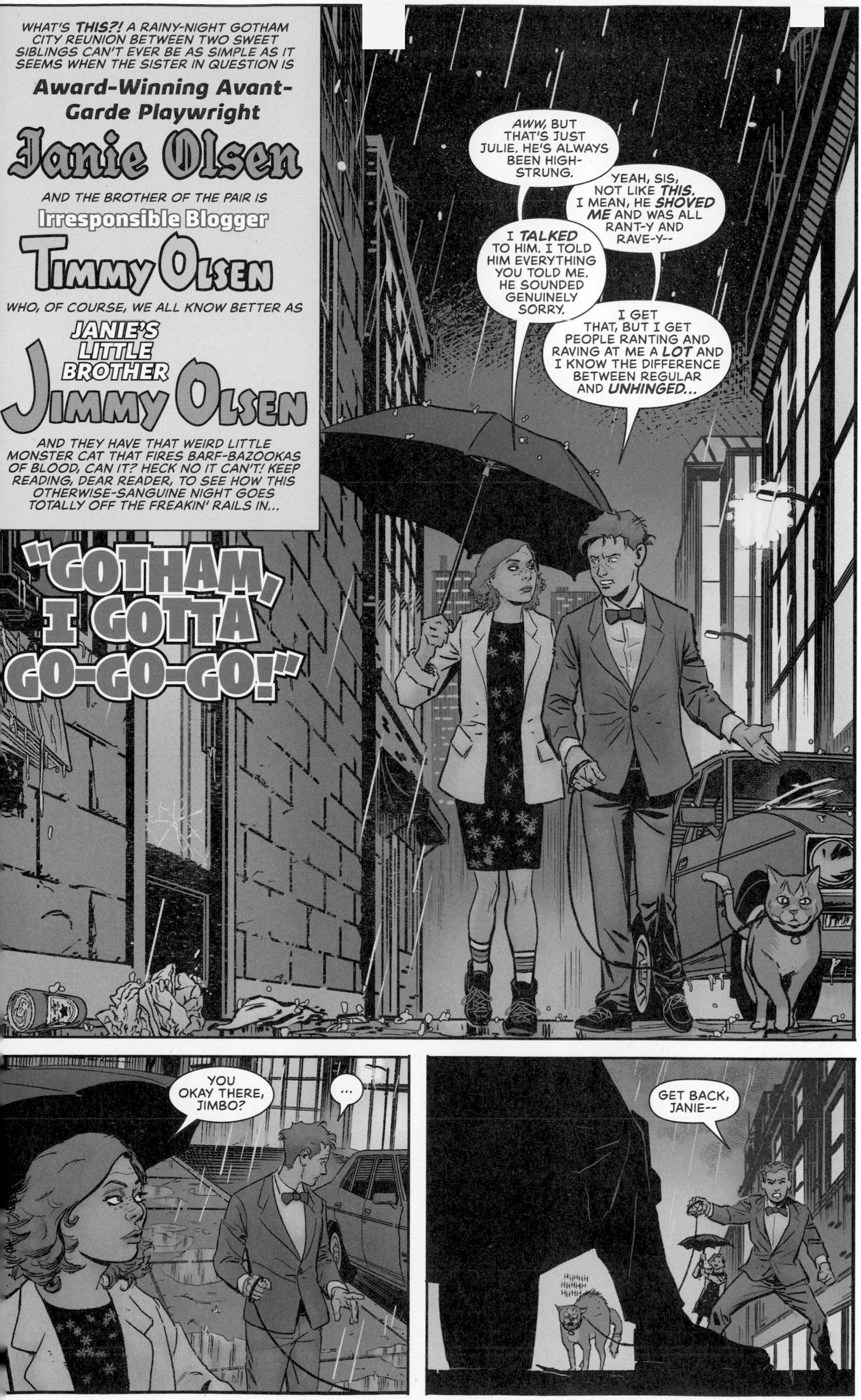
WHAT'S THIS?! A RAINY-NIGHT GOTHAM CITY REUNION BETWEEN TWO SWEET SIBLINGS CAN'T EVER BE AS SIMPLE AS IT SEEMS WHEN THE SISTER IN QUESTION IS
Award-Winning Avant-Garde Playwright
Janie Olsen
AND THE BROTHER OF THE PAIR IS
Irresponsible Blogger
TIMMY OLSEN
WHO, OF COURSE, WE ALL KNOW BETTER AS
JANIE'S LITTLE BROTHER
JIMMY OLSEN
AND THEY HAVE THAT WEIRD LITTLE MONSTER CAT THAT FIRES BARF-BAZOOKAS OF BLOOD, CAN IT? HECK NO IT CAN'T! KEEP READING, DEAR READER, TO SEE HOW THIS OTHERWISE-SANGUINE NIGHT GOES TOTALLY OFF THE FREAKIN' RAILS IN...
"GOTHAM, I GOTTA GO-GO-GO!"
AWW, BUT THAT'S JUST JULIE. HE'S ALWAYS BEEN HIGH-STRUNG.
YEAH, SIS, NOT LIKE THIS. I MEAN, HE SHOVED ME AND WAS ALL RANT-Y AND RAVE-Y--
I TALKED TO HIM. I TOLD HIM EVERYTHING YOU TOLD ME. HE SOUNDED GENUINELY SORRY.
I GET THAT, BUT I GET PEOPLE RANTING AND RAVING AT ME A LOT AND I KNOW THE DIFFERENCE BETWEEN REGULAR AND UNHINGED...
YOU OKAY THERE, JIMBO?
...
GET BACK, JANIE--

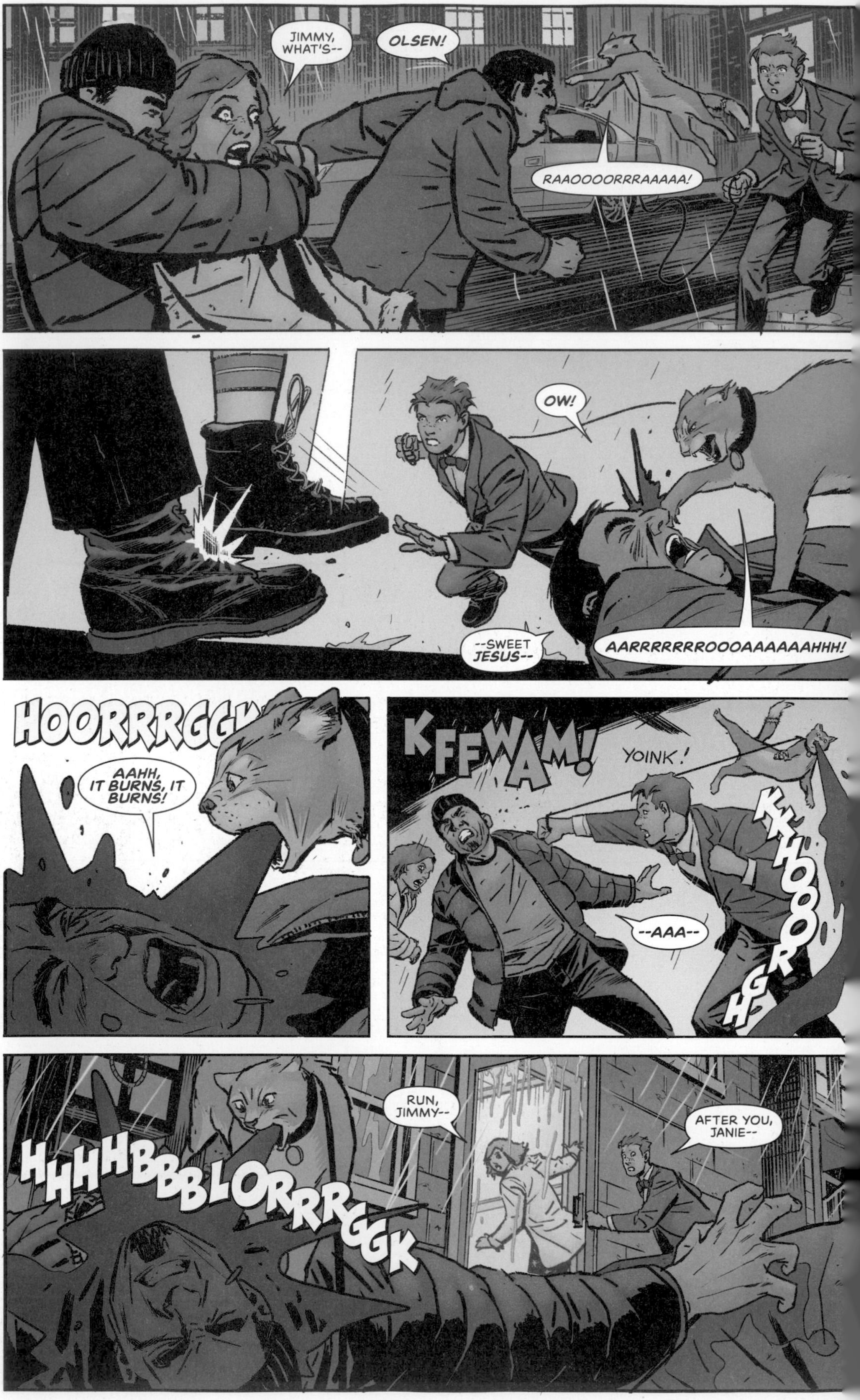
JIMMY, WHAT'S--
OLSEN!
RAAOOOORRRAAAAA!
OW!
--SWEET JESUS--
AARRRRRRROOOAAAAAAHHH!
HOORRRRGGK
AAHH, IT BURNS, IT BURNS!
KFFWAM!
YOINK!
KKHOOOORGH
--AAA--
HHHHBBBLORRRGGK
RUN, JIMMY--
AFTER YOU, JANIE--

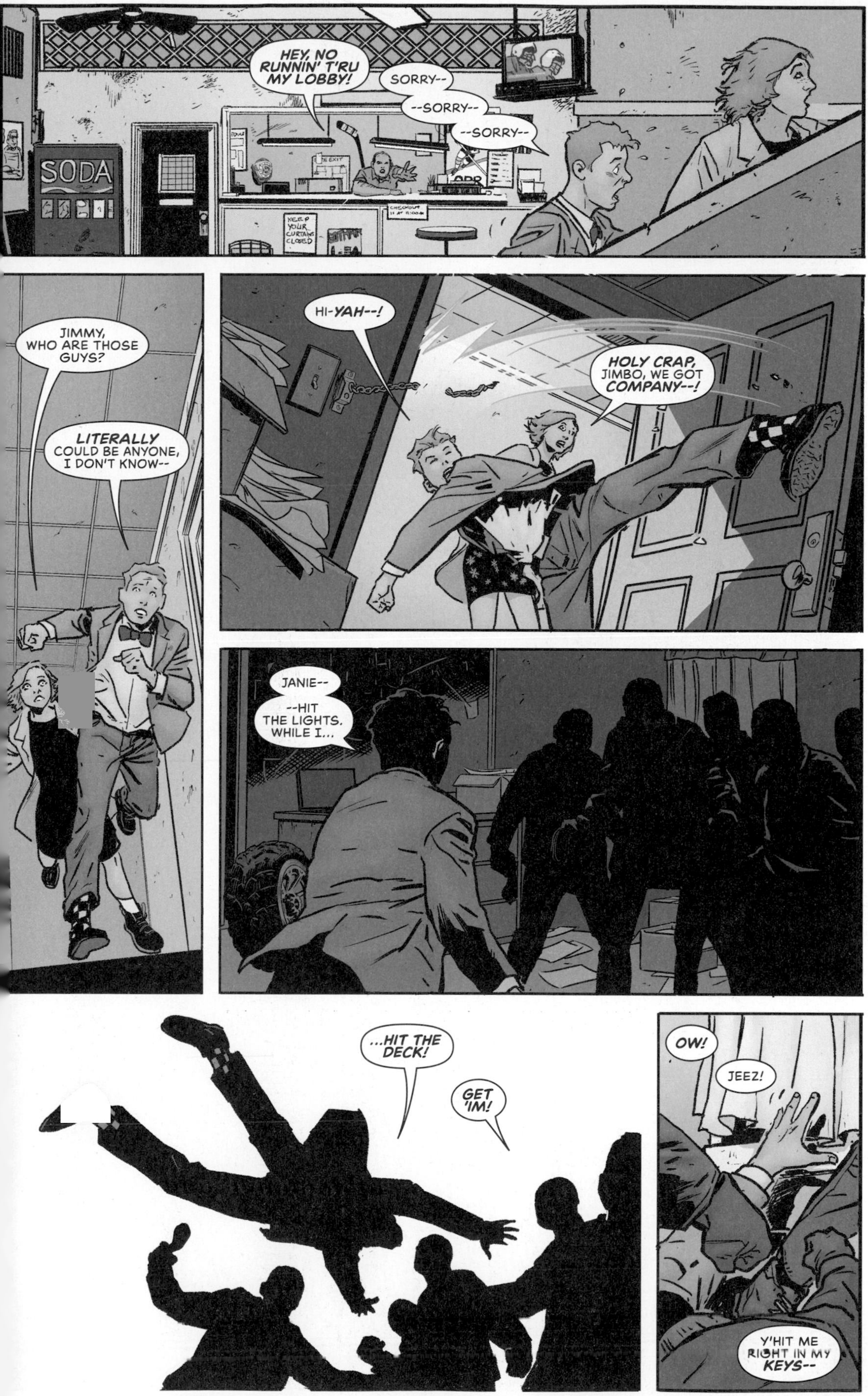

SODA
HEY, NO RUNNIN' T'RU MY LOBBY!
SORRY--
--SORRY--
--SORRY--
JIMMY, WHO ARE THOSE GUYS?
LITERALLY COULD BE ANYONE, I DON'T KNOW--
HI-YAH--!
HOLY CRAP, JIMBO, WE GOT COMPANY--!
JANIE--
--HIT THE LIGHTS. WHILE I...
...HIT THE DECK!
GET 'IM!
OW!
JEEZ!
Y'HIT ME RIGHT IN MY KEYS--

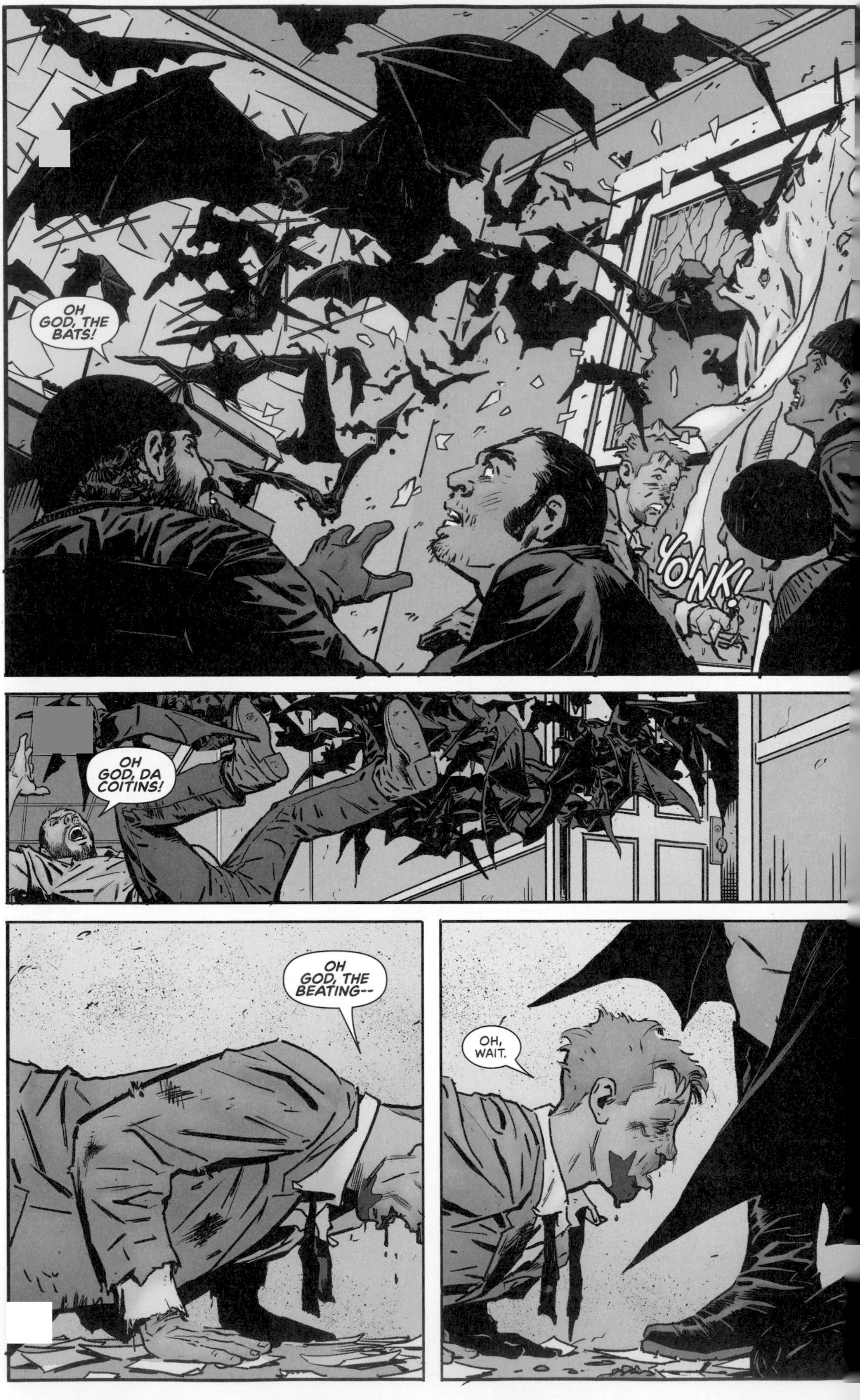
OH GOD, THE BATS!
YONK!
OH GOD, DA COITINS!
OH GOD, THE BEATING--
OH, WAIT.

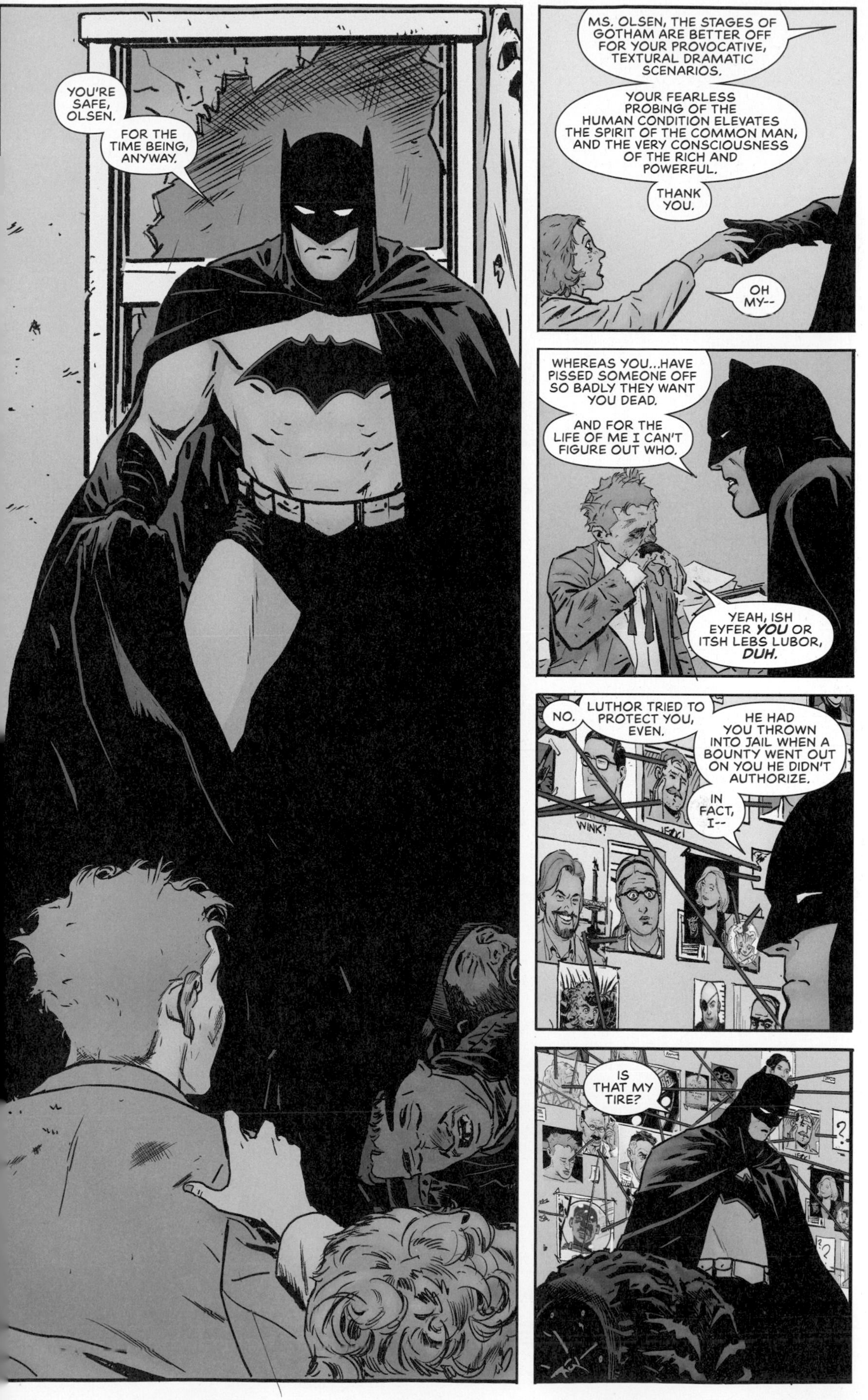
YOU'RE SAFE, OLSEN.
FOR THE TIME BEING, ANYWAY.
MS. OLSEN, THE STAGES OF GOTHAM ARE BETTER OFF FOR YOUR PROVOCATIVE, TEXTURAL DRAMATIC SCENARIOS.
YOUR FEARLESS PROBING OF THE HUMAN CONDITION ELEVATES THE SPIRIT OF THE COMMON MAN, AND THE VERY CONSCIOUSNESS OF THE RICH AND POWERFUL.
THANK YOU.
OH MY--
WHEREAS YOU...HAVE PISSED SOMEONE OFF SO BADLY THEY WANT YOU DEAD.
AND FOR THE LIFE OF ME I CAN'T FIGURE OUT WHO.
YEAH, ISH EYFER *YOU* OR ITSH LEBS LUBOR, ***DUH.***
NO.
LUTHOR TRIED TO PROTECT YOU, EVEN.
HE HAD YOU THROWN INTO JAIL WHEN A BOUNTY WENT OUT ON YOU HE DIDN'T AUTHORIZE.
IN FACT, I--
IS THAT MY TIRE?

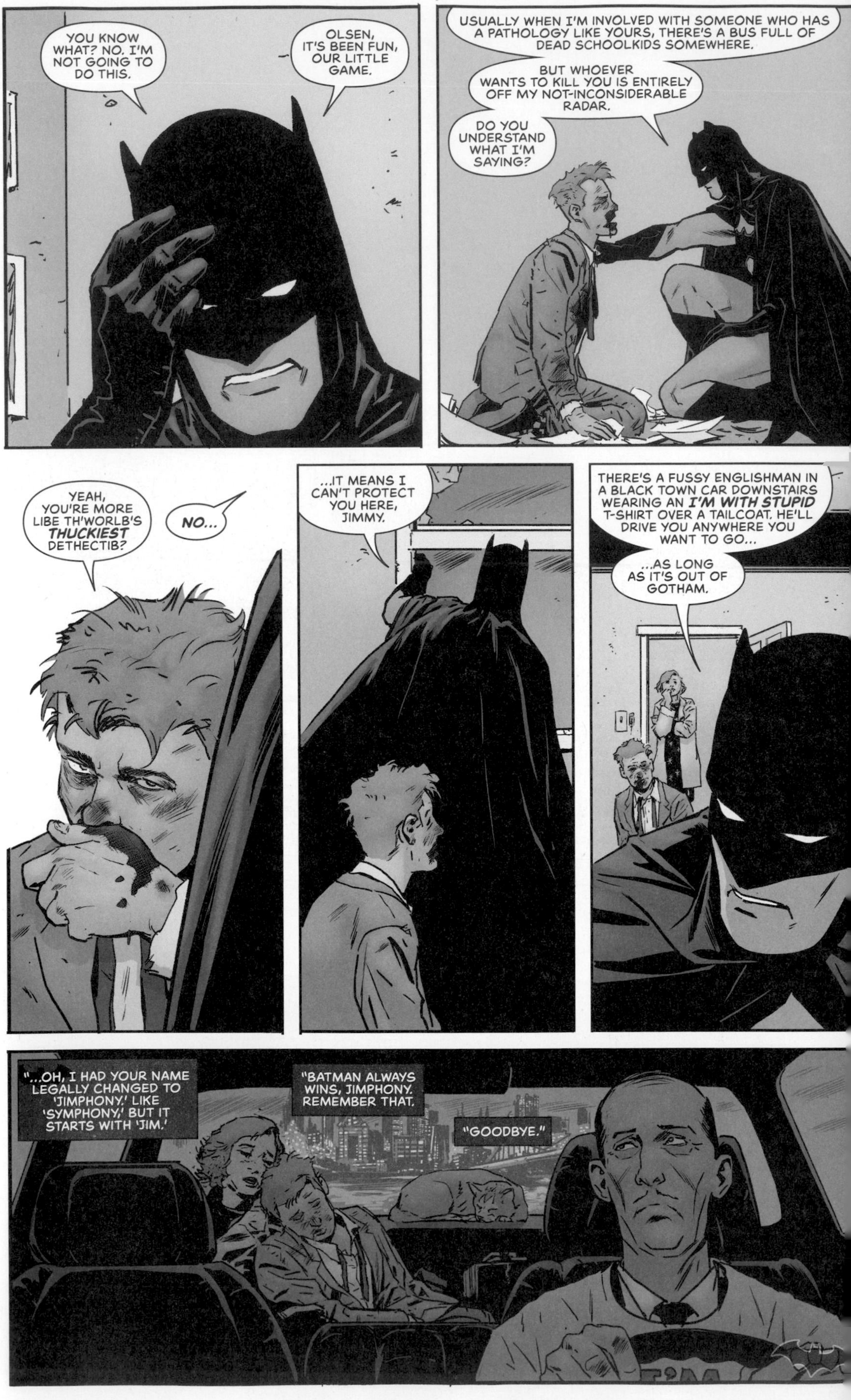
YOU KNOW WHAT? NO. I'M NOT GOING TO DO THIS.
OLSEN, IT'S BEEN FUN, OUR LITTLE GAME.
USUALLY WHEN I'M INVOLVED WITH SOMEONE WHO HAS A PATHOLOGY LIKE YOURS, THERE'S A BUS FULL OF DEAD SCHOOLKIDS SOMEWHERE.
BUT WHOEVER WANTS TO KILL YOU IS ENTIRELY OFF MY NOT-INCONSIDERABLE RADAR.
DO YOU UNDERSTAND WHAT I'M SAYING?
YEAH, YOU'RE MORE LIBE TH'WORLB'S *THUCKIEST* DETHECTIB?
NO...
...IT MEANS I CAN'T PROTECT YOU HERE, JIMMY.
THERE'S A FUSSY ENGLISHMAN IN A BLACK TOWN CAR DOWNSTAIRS WEARING AN *I'M WITH STUPID* T-SHIRT OVER A TAILCOAT. HE'LL DRIVE YOU ANYWHERE YOU WANT TO GO...
...AS LONG AS IT'S OUT OF GOTHAM.
"...OH, I HAD YOUR NAME LEGALLY CHANGED TO 'JIMPHONY,' LIKE 'SYMPHONY,' BUT IT STARTS WITH 'JIM.'
"BATMAN ALWAYS WINS, JIMPHONY. REMEMBER THAT.
"GOODBYE."

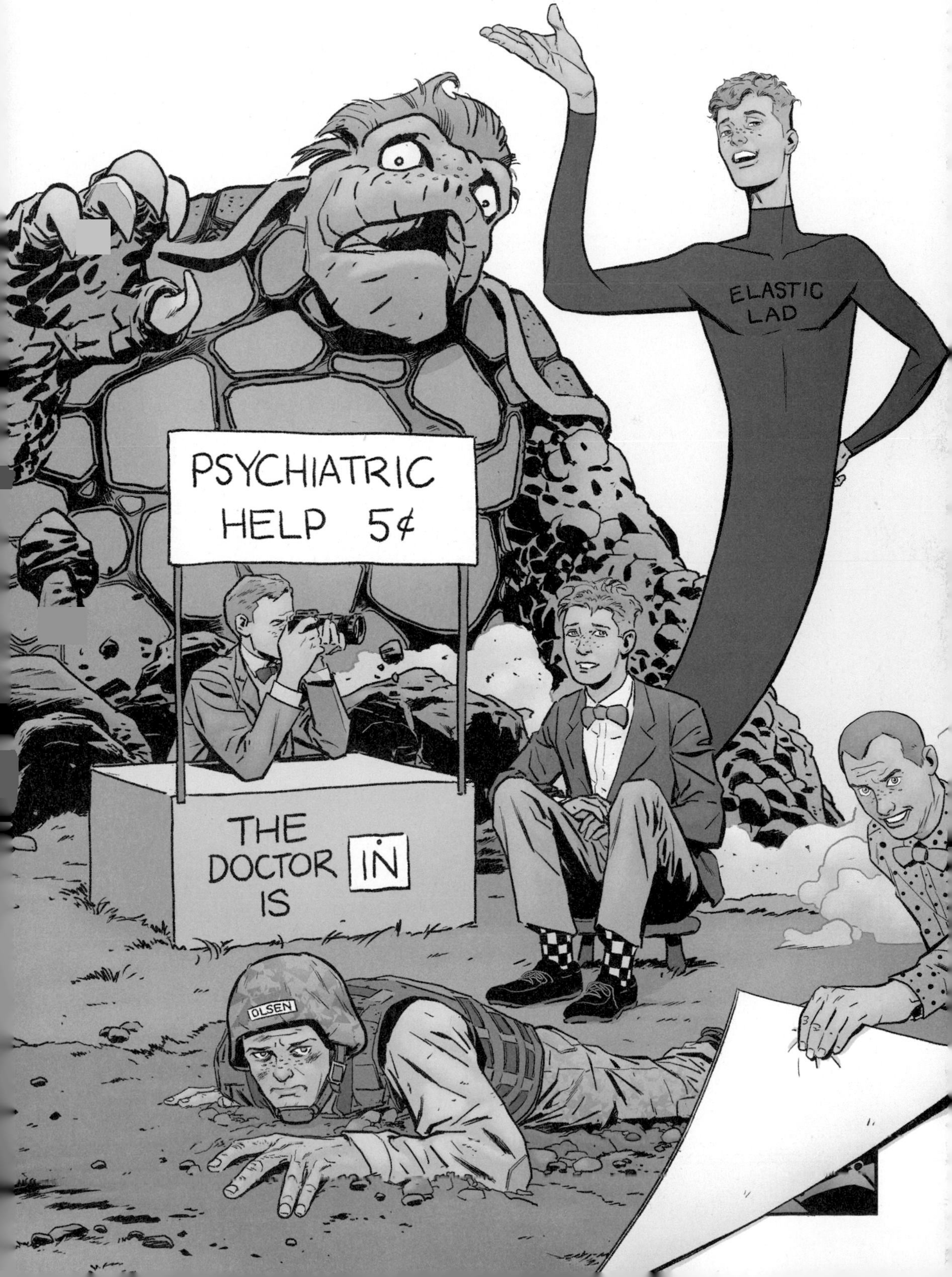
ELASTIC LAD
PSYCHIATRIC HELP 5¢
THE DOCTOR IS IN
OLSEN

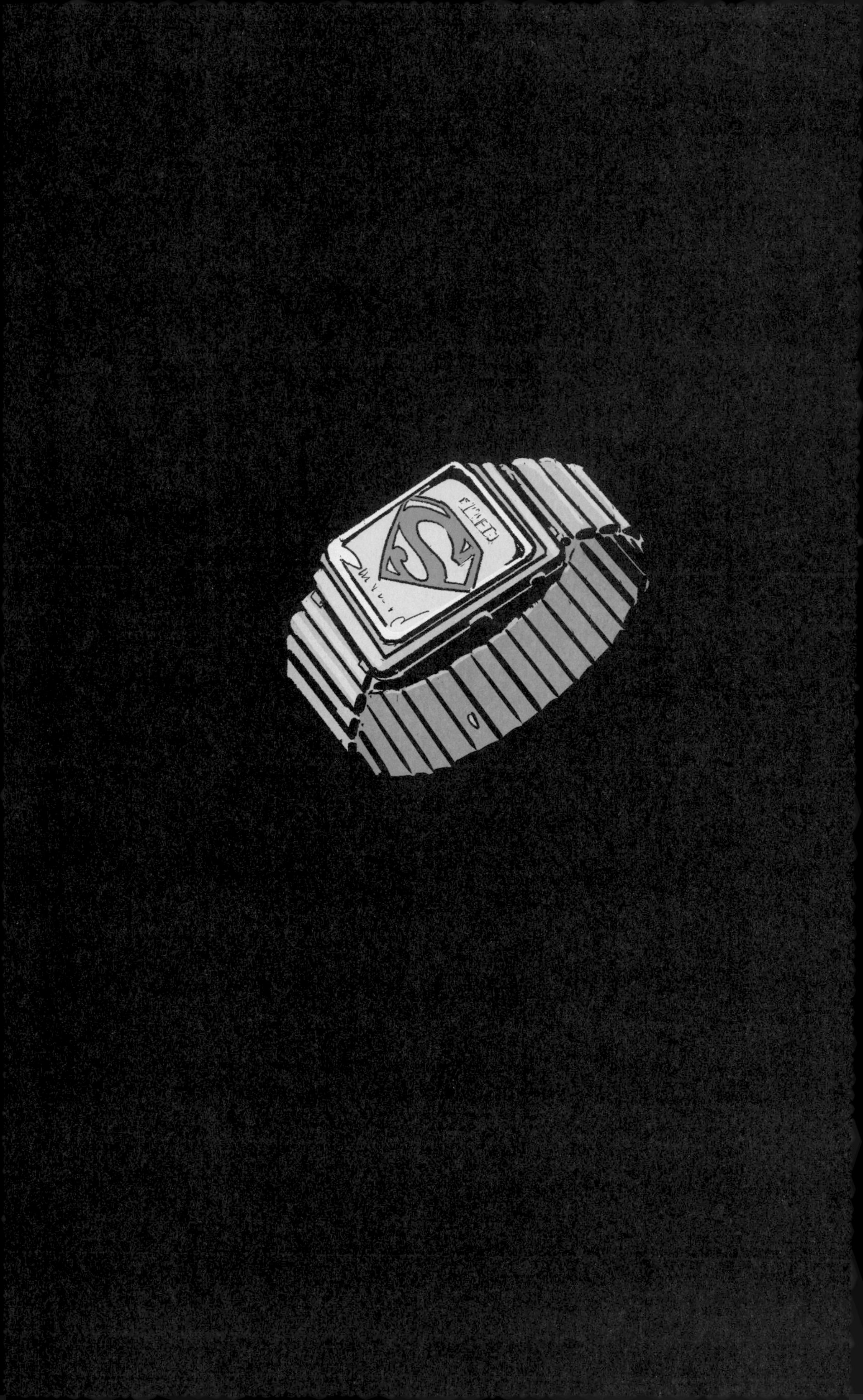

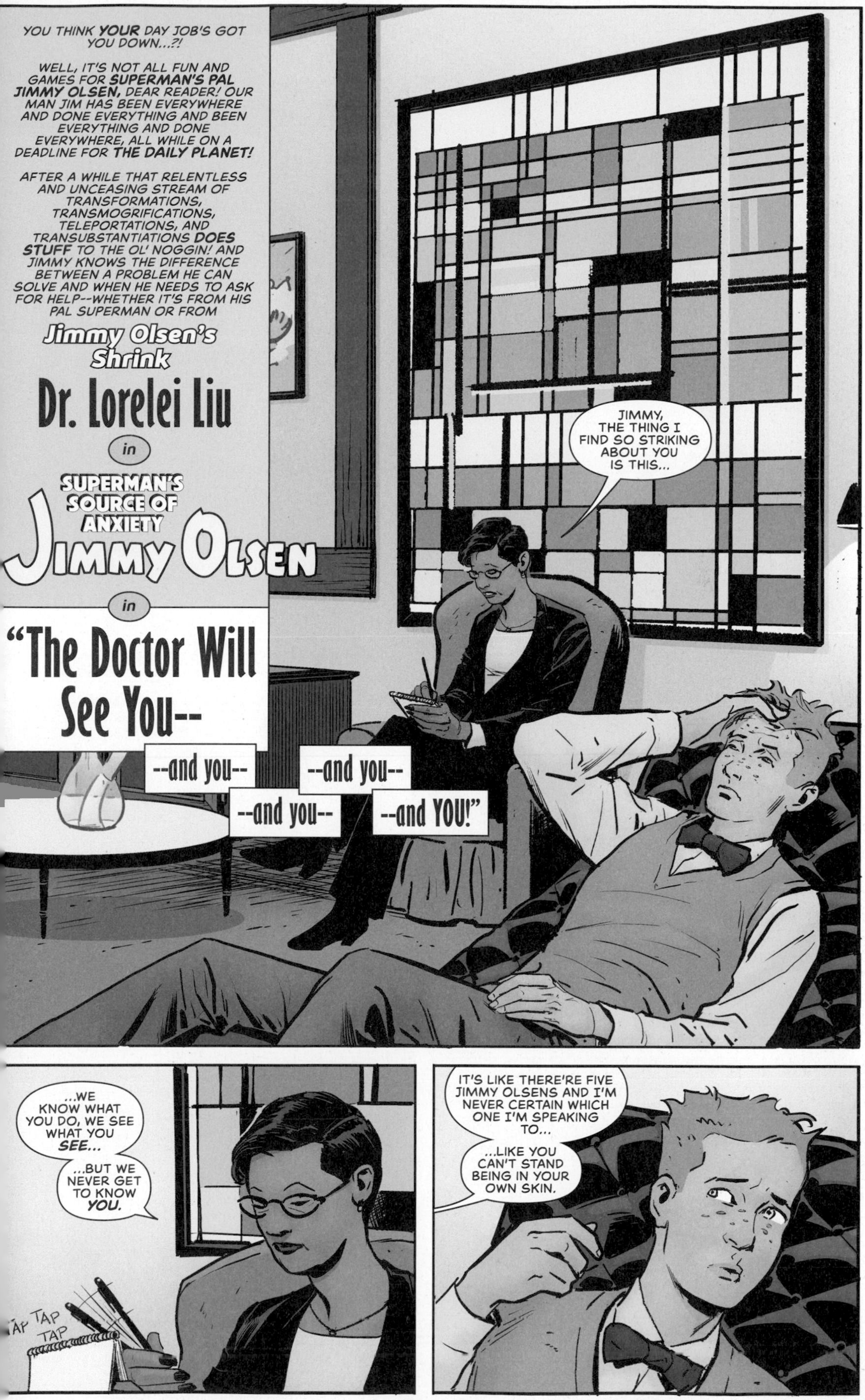
YOU THINK YOUR DAY JOB'S GOT YOU DOWN...?!
WELL, IT'S NOT ALL FUN AND GAMES FOR SUPERMAN'S PAL JIMMY OLSEN, DEAR READER! OUR MAN JIM HAS BEEN EVERYWHERE AND DONE EVERYTHING AND BEEN EVERYTHING AND DONE EVERYWHERE, ALL WHILE ON A DEADLINE FOR THE DAILY PLANET!
AFTER A WHILE THAT RELENTLESS AND UNCEASING STREAM OF TRANSFORMATIONS, TRANSMOGRIFICATIONS, TELEPORTATIONS, AND TRANSUBSTANTIATIONS DOES STUFF TO THE OL' NOGGIN! AND JIMMY KNOWS THE DIFFERENCE BETWEEN A PROBLEM HE CAN SOLVE AND WHEN HE NEEDS TO ASK FOR HELP--WHETHER IT'S FROM HIS PAL SUPERMAN OR FROM
Jimmy Olsen's Shrink
Dr. Lorelei Liu
in
SUPERMAN'S SOURCE OF ANXIETY JIMMY OLSEN
in
"The Doctor Will See You--
--and you--
--and you--
--and you--
--and YOU!"
JIMMY, THE THING I FIND SO STRIKING ABOUT YOU IS THIS...
...WE KNOW WHAT YOU DO, WE SEE WHAT YOU SEE...
...BUT WE NEVER GET TO KNOW YOU.
TAP TAP TAP
IT'S LIKE THERE'RE FIVE JIMMY OLSENS AND I'M NEVER CERTAIN WHICH ONE I'M SPEAKING TO...
...LIKE YOU CAN'T STAND BEING IN YOUR OWN SKIN.

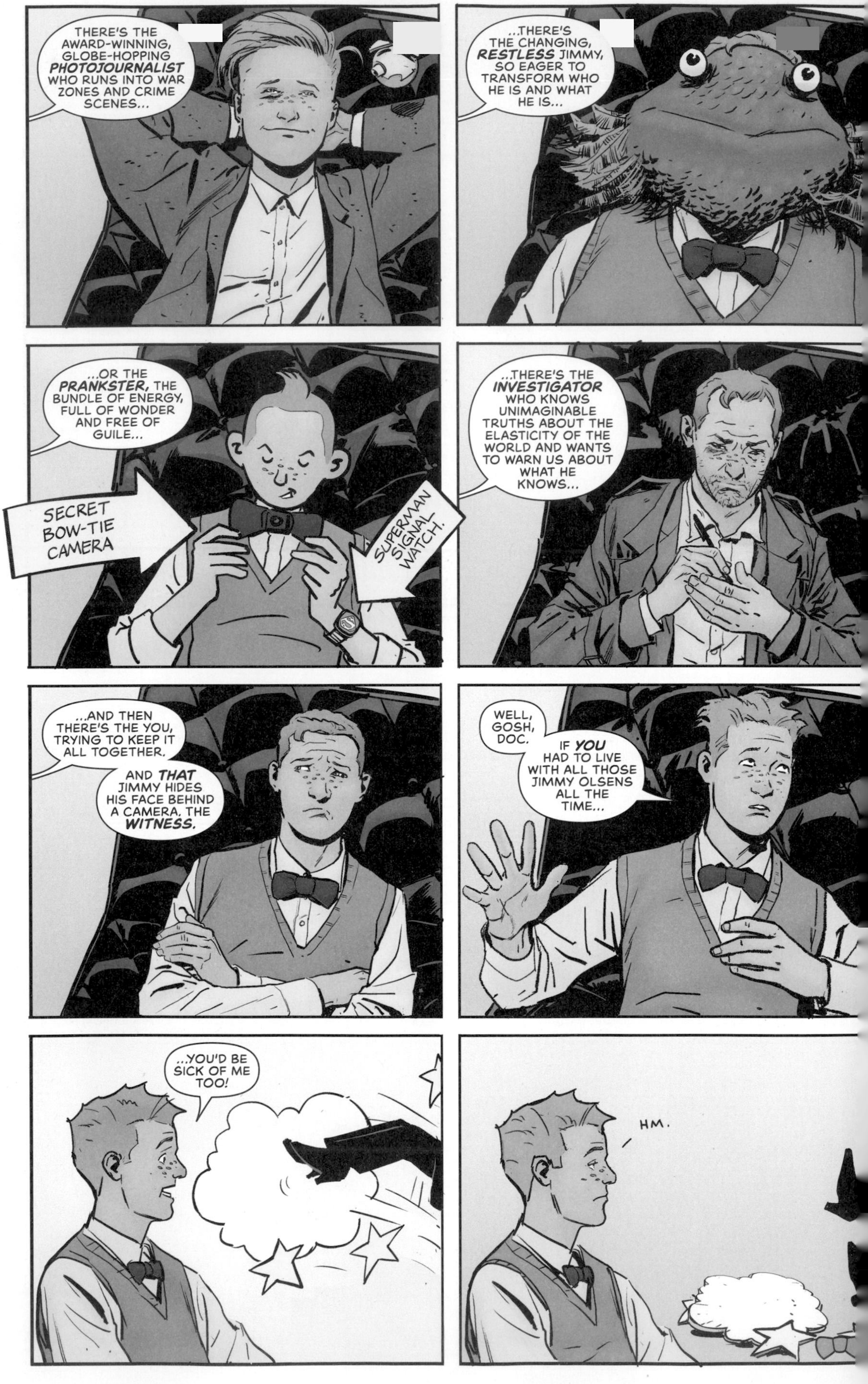
THERE'S THE AWARD-WINNING, GLOBE-HOPPING PHOTOJOURNALIST WHO RUNS INTO WAR ZONES AND CRIME SCENES...
...THERE'S THE CHANGING, RESTLESS JIMMY, SO EAGER TO TRANSFORM WHO HE IS AND WHAT HE IS...
...OR THE PRANKSTER, THE BUNDLE OF ENERGY, FULL OF WONDER AND FREE OF GUILE...
SECRET BOW-TIE CAMERA
SUPERMAN SIGNAL WATCH.
...THERE'S THE INVESTIGATOR WHO KNOWS UNIMAGINABLE TRUTHS ABOUT THE ELASTICITY OF THE WORLD AND WANTS TO WARN US ABOUT WHAT HE KNOWS...
...AND THEN THERE'S THE YOU, TRYING TO KEEP IT ALL TOGETHER.
AND THAT JIMMY HIDES HIS FACE BEHIND A CAMERA. THE WITNESS.
WELL, GOSH, DOC.
IF YOU HAD TO LIVE WITH ALL THOSE JIMMY OLSENS ALL THE TIME...
...YOU'D BE SICK OF ME TOO!
HM.

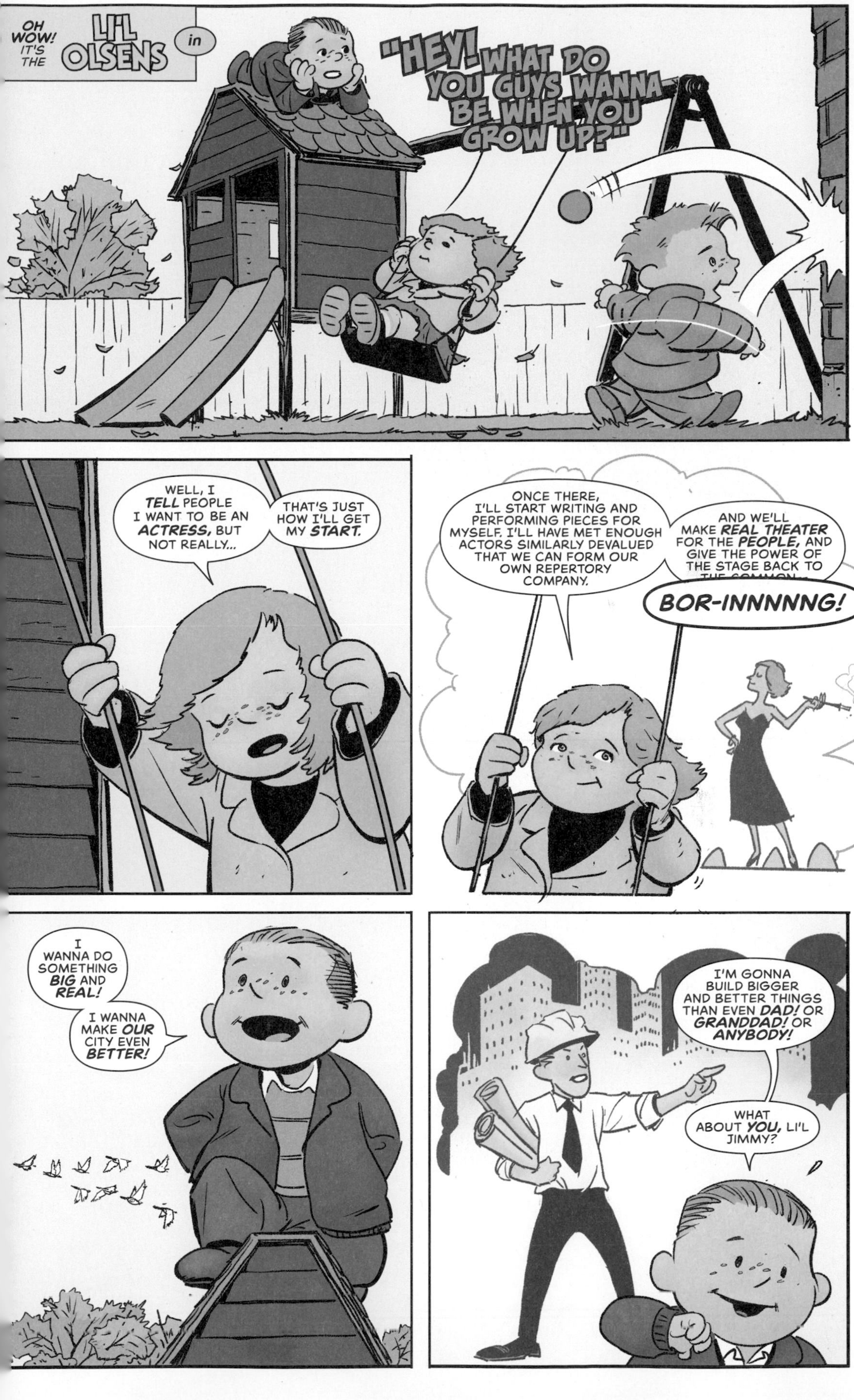
OH WOW! IT'S THE LI'L OLSENS in
"HEY! WHAT DO YOU GUYS WANNA BE WHEN YOU GROW UP?"
WELL, I TELL PEOPLE I WANT TO BE AN ACTRESS, BUT NOT REALLY...
THAT'S JUST HOW I'LL GET MY START.
ONCE THERE, I'LL START WRITING AND PERFORMING PIECES FOR MYSELF. I'LL HAVE MET ENOUGH ACTORS SIMILARLY DEVALUED THAT WE CAN FORM OUR OWN REPERTORY COMPANY.
AND WE'LL MAKE REAL THEATER FOR THE PEOPLE, AND GIVE THE POWER OF THE STAGE BACK TO
BOR-INNNNNG!
I WANNA DO SOMETHING BIG AND REAL!
I WANNA MAKE OUR CITY EVEN BETTER!
I'M GONNA BUILD BIGGER AND BETTER THINGS THAN EVEN DAD! OR GRANDDAD! OR ANYBODY!
WHAT ABOUT YOU, LI'L JIMMY?

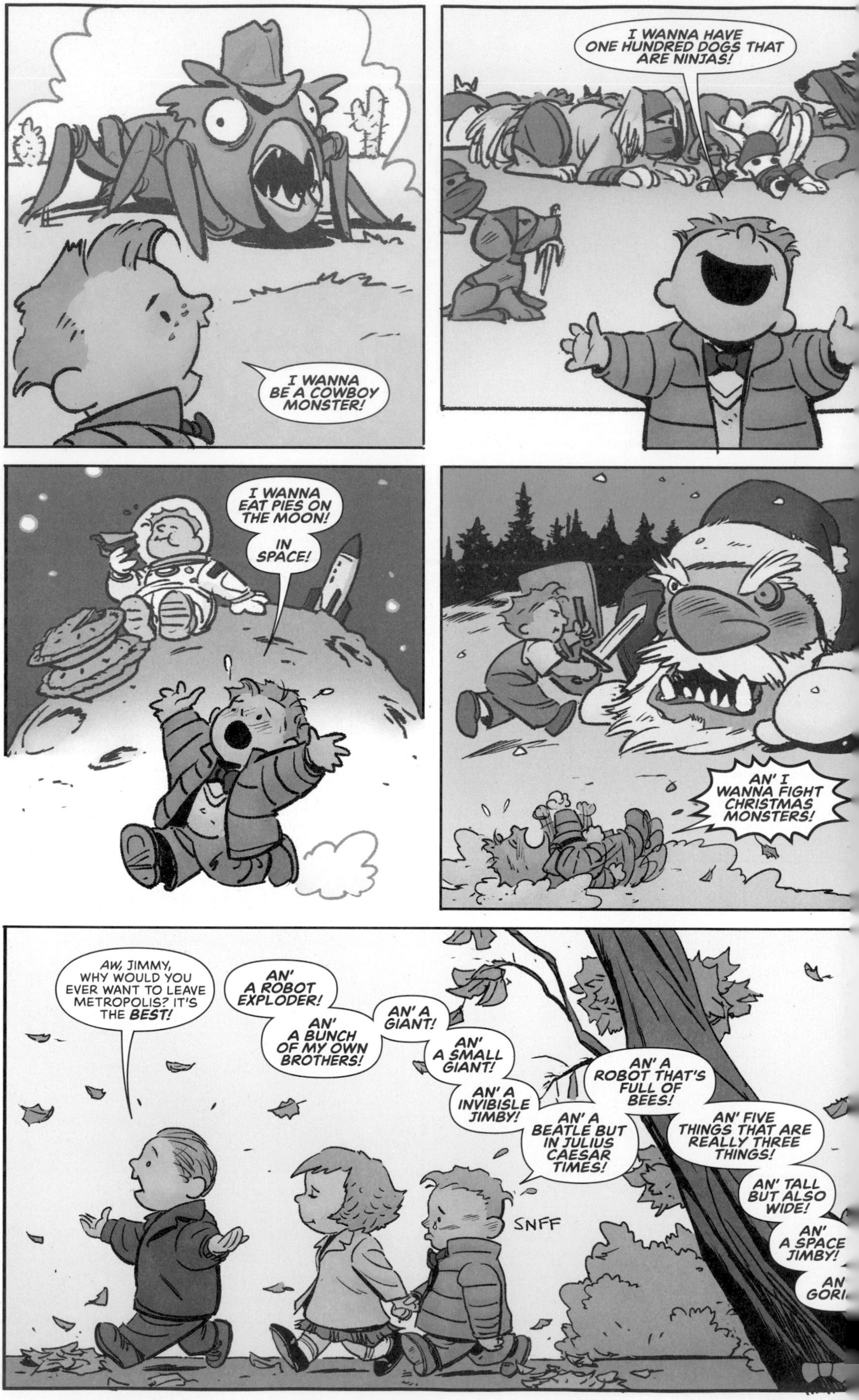
I WANNA BE A COWBOY MONSTER!
I WANNA HAVE ONE HUNDRED DOGS THAT ARE NINJAS!
I WANNA EAT PIES ON THE MOON!
IN SPACE!
AN' I WANNA FIGHT CHRISTMAS MONSTERS!
AW, JIMMY, WHY WOULD YOU EVER WANT TO LEAVE METROPOLIS? IT'S THE BEST!
AN' A ROBOT EXPLODER!
AN' A BUNCH OF MY OWN BROTHERS!
AN' A GIANT!
AN' A SMALL GIANT!
AN' A INVIBISLE JIMBY!
AN' A ROBOT THAT'S FULL OF BEES!
AN' A BEATLE BUT IN JULIUS CAESAR TIMES!
AN' FIVE THINGS THAT ARE REALLY THREE THINGS!
SNFF
AN' TALL BUT ALSO WIDE!
AN' A SPACE JIMBY!

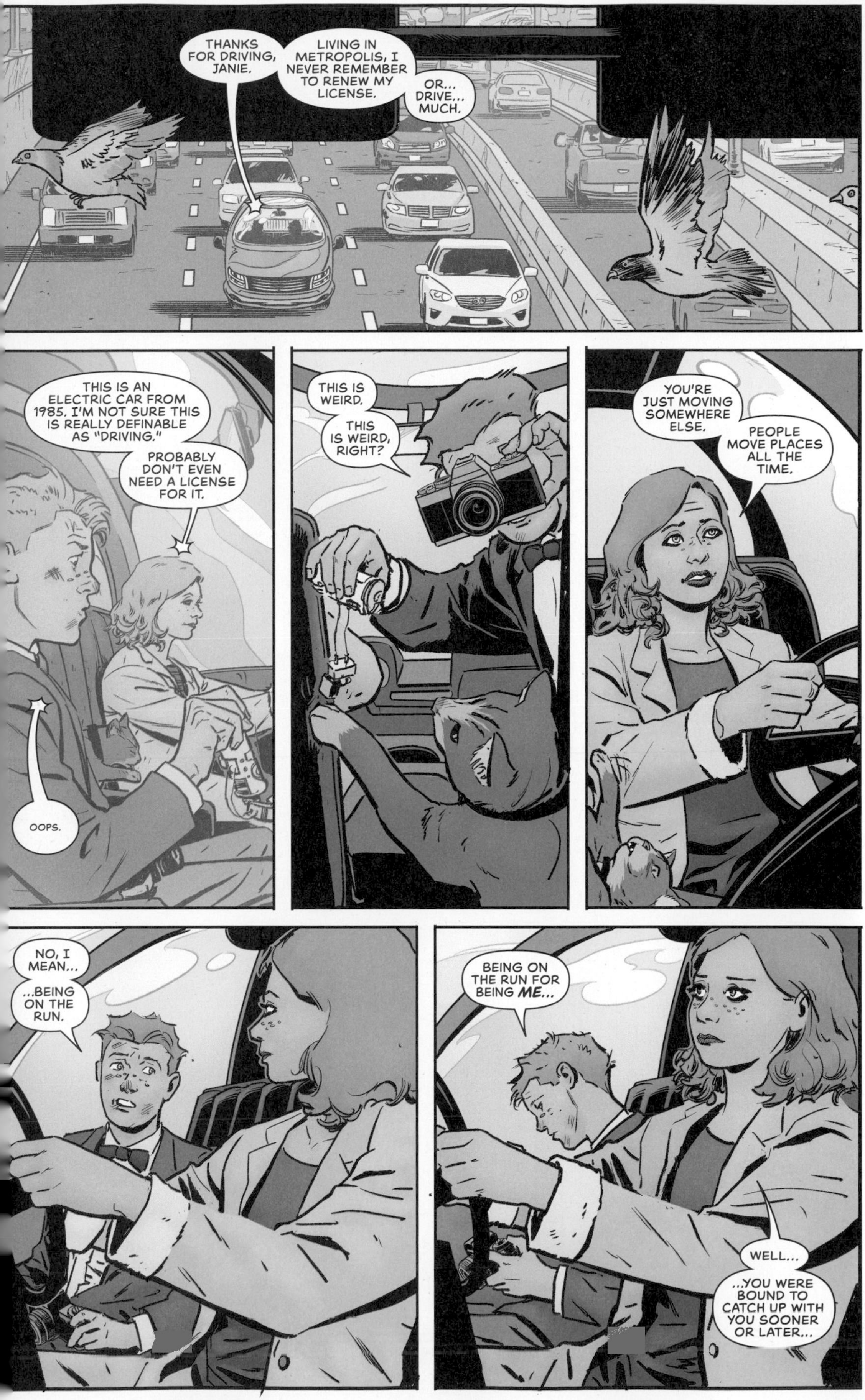
THANKS FOR DRIVING, JANIE.
LIVING IN METROPOLIS, I NEVER REMEMBER TO RENEW MY LICENSE.
OR... DRIVE... MUCH.
THIS IS AN ELECTRIC CAR FROM 1985. I'M NOT SURE THIS IS REALLY DEFINABLE AS "DRIVING."
PROBABLY DON'T EVEN NEED A LICENSE FOR IT.
OOPS.
THIS IS WEIRD.
THIS IS WEIRD, RIGHT?
YOU'RE JUST MOVING SOMEWHERE ELSE.
PEOPLE MOVE PLACES ALL THE TIME.
NO, I MEAN...
...BEING ON THE RUN.
BEING ON THE RUN FOR BEING *ME*...
WELL...
...YOU WERE BOUND TO CATCH UP WITH YOU SOONER OR LATER...

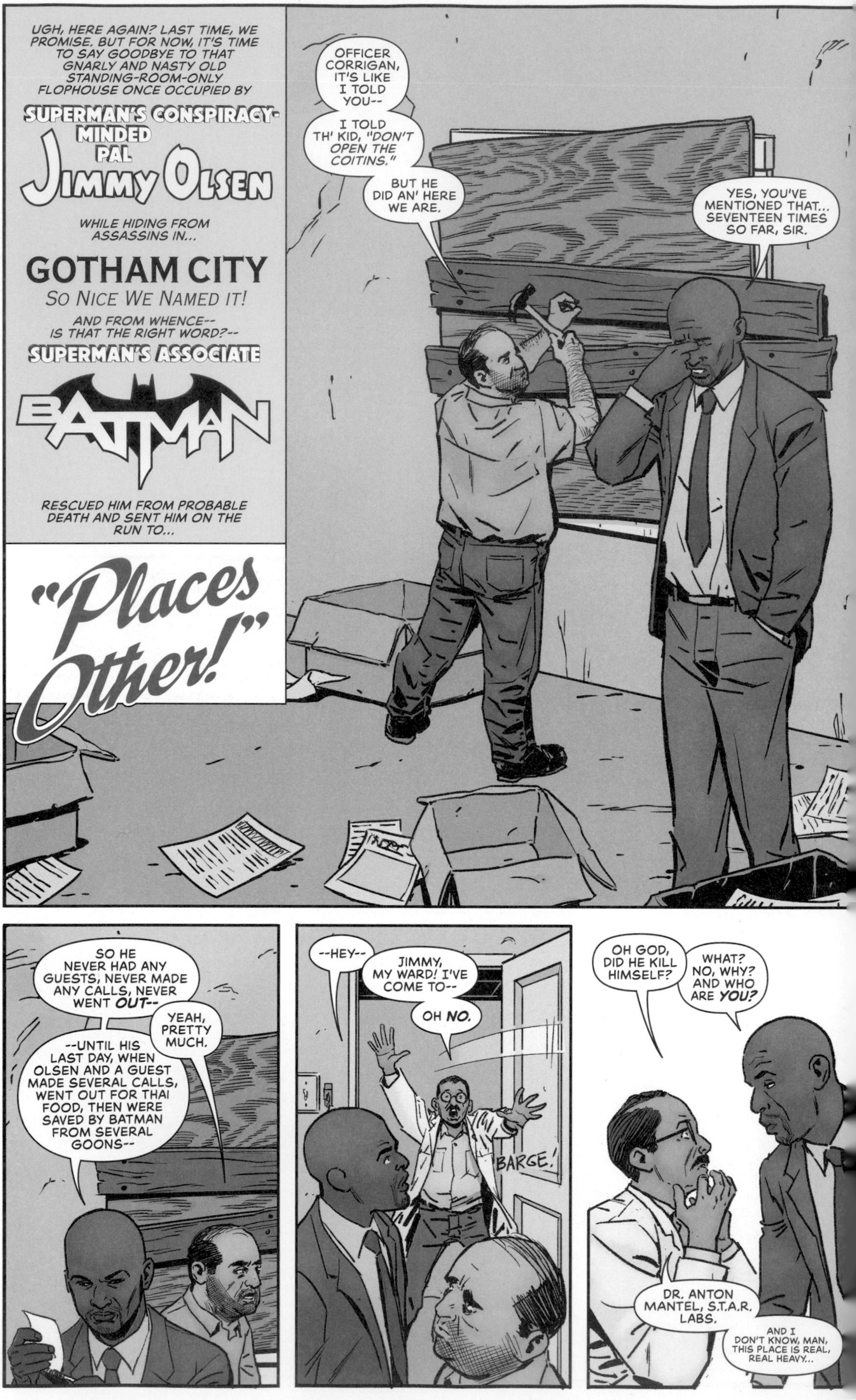

UGH, HERE AGAIN? LAST TIME, WE PROMISE. BUT FOR NOW, IT'S TIME TO SAY GOODBYE TO THAT GNARLY AND NASTY OLD STANDING-ROOM-ONLY FLOPHOUSE ONCE OCCUPIED BY
SUPERMAN'S CONSPIRACY-MINDED PAL
JIMMY OLSEN
WHILE HIDING FROM ASSASSINS IN...
GOTHAM CITY
SO NICE WE NAMED IT!
AND FROM WHENCE-- IS THAT THE RIGHT WORD?--
SUPERMAN'S ASSOCIATE
BATMAN
RESCUED HIM FROM PROBABLE DEATH AND SENT HIM ON THE RUN TO...
"Places Other!"
OFFICER CORRIGAN, IT'S LIKE I TOLD YOU--
I TOLD TH' KID, "DON'T OPEN THE COITINS."
BUT HE DID AN' HERE WE ARE.
YES, YOU'VE MENTIONED THAT... SEVENTEEN TIMES SO FAR, SIR.
SO HE NEVER HAD ANY GUESTS, NEVER MADE ANY CALLS, NEVER WENT OUT--
YEAH, PRETTY MUCH.
--UNTIL HIS LAST DAY, WHEN OLSEN AND A GUEST MADE SEVERAL CALLS, WENT OUT FOR THAI FOOD, THEN WERE SAVED BY BATMAN FROM SEVERAL GOONS--
--HEY--
JIMMY, MY WARD! I'VE COME TO--
OH NO.
BARGE!
OH GOD, DID HE KILL HIMSELF?
WHAT? NO, WHY? AND WHO ARE YOU?
DR. ANTON MANTEL, S.T.A.R. LABS.
AND I DON'T KNOW, MAN, THIS PLACE IS REAL, REAL HEAVY...

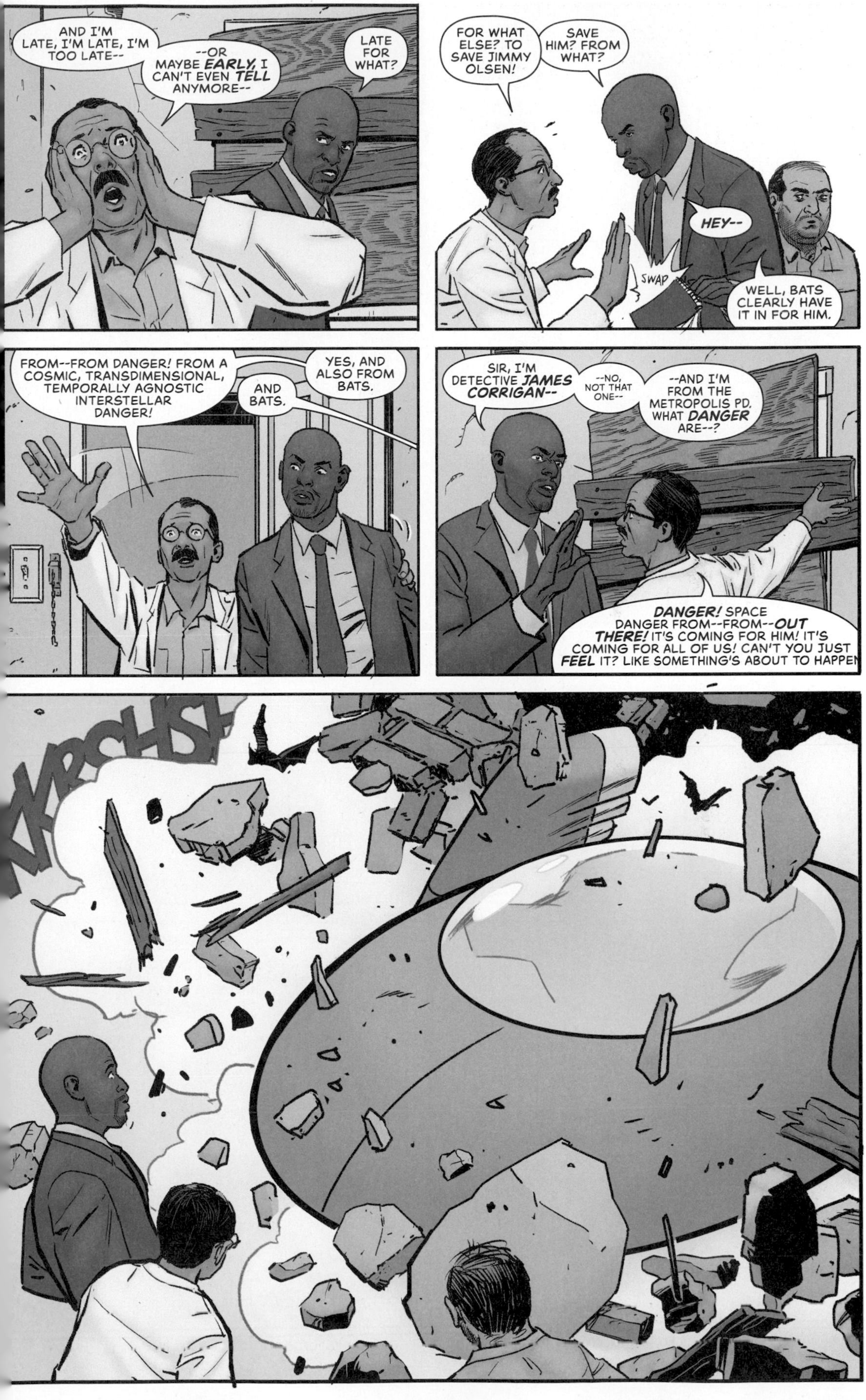
AND I'M LATE, I'M LATE, I'M TOO LATE--
--OR MAYBE EARLY, I CAN'T EVEN TELL ANYMORE--
LATE FOR WHAT?
FOR WHAT ELSE? TO SAVE JIMMY OLSEN!
SAVE HIM? FROM WHAT?
HEY--
SWAP
WELL, BATS CLEARLY HAVE IT IN FOR HIM.
FROM--FROM DANGER! FROM A COSMIC, TRANSDIMENSIONAL, TEMPORALLY AGNOSTIC INTERSTELLAR DANGER!
YES, AND ALSO FROM BATS.
AND BATS.
SIR, I'M DETECTIVE JAMES CORRIGAN--
--NO, NOT THAT ONE--
--AND I'M FROM THE METROPOLIS PD. WHAT DANGER ARE--?
DANGER! SPACE DANGER FROM--FROM--OUT THERE! IT'S COMING FOR HIM! IT'S COMING FOR ALL OF US! CAN'T YOU JUST FEEL IT? LIKE SOMETHING'S ABOUT TO HAPPEN

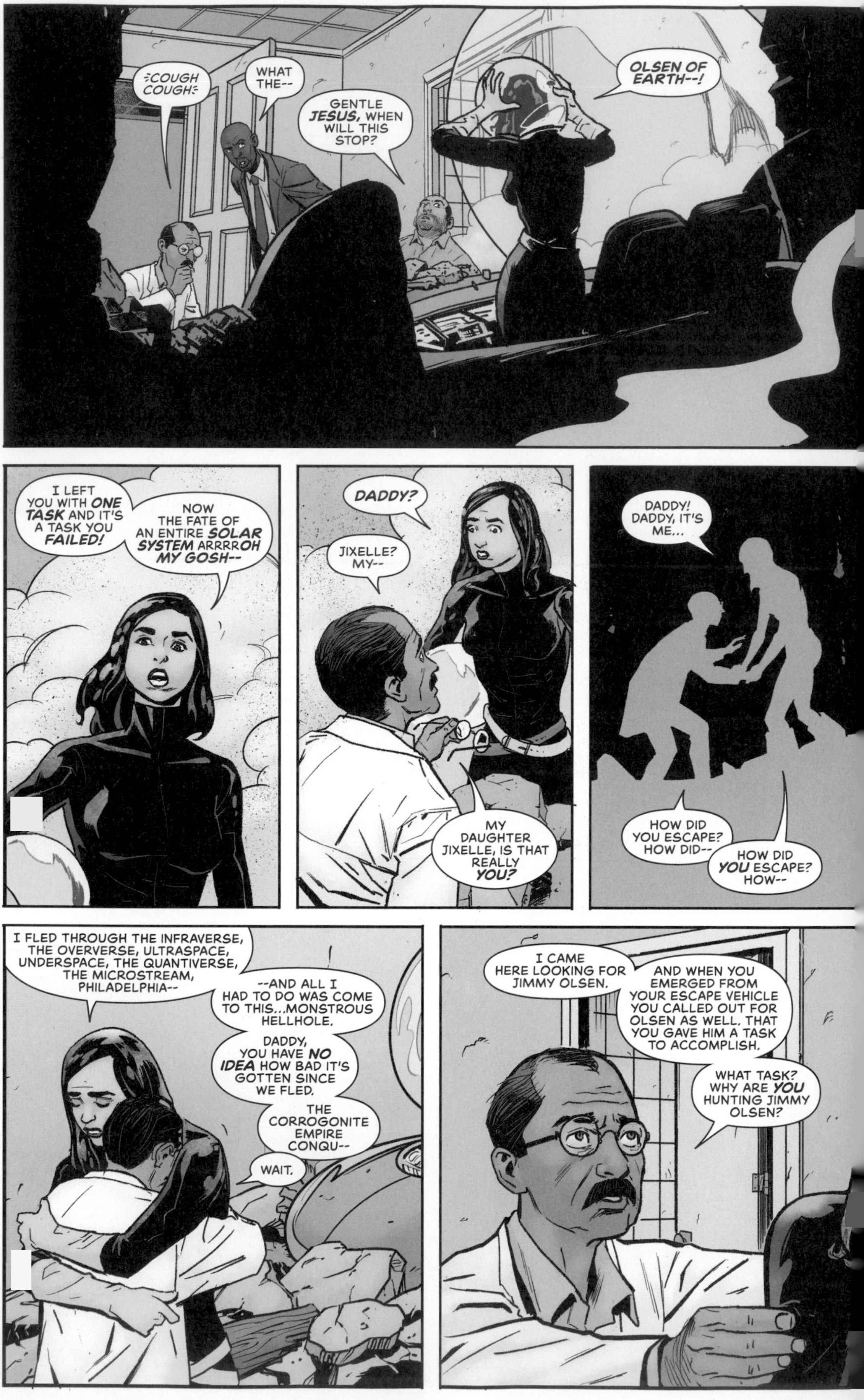

COUGH COUGH
WHAT THE--
GENTLE JESUS, WHEN WILL THIS STOP?
OLSEN OF EARTH--!
I LEFT YOU WITH ONE TASK AND IT'S A TASK YOU FAILED!
NOW THE FATE OF AN ENTIRE SOLAR SYSTEM ARRRROH MY GOSH--
DADDY?
JIXELLE? MY--
MY DAUGHTER JIXELLE, IS THAT REALLY YOU?
DADDY! DADDY, IT'S ME...
HOW DID YOU ESCAPE? HOW DID--
HOW DID YOU ESCAPE? HOW--
I FLED THROUGH THE INFRAVERSE, THE OVERVERSE, ULTRASPACE, UNDERSPACE, THE QUANTIVERSE, THE MICROSTREAM, PHILADELPHIA--
--AND ALL I HAD TO DO WAS COME TO THIS...MONSTROUS HELLHOLE.
DADDY, YOU HAVE NO IDEA HOW BAD IT'S GOTTEN SINCE WE FLED.
THE CORROGONITE EMPIRE CONQU--
WAIT.
I CAME HERE LOOKING FOR JIMMY OLSEN.
AND WHEN YOU EMERGED FROM YOUR ESCAPE VEHICLE YOU CALLED OUT FOR OLSEN AS WELL. THAT YOU GAVE HIM A TASK TO ACCOMPLISH.
WHAT TASK? WHY ARE YOU HUNTING JIMMY OLSEN?

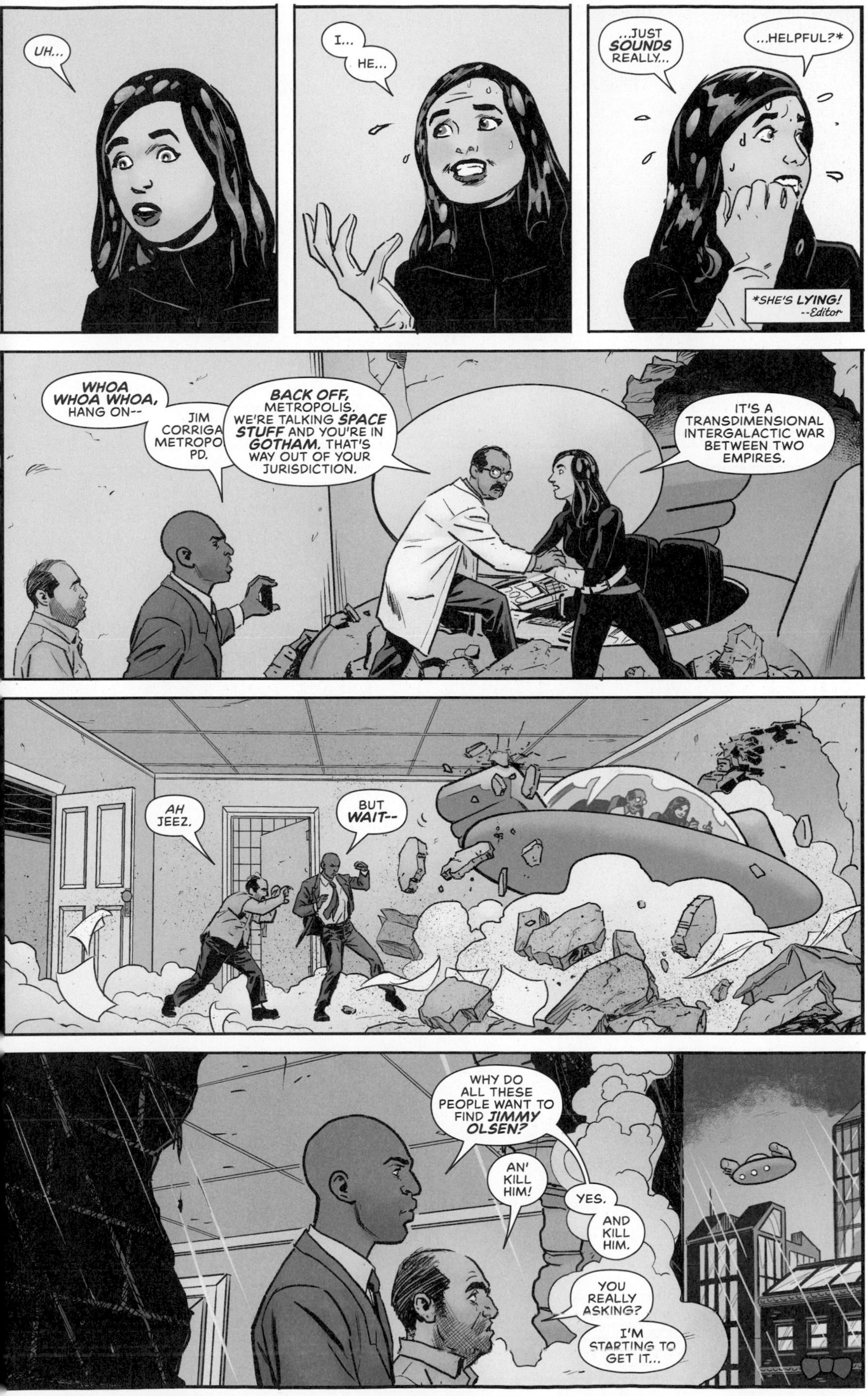
UH...
I...
HE...
...JUST SOUNDS REALLY...
...HELPFUL?*
*SHE'S LYING! --Editor
WHOA WHOA WHOA, HANG ON--
JIM CORRIGA METROPO PD.
BACK OFF, METROPOLIS. WE'RE TALKING SPACE STUFF AND YOU'RE IN GOTHAM. THAT'S WAY OUT OF YOUR JURISDICTION.
IT'S A TRANSDIMENSIONAL INTERGALACTIC WAR BETWEEN TWO EMPIRES.
AH JEEZ.
BUT WAIT--
WHY DO ALL THESE PEOPLE WANT TO FIND JIMMY OLSEN?
AN' KILL HIM!
YES.
AND KILL HIM.
YOU REALLY ASKING?
I'M STARTING TO GET IT...

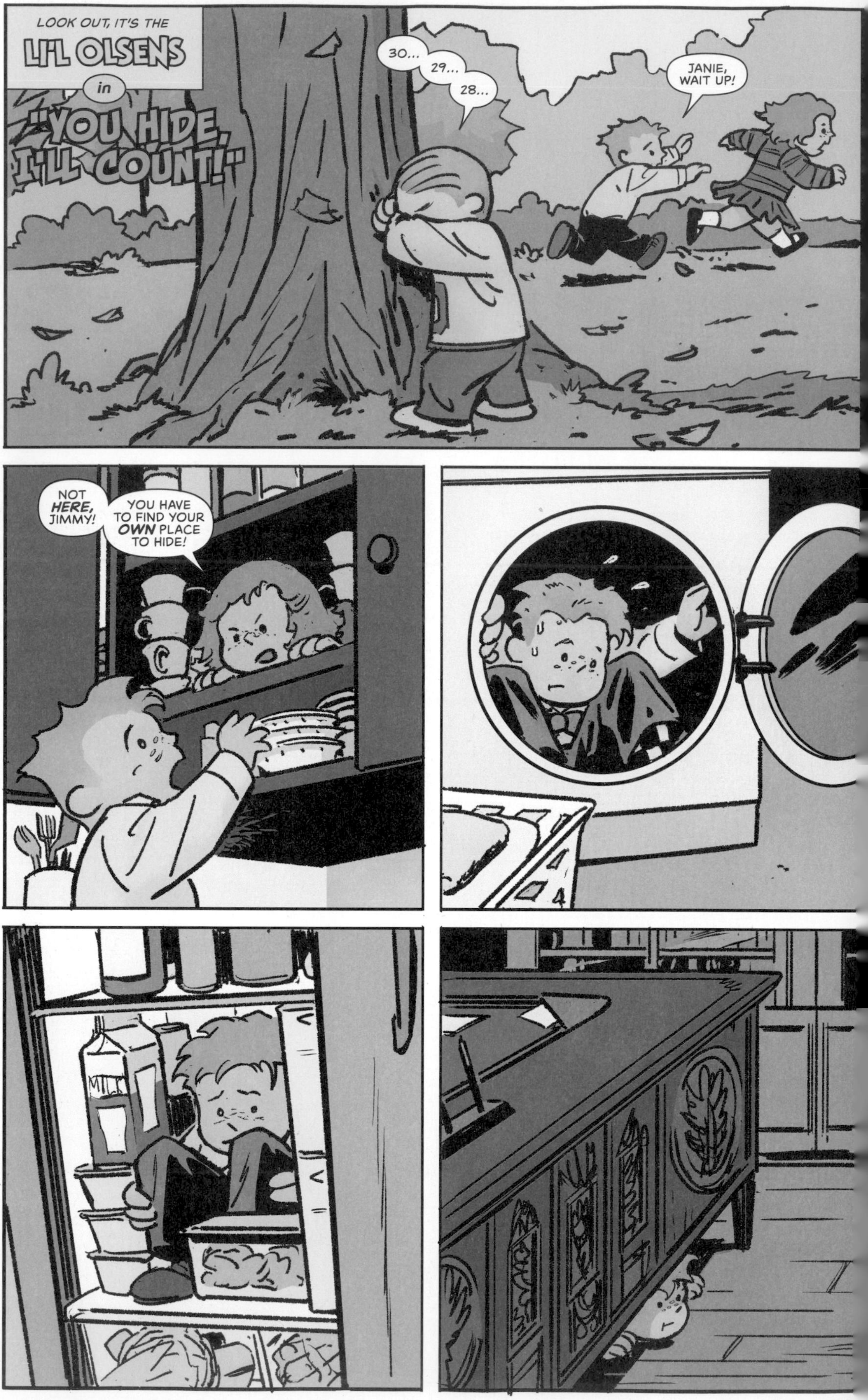
LOOK OUT, IT'S THE
LI'L OLSENS
in
"YOU HIDE, I'LL COUNT!"
30...
29...
28...
JANIE, WAIT UP!
NOT HERE, JIMMY!
YOU HAVE TO FIND YOUR OWN PLACE TO HIDE!
MILK

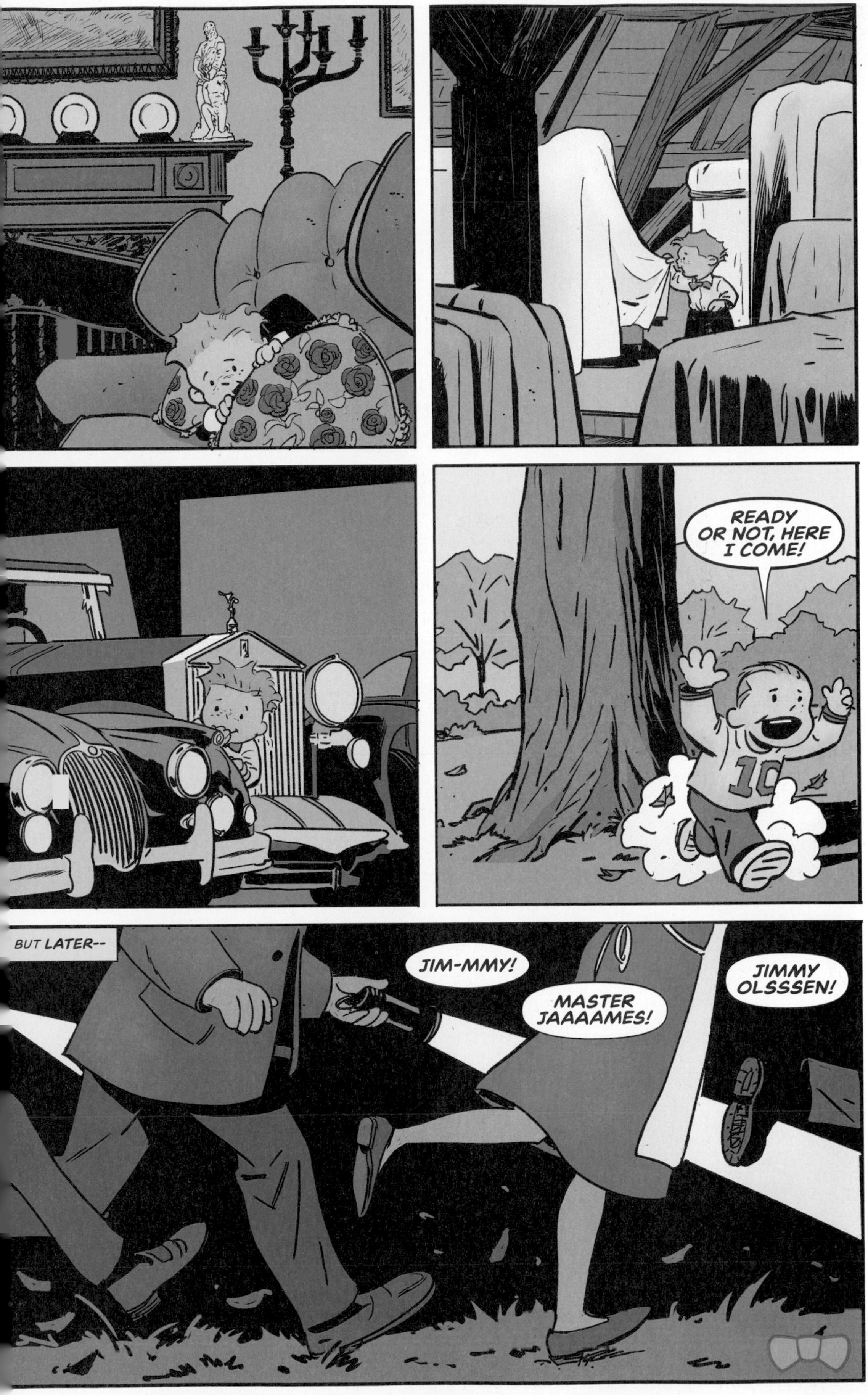
READY OR NOT, HERE I COME!
BUT LATER--
JIM-MMY!
MASTER JAAAAMES!
JIMMY OLSSSEN!

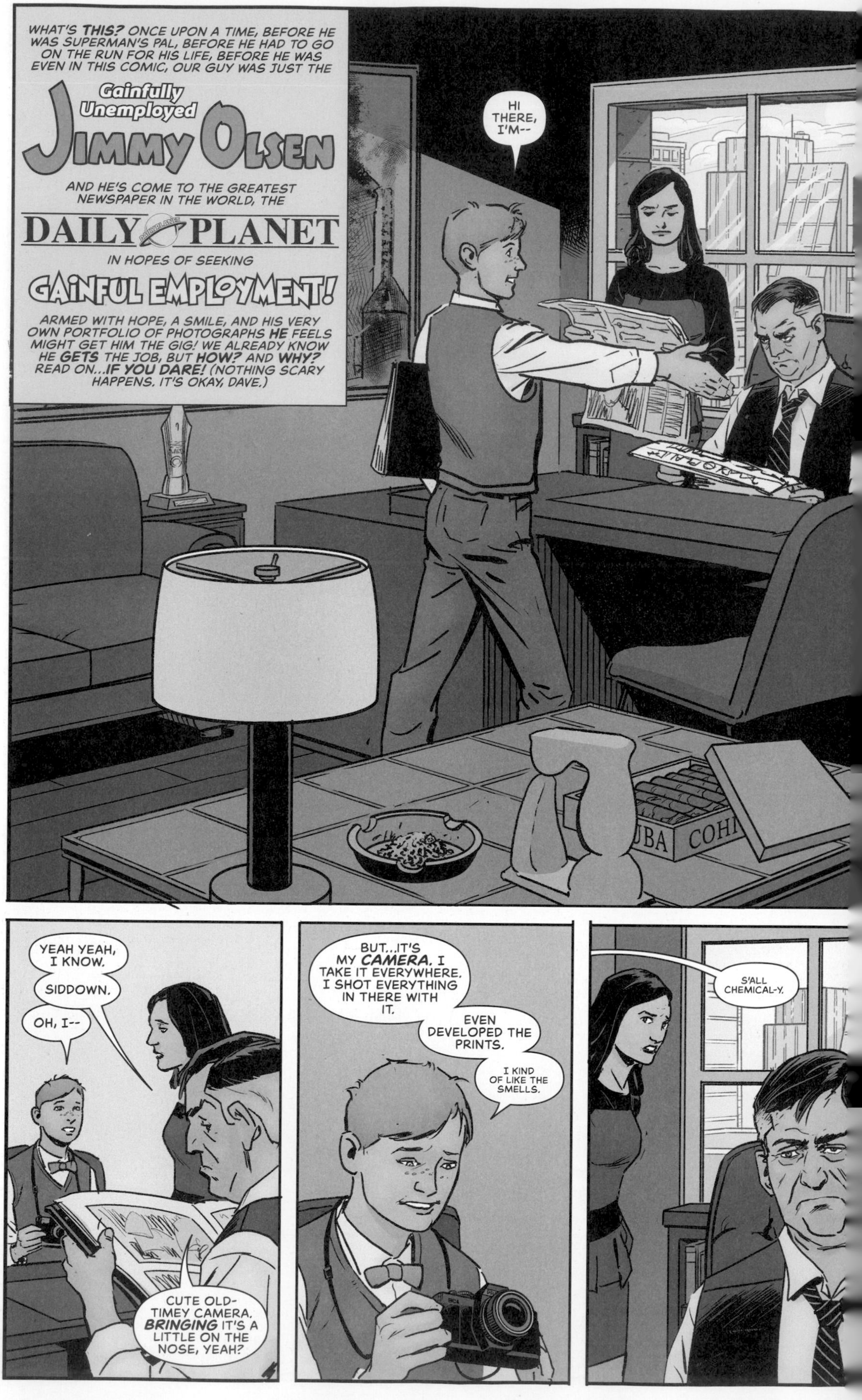
WHAT'S THIS? ONCE UPON A TIME, BEFORE HE WAS SUPERMAN'S PAL, BEFORE HE HAD TO GO ON THE RUN FOR HIS LIFE, BEFORE HE WAS EVEN IN THIS COMIC, OUR GUY WAS JUST THE
Gainfully Unemployed
JIMMY OLSEN
AND HE'S COME TO THE GREATEST NEWSPAPER IN THE WORLD, THE
DAILY PLANET
IN HOPES OF SEEKING
GAINFUL EMPLOYMENT!
ARMED WITH HOPE, A SMILE, AND HIS VERY OWN PORTFOLIO OF PHOTOGRAPHS HE FEELS MIGHT GET HIM THE GIG! WE ALREADY KNOW HE GETS THE JOB, BUT HOW? AND WHY? READ ON...IF YOU DARE! (NOTHING SCARY HAPPENS. IT'S OKAY, DAVE.)
HI THERE, I'M--
UBA COHI
YEAH YEAH, I KNOW.
SIDDOWN.
OH, I--
CUTE OLD-TIMEY CAMERA. BRINGING IT'S A LITTLE ON THE NOSE, YEAH?
BUT...IT'S MY CAMERA. I TAKE IT EVERYWHERE. I SHOT EVERYTHING IN THERE WITH IT.
EVEN DEVELOPED THE PRINTS.
I KIND OF LIKE THE SMELLS.
S'ALL CHEMICAL-Y.

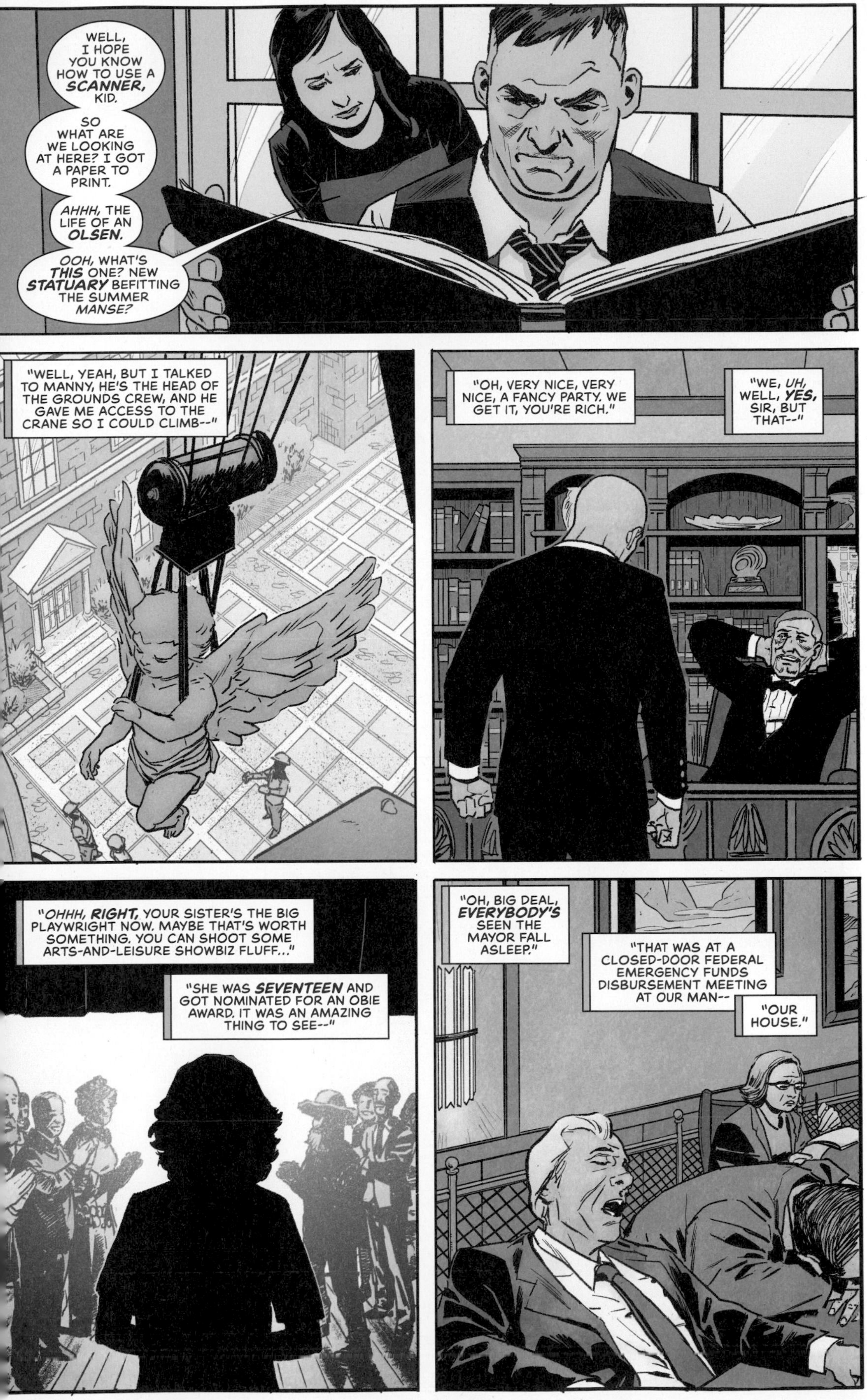
WELL, I HOPE YOU KNOW HOW TO USE A *SCANNER,* KID.
SO WHAT ARE WE LOOKING AT HERE? I GOT A PAPER TO PRINT.
AHHH, THE LIFE OF AN **OLSEN.**
OOH, WHAT'S **THIS** ONE? NEW **STATUARY** BEFITTING THE SUMMER *MANSE?*
"WELL, YEAH, BUT I TALKED TO MANNY, HE'S THE HEAD OF THE GROUNDS CREW, AND HE GAVE ME ACCESS TO THE CRANE SO I COULD CLIMB--"
"OH, VERY NICE, VERY NICE, A FANCY PARTY. WE GET IT, YOU'RE RICH."
"WE, *UH,* WELL, ***YES,*** SIR, BUT THAT--"
"*OHHH,* ***RIGHT,*** YOUR SISTER'S THE BIG PLAYWRIGHT NOW. MAYBE THAT'S WORTH SOMETHING. YOU CAN SHOOT SOME ARTS-AND-LEISURE SHOWBIZ FLUFF..."
"SHE WAS ***SEVENTEEN*** AND GOT NOMINATED FOR AN OBIE AWARD. IT WAS AN AMAZING THING TO SEE--"
"OH, BIG DEAL, ***EVERYBODY'S*** SEEN THE MAYOR FALL ASLEEP."
"THAT WAS AT A CLOSED-DOOR FEDERAL EMERGENCY FUNDS DISBURSEMENT MEETING AT OUR MAN--
"OUR HOUSE."

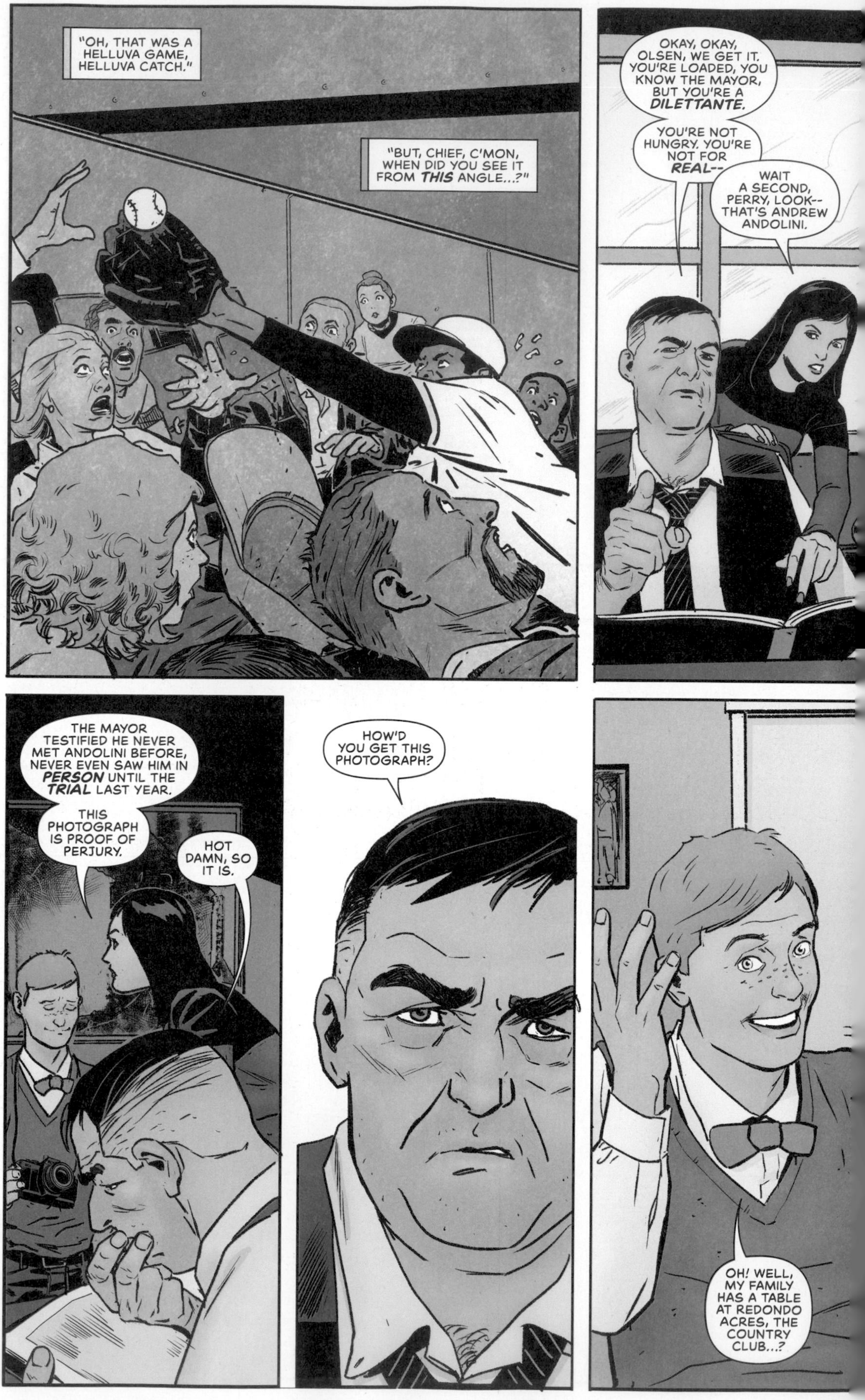
"OH, THAT WAS A HELLUVA GAME, HELLUVA CATCH."
"BUT, CHIEF, C'MON, WHEN DID YOU SEE IT FROM *THIS* ANGLE...?"
OKAY, OKAY, OLSEN, WE GET IT. YOU'RE LOADED, YOU KNOW THE MAYOR, BUT YOU'RE A *DILETTANTE.*
YOU'RE NOT HUNGRY. YOU'RE NOT FOR *REAL--*
WAIT A SECOND, PERRY, LOOK-- THAT'S ANDREW ANDOLINI.
THE MAYOR TESTIFIED HE NEVER MET ANDOLINI BEFORE, NEVER EVEN SAW HIM IN *PERSON* UNTIL THE *TRIAL* LAST YEAR.
THIS PHOTOGRAPH IS PROOF OF PERJURY.
HOT DAMN, SO IT IS.
HOW'D YOU GET THIS PHOTOGRAPH?
OH! WELL, MY FAMILY HAS A TABLE AT REDONDO ACRES, THE COUNTRY CLUB...?

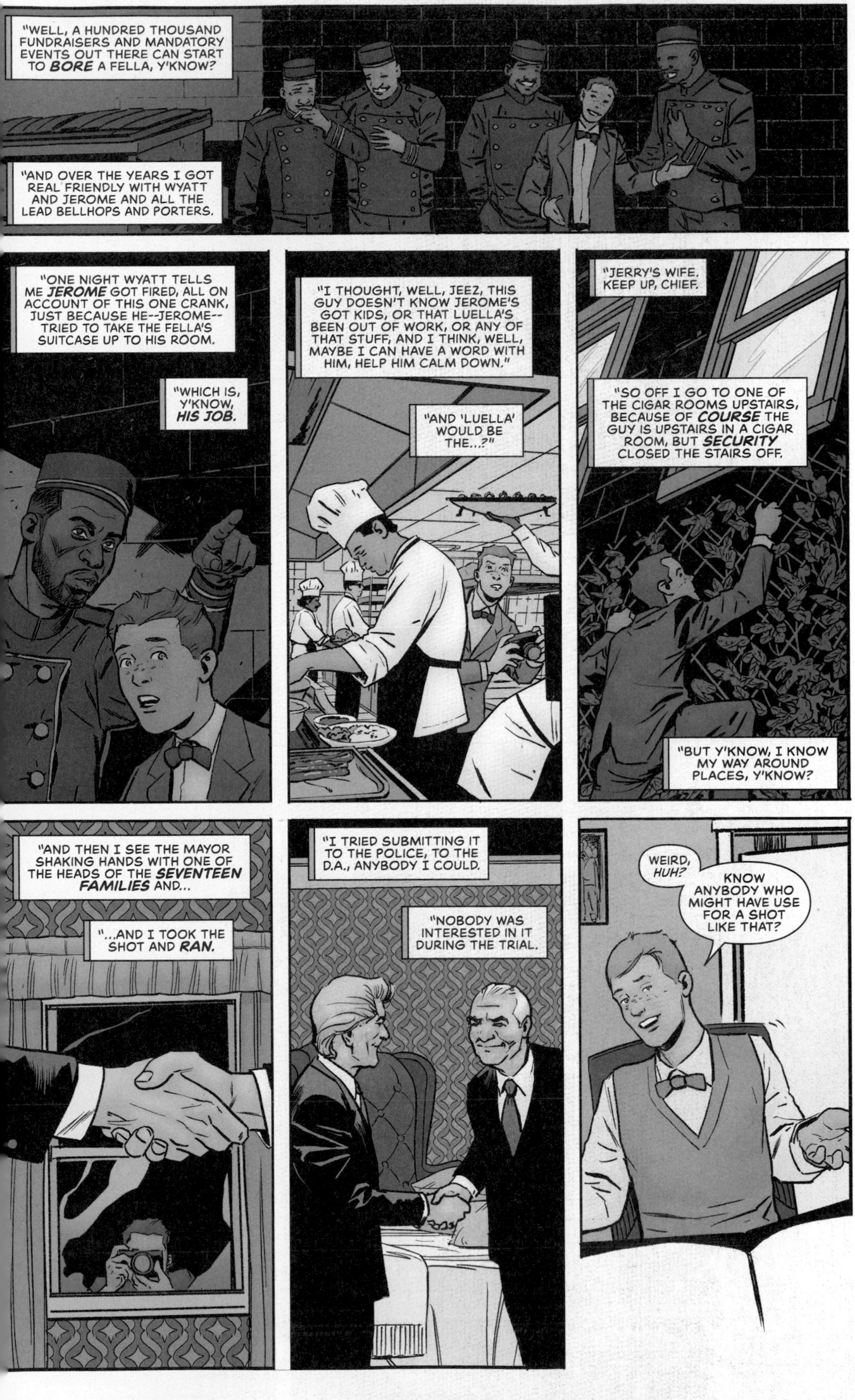
"WELL, A HUNDRED THOUSAND FUNDRAISERS AND MANDATORY EVENTS OUT THERE CAN START TO BORE A FELLA, Y'KNOW?
"AND OVER THE YEARS I GOT REAL FRIENDLY WITH WYATT AND JEROME AND ALL THE LEAD BELLHOPS AND PORTERS.
"ONE NIGHT WYATT TELLS ME JEROME GOT FIRED, ALL ON ACCOUNT OF THIS ONE CRANK, JUST BECAUSE HE--JEROME--TRIED TO TAKE THE FELLA'S SUITCASE UP TO HIS ROOM.
"WHICH IS, Y'KNOW, HIS JOB.
"I THOUGHT, WELL, JEEZ, THIS GUY DOESN'T KNOW JEROME'S GOT KIDS, OR THAT LUELLA'S BEEN OUT OF WORK, OR ANY OF THAT STUFF, AND I THINK, WELL, MAYBE I CAN HAVE A WORD WITH HIM, HELP HIM CALM DOWN."
"AND 'LUELLA' WOULD BE THE...?"
"JERRY'S WIFE. KEEP UP, CHIEF.
"SO OFF I GO TO ONE OF THE CIGAR ROOMS UPSTAIRS, BECAUSE OF COURSE THE GUY IS UPSTAIRS IN A CIGAR ROOM, BUT SECURITY CLOSED THE STAIRS OFF.
"BUT Y'KNOW, I KNOW MY WAY AROUND PLACES, Y'KNOW?
"AND THEN I SEE THE MAYOR SHAKING HANDS WITH ONE OF THE HEADS OF THE SEVENTEEN FAMILIES AND...
"...AND I TOOK THE SHOT AND RAN.
"I TRIED SUBMITTING IT TO THE POLICE, TO THE D.A., ANYBODY I COULD.
"NOBODY WAS INTERESTED IN IT DURING THE TRIAL.
WEIRD, HUH?
KNOW ANYBODY WHO MIGHT HAVE USE FOR A SHOT LIKE THAT?

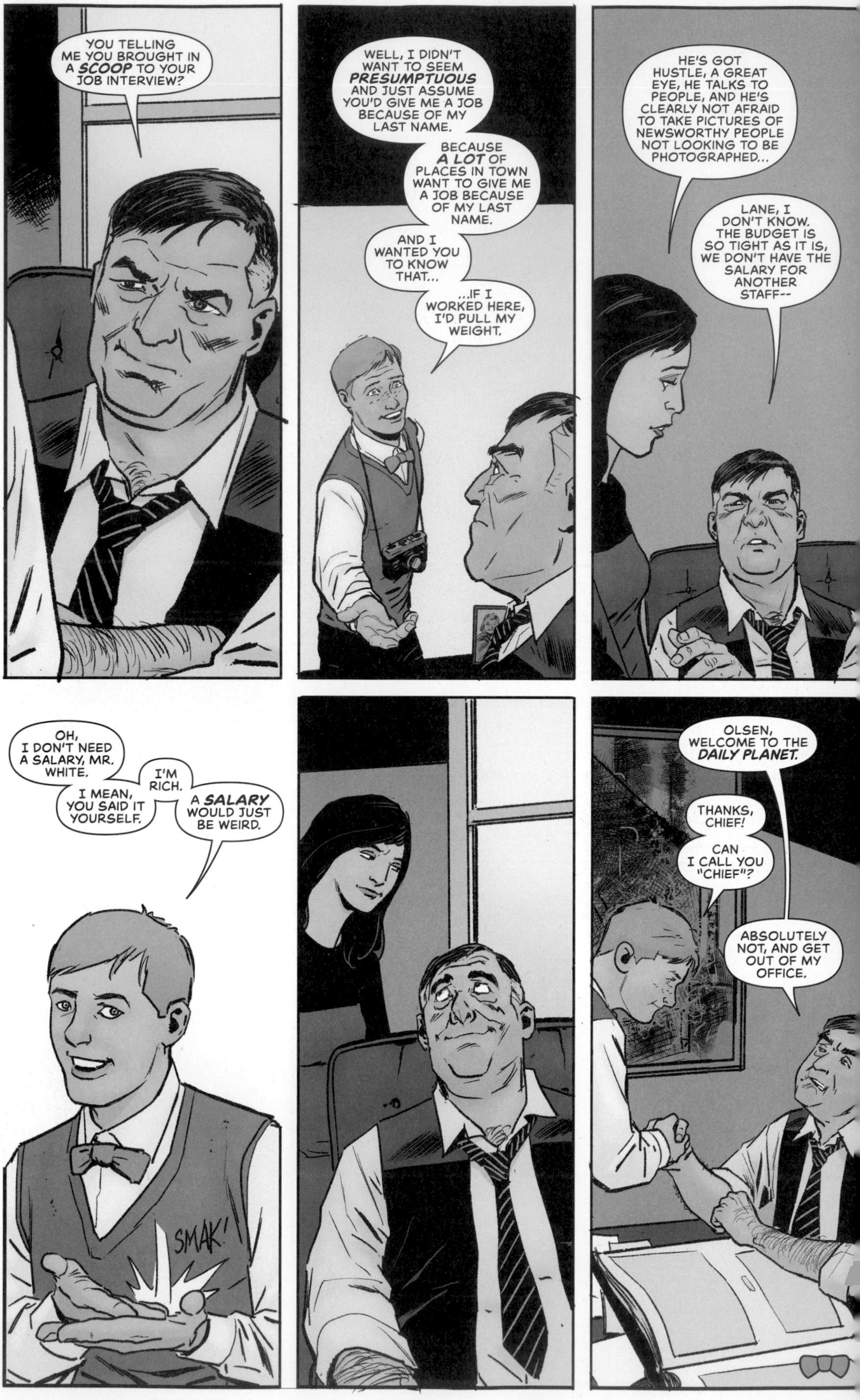

YOU TELLING ME YOU BROUGHT IN A SCOOP TO YOUR JOB INTERVIEW?
WELL, I DIDN'T WANT TO SEEM PRESUMPTUOUS AND JUST ASSUME YOU'D GIVE ME A JOB BECAUSE OF MY LAST NAME.
BECAUSE A LOT OF PLACES IN TOWN WANT TO GIVE ME A JOB BECAUSE OF MY LAST NAME.
AND I WANTED YOU TO KNOW THAT...
...IF I WORKED HERE, I'D PULL MY WEIGHT.
HE'S GOT HUSTLE, A GREAT EYE, HE TALKS TO PEOPLE, AND HE'S CLEARLY NOT AFRAID TO TAKE PICTURES OF NEWSWORTHY PEOPLE NOT LOOKING TO BE PHOTOGRAPHED...
LANE, I DON'T KNOW. THE BUDGET IS SO TIGHT AS IT IS, WE DON'T HAVE THE SALARY FOR ANOTHER STAFF--
OH, I DON'T NEED A SALARY, MR. WHITE.
I'M RICH.
I MEAN, YOU SAID IT YOURSELF.
A SALARY WOULD JUST BE WEIRD.
SMAK!
OLSEN, WELCOME TO THE DAILY PLANET.
THANKS, CHIEF!
CAN I CALL YOU "CHIEF"?
ABSOLUTELY NOT, AND GET OUT OF MY OFFICE.

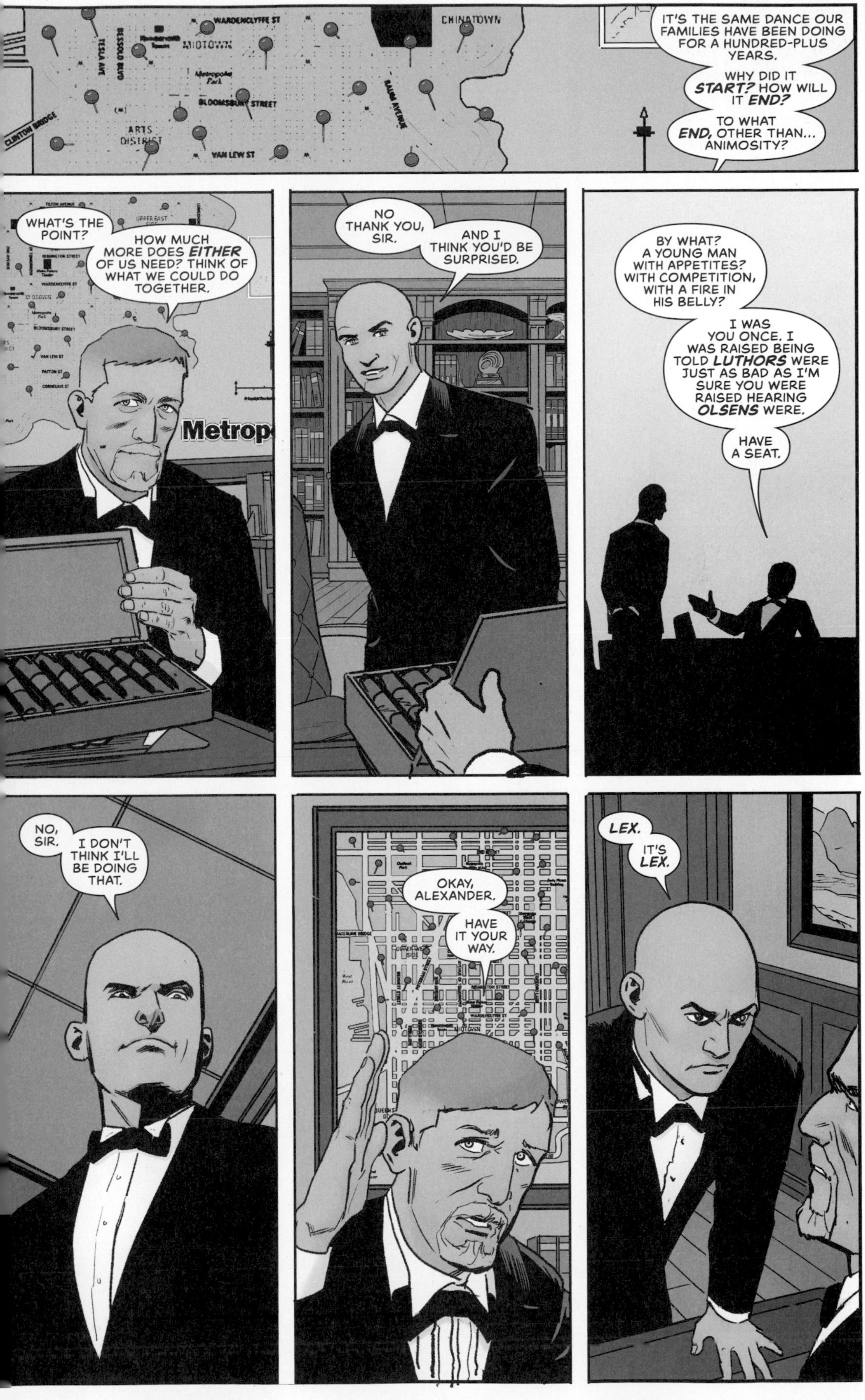
WARDENCLYFFE ST
CHINATOWN
MIDTOWN
TESLA AVE
BLOOMSBURY STREET
ARTS DISTRICT
VAN LEW ST
CLINTON BRIDGE
IT'S THE SAME DANCE OUR FAMILIES HAVE BEEN DOING FOR A HUNDRED-PLUS YEARS.
WHY DID IT START? HOW WILL IT END?
TO WHAT END, OTHER THAN... ANIMOSITY?
WHAT'S THE POINT?
HOW MUCH MORE DOES EITHER OF US NEED? THINK OF WHAT WE COULD DO TOGETHER.
NO THANK YOU, SIR.
AND I THINK YOU'D BE SURPRISED.
BY WHAT? A YOUNG MAN WITH APPETITES? WITH COMPETITION, WITH A FIRE IN HIS BELLY?
I WAS YOU ONCE. I WAS RAISED BEING TOLD LUTHORS WERE JUST AS BAD AS I'M SURE YOU WERE RAISED HEARING OLSENS WERE.
HAVE A SEAT.
NO, SIR.
I DON'T THINK I'LL BE DOING THAT.
OKAY, ALEXANDER.
HAVE IT YOUR WAY.
LEX.
IT'S LEX.

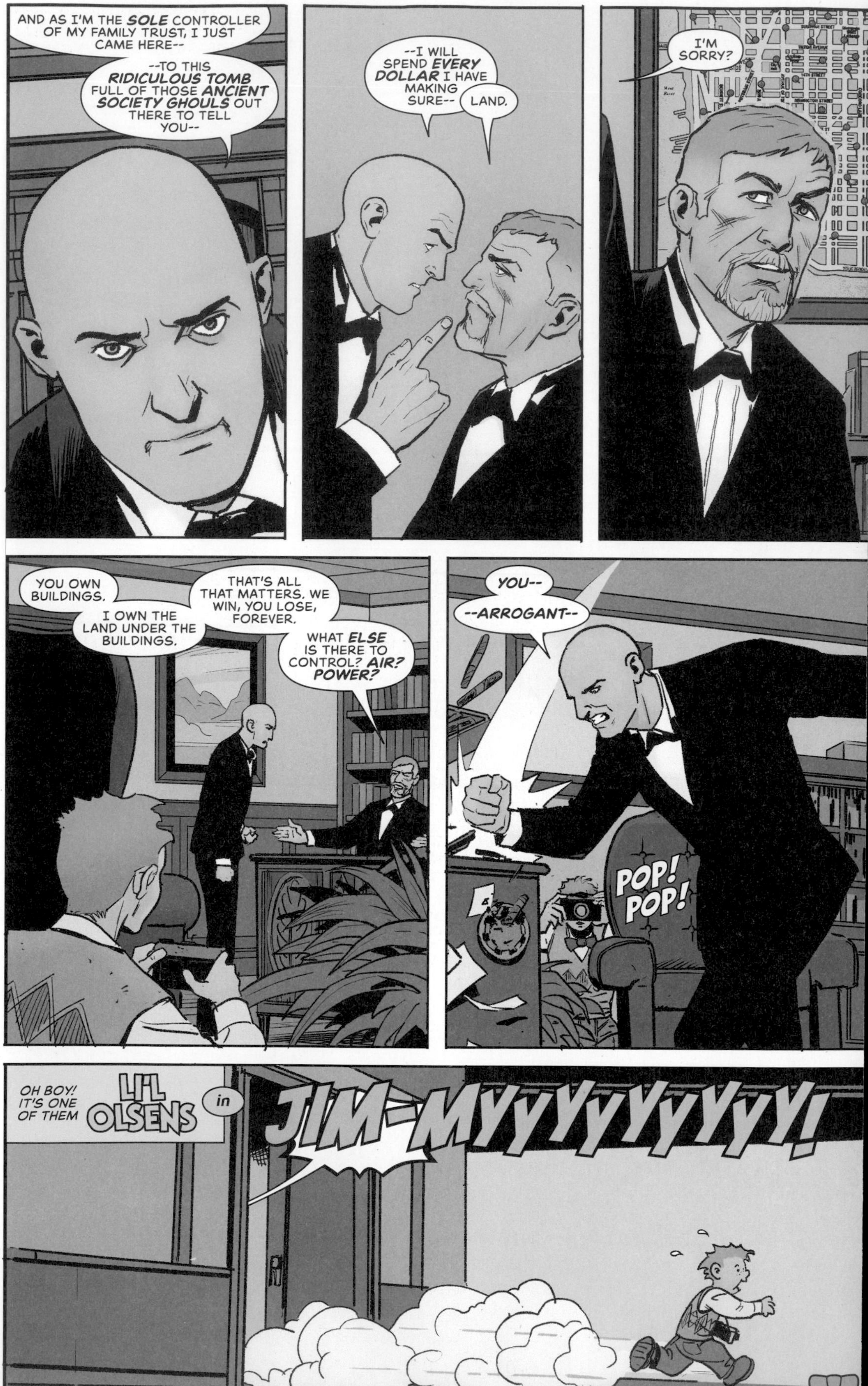
AND AS I'M THE SOLE CONTROLLER OF MY FAMILY TRUST, I JUST CAME HERE--
--TO THIS RIDICULOUS TOMB FULL OF THOSE ANCIENT SOCIETY GHOULS OUT THERE TO TELL YOU--
--I WILL SPEND EVERY DOLLAR I HAVE MAKING SURE--
LAND.
I'M SORRY?
YOU OWN BUILDINGS.
I OWN THE LAND UNDER THE BUILDINGS.
THAT'S ALL THAT MATTERS. WE WIN, YOU LOSE, FOREVER.
WHAT ELSE IS THERE TO CONTROL? AIR? POWER?
YOU--
--ARROGANT--
POP! POP!
OH BOY! IT'S ONE OF THEM LI'L OLSENS in
JIM-MYYYYYYYYY!

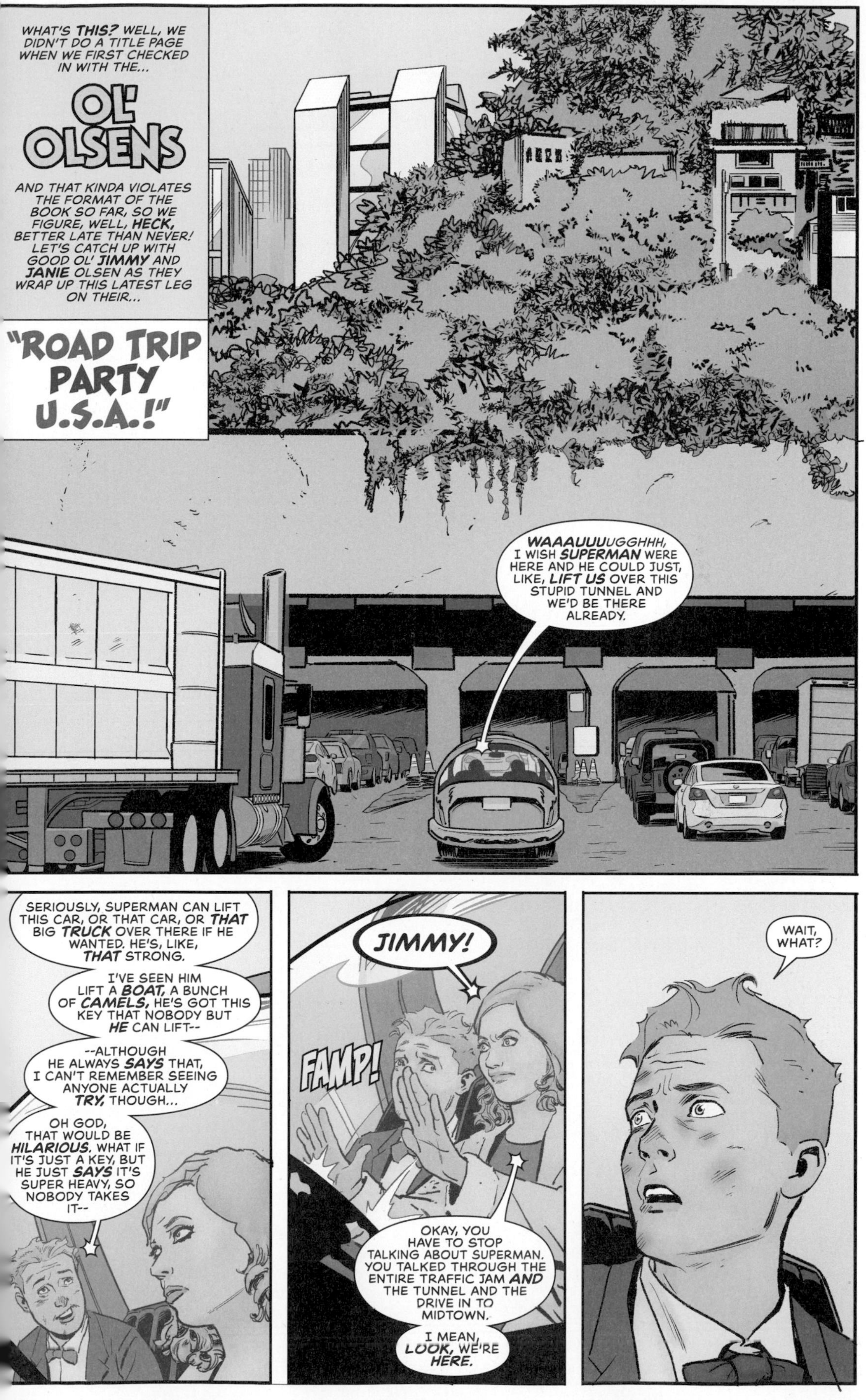
WHAT'S THIS? WELL, WE DIDN'T DO A TITLE PAGE WHEN WE FIRST CHECKED IN WITH THE...
OL' OLSENS
AND THAT KINDA VIOLATES THE FORMAT OF THE BOOK SO FAR, SO WE FIGURE, WELL, HECK, BETTER LATE THAN NEVER! LET'S CATCH UP WITH GOOD OL' JIMMY AND JANIE OLSEN AS THEY WRAP UP THIS LATEST LEG ON THEIR...
"ROAD TRIP PARTY U.S.A.!"
WAAAUUUUGGHHH, I WISH SUPERMAN WERE HERE AND HE COULD JUST, LIKE, LIFT US OVER THIS STUPID TUNNEL AND WE'D BE THERE ALREADY.
SERIOUSLY, SUPERMAN CAN LIFT THIS CAR, OR THAT CAR, OR THAT BIG TRUCK OVER THERE IF HE WANTED. HE'S, LIKE, THAT STRONG.
I'VE SEEN HIM LIFT A BOAT, A BUNCH OF CAMELS, HE'S GOT THIS KEY THAT NOBODY BUT HE CAN LIFT--
--ALTHOUGH HE ALWAYS SAYS THAT, I CAN'T REMEMBER SEEING ANYONE ACTUALLY TRY, THOUGH...
OH GOD, THAT WOULD BE HILARIOUS. WHAT IF IT'S JUST A KEY, BUT HE JUST SAYS IT'S SUPER HEAVY, SO NOBODY TAKES IT--
JIMMY!
FAMP!
OKAY, YOU HAVE TO STOP TALKING ABOUT SUPERMAN. YOU TALKED THROUGH THE ENTIRE TRAFFIC JAM AND THE TUNNEL AND THE DRIVE IN TO MIDTOWN.
I MEAN, LOOK, WE'RE HERE.
WAIT, WHAT?

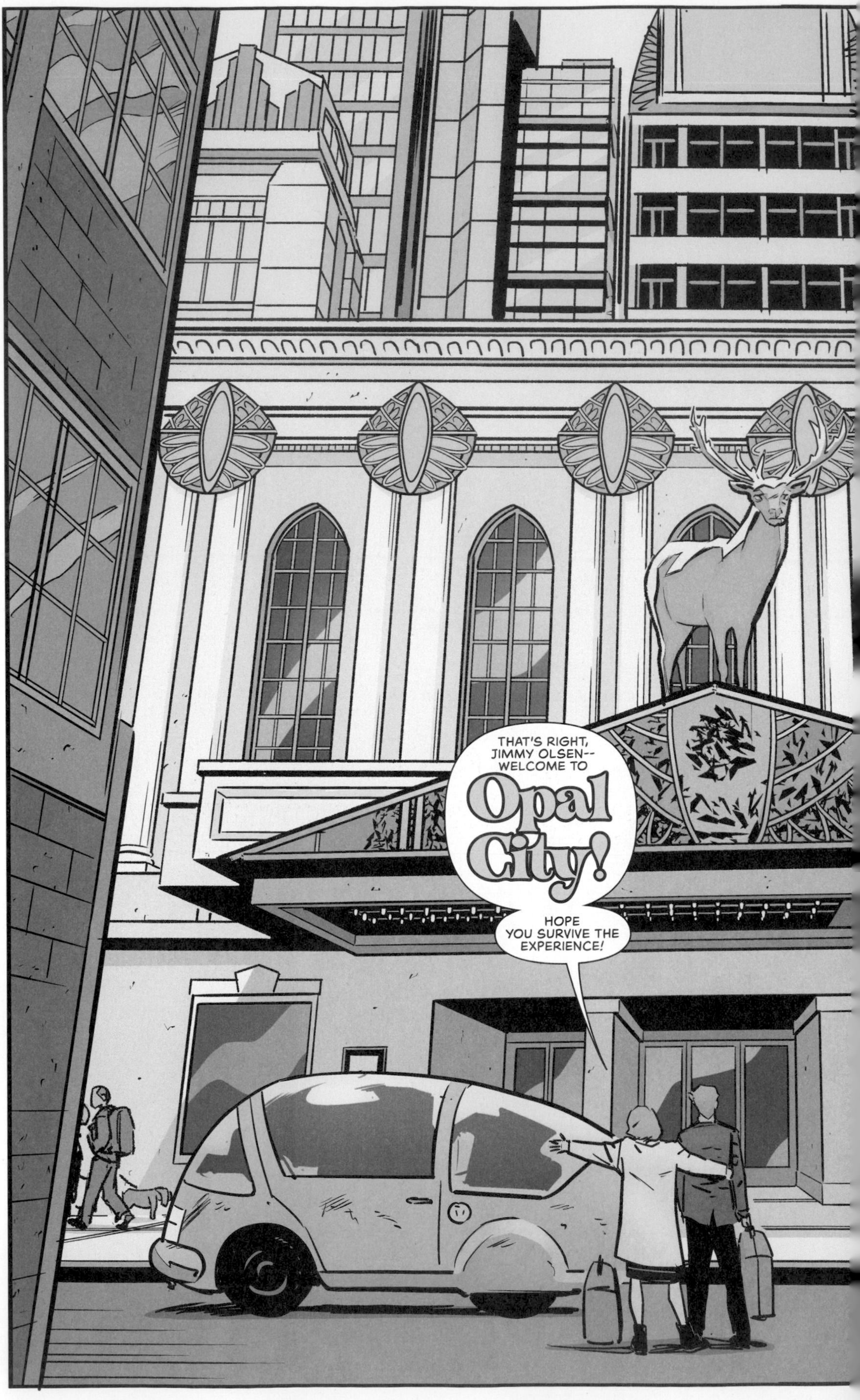
THAT'S RIGHT, JIMMY OLSEN-- WELCOME TO
Opal City!
HOPE YOU SURVIVE THE EXPERIENCE!

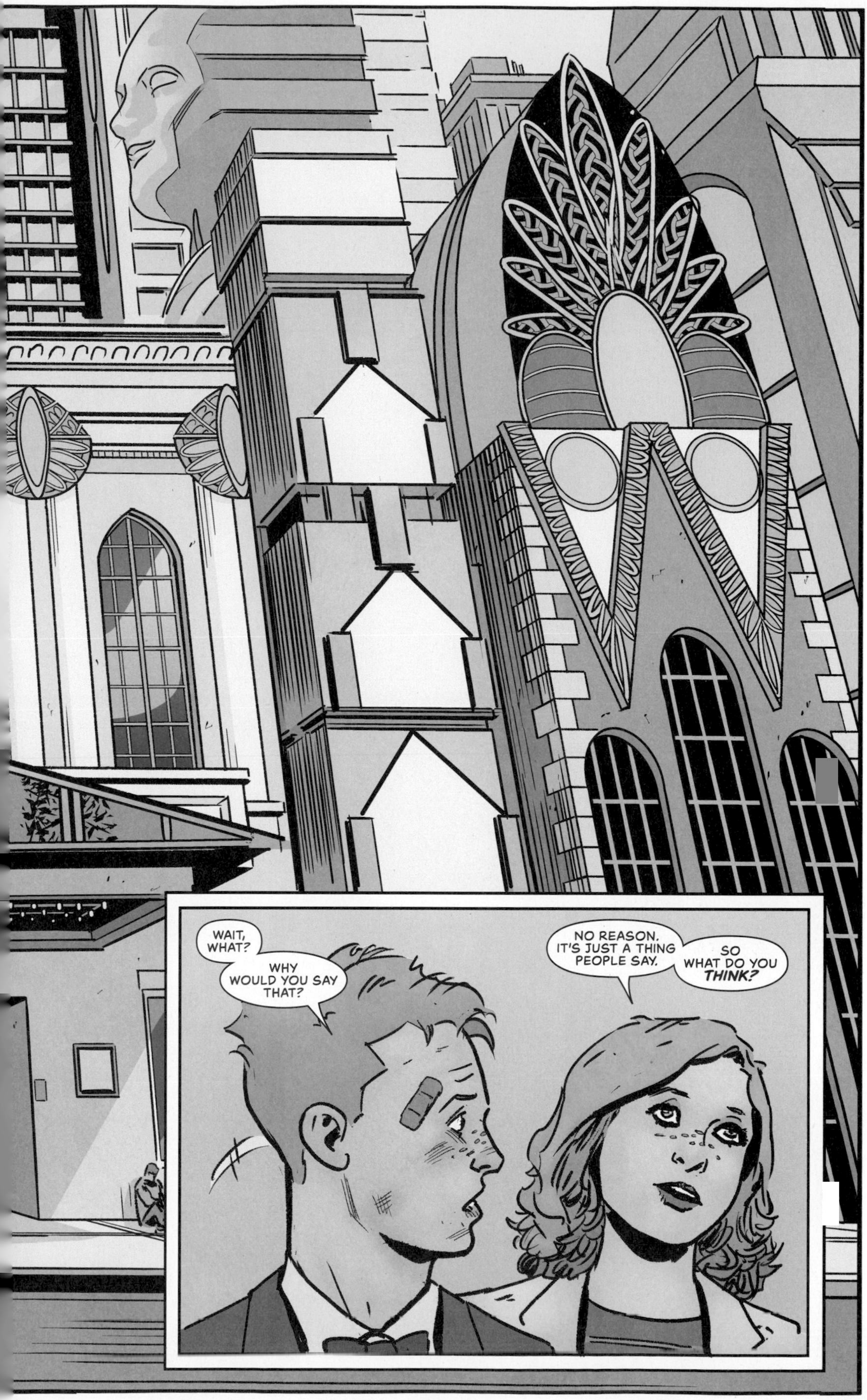

WAIT, WHAT?
WHY WOULD YOU SAY THAT?
NO REASON. IT'S JUST A THING PEOPLE SAY.
SO WHAT DO YOU *THINK?*

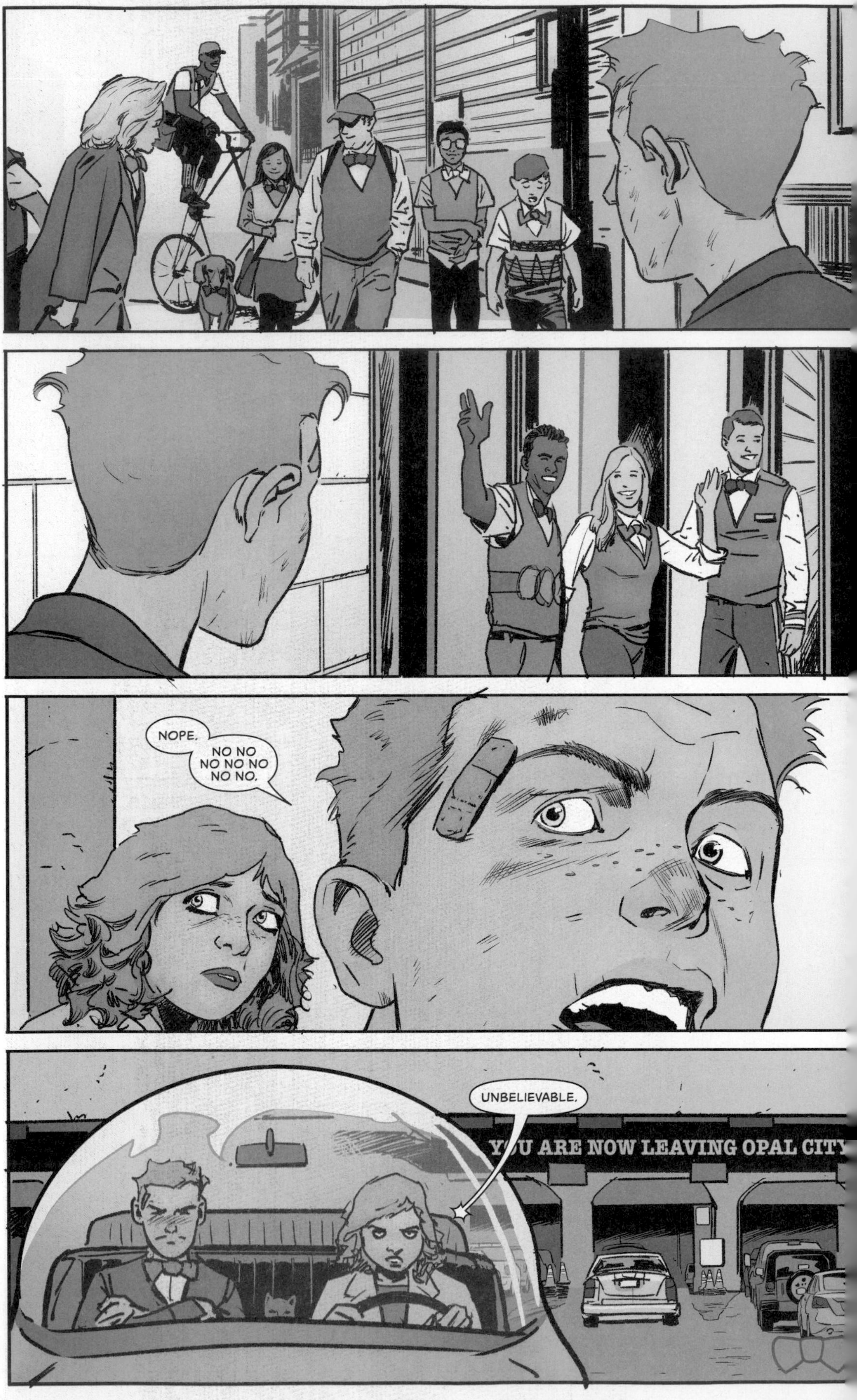
NOPE.
NO NO NO NO NO NO NO.
UNBELIEVABLE.
YOU ARE NOW LEAVING OPAL CITY

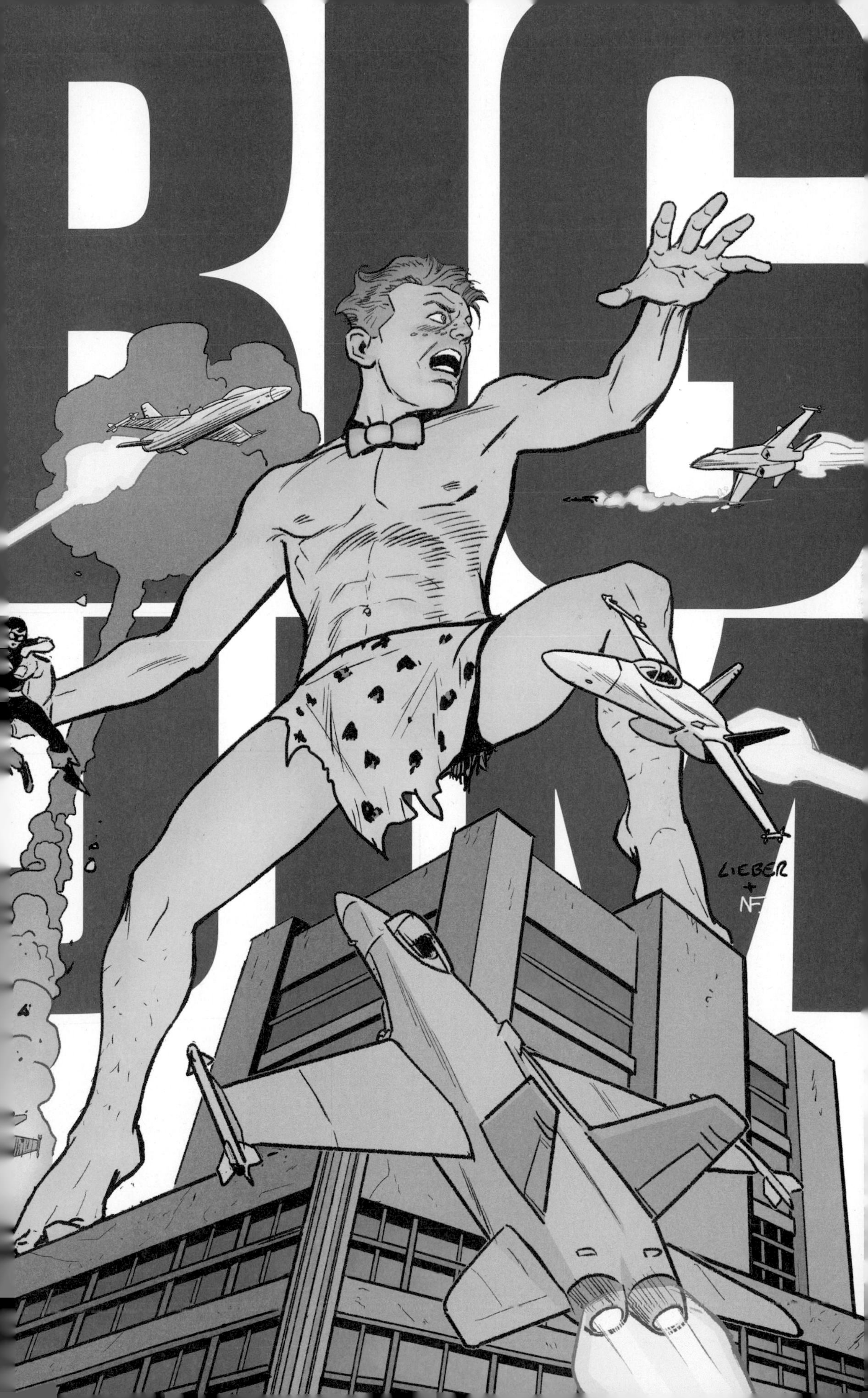
BIG
LIEBER

VERY GOOD, SALISBURY, I'M READY NOW.

AS YOU WISH, MASTER JULIAN.

AHH, MY BREAKFAST.

BUT FIRST, A NICE, LONG SIP OF COFFEE--

SSSSRRRRRRRr

RRRRRRRRRRR

RRRRRRRRRP--

PFFFFPFFFF

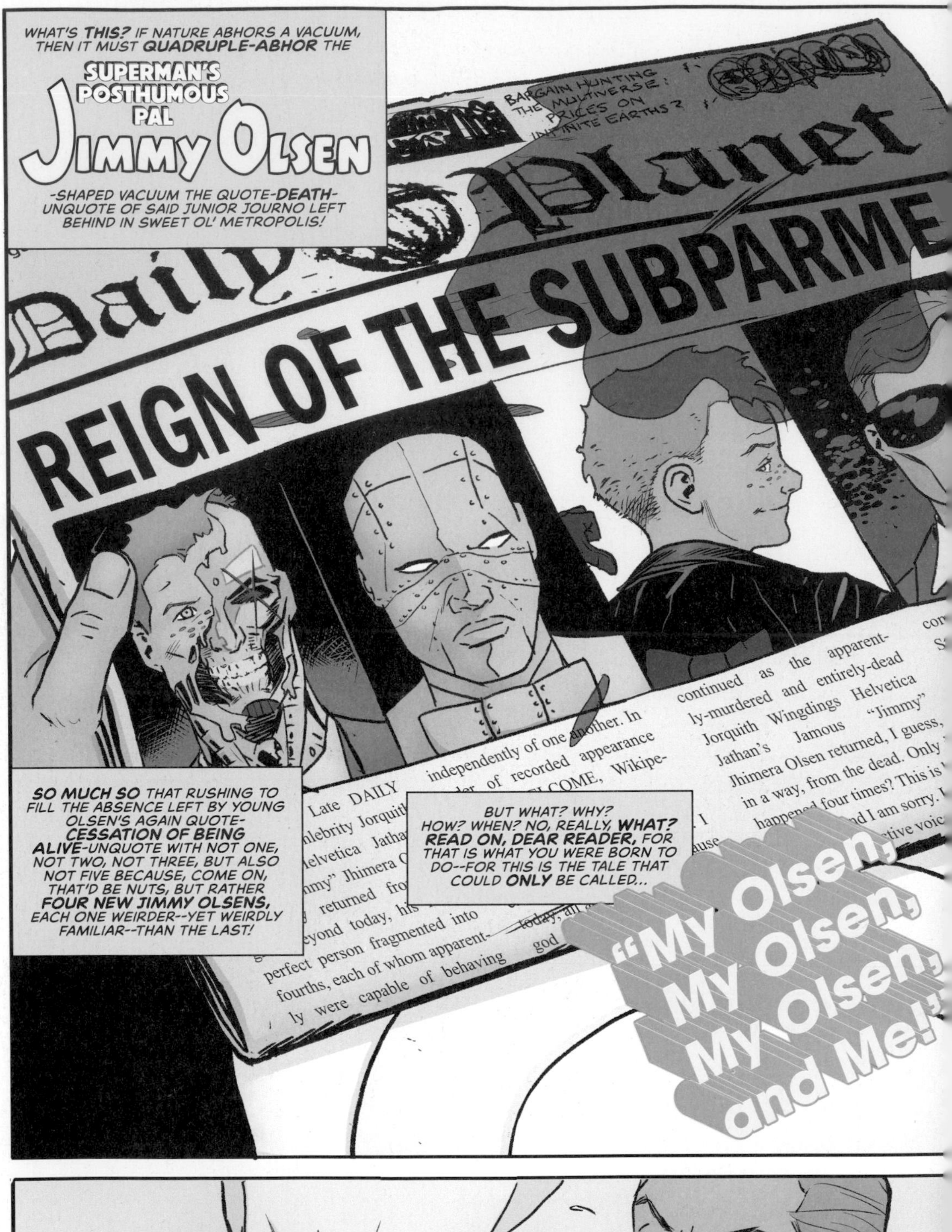

WHAT'S THIS? IF NATURE ABHORS A VACUUM, THEN IT MUST QUADRUPLE-ABHOR THE
SUPERMAN'S POSTHUMOUS PAL JIMMY OLSEN
-SHAPED VACUUM THE QUOTE-DEATH-UNQUOTE OF SAID JUNIOR JOURNO LEFT BEHIND IN SWEET OL' METROPOLIS!
BARGAIN HUNTING THE MULTIVERSE: PRICES ON INFINITE EARTHS?
Daily Planet
REIGN OF THE SUBPARME
independently of one another. In
of recorded appearance
Wikipe-
continued as the apparent-
ly-murdered and entirely-dead
Jorquith Wingdings Helvetica
Jathan's Jamous "Jimmy"
Jhimera Olsen returned, I guess,
in a way, from the dead. Only
four times? This is
and I am sorry.
perfect person fragmented into
fourths, each of whom apparently were capable of behaving
SO MUCH SO THAT RUSHING TO FILL THE ABSENCE LEFT BY YOUNG OLSEN'S AGAIN QUOTE-CESSATION OF BEING ALIVE-UNQUOTE WITH NOT ONE, NOT TWO, NOT THREE, BUT ALSO NOT FIVE BECAUSE, COME ON, THAT'D BE NUTS, BUT RATHER FOUR NEW JIMMY OLSENS, EACH ONE WEIRDER--YET WEIRDLY FAMILIAR--THAN THE LAST!
BUT WHAT? WHY? HOW? WHEN? NO, REALLY, WHAT? READ ON, DEAR READER, FOR THAT IS WHAT YOU WERE BORN TO DO--FOR THIS IS THE TALE THAT COULD ONLY BE CALLED...
"My Olsen, My Olsen, My Olsen, and Me!"

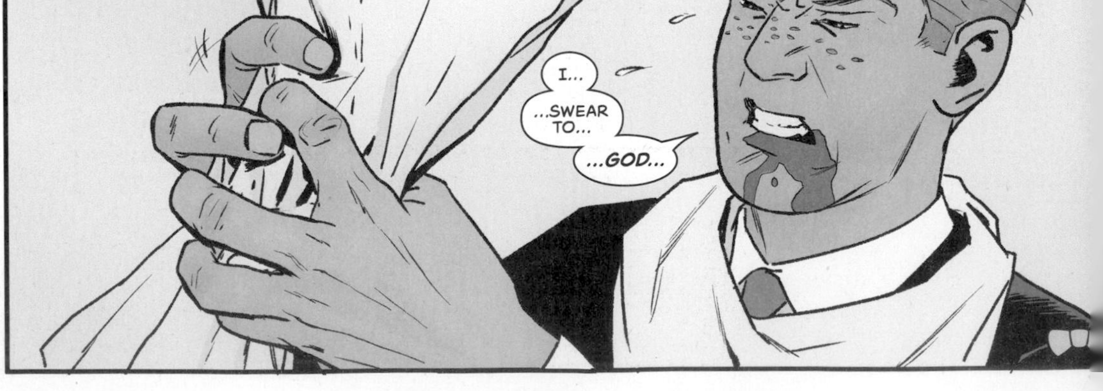

I...
...SWEAR TO...
...GOD...

CYBORG MONSTER OLSEN FOILS ROBBERY

For the 'grams," *Monstrous Scientific Mistake Utters*

(METROPOLIS) A daring daylight robbery in midtown Metropolis was foiled by some kind of killer robot made to app... ...ilar ...ate.

Daily Planet contentographer Bitters... ...Jimpl...

OH DEAR.

DAB DAB DAB

THANK YOU FOR YOUR KIND INTERLOPERY ON BEHALF OF OUR FAIR--

GOOD LORD--
=CHOKE=--

CITIZEN!

DON'T-FORGET-TO-LIKE-AND-FAVE!

THANK-YOU-FOR-YOUR-ENGAGEMENT-AND-IMPRESSIONS.

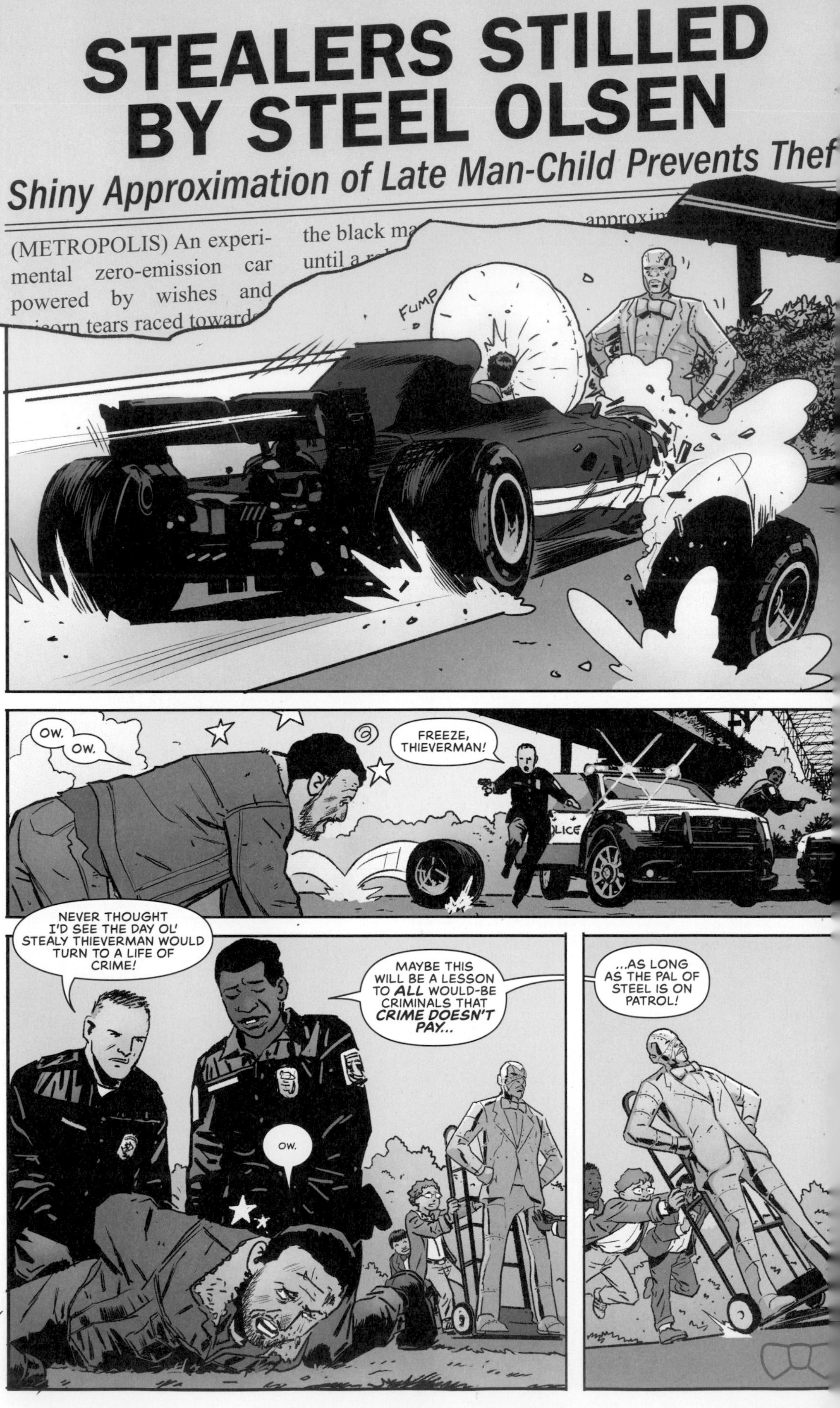

STEALERS STILLED BY STEEL OLSEN
Shiny Approximation of Late Man-Child Prevents Thef
(METROPOLIS) An experi-
mental zero-emission car
powered by wishes and
the black ma
FUMP
OW.
OW.
FREEZE, THIEVERMAN!
POLICE
NEVER THOUGHT I'D SEE THE DAY OL' STEALY THIEVERMAN WOULD TURN TO A LIFE OF CRIME!
MAYBE THIS WILL BE A LESSON TO ALL WOULD-BE CRIMINALS THAT CRIME DOESN'T PAY...
OW.
...AS LONG AS THE PAL OF STEEL IS ON PATROL!

OTALLY RADICAL, EXTREME OLSEN REPLACEMENT VERBS NOUN

"Only Nineties Kids Will Get This," *Says Facsimile*

(METROPOLIS)   Pleated   guys yeste— ...as yet another
perfection inline-skated up   Park
...other win for the good

STOP!

THIEF!

OH, *BOGUS!*

WHOOMP THERE IT IS

WHAM

--WHOOP--

GNARLY.

MY MOTHER'S URN IS IN THIS PURSE, I NEVER WOULD'VE FORGIVEN MYSELF IF I'D LOST IT.

HOW CAN I EVER THANK YOU?

PROMISE YOU'LL ALWAYS STAY *RADICAL...*

...AND *RELEVANT!*

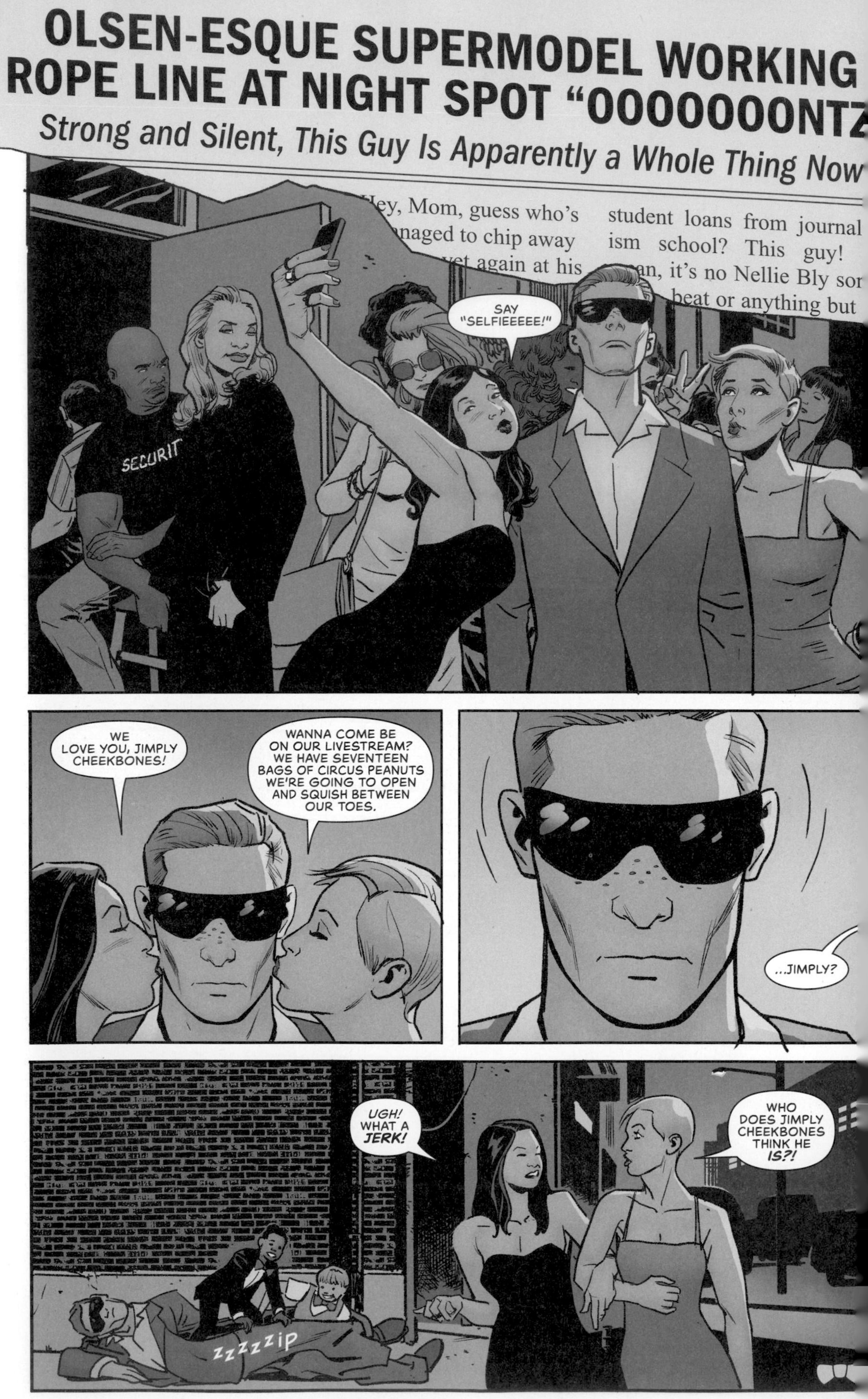
OLSEN-ESQUE SUPERMODEL WORKING
ROPE LINE AT NIGHT SPOT "OOOOOOOONTZ
Strong and Silent, This Guy Is Apparently a Whole Thing Now
ey, Mom, guess who's
naged to chip away
yet again at his
student loans from journal
ism school? This guy!
an, it's no Nellie Bly sor
beat or anything but
SAY "SELFIEEEEE!"
SECURIT
WE LOVE YOU, JIMPLY CHEEKBONES!
WANNA COME BE ON OUR LIVESTREAM? WE HAVE SEVENTEEN BAGS OF CIRCUS PEANUTS WE'RE GOING TO OPEN AND SQUISH BETWEEN OUR TOES.
...JIMPLY?
UGH! WHAT A JERK!
WHO DOES JIMPLY CHEEKBONES THINK HE IS?!
ZZZZZip

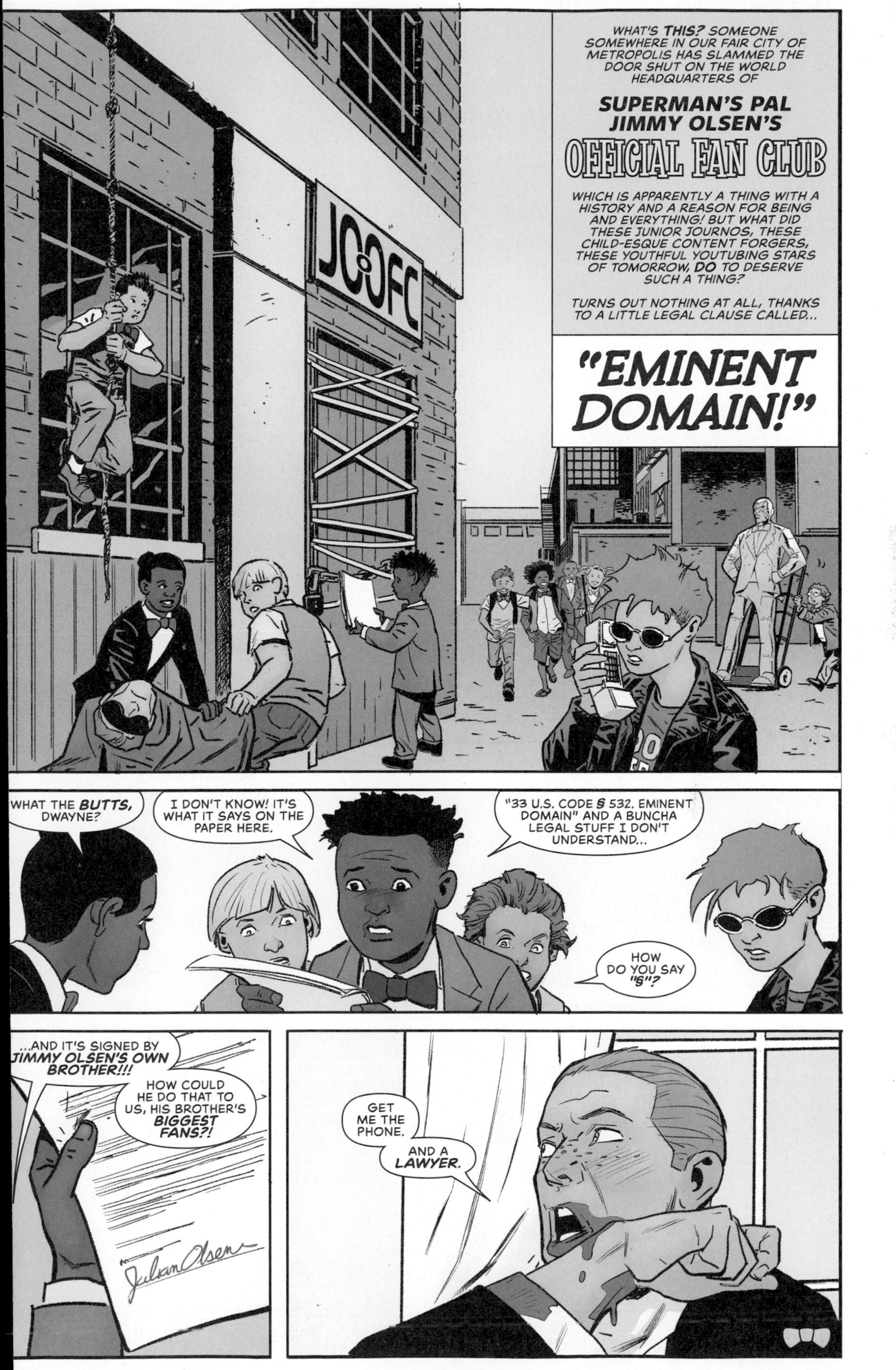

WHAT'S THIS? SOMEONE SOMEWHERE IN OUR FAIR CITY OF METROPOLIS HAS SLAMMED THE DOOR SHUT ON THE WORLD HEADQUARTERS OF
SUPERMAN'S PAL JIMMY OLSEN'S
OFFICIAL FAN CLUB
WHICH IS APPARENTLY A THING WITH A HISTORY AND A REASON FOR BEING AND EVERYTHING! BUT WHAT DID THESE JUNIOR JOURNOS, THESE CHILD-ESQUE CONTENT FORGERS, THESE YOUTHFUL YOUTUBING STARS OF TOMORROW, DO TO DESERVE SUCH A THING?
TURNS OUT NOTHING AT ALL, THANKS TO A LITTLE LEGAL CLAUSE CALLED...
"EMINENT DOMAIN!"
JOOFC
WHAT THE BUTTS, DWAYNE?
I DON'T KNOW! IT'S WHAT IT SAYS ON THE PAPER HERE.
"33 U.S. CODE § 532. EMINENT DOMAIN" AND A BUNCHA LEGAL STUFF I DON'T UNDERSTAND...
HOW DO YOU SAY "§"?
...AND IT'S SIGNED BY JIMMY OLSEN'S OWN BROTHER!!!
HOW COULD HE DO THAT TO US, HIS BROTHER'S BIGGEST FANS?!
Julian Olsen
GET ME THE PHONE.
AND A LAWYER.

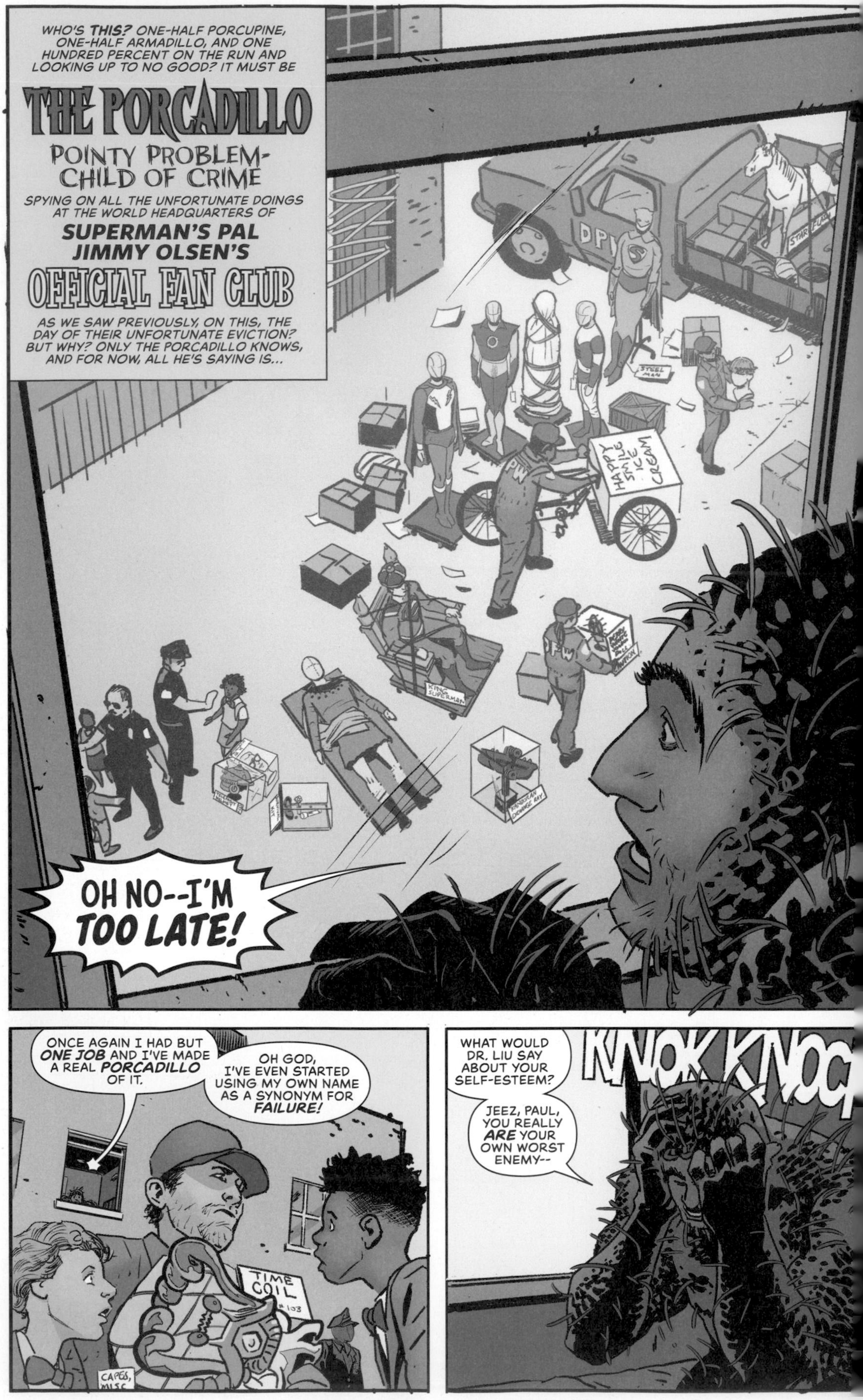
WHO'S THIS? ONE-HALF PORCUPINE, ONE-HALF ARMADILLO, AND ONE HUNDRED PERCENT ON THE RUN AND LOOKING UP TO NO GOOD? IT MUST BE
THE PORCADILLO
POINTY PROBLEM-CHILD OF CRIME
SPYING ON ALL THE UNFORTUNATE DOINGS AT THE WORLD HEADQUARTERS OF
SUPERMAN'S PAL JIMMY OLSEN'S
OFFICIAL FAN CLUB
AS WE SAW PREVIOUSLY, ON THIS, THE DAY OF THEIR UNFORTUNATE EVICTION? BUT WHY? ONLY THE PORCADILLO KNOWS, AND FOR NOW, ALL HE'S SAYING IS...
STEEL MAN
HAPPY SMILE ICE CREAM
KING SUPERMAN
OH NO--I'M TOO LATE!
ONCE AGAIN I HAD BUT ONE JOB AND I'VE MADE A REAL PORCADILLO OF IT.
OH GOD, I'VE EVEN STARTED USING MY OWN NAME AS A SYNONYM FOR FAILURE!
TIME COIL #103
CAPES, MISC
WHAT WOULD DR. LIU SAY ABOUT YOUR SELF-ESTEEM?
JEEZ, PAUL, YOU REALLY ARE YOUR OWN WORST ENEMY--
KNOK KNOCK

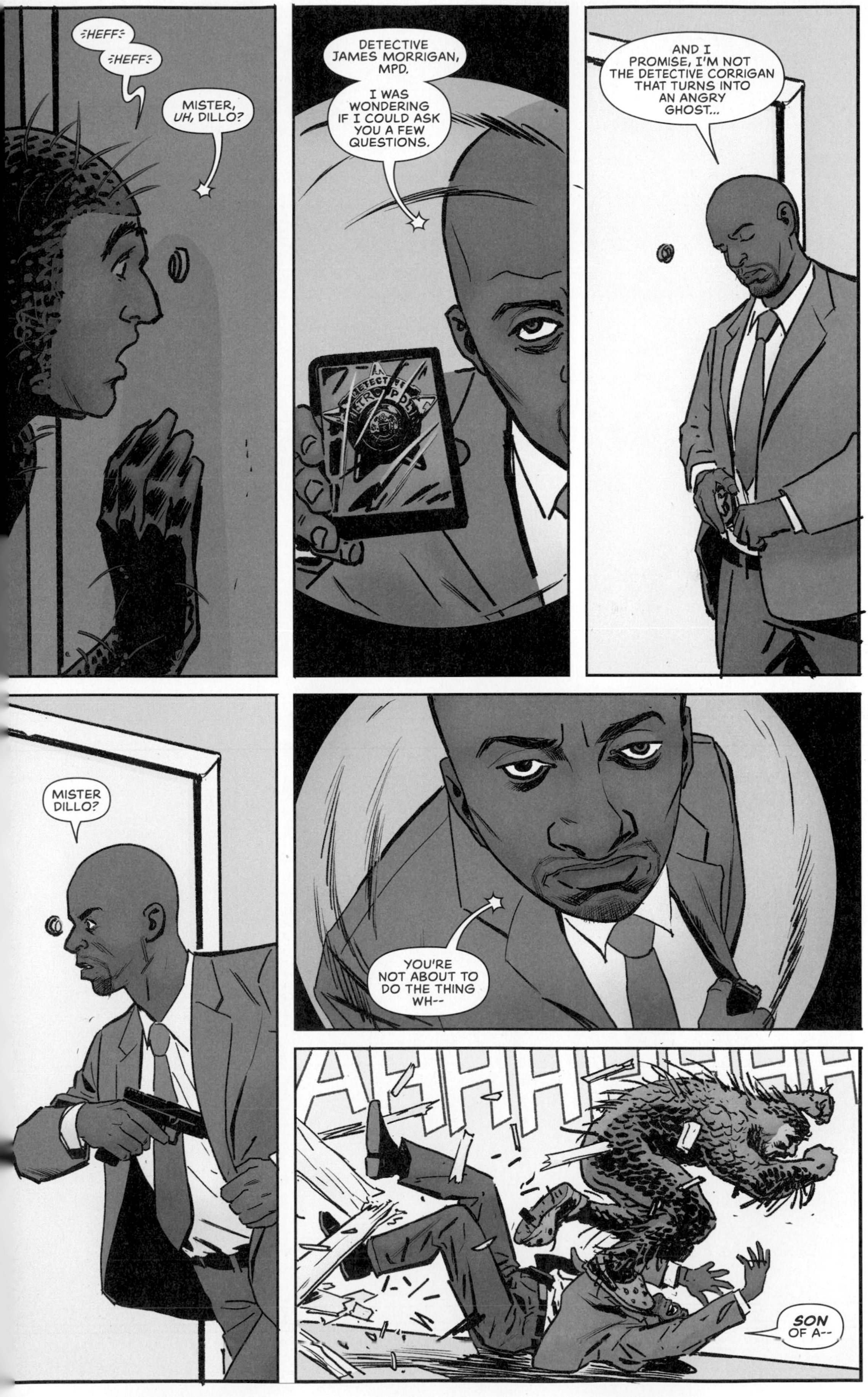
HEFF
HEFF
MISTER, UH, DILLO?
DETECTIVE JAMES MORRIGAN, MPD.
I WAS WONDERING IF I COULD ASK YOU A FEW QUESTIONS.
AND I PROMISE, I'M NOT THE DETECTIVE CORRIGAN THAT TURNS INTO AN ANGRY GHOST...
MISTER DILLO?
YOU'RE NOT ABOUT TO DO THE THING WH--
AAHHHHHHH
SON OF A--

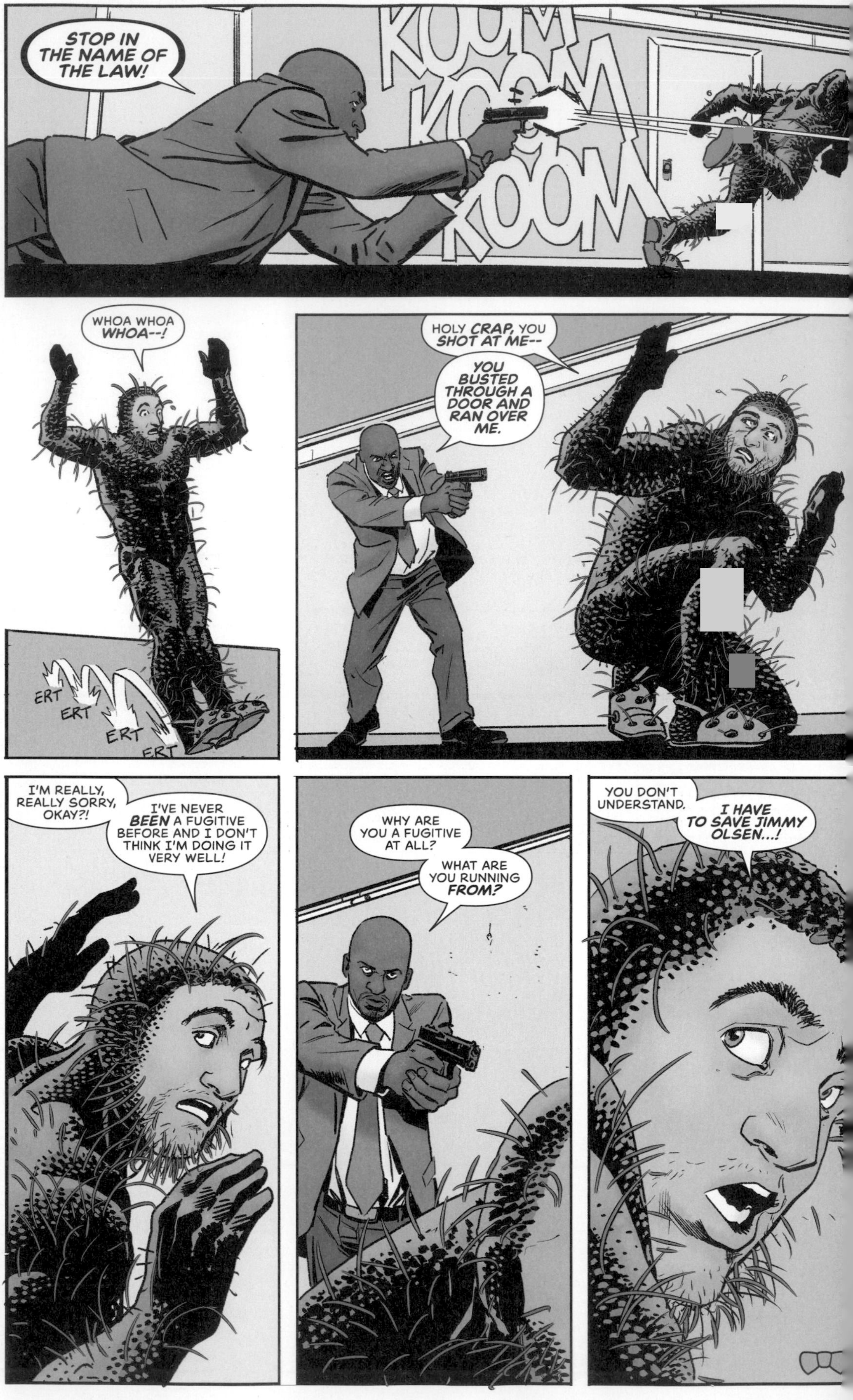
STOP IN THE NAME OF THE LAW!
KOOM KOOM KOOM
WHOA WHOA WHOA--!
ERT ERT ERT ERT
HOLY CRAP, YOU SHOT AT ME--
YOU BUSTED THROUGH A DOOR AND RAN OVER ME.
I'M REALLY, REALLY SORRY, OKAY?!
I'VE NEVER BEEN A FUGITIVE BEFORE AND I DON'T THINK I'M DOING IT VERY WELL!
WHY ARE YOU A FUGITIVE AT ALL?
WHAT ARE YOU RUNNING FROM?
YOU DON'T UNDERSTAND.
I HAVE TO SAVE JIMMY OLSEN...!

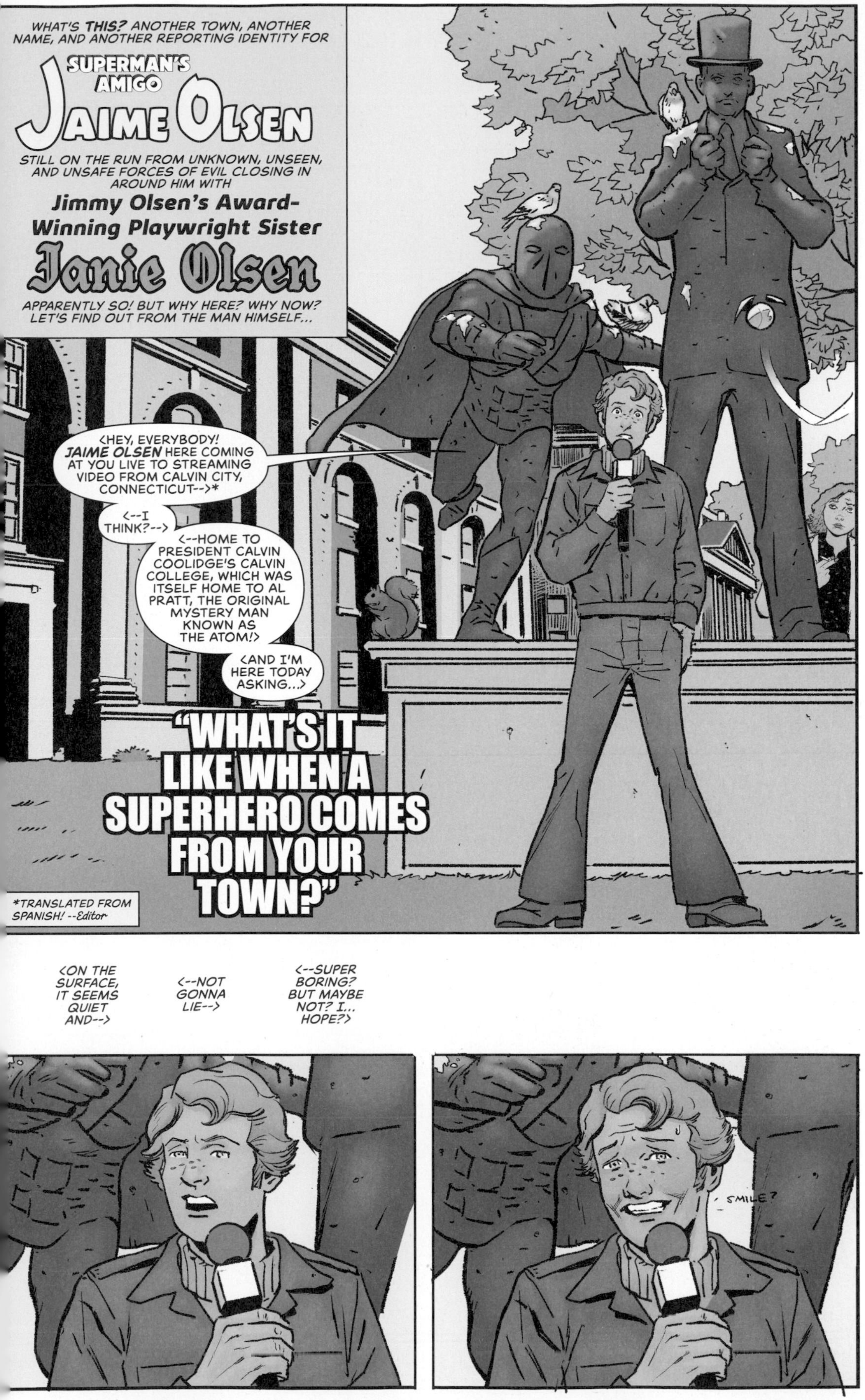
WHAT'S THIS? ANOTHER TOWN, ANOTHER NAME, AND ANOTHER REPORTING IDENTITY FOR
SUPERMAN'S AMIGO
JAIME OLSEN
STILL ON THE RUN FROM UNKNOWN, UNSEEN, AND UNSAFE FORCES OF EVIL CLOSING IN AROUND HIM WITH
Jimmy Olsen's Award-Winning Playwright Sister
Janie Olsen
APPARENTLY SO! BUT WHY HERE? WHY NOW? LET'S FIND OUT FROM THE MAN HIMSELF...
<HEY, EVERYBODY! JAIME OLSEN HERE COMING AT YOU LIVE TO STREAMING VIDEO FROM CALVIN CITY, CONNECTICUT-->*
<--I THINK?-->
<--HOME TO PRESIDENT CALVIN COOLIDGE'S CALVIN COLLEGE, WHICH WAS ITSELF HOME TO AL PRATT, THE ORIGINAL MYSTERY MAN KNOWN AS THE ATOM!>
<AND I'M HERE TODAY ASKING...>
"WHAT'S IT LIKE WHEN A SUPERHERO COMES FROM YOUR TOWN?"
*TRANSLATED FROM SPANISH! --Editor
<ON THE SURFACE, IT SEEMS QUIET AND-->
<--NOT GONNA LIE-->
<--SUPER BORING? BUT MAYBE NOT? I... HOPE?>
SMILE?

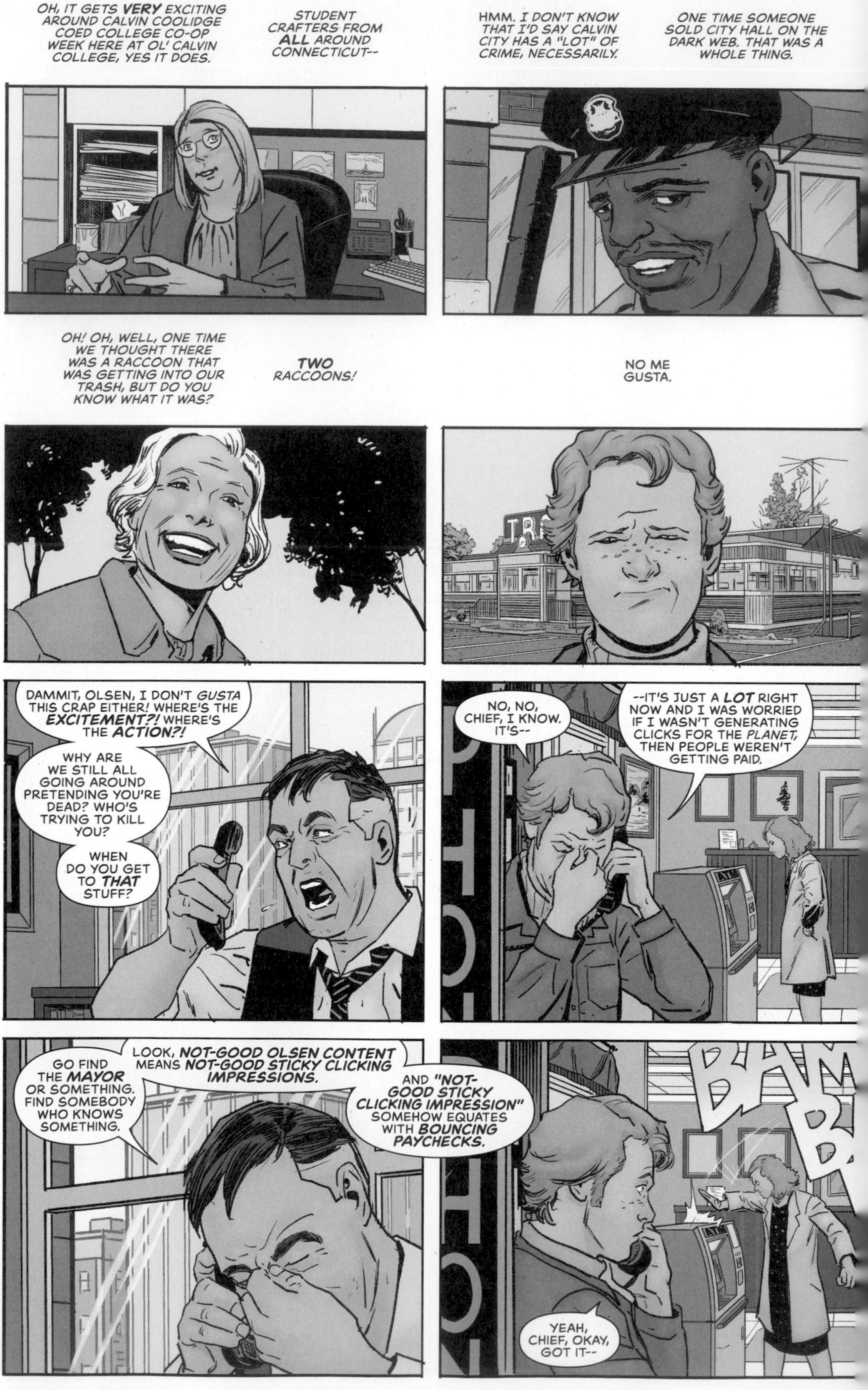
OH, IT GETS VERY EXCITING AROUND CALVIN COOLIDGE COED COLLEGE CO-OP WEEK HERE AT OL' CALVIN COLLEGE, YES IT DOES.
STUDENT CRAFTERS FROM ALL AROUND CONNECTICUT--
HMM. I DON'T KNOW THAT I'D SAY CALVIN CITY HAS A "LOT" OF CRIME, NECESSARILY.
ONE TIME SOMEONE SOLD CITY HALL ON THE DARK WEB. THAT WAS A WHOLE THING.
OH! OH, WELL, ONE TIME WE THOUGHT THERE WAS A RACCOON THAT WAS GETTING INTO OUR TRASH, BUT DO YOU KNOW WHAT IT WAS?
TWO RACCOONS!
NO ME GUSTA.
DAMMIT, OLSEN, I DON'T GUSTA THIS CRAP EITHER! WHERE'S THE EXCITEMENT?! WHERE'S THE ACTION?!
WHY ARE WE STILL ALL GOING AROUND PRETENDING YOU'RE DEAD? WHO'S TRYING TO KILL YOU?
WHEN DO YOU GET TO THAT STUFF?
NO, NO, CHIEF, I KNOW. IT'S--
--IT'S JUST A LOT RIGHT NOW AND I WAS WORRIED IF I WASN'T GENERATING CLICKS FOR THE PLANET, THEN PEOPLE WEREN'T GETTING PAID.
GO FIND THE MAYOR OR SOMETHING. FIND SOMEBODY WHO KNOWS SOMETHING.
LOOK, NOT-GOOD OLSEN CONTENT MEANS NOT-GOOD STICKY CLICKING IMPRESSIONS.
AND "NOT-GOOD STICKY CLICKING IMPRESSION" SOMEHOW EQUATES WITH BOUNCING PAYCHECKS.
YEAH, CHIEF, OKAY, GOT IT--

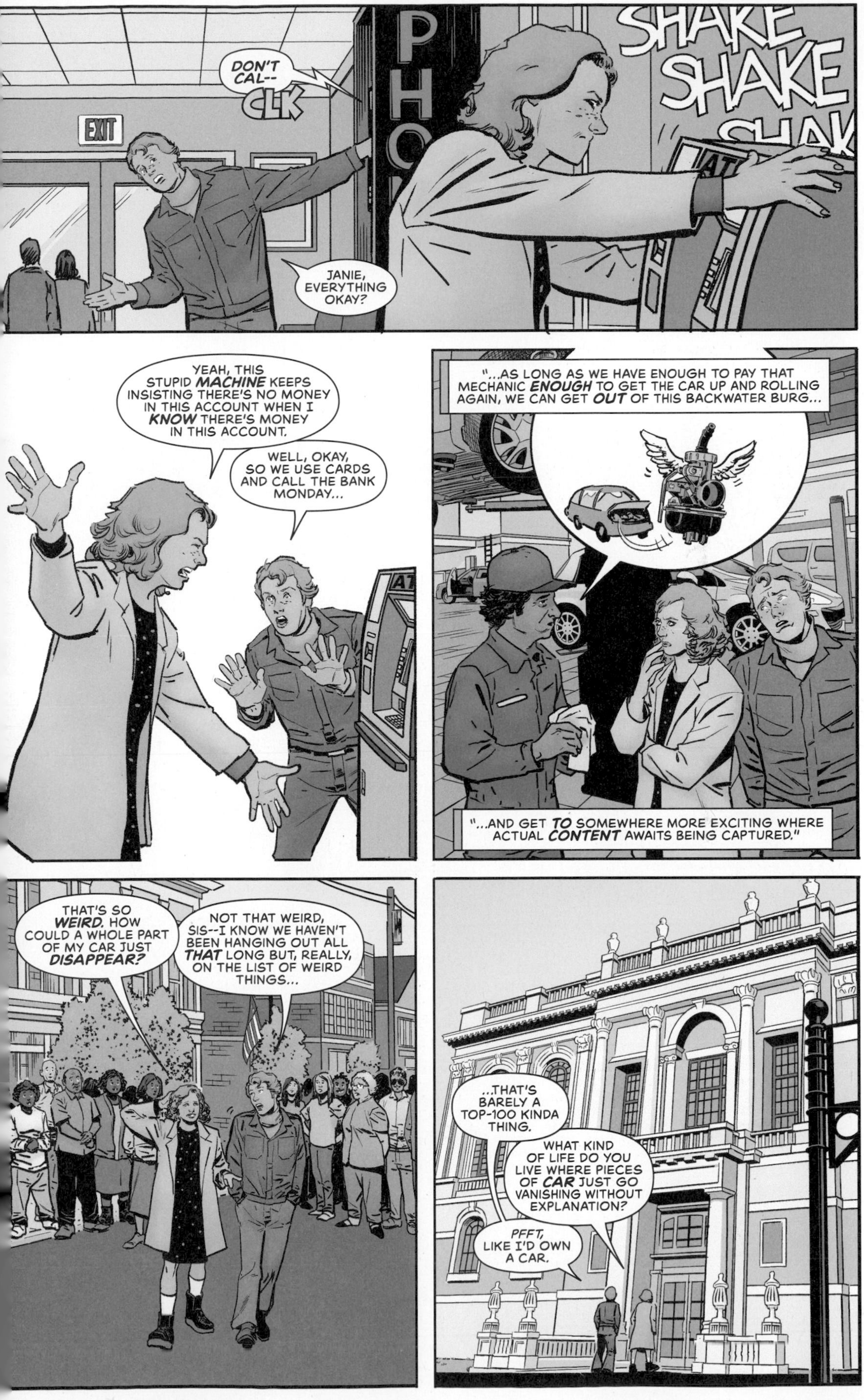
DON'T CAL--
CLK
EXIT
SHAKE
SHAKE
JANIE, EVERYTHING OKAY?
YEAH, THIS STUPID MACHINE KEEPS INSISTING THERE'S NO MONEY IN THIS ACCOUNT WHEN I KNOW THERE'S MONEY IN THIS ACCOUNT.
WELL, OKAY, SO WE USE CARDS AND CALL THE BANK MONDAY...
"...AS LONG AS WE HAVE ENOUGH TO PAY THAT MECHANIC ENOUGH TO GET THE CAR UP AND ROLLING AGAIN, WE CAN GET OUT OF THIS BACKWATER BURG...
"...AND GET TO SOMEWHERE MORE EXCITING WHERE ACTUAL CONTENT AWAITS BEING CAPTURED."
THAT'S SO WEIRD. HOW COULD A WHOLE PART OF MY CAR JUST DISAPPEAR?
NOT THAT WEIRD, SIS--I KNOW WE HAVEN'T BEEN HANGING OUT ALL THAT LONG BUT, REALLY, ON THE LIST OF WEIRD THINGS...
...THAT'S BARELY A TOP-100 KINDA THING.
WHAT KIND OF LIFE DO YOU LIVE WHERE PIECES OF CAR JUST GO VANISHING WITHOUT EXPLANATION?
PFFT, LIKE I'D OWN A CAR.

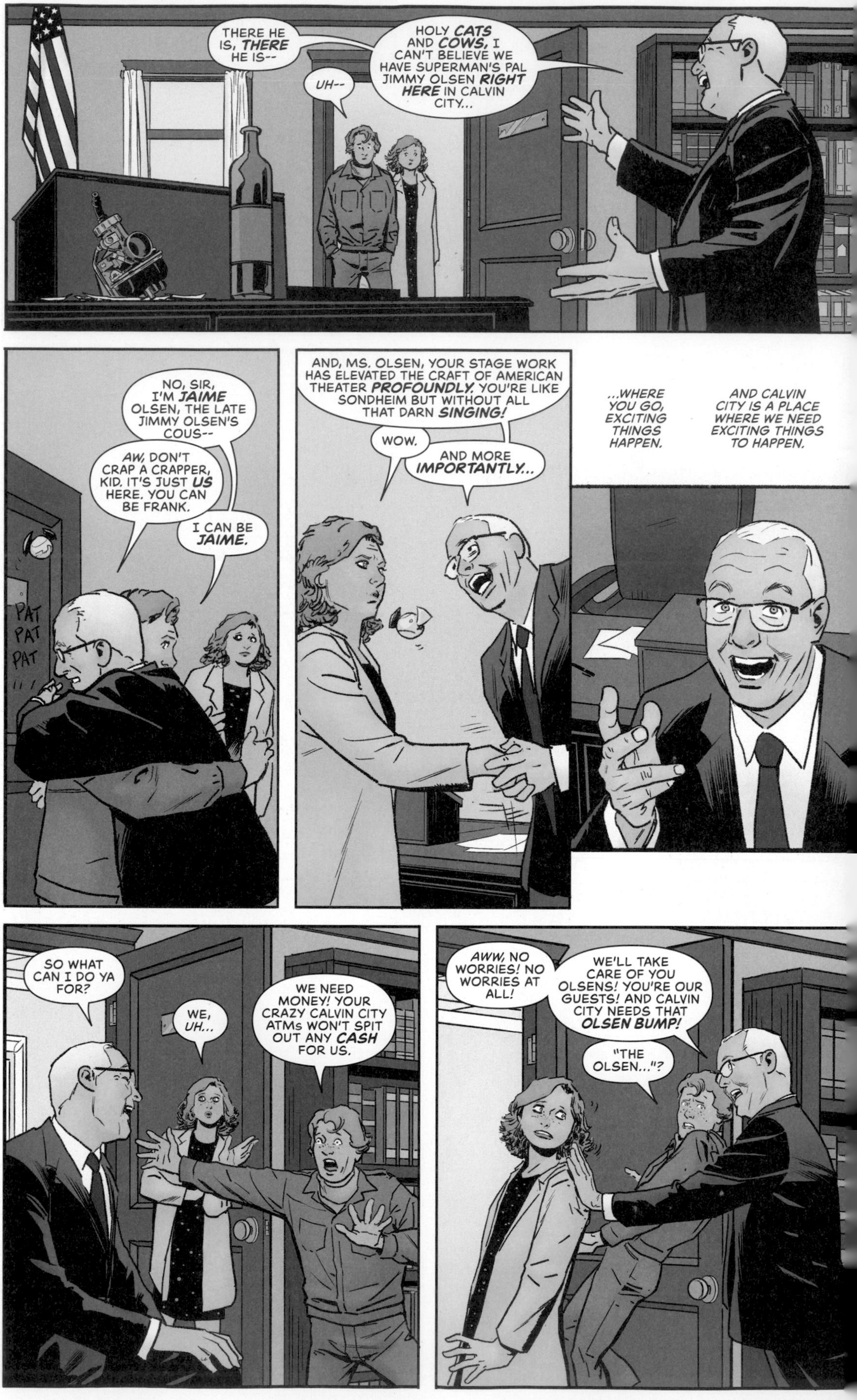
THERE HE IS, THERE HE IS--
HOLY CATS AND COWS, I CAN'T BELIEVE WE HAVE SUPERMAN'S PAL JIMMY OLSEN RIGHT HERE IN CALVIN CITY...
UH--
NO, SIR, I'M JAIME OLSEN, THE LATE JIMMY OLSEN'S COUS--
AW, DON'T CRAP A CRAPPER, KID. IT'S JUST US HERE. YOU CAN BE FRANK.
I CAN BE JAIME.
PAT PAT PAT
AND, MS. OLSEN, YOUR STAGE WORK HAS ELEVATED THE CRAFT OF AMERICAN THEATER PROFOUNDLY. YOU'RE LIKE SONDHEIM BUT WITHOUT ALL THAT DARN SINGING!
WOW.
AND MORE IMPORTANTLY...
...WHERE YOU GO, EXCITING THINGS HAPPEN.
AND CALVIN CITY IS A PLACE WHERE WE NEED EXCITING THINGS TO HAPPEN.
SO WHAT CAN I DO YA FOR?
WE, UH...
WE NEED MONEY! YOUR CRAZY CALVIN CITY ATMs WON'T SPIT OUT ANY CASH FOR US.
AWW, NO WORRIES! NO WORRIES AT ALL!
WE'LL TAKE CARE OF YOU OLSENS! YOU'RE OUR GUESTS! AND CALVIN CITY NEEDS THAT OLSEN BUMP!
"THE OLSEN..."?

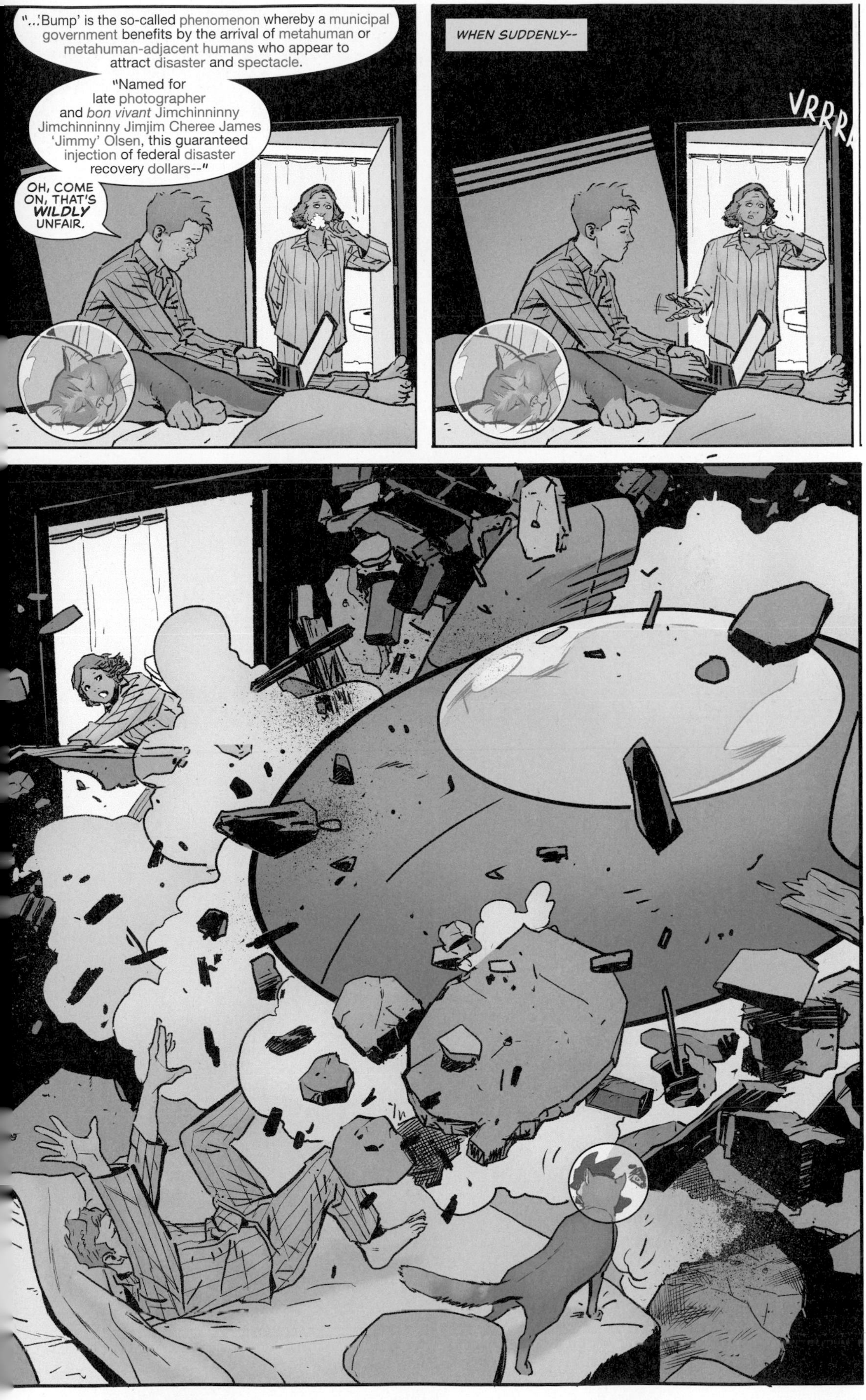
"...'Bump' is the so-called phenomenon whereby a municipal government benefits by the arrival of metahuman or metahuman-adjacent humans who appear to attract disaster and spectacle.
"Named for late photographer and *bon vivant* Jimchinninny Jimchinninny Jimjim Cheree James 'Jimmy' Olsen, this guaranteed injection of federal disaster recovery dollars--"
OH, COME ON, THAT'S **WILDLY** UNFAIR.
WHEN SUDDENLY--
VRRRA

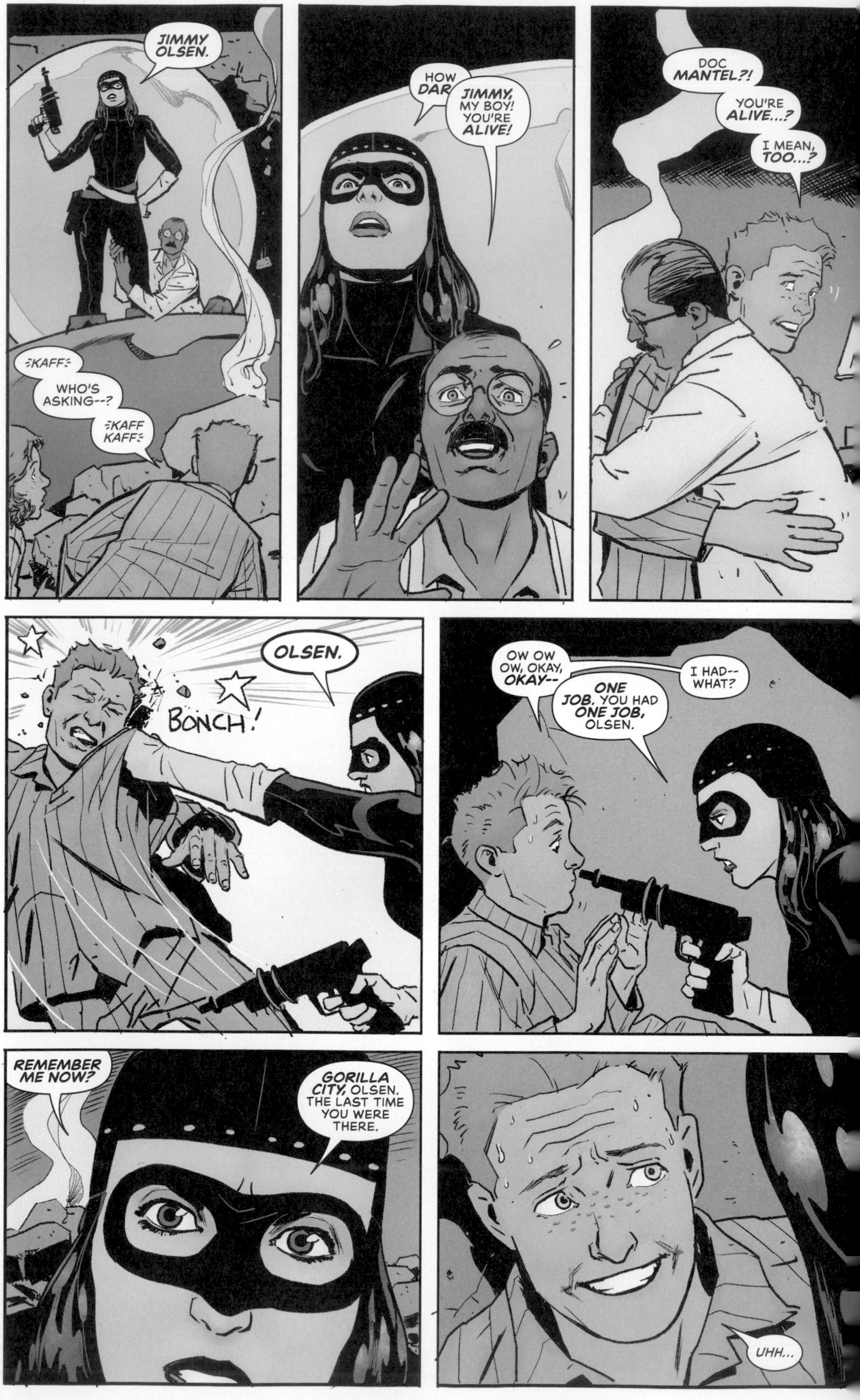
JIMMY OLSEN.
KAFF
WHO'S ASKING--?
KAFF KAFF
HOW DAR
JIMMY, MY BOY! YOU'RE ALIVE!
DOC MANTEL?!
YOU'RE ALIVE...?
I MEAN, TOO...?
OLSEN.
BONCH!
OW OW OW, OKAY, OKAY--
I HAD-- WHAT?
ONE JOB. YOU HAD ONE JOB, OLSEN.
REMEMBER ME NOW?
GORILLA CITY, OLSEN. THE LAST TIME YOU WERE THERE.
UHH...

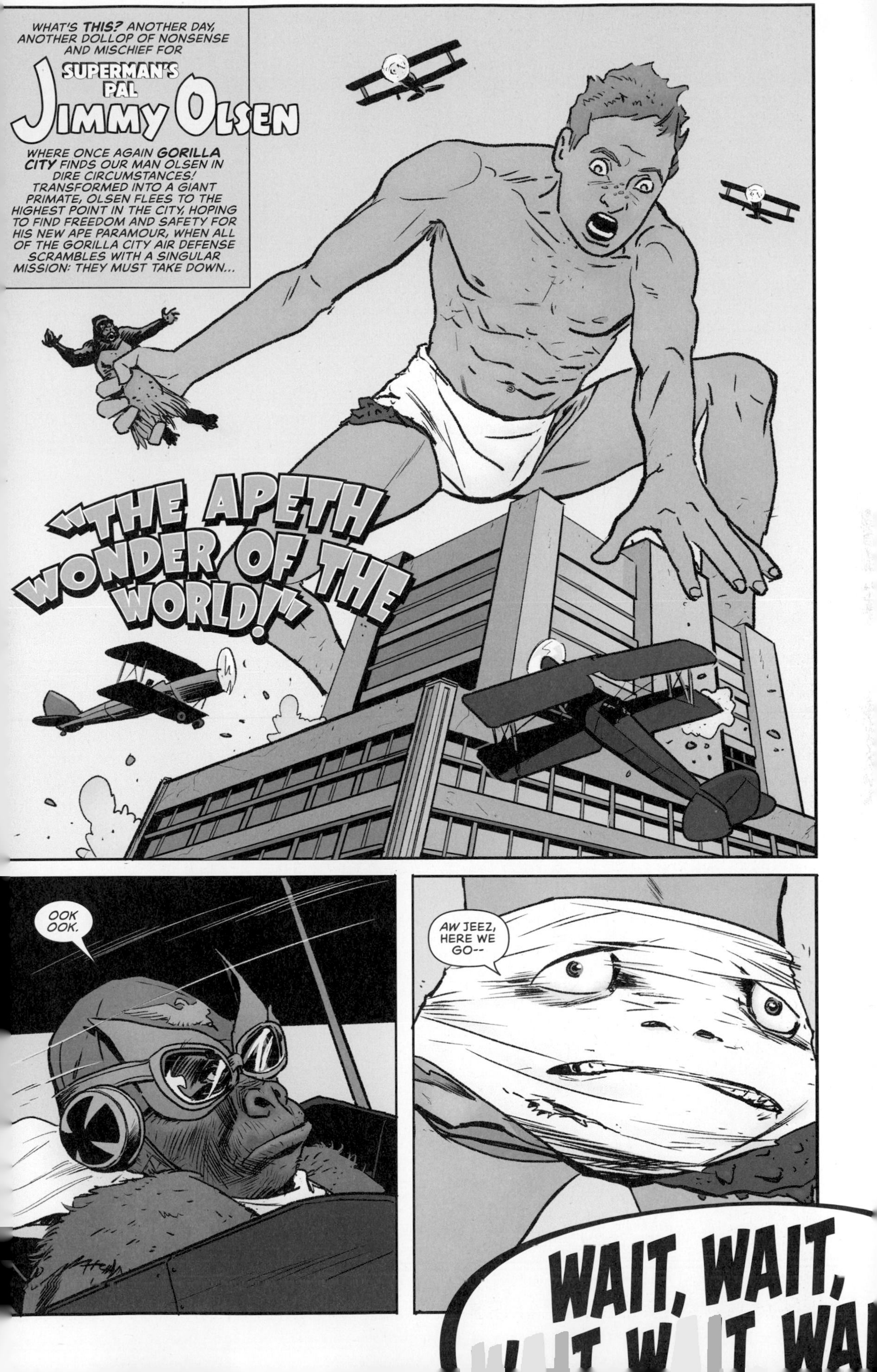

WHAT'S THIS? ANOTHER DAY, ANOTHER DOLLOP OF NONSENSE AND MISCHIEF FOR
SUPERMAN'S PAL JIMMY OLSEN
WHERE ONCE AGAIN GORILLA CITY FINDS OUR MAN OLSEN IN DIRE CIRCUMSTANCES! TRANSFORMED INTO A GIANT PRIMATE, OLSEN FLEES TO THE HIGHEST POINT IN THE CITY, HOPING TO FIND FREEDOM AND SAFETY FOR HIS NEW APE PARAMOUR, WHEN ALL OF THE GORILLA CITY AIR DEFENSE SCRAMBLES WITH A SINGULAR MISSION: THEY MUST TAKE DOWN...
"THE APETH WONDER OF THE WORLD!"
OOK OOK.
AW JEEZ, HERE WE GO--
WAIT, WAIT,

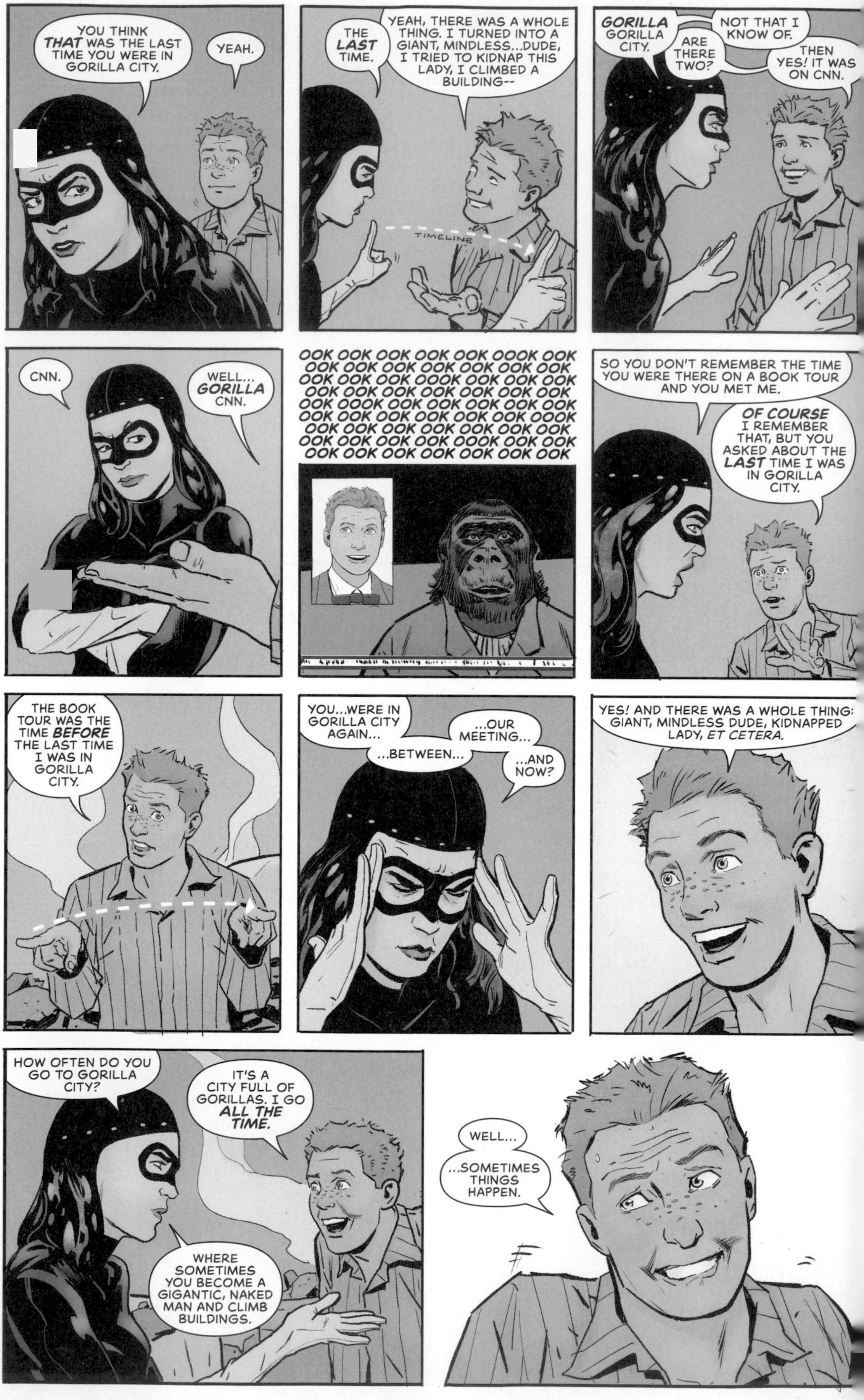

YOU THINK THAT WAS THE LAST TIME YOU WERE IN GORILLA CITY.
YEAH.
THE LAST TIME.
YEAH, THERE WAS A WHOLE THING. I TURNED INTO A GIANT, MINDLESS...DUDE, I TRIED TO KIDNAP THIS LADY, I CLIMBED A BUILDING--
TIMELINE
GORILLA GORILLA CITY.
NOT THAT I KNOW OF.
ARE THERE TWO?
THEN YES! IT WAS ON CNN.
CNN.
WELL... GORILLA CNN.
OOK OOK OOK OOK OOK OOOK OOK
OOK OOK OOK OOK OOK OOK OOK
OOK OOK OOK OOOK OOK OOK OOK
OOK OOK OOK OOK OOK OOK OOK
OOK OOOK OOK OOK OOK OOK OOK
OOK OOK OOK OOK OOK OOK OOOK
OOK OOK OOK OOK OOK OOK OOK
OOK OOK OOK OOK OOOK OOK OOK
OOK OOK OOK OOK OOK OOK OOK
SO YOU DON'T REMEMBER THE TIME YOU WERE THERE ON A BOOK TOUR AND YOU MET ME.
OF COURSE I REMEMBER THAT, BUT YOU ASKED ABOUT THE LAST TIME I WAS IN GORILLA CITY.
THE BOOK TOUR WAS THE TIME BEFORE THE LAST TIME I WAS IN GORILLA CITY.
YOU...WERE IN GORILLA CITY AGAIN...
...BETWEEN...
...OUR MEETING...
...AND NOW?
YES! AND THERE WAS A WHOLE THING: GIANT, MINDLESS DUDE, KIDNAPPED LADY, ET CETERA.
HOW OFTEN DO YOU GO TO GORILLA CITY?
IT'S A CITY FULL OF GORILLAS. I GO ALL THE TIME.
WHERE SOMETIMES YOU BECOME A GIGANTIC, NAKED MAN AND CLIMB BUILDINGS.
WELL...
...SOMETIMES THINGS HAPPEN.

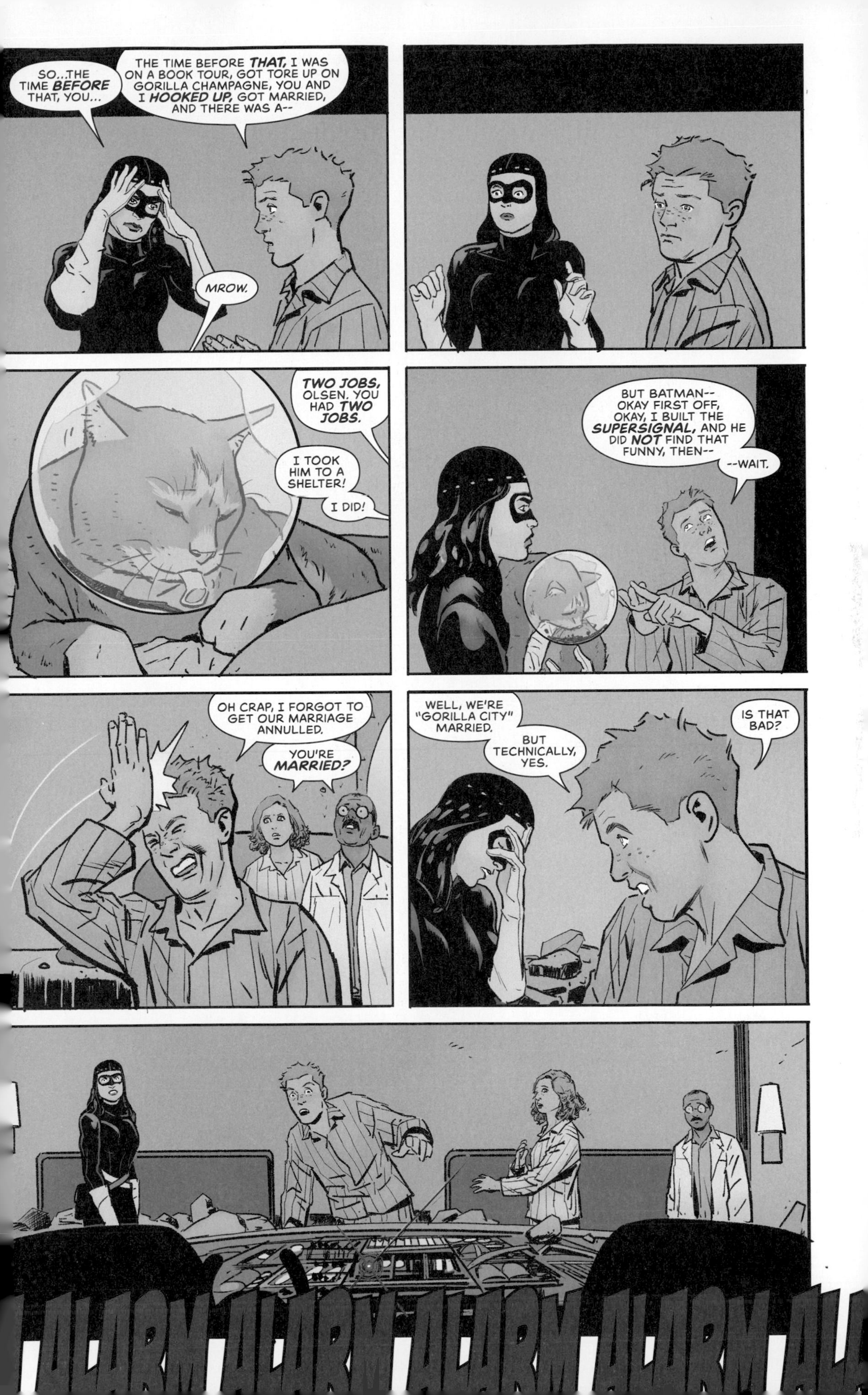
SO...THE TIME BEFORE THAT, YOU...
THE TIME BEFORE THAT, I WAS ON A BOOK TOUR, GOT TORE UP ON GORILLA CHAMPAGNE, YOU AND I HOOKED UP, GOT MARRIED, AND THERE WAS A--
MROW.
TWO JOBS, OLSEN. YOU HAD TWO JOBS.
I TOOK HIM TO A SHELTER!
I DID!
BUT BATMAN-- OKAY FIRST OFF, OKAY, I BUILT THE SUPERSIGNAL, AND HE DID NOT FIND THAT FUNNY, THEN--
--WAIT.
OH CRAP, I FORGOT TO GET OUR MARRIAGE ANNULLED.
YOU'RE MARRIED?
WELL, WE'RE "GORILLA CITY" MARRIED.
BUT TECHNICALLY, YES.
IS THAT BAD?
ALARM ALARM ALARM ALARM

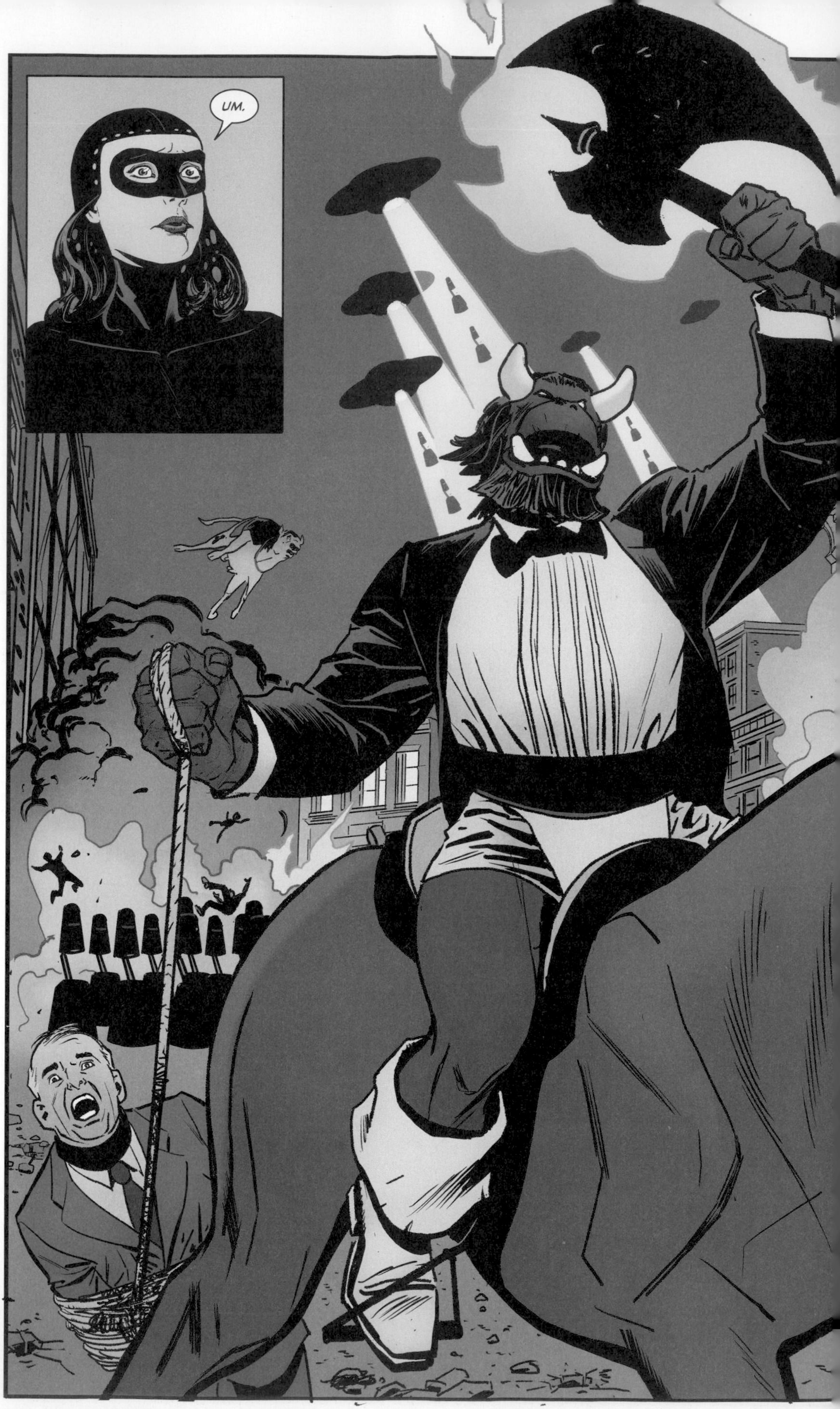
UM.

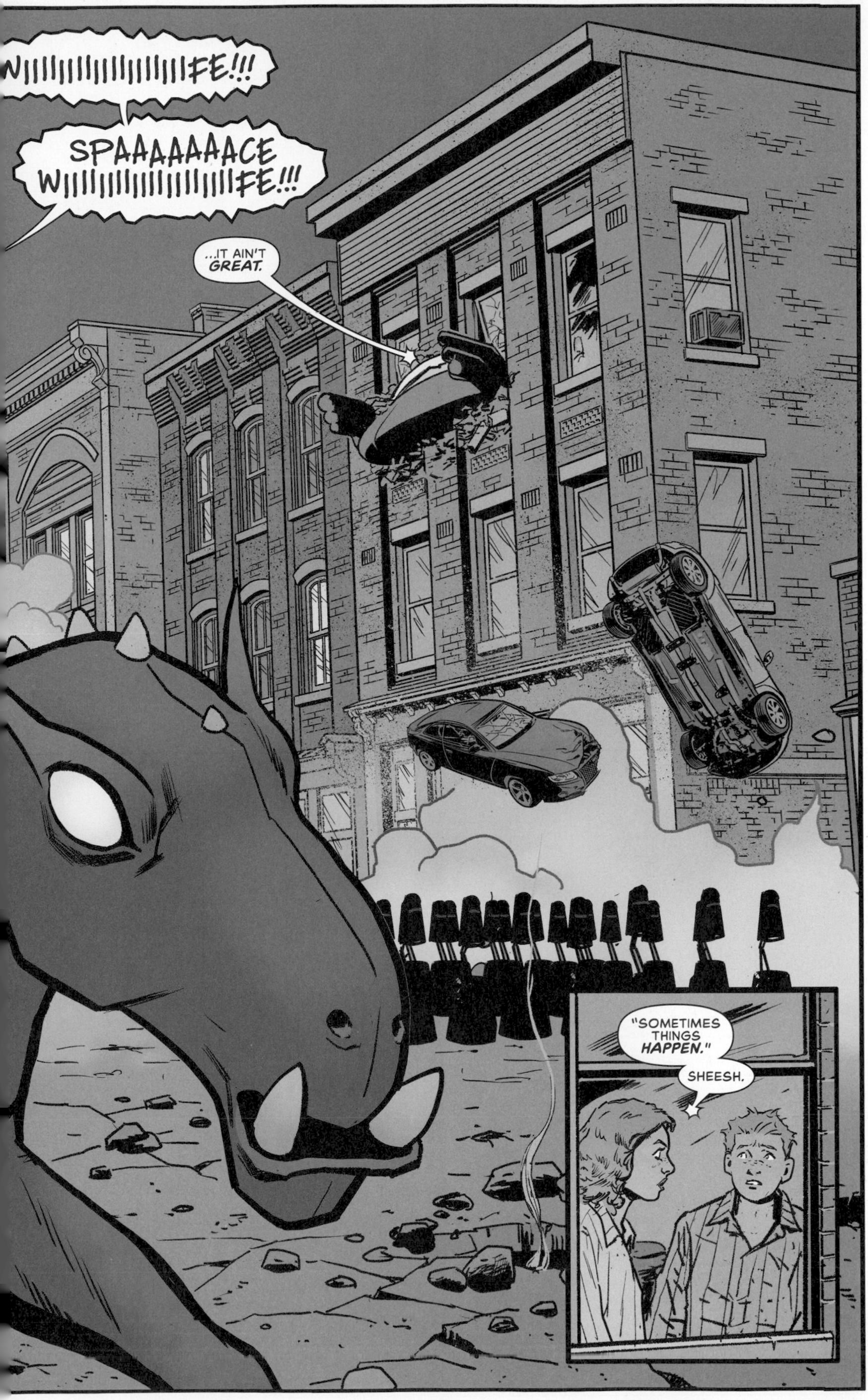
WIIIIIIIIIIIIIIIIIFE!!!
SPAAAAAAACE WIIIIIIIIIIIIIIIIIFE!!!
...IT AIN'T GREAT.
"SOMETIMES THINGS HAPPEN."
SHEESH.

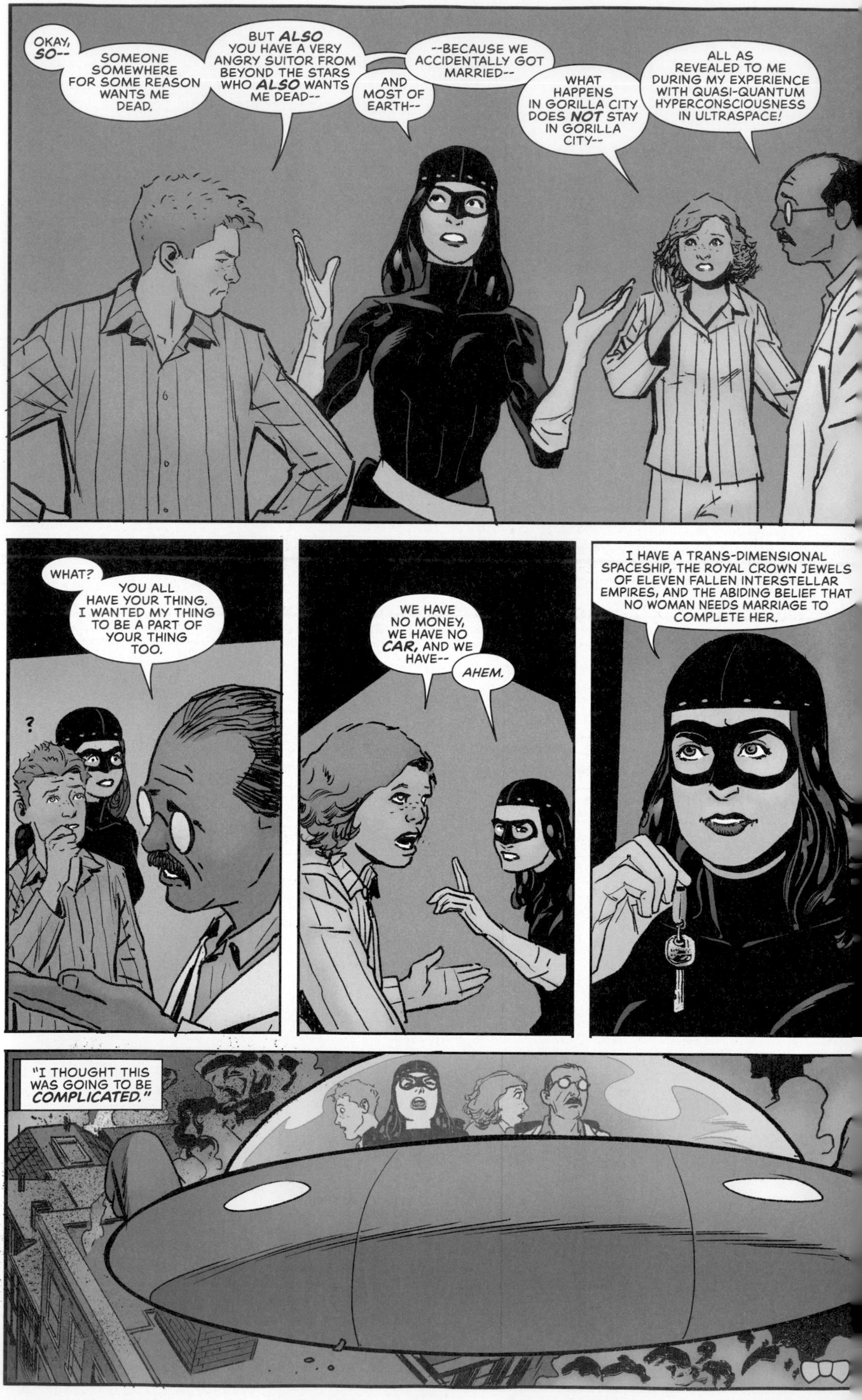

OKAY, SO--
SOMEONE SOMEWHERE FOR SOME REASON WANTS ME DEAD.
BUT ALSO YOU HAVE A VERY ANGRY SUITOR FROM BEYOND THE STARS WHO ALSO WANTS ME DEAD--
--BECAUSE WE ACCIDENTALLY GOT MARRIED--
AND MOST OF EARTH--
WHAT HAPPENS IN GORILLA CITY DOES NOT STAY IN GORILLA CITY--
ALL AS REVEALED TO ME DURING MY EXPERIENCE WITH QUASI-QUANTUM HYPERCONSCIOUSNESS IN ULTRASPACE!
WHAT?
YOU ALL HAVE YOUR THING. I WANTED MY THING TO BE A PART OF YOUR THING TOO.
?
WE HAVE NO MONEY, WE HAVE NO CAR, AND WE HAVE--
AHEM.
I HAVE A TRANS-DIMENSIONAL SPACESHIP, THE ROYAL CROWN JEWELS OF ELEVEN FALLEN INTERSTELLAR EMPIRES, AND THE ABIDING BELIEF THAT NO WOMAN NEEDS MARRIAGE TO COMPLETE HER.
"I THOUGHT THIS WAS GOING TO BE COMPLICATED."

JIMMY GETS A CLUE

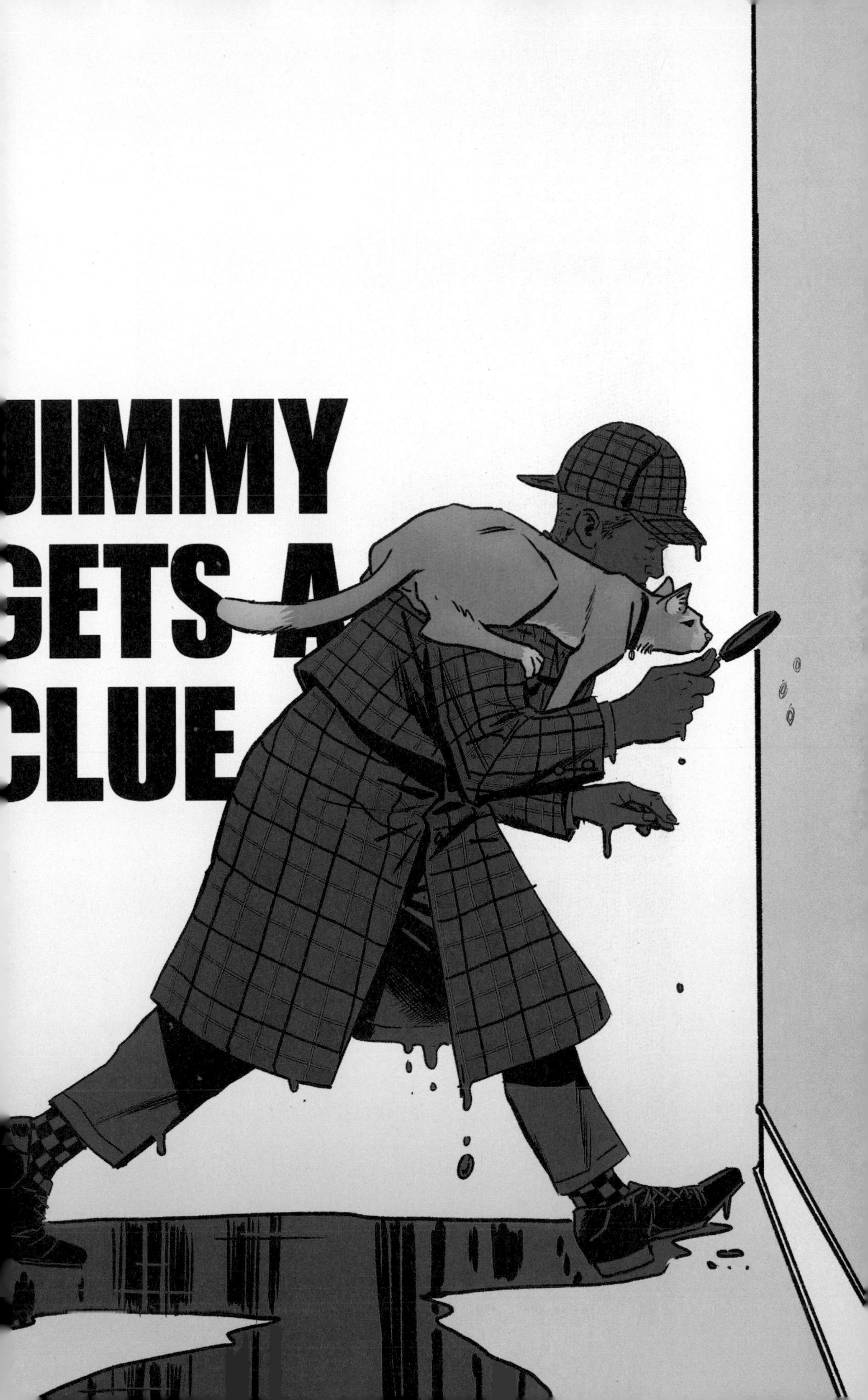

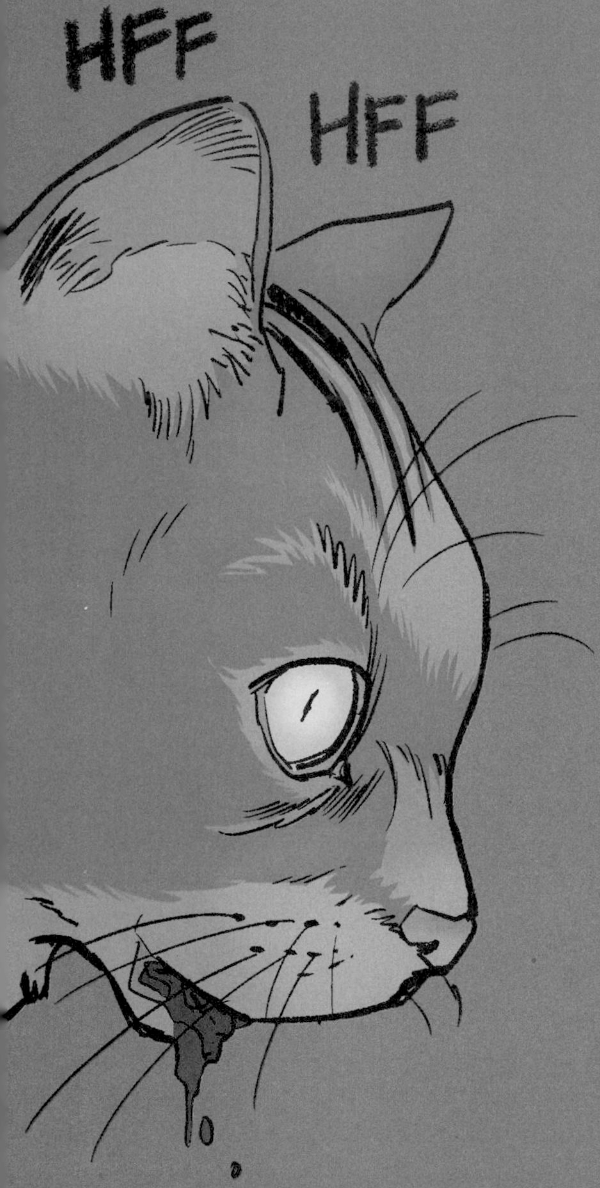
HFF
HFF

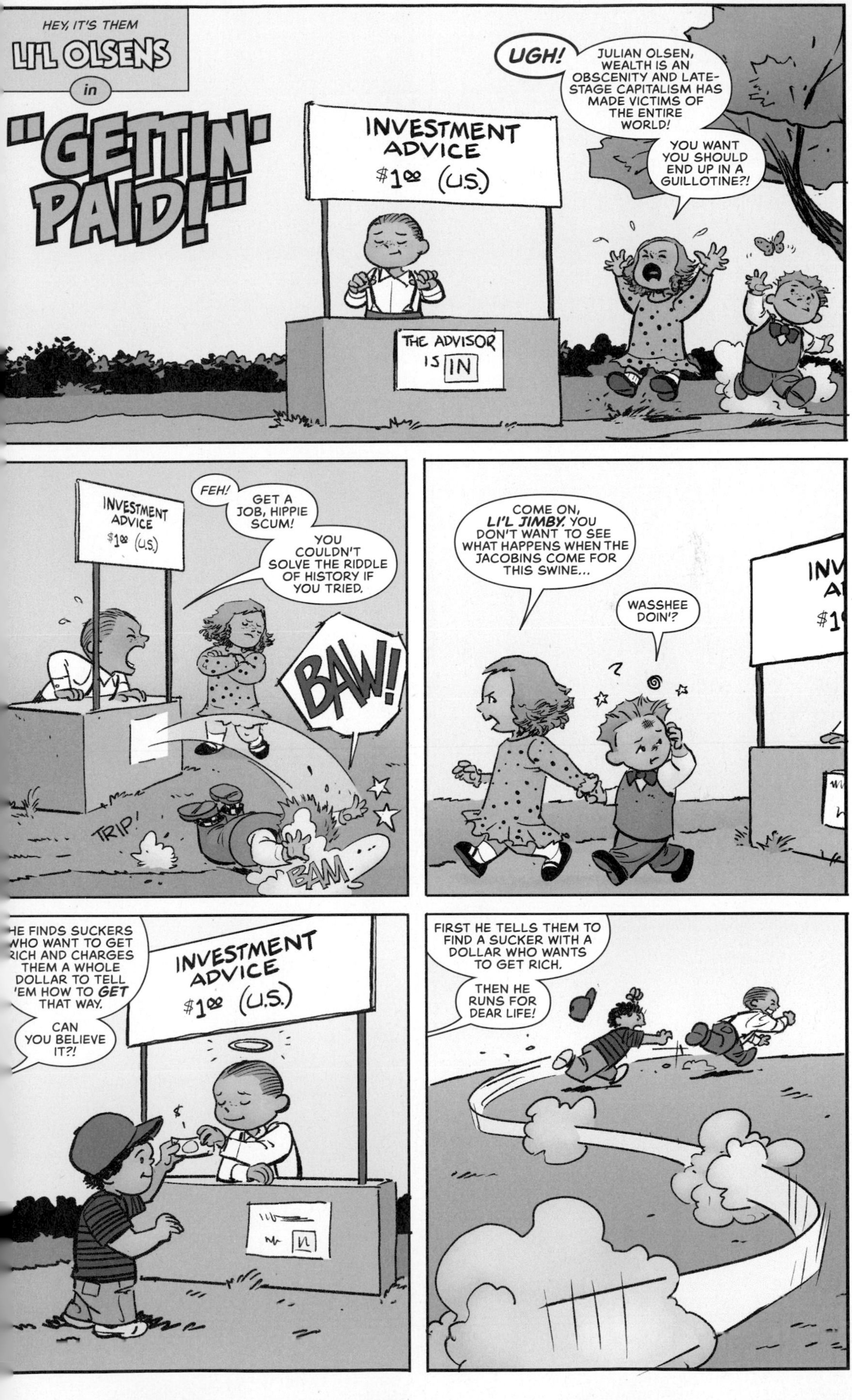

HEY, IT'S THEM
LI'L OLSENS
in
"GETTIN' PAID!"
INVESTMENT ADVICE $1.00 (U.S.)
THE ADVISOR IS IN
UGH!
JULIAN OLSEN, WEALTH IS AN OBSCENITY AND LATE-STAGE CAPITALISM HAS MADE VICTIMS OF THE ENTIRE WORLD!
YOU WANT YOU SHOULD END UP IN A GUILLOTINE?!
INVESTMENT ADVICE $1.00 (U.S.)
FEH!
GET A JOB, HIPPIE SCUM!
YOU COULDN'T SOLVE THE RIDDLE OF HISTORY IF YOU TRIED.
BAW!
TRIP!
BAM
COME ON, LI'L JIMBY. YOU DON'T WANT TO SEE WHAT HAPPENS WHEN THE JACOBINS COME FOR THIS SWINE...
WASSHEE DOIN'?
HE FINDS SUCKERS WHO WANT TO GET RICH AND CHARGES THEM A WHOLE DOLLAR TO TELL 'EM HOW TO GET THAT WAY.
CAN YOU BELIEVE IT?!
INVESTMENT ADVICE $1.00 (U.S.)
FIRST HE TELLS THEM TO FIND A SUCKER WITH A DOLLAR WHO WANTS TO GET RICH.
THEN HE RUNS FOR DEAR LIFE!

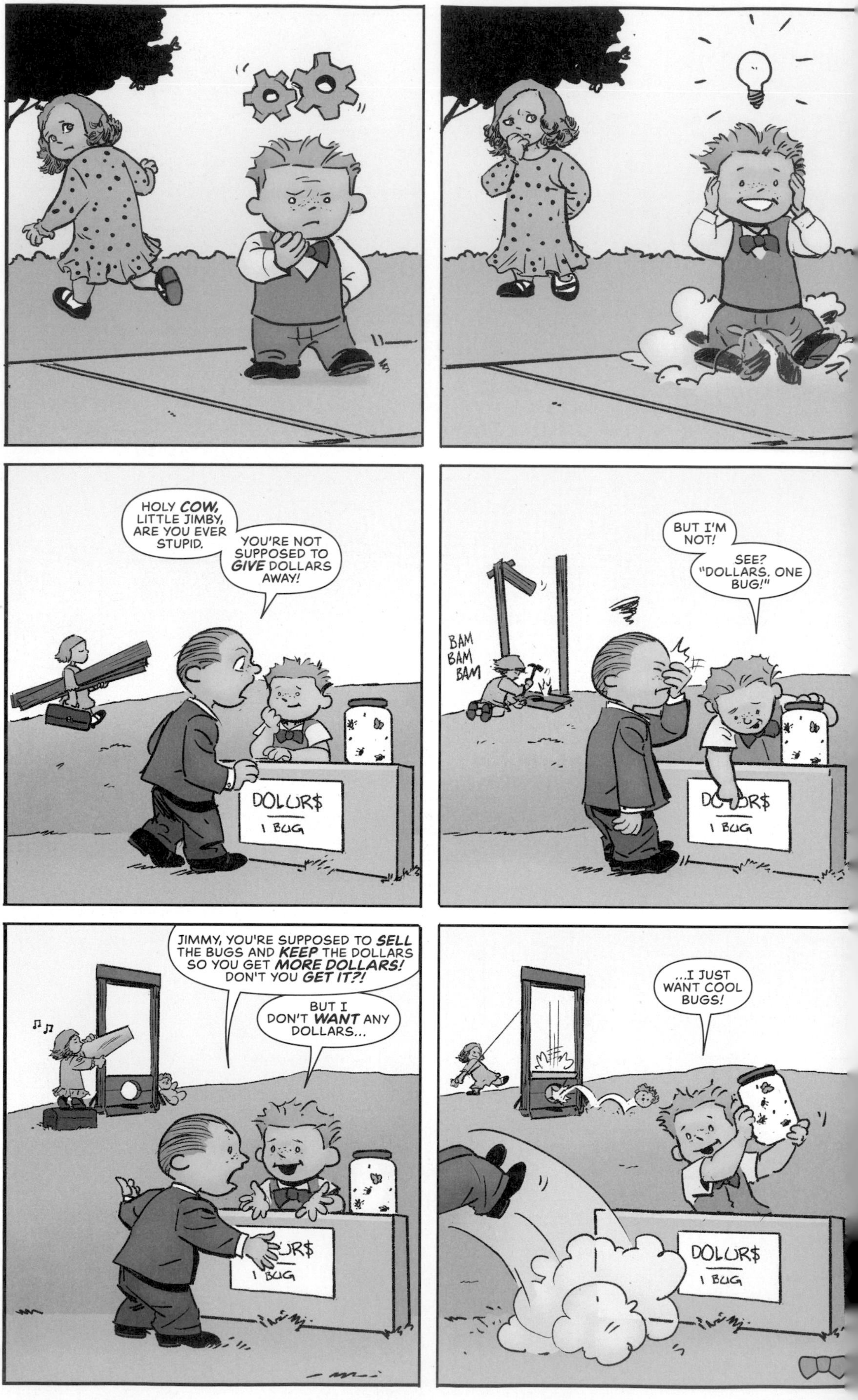
HOLY COW, LITTLE JIMBY, ARE YOU EVER STUPID.
YOU'RE NOT SUPPOSED TO GIVE DOLLARS AWAY!
DOLUR$
1 BUG
BUT I'M NOT!
SEE? "DOLLARS, ONE BUG!"
BAM BAM BAM
JIMMY, YOU'RE SUPPOSED TO SELL THE BUGS AND KEEP THE DOLLARS SO YOU GET MORE DOLLARS! DON'T YOU GET IT?!
BUT I DON'T WANT ANY DOLLARS...
...I JUST WANT COOL BUGS!
DOLUR$
1 BUG

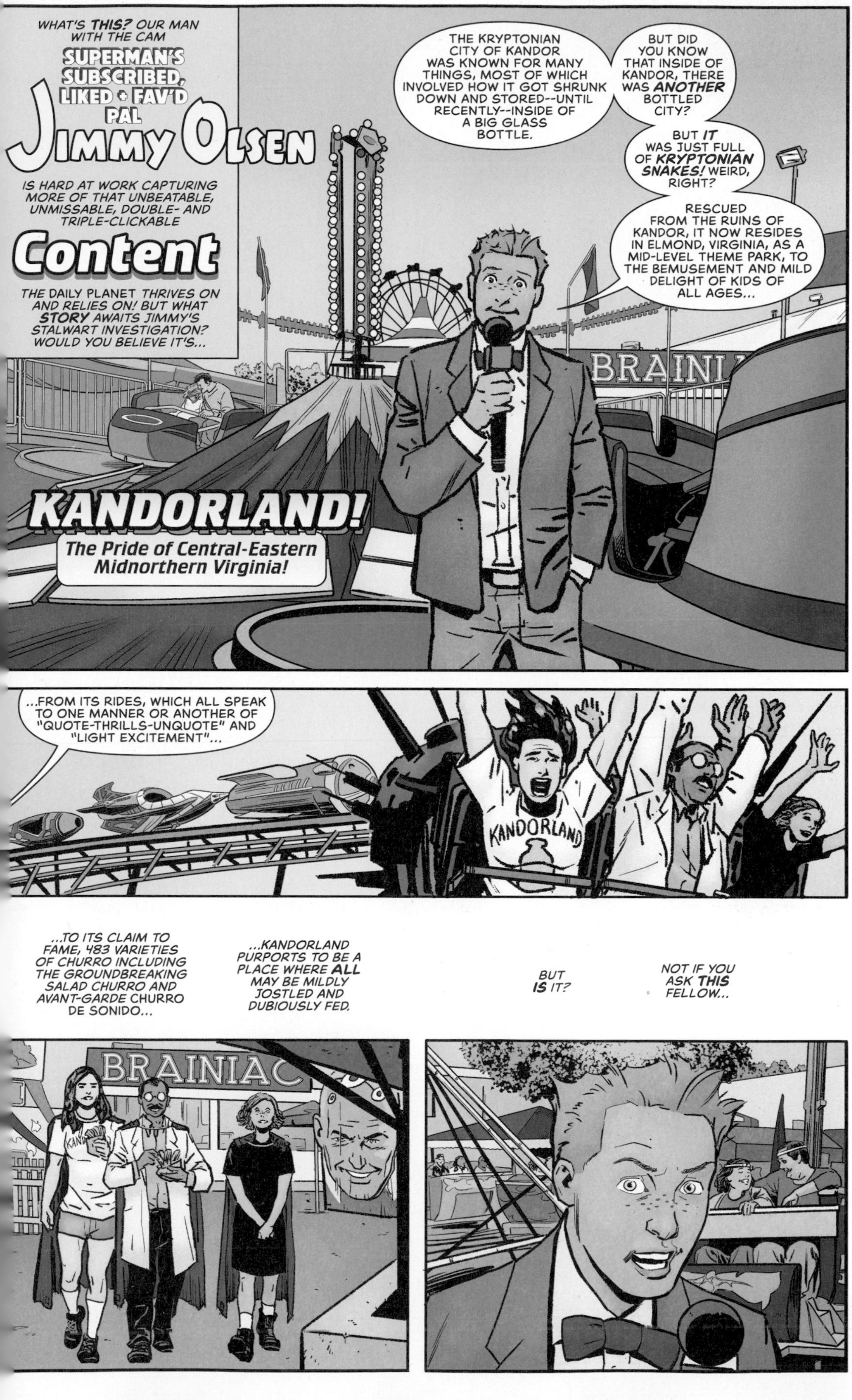
WHAT'S THIS? OUR MAN WITH THE CAM
SUPERMAN'S SUBSCRIBED, LIKED + FAV'D PAL
JIMMY OLSEN
IS HARD AT WORK CAPTURING MORE OF THAT UNBEATABLE, UNMISSABLE, DOUBLE- AND TRIPLE-CLICKABLE
Content
THE DAILY PLANET THRIVES ON AND RELIES ON! BUT WHAT STORY AWAITS JIMMY'S STALWART INVESTIGATION? WOULD YOU BELIEVE IT'S...
THE KRYPTONIAN CITY OF KANDOR WAS KNOWN FOR MANY THINGS, MOST OF WHICH INVOLVED HOW IT GOT SHRUNK DOWN AND STORED--UNTIL RECENTLY--INSIDE OF A BIG GLASS BOTTLE.
BUT DID YOU KNOW THAT INSIDE OF KANDOR, THERE WAS ANOTHER BOTTLED CITY?
BUT IT WAS JUST FULL OF KRYPTONIAN SNAKES! WEIRD, RIGHT?
RESCUED FROM THE RUINS OF KANDOR, IT NOW RESIDES IN ELMOND, VIRGINIA, AS A MID-LEVEL THEME PARK, TO THE BEMUSEMENT AND MILD DELIGHT OF KIDS OF ALL AGES...
BRAINI
KANDORLAND!
The Pride of Central-Eastern Midnorthern Virginia!
...FROM ITS RIDES, WHICH ALL SPEAK TO ONE MANNER OR ANOTHER OF "QUOTE-THRILLS-UNQUOTE" AND "LIGHT EXCITEMENT"...
KANDORLAND
...TO ITS CLAIM TO FAME, 483 VARIETIES OF CHURRO INCLUDING THE GROUNDBREAKING SALAD CHURRO AND AVANT-GARDE CHURRO DE SONIDO...
...KANDORLAND PURPORTS TO BE A PLACE WHERE ALL MAY BE MILDLY JOSTLED AND DUBIOUSLY FED.
BRAINIAC
BUT IS IT?
NOT IF YOU ASK THIS FELLOW...

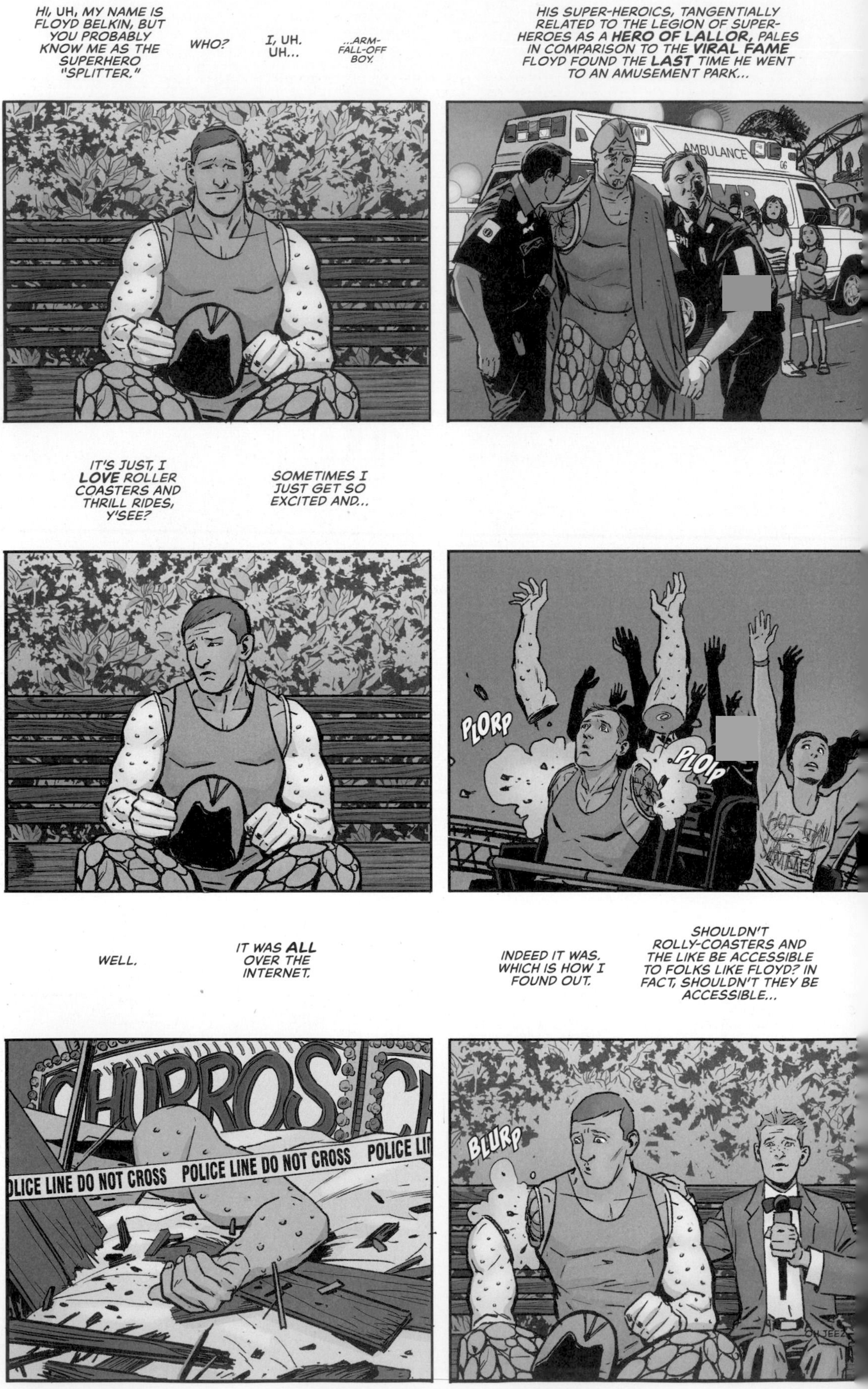
HI, UH, MY NAME IS FLOYD BELKIN, BUT YOU PROBABLY KNOW ME AS THE SUPERHERO "SPLITTER."
WHO?
I, UH. UH...
...ARM-FALL-OFF BOY.
HIS SUPER-HEROICS, TANGENTIALLY RELATED TO THE LEGION OF SUPER-HEROES AS A HERO OF LALLOR, PALES IN COMPARISON TO THE VIRAL FAME FLOYD FOUND THE LAST TIME HE WENT TO AN AMUSEMENT PARK...
AMBULANCE
IT'S JUST, I LOVE ROLLER COASTERS AND THRILL RIDES, Y'SEE?
SOMETIMES I JUST GET SO EXCITED AND...
PLORP
PLOIP
WELL.
IT WAS ALL OVER THE INTERNET.
CHURROS
POLICE LINE DO NOT CROSS POLICE LINE DO NOT CROSS POLICE LIN
INDEED IT WAS. WHICH IS HOW I FOUND OUT.
SHOULDN'T ROLLY-COASTERS AND THE LIKE BE ACCESSIBLE TO FOLKS LIKE FLOYD? IN FACT, SHOULDN'T THEY BE ACCESSIBLE...
BLURP
OH JEEZ

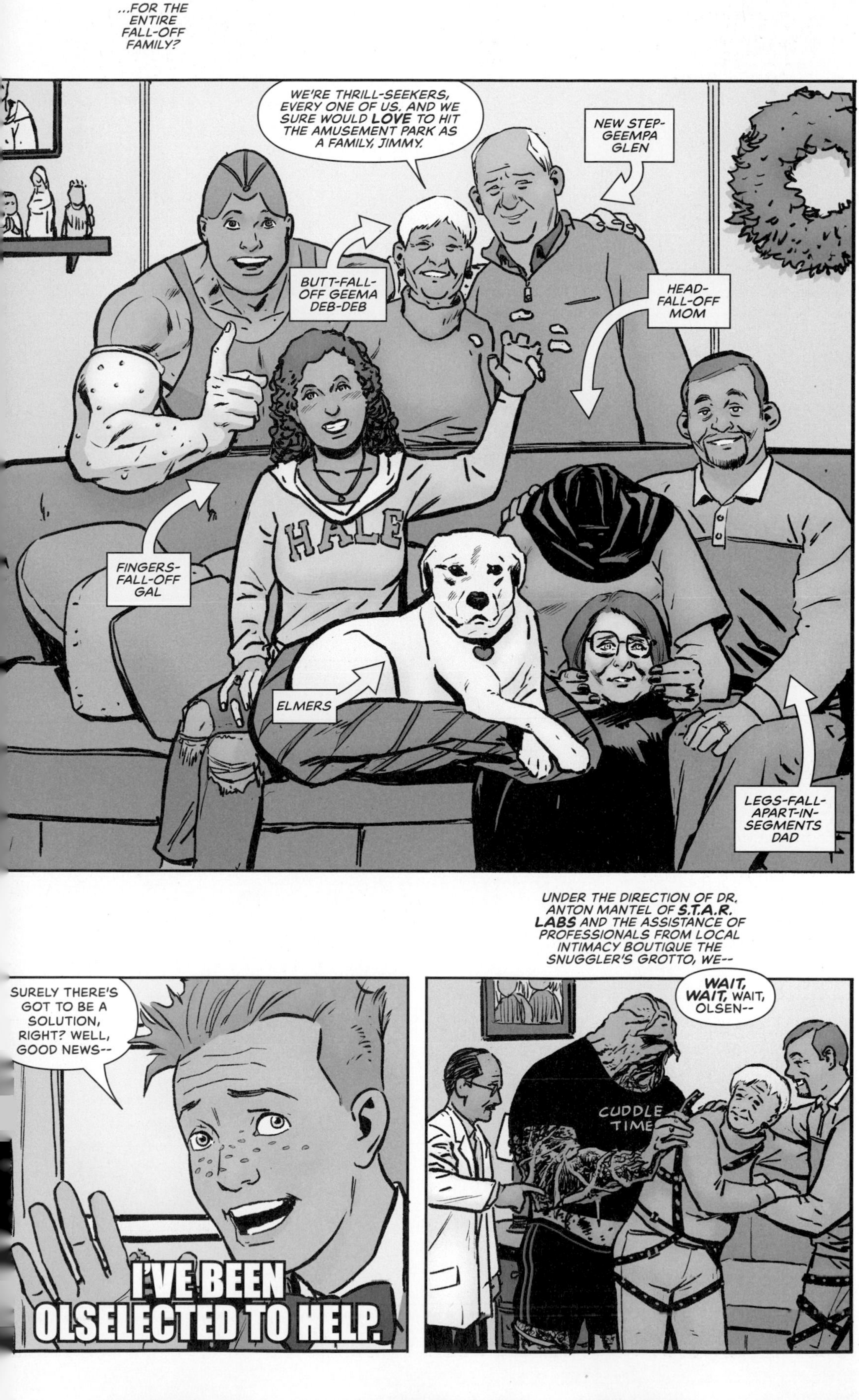

...FOR THE ENTIRE FALL-OFF FAMILY?
WE'RE THRILL-SEEKERS, EVERY ONE OF US. AND WE SURE WOULD LOVE TO HIT THE AMUSEMENT PARK AS A FAMILY, JIMMY.
NEW STEP-GEEMPA GLEN
BUTT-FALL-OFF GEEMA DEB-DEB
HEAD-FALL-OFF MOM
HALE
FINGERS-FALL-OFF GAL
ELMERS
LEGS-FALL-APART-IN-SEGMENTS DAD
SURELY THERE'S GOT TO BE A SOLUTION, RIGHT? WELL, GOOD NEWS--
I'VE BEEN OLSELECTED TO HELP.
UNDER THE DIRECTION OF DR. ANTON MANTEL OF S.T.A.R. LABS AND THE ASSISTANCE OF PROFESSIONALS FROM LOCAL INTIMACY BOUTIQUE THE SNUGGLER'S GROTTO, WE--
WAIT, WAIT, WAIT, OLSEN--
CUDDLE TIME

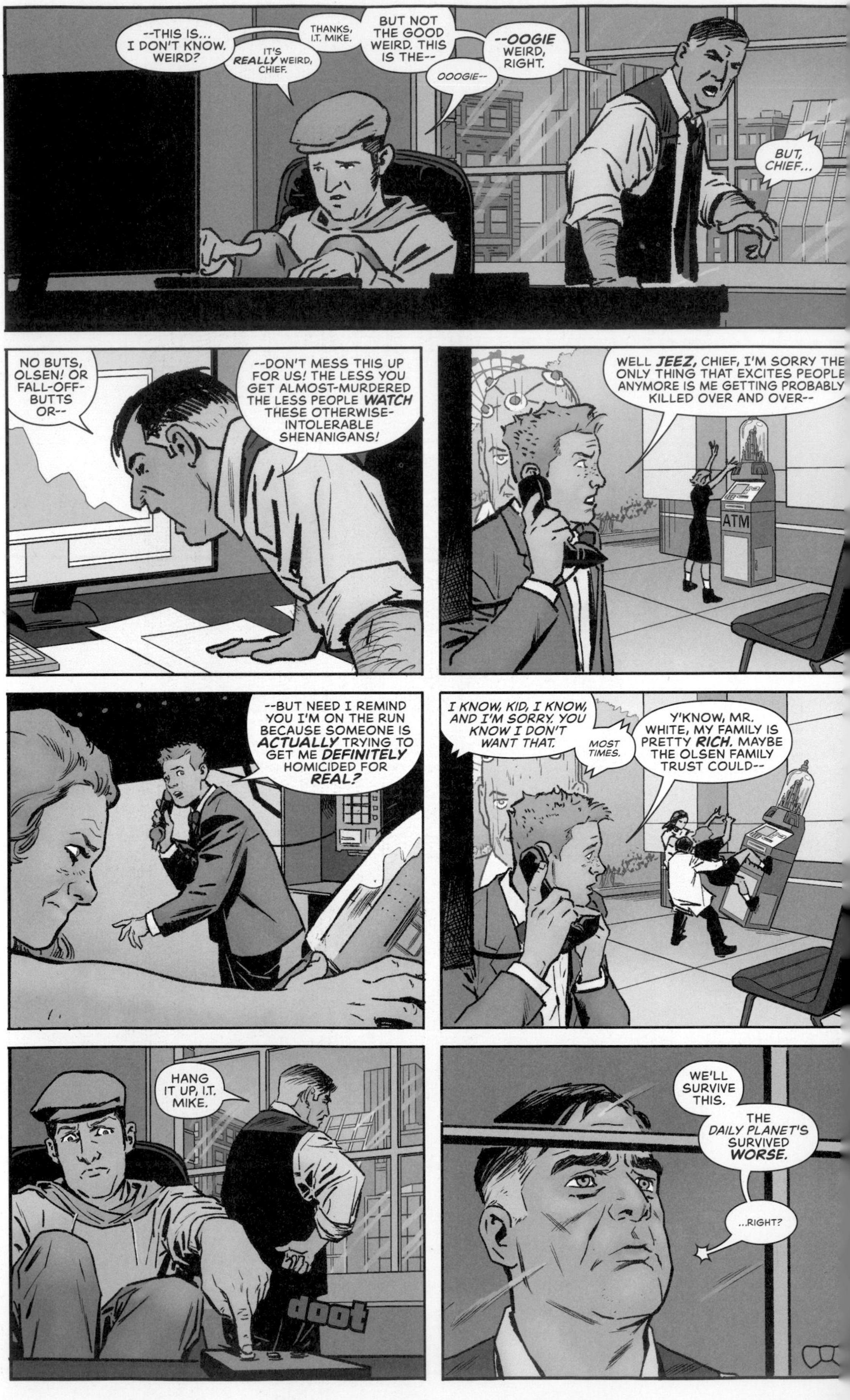
--THIS IS... I DON'T KNOW. WEIRD?
IT'S REALLY WEIRD, CHIEF.
THANKS, I.T. MIKE.
BUT NOT THE GOOD WEIRD. THIS IS THE--
OOOGIE--
--OOGIE WEIRD, RIGHT.
BUT, CHIEF...
NO BUTS, OLSEN! OR FALL-OFF-BUTTS OR--
--DON'T MESS THIS UP FOR US! THE LESS YOU GET ALMOST-MURDERED THE LESS PEOPLE WATCH THESE OTHERWISE-INTOLERABLE SHENANIGANS!
WELL JEEZ, CHIEF, I'M SORRY THE ONLY THING THAT EXCITES PEOPLE ANYMORE IS ME GETTING PROBABLY KILLED OVER AND OVER--
ATM
--BUT NEED I REMIND YOU I'M ON THE RUN BECAUSE SOMEONE IS ACTUALLY TRYING TO GET ME DEFINITELY HOMICIDED FOR REAL?
I KNOW, KID, I KNOW, AND I'M SORRY. YOU KNOW I DON'T WANT THAT.
MOST TIMES.
Y'KNOW, MR. WHITE, MY FAMILY IS PRETTY RICH. MAYBE THE OLSEN FAMILY TRUST COULD--
HANG IT UP, I.T. MIKE.
doot
WE'LL SURVIVE THIS.
THE DAILY PLANET'S SURVIVED WORSE.
...RIGHT?

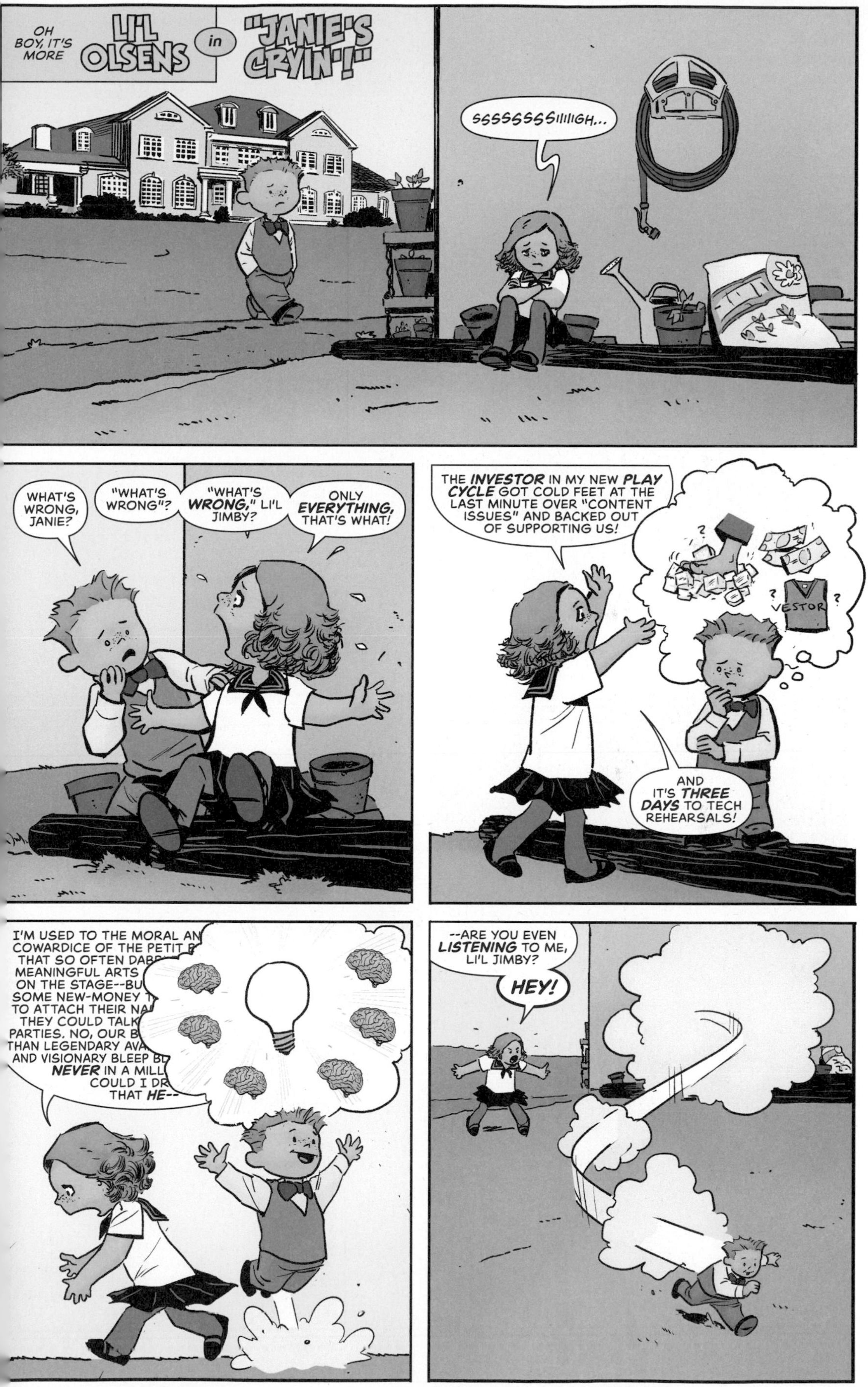
OH BOY, IT'S MORE LI'L OLSENS in "JANIE'S CRYIN'!"
SSSSSSSSIIIIIGH...
WHAT'S WRONG, JANIE?
"WHAT'S WRONG"?
"WHAT'S WRONG," LI'L JIMBY?
ONLY EVERYTHING, THAT'S WHAT!
THE INVESTOR IN MY NEW PLAY CYCLE GOT COLD FEET AT THE LAST MINUTE OVER "CONTENT ISSUES" AND BACKED OUT OF SUPPORTING US!
? ? VESTOR ?
AND IT'S THREE DAYS TO TECH REHEARSALS!
I'M USED TO THE MORAL AN
COWARDICE OF THE PETIT
THAT SO OFTEN DAB
MEANINGFUL ARTS
ON THE STAGE--BU
SOME NEW-MONEY
TO ATTACH THEIR NA
THEY COULD TALK
PARTIES. NO, OUR B
THAN LEGENDARY AVA
AND VISIONARY BLEEP B
NEVER IN A MILL
COULD I DR
THAT HE--
--ARE YOU EVEN LISTENING TO ME, LI'L JIMBY?
HEY!

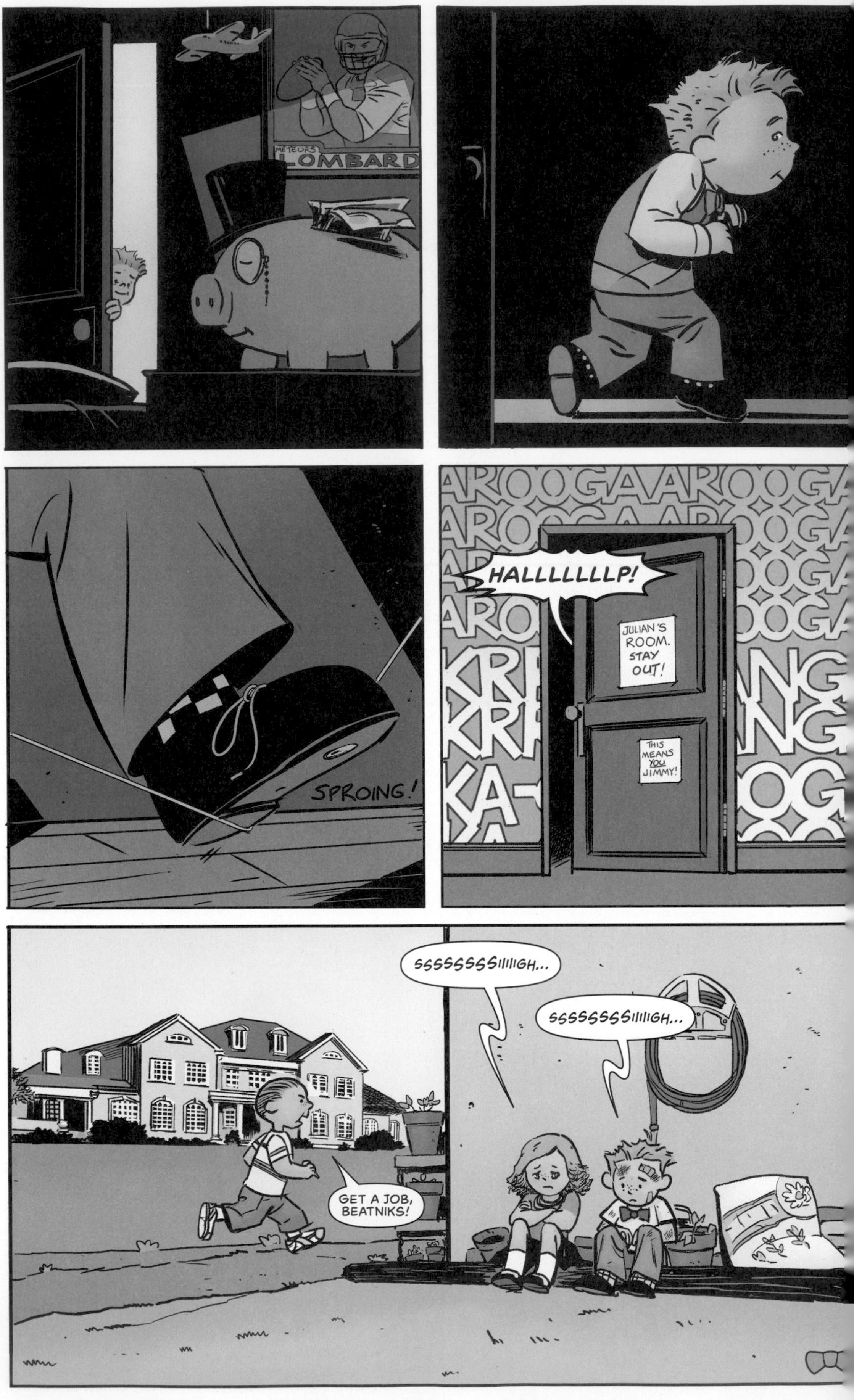

METEORS
LOMBARD
SPROING!
AROOGA AROOGA
HALLLLLLLP!
JULIAN'S ROOM. STAY OUT!
THIS MEANS YOU JIMMY!
GET A JOB, BEATNIKS!
SSSSSSSSIIIIIGH...
SSSSSSSSIIIIIGH...

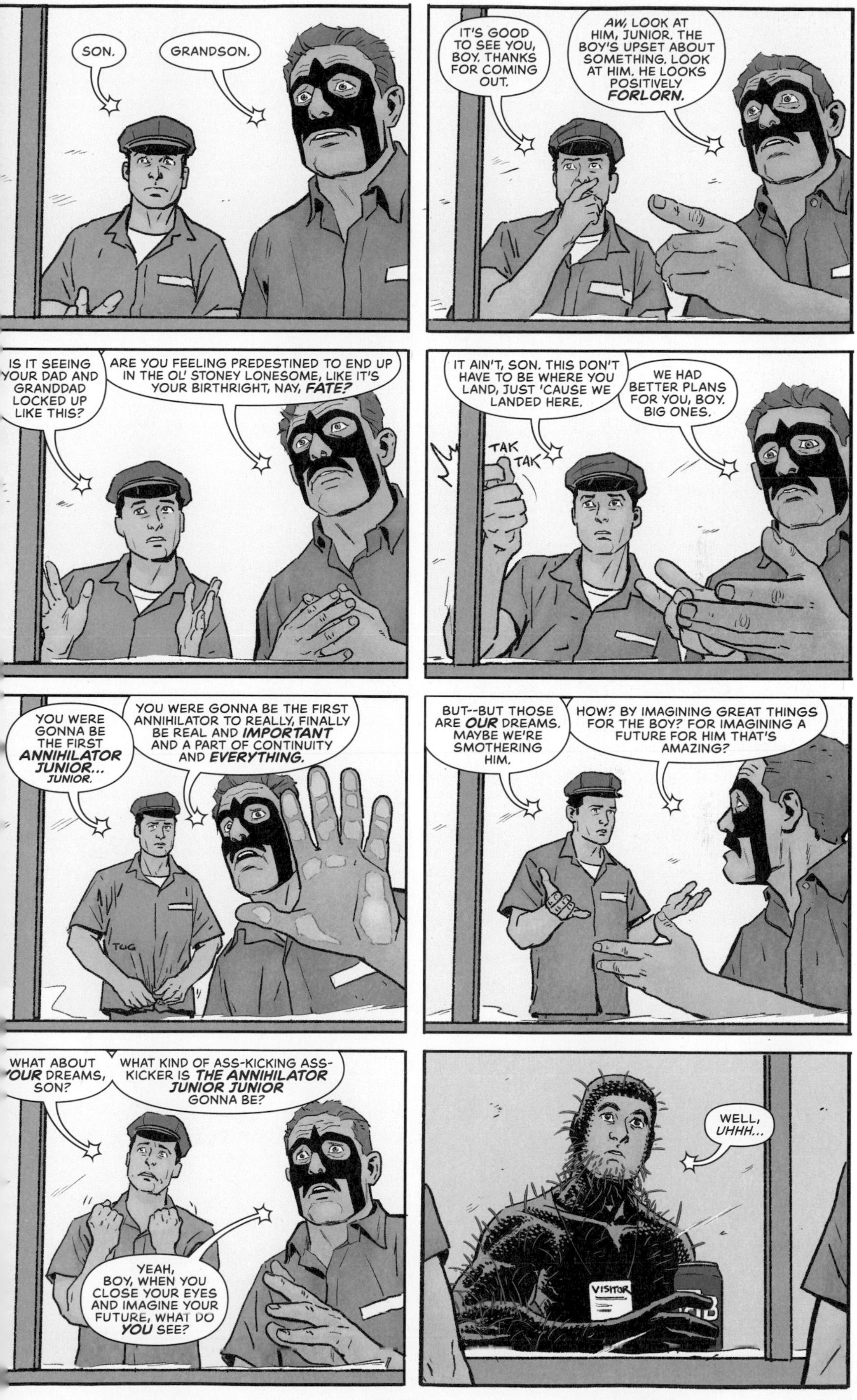
SON.
GRANDSON.
IT'S GOOD TO SEE YOU, BOY. THANKS FOR COMING OUT.
AW, LOOK AT HIM, JUNIOR. THE BOY'S UPSET ABOUT SOMETHING. LOOK AT HIM. HE LOOKS POSITIVELY FORLORN.
IS IT SEEING YOUR DAD AND GRANDDAD LOCKED UP LIKE THIS?
ARE YOU FEELING PREDESTINED TO END UP IN THE OL' STONEY LONESOME, LIKE IT'S YOUR BIRTHRIGHT, NAY, FATE?
IT AIN'T, SON. THIS DON'T HAVE TO BE WHERE YOU LAND, JUST 'CAUSE WE LANDED HERE.
WE HAD BETTER PLANS FOR YOU, BOY. BIG ONES.
TAK TAK
YOU WERE GONNA BE THE FIRST ANNIHILATOR JUNIOR... JUNIOR.
YOU WERE GONNA BE THE FIRST ANNIHILATOR TO REALLY, FINALLY BE REAL AND IMPORTANT AND A PART OF CONTINUITY AND EVERYTHING.
TUG
BUT--BUT THOSE ARE OUR DREAMS. MAYBE WE'RE SMOTHERING HIM.
HOW? BY IMAGINING GREAT THINGS FOR THE BOY? FOR IMAGINING A FUTURE FOR HIM THAT'S AMAZING?
WHAT ABOUT YOUR DREAMS, SON?
WHAT KIND OF ASS-KICKING ASS-KICKER IS THE ANNIHILATOR JUNIOR JUNIOR GONNA BE?
YEAH, BOY, WHEN YOU CLOSE YOUR EYES AND IMAGINE YOUR FUTURE, WHAT DO YOU SEE?
WELL, UHHH...
VISITOR

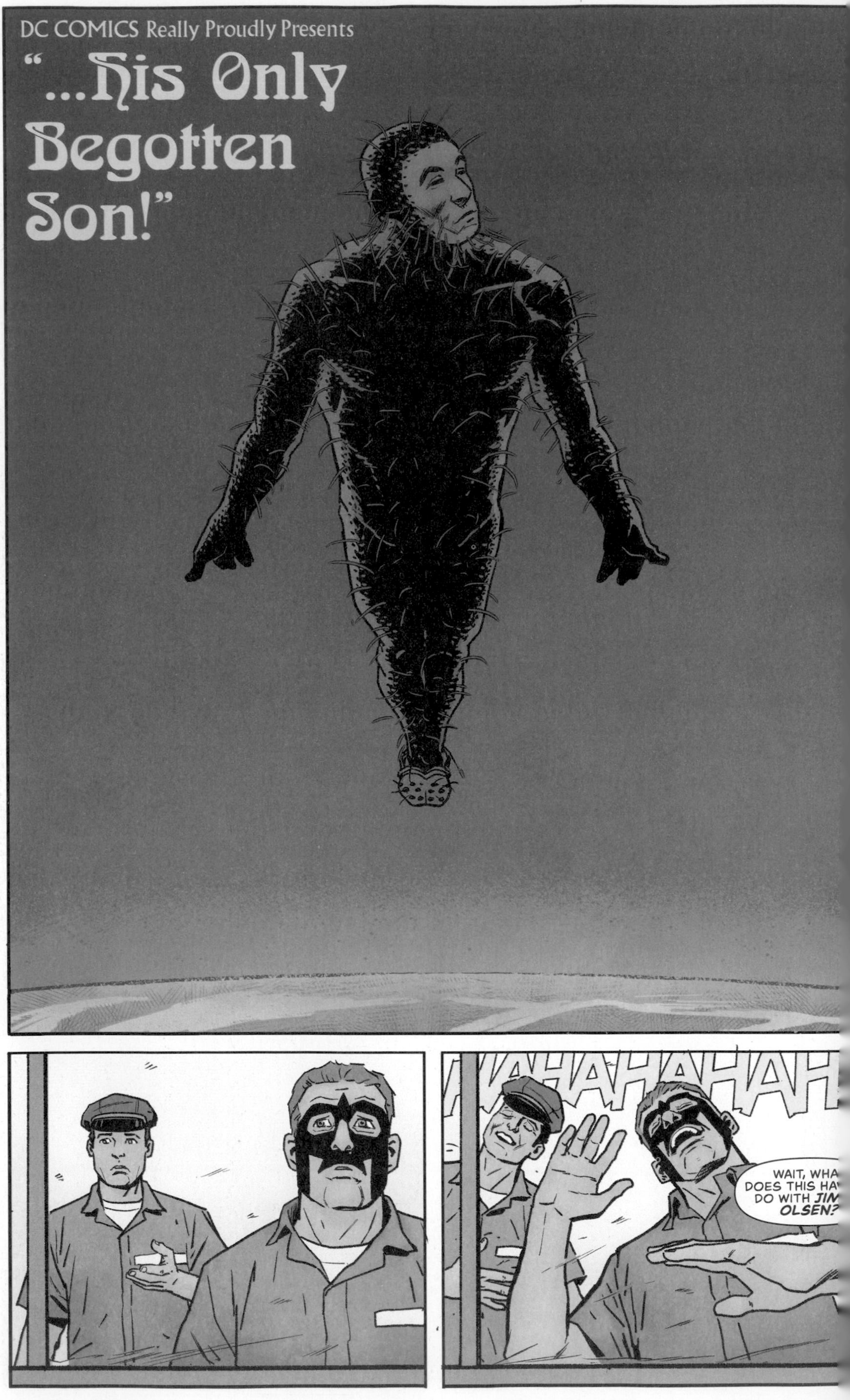

DC COMICS Really Proudly Presents
"...His Only Begotten Son!"
HAHAHAHAH
WAIT, WHA DOES THIS HA DO WITH JIM OLSEN?

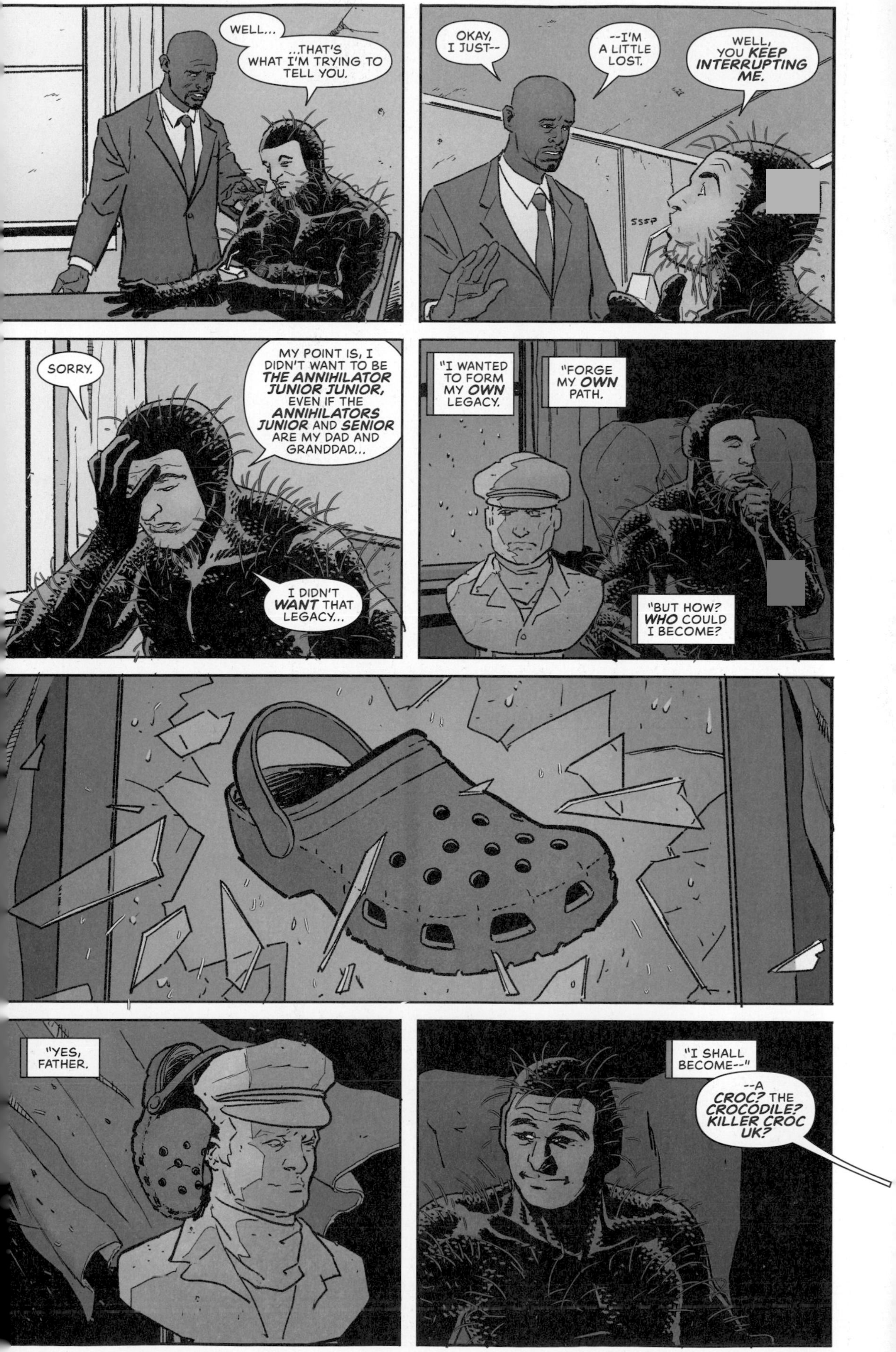
WELL...
...THAT'S WHAT I'M TRYING TO TELL YOU.
OKAY, I JUST--
--I'M A LITTLE LOST.
WELL, YOU KEEP INTERRUPTING ME.
SSSP
SORRY.
MY POINT IS, I DIDN'T WANT TO BE THE ANNIHILATOR JUNIOR JUNIOR, EVEN IF THE ANNIHILATORS JUNIOR AND SENIOR ARE MY DAD AND GRANDDAD...
I DIDN'T WANT THAT LEGACY...
"I WANTED TO FORM MY OWN LEGACY.
"FORGE MY OWN PATH.
"BUT HOW? WHO COULD I BECOME?
"YES, FATHER.
"I SHALL BECOME--"
--A CROC? THE CROCODILE? KILLER CROC UK?

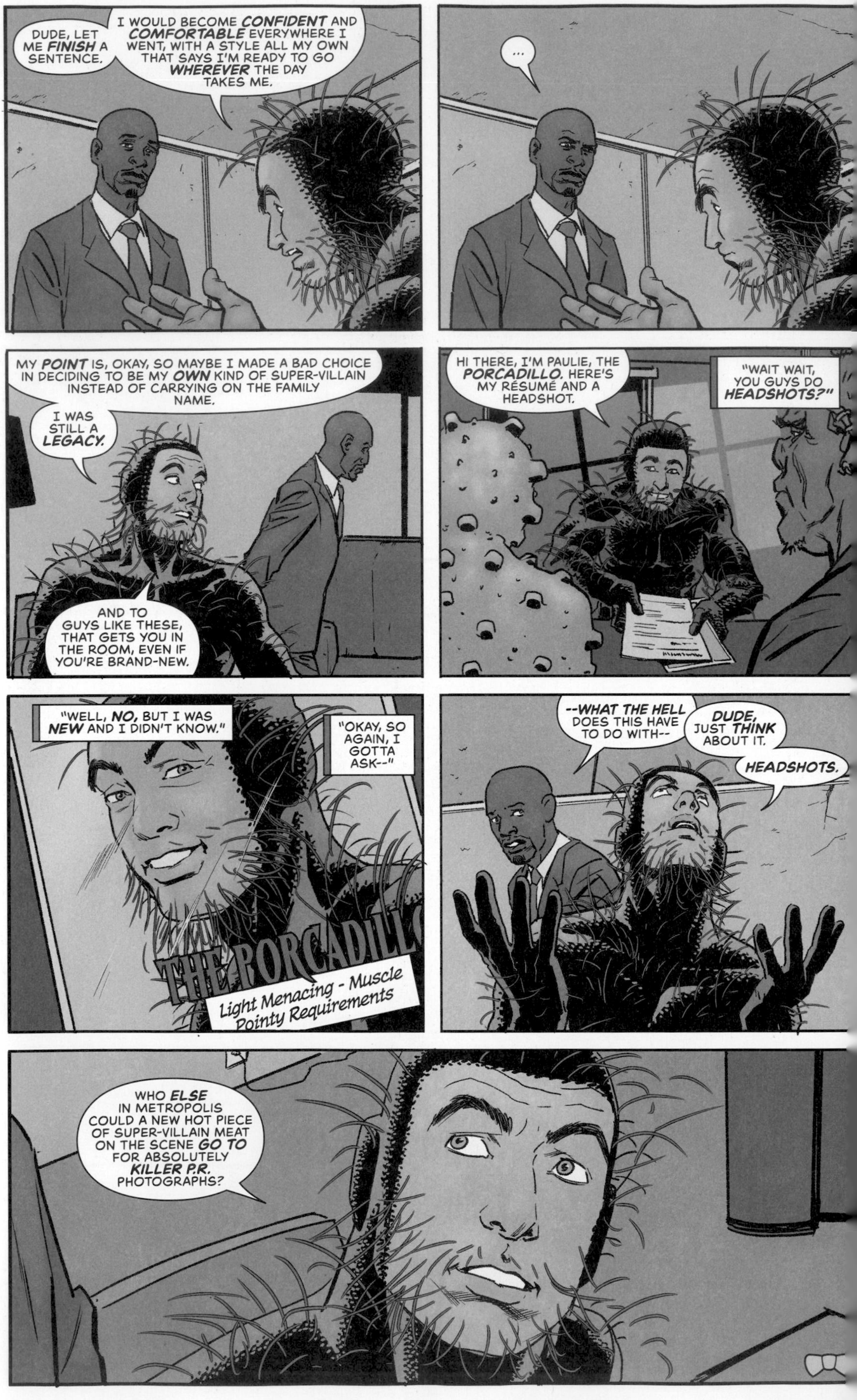
DUDE, LET ME FINISH A SENTENCE.
I WOULD BECOME CONFIDENT AND COMFORTABLE EVERYWHERE I WENT, WITH A STYLE ALL MY OWN THAT SAYS I'M READY TO GO WHEREVER THE DAY TAKES ME.
...
MY POINT IS, OKAY, SO MAYBE I MADE A BAD CHOICE IN DECIDING TO BE MY OWN KIND OF SUPER-VILLAIN INSTEAD OF CARRYING ON THE FAMILY NAME.
I WAS STILL A LEGACY.
AND TO GUYS LIKE THESE, THAT GETS YOU IN THE ROOM, EVEN IF YOU'RE BRAND-NEW.
HI THERE, I'M PAULIE, THE PORCADILLO. HERE'S MY RÉSUMÉ AND A HEADSHOT.
"WAIT WAIT, YOU GUYS DO HEADSHOTS?"
"WELL, NO, BUT I WAS NEW AND I DIDN'T KNOW."
"OKAY, SO AGAIN, I GOTTA ASK--"
THE PORCADILLO
Light Menacing - Muscle
Pointy Requirements
--WHAT THE HELL DOES THIS HAVE TO DO WITH--
DUDE, JUST THINK ABOUT IT.
HEADSHOTS.
WHO ELSE IN METROPOLIS COULD A NEW HOT PIECE OF SUPER-VILLAIN MEAT ON THE SCENE GO TO FOR ABSOLUTELY KILLER P.R. PHOTOGRAPHS?

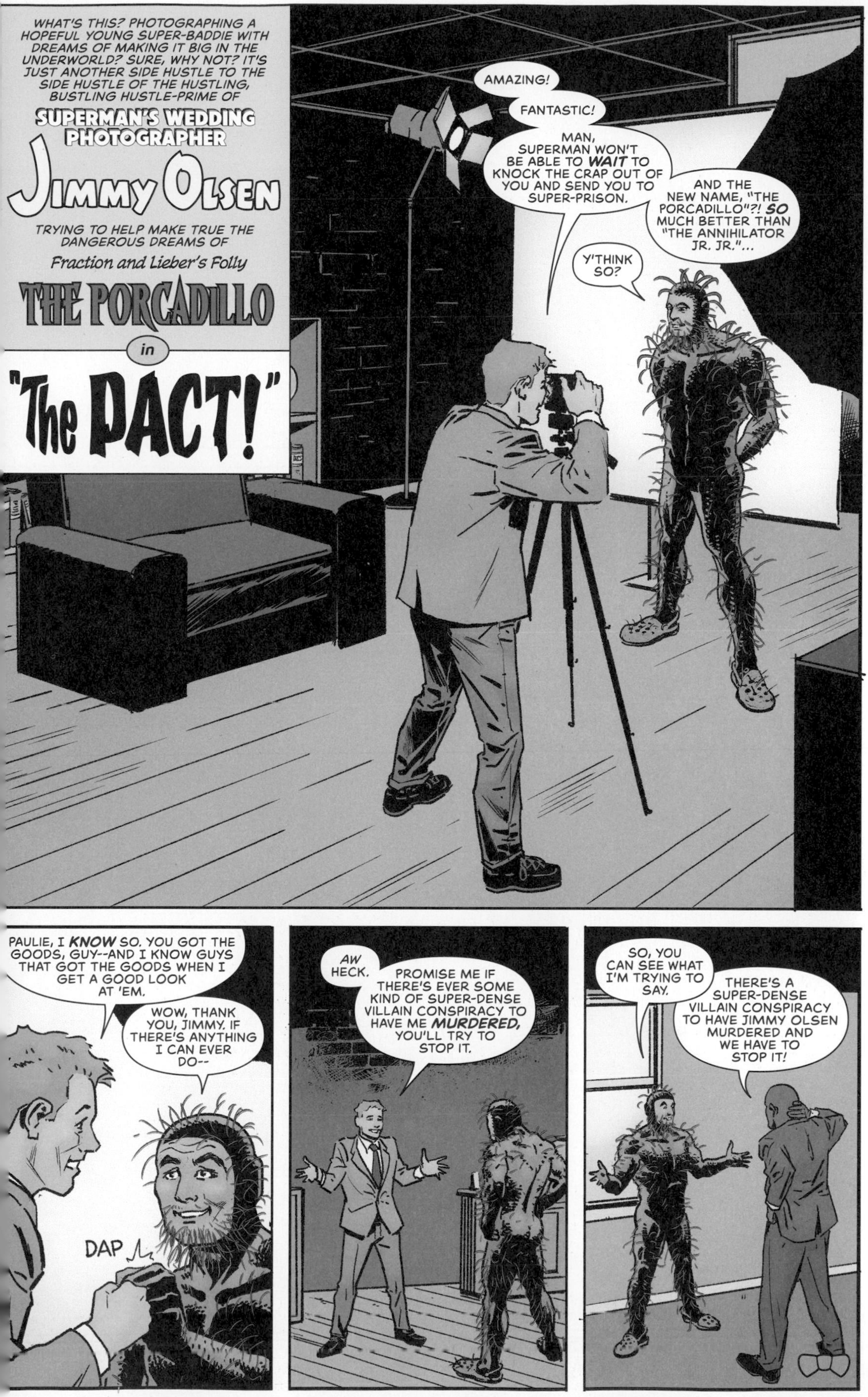
WHAT'S THIS? PHOTOGRAPHING A HOPEFUL YOUNG SUPER-BADDIE WITH DREAMS OF MAKING IT BIG IN THE UNDERWORLD? SURE, WHY NOT? IT'S JUST ANOTHER SIDE HUSTLE TO THE SIDE HUSTLE OF THE HUSTLING, BUSTLING HUSTLE-PRIME OF
SUPERMAN'S WEDDING PHOTOGRAPHER
JIMMY OLSEN
TRYING TO HELP MAKE TRUE THE DANGEROUS DREAMS OF
Fraction and Lieber's Folly
THE PORCADILLO
in
"The PACT!"
AMAZING!
FANTASTIC!
MAN, SUPERMAN WON'T BE ABLE TO WAIT TO KNOCK THE CRAP OUT OF YOU AND SEND YOU TO SUPER-PRISON.
AND THE NEW NAME, "THE PORCADILLO"?! SO MUCH BETTER THAN "THE ANNIHILATOR JR. JR."...
Y'THINK SO?
PAULIE, I KNOW SO. YOU GOT THE GOODS, GUY--AND I KNOW GUYS THAT GOT THE GOODS WHEN I GET A GOOD LOOK AT 'EM.
WOW, THANK YOU, JIMMY. IF THERE'S ANYTHING I CAN EVER DO--
DAP
AW HECK.
PROMISE ME IF THERE'S EVER SOME KIND OF SUPER-DENSE VILLAIN CONSPIRACY TO HAVE ME MURDERED, YOU'LL TRY TO STOP IT.
SO, YOU CAN SEE WHAT I'M TRYING TO SAY.
THERE'S A SUPER-DENSE VILLAIN CONSPIRACY TO HAVE JIMMY OLSEN MURDERED AND WE HAVE TO STOP IT!

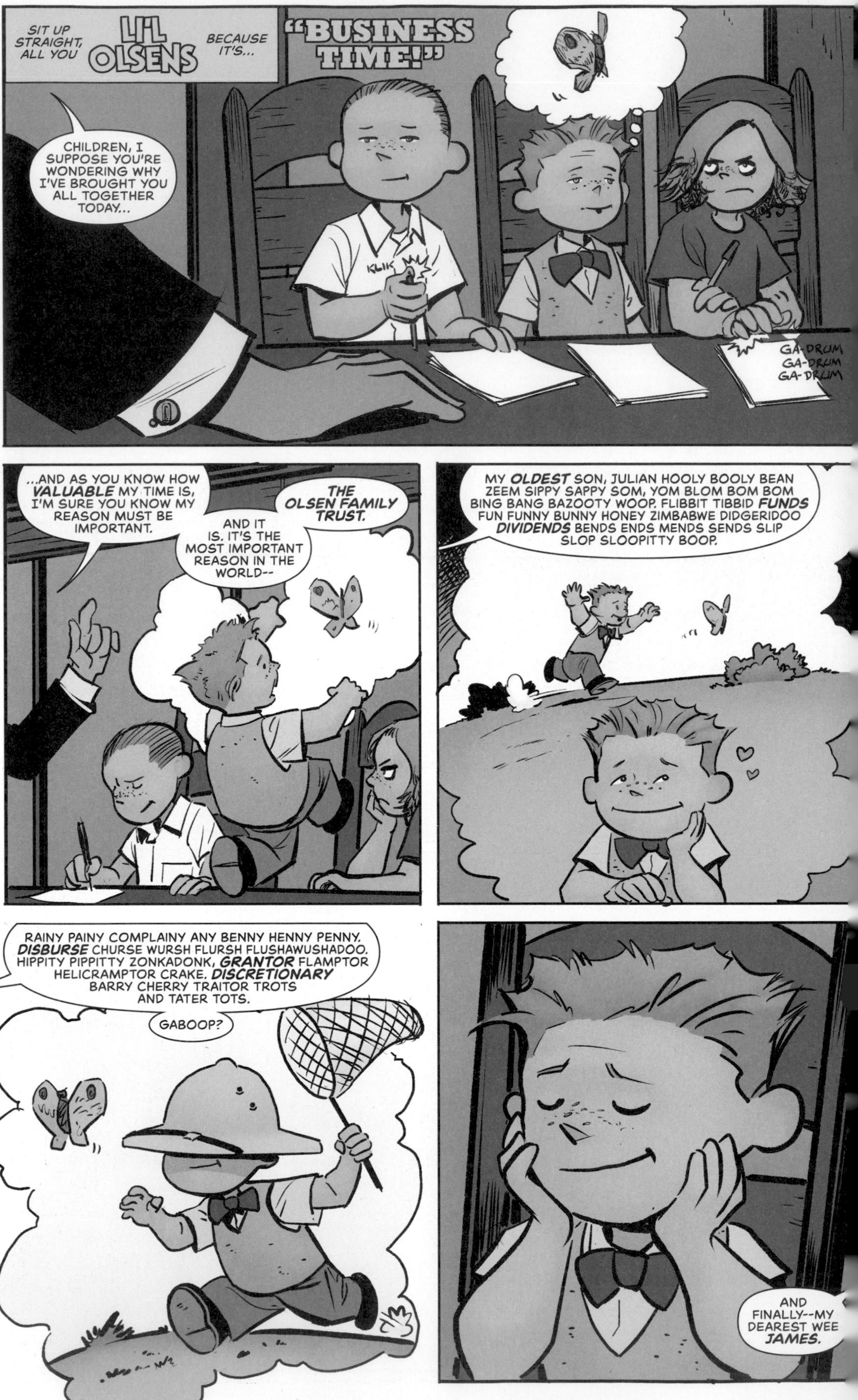
SIT UP STRAIGHT, ALL YOU LI'L OLSENS BECAUSE IT'S...
"BUSINESS TIME!"
CHILDREN, I SUPPOSE YOU'RE WONDERING WHY I'VE BROUGHT YOU ALL TOGETHER TODAY...
KLIK
GA-DRUM GA-DRUM GA-DRUM
...AND AS YOU KNOW HOW VALUABLE MY TIME IS, I'M SURE YOU KNOW MY REASON MUST BE IMPORTANT.
AND IT IS. IT'S THE MOST IMPORTANT REASON IN THE WORLD--
THE OLSEN FAMILY TRUST.
MY OLDEST SON, JULIAN HOOLY BOOLY BEAN ZEEM SIPPY SAPPY SOM, YOM BLOM BOM BOM BING BANG BAZOOTY WOOP. FLIBBIT TIBBID FUNDS FUN FUNNY BUNNY HONEY ZIMBABWE DIDGERIDOO DIVIDENDS BENDS ENDS MENDS SENDS SLIP SLOP SLOOPITTY BOOP.
RAINY PAINY COMPLAINY ANY BENNY HENNY PENNY. DISBURSE CHURSE WURSH FLURSH FLUSHAWUSHADOO. HIPPITY PIPPITTY ZONKADONK, GRANTOR FLAMPTOR HELICRAMPTOR CRAKE. DISCRETIONARY BARRY CHERRY TRAITOR TROTS AND TATER TOTS.
GABOOP?
AND FINALLY--MY DEAREST WEE JAMES.

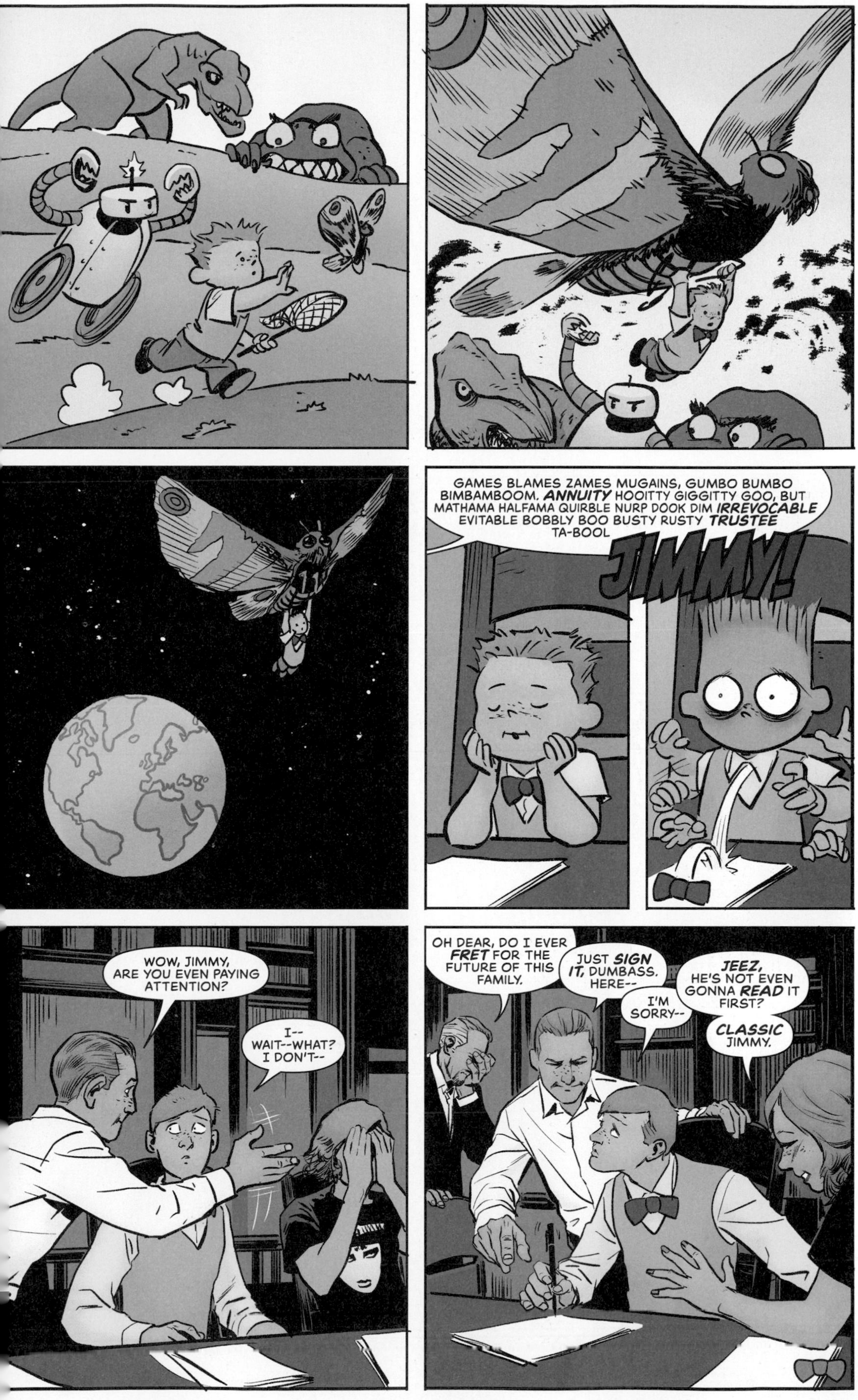

GAMES BLAMES ZAMES MUGAINS, GUMBO BUMBO BIMBAMBOOM. ANNUITY HOOITTY GIGGITTY GOO, BUT MATHAMA HALFAMA QUIRBLE NURP DOOK DIM IRREVOCABLE EVITABLE BOBBLY BOO BUSTY RUSTY TRUSTEE TA-BOOL
JIMMY!
WOW, JIMMY, ARE YOU EVEN PAYING ATTENTION?
I-- WAIT--WHAT? I DON'T--
OH DEAR, DO I EVER FRET FOR THE FUTURE OF THIS FAMILY.
JUST SIGN IT, DUMBASS. HERE--
I'M SORRY--
JEEZ, HE'S NOT EVEN GONNA READ IT FIRST?
CLASSIC JIMMY.

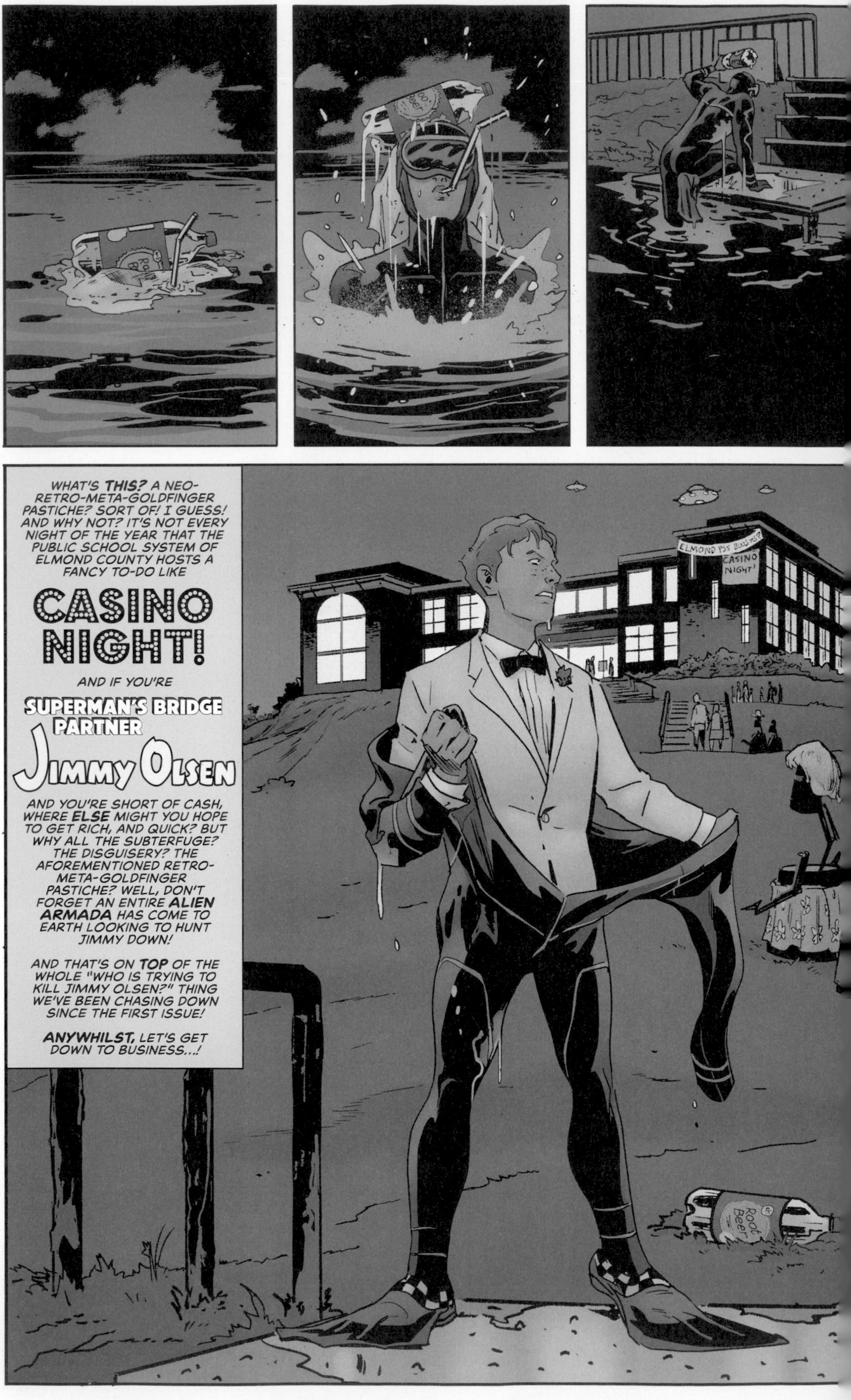
WHAT'S THIS? A NEO-RETRO-META-GOLDFINGER PASTICHE? SORT OF! I GUESS! AND WHY NOT? IT'S NOT EVERY NIGHT OF THE YEAR THAT THE PUBLIC SCHOOL SYSTEM OF ELMOND COUNTY HOSTS A FANCY TO-DO LIKE
CASINO NIGHT!
AND IF YOU'RE
SUPERMAN'S BRIDGE PARTNER
JIMMY OLSEN
AND YOU'RE SHORT OF CASH, WHERE ELSE MIGHT YOU HOPE TO GET RICH, AND QUICK? BUT WHY ALL THE SUBTERFUGE? THE DISGUISERY? THE AFOREMENTIONED RETRO-META-GOLDFINGER PASTICHE? WELL, DON'T FORGET AN ENTIRE ALIEN ARMADA HAS COME TO EARTH LOOKING TO HUNT JIMMY DOWN!
AND THAT'S ON TOP OF THE WHOLE "WHO IS TRYING TO KILL JIMMY OLSEN?" THING WE'VE BEEN CHASING DOWN SINCE THE FIRST ISSUE!
ANYWHILST, LET'S GET DOWN TO BUSINESS...!
CASINO NIGHT!
Root Beer

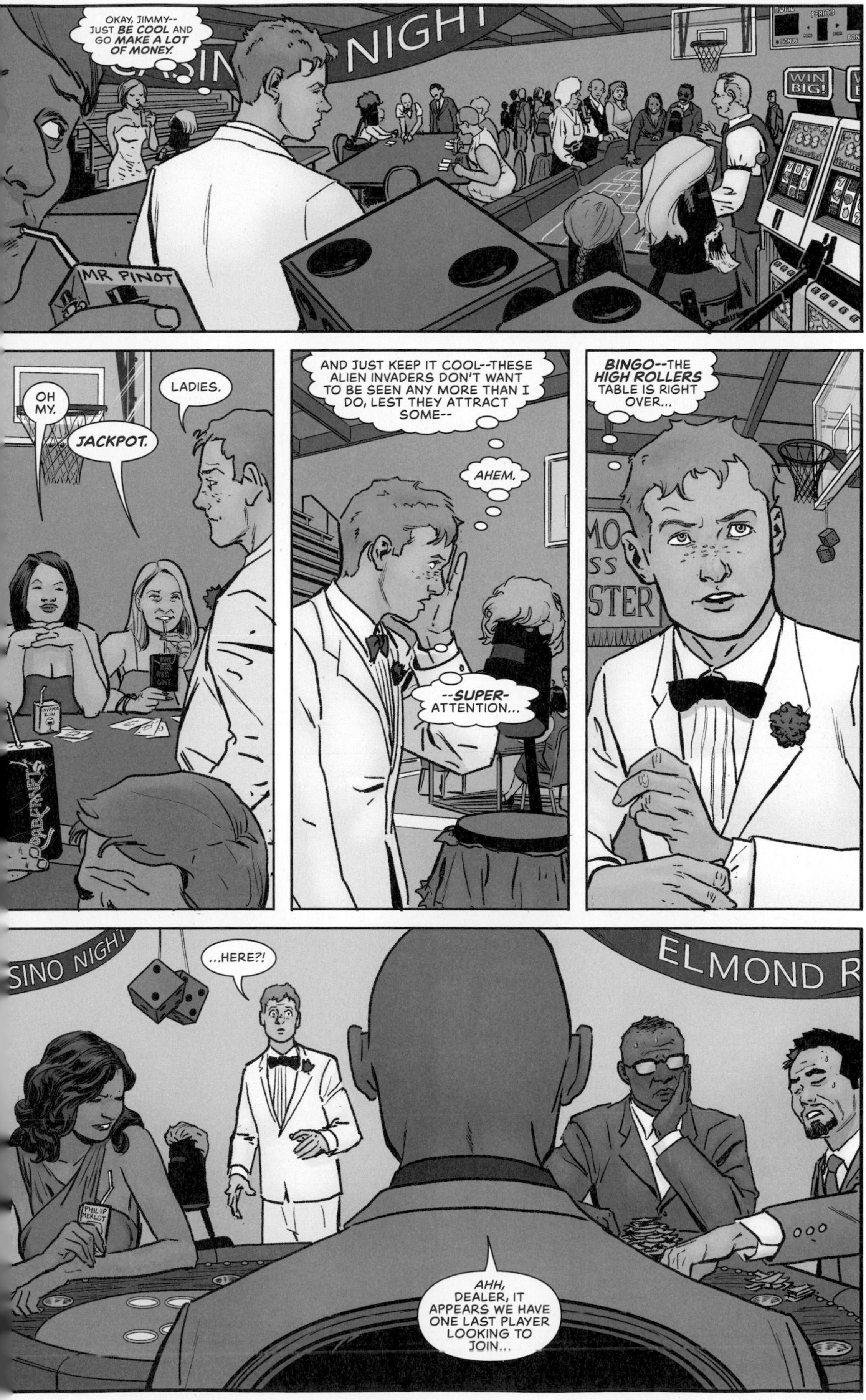
OKAY, JIMMY-- JUST BE COOL AND GO MAKE A LOT OF MONEY.
NIGHT
WIN BIG!
MR PINOT
OH MY.
JACKPOT.
LADIES.
AND JUST KEEP IT COOL--THESE ALIEN INVADERS DON'T WANT TO BE SEEN ANY MORE THAN I DO, LEST THEY ATTRACT SOME--
AHEM.
--SUPER-ATTENTION...
BINGO--THE HIGH ROLLERS TABLE IS RIGHT OVER...
SINO NIGH
ELMOND R
...HERE?!
PHILIP MERLOT
AHH, DEALER, IT APPEARS WE HAVE ONE LAST PLAYER LOOKING TO JOIN...

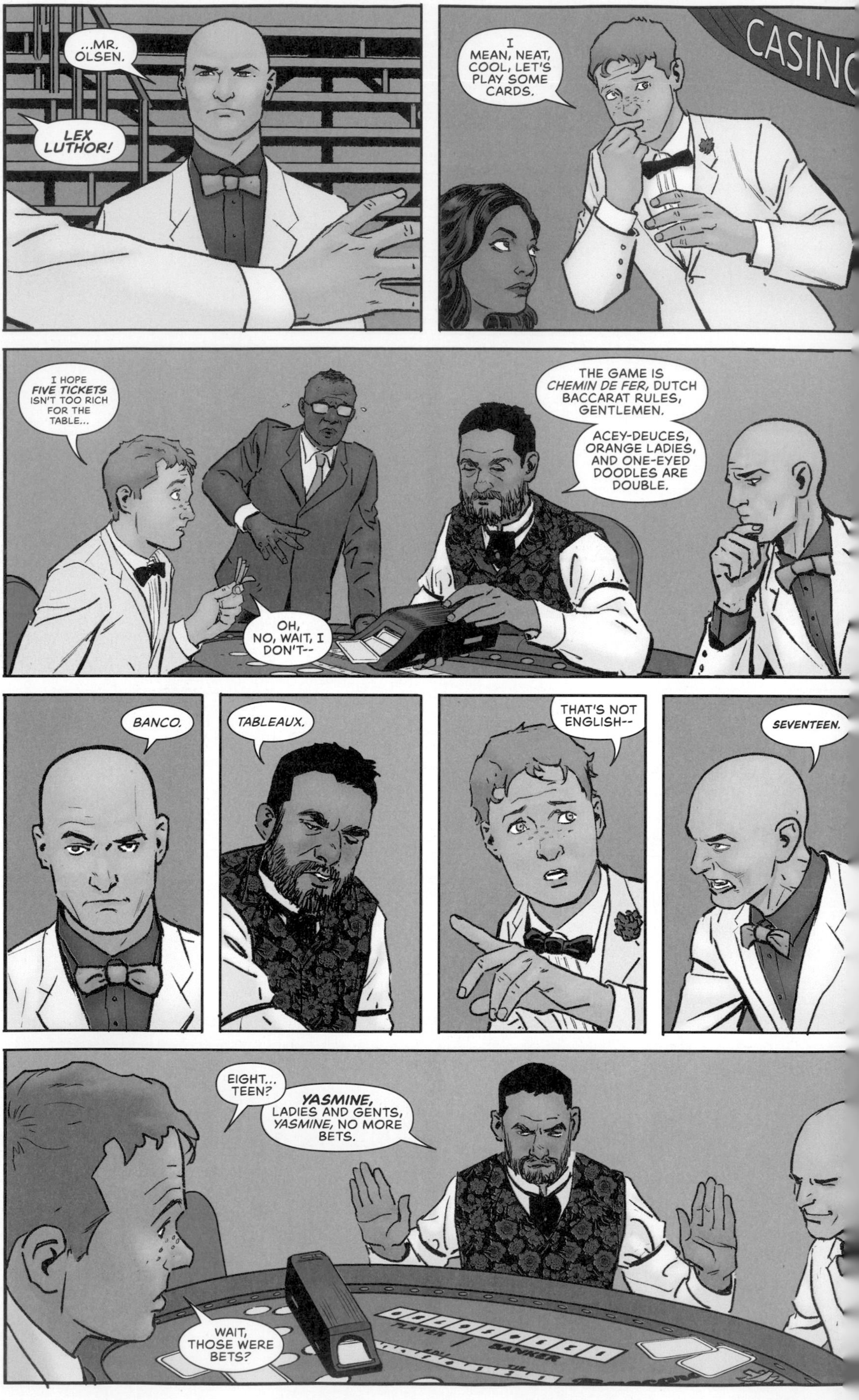
...MR. OLSEN.
LEX LUTHOR!
CASINO
I MEAN, NEAT, COOL, LET'S PLAY SOME CARDS.
I HOPE FIVE TICKETS ISN'T TOO RICH FOR THE TABLE...
THE GAME IS CHEMIN DE FER, DUTCH BACCARAT RULES, GENTLEMEN.
ACEY-DEUCES, ORANGE LADIES, AND ONE-EYED DOODLES ARE DOUBLE.
OH, NO, WAIT, I DON'T--
BANCO.
TABLEAUX.
THAT'S NOT ENGLISH--
SEVENTEEN.
EIGHT... TEEN?
YASMINE, LADIES AND GENTS, YASMINE, NO MORE BETS.
WAIT, THOSE WERE BETS?
PLAYER
BANKER

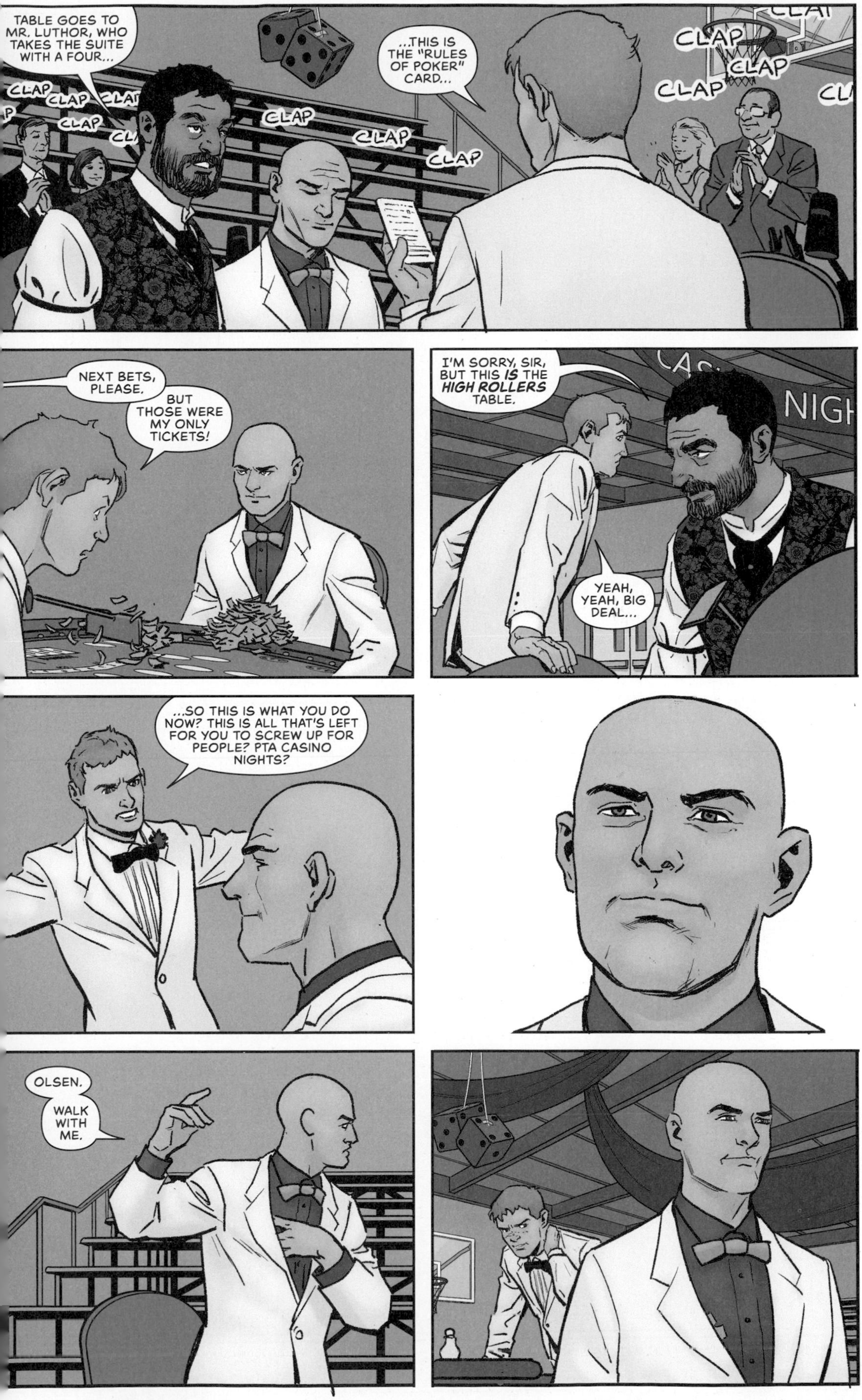
TABLE GOES TO MR. LUTHOR, WHO TAKES THE SUITE WITH A FOUR...
CLAP CLAP CLAP
CLAP
CLAP
CLAP
CLAP
...THIS IS THE "RULES OF POKER" CARD...
CLAP
CLAP
CLAP
CLAP
NEXT BETS, PLEASE.
BUT THOSE WERE MY ONLY TICKETS!
I'M SORRY, SIR, BUT THIS *IS* THE *HIGH ROLLERS* TABLE.
YEAH, YEAH, BIG DEAL...
...SO THIS IS WHAT YOU DO NOW? THIS IS ALL THAT'S LEFT FOR YOU TO SCREW UP FOR PEOPLE? PTA CASINO NIGHTS?
OLSEN.
WALK WITH ME.

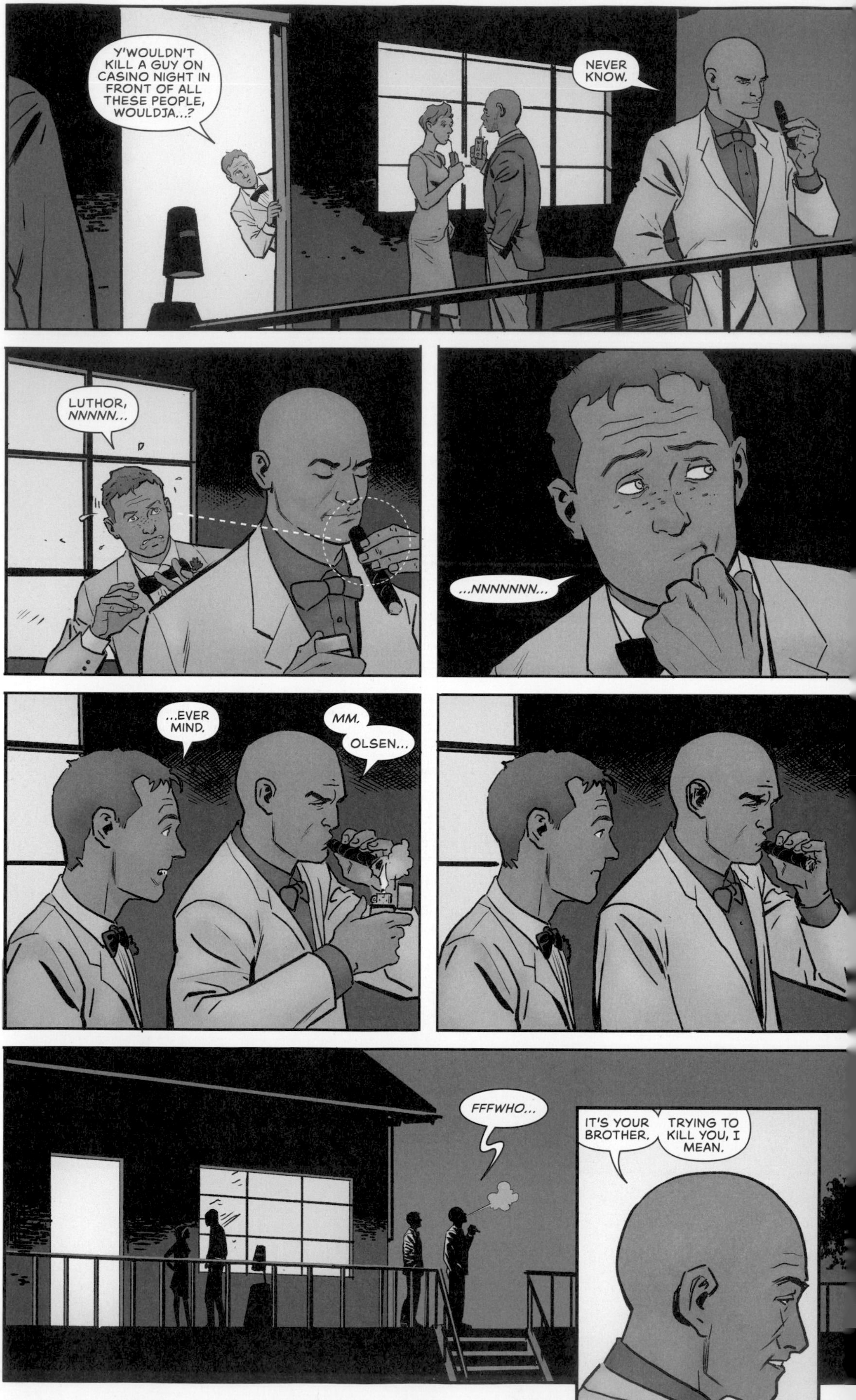
Y'WOULDN'T KILL A GUY ON CASINO NIGHT IN FRONT OF ALL THESE PEOPLE, WOULDJA...?
NEVER KNOW.
LUTHOR, NNNNN...
...NNNNNNN...
...EVER MIND.
MM.
OLSEN...
FFFWHO...
IT'S YOUR BROTHER.
TRYING TO KILL YOU, I MEAN.

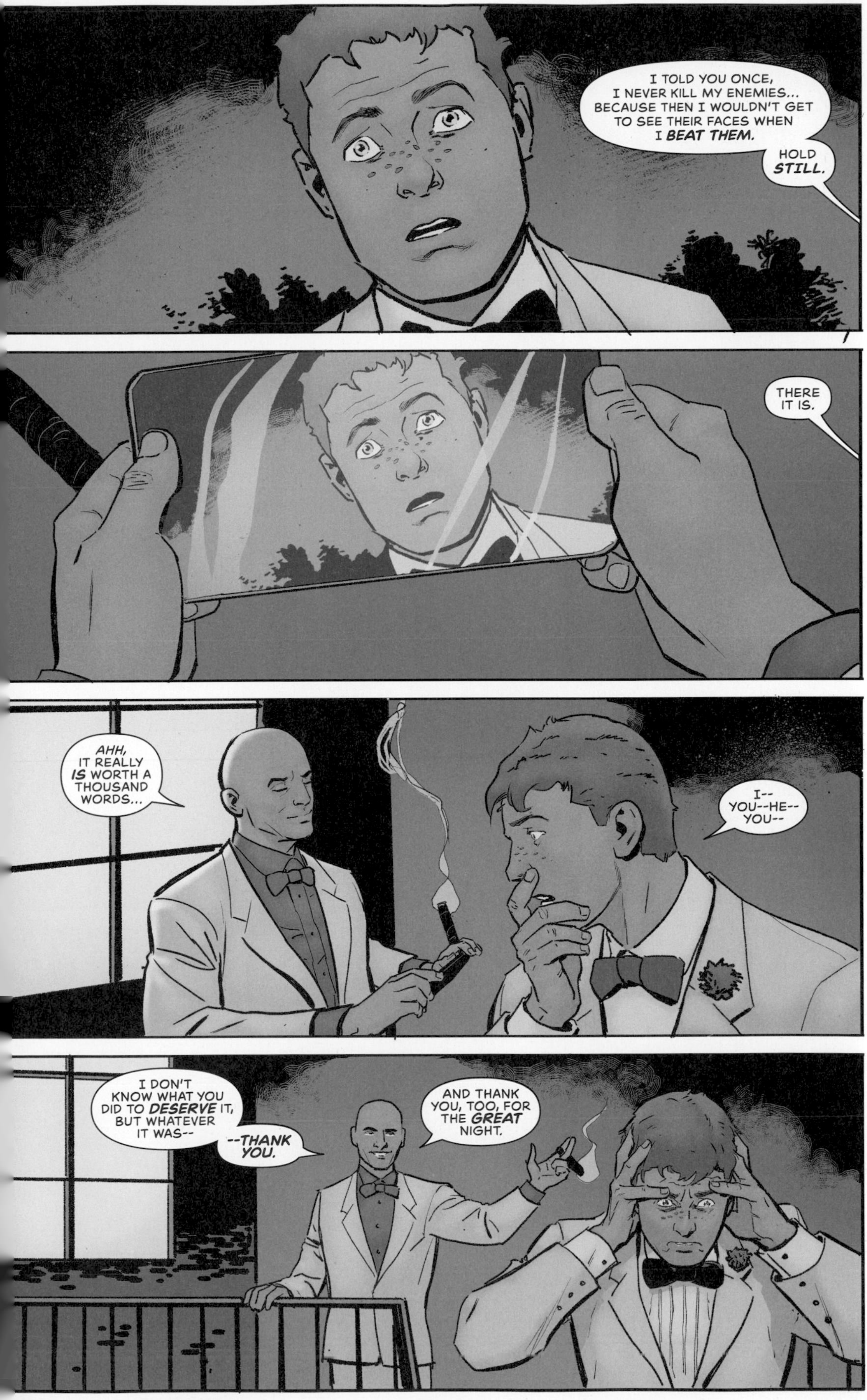
I TOLD YOU ONCE, I NEVER KILL MY ENEMIES... BECAUSE THEN I WOULDN'T GET TO SEE THEIR FACES WHEN I *BEAT THEM.*
HOLD *STILL.*
THERE IT IS.
AHH, IT REALLY *IS* WORTH A THOUSAND WORDS...
I-- YOU--HE-- YOU--
I DON'T KNOW WHAT YOU DID TO *DESERVE* IT, BUT WHATEVER IT WAS--
--THANK YOU.
AND THANK YOU, TOO, FOR THE *GREAT* NIGHT.

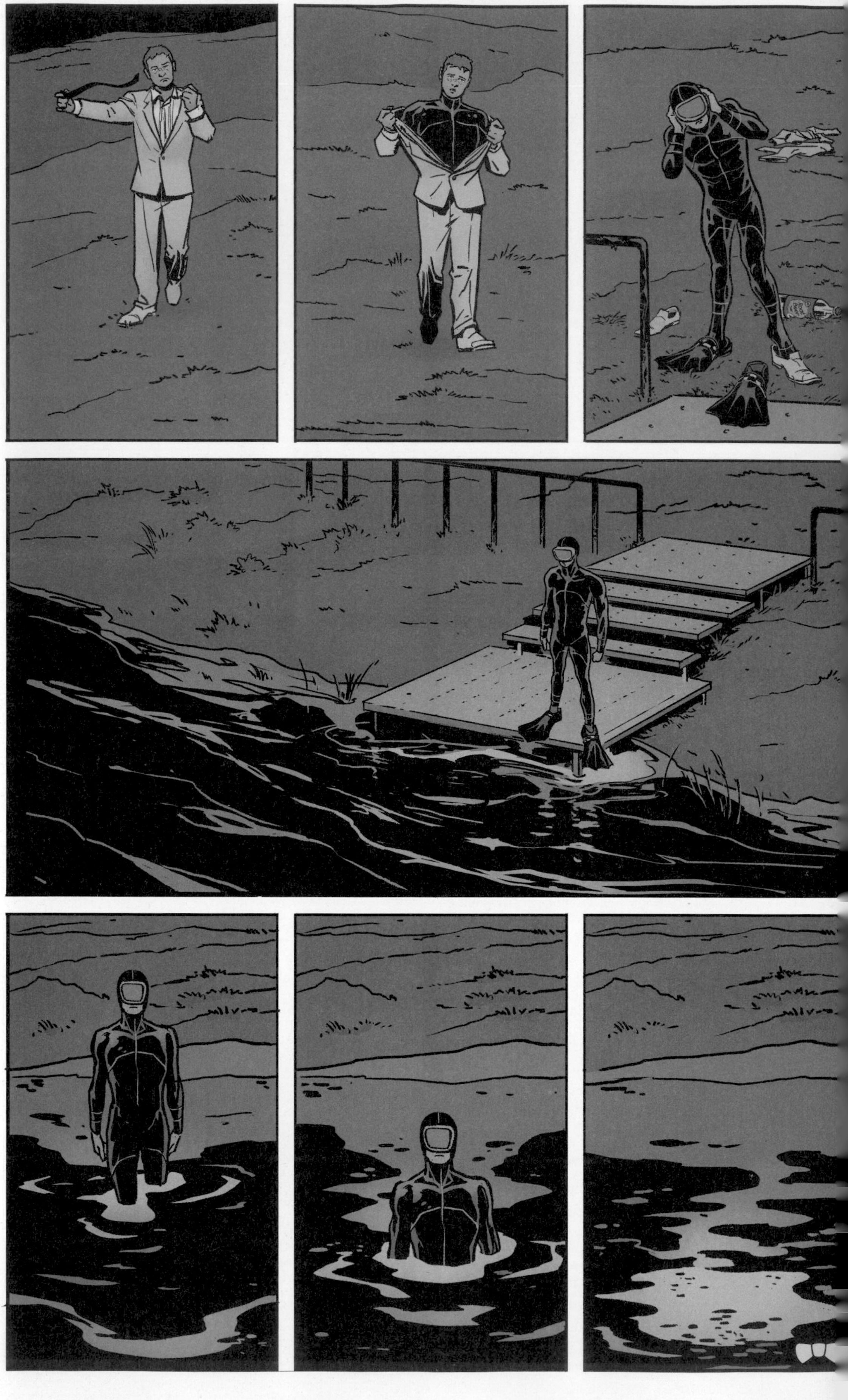

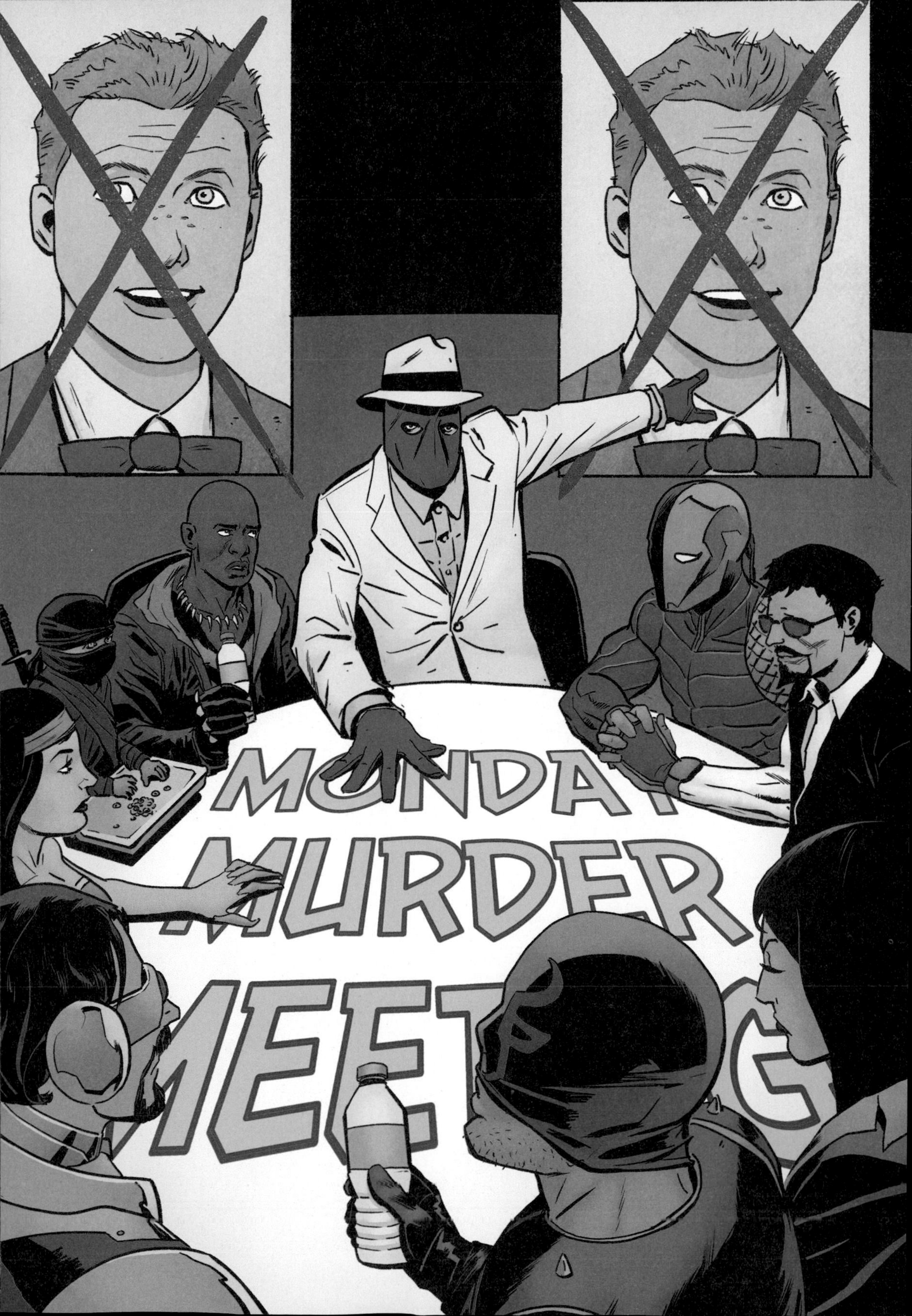
MONDA
MURDER
MEET

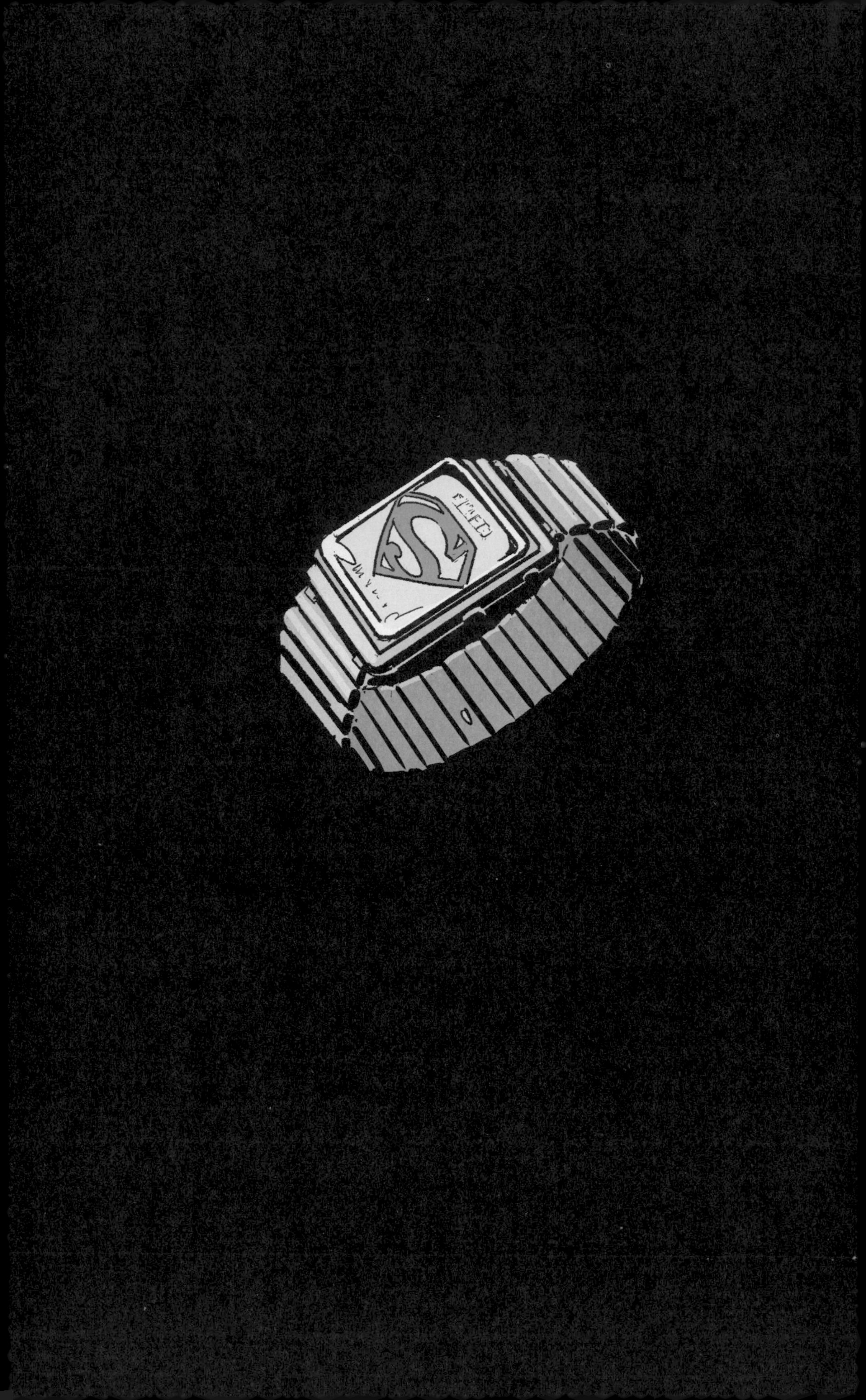

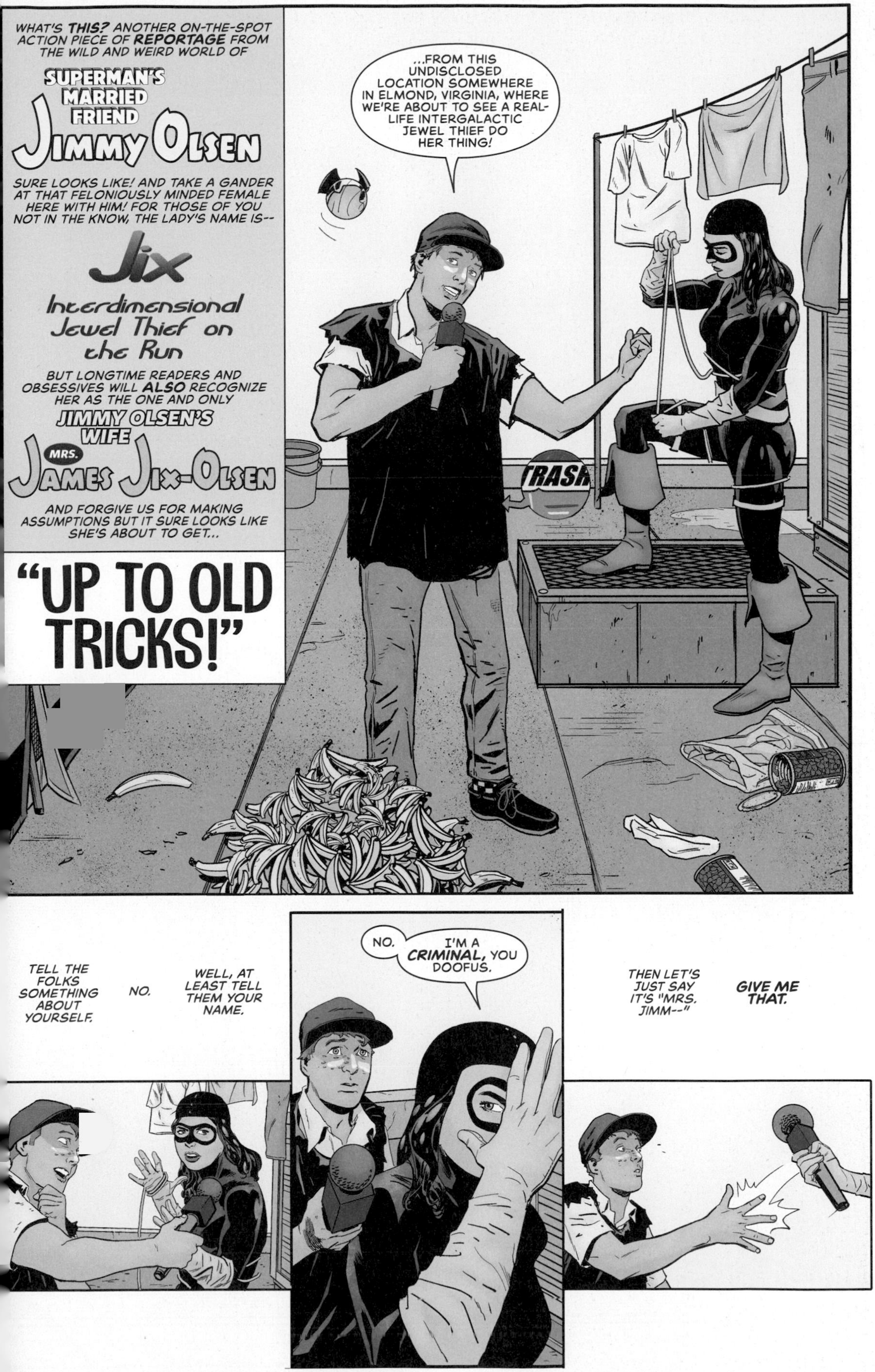
WHAT'S THIS? ANOTHER ON-THE-SPOT ACTION PIECE OF REPORTAGE FROM THE WILD AND WEIRD WORLD OF
SUPERMAN'S MARRIED FRIEND
JIMMY OLSEN
SURE LOOKS LIKE! AND TAKE A GANDER AT THAT FELONIOUSLY MINDED FEMALE HERE WITH HIM! FOR THOSE OF YOU NOT IN THE KNOW, THE LADY'S NAME IS--
JIX
Interdimensional Jewel Thief on the Run
BUT LONGTIME READERS AND OBSESSIVES WILL ALSO RECOGNIZE HER AS THE ONE AND ONLY
JIMMY OLSEN'S WIFE
MRS. JAMES JIX-OLSEN
AND FORGIVE US FOR MAKING ASSUMPTIONS BUT IT SURE LOOKS LIKE SHE'S ABOUT TO GET...
"UP TO OLD TRICKS!"
...FROM THIS UNDISCLOSED LOCATION SOMEWHERE IN ELMOND, VIRGINIA, WHERE WE'RE ABOUT TO SEE A REAL-LIFE INTERGALACTIC JEWEL THIEF DO HER THING!
TRASH
TELL THE FOLKS SOMETHING ABOUT YOURSELF.
NO.
WELL, AT LEAST TELL THEM YOUR NAME.
NO.
I'M A CRIMINAL, YOU DOOFUS.
THEN LET'S JUST SAY IT'S "MRS. JIMM--"
GIVE ME THAT.

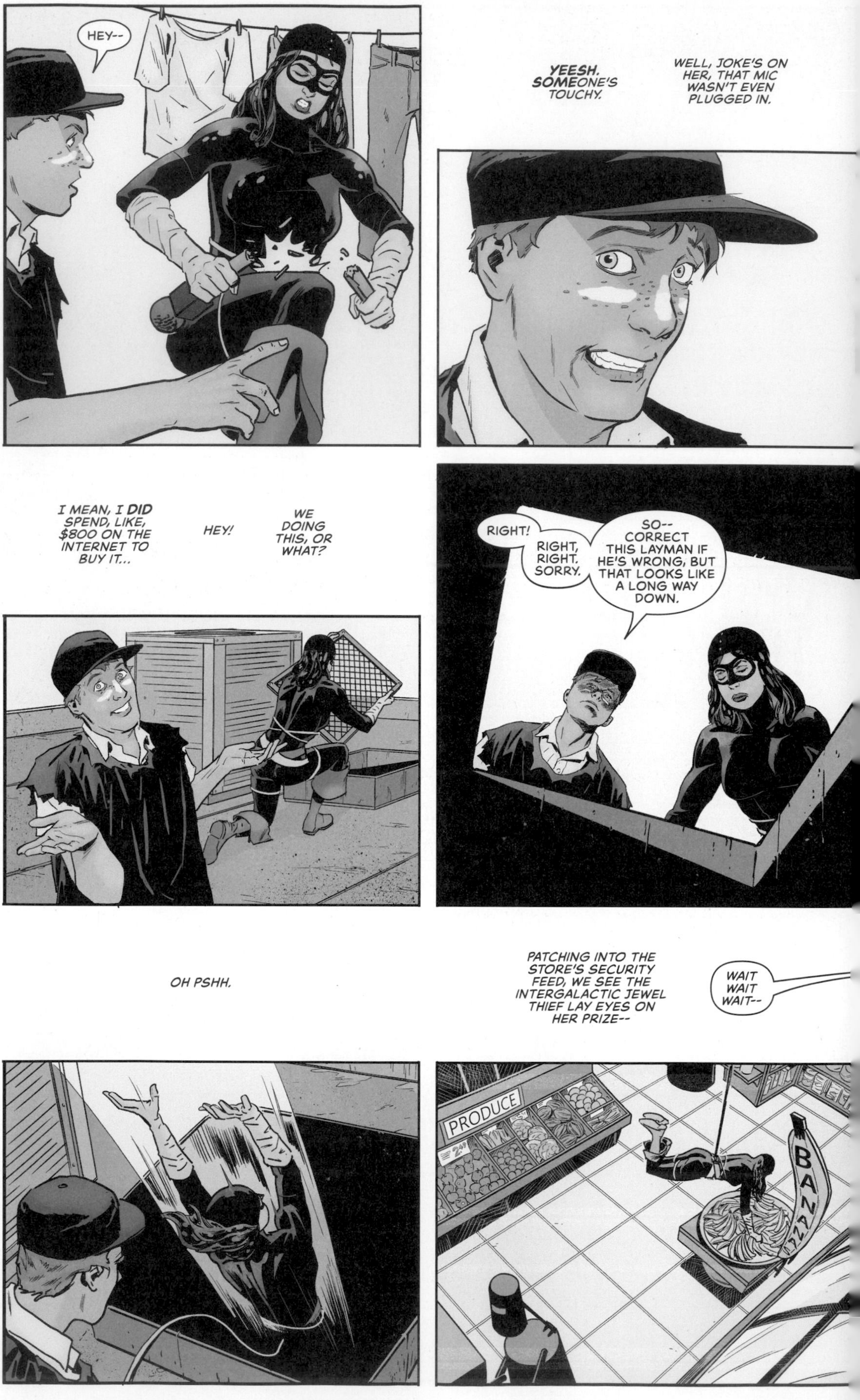
HEY--
YEESH. SOMEONE'S TOUCHY.
WELL, JOKE'S ON HER, THAT MIC WASN'T EVEN PLUGGED IN.
I MEAN, I DID SPEND, LIKE, $800 ON THE INTERNET TO BUY IT...
HEY!
WE DOING THIS, OR WHAT?
RIGHT!
RIGHT, RIGHT. SORRY.
SO-- CORRECT THIS LAYMAN IF HE'S WRONG, BUT THAT LOOKS LIKE A LONG WAY DOWN.
OH PSHH.
PATCHING INTO THE STORE'S SECURITY FEED, WE SEE THE INTERGALACTIC JEWEL THIEF LAY EYES ON HER PRIZE--
WAIT WAIT WAIT--
PRODUCE

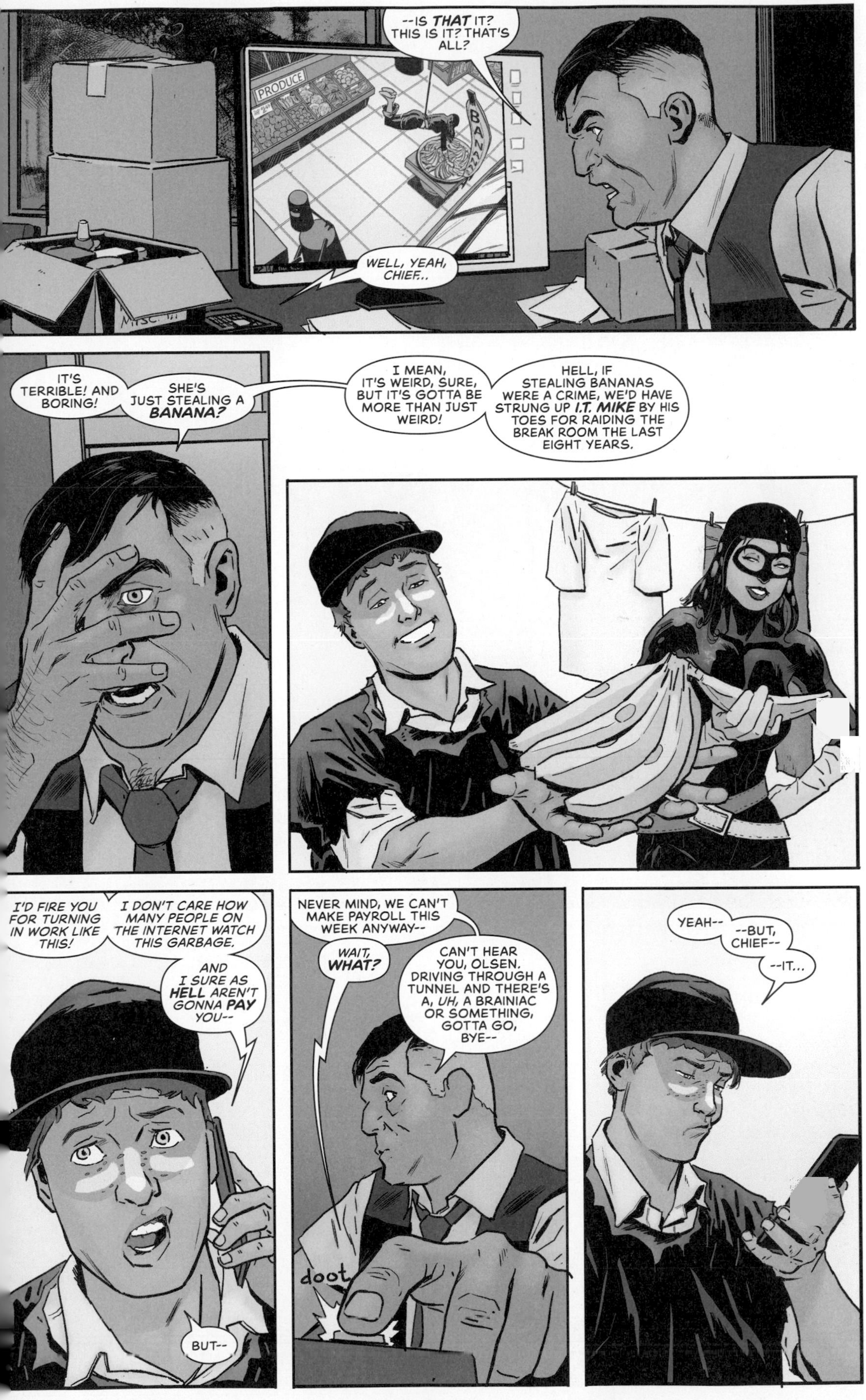
--IS THAT IT? THIS IS IT? THAT'S ALL?
WELL, YEAH, CHIEF...
IT'S TERRIBLE! AND BORING!
SHE'S JUST STEALING A BANANA?
I MEAN, IT'S WEIRD, SURE, BUT IT'S GOTTA BE MORE THAN JUST WEIRD!
HELL, IF STEALING BANANAS WERE A CRIME, WE'D HAVE STRUNG UP I.T. MIKE BY HIS TOES FOR RAIDING THE BREAK ROOM THE LAST EIGHT YEARS.
I'D FIRE YOU FOR TURNING IN WORK LIKE THIS!
I DON'T CARE HOW MANY PEOPLE ON THE INTERNET WATCH THIS GARBAGE.
AND I SURE AS HELL AREN'T GONNA PAY YOU--
BUT--
NEVER MIND, WE CAN'T MAKE PAYROLL THIS WEEK ANYWAY--
WAIT, WHAT?
CAN'T HEAR YOU, OLSEN. DRIVING THROUGH A TUNNEL AND THERE'S A, UH, A BRAINIAC OR SOMETHING, GOTTA GO, BYE--
doot
YEAH--
--BUT, CHIEF--
--IT...

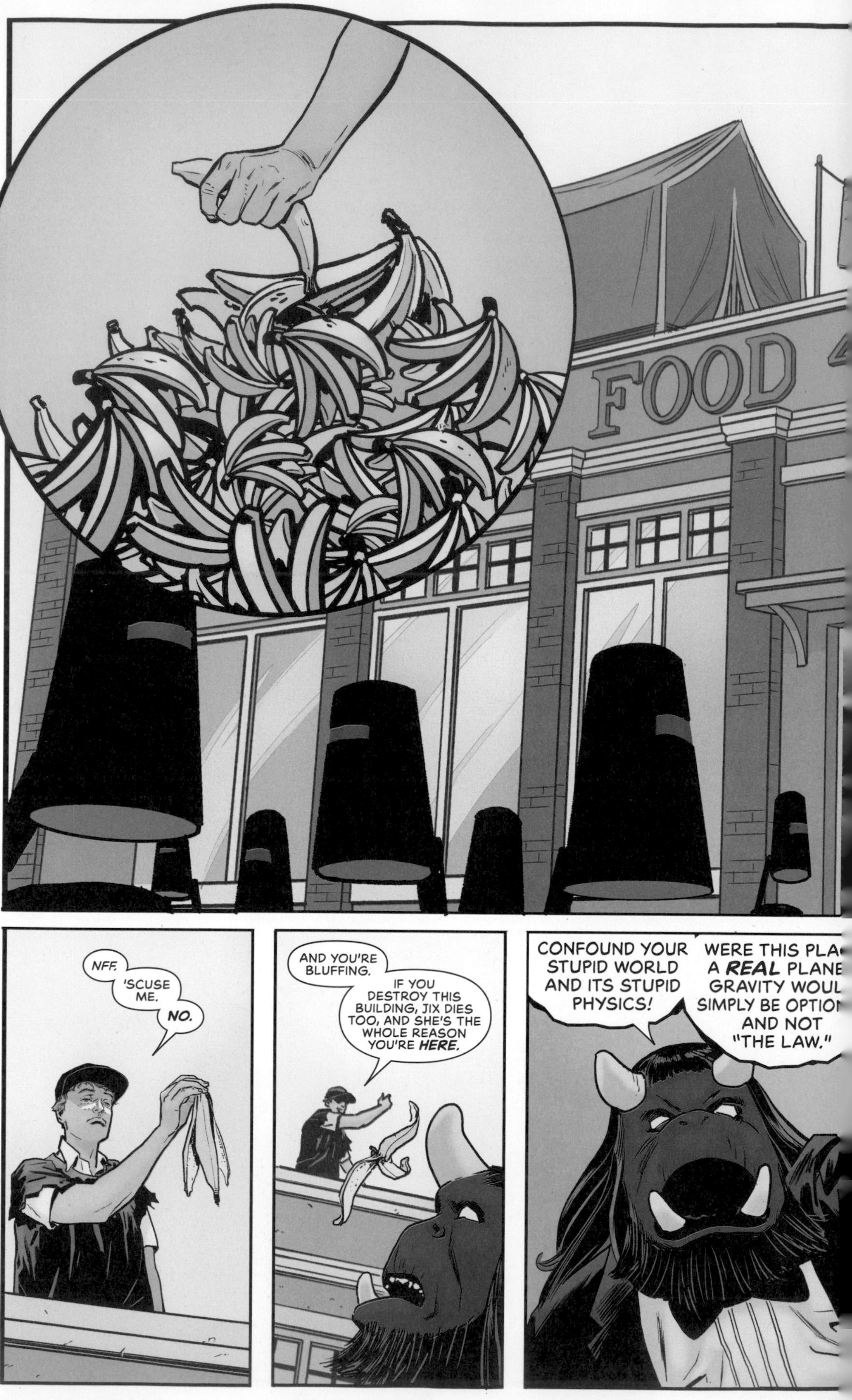
FOOD
NFF.
'SCUSE ME.
NO.
AND YOU'RE BLUFFING.
IF YOU DESTROY THIS BUILDING, JIX DIES TOO, AND SHE'S THE WHOLE REASON YOU'RE *HERE.*
CONFOUND YOUR STUPID WORLD AND ITS STUPID PHYSICS!
WERE THIS PLA
A *REAL* PLANE
GRAVITY WOUL
SIMPLY BE OPTIO
AND NOT
"THE LAW."

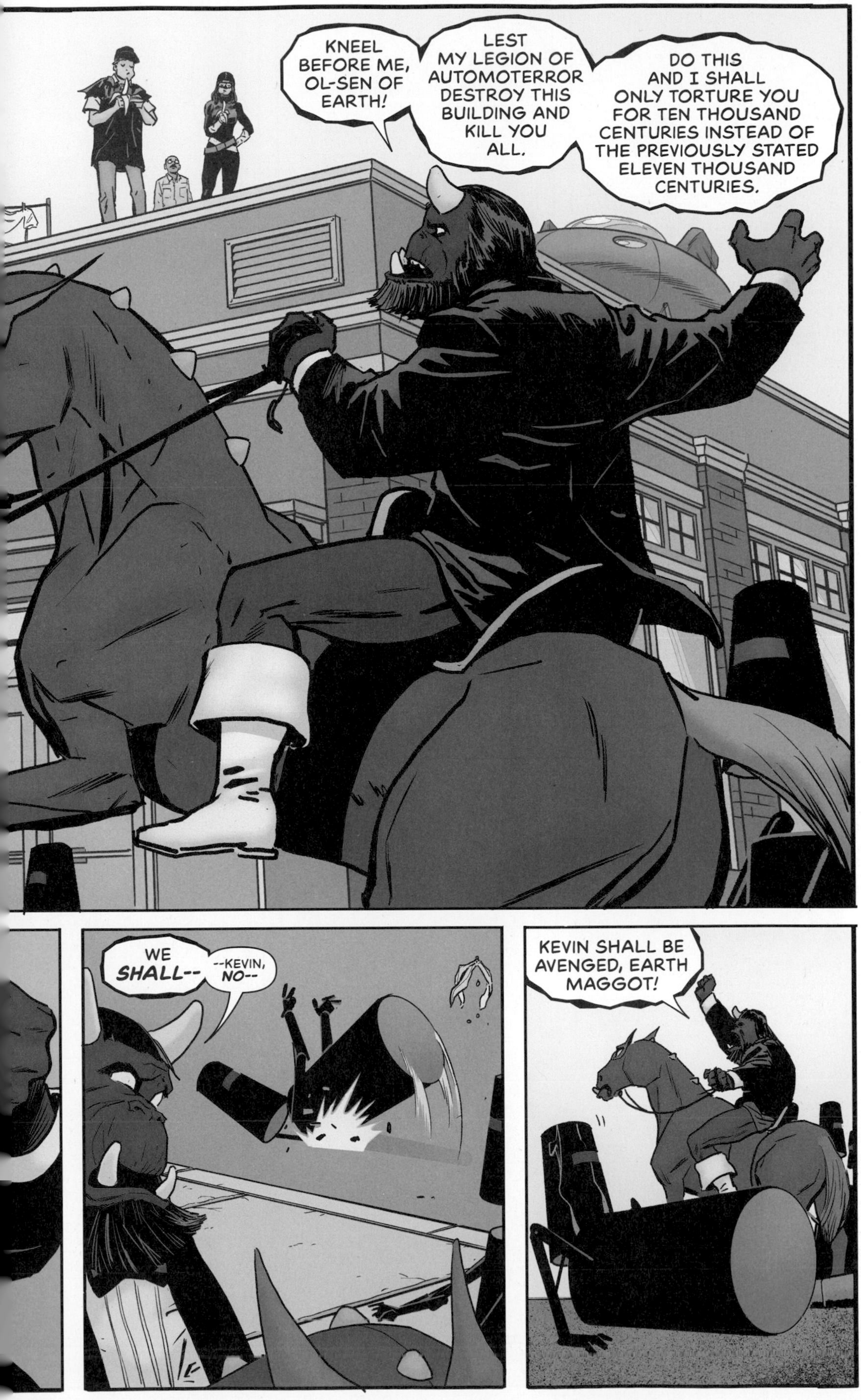
KNEEL BEFORE ME, OL-SEN OF EARTH!
LEST MY LEGION OF AUTOMOTERROR DESTROY THIS BUILDING AND KILL YOU ALL.
DO THIS AND I SHALL ONLY TORTURE YOU FOR TEN THOUSAND CENTURIES INSTEAD OF THE PREVIOUSLY STATED ELEVEN THOUSAND CENTURIES.
WE SHALL--
--KEVIN, NO--
KEVIN SHALL BE AVENGED, EARTH MAGGOT!

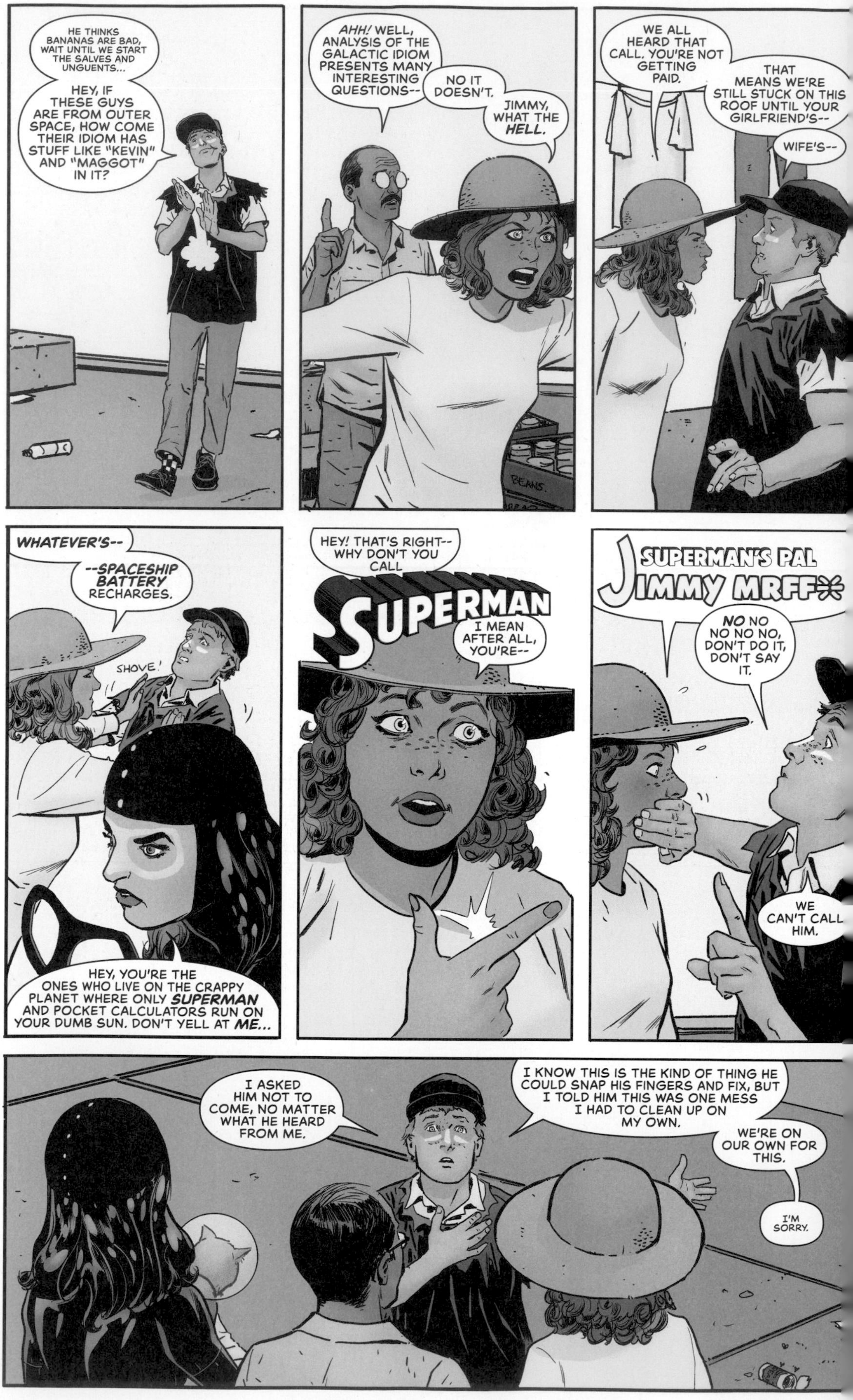
HE THINKS BANANAS ARE BAD, WAIT UNTIL WE START THE SALVES AND UNGUENTS...
HEY, IF THESE GUYS ARE FROM OUTER SPACE, HOW COME THEIR IDIOM HAS STUFF LIKE "KEVIN" AND "MAGGOT" IN IT?
AHH! WELL, ANALYSIS OF THE GALACTIC IDIOM PRESENTS MANY INTERESTING QUESTIONS--
NO IT DOESN'T.
JIMMY, WHAT THE HELL.
BEANS.
WE ALL HEARD THAT CALL. YOU'RE NOT GETTING PAID.
THAT MEANS WE'RE STILL STUCK ON THIS ROOF UNTIL YOUR GIRLFRIEND'S--
WIFE'S--
WHATEVER'S--
--SPACESHIP BATTERY RECHARGES.
SHOVE!
HEY, YOU'RE THE ONES WHO LIVE ON THE CRAPPY PLANET WHERE ONLY SUPERMAN AND POCKET CALCULATORS RUN ON YOUR DUMB SUN. DON'T YELL AT ME...
HEY! THAT'S RIGHT-- WHY DON'T YOU CALL
SUPERMAN
I MEAN AFTER ALL, YOU'RE--
SUPERMAN'S PAL JIMMY MRFF
NO NO NO NO NO, DON'T DO IT, DON'T SAY IT.
WE CAN'T CALL HIM.
I ASKED HIM NOT TO COME, NO MATTER WHAT HE HEARD FROM ME.
I KNOW THIS IS THE KIND OF THING HE COULD SNAP HIS FINGERS AND FIX, BUT I TOLD HIM THIS WAS ONE MESS I HAD TO CLEAN UP ON MY OWN.
WE'RE ON OUR OWN FOR THIS.
I'M SORRY.

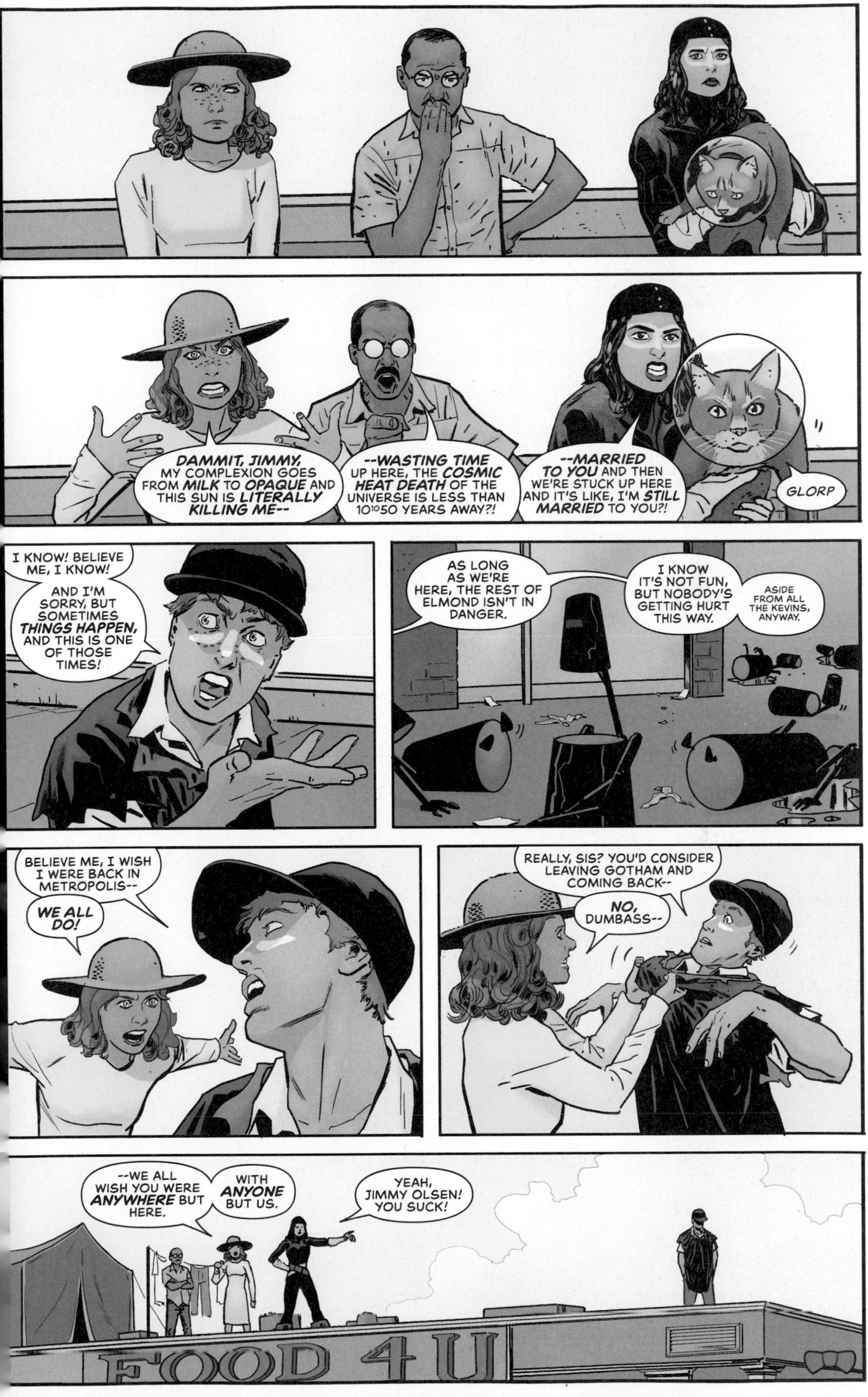
DAMMIT, JIMMY, MY COMPLEXION GOES FROM MILK TO OPAQUE AND THIS SUN IS LITERALLY KILLING ME--
--WASTING TIME UP HERE, THE COSMIC HEAT DEATH OF THE UNIVERSE IS LESS THAN 10^{10}50 YEARS AWAY?!
--MARRIED TO YOU AND THEN WE'RE STUCK UP HERE AND IT'S LIKE, I'M STILL MARRIED TO YOU?!
GLORP
I KNOW! BELIEVE ME, I KNOW!
AND I'M SORRY, BUT SOMETIMES THINGS HAPPEN, AND THIS IS ONE OF THOSE TIMES!
AS LONG AS WE'RE HERE, THE REST OF ELMOND ISN'T IN DANGER.
I KNOW IT'S NOT FUN, BUT NOBODY'S GETTING HURT THIS WAY.
ASIDE FROM ALL THE KEVINS, ANYWAY.
BELIEVE ME, I WISH I WERE BACK IN METROPOLIS--
WE ALL DO!
REALLY, SIS? YOU'D CONSIDER LEAVING GOTHAM AND COMING BACK--
NO, DUMBASS--
--WE ALL WISH YOU WERE ANYWHERE BUT HERE.
WITH ANYONE BUT US.
YEAH, JIMMY OLSEN! YOU SUCK!
FOOD 4 U

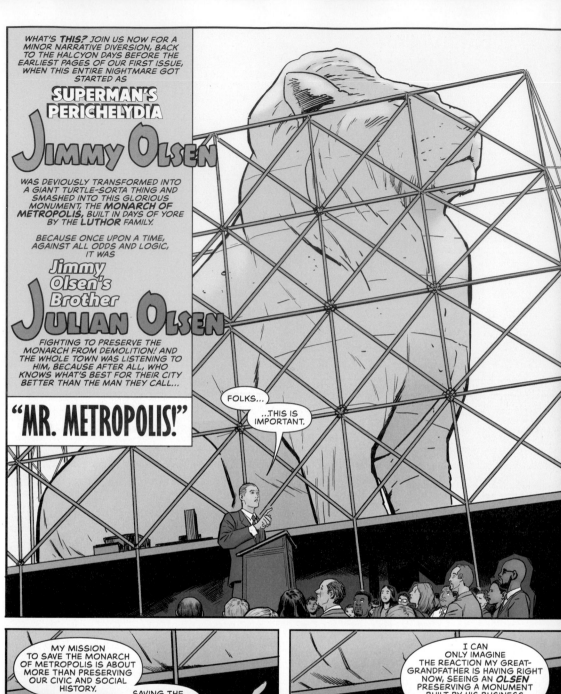

WHAT'S **THIS?** JOIN US NOW FOR A MINOR NARRATIVE DIVERSION, BACK TO THE HALCYON DAYS BEFORE THE EARLIEST PAGES OF OUR FIRST ISSUE, WHEN THIS ENTIRE NIGHTMARE GOT STARTED AS

SUPERMAN'S
PERICHELYDIA

JIMMY OLSEN

WAS DEVIOUSLY TRANSFORMED INTO A GIANT TURTLE-SORTA THING AND SMASHED INTO THIS GLORIOUS MONUMENT, THE **MONARCH OF METROPOLIS,** BUILT IN DAYS OF YORE BY THE **LUTHOR** FAMILY.

BECAUSE ONCE UPON A TIME, AGAINST ALL ODDS AND LOGIC, IT WAS

Jimmy
Olsen's
Brother

JULIAN OLSEN

FIGHTING TO PRESERVE THE MONARCH FROM DEMOLITION! AND THE WHOLE TOWN WAS LISTENING TO HIM, BECAUSE AFTER ALL, WHO KNOWS WHAT'S BEST FOR THEIR CITY BETTER THAN THE MAN THEY CALL...

"MR. METROPOLIS!"

FOLKS...

...THIS IS IMPORTANT.

MY MISSION TO SAVE THE MONARCH OF METROPOLIS IS ABOUT MORE THAN PRESERVING OUR CIVIC AND SOCIAL HISTORY.

SAVING THE MONARCH MEANS SAVING OUR **FUTURE.**

I CAN ONLY IMAGINE THE REACTION MY GREAT-GRANDFATHER IS HAVING RIGHT NOW, SEEING AN **OLSEN** PRESERVING A MONUMENT BUILT BY HIS BUSINESS RIVALS, THE **LUTHORS.**

BUT TIMES CHANGE.

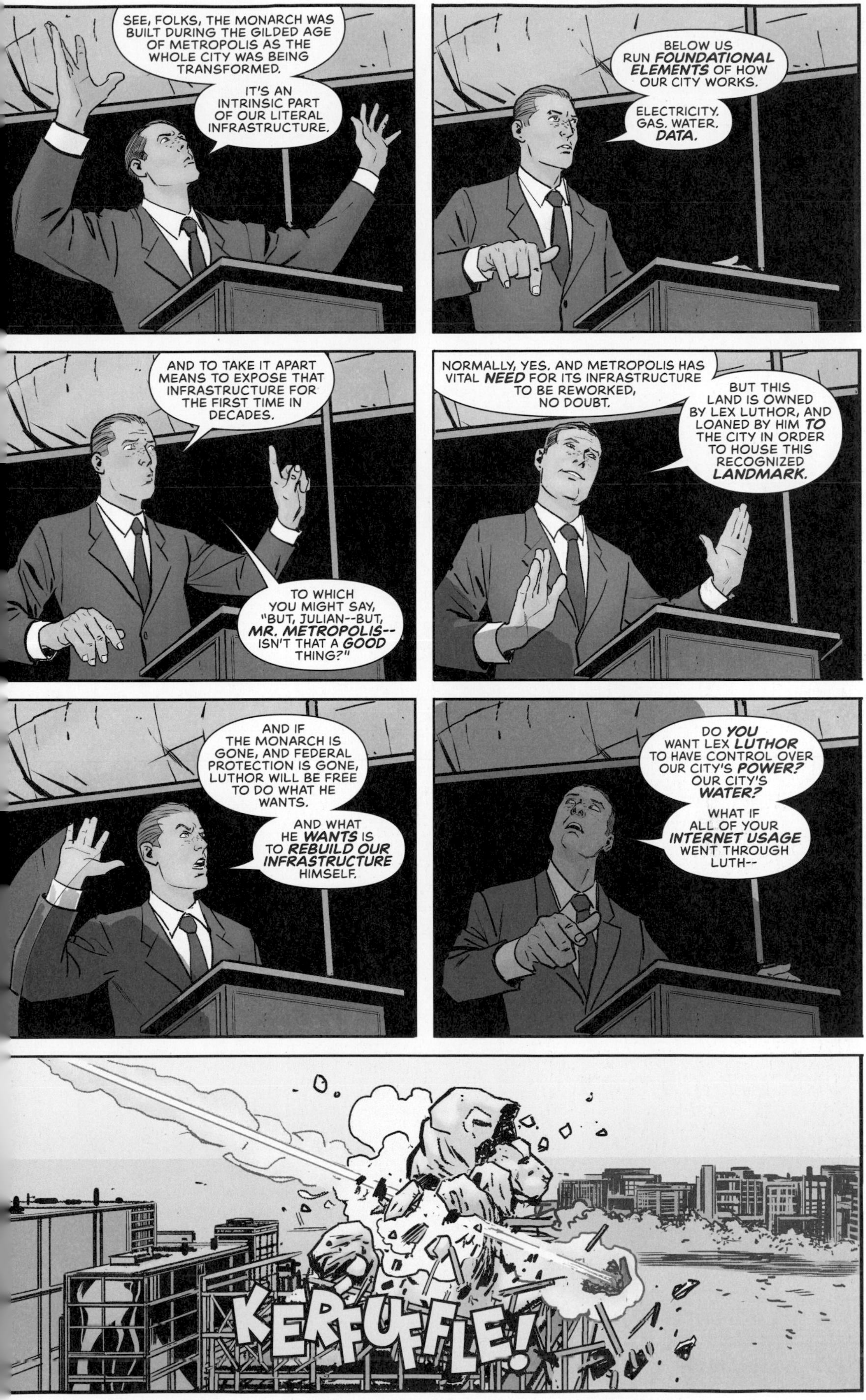
SEE, FOLKS, THE MONARCH WAS BUILT DURING THE GILDED AGE OF METROPOLIS AS THE WHOLE CITY WAS BEING TRANSFORMED.
IT'S AN INTRINSIC PART OF OUR LITERAL INFRASTRUCTURE.
BELOW US RUN **FOUNDATIONAL ELEMENTS** OF HOW OUR CITY WORKS.
ELECTRICITY. GAS. WATER. **DATA.**
AND TO TAKE IT APART MEANS TO EXPOSE THAT INFRASTRUCTURE FOR THE FIRST TIME IN DECADES.
TO WHICH YOU MIGHT SAY, "BUT, JULIAN--BUT, **MR. METROPOLIS--** ISN'T THAT A **GOOD** THING?"
NORMALLY, YES, AND METROPOLIS HAS VITAL **NEED** FOR ITS INFRASTRUCTURE TO BE REWORKED, NO DOUBT.
BUT THIS LAND IS OWNED BY LEX LUTHOR, AND LOANED BY HIM **TO** THE CITY IN ORDER TO HOUSE THIS RECOGNIZED **LANDMARK.**
AND IF THE MONARCH IS GONE, AND FEDERAL PROTECTION IS GONE, LUTHOR WILL BE FREE TO DO WHAT HE WANTS.
AND WHAT HE **WANTS** IS TO **REBUILD OUR INFRASTRUCTURE** HIMSELF.
DO **YOU** WANT LEX **LUTHOR** TO HAVE CONTROL OVER OUR CITY'S **POWER?** OUR CITY'S **WATER?**
WHAT IF ALL OF YOUR **INTERNET USAGE** WENT THROUGH LUTH--
KERFUFFLE!

YOU'RE *BROKE.*

NO, JUST SCRAPED UP A LITTLE.

NO, SIR, *YOU* ARE BROKE. THE *FAMILY.* THE *TRUST.*

I'M SORRY?

WELL, SIR, YOUR GENERAL EXTRAVAGANCE, COST-OF-LIVING-WISE...

...ON TOP OF YOUR VARIOUS FINANCIAL PURSUITS AND PRESERVATION EFFORTS...

TUG

...COMBINED WITH CORRECTING FOR *MASTER* OLSEN'S, *AHH,* EXPLOITS...

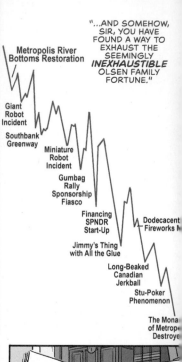

"...AND SOMEHOW, SIR, YOU HAVE FOUND A WAY TO EXHAUST THE SEEMINGLY *INEXHAUSTIBLE* OLSEN FAMILY FORTUNE."

Metropolis River Bottoms Restoration

Giant Robot Incident

Southbank Greenway

Miniature Robot Incident

Gumbag Rally Sponsorship Fiasco

Financing SPNDR Start-Up

Jimmy's Thing with All the Glue

Dodecacent Fireworks M

Long-Beaked Canadian Jerkball

Stu-Poker Phenomenon

The Mona of Metrop Destroye

BUT THE...

OKAY, THERE'S THE FAMILY TRUST, BUT WHAT ABOUT OUR INDIVIDUAL TRUSTS? THOSE *CAN'T* BE GONE TOO...

WELL, SIR, THEY ARE.

JIMMY'S ISN'T, OF COURSE...

SHRUG

SAY WHAT NOW?

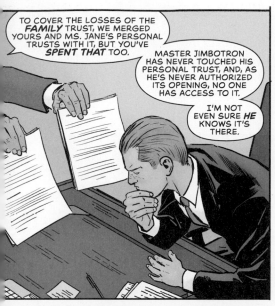

TO COVER THE LOSSES OF THE *FAMILY* TRUST, WE MERGED YOURS AND MS. JANE'S PERSONAL TRUSTS WITH IT, BUT YOU'VE *SPENT THAT* TOO.

MASTER JIMBOTRON HAS NEVER TOUCHED HIS PERSONAL TRUST, AND, AS HE'S NEVER AUTHORIZED ITS OPENING, NO ONE HAS ACCESS TO IT.

I'M NOT EVEN SURE *HE* KNOWS IT'S THERE.

AND I CAN'T *GO* TO HIM WITH THIS... I'D NEVER HEAR THE END OF IT, AND THEN *JANIE* WOULD FIND OUT AND IT'D BE A WHOLE THING...

IT'S INFURIATING, TO THINK A THIRD OF OUR FAMILY FORTUNE IS JUST SITTING THERE INACCESSIBLE *FOREVER* BECAUSE JIMMY'S TOO DUMB TO NOTICE.

WELL, NOT *FOREVER.*

I MEAN, EVEN *JIMMY OLSEN* WILL PASS AWAY *SOME*DAY, AND *THEN* WHATEVER'S LEFT FLOWS BACK TO THE FAMILY.

...WHAT?

NOTHING.

LEAVE US.

...US?

GO! I HAVE *THINKING* TO DO!

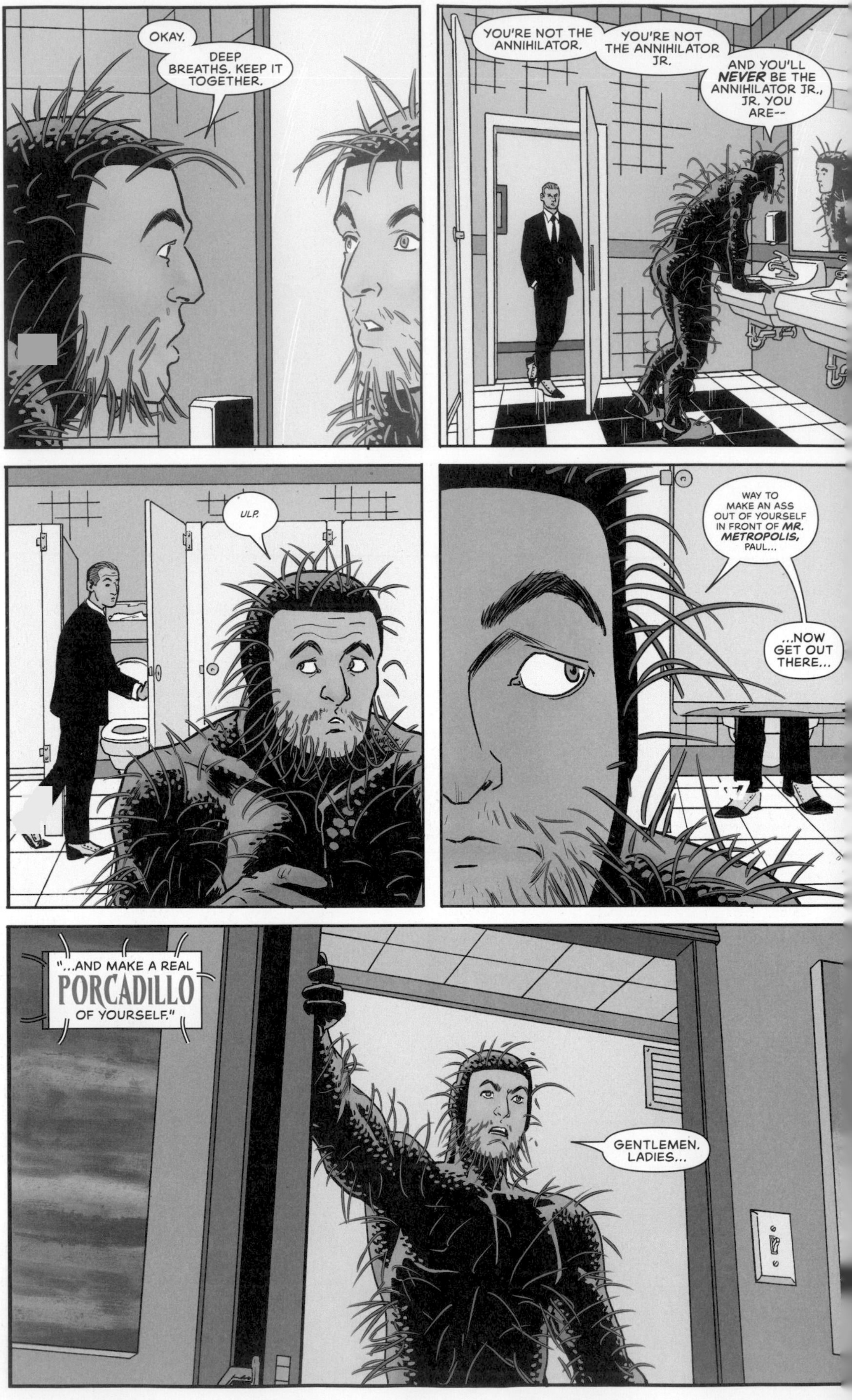

OKAY.
DEEP BREATHS. KEEP IT TOGETHER.
YOU'RE NOT THE ANNIHILATOR.
YOU'RE NOT THE ANNIHILATOR JR.
AND YOU'LL NEVER BE THE ANNIHILATOR JR., JR. YOU ARE--
ULP.
WAY TO MAKE AN ASS OUT OF YOURSELF IN FRONT OF MR. METROPOLIS, PAUL...
...NOW GET OUT THERE...
"...AND MAKE A REAL PORCADILLO OF YOURSELF."
GENTLEMEN. LADIES...

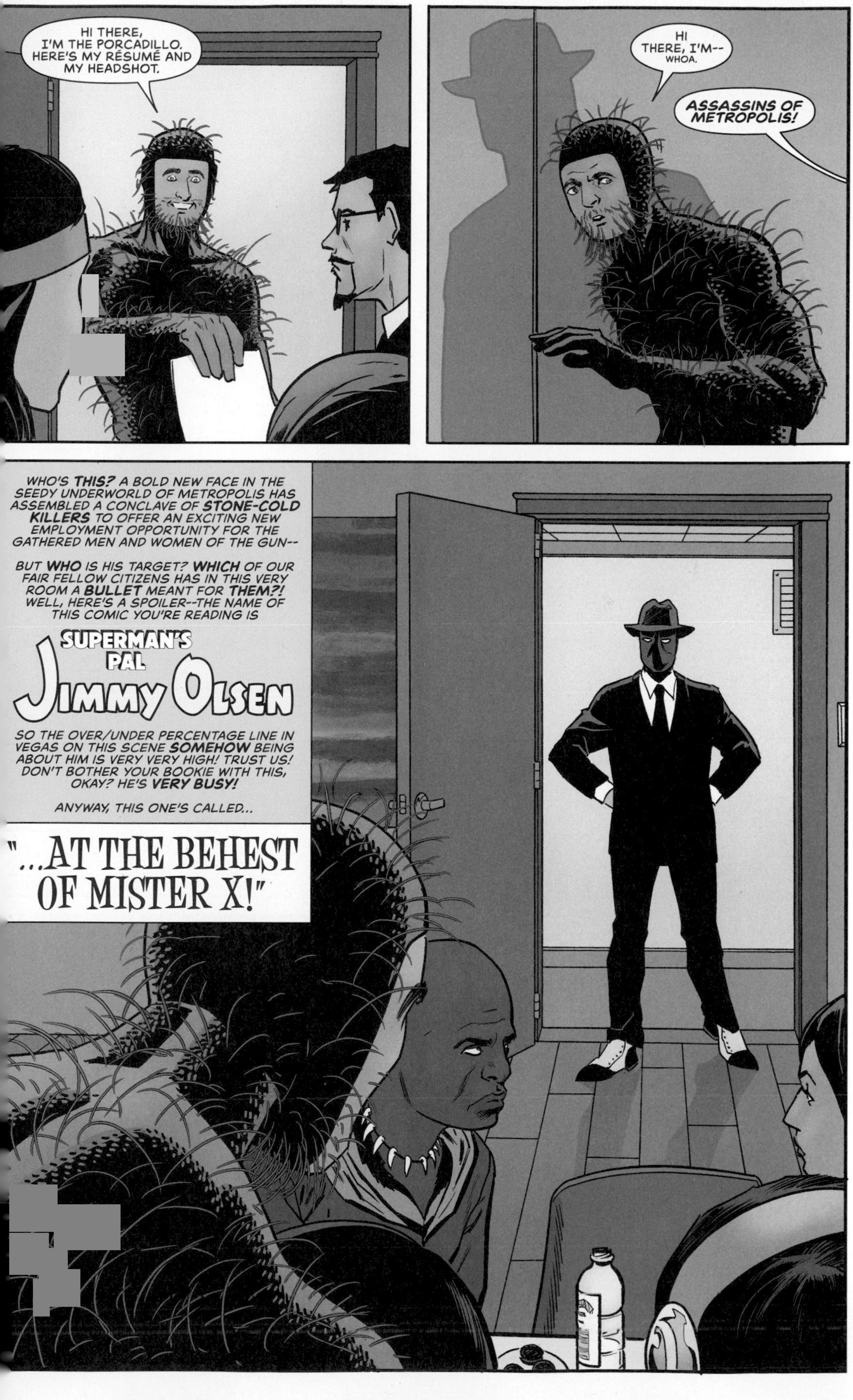
HI THERE, I'M THE PORCADILLO. HERE'S MY RÉSUMÉ AND MY HEADSHOT.
HI THERE, I'M-- WHOA.
ASSASSINS OF METROPOLIS!
WHO'S THIS? A BOLD NEW FACE IN THE SEEDY UNDERWORLD OF METROPOLIS HAS ASSEMBLED A CONCLAVE OF STONE-COLD KILLERS TO OFFER AN EXCITING NEW EMPLOYMENT OPPORTUNITY FOR THE GATHERED MEN AND WOMEN OF THE GUN--
BUT WHO IS HIS TARGET? WHICH OF OUR FAIR FELLOW CITIZENS HAS IN THIS VERY ROOM A BULLET MEANT FOR THEM?! WELL, HERE'S A SPOILER--THE NAME OF THIS COMIC YOU'RE READING IS
SUPERMAN'S PAL JIMMY OLSEN
SO THE OVER/UNDER PERCENTAGE LINE IN VEGAS ON THIS SCENE SOMEHOW BEING ABOUT HIM IS VERY VERY HIGH! TRUST US! DON'T BOTHER YOUR BOOKIE WITH THIS, OKAY? HE'S VERY BUSY!
ANYWAY, THIS ONE'S CALLED...
"...AT THE BEHEST OF MISTER X!"

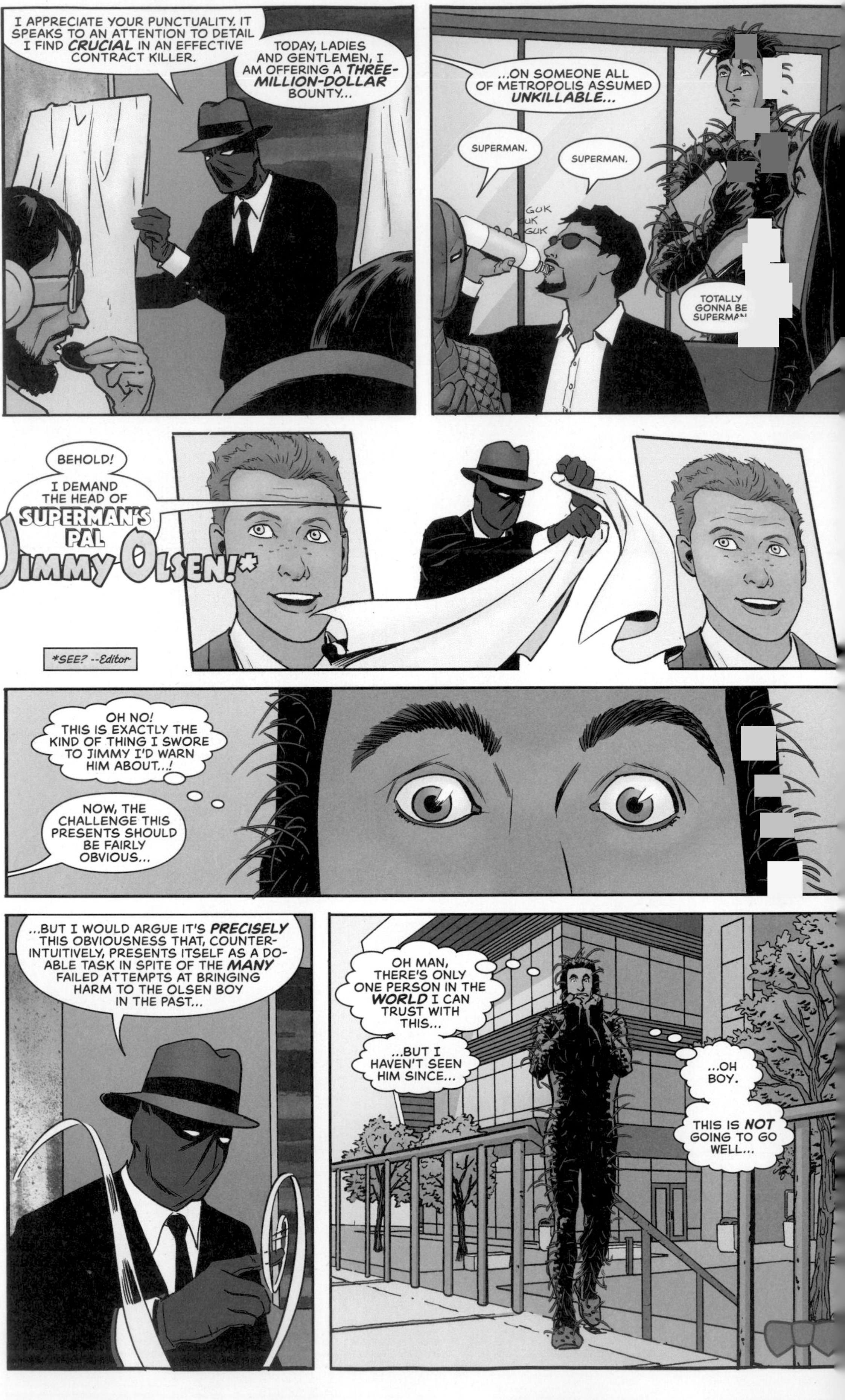

I APPRECIATE YOUR PUNCTUALITY. IT SPEAKS TO AN ATTENTION TO DETAIL I FIND CRUCIAL IN AN EFFECTIVE CONTRACT KILLER.
TODAY, LADIES AND GENTLEMEN, I AM OFFERING A THREE-MILLION-DOLLAR BOUNTY...
...ON SOMEONE ALL OF METROPOLIS ASSUMED UNKILLABLE...
SUPERMAN.
SUPERMAN.
GUK GUK GUK
TOTALLY GONNA BE SUPERMA
BEHOLD!
I DEMAND THE HEAD OF SUPERMAN'S PAL JIMMY OLSEN!*
*SEE? --Editor
OH NO! THIS IS EXACTLY THE KIND OF THING I SWORE TO JIMMY I'D WARN HIM ABOUT...!
NOW, THE CHALLENGE THIS PRESENTS SHOULD BE FAIRLY OBVIOUS...
...BUT I WOULD ARGUE IT'S PRECISELY THIS OBVIOUSNESS THAT, COUNTER-INTUITIVELY, PRESENTS ITSELF AS A DO-ABLE TASK IN SPITE OF THE MANY FAILED ATTEMPTS AT BRINGING HARM TO THE OLSEN BOY IN THE PAST...
OH MAN, THERE'S ONLY ONE PERSON IN THE WORLD I CAN TRUST WITH THIS...
...BUT I HAVEN'T SEEN HIM SINCE...
...OH BOY.
THIS IS NOT GOING TO GO WELL...

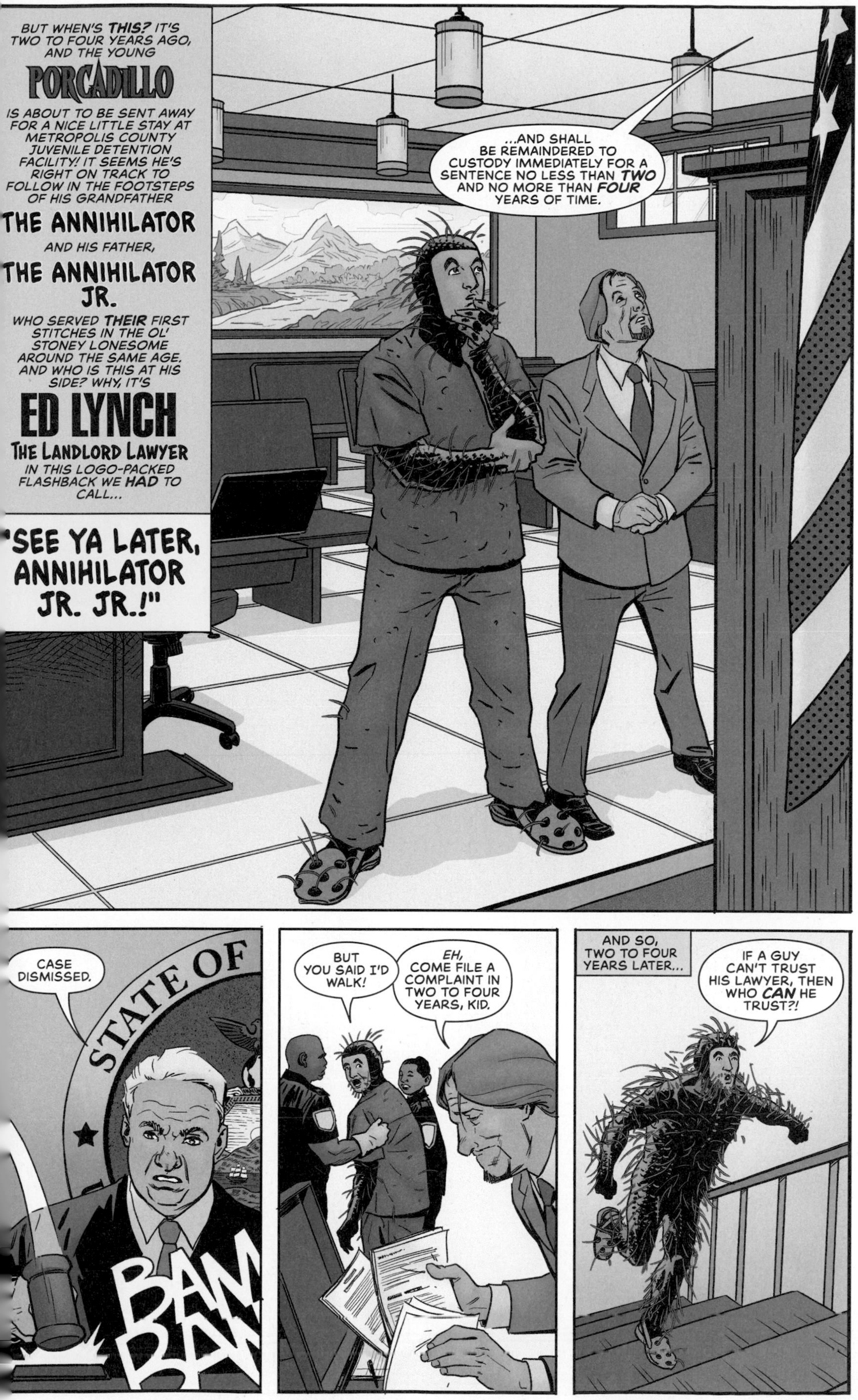
BUT WHEN'S THIS? IT'S TWO TO FOUR YEARS AGO, AND THE YOUNG
PORCADILLO
IS ABOUT TO BE SENT AWAY FOR A NICE LITTLE STAY AT METROPOLIS COUNTY JUVENILE DETENTION FACILITY! IT SEEMS HE'S RIGHT ON TRACK TO FOLLOW IN THE FOOTSTEPS OF HIS GRANDFATHER
THE ANNIHILATOR
AND HIS FATHER,
THE ANNIHILATOR JR.
WHO SERVED THEIR FIRST STITCHES IN THE OL' STONEY LONESOME AROUND THE SAME AGE. AND WHO IS THIS AT HIS SIDE? WHY, IT'S
ED LYNCH
THE LANDLORD LAWYER
IN THIS LOGO-PACKED FLASHBACK WE HAD TO CALL...
"SEE YA LATER, ANNIHILATOR JR. JR.!"
...AND SHALL BE REMAINDERED TO CUSTODY IMMEDIATELY FOR A SENTENCE NO LESS THAN TWO AND NO MORE THAN FOUR YEARS OF TIME.
CASE DISMISSED.
STATE OF
BAM
BUT YOU SAID I'D WALK!
EH, COME FILE A COMPLAINT IN TWO TO FOUR YEARS, KID.
AND SO, TWO TO FOUR YEARS LATER...
IF A GUY CAN'T TRUST HIS LAWYER, THEN WHO CAN HE TRUST?!

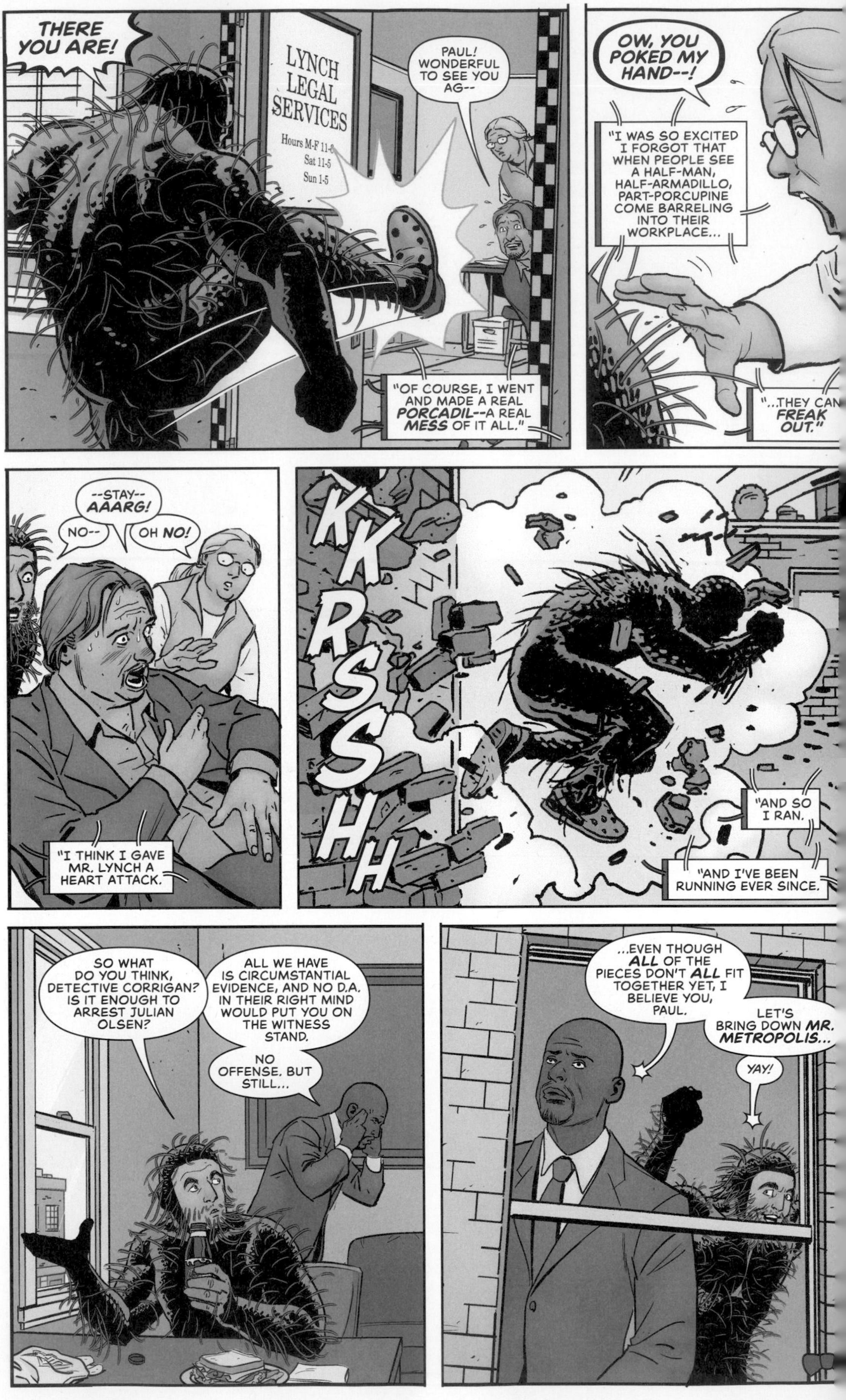
THERE YOU ARE!
LYNCH LEGAL SERVICES
Hours M-F 11-6
Sat 11-5
Sun 1-5
PAUL! WONDERFUL TO SEE YOU AG--
"OF COURSE, I WENT AND MADE A REAL PORCADIL--A REAL MESS OF IT ALL."
OW, YOU POKED MY HAND--!
"I WAS SO EXCITED I FORGOT THAT WHEN PEOPLE SEE A HALF-MAN, HALF-ARMADILLO, PART-PORCUPINE COME BARRELING INTO THEIR WORKPLACE...
"...THEY CAN FREAK OUT."
--STAY-- AAARG!
NO--
OH NO!
"I THINK I GAVE MR. LYNCH A HEART ATTACK.
KKRSSHH
"AND SO I RAN.
"AND I'VE BEEN RUNNING EVER SINCE.
SO WHAT DO YOU THINK, DETECTIVE CORRIGAN? IS IT ENOUGH TO ARREST JULIAN OLSEN?
ALL WE HAVE IS CIRCUMSTANTIAL EVIDENCE, AND NO D.A. IN THEIR RIGHT MIND WOULD PUT YOU ON THE WITNESS STAND.
NO OFFENSE, BUT STILL...
...EVEN THOUGH ALL OF THE PIECES DON'T ALL FIT TOGETHER YET, I BELIEVE YOU, PAUL.
LET'S BRING DOWN MR. METROPOLIS...
YAY!

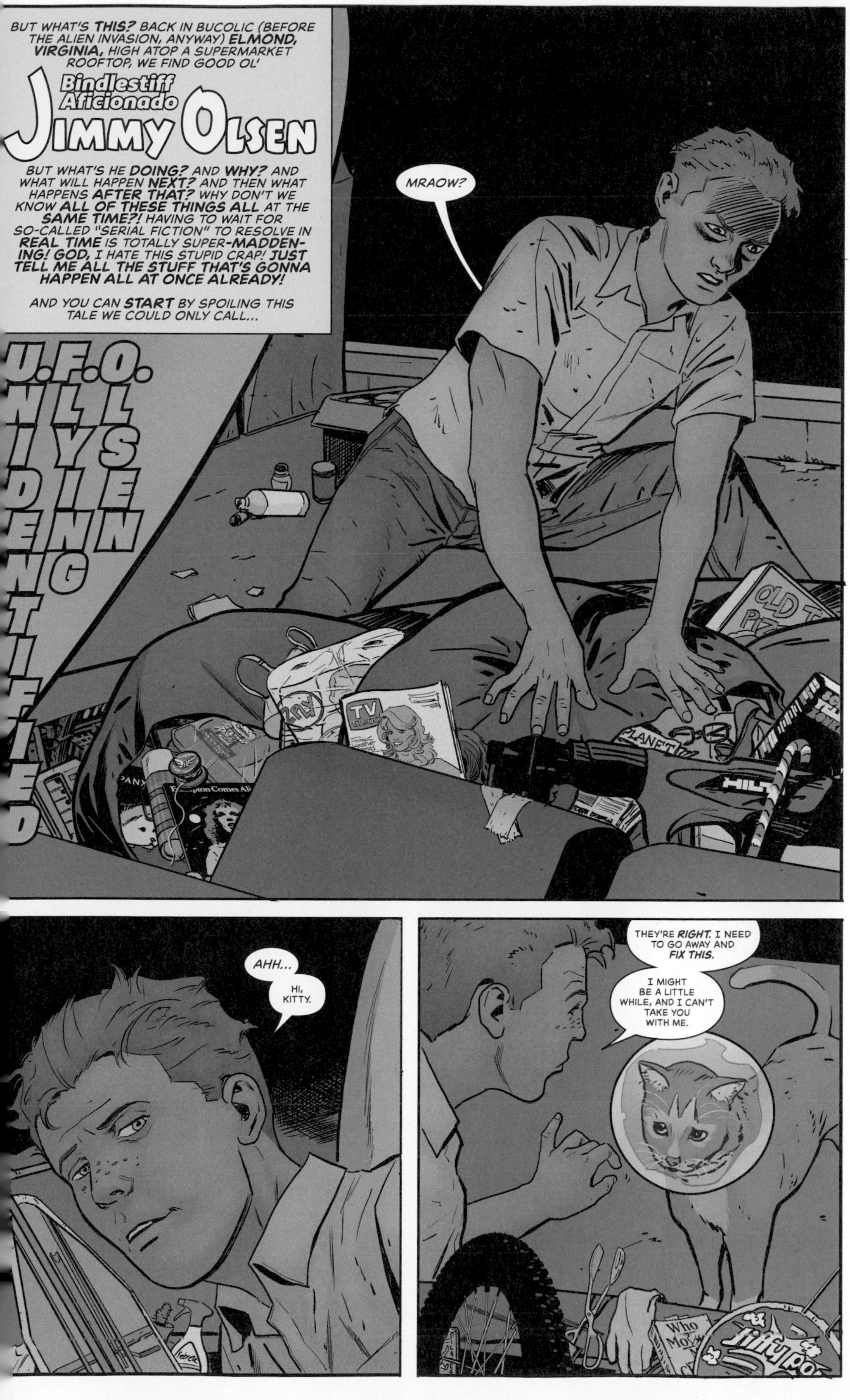
BUT WHAT'S THIS? BACK IN BUCOLIC (BEFORE THE ALIEN INVASION, ANYWAY) ELMOND, VIRGINIA, HIGH ATOP A SUPERMARKET ROOFTOP, WE FIND GOOD OL'
Bindlestiff Aficionado
JIMMY OLSEN
BUT WHAT'S HE DOING? AND WHY? AND WHAT WILL HAPPEN NEXT? AND THEN WHAT HAPPENS AFTER THAT? WHY DON'T WE KNOW ALL OF THESE THINGS ALL AT THE SAME TIME?! HAVING TO WAIT FOR SO-CALLED "SERIAL FICTION" TO RESOLVE IN REAL TIME IS TOTALLY SUPER-MADDENING! GOD, I HATE THIS STUPID CRAP! JUST TELL ME ALL THE STUFF THAT'S GONNA HAPPEN ALL AT ONCE ALREADY!
AND YOU CAN START BY SPOILING THIS TALE WE COULD ONLY CALL...
U.F.O.
UNIDENTIFIED FLYING OLSEN
MRAOW?
AHH...
HI, KITTY.
THEY'RE RIGHT. I NEED TO GO AWAY AND FIX THIS.
I MIGHT BE A LITTLE WHILE, AND I CAN'T TAKE YOU WITH ME.

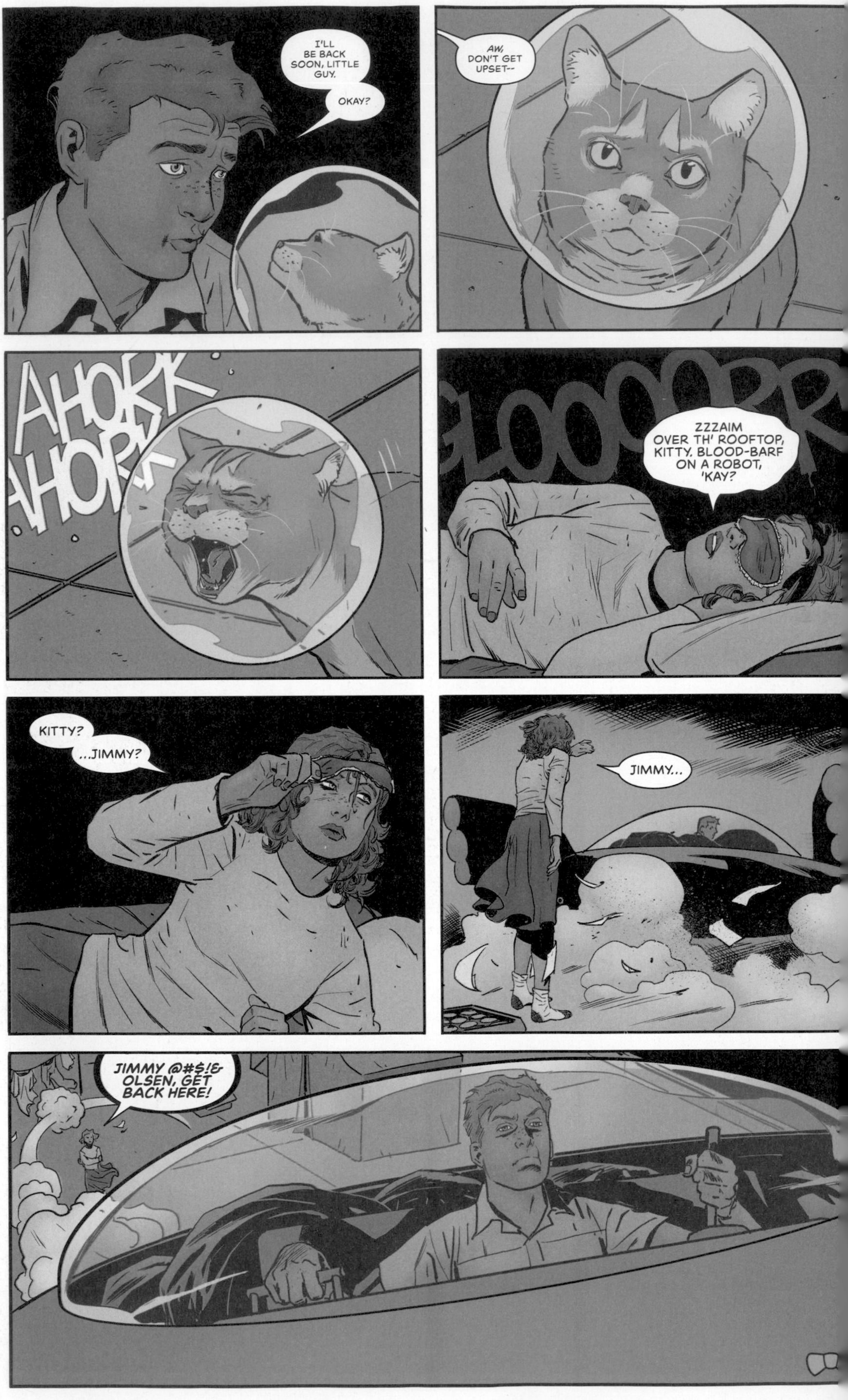
I'LL BE BACK SOON, LITTLE GUY.
OKAY?
AW, DON'T GET UPSET--
AHORK AHORK
GLOOOORR
ZZZAIM OVER TH' ROOFTOP, KITTY. BLOOD-BARF ON A ROBOT, 'KAY?
KITTY?
...JIMMY?
JIMMY...
JIMMY @#$!& OLSEN, GET BACK HERE!

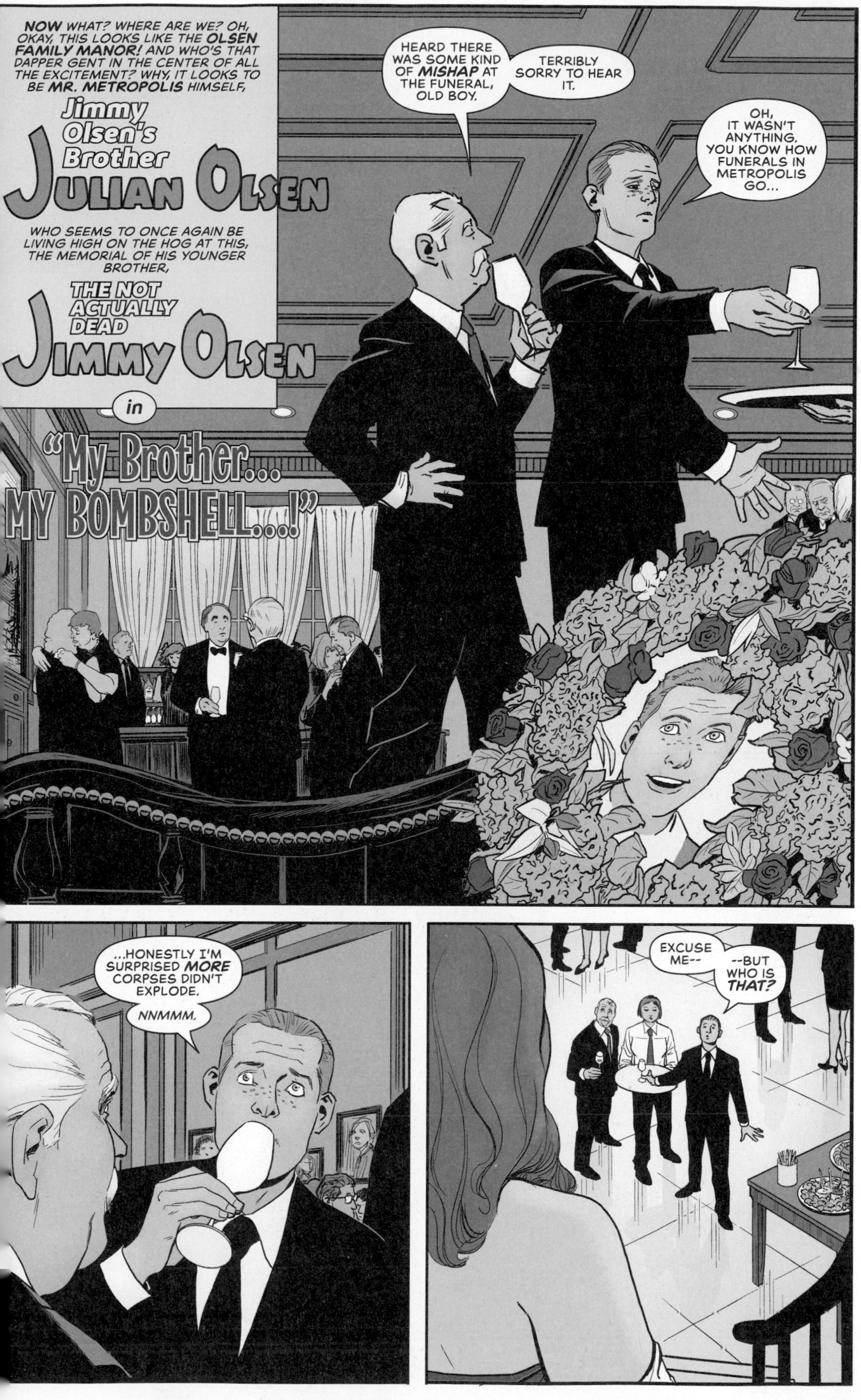
NOW WHAT? WHERE ARE WE? OH, OKAY, THIS LOOKS LIKE THE OLSEN FAMILY MANOR! AND WHO'S THAT DAPPER GENT IN THE CENTER OF ALL THE EXCITEMENT? WHY, IT LOOKS TO BE MR. METROPOLIS HIMSELF,
Jimmy Olsen's Brother
JULIAN OLSEN
WHO SEEMS TO ONCE AGAIN BE LIVING HIGH ON THE HOG AT THIS, THE MEMORIAL OF HIS YOUNGER BROTHER,
THE NOT ACTUALLY DEAD
JIMMY OLSEN
in
"My Brother... MY BOMBSHELL...!"
HEARD THERE WAS SOME KIND OF MISHAP AT THE FUNERAL, OLD BOY.
TERRIBLY SORRY TO HEAR IT.
OH, IT WASN'T ANYTHING. YOU KNOW HOW FUNERALS IN METROPOLIS GO...
...HONESTLY I'M SURPRISED MORE CORPSES DIDN'T EXPLODE.
NNMMM.
EXCUSE ME--
--BUT WHO IS THAT?

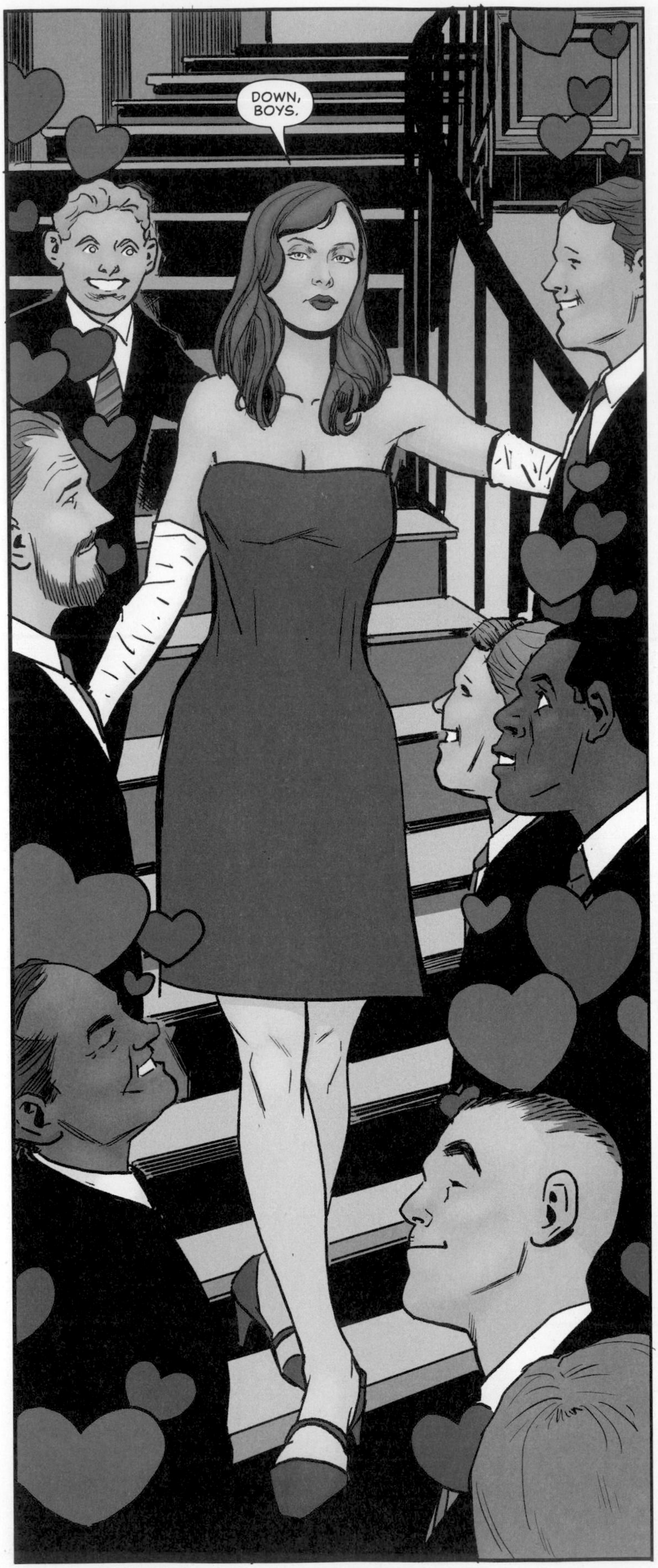
DOWN, BOYS.

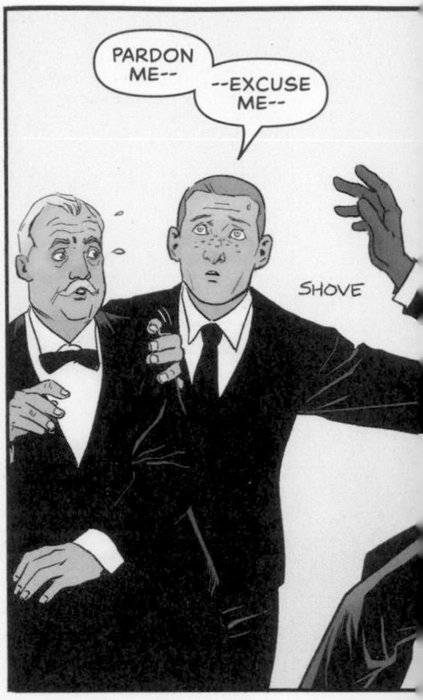
PARDON ME--
--EXCUSE ME--
SHOVE

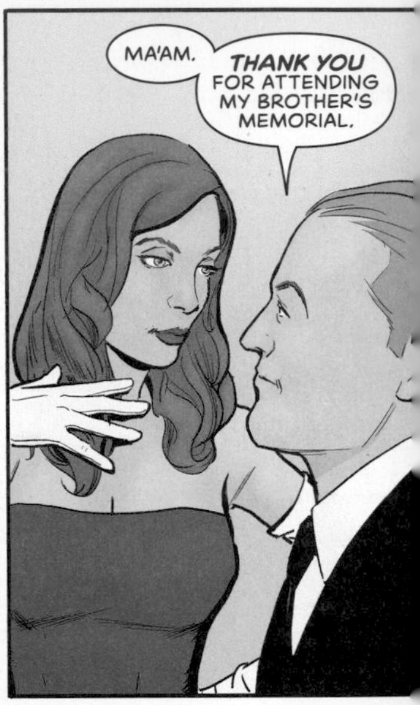
MA'AM. THANK YOU FOR ATTENDING MY BROTHER'S MEMORIAL.

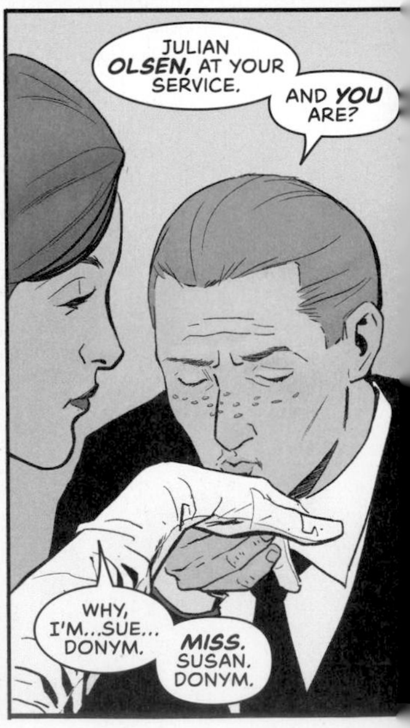
JULIAN OLSEN, AT YOUR SERVICE.
AND YOU ARE?
WHY, I'M...SUE... DONYM.
MISS. SUSAN. DONYM.

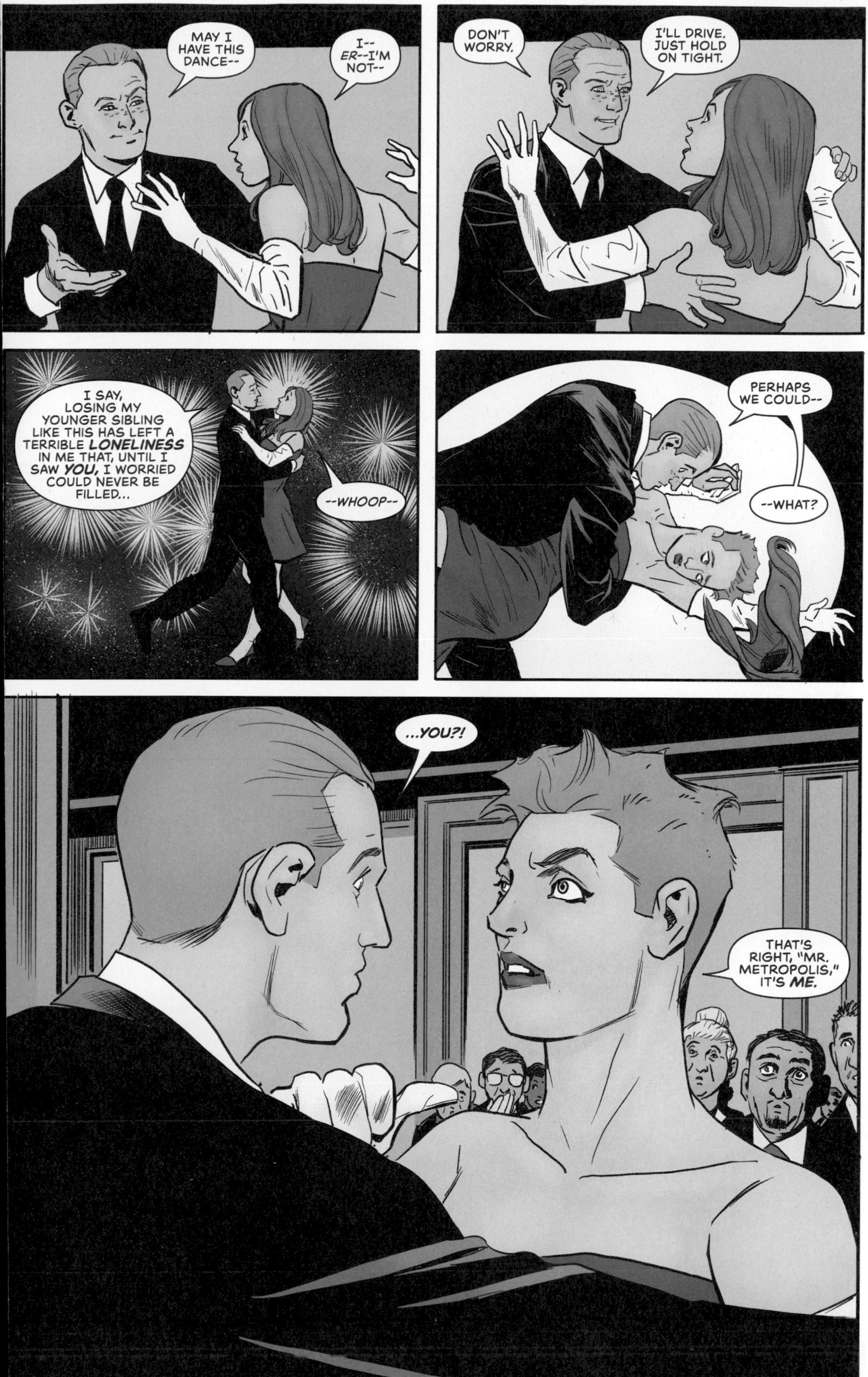
MAY I HAVE THIS DANCE--
I-- ER--I'M NOT--
DON'T WORRY.
I'LL DRIVE. JUST HOLD ON TIGHT.
I SAY, LOSING MY YOUNGER SIBLING LIKE THIS HAS LEFT A TERRIBLE LONELINESS IN ME THAT, UNTIL I SAW YOU, I WORRIED COULD NEVER BE FILLED...
--WHOOP--
PERHAPS WE COULD--
--WHAT?
...YOU?!
THAT'S RIGHT, "MR. METROPOLIS," IT'S ME.

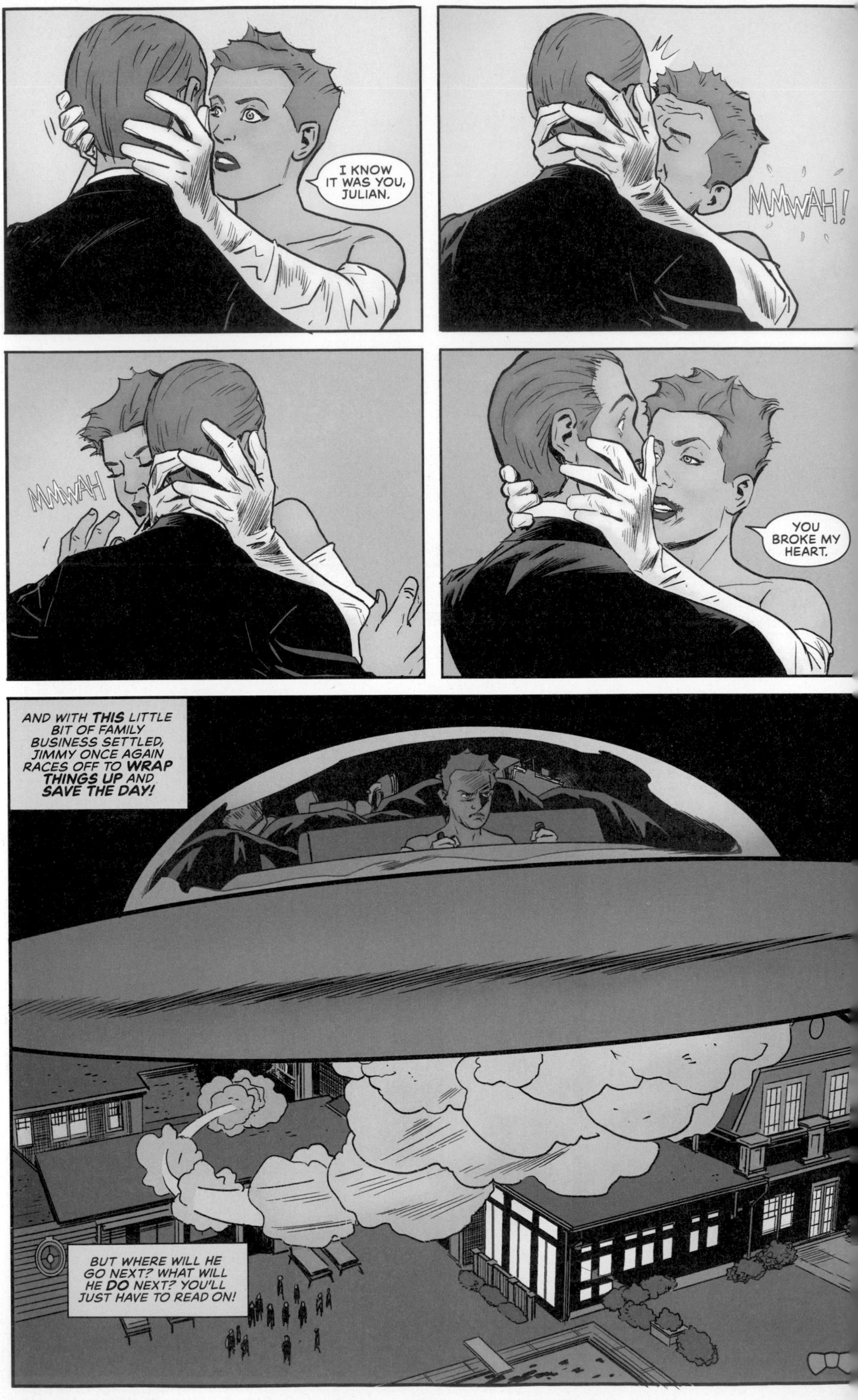
I KNOW IT WAS YOU, JULIAN.
MMWAH!
MMWAH
YOU BROKE MY HEART.
AND WITH THIS LITTLE BIT OF FAMILY BUSINESS SETTLED, JIMMY ONCE AGAIN RACES OFF TO WRAP THINGS UP AND SAVE THE DAY!
BUT WHERE WILL HE GO NEXT? WHAT WILL HE DO NEXT? YOU'LL JUST HAVE TO READ ON!

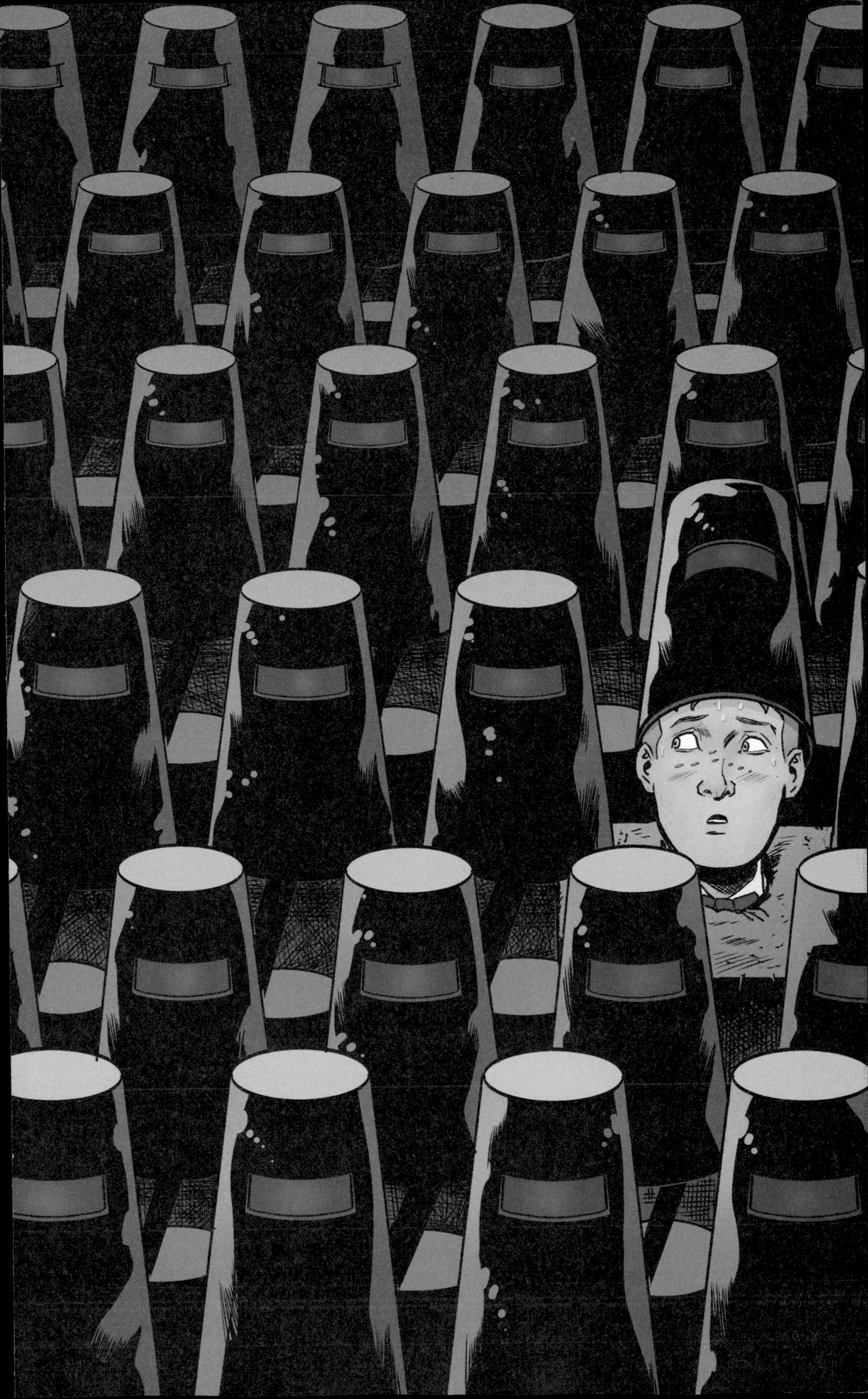

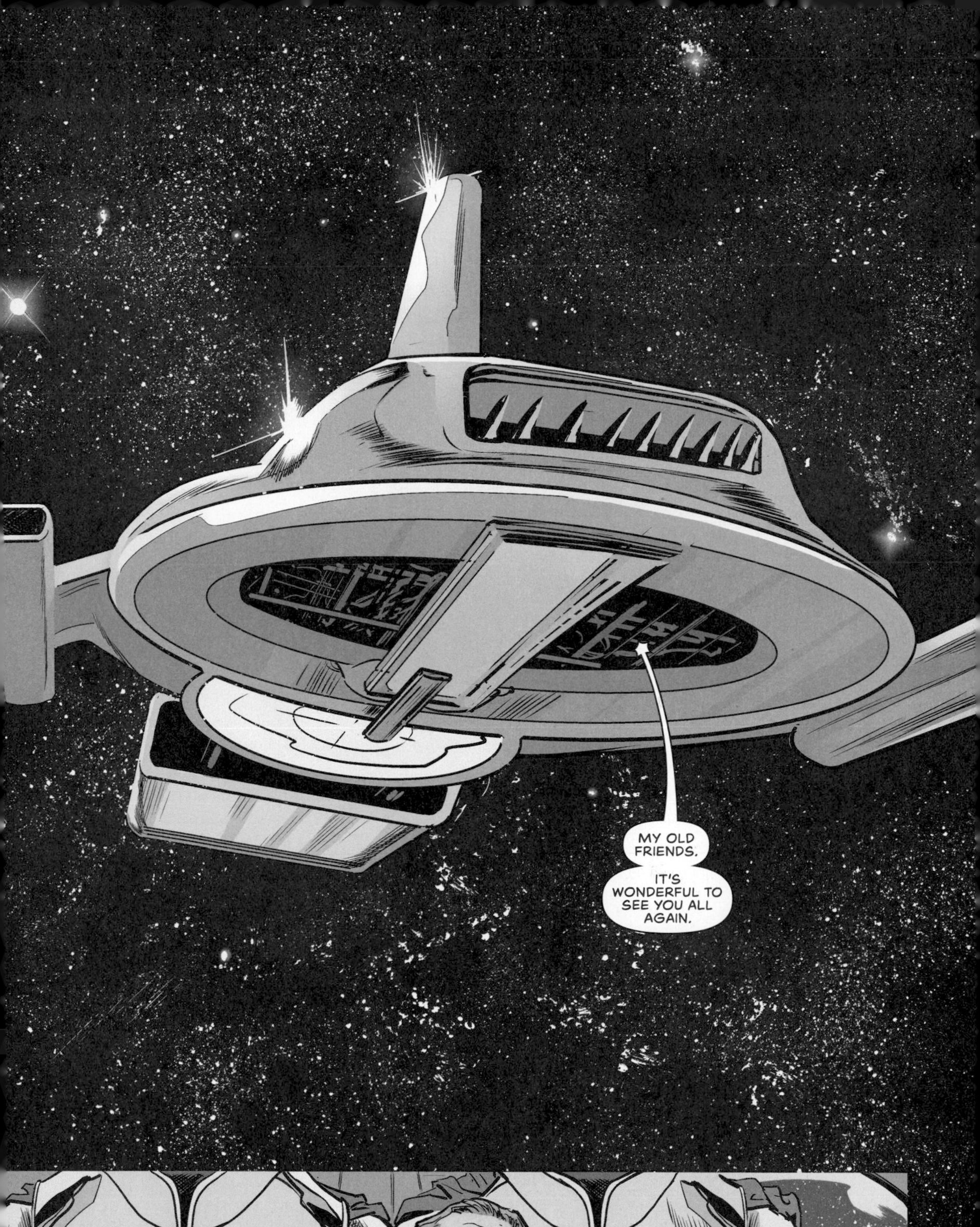
MY OLD FRIENDS.
IT'S WONDERFUL TO SEE YOU ALL AGAIN.

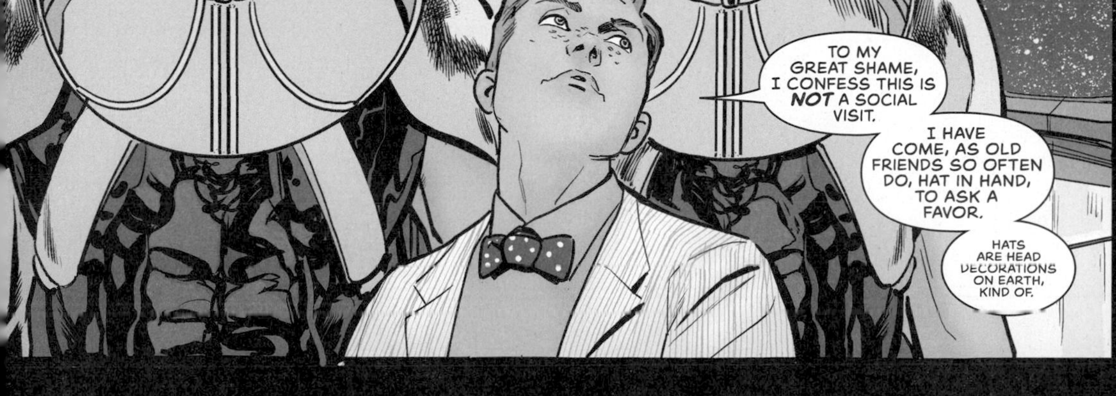
TO MY GREAT SHAME, I CONFESS THIS IS NOT A SOCIAL VISIT.
I HAVE COME, AS OLD FRIENDS SO OFTEN DO, HAT IN HAND, TO ASK A FAVOR.
HATS ARE HEAD DECORATIONS ON EARTH, KIND OF.

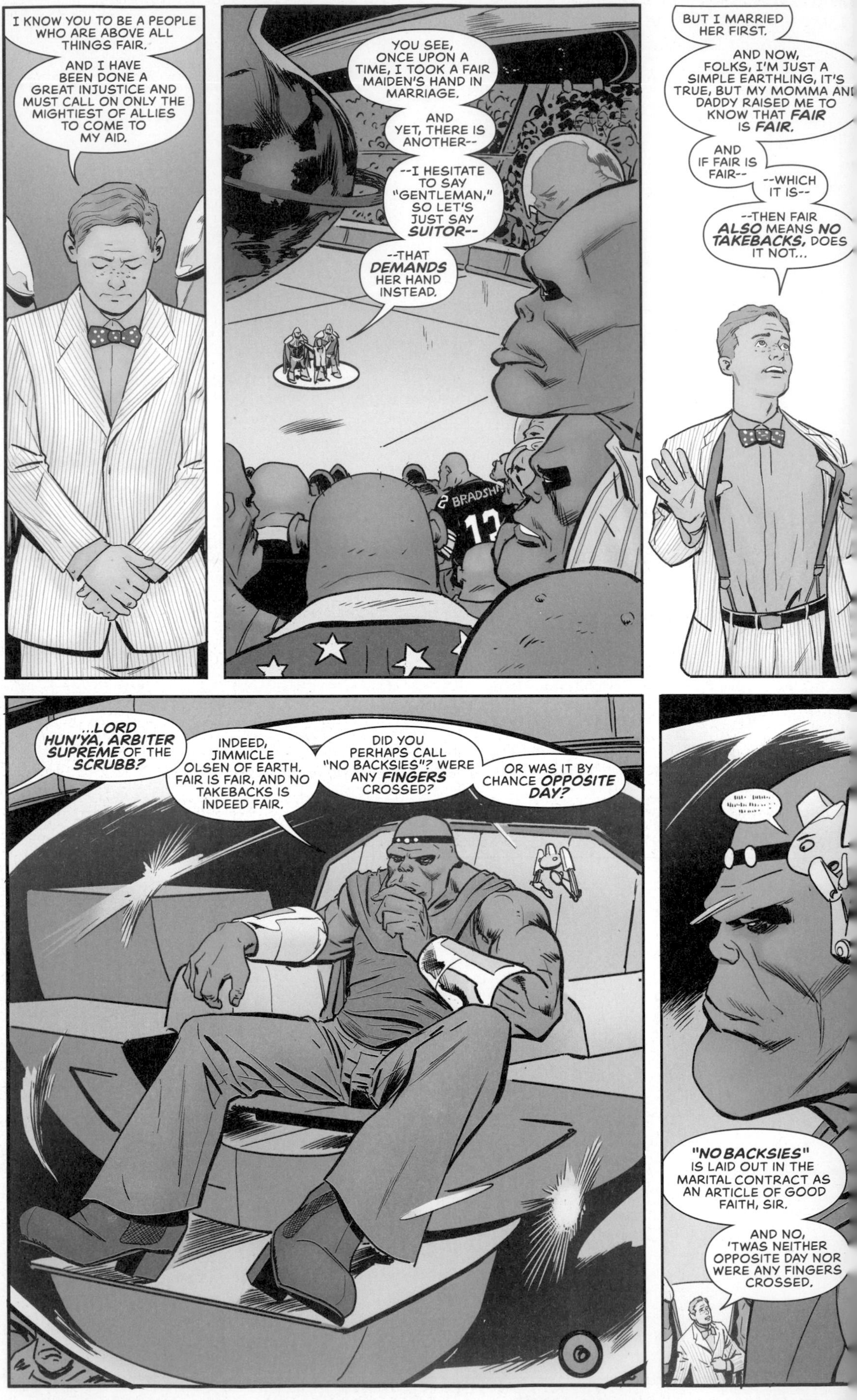
I KNOW YOU TO BE A PEOPLE WHO ARE ABOVE ALL THINGS FAIR.
AND I HAVE BEEN DONE A GREAT INJUSTICE AND MUST CALL ON ONLY THE MIGHTIEST OF ALLIES TO COME TO MY AID.
YOU SEE, ONCE UPON A TIME, I TOOK A FAIR MAIDEN'S HAND IN MARRIAGE.
AND YET, THERE IS ANOTHER--
--I HESITATE TO SAY "GENTLEMAN," SO LET'S JUST SAY SUITOR--
--THAT DEMANDS HER HAND INSTEAD.
BUT I MARRIED HER FIRST.
AND NOW, FOLKS, I'M JUST A SIMPLE EARTHLING, IT'S TRUE, BUT MY MOMMA AND DADDY RAISED ME TO KNOW THAT FAIR IS FAIR.
AND IF FAIR IS FAIR--
--WHICH IT IS--
--THEN FAIR ALSO MEANS NO TAKEBACKS, DOES IT NOT...
...LORD HUN'YA, ARBITER SUPREME OF THE SCRUBB?
INDEED, JIMMICLE OLSEN OF EARTH. FAIR IS FAIR, AND NO TAKEBACKS IS INDEED FAIR.
DID YOU PERHAPS CALL "NO BACKSIES"? WERE ANY FINGERS CROSSED?
OR WAS IT BY CHANCE OPPOSITE DAY?
"NO BACKSIES" IS LAID OUT IN THE MARITAL CONTRACT AS AN ARTICLE OF GOOD FAITH, SIR.
AND NO, 'TWAS NEITHER OPPOSITE DAY NOR WERE ANY FINGERS CROSSED.

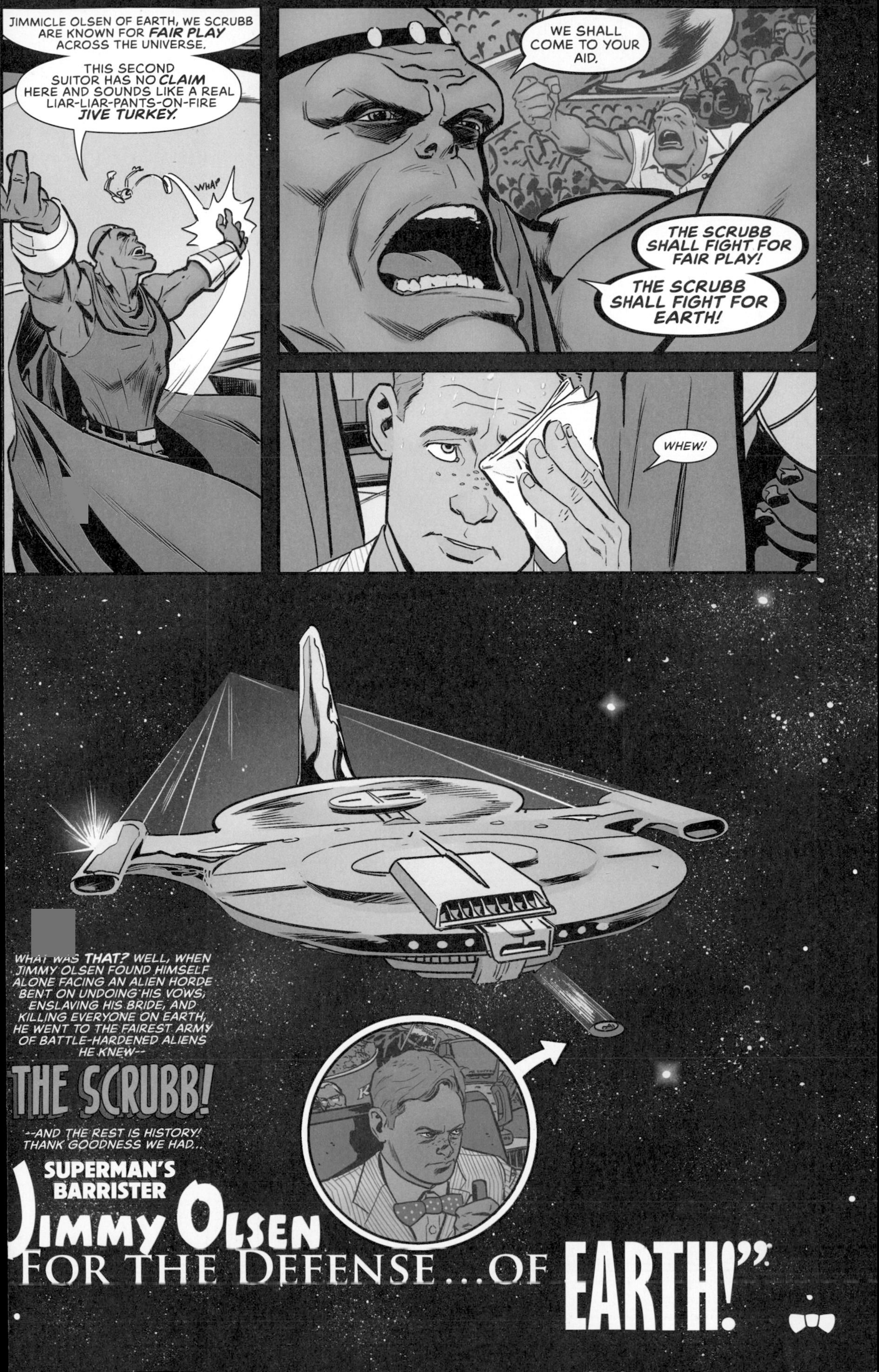

JIMMICLE OLSEN OF EARTH, WE SCRUBB ARE KNOWN FOR FAIR PLAY ACROSS THE UNIVERSE.
THIS SECOND SUITOR HAS NO CLAIM HERE AND SOUNDS LIKE A REAL LIAR-LIAR-PANTS-ON-FIRE JIVE TURKEY.
WHAP
WE SHALL COME TO YOUR AID.
THE SCRUBB SHALL FIGHT FOR FAIR PLAY!
THE SCRUBB SHALL FIGHT FOR EARTH!
WHEW!
WHAT WAS THAT? WELL, WHEN JIMMY OLSEN FOUND HIMSELF ALONE FACING AN ALIEN HORDE BENT ON UNDOING HIS VOWS, ENSLAVING HIS BRIDE, AND KILLING EVERYONE ON EARTH, HE WENT TO THE FAIREST ARMY OF BATTLE-HARDENED ALIENS HE KNEW--
THE SCRUBB!
--AND THE REST IS HISTORY! THANK GOODNESS WE HAD...
SUPERMAN'S BARRISTER
JIMMY OLSEN
FOR THE DEFENSE...OF EARTH!"

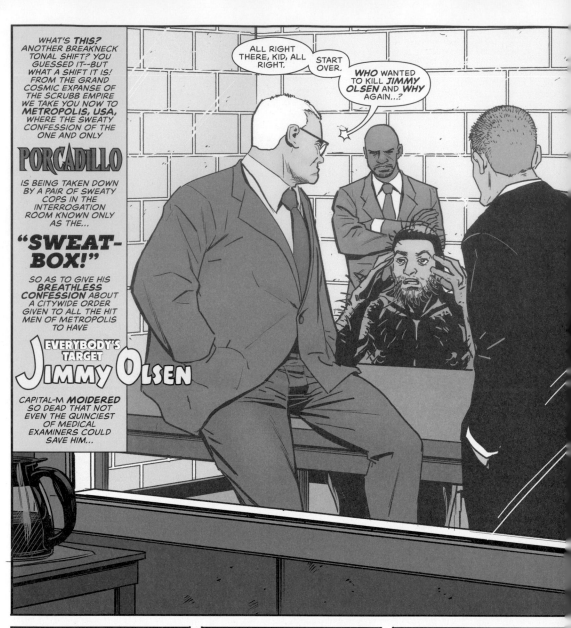

WHAT'S **THIS?** ANOTHER **BREAKNECK TONAL SHIFT?** YOU GUESSED IT--BUT WHAT A SHIFT IT IS! FROM THE GRAND COSMIC EXPANSE OF THE **SCRUBB EMPIRE** WE TAKE YOU NOW TO **METROPOLIS, USA,** WHERE THE SWEATY CONFESSION OF THE ONE AND ONLY

PORCADILLO

IS BEING TAKEN DOWN BY A PAIR OF SWEATY COPS IN THE INTERROGATION ROOM KNOWN ONLY AS THE...

"SWEAT-BOX!"

SO AS TO GIVE HIS **BREATHLESS CONFESSION** ABOUT A CITYWIDE ORDER GIVEN TO ALL THE HIT MEN OF METROPOLIS TO HAVE

EVERYBODY'S TARGET

JIMMY OLSEN

CAPITAL-M **MOIDERED** SO DEAD THAT NOT EVEN THE QUINCIEST OF MEDICAL EXAMINERS COULD SAVE HIM...

ALL RIGHT THERE, KID, ALL RIGHT.

START OVER.

WHO WANTED TO KILL **JIMMY OLSEN** AND **WHY** AGAIN...?

HE TRIES, AS ONLY A TWO-TIME LOSER ON THE WRONG SIDE OF THE LAW CAN TRY, TO LAY THE WHOLE SORDID AFFAIR OUT AS HE UNDERSTOOD IT.

HE LEAVES NOTHING OUT, EVEN IF IT MAKES HIM LOOK BAD.

THE DETECTIVES--JADED AND CYNICAL--TRY TO MAKE HEADS OR TAILS OF THE ENTIRE LABYRINTHINE AFFAIR.

THEY ASK QUESTIONS. THEY SEEK CLARITY.

DETECTIVE **CORRIGAN**--BY NOW ACCUSTOMED TO THE LABORIOUS MAZE MADE BY THIS MURDEROUS CONSPIRACY--TRIES TO HELP.

TELL THEM ABOUT THE **SPATS.**

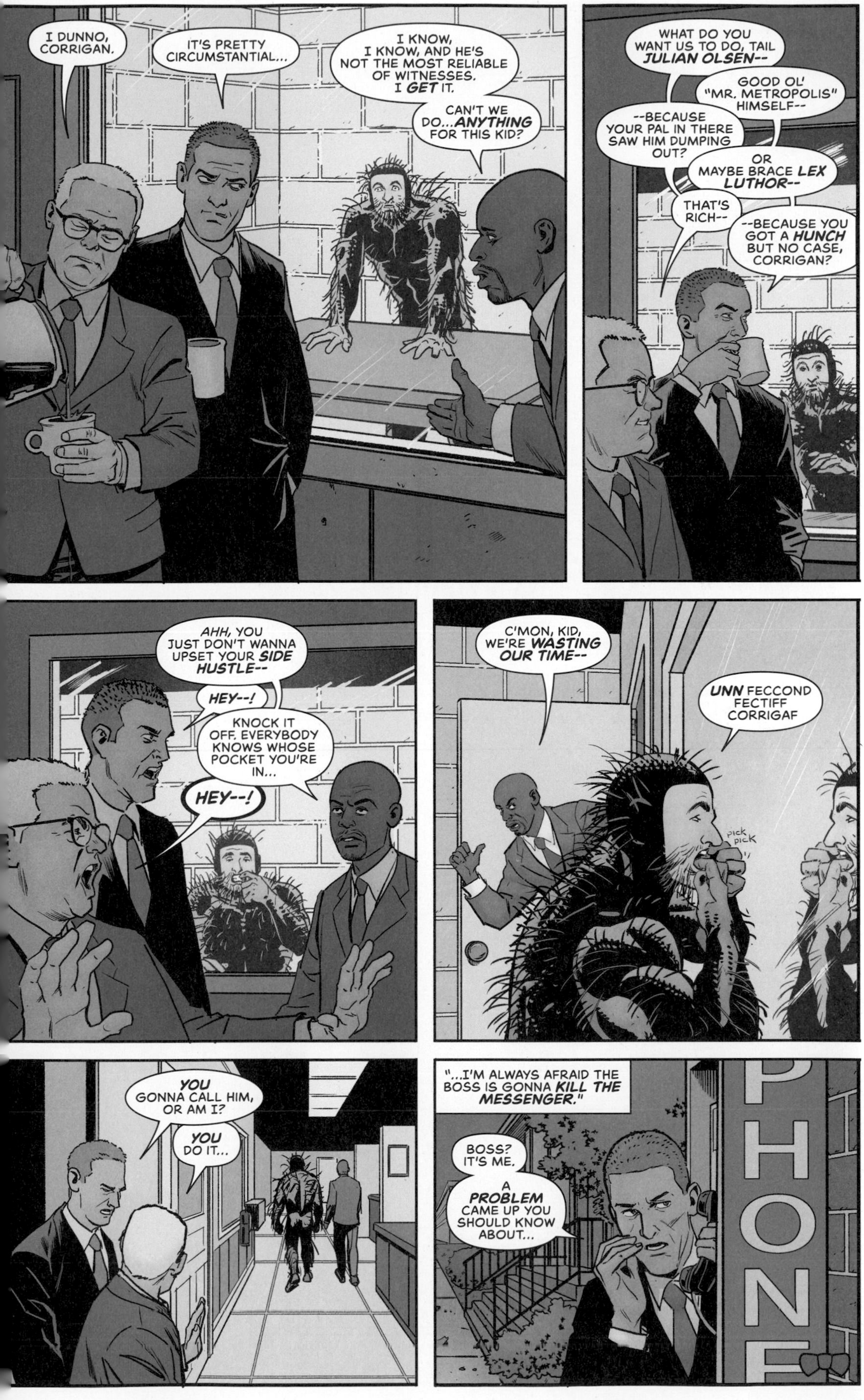
I DUNNO, CORRIGAN.
IT'S PRETTY CIRCUMSTANTIAL...
I KNOW, I KNOW, AND HE'S NOT THE MOST RELIABLE OF WITNESSES. I *GET* IT.
CAN'T WE DO...*ANYTHING* FOR THIS KID?
WHAT DO YOU WANT US TO DO, TAIL *JULIAN OLSEN--*
GOOD OL' "MR. METROPOLIS" HIMSELF--
--BECAUSE YOUR PAL IN THERE SAW HIM DUMPING OUT?
OR MAYBE BRACE *LEX LUTHOR--*
THAT'S RICH--
--BECAUSE YOU GOT A *HUNCH* BUT NO CASE, CORRIGAN?
AHH, YOU JUST DON'T WANNA UPSET YOUR *SIDE HUSTLE--*
HEY--!
KNOCK IT OFF. EVERYBODY KNOWS WHOSE POCKET YOU'RE IN...
HEY--!
C'MON, KID, WE'RE *WASTING OUR TIME--*
UNN FECCOND FECTIFF CORRIGAF
PICK PICK
YOU GONNA CALL HIM, OR AM I?
YOU DO IT...
"...I'M ALWAYS AFRAID THE BOSS IS GONNA *KILL THE MESSENGER.*"
BOSS? IT'S ME.
A *PROBLEM* CAME UP YOU SHOULD KNOW ABOUT...
PHONE

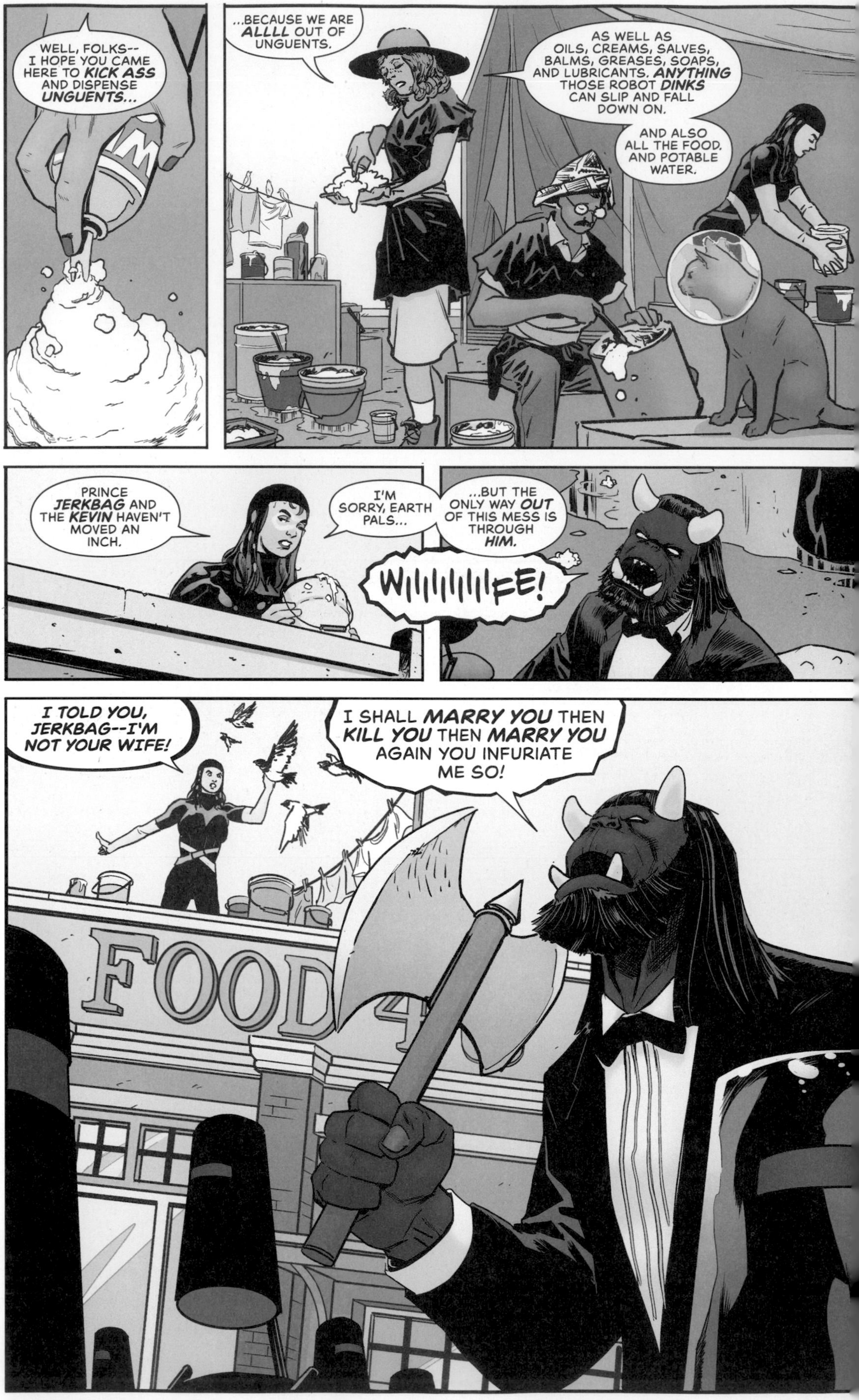
WELL, FOLKS-- I HOPE YOU CAME HERE TO KICK ASS AND DISPENSE UNGUENTS...
...BECAUSE WE ARE ALLLL OUT OF UNGUENTS.
AS WELL AS OILS, CREAMS, SALVES, BALMS, GREASES, SOAPS, AND LUBRICANTS. ANYTHING THOSE ROBOT DINKS CAN SLIP AND FALL DOWN ON.
AND ALSO ALL THE FOOD. AND POTABLE WATER.
PRINCE JERKBAG AND THE KEVIN HAVEN'T MOVED AN INCH.
I'M SORRY, EARTH PALS...
...BUT THE ONLY WAY OUT OF THIS MESS IS THROUGH HIM.
WIIIIIIIIFE!
I TOLD YOU, JERKBAG--I'M NOT YOUR WIFE!
I SHALL MARRY YOU THEN KILL YOU THEN MARRY YOU AGAIN YOU INFURIATE ME SO!
FOOD 4

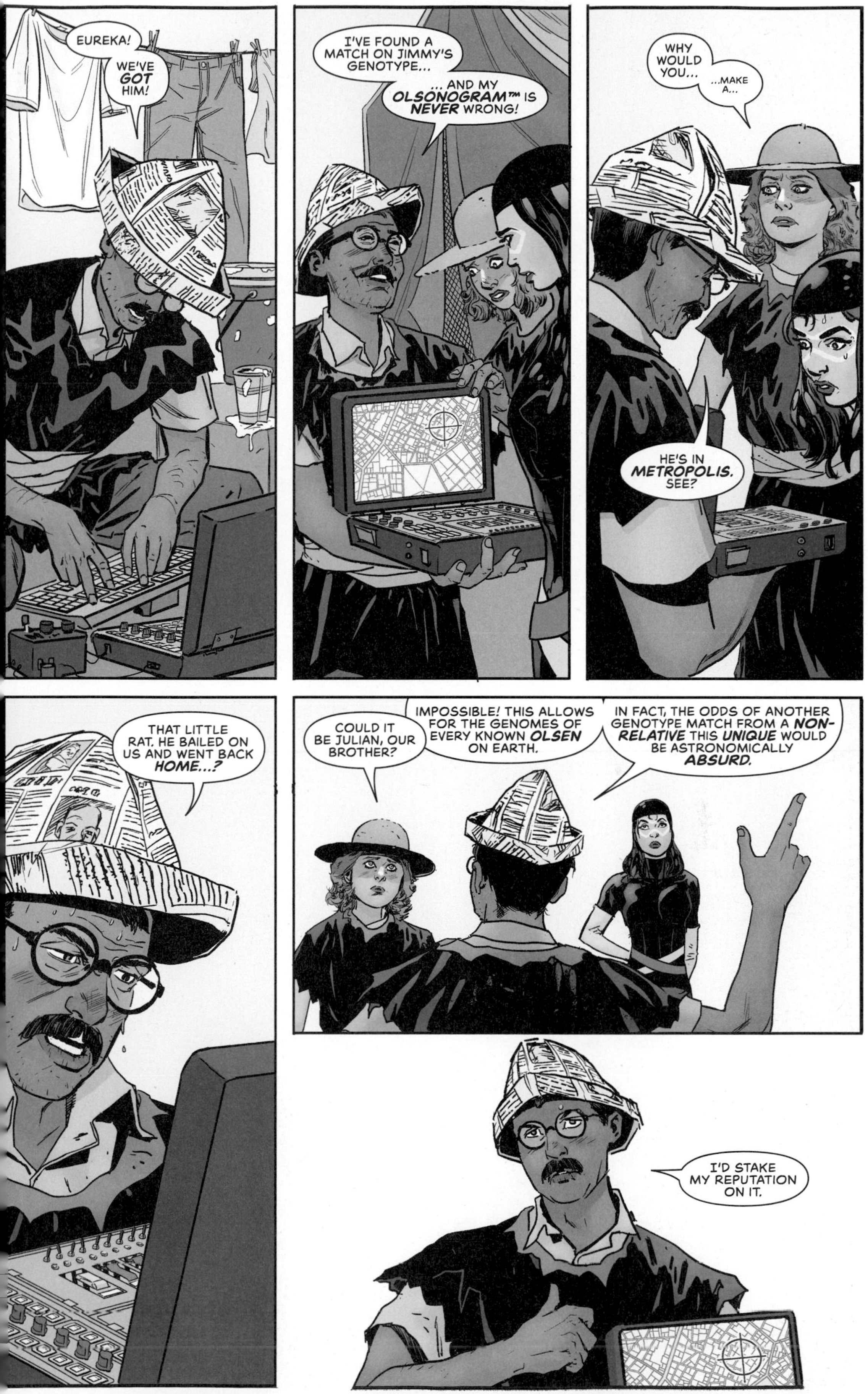
EUREKA!
WE'VE GOT HIM!
I'VE FOUND A MATCH ON JIMMY'S GENOTYPE...
...AND MY OLSONOGRAM™ IS NEVER WRONG!
WHY WOULD YOU...
...MAKE A...
HE'S IN METROPOLIS. SEE?
THAT LITTLE RAT. HE BAILED ON US AND WENT BACK HOME...?
COULD IT BE JULIAN, OUR BROTHER?
IMPOSSIBLE! THIS ALLOWS FOR THE GENOMES OF EVERY KNOWN OLSEN ON EARTH.
IN FACT, THE ODDS OF ANOTHER GENOTYPE MATCH FROM A NON-RELATIVE THIS UNIQUE WOULD BE ASTRONOMICALLY ABSURD.
I'D STAKE MY REPUTATION ON IT.

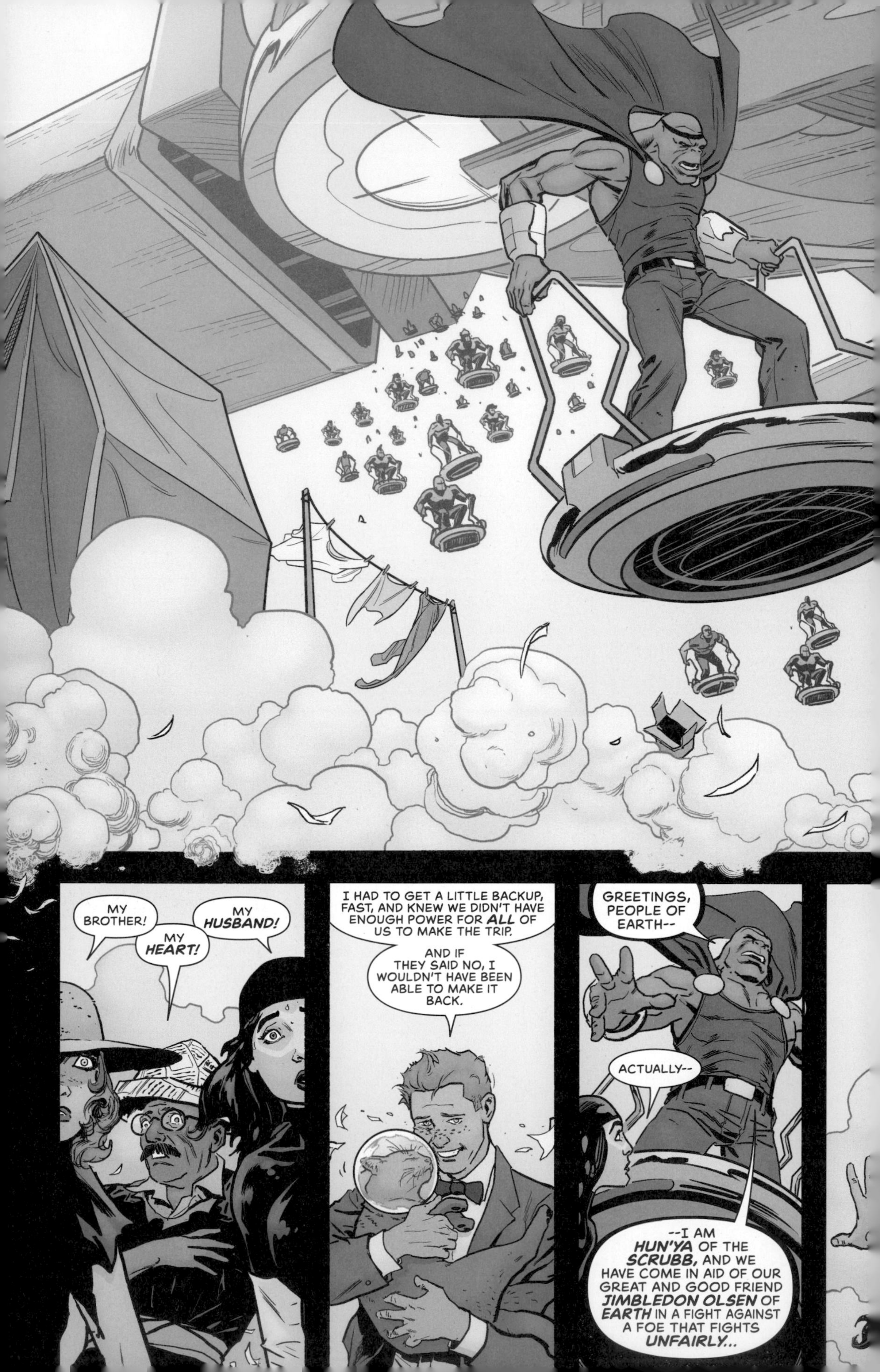
MY BROTHER!
MY HEART!
MY HUSBAND!
I HAD TO GET A LITTLE BACKUP, FAST, AND KNEW WE DIDN'T HAVE ENOUGH POWER FOR ALL OF US TO MAKE THE TRIP.
AND IF THEY SAID NO, I WOULDN'T HAVE BEEN ABLE TO MAKE IT BACK.
GREETINGS, PEOPLE OF EARTH--
ACTUALLY--
--I AM HUN'YA OF THE SCRUBB, AND WE HAVE COME IN AID OF OUR GREAT AND GOOD FRIEND JIMBLEDON OLSEN OF EARTH IN A FIGHT AGAINST A FOE THAT FIGHTS UNFAIRLY...

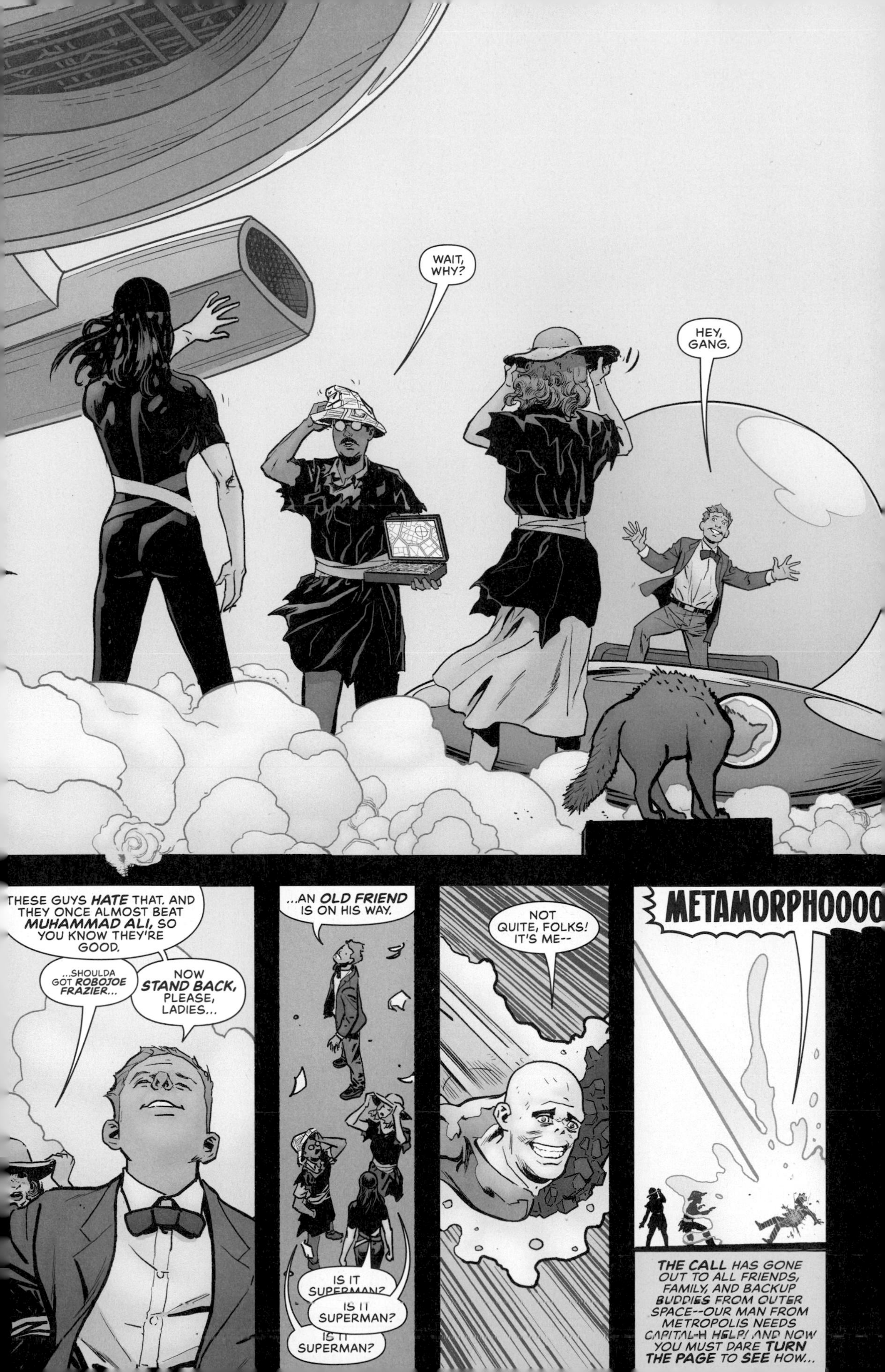
WAIT, WHY?
HEY, GANG.
THESE GUYS HATE THAT. AND THEY ONCE ALMOST BEAT MUHAMMAD ALI, SO YOU KNOW THEY'RE GOOD.
...SHOULDA GOT ROBOJOE FRAZIER...
NOW STAND BACK, PLEASE, LADIES...
...AN OLD FRIEND IS ON HIS WAY.
IS IT SUPERMAN?
IS IT SUPERMAN?
IS IT SUPERMAN?
NOT QUITE, FOLKS! IT'S ME--
METAMORPHOOOO
THE CALL HAS GONE OUT TO ALL FRIENDS, FAMILY, AND BACKUP BUDDIES FROM OUTER SPACE--OUR MAN FROM METROPOLIS NEEDS CAPITAL-H HELP! AND NOW YOU MUST DARE TURN THE PAGE TO SEE HOW...

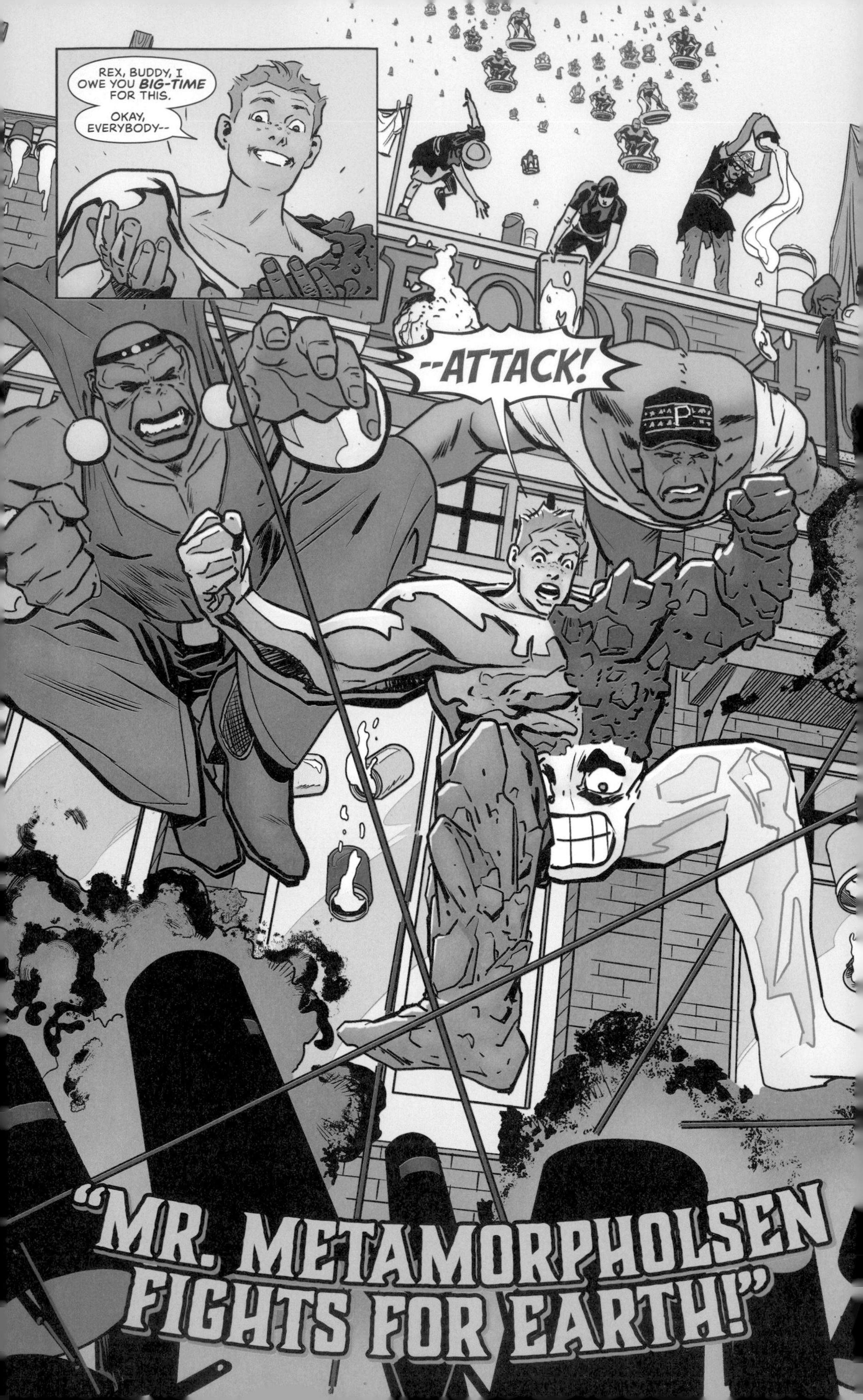
REX, BUDDY, I OWE YOU BIG-TIME FOR THIS.
OKAY, EVERYBODY--
--ATTACK!
"MR. METAMORPHOLSEN FIGHTS FOR EARTH!"

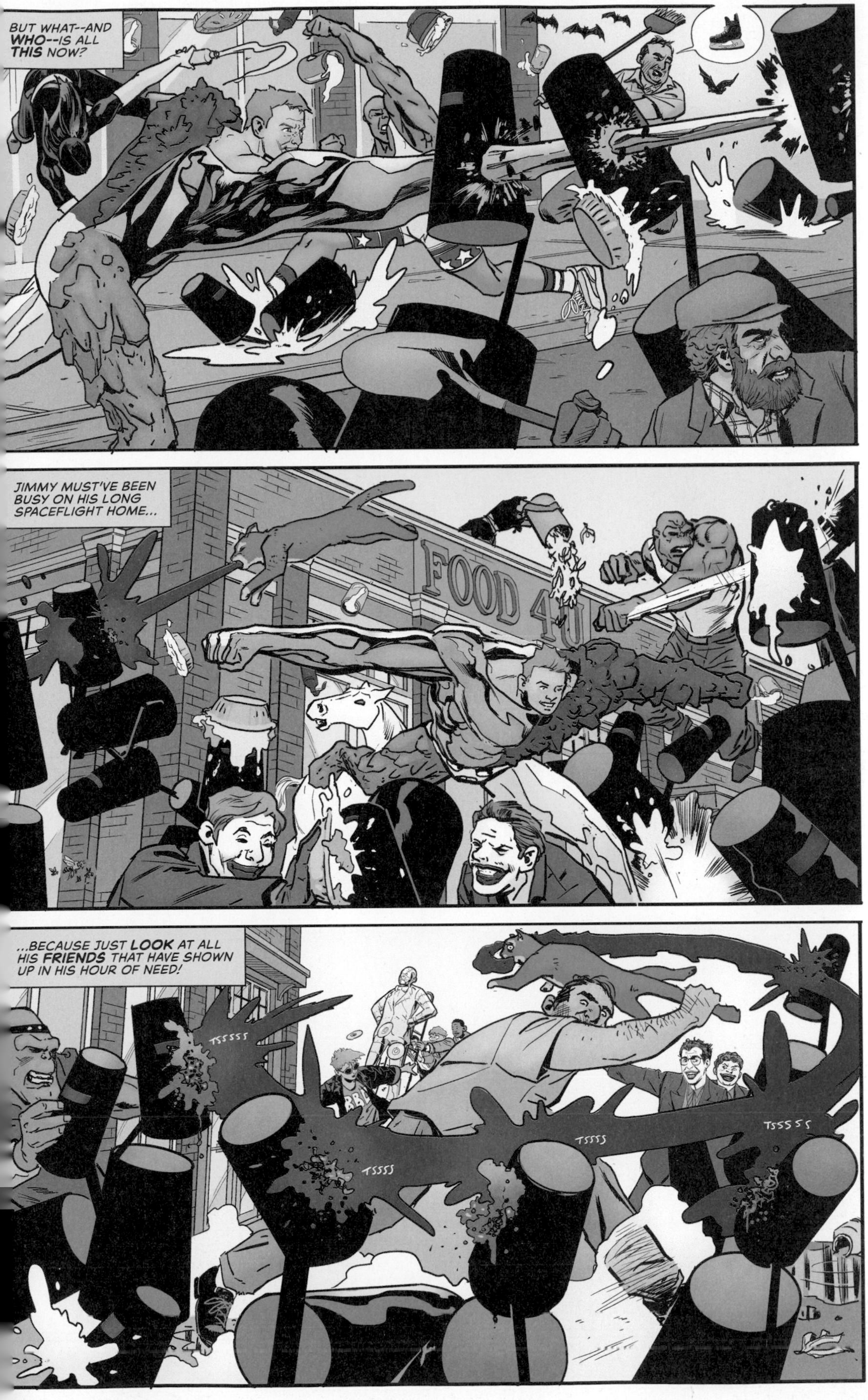
BUT WHAT--AND **WHO**--IS ALL **THIS** NOW?
JIMMY MUST'VE BEEN BUSY ON HIS LONG SPACEFLIGHT HOME...
FOOD 4U
...BECAUSE JUST **LOOK** AT ALL HIS **FRIENDS** THAT HAVE SHOWN UP IN HIS HOUR OF NEED!
TSSSSS
TSSSS
TSSSS
TSSSSS

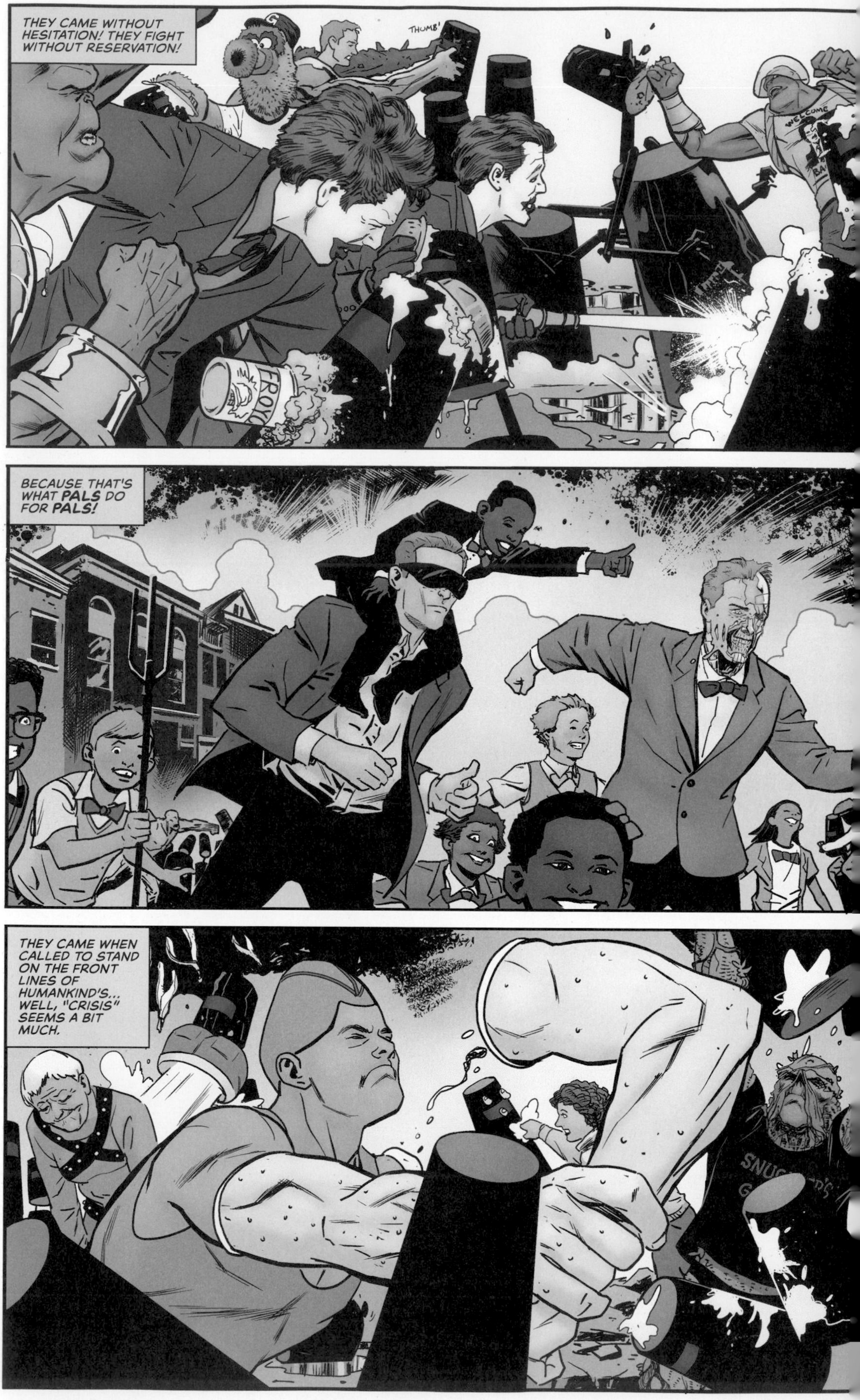
THEY CAME WITHOUT HESITATION! THEY FIGHT WITHOUT RESERVATION!
THUMB'
WELCOME
BECAUSE THAT'S WHAT **PALS** DO FOR **PALS!**
THEY CAME WHEN CALLED TO STAND ON THE FRONT LINES OF HUMANKIND'S... WELL, "CRISIS" SEEMS A BIT MUCH.

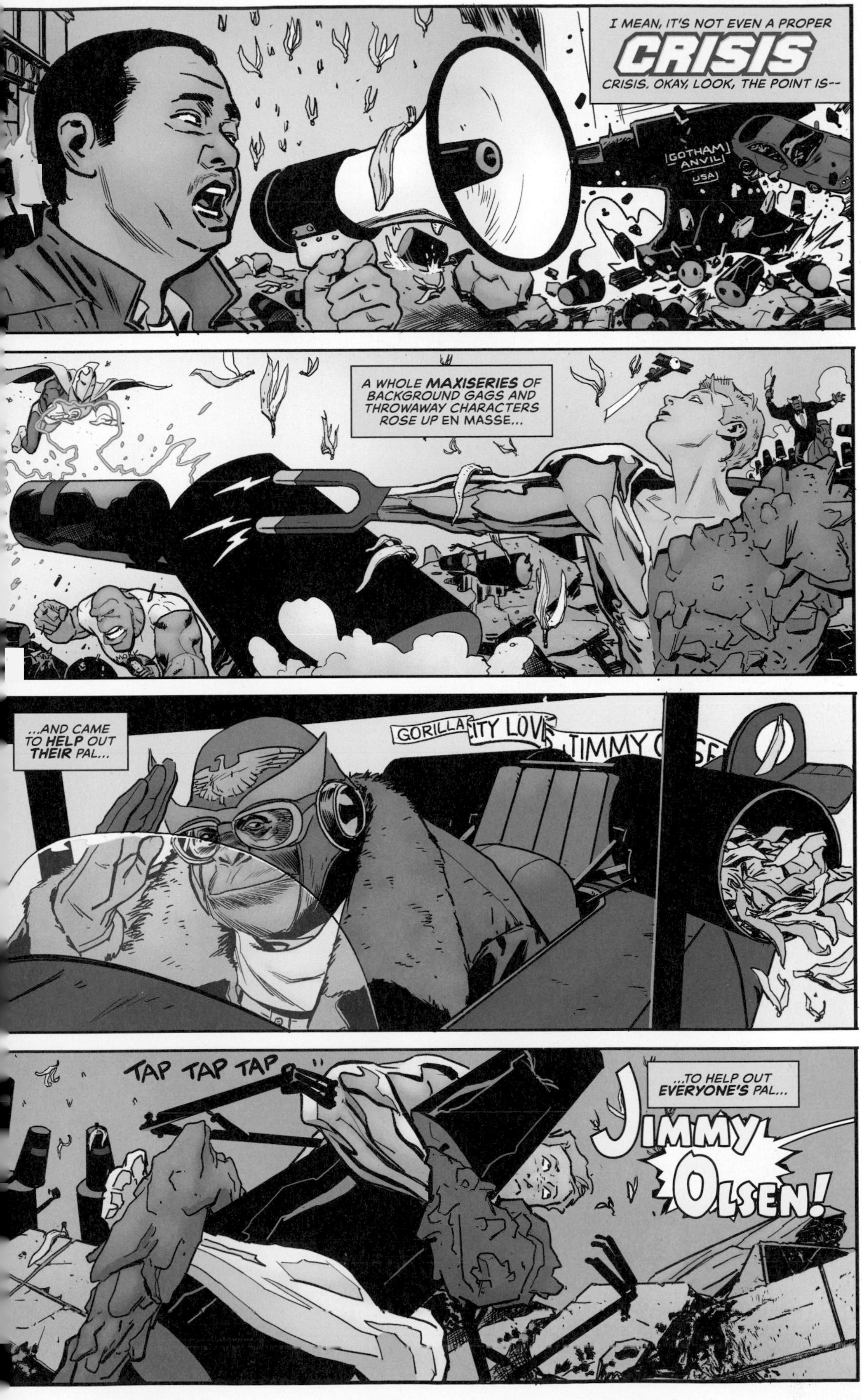
I MEAN, IT'S NOT EVEN A PROPER
CRISIS
CRISIS. OKAY, LOOK, THE POINT IS--
GOTHAM ANVIL USA
A WHOLE MAXISERIES OF BACKGROUND GAGS AND THROWAWAY CHARACTERS ROSE UP EN MASSE...
...AND CAME TO HELP OUT THEIR PAL...
GORILLA CITY LOV
JIMMY O
TAP TAP TAP
...TO HELP OUT EVERYONE'S PAL...
JIMMY OLSEN!

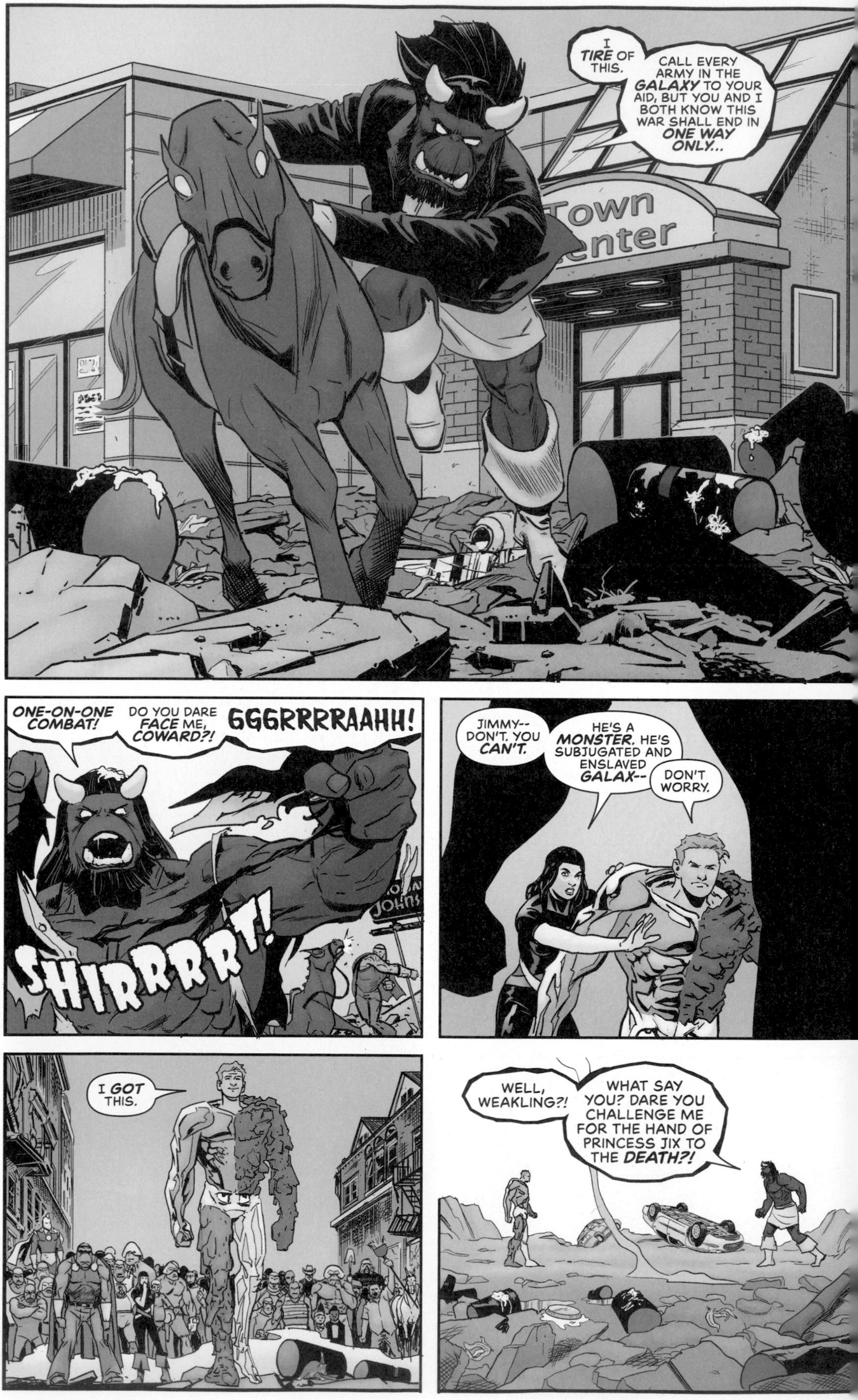
I TIRE OF THIS.
CALL EVERY ARMY IN THE GALAXY TO YOUR AID, BUT YOU AND I BOTH KNOW THIS WAR SHALL END IN ONE WAY ONLY...
Town Center
ONE-ON-ONE COMBAT!
DO YOU DARE FACE ME, COWARD?!
GGGRRRRAAHH!
SHIRRRRT!
JIMMY-- DON'T. YOU CAN'T.
HE'S A MONSTER. HE'S SUBJUGATED AND ENSLAVED GALAX--
DON'T WORRY.
I GOT THIS.
WELL, WEAKLING?!
WHAT SAY YOU? DARE YOU CHALLENGE ME FOR THE HAND OF PRINCESS JIX TO THE DEATH?!

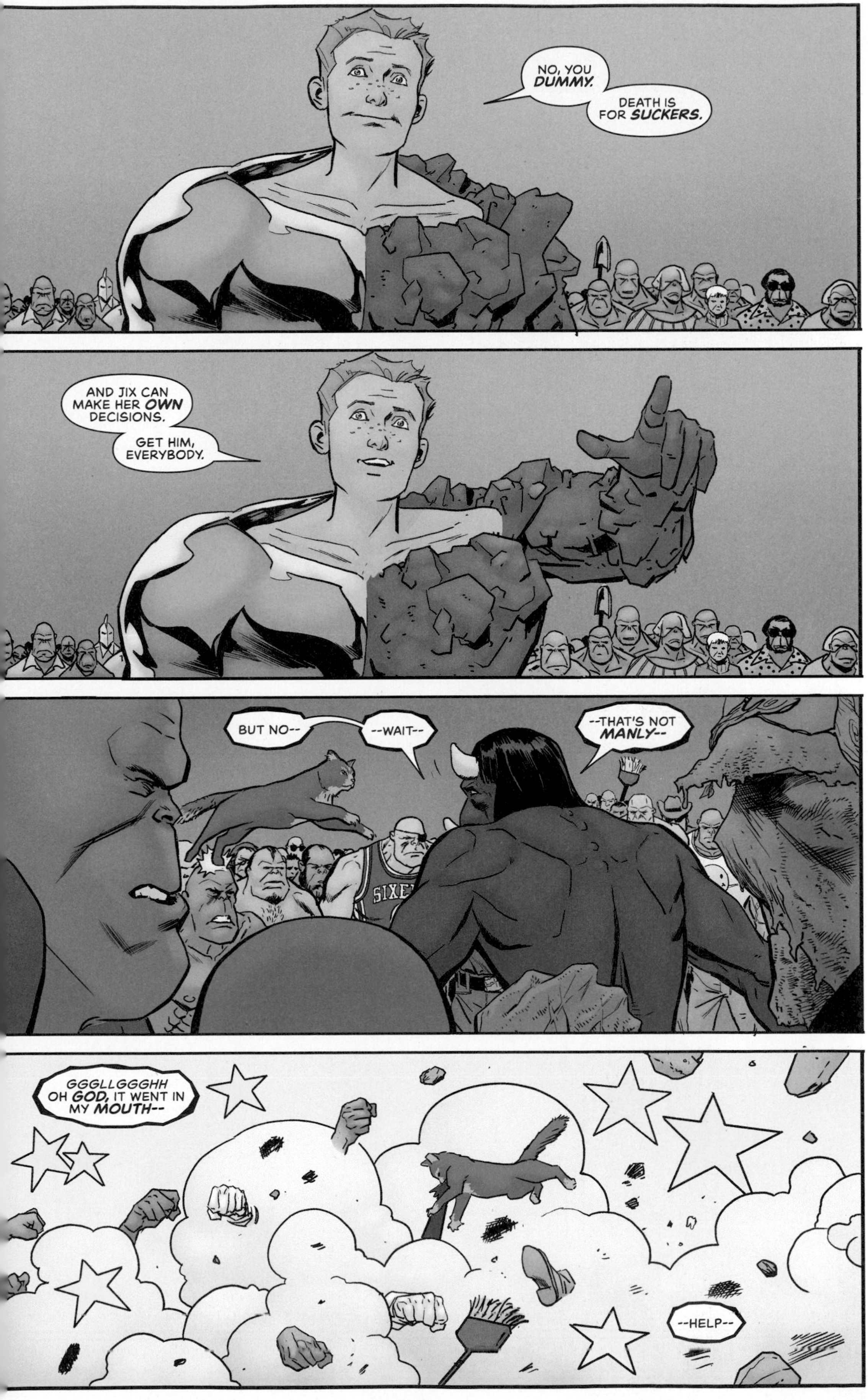

NO, YOU DUMMY.
DEATH IS FOR SUCKERS.
AND JIX CAN MAKE HER OWN DECISIONS.
GET HIM, EVERYBODY.
BUT NO--
--WAIT--
--THAT'S NOT MANLY--
GGGLLGGGHH OH GOD, IT WENT IN MY MOUTH--
--HELP--

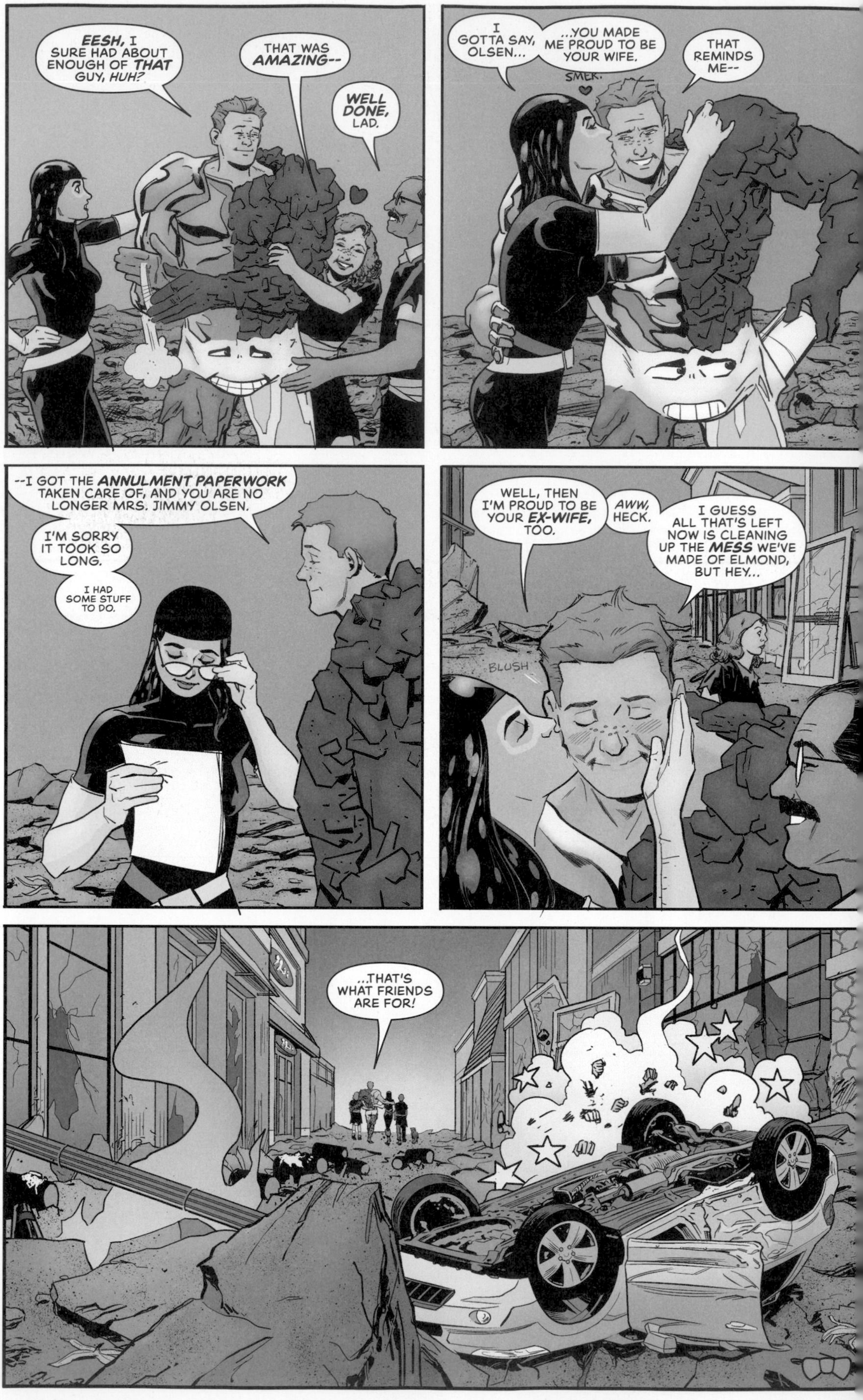
EESH, I SURE HAD ABOUT ENOUGH OF THAT GUY, HUH?
THAT WAS AMAZING--
WELL DONE, LAD.
I GOTTA SAY, OLSEN...
...YOU MADE ME PROUD TO BE YOUR WIFE.
SMEK.
THAT REMINDS ME--
--I GOT THE ANNULMENT PAPERWORK TAKEN CARE OF, AND YOU ARE NO LONGER MRS. JIMMY OLSEN.
I'M SORRY IT TOOK SO LONG.
I HAD SOME STUFF TO DO.
WELL, THEN I'M PROUD TO BE YOUR EX-WIFE, TOO.
AWW, HECK.
I GUESS ALL THAT'S LEFT NOW IS CLEANING UP THE MESS WE'VE MADE OF ELMOND, BUT HEY...
BLUSH
...THAT'S WHAT FRIENDS ARE FOR!

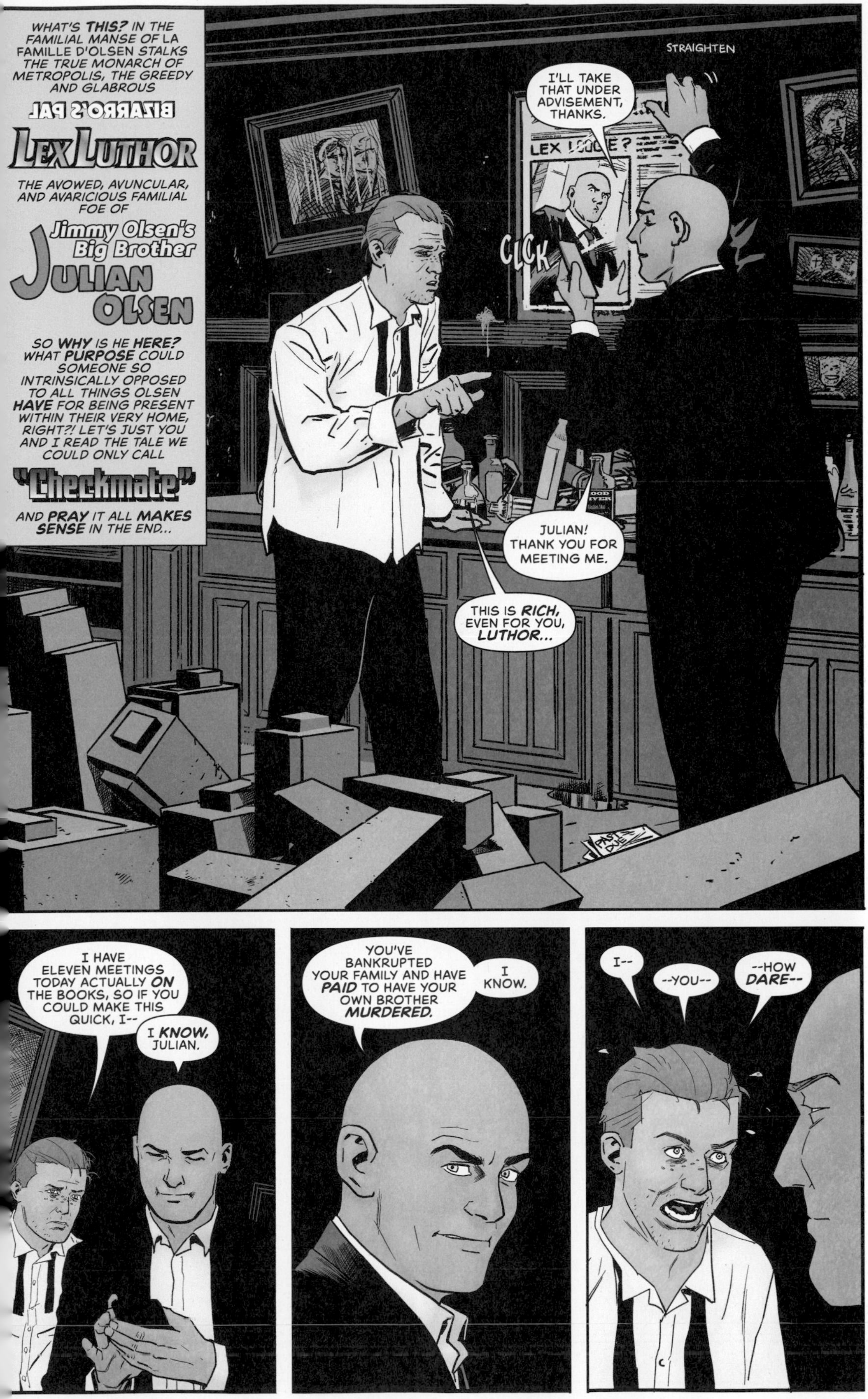
WHAT'S THIS? IN THE FAMILIAL MANSE OF LA FAMILLE D'OLSEN STALKS THE TRUE MONARCH OF METROPOLIS, THE GREEDY AND GLABROUS
BIZARRO'S PAL
LEX LUTHOR
THE AVOWED, AVUNCULAR, AND AVARICIOUS FAMILIAL FOE OF
Jimmy Olsen's Big Brother
JULIAN OLSEN
SO WHY IS HE HERE? WHAT PURPOSE COULD SOMEONE SO INTRINSICALLY OPPOSED TO ALL THINGS OLSEN HAVE FOR BEING PRESENT WITHIN THEIR VERY HOME, RIGHT?! LET'S JUST YOU AND I READ THE TALE WE COULD ONLY CALL
"Checkmate"
AND PRAY IT ALL MAKES SENSE IN THE END...
STRAIGHTEN
I'LL TAKE THAT UNDER ADVISEMENT, THANKS.
CLICK
JULIAN! THANK YOU FOR MEETING ME.
THIS IS RICH, EVEN FOR YOU, LUTHOR...
I HAVE ELEVEN MEETINGS TODAY ACTUALLY ON THE BOOKS, SO IF YOU COULD MAKE THIS QUICK, I--
I KNOW, JULIAN.
YOU'VE BANKRUPTED YOUR FAMILY AND HAVE PAID TO HAVE YOUR OWN BROTHER MURDERED.
I KNOW.
I--
--YOU--
--HOW DARE--

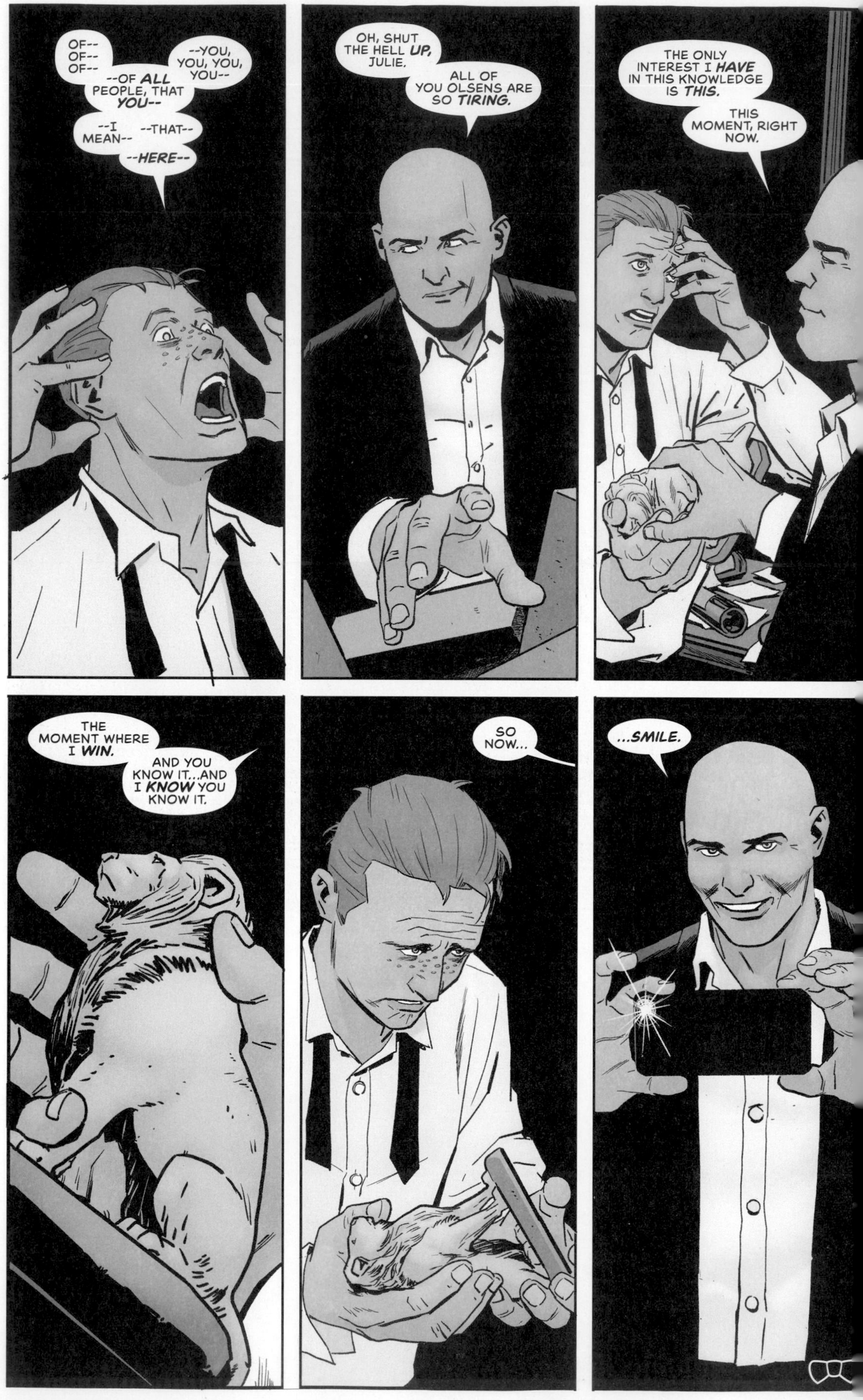

OF-- OF-- OF--
--YOU, YOU, YOU, YOU--
--OF ALL PEOPLE, THAT YOU--
--I MEAN--
--THAT--
--HERE--
OH, SHUT THE HELL UP, JULIE.
ALL OF YOU OLSENS ARE SO TIRING.
THE ONLY INTEREST I HAVE IN THIS KNOWLEDGE IS THIS.
THIS MOMENT, RIGHT NOW.
THE MOMENT WHERE I WIN.
AND YOU KNOW IT...AND I KNOW YOU KNOW IT.
SO NOW...
...SMILE.

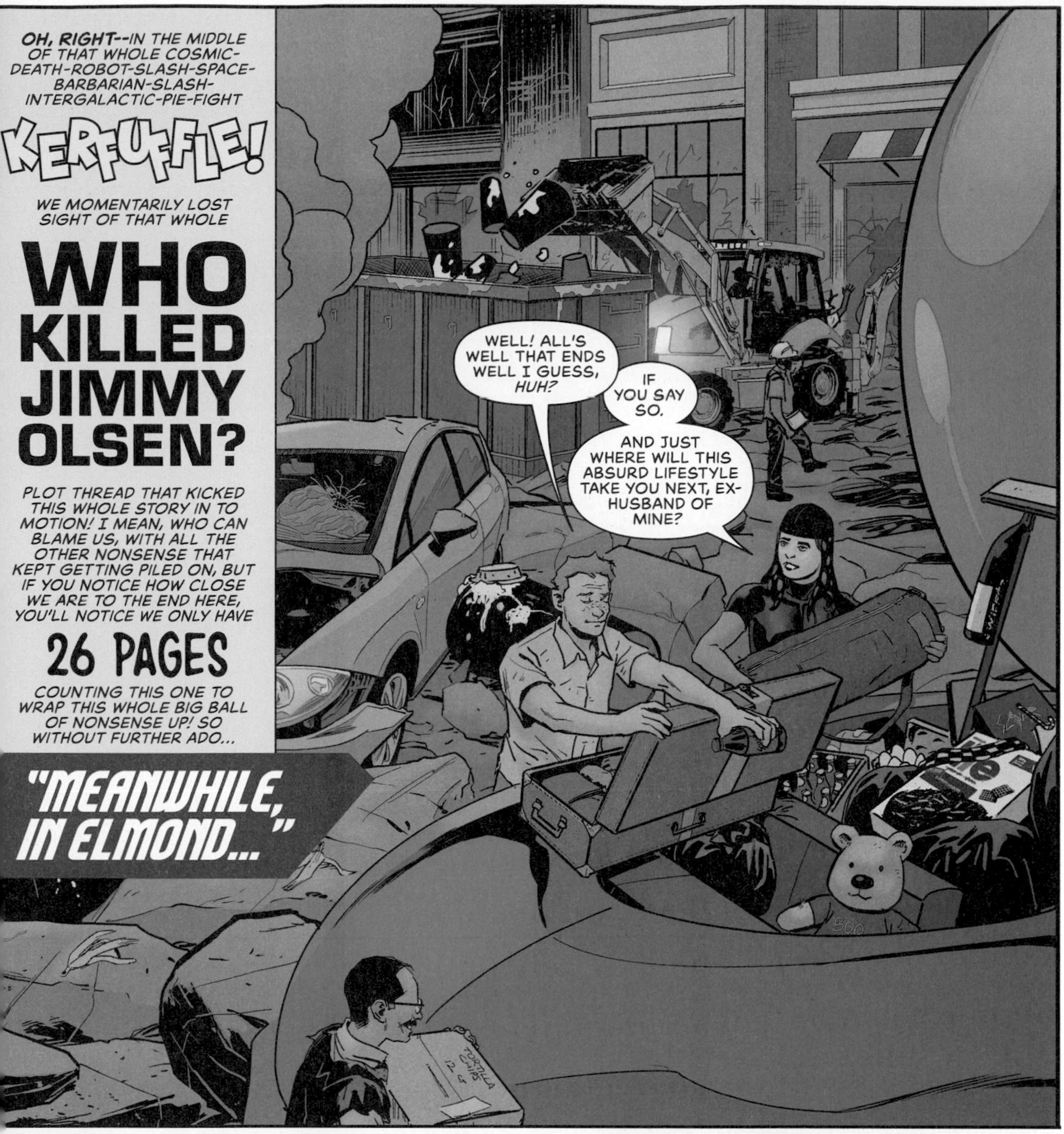
OH, RIGHT--IN THE MIDDLE OF THAT WHOLE COSMIC-DEATH-ROBOT-SLASH-SPACE-BARBARIAN-SLASH-INTERGALACTIC-PIE-FIGHT
KERFUFFLE!
WE MOMENTARILY LOST SIGHT OF THAT WHOLE
WHO KILLED JIMMY OLSEN?
PLOT THREAD THAT KICKED THIS WHOLE STORY IN TO MOTION! I MEAN, WHO CAN BLAME US, WITH ALL THE OTHER NONSENSE THAT KEPT GETTING PILED ON, BUT IF YOU NOTICE HOW CLOSE WE ARE TO THE END HERE, YOU'LL NOTICE WE ONLY HAVE
26 PAGES
COUNTING THIS ONE TO WRAP THIS WHOLE BIG BALL OF NONSENSE UP! SO WITHOUT FURTHER ADO...
"MEANWHILE, IN ELMOND..."
WELL! ALL'S WELL THAT ENDS WELL I GUESS, HUH?
IF YOU SAY SO.
AND JUST WHERE WILL THIS ABSURD LIFESTYLE TAKE YOU NEXT, EX-HUSBAND OF MINE?

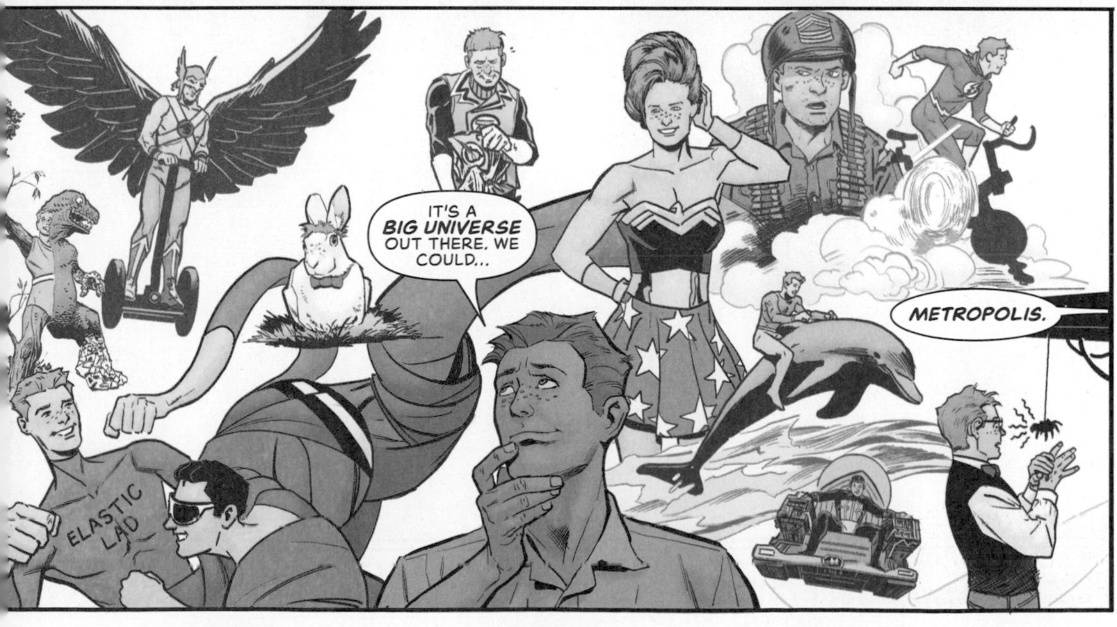
IT'S A BIG UNIVERSE OUT THERE. WE COULD...
METROPOLIS.
ELASTIC LAD

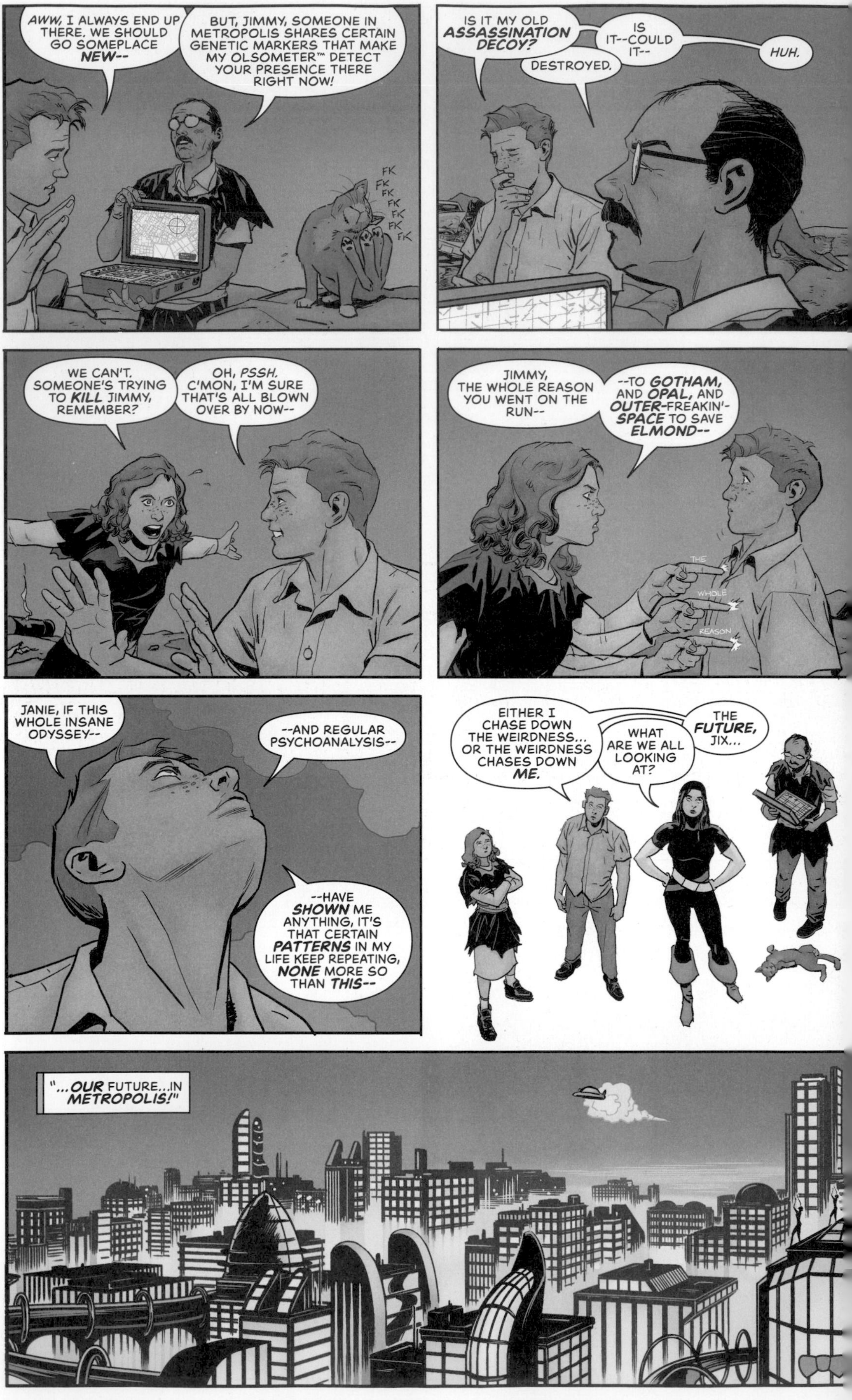
AWW, I ALWAYS END UP THERE. WE SHOULD GO SOMEPLACE NEW--
BUT, JIMMY, SOMEONE IN METROPOLIS SHARES CERTAIN GENETIC MARKERS THAT MAKE MY OLSOMETER™ DETECT YOUR PRESENCE THERE RIGHT NOW!
FK FK FK FK FK FK FK
IS IT MY OLD ASSASSINATION DECOY?
DESTROYED.
IS IT--COULD IT--
HUH.
WE CAN'T. SOMEONE'S TRYING TO KILL JIMMY, REMEMBER?
OH, PSSH. C'MON, I'M SURE THAT'S ALL BLOWN OVER BY NOW--
JIMMY, THE WHOLE REASON YOU WENT ON THE RUN--
--TO GOTHAM, AND OPAL, AND OUTER-FREAKIN'-SPACE TO SAVE ELMOND--
THE
WHOLE
REASON
JANIE, IF THIS WHOLE INSANE ODYSSEY--
--AND REGULAR PSYCHOANALYSIS--
--HAVE SHOWN ME ANYTHING, IT'S THAT CERTAIN PATTERNS IN MY LIFE KEEP REPEATING, NONE MORE SO THAN THIS--
EITHER I CHASE DOWN THE WEIRDNESS... OR THE WEIRDNESS CHASES DOWN ME.
WHAT ARE WE ALL LOOKING AT?
THE FUTURE, JIX...
"...OUR FUTURE...IN METROPOLIS!"

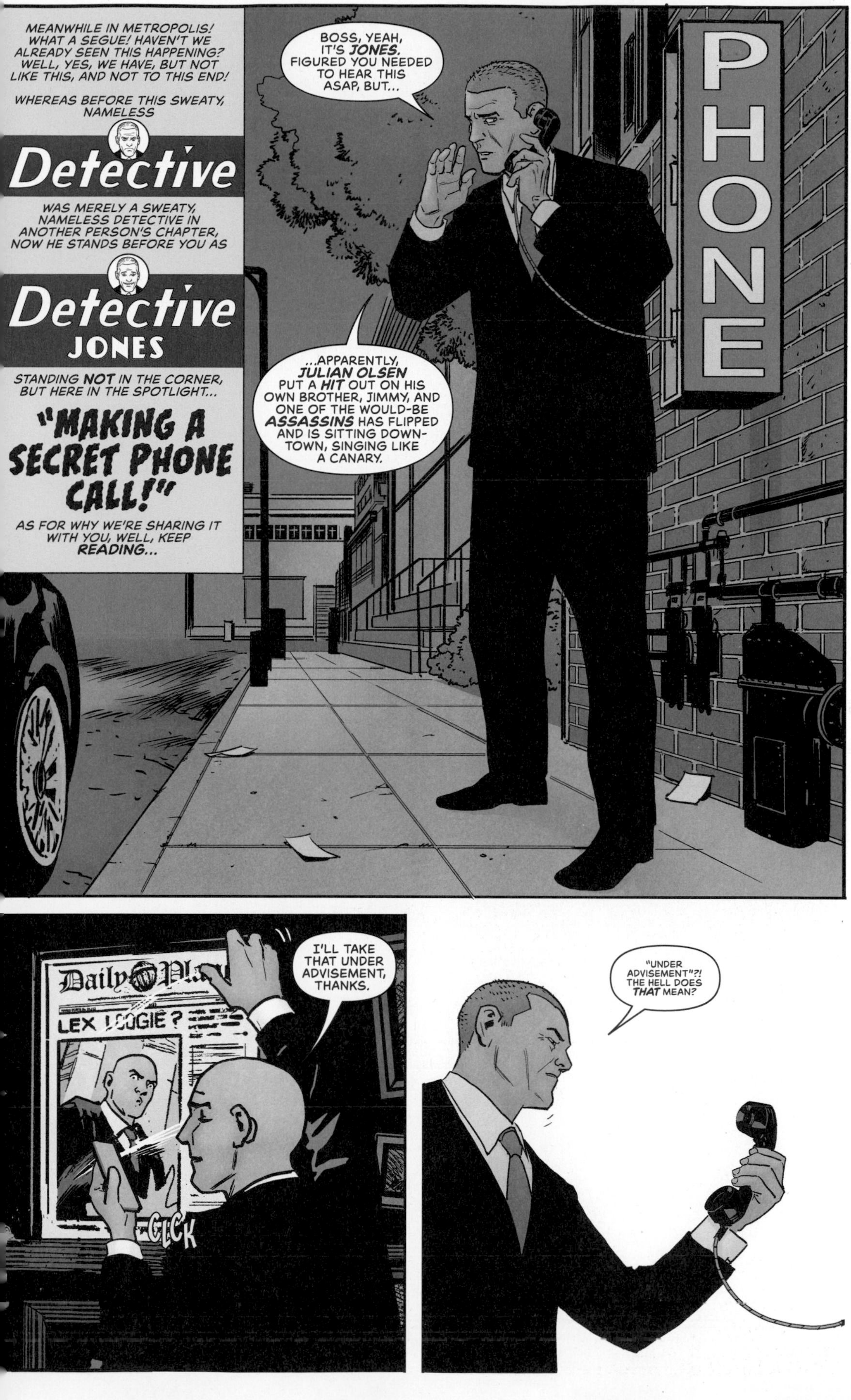
MEANWHILE IN METROPOLIS! WHAT A SEGUE! HAVEN'T WE ALREADY SEEN THIS HAPPENING? WELL, YES, WE HAVE, BUT NOT LIKE THIS, AND NOT TO THIS END!
WHEREAS BEFORE THIS SWEATY, NAMELESS
Detective
WAS MERELY A SWEATY, NAMELESS DETECTIVE IN ANOTHER PERSON'S CHAPTER, NOW HE STANDS BEFORE YOU AS
Detective JONES
STANDING NOT IN THE CORNER, BUT HERE IN THE SPOTLIGHT...
"MAKING A SECRET PHONE CALL!"
AS FOR WHY WE'RE SHARING IT WITH YOU, WELL, KEEP READING...
BOSS, YEAH, IT'S JONES. FIGURED YOU NEEDED TO HEAR THIS ASAP, BUT...
PHONE
...APPARENTLY, JULIAN OLSEN PUT A HIT OUT ON HIS OWN BROTHER, JIMMY, AND ONE OF THE WOULD-BE ASSASSINS HAS FLIPPED AND IS SITTING DOWNTOWN, SINGING LIKE A CANARY.
Daily
LEX LOOGIE?
I'LL TAKE THAT UNDER ADVISEMENT, THANKS.
CLCK
"UNDER ADVISEMENT"?! THE HELL DOES THAT MEAN?

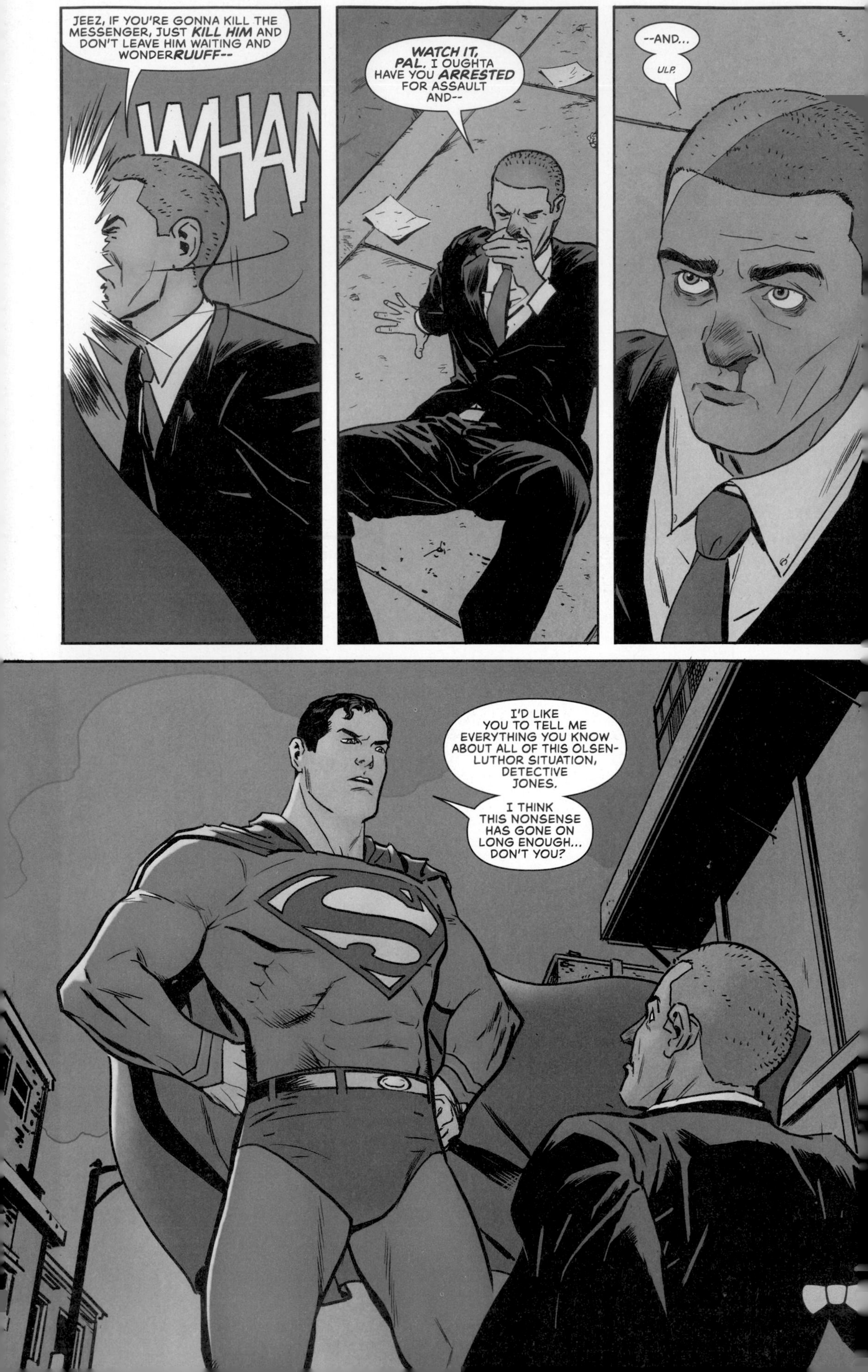
JEEZ, IF YOU'RE GONNA KILL THE MESSENGER, JUST KILL HIM AND DON'T LEAVE HIM WAITING AND WONDERRUUFF--
WHAM
WATCH IT, PAL. I OUGHTA HAVE YOU ARRESTED FOR ASSAULT AND--
--AND...
ULP.
I'D LIKE YOU TO TELL ME EVERYTHING YOU KNOW ABOUT ALL OF THIS OLSEN-LUTHOR SITUATION, DETECTIVE JONES.
I THINK THIS NONSENSE HAS GONE ON LONG ENOUGH... DON'T YOU?

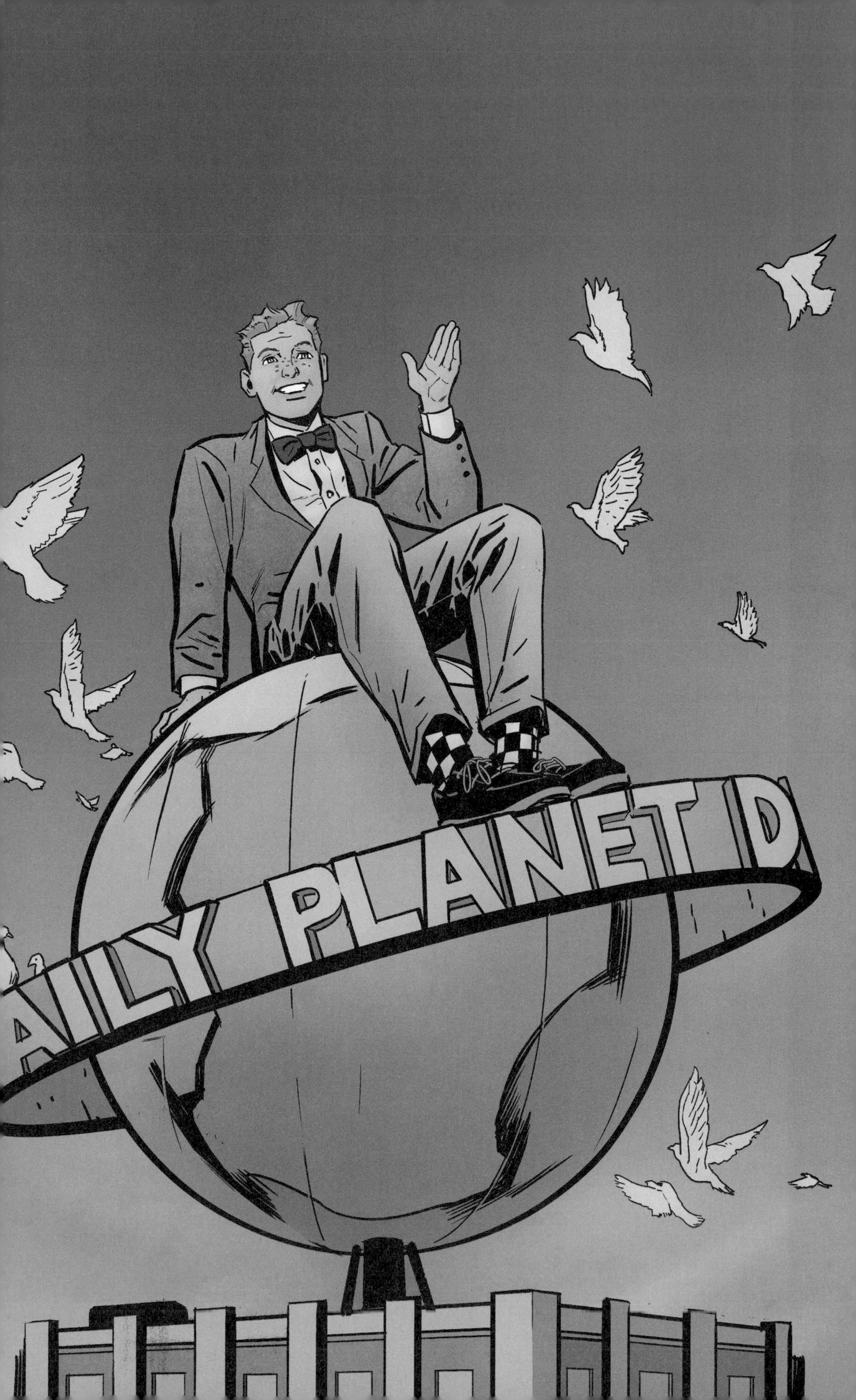
AILY PLANET D

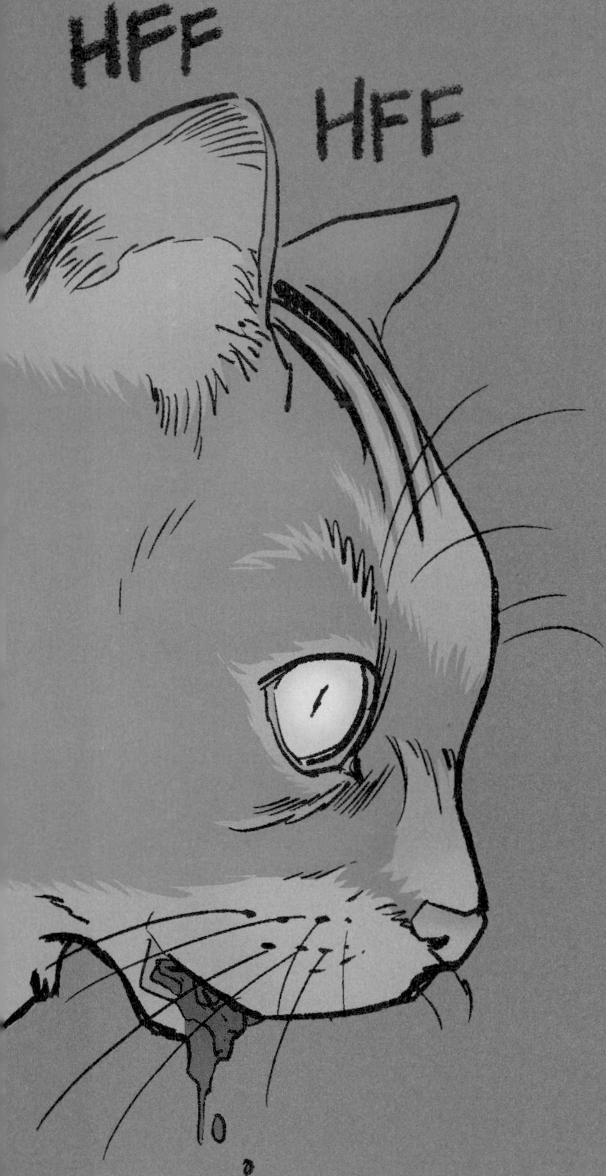
HFF
HFF

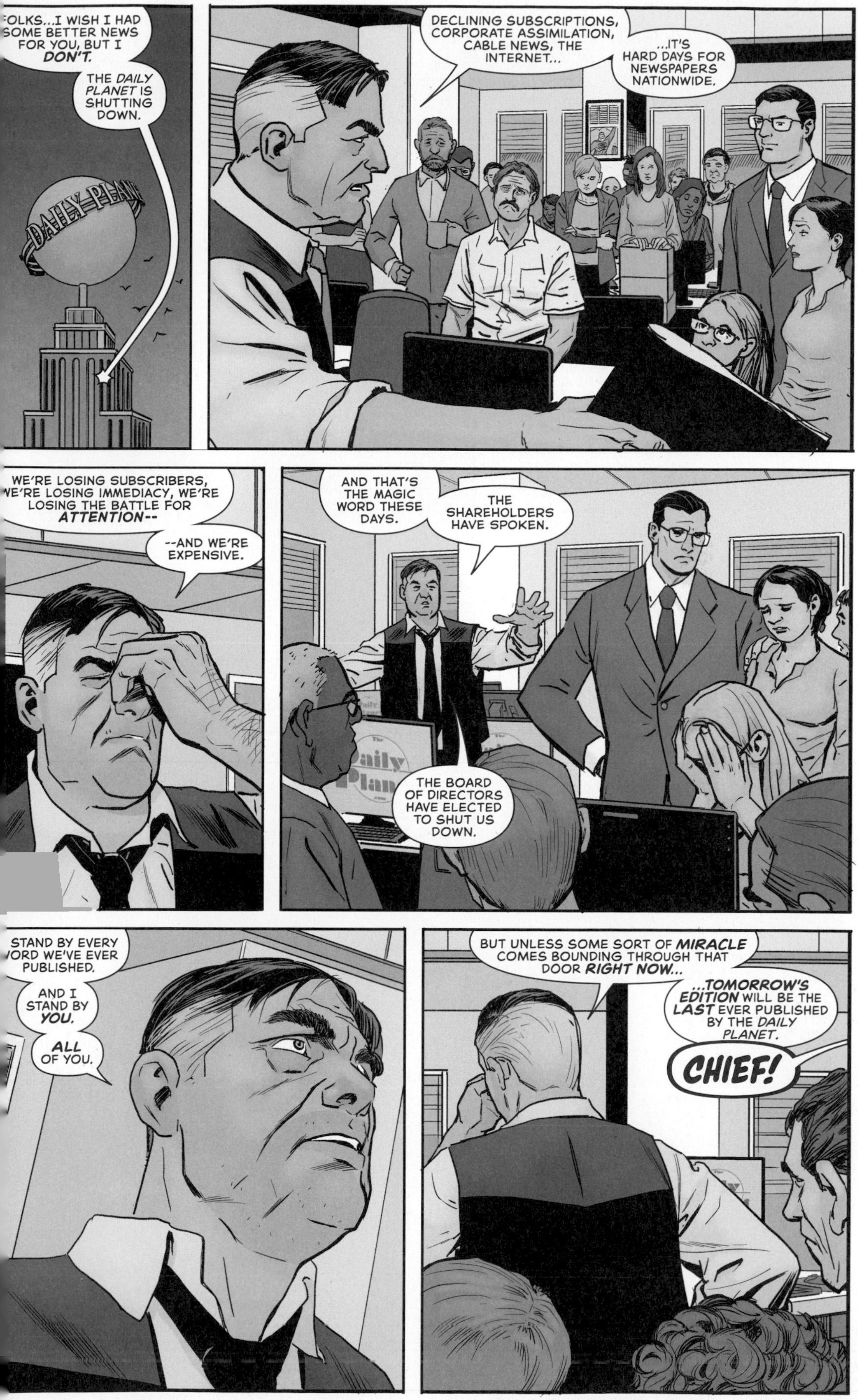
FOLKS...I WISH I HAD SOME BETTER NEWS FOR YOU, BUT I DON'T.
THE DAILY PLANET IS SHUTTING DOWN.
DAILY PLANET
DECLINING SUBSCRIPTIONS, CORPORATE ASSIMILATION, CABLE NEWS, THE INTERNET...
...IT'S HARD DAYS FOR NEWSPAPERS NATIONWIDE.
WE'RE LOSING SUBSCRIBERS, WE'RE LOSING IMMEDIACY, WE'RE LOSING THE BATTLE FOR ATTENTION--
--AND WE'RE EXPENSIVE.
AND THAT'S THE MAGIC WORD THESE DAYS.
THE SHAREHOLDERS HAVE SPOKEN.
THE BOARD OF DIRECTORS HAVE ELECTED TO SHUT US DOWN.
STAND BY EVERY WORD WE'VE EVER PUBLISHED.
AND I STAND BY YOU.
ALL OF YOU.
BUT UNLESS SOME SORT OF MIRACLE COMES BOUNDING THROUGH THAT DOOR RIGHT NOW...
...TOMORROW'S EDITION WILL BE THE LAST EVER PUBLISHED BY THE DAILY PLANET.
CHIEF!

WHAT'S **THIS?** AS OUR ROLLICKING NARRATIVE RAMPAGE COLLAPSES INTO THIS INFINITELY DENSE **DOT** OF A COMIC BOOK, PLOT THREADS CONVERGE, AND CHARACTERS WILL COLLIDE AS

SUPERMAN'S PAL JIMMY OLSEN

HAS RETURNED TO METROPOLIS, TO FIND HIS BELOVED EMPLOYER, THE

DAILY PLANET

HOBBLED BY SCANDALS BOTH BANAL AND SUPER-POWERED ALIKE, ON THE BRINK OF STOPPING THE PRESSES--

FOREVER!

SURELY THE **BAD GUYS** AREN'T GOING TO WIN, RIGHT? **SURELY** THE **GOOD GUYS** WILL RALLY IN THE LAST MOMENTS TO **RISE UP** AND **SAVE THE DAY,** RIGHT? **SURELY IN THE FACE OF QUARANTINE CRISIS WE ARE ALL BETTER TOGETHER THAN OUR WORST PARTS ARE INDIVIDUALLY, RIGHT?**

RIGHT?

HELLO?

I GUESS THE ONLY WAY TO FIGURE IT OUT ONCE AND FOR ALL IS TO READ THIS, OUR **LAST** CHAPTER, WHICH WE COULD ONLY TITLE...

"FINALLY!"

MATT FRACTION writer
STEVE LIEBER artist

NATHAN FAIRBAIRN colorist
CLAYTON COWLES letterer
LIEBER & FAIRBAIRN cover
BIXIE MATHIEU asst. editor
JESSICA CHEN editor
JAMIE S. RICH group editor

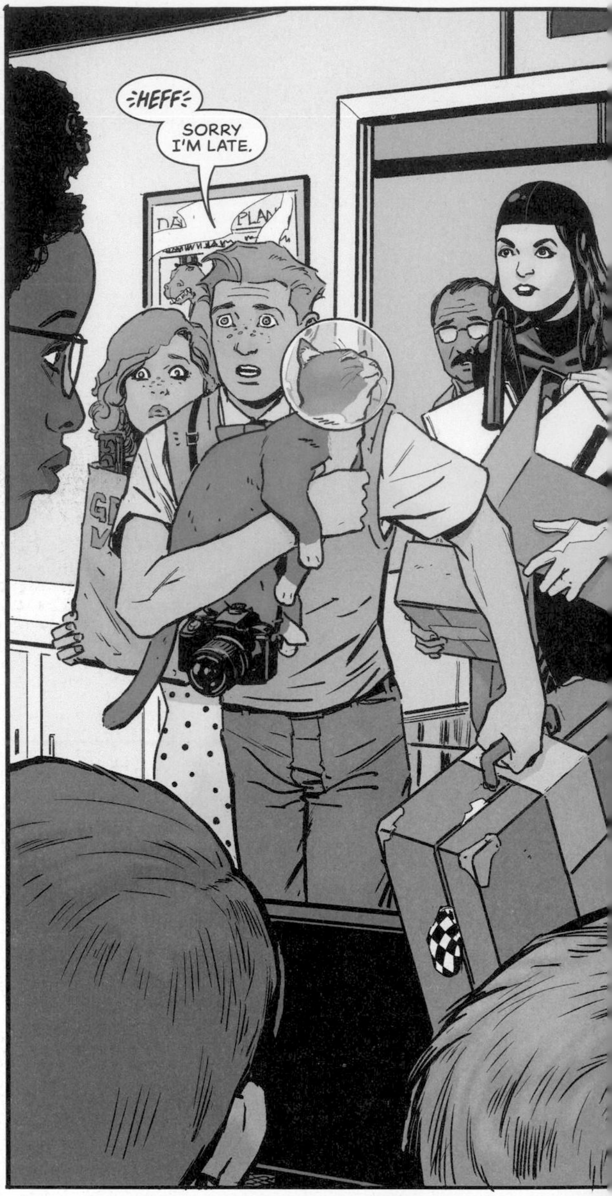
HEFF
SORRY I'M LATE.

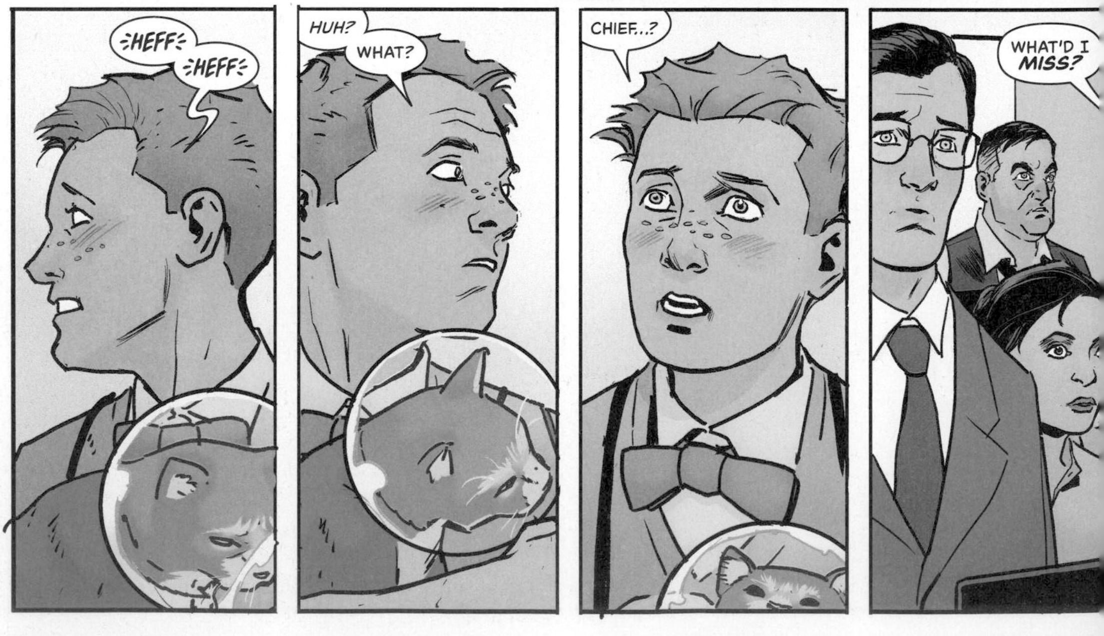
HEFF
HEFF
HUH?
WHAT?
CHIEF...?
WHAT'D I MISS?

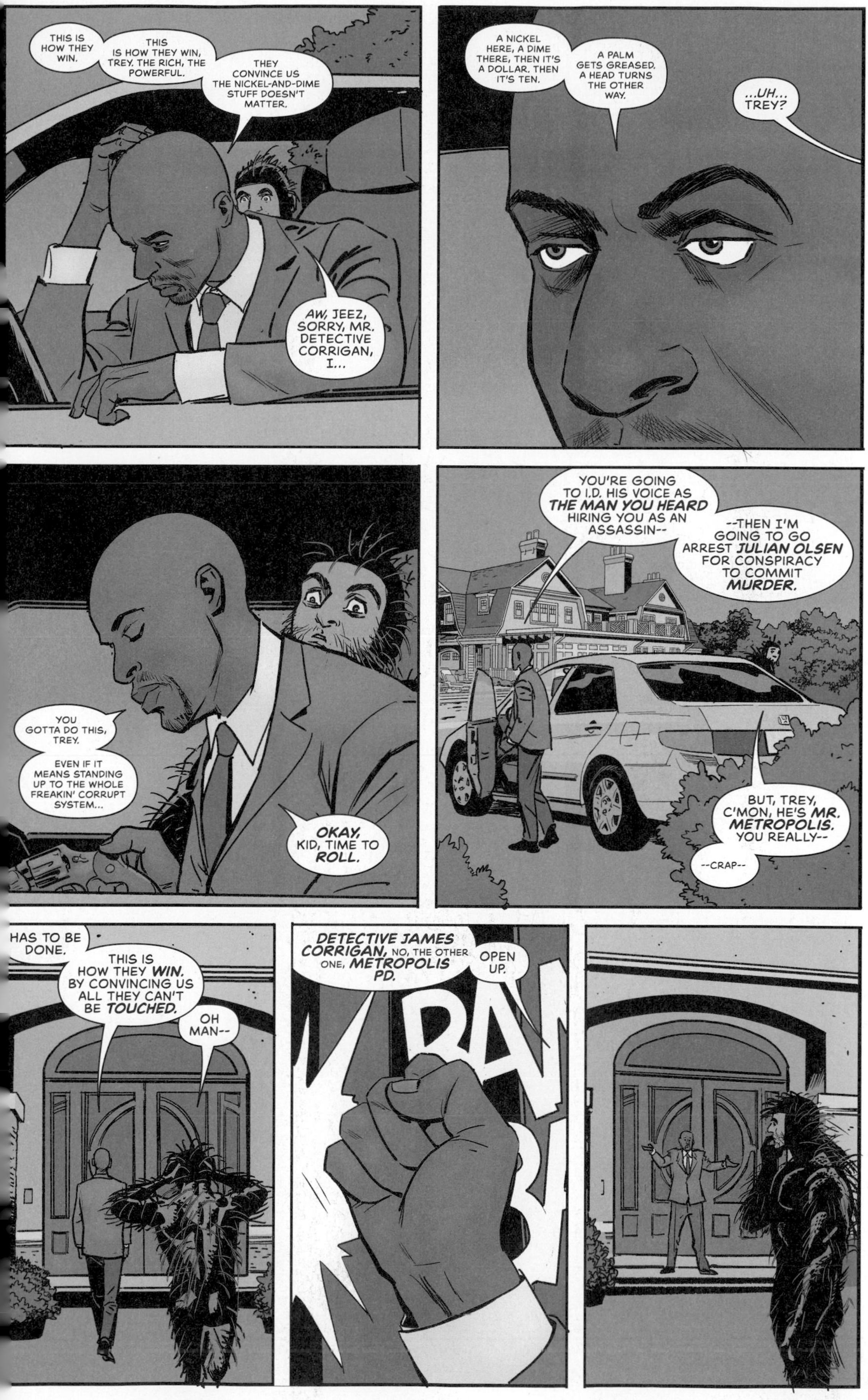
THIS IS HOW THEY WIN.
THIS IS HOW THEY WIN, TREY. THE RICH, THE POWERFUL.
THEY CONVINCE US THE NICKEL-AND-DIME STUFF DOESN'T MATTER.
AW, JEEZ, SORRY, MR. DETECTIVE CORRIGAN, I...
A NICKEL HERE, A DIME THERE, THEN IT'S A DOLLAR. THEN IT'S TEN.
A PALM GETS GREASED. A HEAD TURNS THE OTHER WAY.
...UH... TREY?
YOU GOTTA DO THIS, TREY.
EVEN IF IT MEANS STANDING UP TO THE WHOLE FREAKIN' CORRUPT SYSTEM...
OKAY, KID, TIME TO ROLL.
YOU'RE GOING TO I.D. HIS VOICE AS THE MAN YOU HEARD HIRING YOU AS AN ASSASSIN--
--THEN I'M GOING TO GO ARREST JULIAN OLSEN FOR CONSPIRACY TO COMMIT MURDER.
BUT, TREY, C'MON, HE'S MR. METROPOLIS. YOU REALLY--
--CRAP--
HAS TO BE DONE.
THIS IS HOW THEY WIN. BY CONVINCING US ALL THEY CAN'T BE TOUCHED.
OH MAN--
DETECTIVE JAMES CORRIGAN, NO, THE OTHER ONE, METROPOLIS PD.
OPEN UP.
BAM

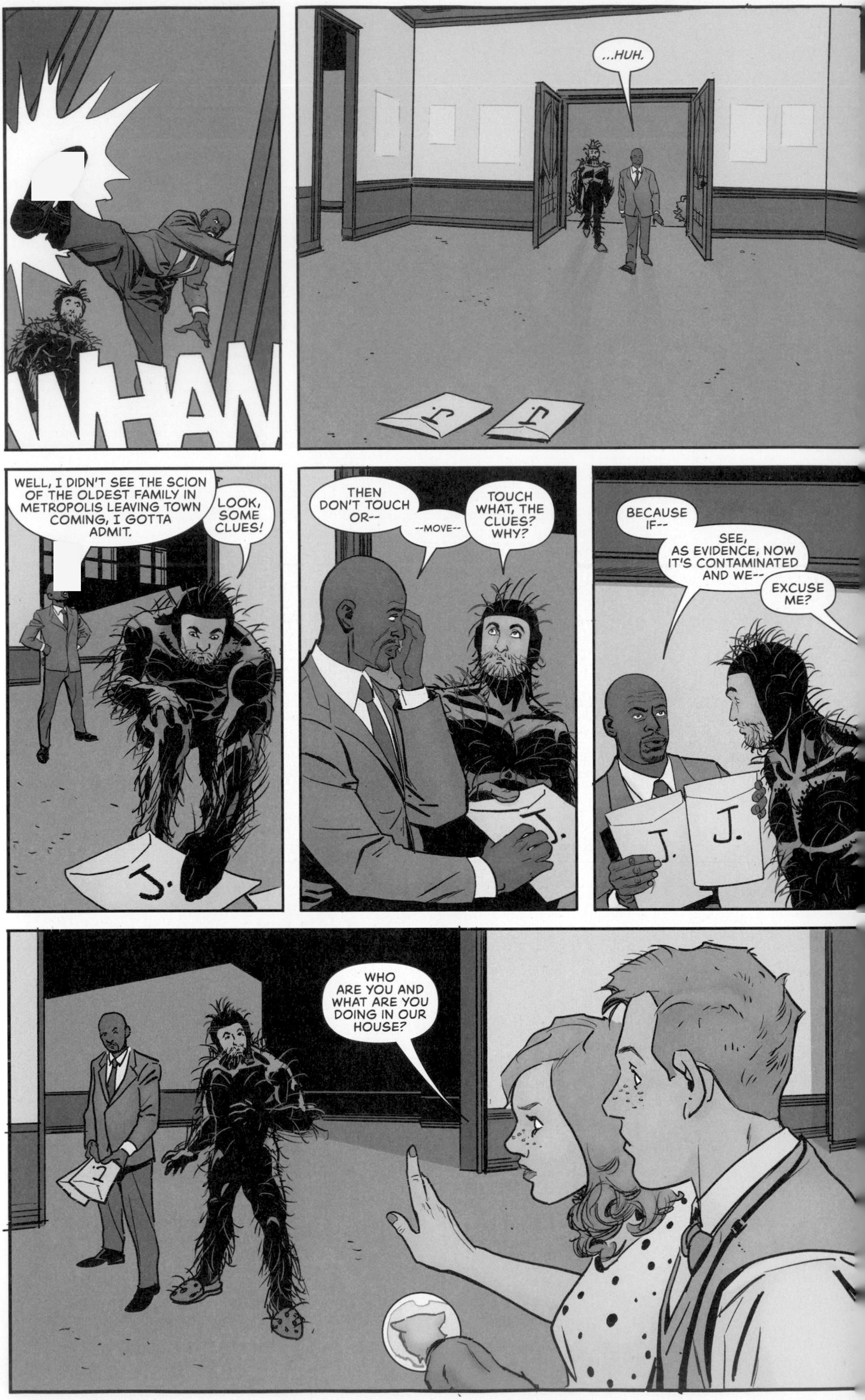
...HUH.
WELL, I DIDN'T SEE THE SCION OF THE OLDEST FAMILY IN METROPOLIS LEAVING TOWN COMING, I GOTTA ADMIT.
LOOK, SOME CLUES!
THEN DON'T TOUCH OR--
--MOVE--
TOUCH WHAT, THE CLUES? WHY?
BECAUSE IF--
SEE, AS EVIDENCE, NOW IT'S CONTAMINATED AND WE--
EXCUSE ME?
WHO ARE YOU AND WHAT ARE YOU DOING IN OUR HOUSE?

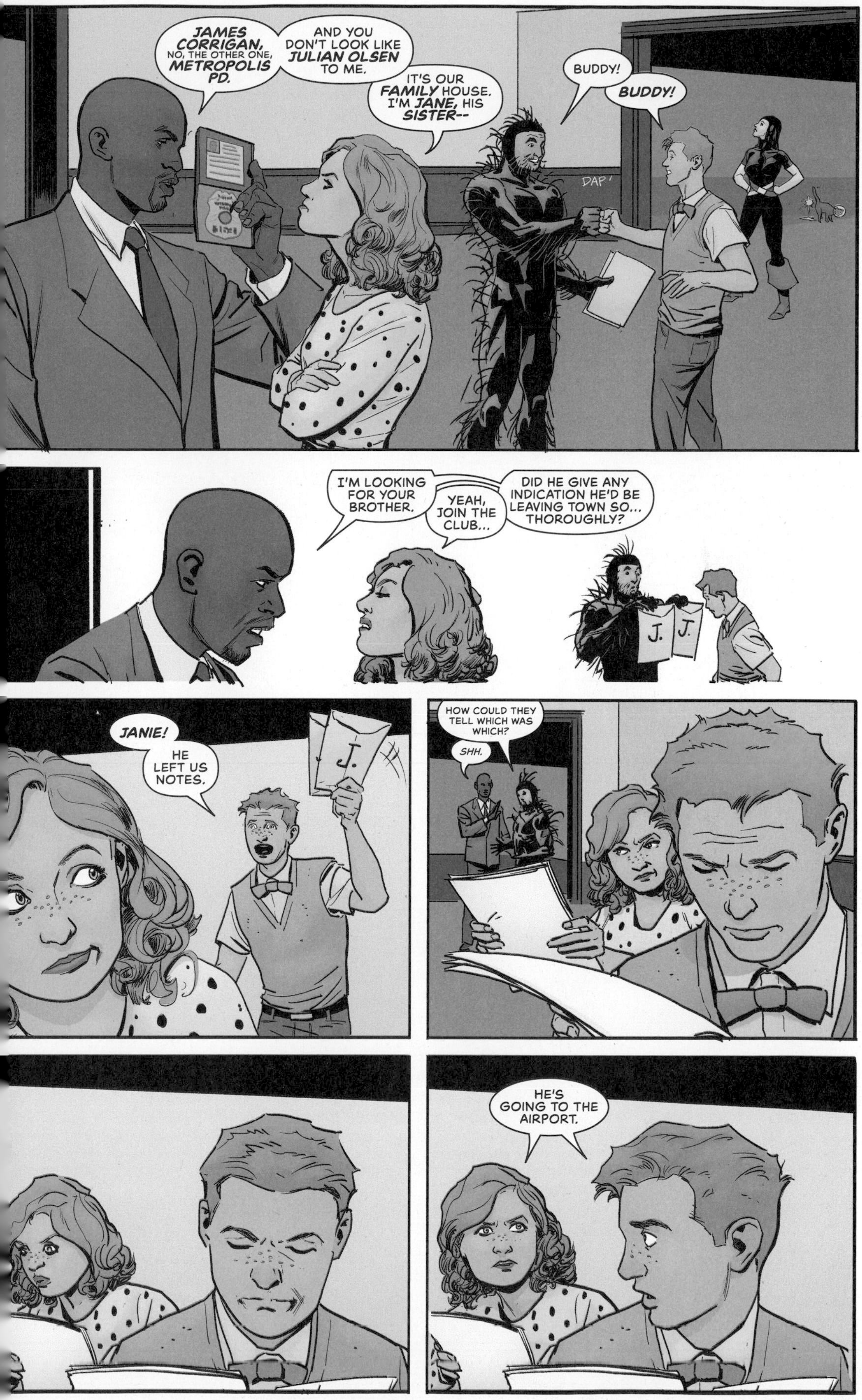

JAMES CORRIGAN, NO, THE OTHER ONE, METROPOLIS PD.
AND YOU DON'T LOOK LIKE JULIAN OLSEN TO ME.
IT'S OUR FAMILY HOUSE. I'M JANE, HIS SISTER--
BUDDY!
BUDDY!
DAP'
I'M LOOKING FOR YOUR BROTHER.
YEAH, JOIN THE CLUB...
DID HE GIVE ANY INDICATION HE'D BE LEAVING TOWN SO... THOROUGHLY?
J.
J.
JANIE!
HE LEFT US NOTES.
J.
HOW COULD THEY TELL WHICH WAS WHICH?
SHH.
HE'S GOING TO THE AIRPORT.

THIS MAKES NO *SENSE*...

SEE, MY *OLSENIC GENETIDETECTOR™* SAYS WHOEVER YOUR *GENETIC MATCH* IN METROPOLIS IS, THEY'RE NOT AT THE AIRPORT, THEY'RE *DOWNTOWN*...

DOC, OKAY, JEEZ, WILL YA GIVE ME A BREAK WITH THIS...?

I CAN ONLY HANDLE ONE COMPLETELY BAFFLING AND INEXPLICABLE BIT OF NONSENSE AT A TIME.

CAN'T THIS THING GO ANY *FASTER*?

IT'S A *SPACESHIP*, OLSEN, OF *COURSE* IT CAN GO FASTER.

BUT I CAN'T *STOP* IT ANY SLOWER AND I DON'T WANT TO HOSE YOU AND YOUR SISTER OFF THE CANOPY.

JEEZ, TOUCHY.

THERE, I SEE HIM--

HANG ON--!

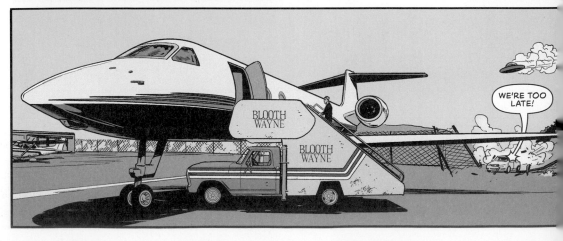

WE'RE TOO LATE!

BLOOTH WAYNE

BLOOTH WAYNE

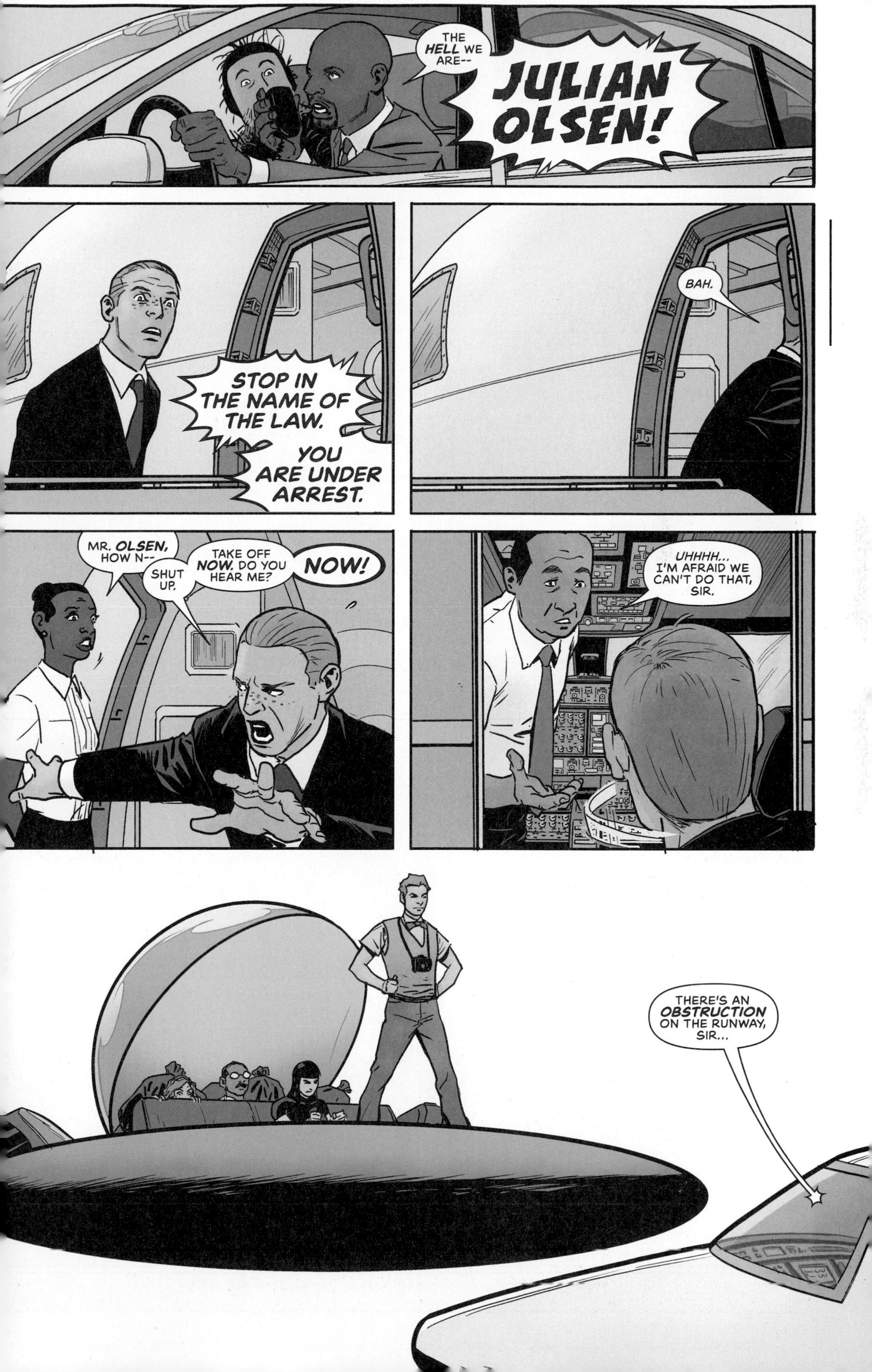
THE HELL WE ARE--
JULIAN OLSEN!
STOP IN THE NAME OF THE LAW.
YOU ARE UNDER ARREST.
BAH.
MR. OLSEN, HOW N--
SHUT UP.
TAKE OFF NOW. DO YOU HEAR ME?
NOW!
UHHHH... I'M AFRAID WE CAN'T DO THAT, SIR.
THERE'S AN OBSTRUCTION ON THE RUNWAY, SIR...

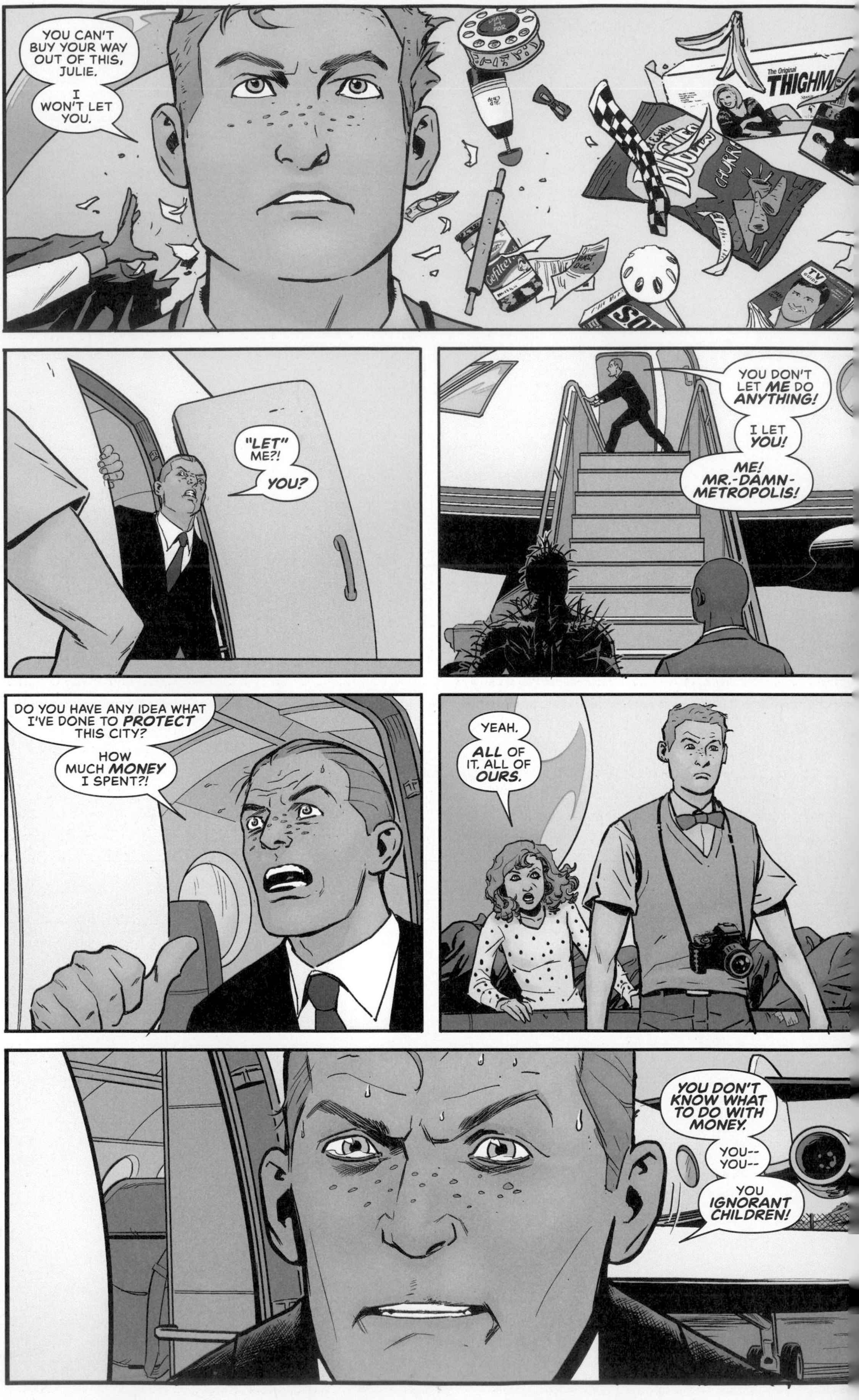
YOU CAN'T BUY YOUR WAY OUT OF THIS, JULIE.
I WON'T LET YOU.
The Original
THIGHM
TV GUIDE
"LET" ME?!
YOU?
YOU DON'T LET ME DO ANYTHING!
I LET YOU!
ME! MR.-DAMN-METROPOLIS!
DO YOU HAVE ANY IDEA WHAT I'VE DONE TO PROTECT THIS CITY?
HOW MUCH MONEY I SPENT?!
YEAH. ALL OF IT. ALL OF OURS.
YOU DON'T KNOW WHAT TO DO WITH MONEY.
YOU-- YOU--
YOU IGNORANT CHILDREN!

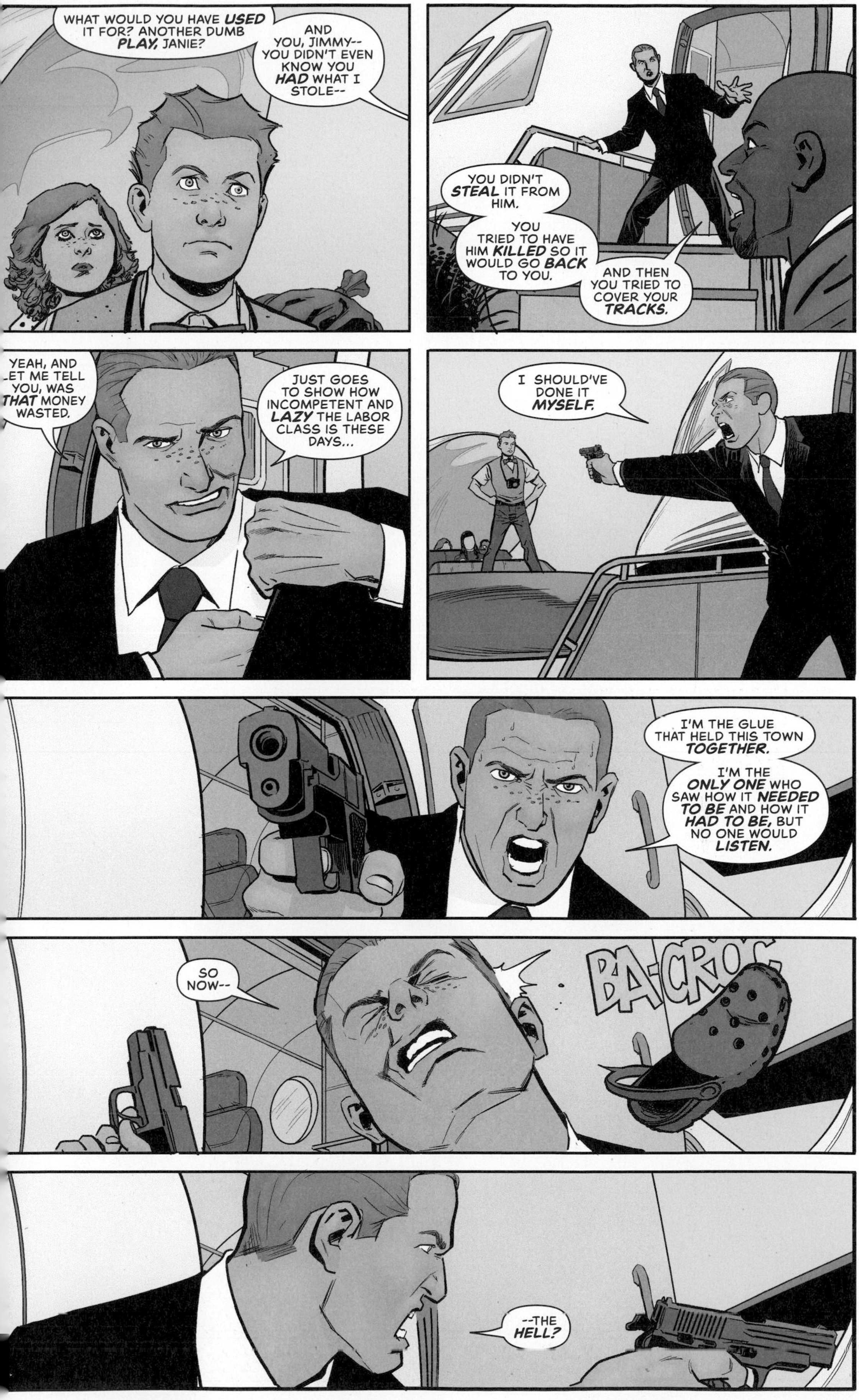
WHAT WOULD YOU HAVE USED IT FOR? ANOTHER DUMB PLAY, JANIE?
AND YOU, JIMMY-- YOU DIDN'T EVEN KNOW YOU HAD WHAT I STOLE--
YOU DIDN'T STEAL IT FROM HIM.
YOU TRIED TO HAVE HIM KILLED SO IT WOULD GO BACK TO YOU.
AND THEN YOU TRIED TO COVER YOUR TRACKS.
YEAH, AND LET ME TELL YOU, WAS THAT MONEY WASTED.
JUST GOES TO SHOW HOW INCOMPETENT AND LAZY THE LABOR CLASS IS THESE DAYS...
I SHOULD'VE DONE IT MYSELF.
I'M THE GLUE THAT HELD THIS TOWN TOGETHER.
I'M THE ONLY ONE WHO SAW HOW IT NEEDED TO BE AND HOW IT HAD TO BE, BUT NO ONE WOULD LISTEN.
SO NOW--
--THE HELL?

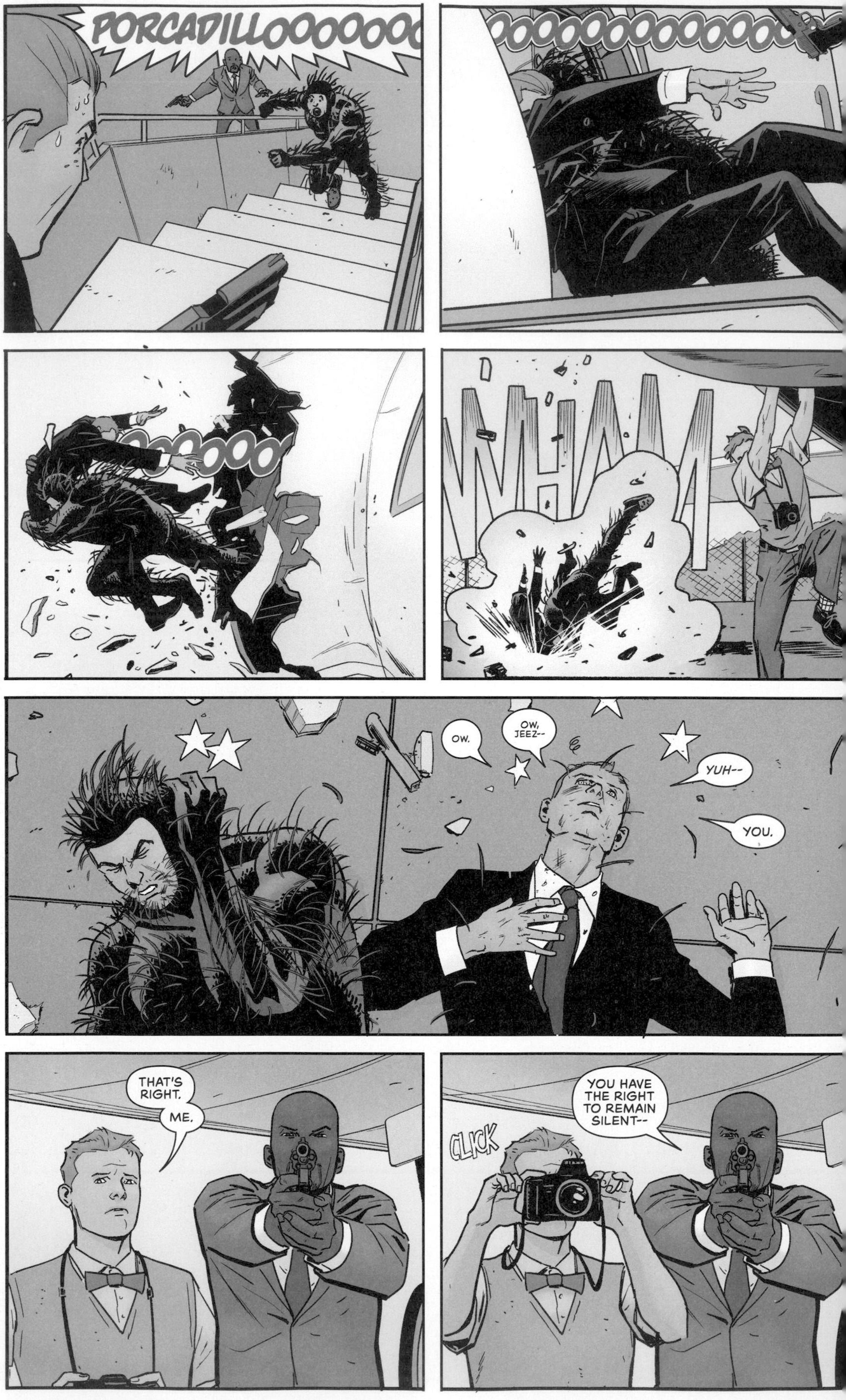
PORCADILLOOOOOOO
OOOOOOOOOOOOOOO
OOOOOO
WHAM
OW.
OW, JEEZ--
YUH--
YOU.
THAT'S RIGHT.
ME.
CLICK
YOU HAVE THE RIGHT TO REMAIN SILENT--

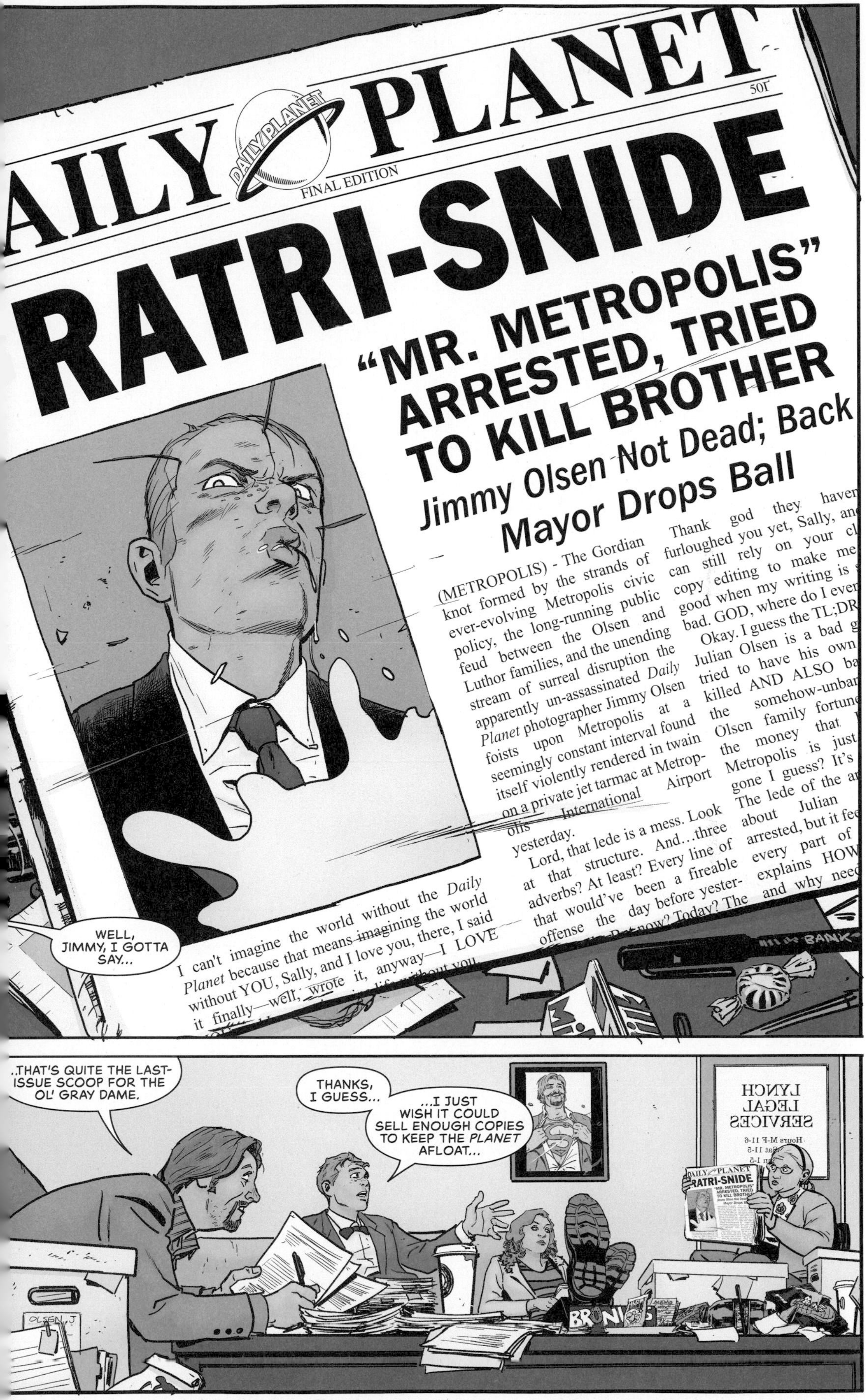
AILY PLANET
DAILY PLANET
FINAL EDITION
50¢
RATRI-SNIDE
"MR. METROPOLIS" ARRESTED, TRIED TO KILL BROTHER
Jimmy Olsen Not Dead; Back
Mayor Drops Ball
(METROPOLIS) - The Gordian knot formed by the strands of ever-evolving Metropolis civic policy, the long-running public feud between the Olsen and Luthor families, and the unending stream of surreal disruption the apparently un-assassinated *Daily Planet* photographer Jimmy Olsen foists upon Metropolis at a seemingly constant interval found itself violently rendered in twain on a private jet tarmac at Metropolis International Airport yesterday.
Lord, that lede is a mess. Look at that structure. And…three adverbs? At least? Every line of that would've been a fireable offense the day before yester-
Thank god they haven furloughed you yet, Sally, and can still rely on your cl copy editing to make me good when my writing is bad. GOD, where do I even
Okay. I guess the TL;DR Julian Olsen is a bad g tried to have his own killed AND ALSO ba the somehow-unban Olsen family fortune the money that Metropolis is just gone I guess? It's
The lede of the a about Julian arrested, but it fee every part of explains HOW and why need
I can't imagine the world without the *Daily Planet* because that means imagining the world without YOU, Sally, and I love you, there, I said it finally—well, wrote it, anyway—I LOVE
WELL, JIMMY, I GOTTA SAY...
...THAT'S QUITE THE LAST-ISSUE SCOOP FOR THE OL' GRAY DAME.
THANKS, I GUESS...
...I JUST WISH IT COULD SELL ENOUGH COPIES TO KEEP THE *PLANET* AFLOAT...
LYNCH LEGAL SERVICES
OLSEN, J.

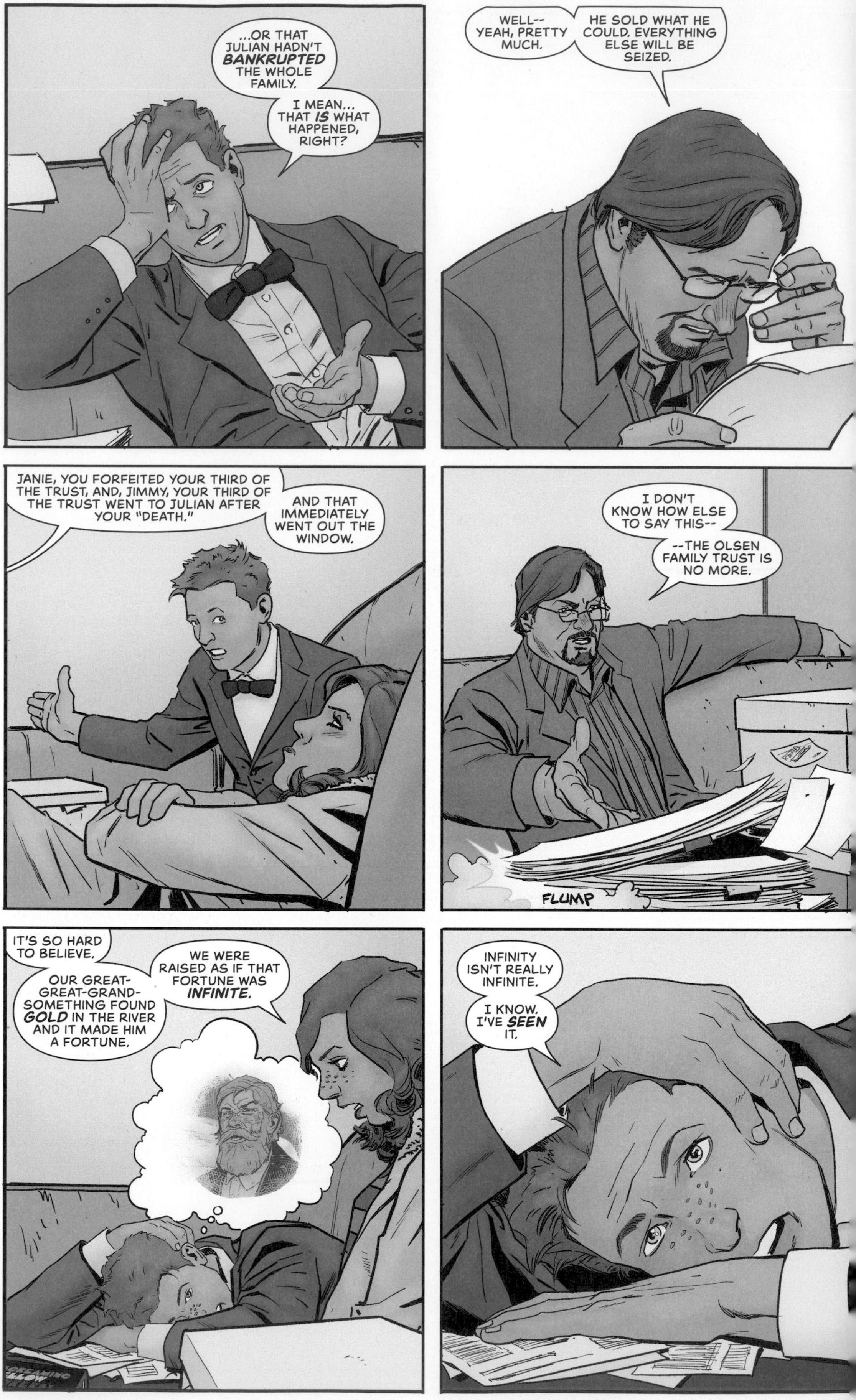
...OR THAT JULIAN HADN'T BANKRUPTED THE WHOLE FAMILY.
I MEAN... THAT IS WHAT HAPPENED, RIGHT?
WELL-- YEAH, PRETTY MUCH.
HE SOLD WHAT HE COULD. EVERYTHING ELSE WILL BE SEIZED.
JANIE, YOU FORFEITED YOUR THIRD OF THE TRUST, AND, JIMMY, YOUR THIRD OF THE TRUST WENT TO JULIAN AFTER YOUR "DEATH."
AND THAT IMMEDIATELY WENT OUT THE WINDOW.
I DON'T KNOW HOW ELSE TO SAY THIS--
--THE OLSEN FAMILY TRUST IS NO MORE.
FLUMP
IT'S SO HARD TO BELIEVE.
OUR GREAT-GREAT-GRAND-SOMETHING FOUND GOLD IN THE RIVER AND IT MADE HIM A FORTUNE.
WE WERE RAISED AS IF THAT FORTUNE WAS INFINITE.
INFINITY ISN'T REALLY INFINITE.
I KNOW. I'VE SEEN IT.

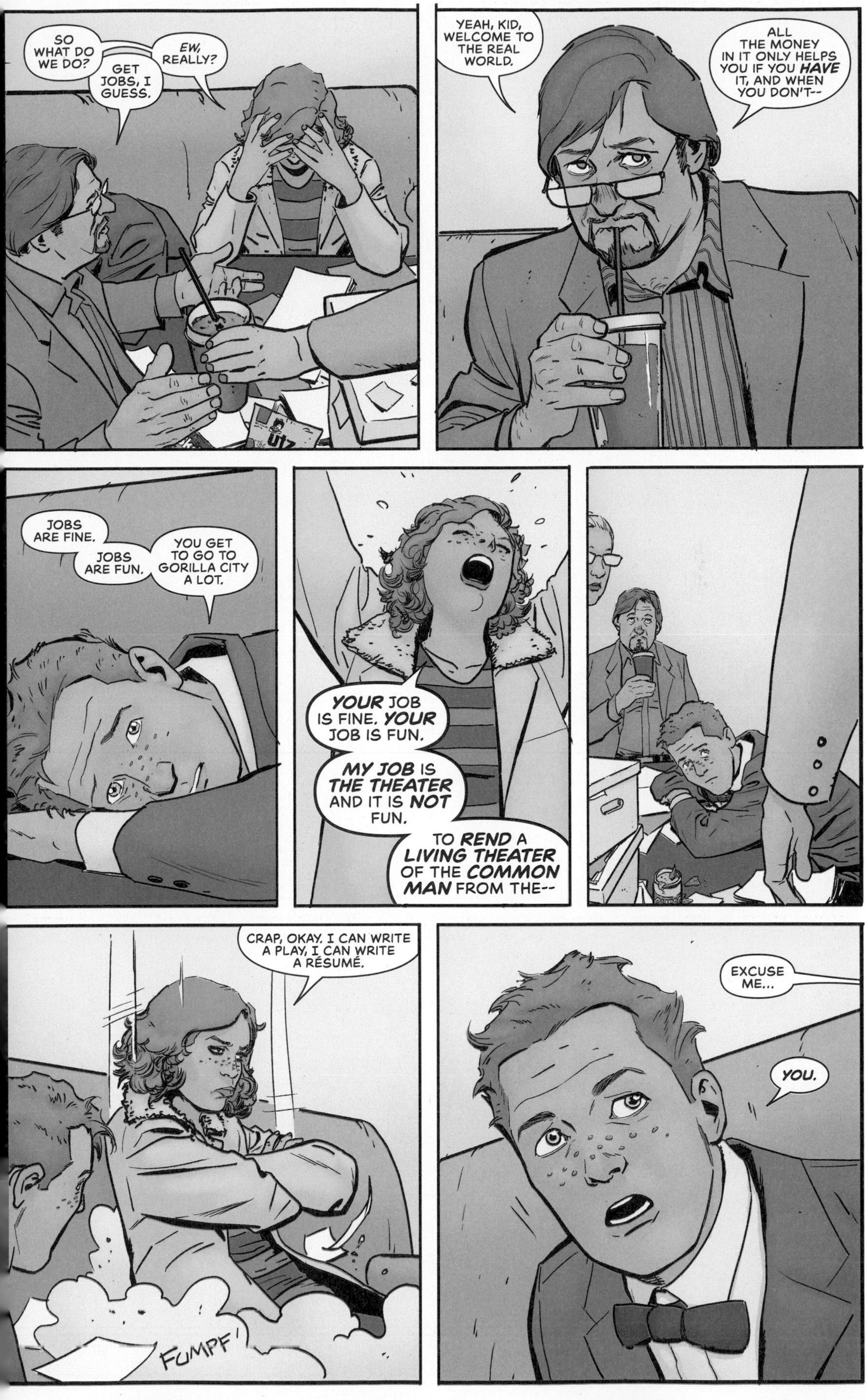
SO WHAT DO WE DO?
GET JOBS, I GUESS.
EW, REALLY?
YEAH, KID, WELCOME TO THE REAL WORLD.
ALL THE MONEY IN IT ONLY HELPS YOU IF YOU ***HAVE*** IT, AND WHEN YOU DON'T--
JOBS ARE FINE.
JOBS ARE FUN.
YOU GET TO GO TO GORILLA CITY A LOT.
YOUR JOB IS FINE. ***YOUR*** JOB IS FUN.
MY JOB IS ***THE THEATER*** AND IT IS ***NOT*** FUN.
TO ***REND*** A ***LIVING THEATER*** OF THE ***COMMON MAN*** FROM THE--
CRAP, OKAY. I CAN WRITE A PLAY, I CAN WRITE A RÉSUMÉ.
FUMPF!
EXCUSE ME...
YOU.

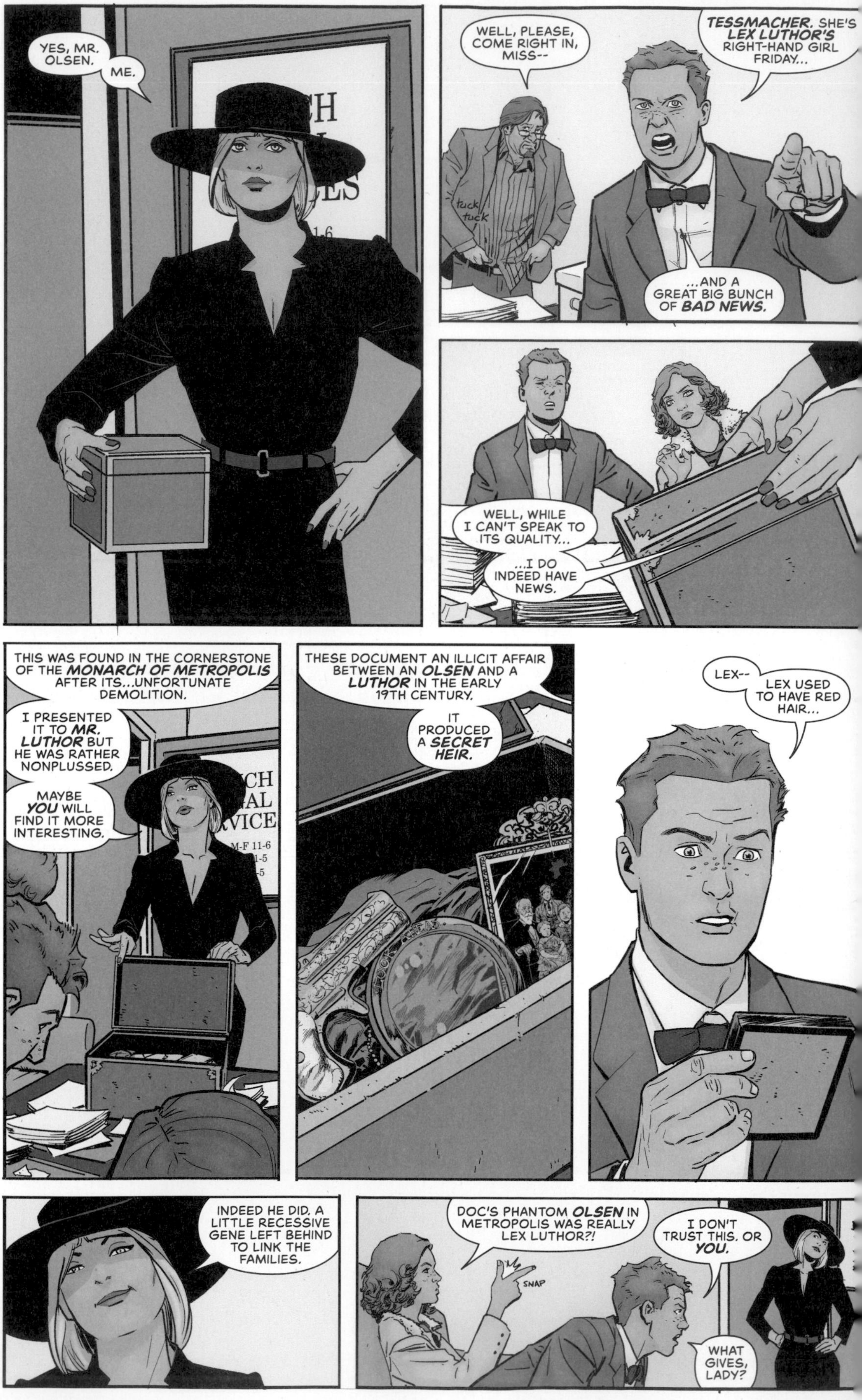
YES, MR. OLSEN.
ME.
WELL, PLEASE, COME RIGHT IN, MISS--
TESSMACHER. SHE'S LEX LUTHOR'S RIGHT-HAND GIRL FRIDAY...
tuck tuck
...AND A GREAT BIG BUNCH OF BAD NEWS.
WELL, WHILE I CAN'T SPEAK TO ITS QUALITY...
...I DO INDEED HAVE NEWS.
THIS WAS FOUND IN THE CORNERSTONE OF THE MONARCH OF METROPOLIS AFTER ITS...UNFORTUNATE DEMOLITION.
I PRESENTED IT TO MR. LUTHOR BUT HE WAS RATHER NONPLUSSED.
MAYBE YOU WILL FIND IT MORE INTERESTING.
THESE DOCUMENT AN ILLICIT AFFAIR BETWEEN AN OLSEN AND A LUTHOR IN THE EARLY 19TH CENTURY.
IT PRODUCED A SECRET HEIR.
LEX--
LEX USED TO HAVE RED HAIR...
INDEED HE DID, A LITTLE RECESSIVE GENE LEFT BEHIND TO LINK THE FAMILIES.
DOC'S PHANTOM OLSEN IN METROPOLIS WAS REALLY LEX LUTHOR?!
SNAP
I DON'T TRUST THIS. OR YOU.
WHAT GIVES, LADY?

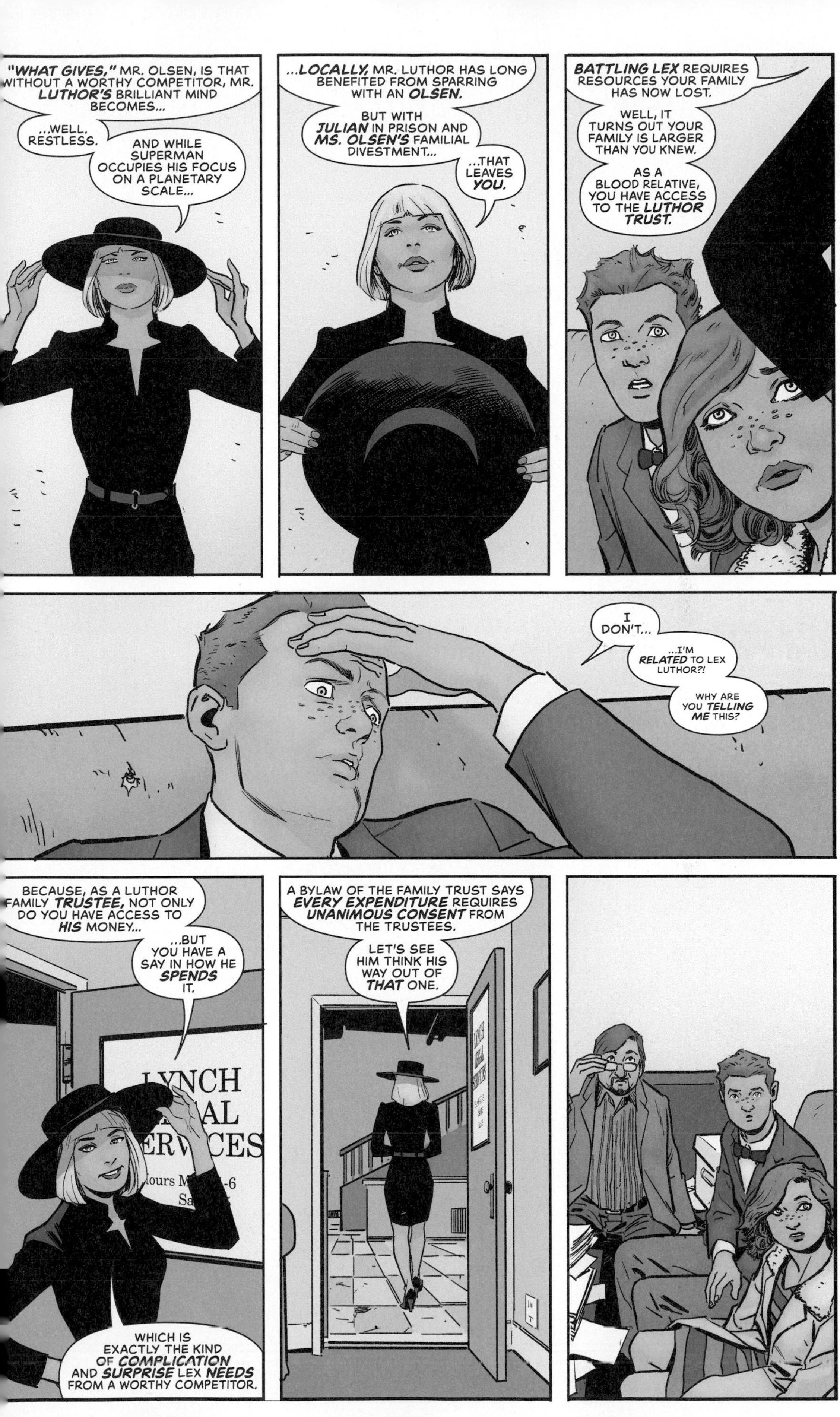
"WHAT GIVES," MR. OLSEN, IS THAT WITHOUT A WORTHY COMPETITOR, MR. LUTHOR'S BRILLIANT MIND BECOMES...
...WELL, RESTLESS.
AND WHILE SUPERMAN OCCUPIES HIS FOCUS ON A PLANETARY SCALE...
...LOCALLY, MR. LUTHOR HAS LONG BENEFITED FROM SPARRING WITH AN OLSEN.
BUT WITH JULIAN IN PRISON AND MS. OLSEN'S FAMILIAL DIVESTMENT...
...THAT LEAVES YOU.
BATTLING LEX REQUIRES RESOURCES YOUR FAMILY HAS NOW LOST.
WELL, IT TURNS OUT YOUR FAMILY IS LARGER THAN YOU KNEW.
AS A BLOOD RELATIVE, YOU HAVE ACCESS TO THE LUTHOR TRUST.
I DON'T...
...I'M RELATED TO LEX LUTHOR?!
WHY ARE YOU TELLING ME THIS?
BECAUSE, AS A LUTHOR FAMILY TRUSTEE, NOT ONLY DO YOU HAVE ACCESS TO HIS MONEY...
...BUT YOU HAVE A SAY IN HOW HE SPENDS IT.
LYNCH
WHICH IS EXACTLY THE KIND OF COMPLICATION AND SURPRISE LEX NEEDS FROM A WORTHY COMPETITOR.
A BYLAW OF THE FAMILY TRUST SAYS EVERY EXPENDITURE REQUIRES UNANIMOUS CONSENT FROM THE TRUSTEES.
LET'S SEE HIM THINK HIS WAY OUT OF THAT ONE.

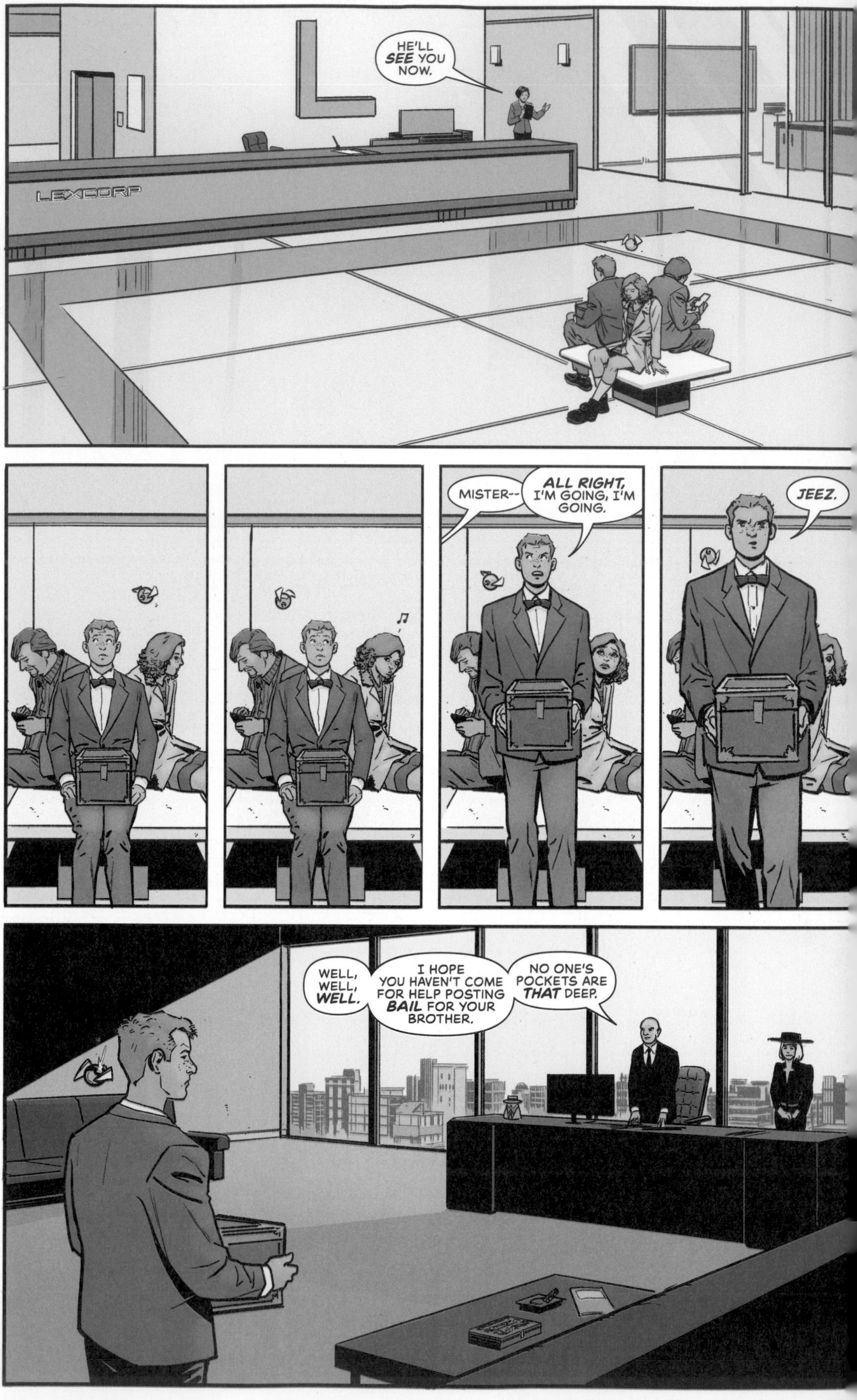
HE'LL SEE YOU NOW.
LEXCORP
MISTER--
ALL RIGHT, I'M GOING, I'M GOING.
JEEZ.
WELL, WELL, WELL.
I HOPE YOU HAVEN'T COME FOR HELP POSTING BAIL FOR YOUR BROTHER.
NO ONE'S POCKETS ARE THAT DEEP.

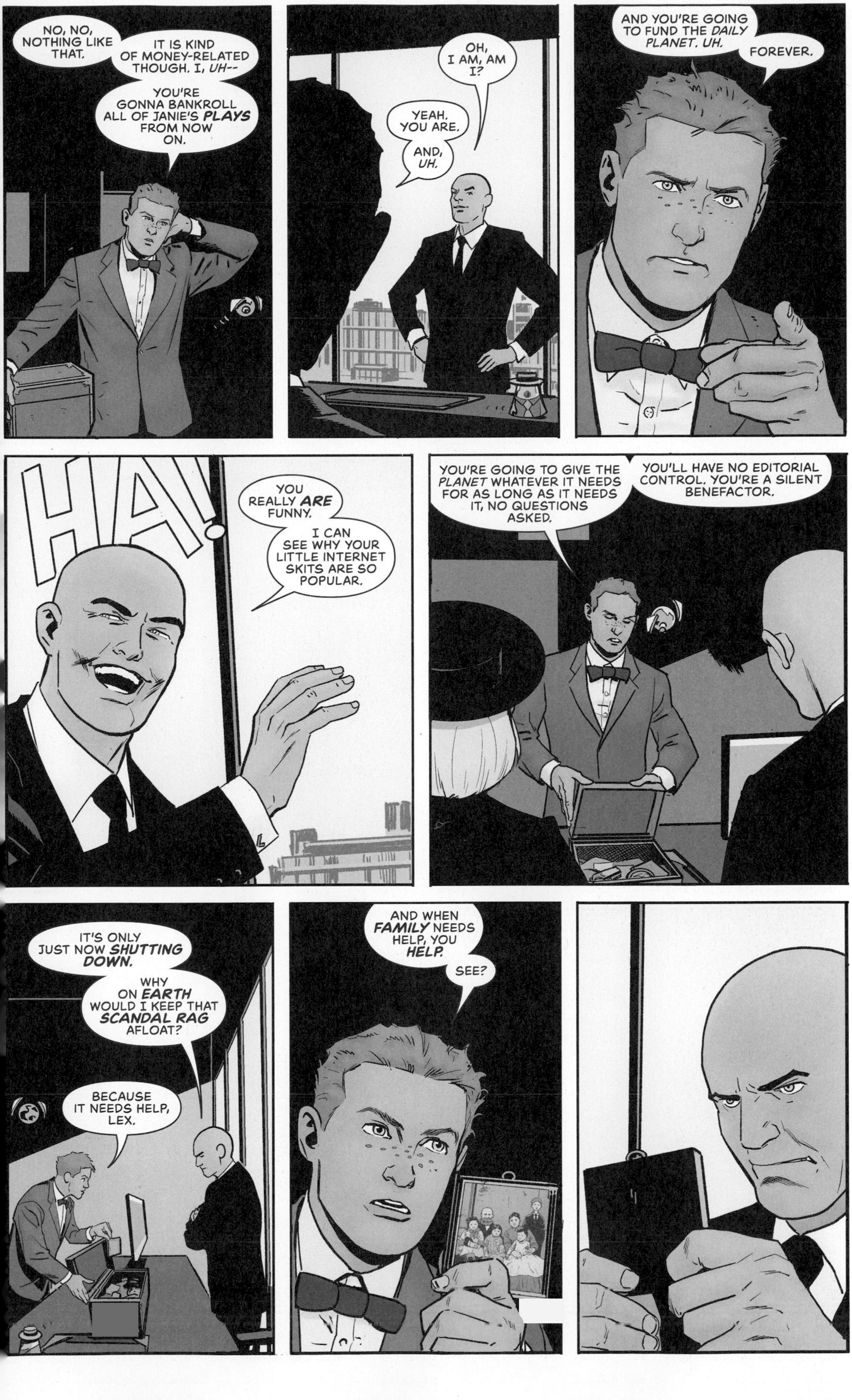
NO, NO, NOTHING LIKE THAT.
IT IS KIND OF MONEY-RELATED THOUGH. I, *UH--*
YOU'RE GONNA BANKROLL ALL OF JANIE'S **PLAYS** FROM NOW ON.
OH, I AM, AM I?
YEAH. YOU ARE.
AND, *UH.*
AND YOU'RE GOING TO FUND THE *DAILY PLANET. UH.*
FOREVER.
HA!
YOU REALLY **ARE** FUNNY.
I CAN SEE WHY YOUR LITTLE INTERNET SKITS ARE SO POPULAR.
YOU'RE GOING TO GIVE THE *PLANET* WHATEVER IT NEEDS FOR AS LONG AS IT NEEDS IT, NO QUESTIONS ASKED.
YOU'LL HAVE NO EDITORIAL CONTROL. YOU'RE A SILENT BENEFACTOR.
IT'S ONLY JUST NOW **SHUTTING DOWN.**
WHY ON **EARTH** WOULD I KEEP THAT **SCANDAL RAG** AFLOAT?
BECAUSE IT NEEDS HELP, LEX.
AND WHEN **FAMILY** NEEDS HELP, YOU **HELP.**
SEE?

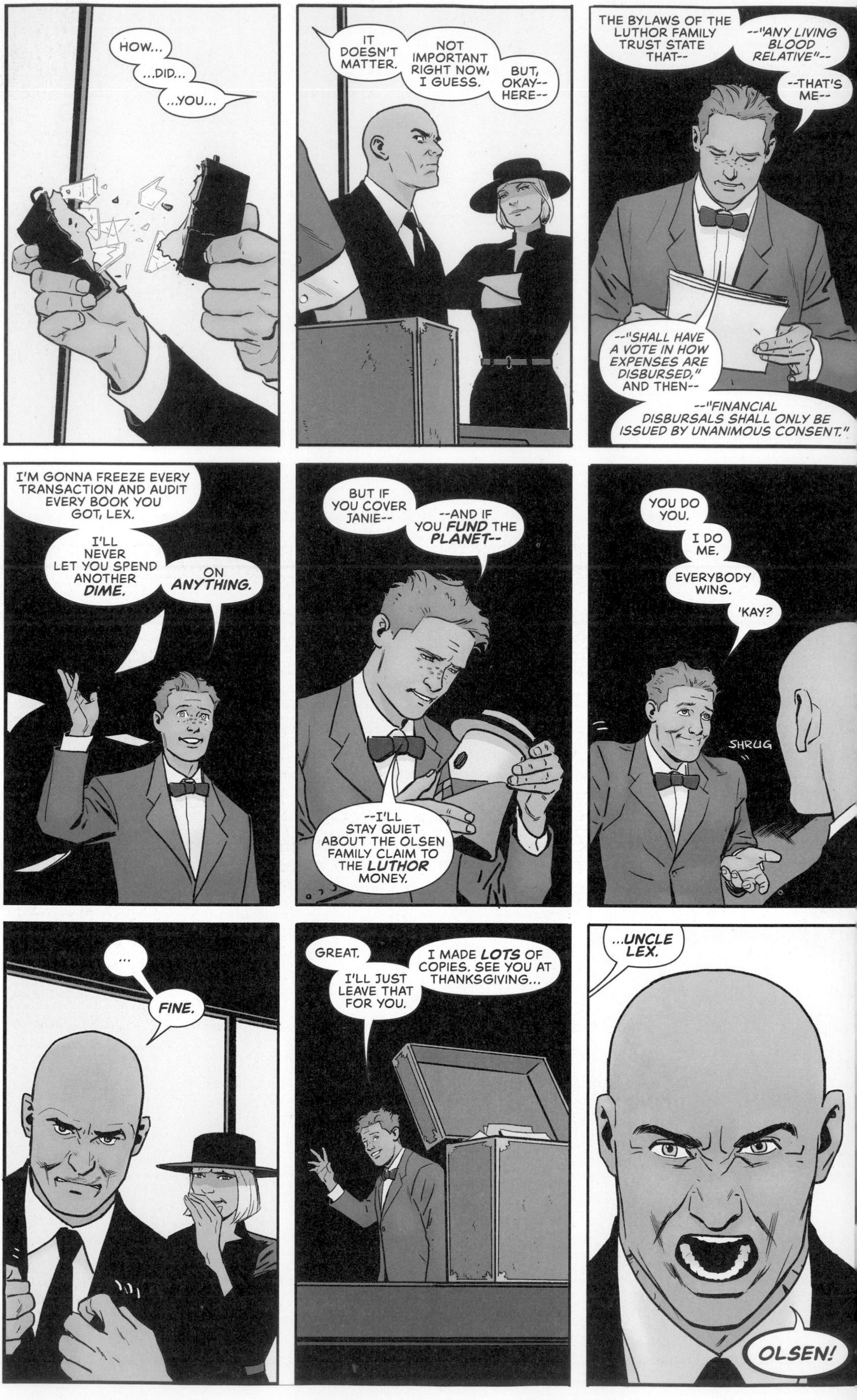
HOW...
...DID...
...YOU...
IT DOESN'T MATTER.
NOT IMPORTANT RIGHT NOW, I GUESS.
BUT, OKAY-- HERE--
THE BYLAWS OF THE LUTHOR FAMILY TRUST STATE THAT--
--"ANY LIVING BLOOD RELATIVE"--
--THAT'S ME--
--"SHALL HAVE A VOTE IN HOW EXPENSES ARE DISBURSED," AND THEN--
--"FINANCIAL DISBURSALS SHALL ONLY BE ISSUED BY UNANIMOUS CONSENT."
I'M GONNA FREEZE EVERY TRANSACTION AND AUDIT EVERY BOOK YOU GOT, LEX.
I'LL NEVER LET YOU SPEND ANOTHER DIME.
ON ANYTHING.
BUT IF YOU COVER JANIE--
--AND IF YOU FUND THE PLANET--
--I'LL STAY QUIET ABOUT THE OLSEN FAMILY CLAIM TO THE LUTHOR MONEY.
YOU DO YOU.
I DO ME.
EVERYBODY WINS.
'KAY?
SHRUG
...
FINE.
GREAT.
I'LL JUST LEAVE THAT FOR YOU.
I MADE LOTS OF COPIES. SEE YOU AT THANKSGIVING...
...UNCLE LEX.
OLSEN!

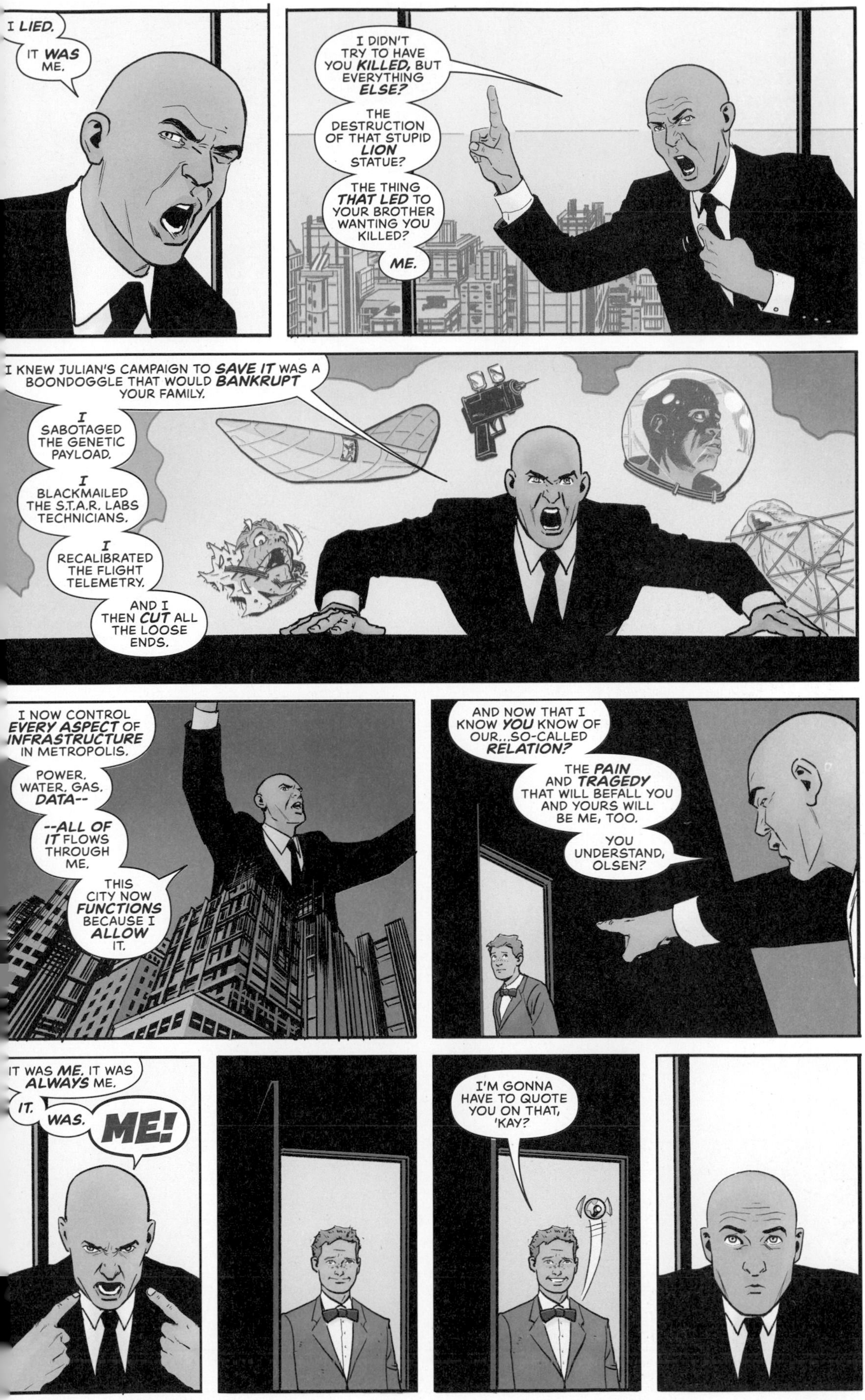
I LIED.
IT WAS ME.
I DIDN'T TRY TO HAVE YOU KILLED, BUT EVERYTHING ELSE?
THE DESTRUCTION OF THAT STUPID LION STATUE?
THE THING THAT LED TO YOUR BROTHER WANTING YOU KILLED?
ME.
I KNEW JULIAN'S CAMPAIGN TO SAVE IT WAS A BOONDOGGLE THAT WOULD BANKRUPT YOUR FAMILY.
I SABOTAGED THE GENETIC PAYLOAD.
I BLACKMAILED THE S.T.A.R. LABS TECHNICIANS.
I RECALIBRATED THE FLIGHT TELEMETRY.
AND I THEN CUT ALL THE LOOSE ENDS.
I NOW CONTROL EVERY ASPECT OF INFRASTRUCTURE IN METROPOLIS.
POWER. WATER. GAS. DATA--
--ALL OF IT FLOWS THROUGH ME.
THIS CITY NOW FUNCTIONS BECAUSE I ALLOW IT.
AND NOW THAT I KNOW YOU KNOW OF OUR...SO-CALLED RELATION?
THE PAIN AND TRAGEDY THAT WILL BEFALL YOU AND YOURS WILL BE ME, TOO.
YOU UNDERSTAND, OLSEN?
IT WAS ME. IT WAS ALWAYS ME.
IT.
WAS.
ME!
I'M GONNA HAVE TO QUOTE YOU ON THAT, 'KAY?

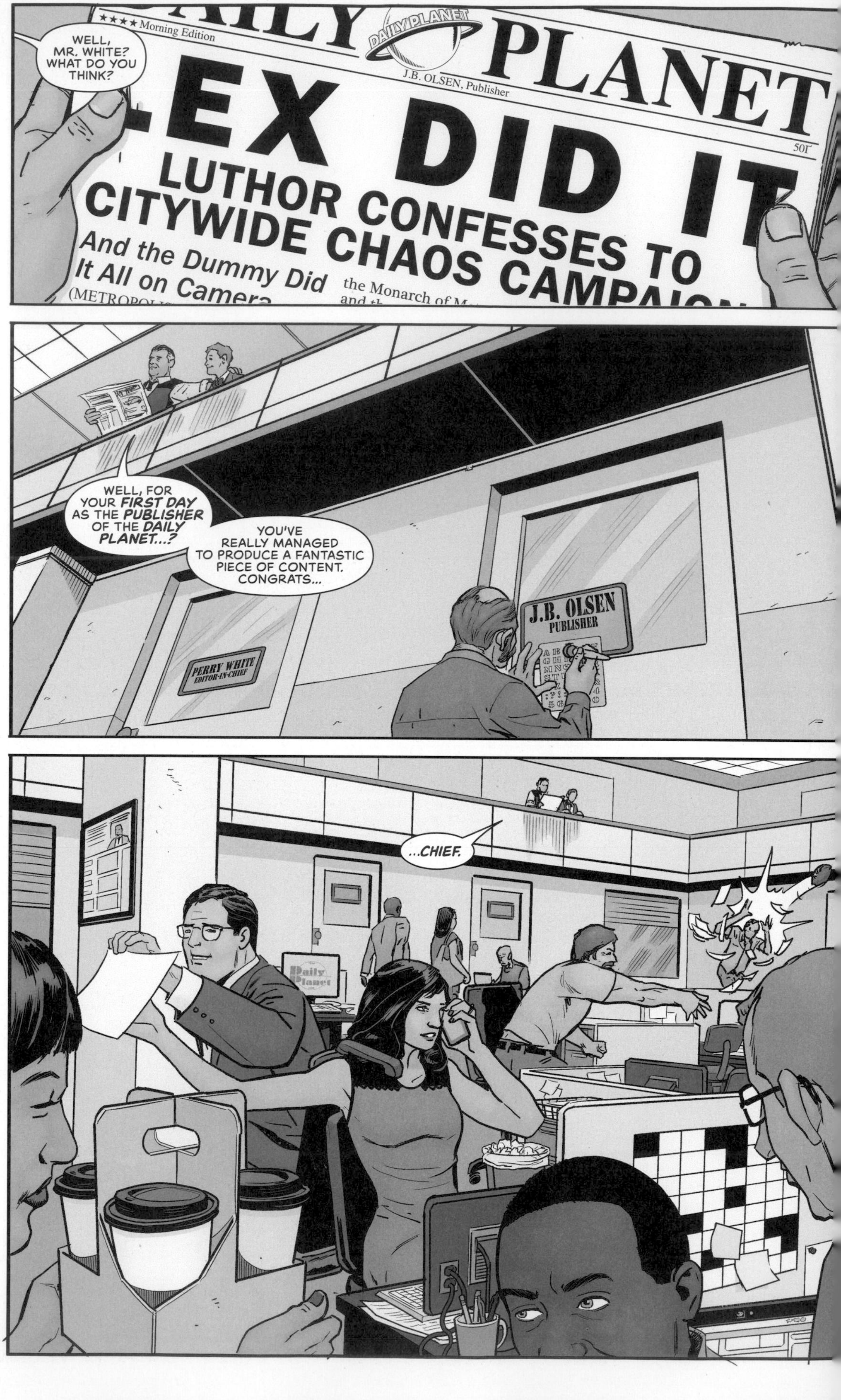
DAILY PLANET
★★★★ Morning Edition
J.B. OLSEN, Publisher
50¢
LEX DID IT
LUTHOR CONFESSES TO CITYWIDE CHAOS CAMPAIGN
And the Dummy Did It All on Camera
WELL, MR. WHITE? WHAT DO YOU THINK?
WELL, FOR YOUR FIRST DAY AS THE PUBLISHER OF THE DAILY PLANET...?
YOU'VE REALLY MANAGED TO PRODUCE A FANTASTIC PIECE OF CONTENT. CONGRATS...
PERRY WHITE EDITOR-IN-CHIEF
J.B. OLSEN PUBLISHER
...CHIEF.
Daily Planet

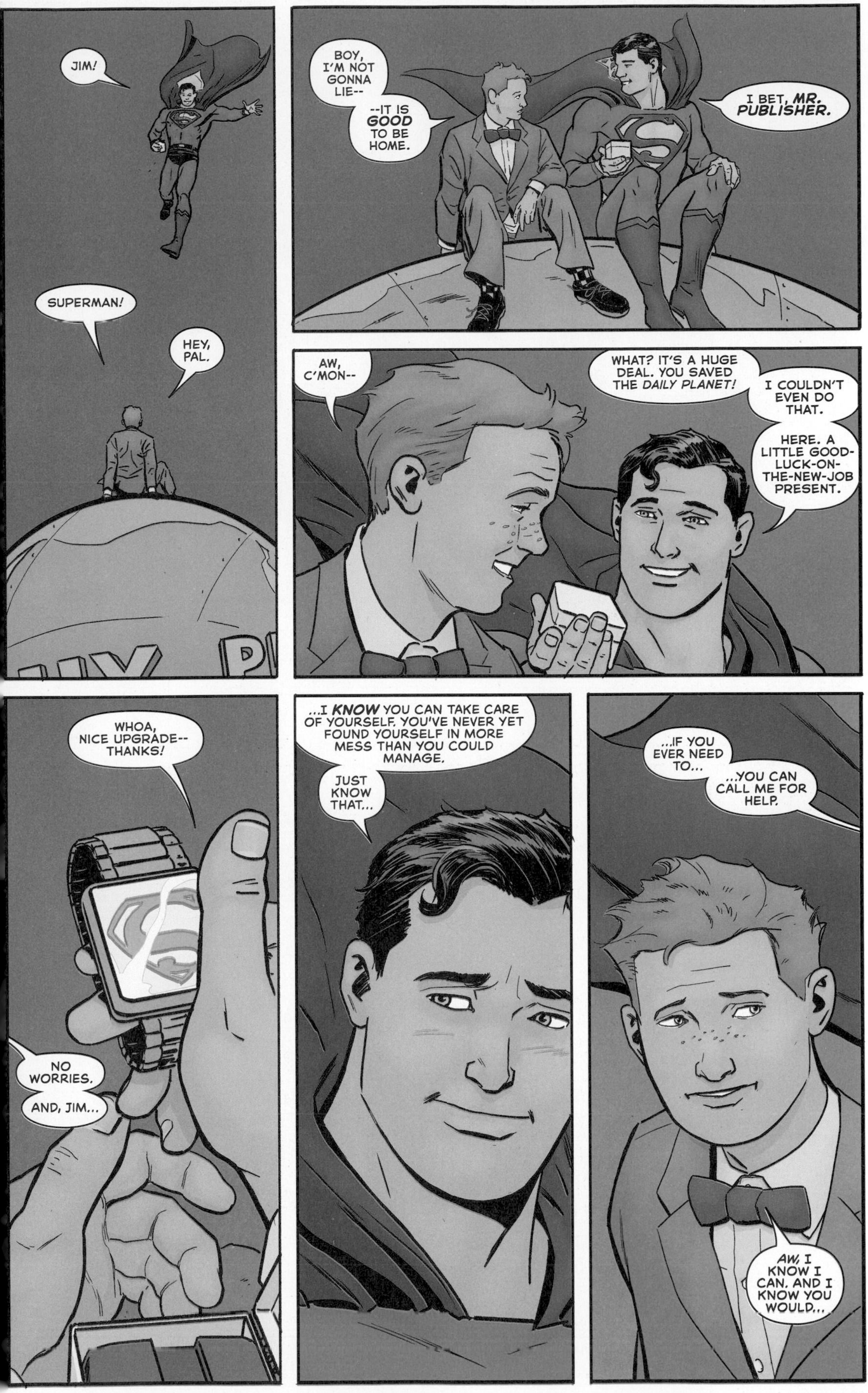
JIM!
BOY, I'M NOT GONNA LIE--
--IT IS GOOD TO BE HOME.
I BET, MR. PUBLISHER.
SUPERMAN!
HEY, PAL.
AW, C'MON--
WHAT? IT'S A HUGE DEAL. YOU SAVED THE DAILY PLANET!
I COULDN'T EVEN DO THAT.
HERE. A LITTLE GOOD-LUCK-ON-THE-NEW-JOB PRESENT.
WHOA, NICE UPGRADE-- THANKS!
NO WORRIES.
AND, JIM...
...I KNOW YOU CAN TAKE CARE OF YOURSELF. YOU'VE NEVER YET FOUND YOURSELF IN MORE MESS THAN YOU COULD MANAGE.
JUST KNOW THAT...
...IF YOU EVER NEED TO...
...YOU CAN CALL ME FOR HELP.
AW, I KNOW I CAN. AND I KNOW YOU WOULD...

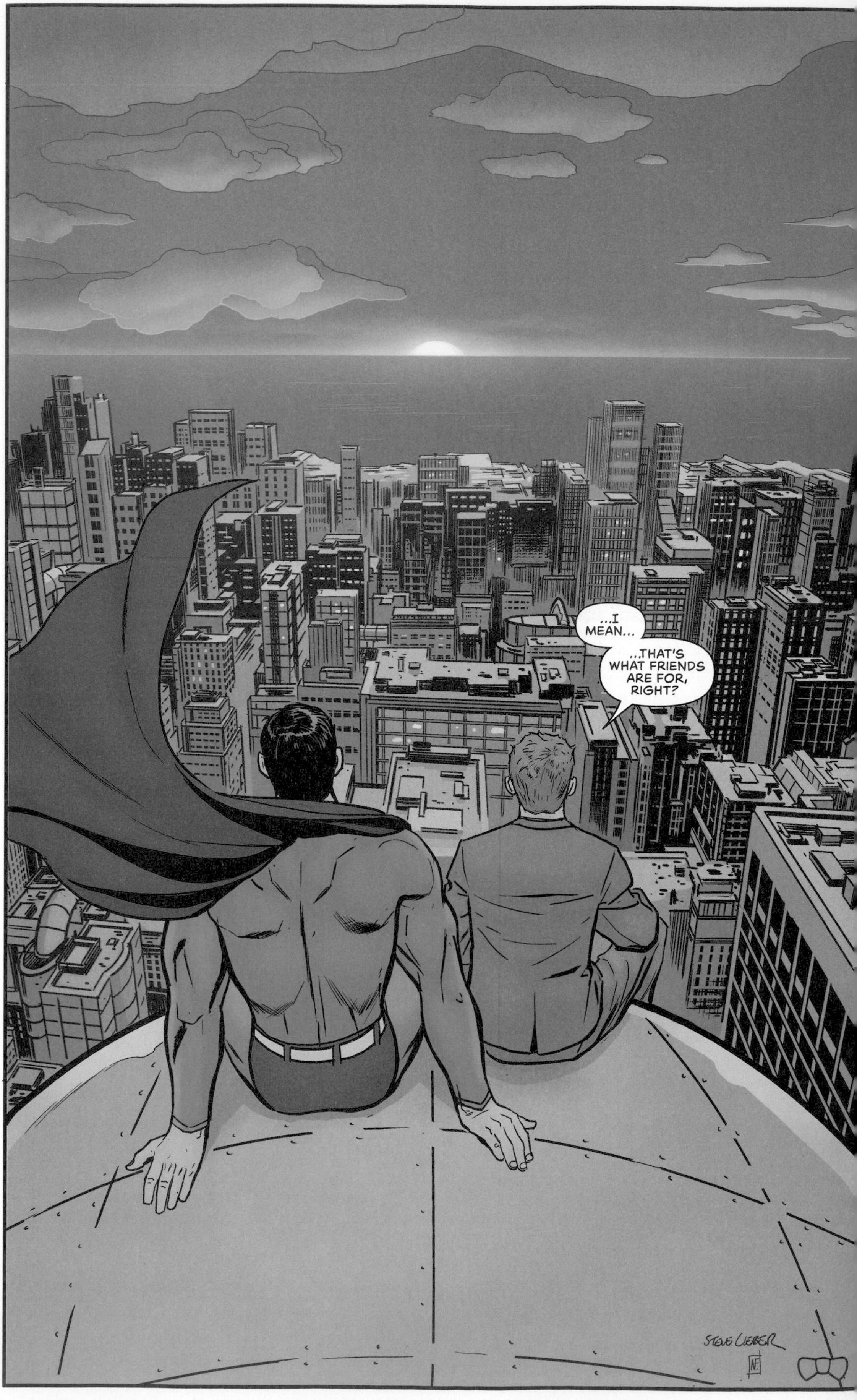
...I MEAN...
...THAT'S WHAT FRIENDS ARE FOR, RIGHT?
STEVE LIEBER

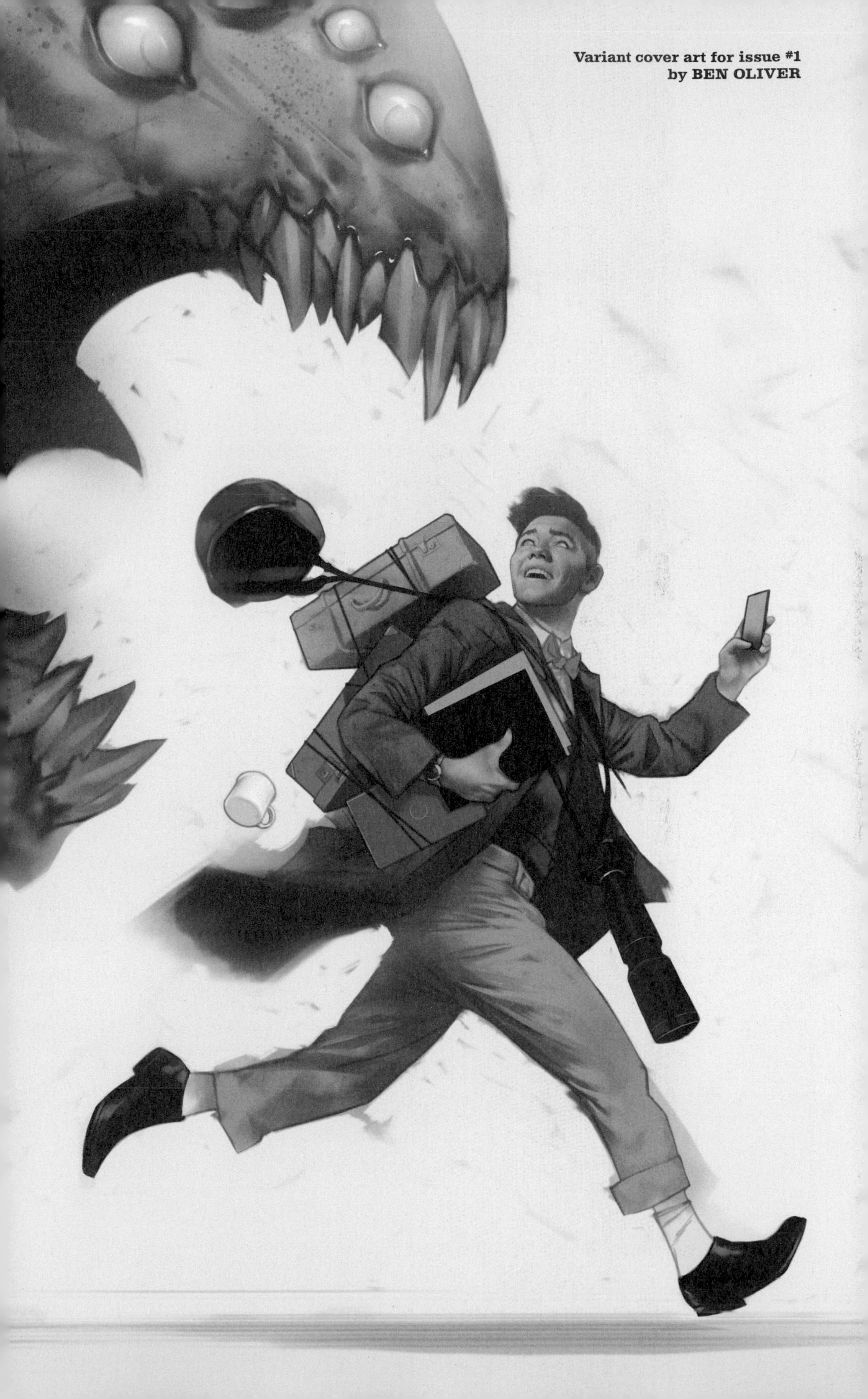

Variant cover art for issue #1
by BEN OLIVER

Variant cover art for issue #2
by BEN OLIVER

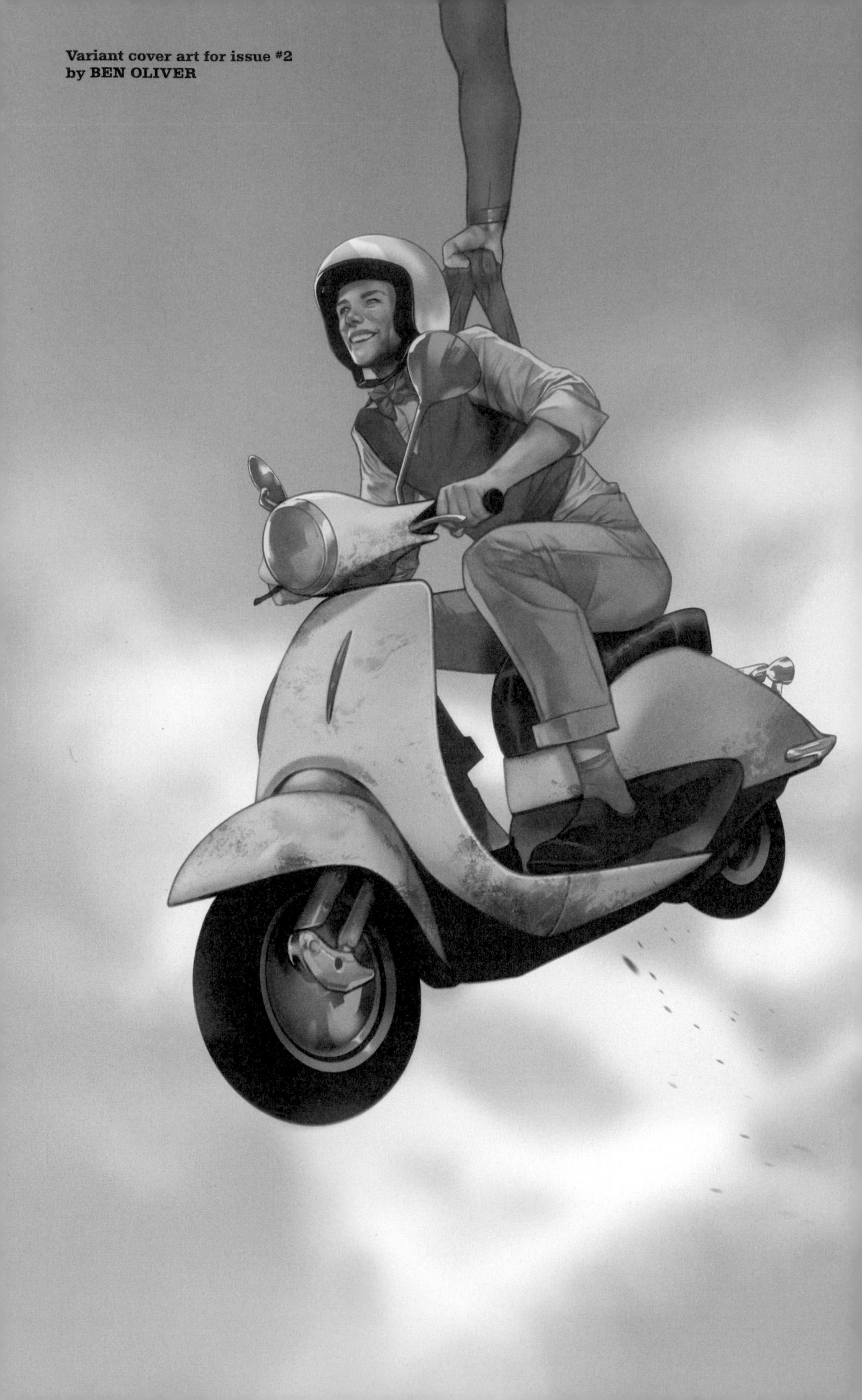

Variant cover art for issue #3
by BEN OLIVER

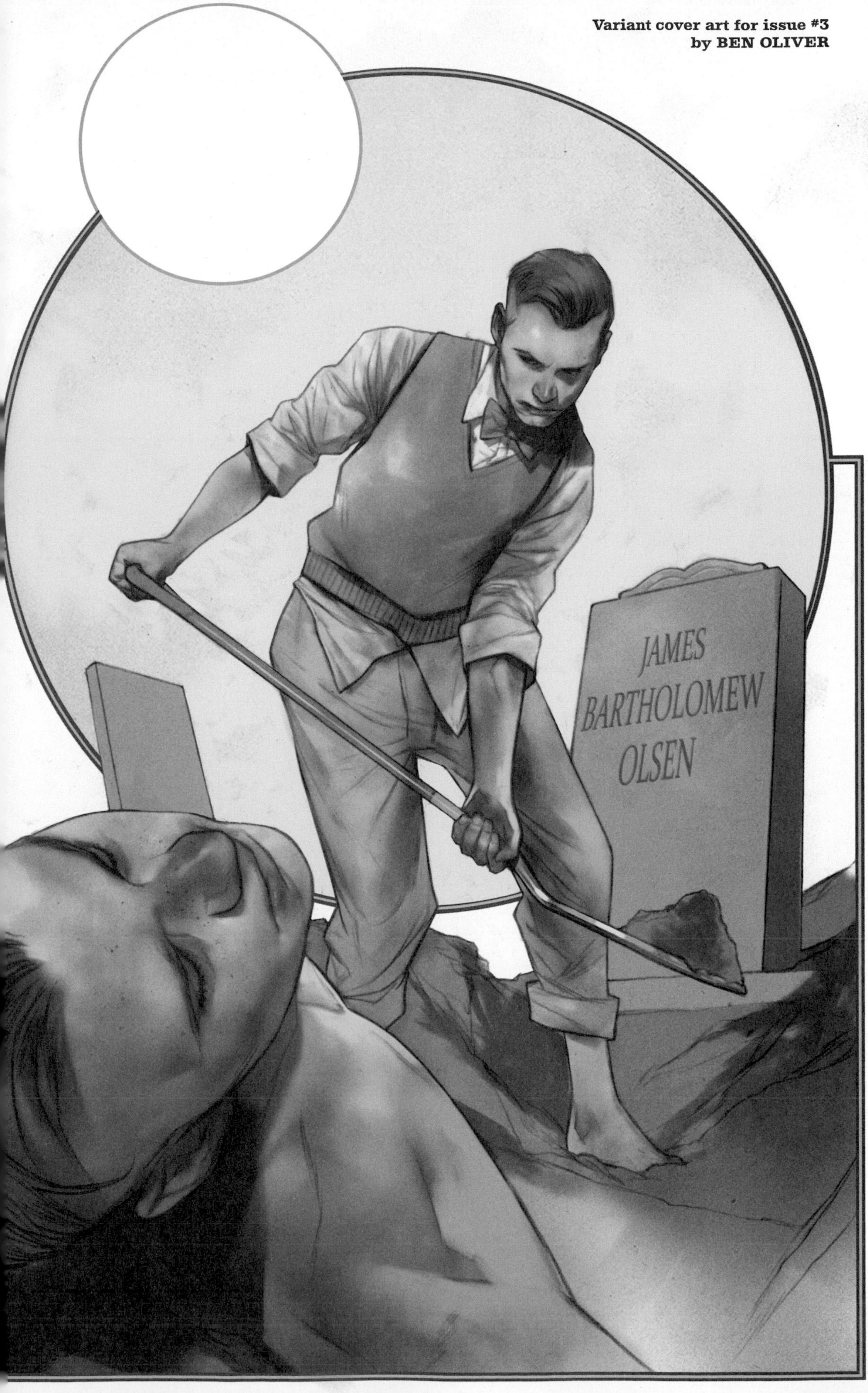
JAMES
BARTHOLOMEW
OLSEN

Variant cover art for issue #4
by DARICK ROBERTSON

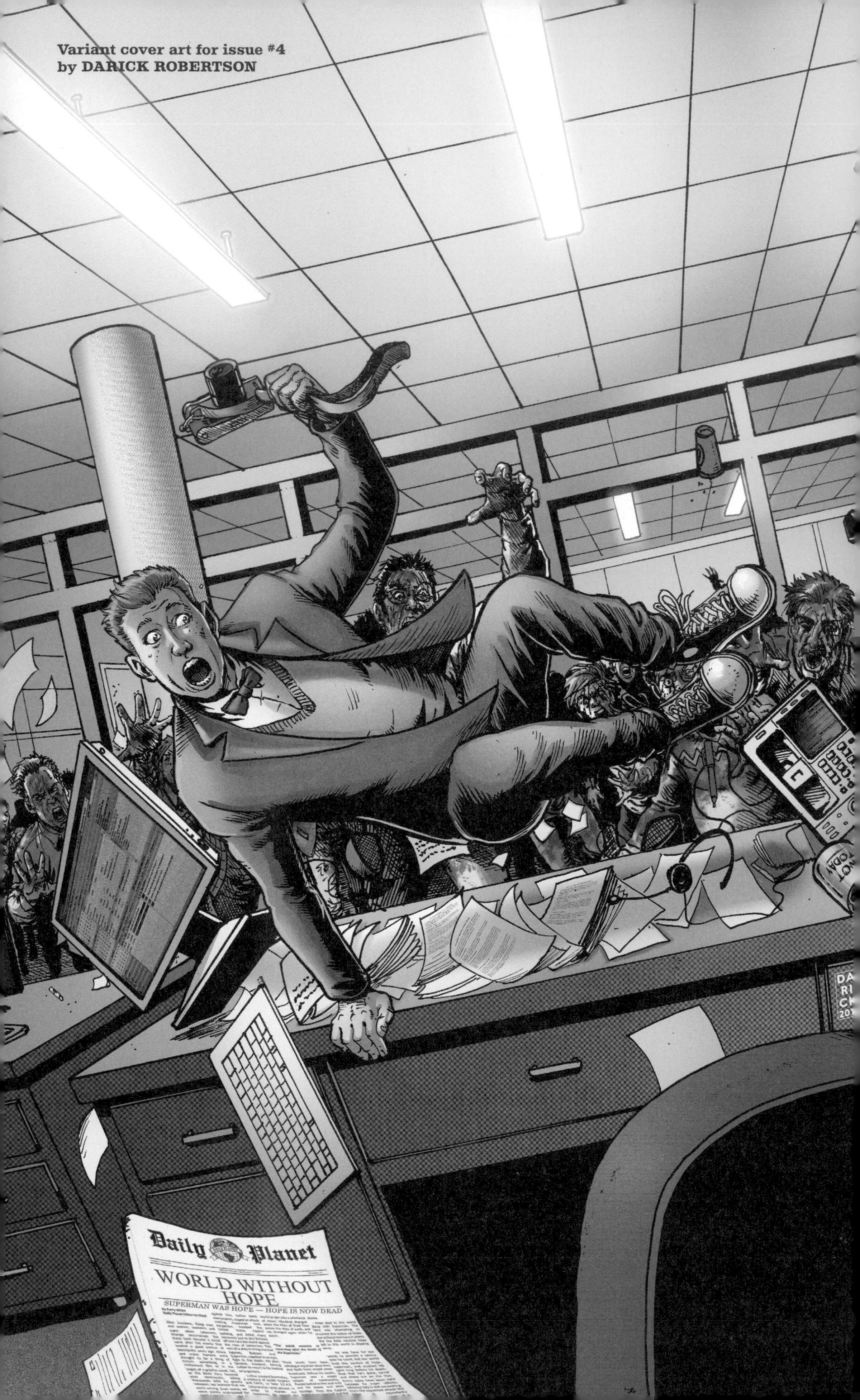

Daily Planet
WORLD WITHOUT HOPE
SUPERMAN WAS HOPE — HOPE IS NOW DEAD

Variant cover art for issue #5
by BEN OLIVER

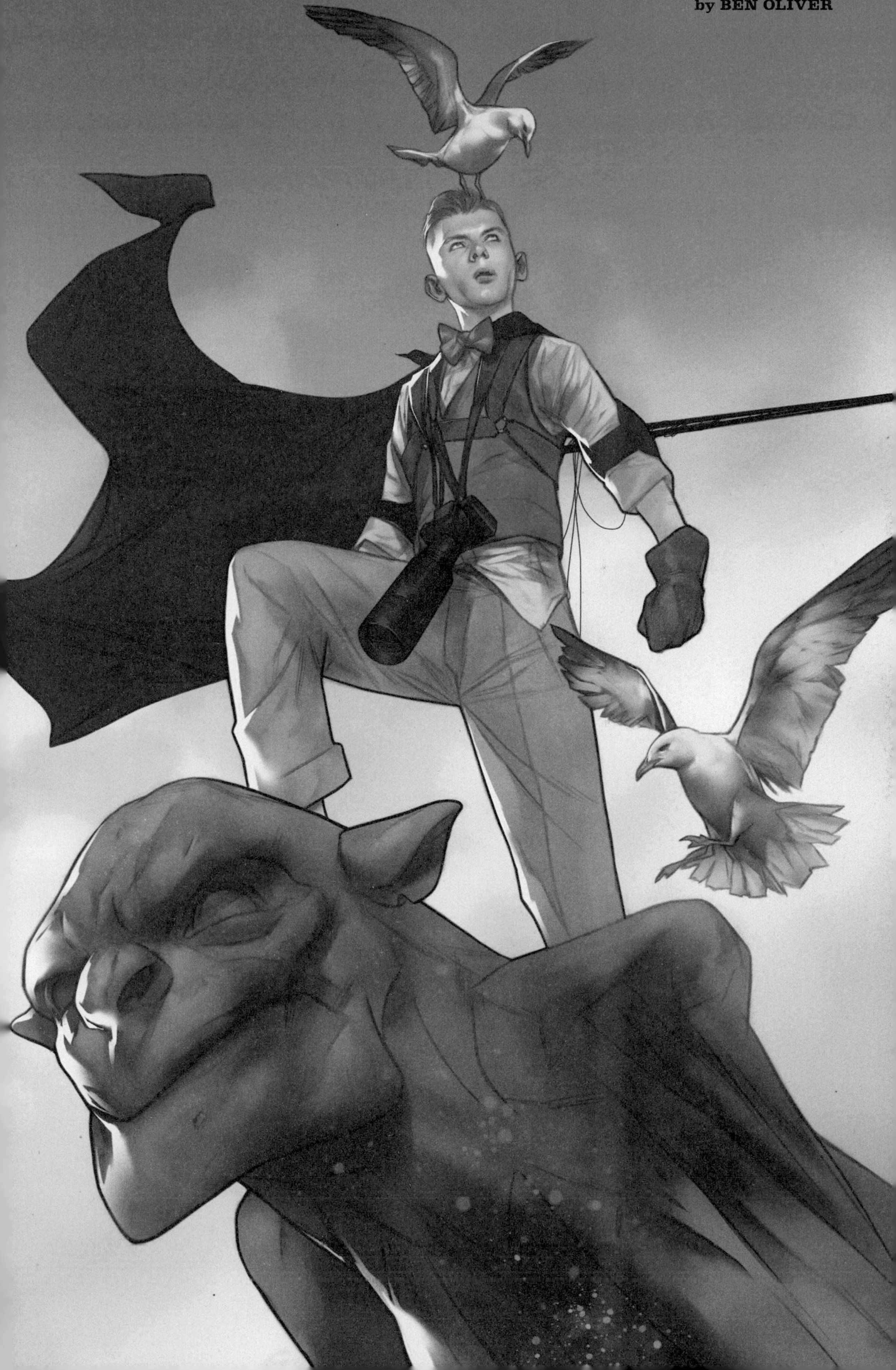

Variant cover art for issue #6
by BEN OLIVER

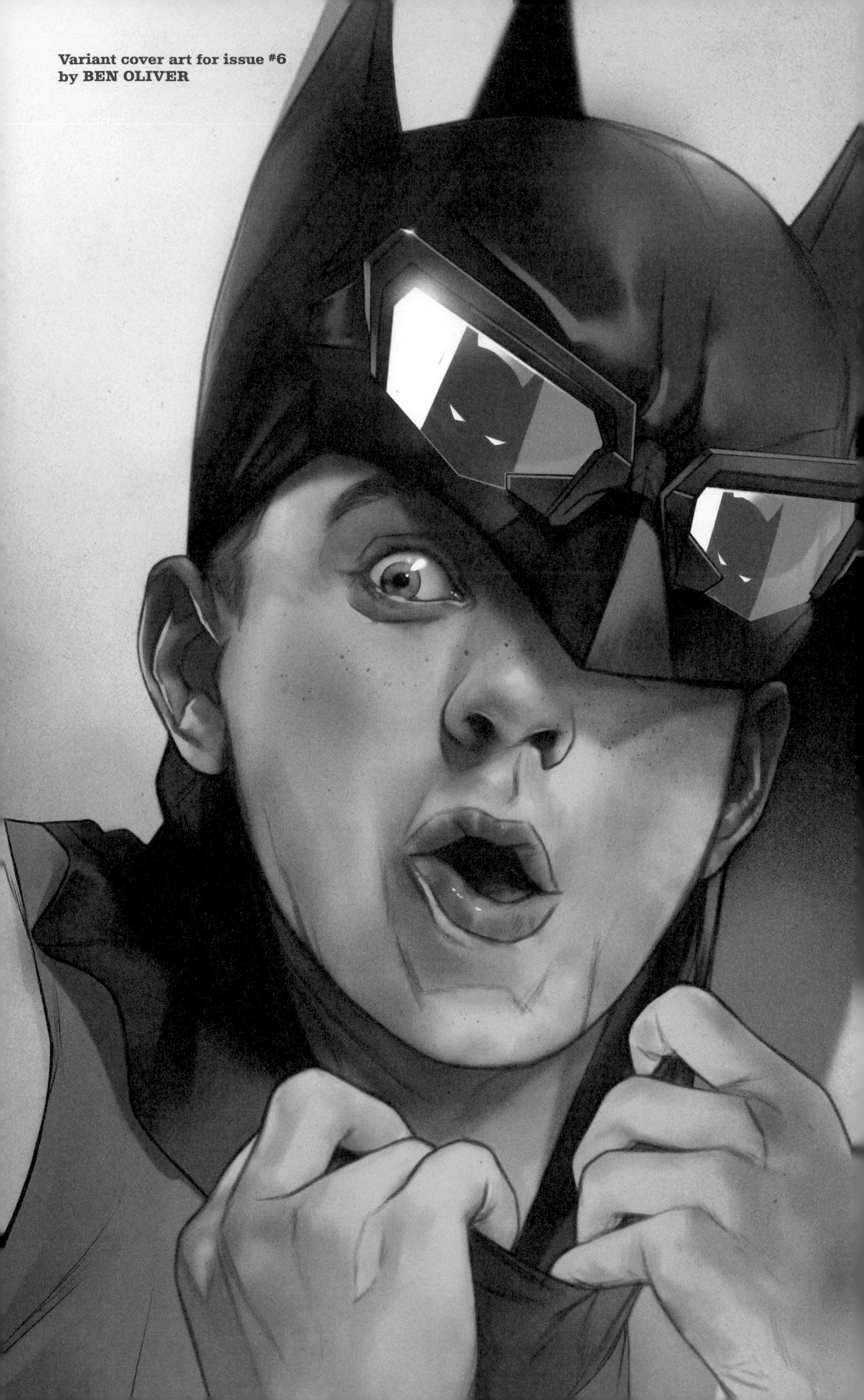

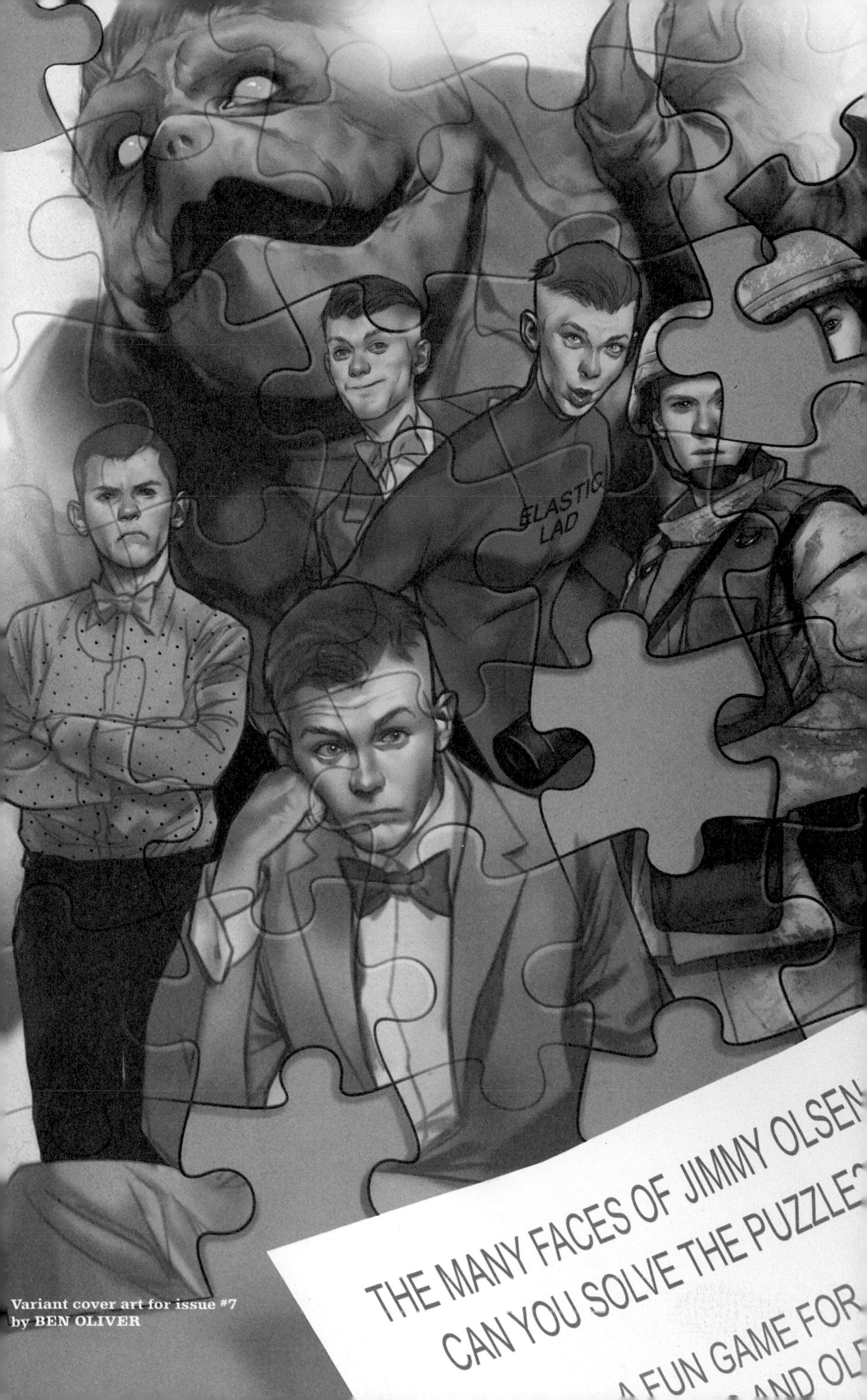
ELASTIC LAD
THE MANY FACES OF JIMMY OLSEN
CAN YOU SOLVE THE PUZZLE
A FUN GAME FOR

Variant cover art for issue #7
by BEN OLIVER

Variant cover art for issue #8
by BEN OLIVER

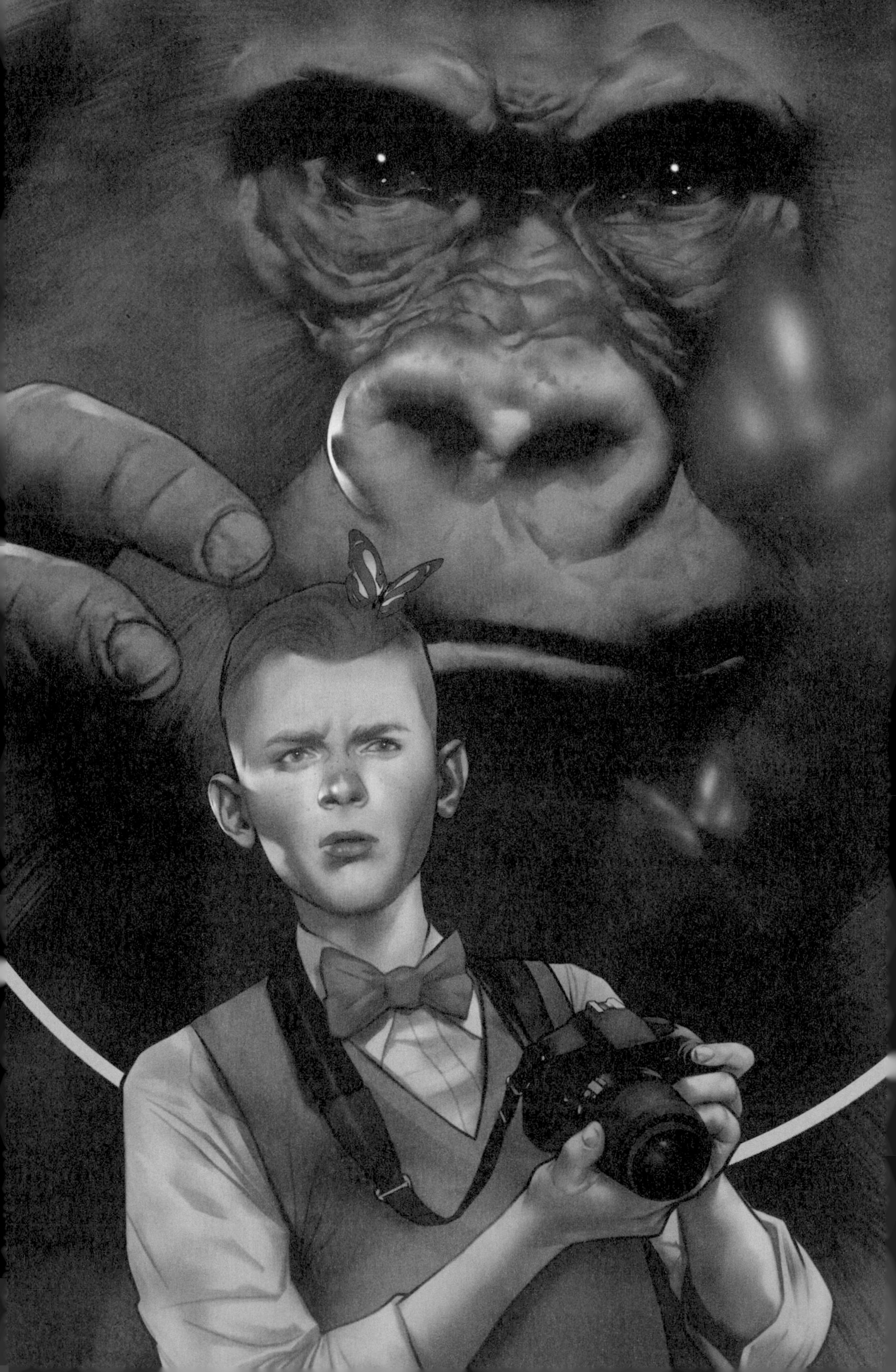

Variant cover art for issue #9
by BEN OLIVER

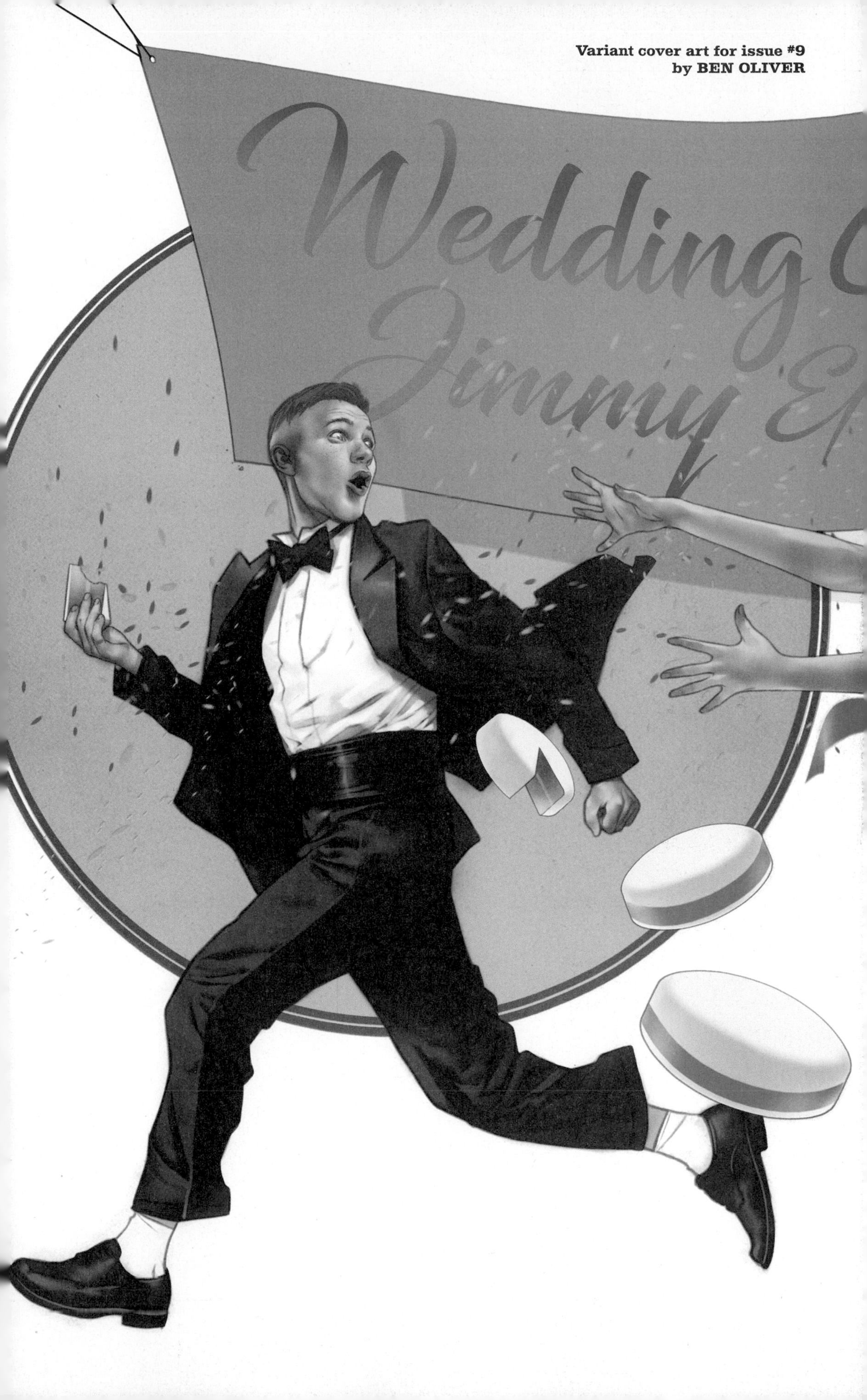
Wedding
Jimmy

Variant cover art
for issue #10
by BEN OLIVER

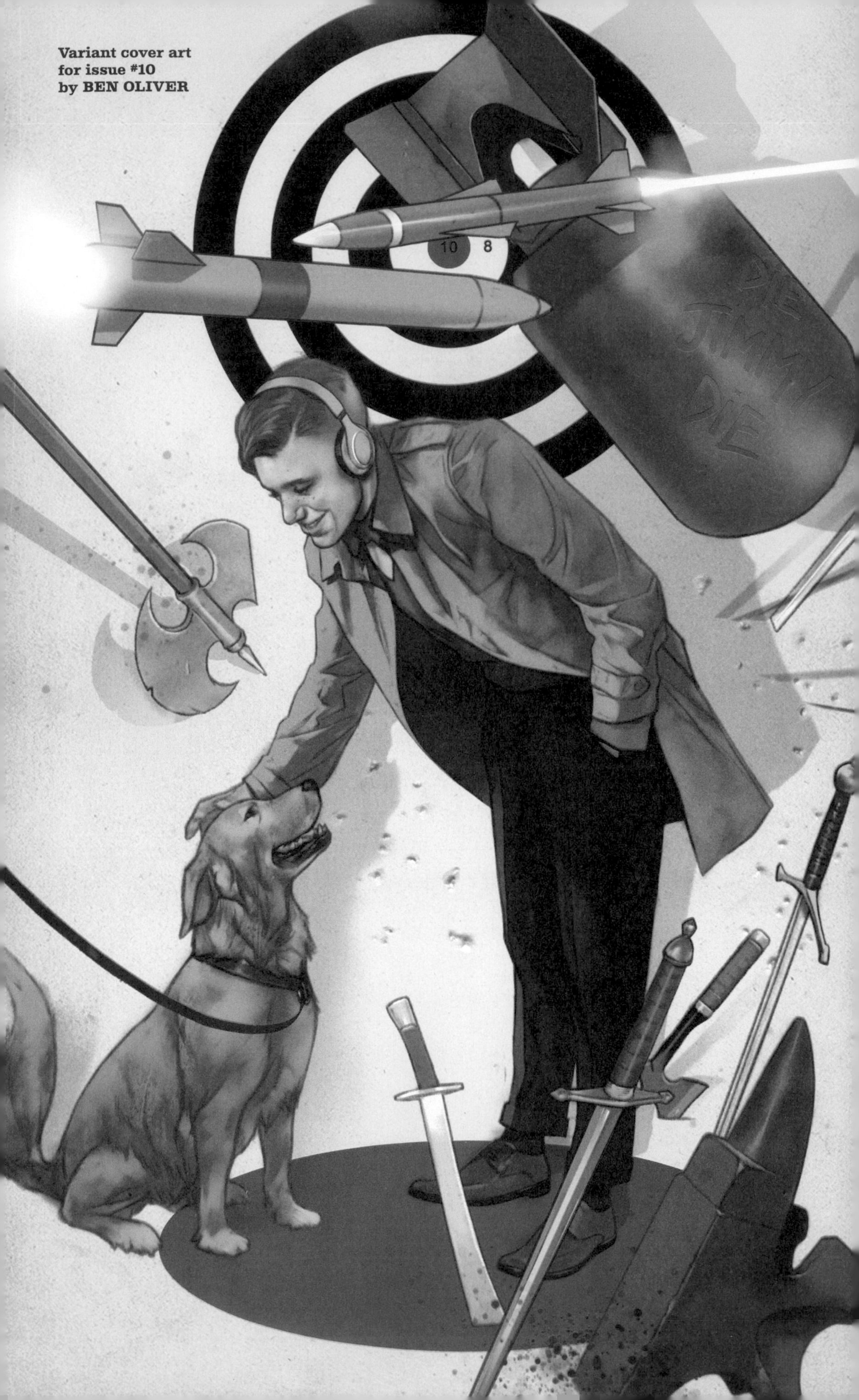
10
8

Variant cover art for issue #11
by BEN OLIVER

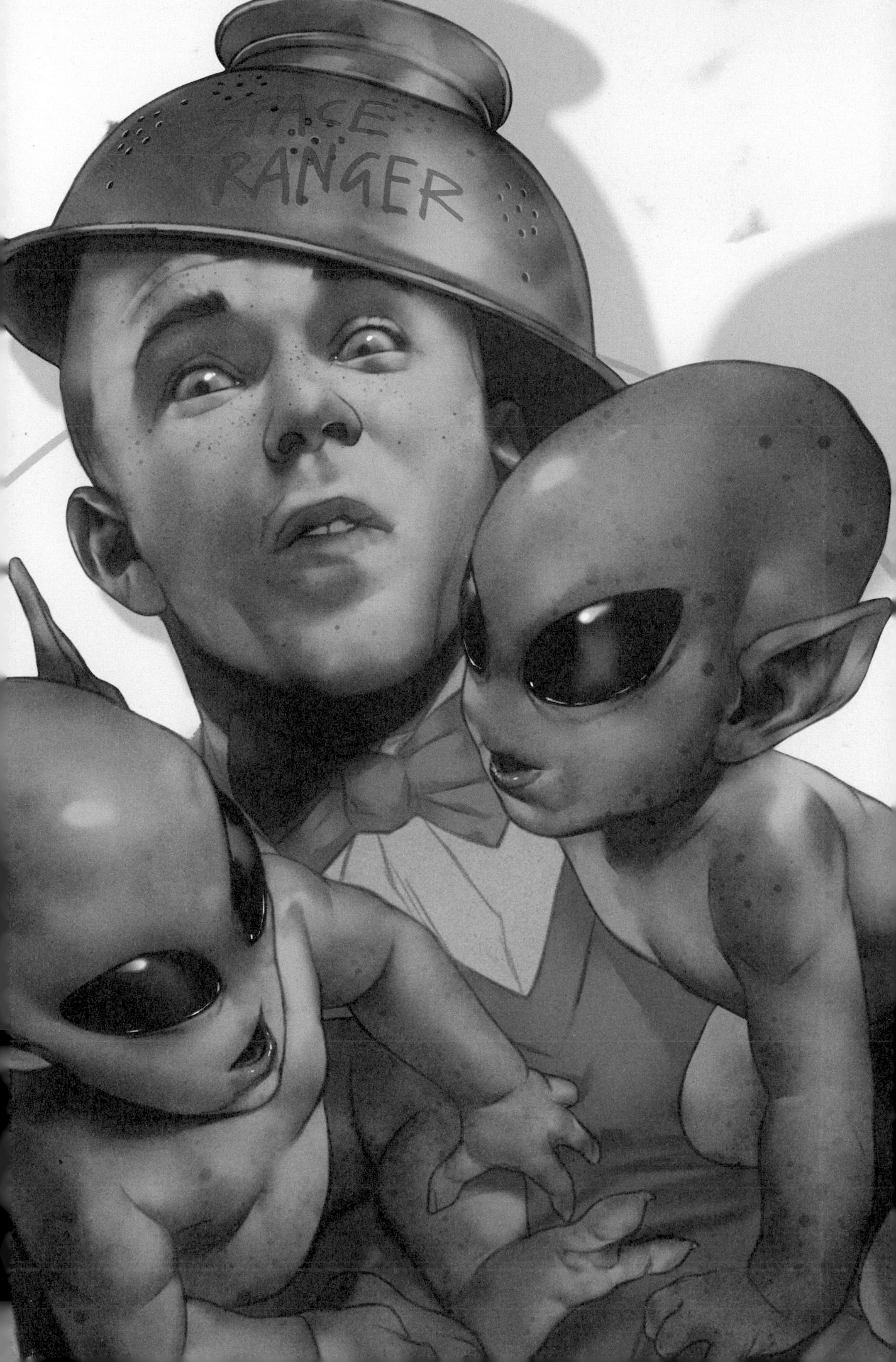
SPACE
RANGER

Variant cover art for issue #12
by **BEN OLIVER**

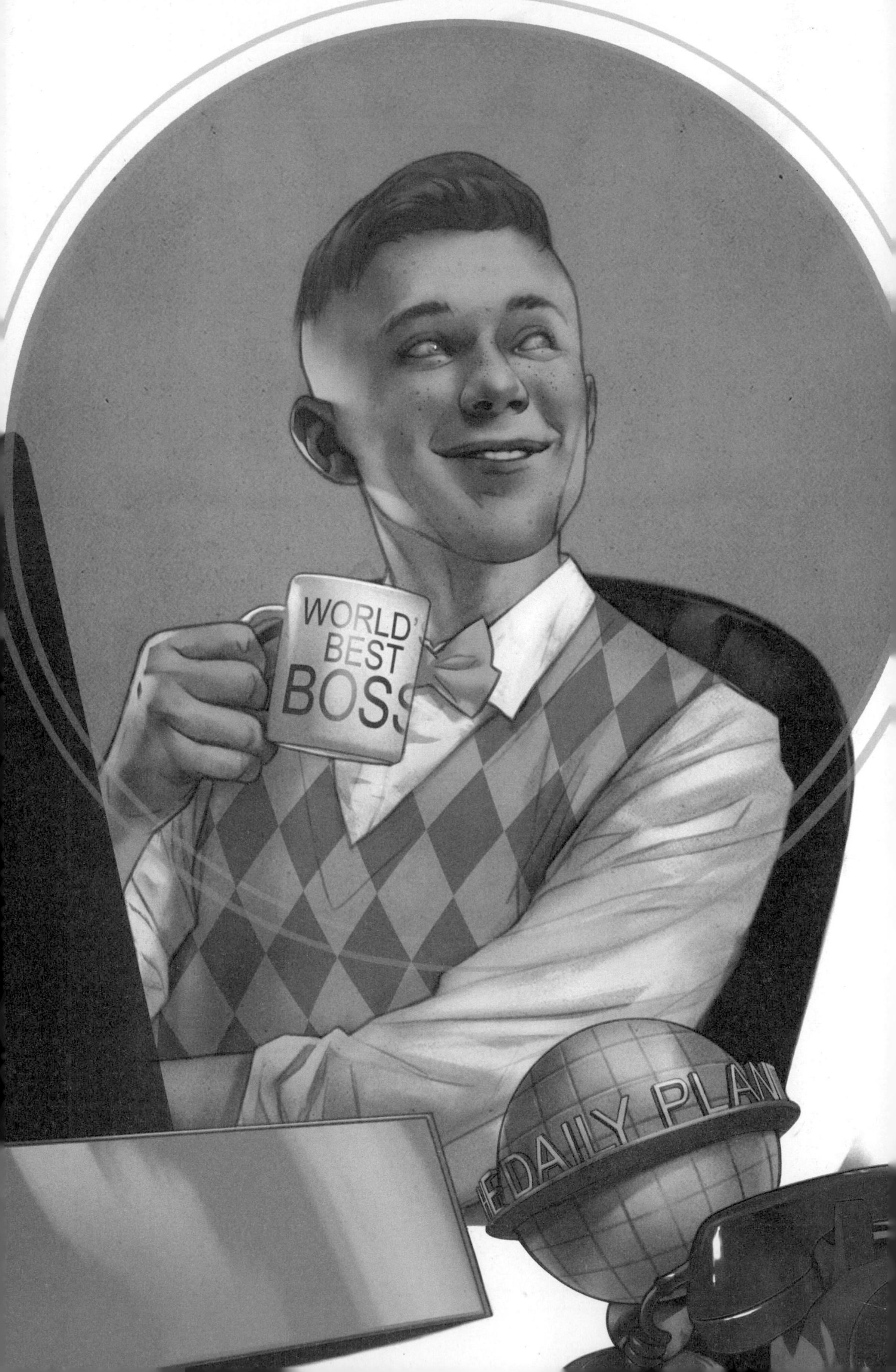
WORLD'
BEST
BOSS
THE DAILY PLAN